D0066583

Teach...
Inspire...
Lead...

**With REA's TExES®
191 Generalist EC–6 test prep,
you'll be in a class all your own.**

We'd like to hear from you!
Visit **www.rea.com** *to send us your comments
or e-mail us at* **info@rea.com.**

Research & Education Association

The Best Teachers' Test Preparation for the

TExES®

191 Generalist EC–6

Luis A. Rosado, Ed.D.

Professor
Director of Center for Bilingual and ESL Education
The University of Texas at Arlington
Arlington, Texas

For updates to the test and this book visit:
www.rea.com/TExES/191Generalist.htm

Planet Friendly Publishing
✔ Made in the United States
✔ Printed on Recycled Paper
  Text: 30%   Cover: 10%
  Learn more: www.greenedition.org

At REA we're committed to producing books in an Earth-friendly manner and to helping our customers make greener choices.

Manufacturing books in the United States ensures compliance with strict environmental laws and eliminates the need for international freight shipping, a major contributor to global air pollution.

And printing on recycled paper helps minimize our consumption of trees, water and fossil fuels. This book was printed on paper made with **30% post-consumer waste**, and the cover was printed on paper made with **10% post-consumer waste**. According to Environmental Defense's Paper Calculator, by using this innovative paper instead of conventional papers, we achieved the following environmental benefits:

Trees Saved: 27 • Air Emissions Eliminated: 6196 pounds
Water Saved: 5159 gallons • Solid Waste Eliminated: 1830 pounds

For more information on our environmental practices, please visit us online at **www.rea.com/green**

Research & Education Association

61 Ethel Road West
Piscataway, New Jersey 08854
E-mail: info@rea.com

The Best Teachers' Test Preparation for the TExES® 191 Generalist EC–6 Test

Copyright © 2010 by Research & Education Association, Inc. All rights reserved. No part of this book may be reproduced in any form without permission of the publisher.

Printed in the United States of America

Library of Congress Control Number 2009938668

ISBN-13: 978-0-7386-0686-6
ISBN-10: 0-7386-0686-3

The competencies presented in this book were created and implemented by the Texas Education Agency and Educational Testing Service (ETS®).

LIMIT OF LIABILITY/DISCLAIMER OF WARRANTY: Publication of this work is for the purpose of test preparation and related use and subjects as set forth herein. While every effort has been made to achieve a work of high quality, neither Research & Education Association, Inc., nor the authors and other contributors of this work guarantee the accuracy or completeness of or assume any liability in connection with the information and opinions contained herein. REA and the authors and other contributors shall in no event be liable for any personal injury, property or other damages of any nature whatsoever, whether special, indirect, consequential or compensatory, directly or indirectly resulting from the publication, use or reliance upon this work.

REA® is a registered trademark of Research & Education Association, Inc.

Contents

CONTENTS

Author's Dedication

This book is dedicated to Kelly, Koko, and Alex, because through their natural behavior and development, they guided me to see the connection between theory and practice.

About the Author

Dr. Luis A. Rosado is the Director of the Center for Bilingual and ESL Education and Professor in the College of Education at the University of Texas at Arlington. He holds degrees from the University of Puerto Rico, Boston State College, and Texas A&M University–Kingsville. He has published in the areas of pedagogy and professional responsibilities, parental involvement, cross-cultural communication, and Spanish linguistics and Spanish for bilingual teachers. Dr. Rosado has over 25 years of teaching experience at the elementary, high school, and college levels. He has taught in Puerto Rico, Massachusetts, and Texas.

About the Contributing Authors

English Language Arts and Reading

Dr. Carla Amaro-Jiménez is a Visiting Assistant Professor of Bilingual/ESL Education at the University of Texas at Arlington (UTA). She holds degrees from the Universidad Latina de Costa Rica and the University of Cincinnati. Prior to coming to UTA, she taught in bilingual and dual language early childhood classrooms both in Costa Rica and Ohio. Her research interests include pre- and in-service teacher preparation for culturally and linguistically diverse environments, equity issues related to the schooling (instruction, learning and assessment) of Latino English language learners, and implementation of technology for content-based second language learning and teaching.

Dr. Peggy Semingson is an Assistant Professor of Literacy Studies in the College of Education at the University of Texas at Arlington. She holds degrees from the University of Texas at Austin, Texas State University, San Marcos, and the University of California, Santa Barbara. She taught bilingual students for eight years in both Southern California and Texas. She has taught fifth grade, third grade, and was a bilingual reading specialist. Dr. Semingson presents at local, state, and national conferences on topics that include: literacy learning, bilingual best practices, and parental involvement.

Mathematics

Dr. Dora Salazar is the Assistant Director of the Center for Research in Leadership and Education, Program Director of Project TEACH, and Assistant Professor in the College of Education at Texas Tech University. She holds degrees from Texas Tech University in Lubbock, Texas. Dr. Salazar has held university faculty appointments at Texas Woman's University and the University of Texas—Pan American. Her research interests include online teacher preparation program models, and certification issues regarding out-of-state and foreign credential teachers. Dr. Salazar has received several grants to prepare bilingual and ESL teachers in Texas. Dr. Salazar has a combined 20 years of teaching experience in bilingual classrooms and at the college level.

Mr. Jason L. Wardlaw is a Ph.D. student in Electrical Engineering at Texas A&M University-College Station. He holds degrees from Tarrant County College and Texas A&M University-College Station. Mr. Wardlaw has been a Teaching Assistant and Assistant Lecturer for the Department of Electrical and Computer Engineering at Texas A&M University from 2005-2008. During the 2008–2009 academic year, he was involved in a National Science Foundation (NSF) GK-12 program for enhancing Science, Technology, Engineering, and Mathematics (STEM) awareness in rural middle school classes.

Social Studies

Dr. Annette Torres Elías is an Assistant Professor of Bilingual/ESL Education at the Texas Wesleyan University in Fort Worth. Dr. Torres Elías holds degrees from the University of Puerto Rico and Texas Woman's University. She has over 15 years of experience as an educator serving students, parents, and educators as a Bilingual/ESL teacher, Bilingual/ESL PK-12th district coordinator, early literacy program coordinator, and university instructor. She is interested in issues dealing with Bilingual/ESL education, teacher preparation, professional development, language acquisition, and early literacy.

Science

Dr. Ann Cavallo is a Professor and Associate Dean of Teacher of Education at the University of Texas at Arlington, and Director of science education programs in the College of Education. She holds degrees from Niagara University and Syracuse University. She taught middle and high school science prior to earning her graduate degrees. She has held university faculty appointments at the University of Oklahoma, the University of California-Davis, and Wayne State University. Dr. Cavallo has over 30 publications in internationally and nationally refereed journals, a book and several book chapters. Dr. Cavallo has made over 60 presentations at professional conferences, and has secured more than $3 million in grants to support her work.

Dr. Patricia A. Gómez is an Assistant Professor in the College of Education Department of Bilingual Education at Texas A&M University-Kingsville. She holds degrees from Texas A&M University-Corpus Christi in Corpus Christi, and Texas A&M University-Kingsville. She has published in the areas of dual literacy instruction, dual language program implementation and science education for English language learners. Dr. Gómez has over 20 years of teaching experience at the elementary, high school, and college levels. She has taught in Spain and Texas.

Visual Arts

Dr. Jill Fox is an Associate Professor and Director of the EC-6 program in the College of Education at the University of Texas at Arlington. She holds degrees from Western Kentucky University, Texas Woman's University and University of North Texas. Prior to coming to the University of Texas at Arlington, Dr. Fox held university a faculty appointments at Virginia Commonwealth University. She has to her credit several journal articles, books and book chapters at the national and international levels. Her research interests include visual art and young children, program development and school-university partnerships. Dr. Fox has been a teacher educator in both Virginia and Texas.

Music

Dr. Diane Lange is an Associate Professor and Area Coordinator of Music Education at The University of Texas at Arlington where she oversees the music education area and teaches courses in Early Childhood and Elementary Music Education. She holds degrees from Michigan State University and Central Michigan University. She has published the book Together in Harmony: Combining Orff Schulwerk and Music Learning Theory, a chapter on combining Music Learning Theory and Orff Schulwerk that appeared in Music Learning Theory: Theory in Practice and several articles in General Music Today. Also, she is a co-author for Jump Right in: the Elementary Music Curriculum, Grades Kindergarten and 5. Dr. Lange has taught elementary and college music for over twenty years in Michigan, Nevada, and Texas.

Health and Physical Education

Dr. Larry P. Nelson is an Assistant Professor at the University of Texas at Arlington and the All-Level Teacher Certification Program Director in the Department of Kinesiology. He holds degrees from Colorado State University and the University of Northern Colorado. He has published in the areas of Physical Education Teacher Efficacy, Program Measurement and Evaluation, Resiliency Profiling, and Service-Learning. In his 13 years of service, Dr. Nelson has procured over $350,000 of grants and contracts, and has won numerous teaching awards.

About Research & Education Association

Founded in 1959, Research & Education Association is dedicated to publishing the finest and most effective educational materials—including software, study guides, and test preps—for students in middle school, high school, college, graduate school, and beyond.

REA's Test Preparation series includes books and software for all academic levels in almost all disciplines. Research & Education Association publishes test preps for students who have not yet entered high school, as well as for high school students preparing to enter college. Students from countries around the world seeking to attend college in the United States will find the assistance they need in REA's publications. For college students seeking advanced degrees, REA publishes test preps for many major graduate school admission examinations in a wide variety of disciplines, including engineering, law, and medicine. Students at every level, in every field, with every ambition can find what they are looking for among REA's publications.

REA's practice tests are always based upon the most recently administered exams and include every type of question that you can expect on the actual exams.

Today REA's wide-ranging catalog is a leading resource for teachers, students, and professionals.

We invite you to visit us at *www.rea.com* to find out how "REA is making the world smarter."

REA Acknowledgments

We would like to thank REA's Larry B. Kling, Vice President, Editorial, for supervising development; Pam Weston, Vice President, Publishing, for setting the quality standards for production integrity and managing the publication to completion; Alice Leonard, Senior Editor, for project management and preflight editorial review; Diane Goldschmidt, and Kathleen Casey, Senior Editors, for post-production quality assurance; Stephanie Reymann for indexing; Ellen Gong for proofreading; Christine Saul, Senior Graphic Artist, for cover design; and Kathy Caratozzolo of Caragraphics for typesetting.

Author's Acknowledgments

I wish to thank teacher candidates throughout Texas and especially teacher candidates from the University of Texas at Arlington who motivated me to undertake this project. I would like to thank my colleagues from universities across Texas whose collective wisdom and experiences made this book possible. I would also like to acknowledge the support and guidance of Alice Leonard, REA Senior Editor, who kept me focused.

Introduction

About This Book

REA's *The Best Teachers' Preparation for the TExES 191 Generalist EC–6* is a comprehensive guide designed to assist you in passing the TExES 191 Generalist EC–6 test and thus giving you a springboard to being certified to teach in Texas.

To enhance your chances of success in this important step toward your career as a teacher in Texas schools, this test guide:

- Presents an accurate and complete overview of the TExES 191 Generalist EC–6 examination.

- Identifies all of the important information and its representation on the exam.

- Provides a comprehensive review of every domain.

- Presents sample questions in the actual test format.

- Provides diagnostic tools to identify areas of strength and weakness.

- Provides a diagnostic test and two full-length practice tests based on the most recently administered TExES.

- Replicates the format of the official exam, including level of difficulty.

• Supplies the correct answer and detailed explanations for each question on the practice test, which enables you to pinpoint your strengths and weaknesses.

This guide is the result of analyses of multiple resources. The editors considered the most recent test administrations and professional standards. They also researched information from the Texas Education Agency, professional journals, textbooks, and educators. This guide includes the best test preparation materials based on the latest information available.

About the Test

Below are the domains used as the basis for the TExES 191 Generalist EC–6 examination, as well as the percentage of the total test that each domain occupies. These domains and the competencies rooted in them represent the knowledge that teams of teachers, subject area specialists, and district-level educators have determined to be important for beginning teachers.

Domain Percentage

1. English Language Arts and Reading 32%

2. Mathematics 19%

3. Social Studies 19%

4. Science 18%

5. Fine Arts, Health, and Physical Education 12%

Format of the TExES

The TExES 191 Generalist EC–6 test includes 125 scorable multiple-choice items and approximately 15 non-scorable items used for field testing. Your final scaled score will be based only on scorable items. Do not leave any item unanswered, since you are not penalized for guessing. All multiple-choice questions are designed to assess your knowledge of the domains and related skills mentioned above and reviewed in this book. In general, the multiple-choice questions are intended to make you think logically. You are expected in most cases to demonstrate more than an ability to recall factual information; you may be asked to think critically about the information, analyze it, consider it carefully, compare it with knowledge you have, or make a judgment about it.

Answering the multiple-choice questions is straightforward. You will have four choices labeled A, B, C, and D. You must mark your choice on a separate answer sheet, or, on the computer-based version, directly below each test item. You should have plenty of time in which to complete the test, but be aware of the amount of time you are spending on each question so that you allow yourself time to complete the whole test. Although speed is not very important, a steady pace should be maintained when answering questions. Using the practice tests will help you prepare for this task.

When Should the TExES Be Taken?

Traditionally, teacher preparation programs determine when their candidates take the various tests required for teacher certification. These programs will also clear you to take the examinations and make final recommendations for certification to the State Board for Educator Certification (SBEC). For those seeking certification right out of school, the test is generally taken just before graduation. Taking all TExES examinations is a requirement to teach in Texas, so if you are planning on being an educator, you must take and pass these tests.

The TExES is available in paper-based or computer-based formats. The former is usually administered five times a year at several locations throughout Texas. The usual testing day is Saturday, but the test may be taken on an alternate day if a conflict, such as a religious obligation, exists. The computer-based examinations are also available several times a year at specific locations.

The TExES Registration Bulletin offers information about test dates and locations, as well as registration information and how to make testing accommodations for those with special needs. The registration bulletin is available at *http://texes.ets. org/registrationBulletin/*

Registration bulletins are also available at the education departments of Texas colleges and universities. To address issues that cannot be solved at the teacher preparation program level, you can contact the offices of SBEC at (888) 863-5880 or (512) 469-8400. You can also find information about the test and registration on the SBEC website at *http://texes.ets.org*.

Is There a Registration Fee?

To take the TExES, you must pay a registration fee. If you are using the registration form, all fees must be paid in full by personal check, cashier's check, or money order payable to ETS. All payments must be made in U.S. dollars. Cash will not be accepted. If you are registering via the Internet or phone during the emergency registration period, payment must be made by VISA or MasterCard.

How to Use This Book

How Do I Begin Studying?

Review the organization of this test preparation guide.

1. To best utilize your study time, follow our TExES Independent Study Schedule elsewhere in this introduction. The schedule is based on a seven-week program, but it can be condensed to four weeks if necessary.

2. Take the diagnostic test.

3. Review the format of the TExES.

4. Review the test-taking advice and suggestions presented later in this chapter.

5. Study the information related to the domains, competencies, and topics on the test.

6. Spend time reviewing topics that stand out as needing more study. Pay special attention to the terminology used in each of the content areas.

7. Take the practice test and then review the explanations carefully. Study the competencies that your scores indicate need further review.

8. Follow the suggestions at the end of this chapter for the day before and the day of the test.

When Should I Start Studying?

It is never too early to start studying for the TExES. The earlier you begin, the more time you will have to sharpen your skills. Do not procrastinate! Cramming is not an effective way to study, since it does not allow you the time needed to learn the test material.

Studying for the TExES 191 Generalist EC–6

It is very important for you to choose the time and place for studying that works best for you. Some individuals may set aside a certain number of hours every morning to study, while others may choose to study at night before going to sleep. Other people may study during the day, while waiting in line, or even while eating lunch. Only you can determine when and where your study time will be most effective. Be consistent and use your time wisely. Work out a study routine and stick to it.

When you take the practice tests, simulate the conditions of the actual test as closely as possible. Turn your television and radio off, and sit down at a quiet table free from distraction. As you complete each practice test, score your test and thoroughly review the explanations to the questions you answered incorrectly; however, do not review too much at any one time. Concentrate on one problem area at a time by reviewing the question and explanation, and by studying our review until you are confident that you have mastered the material.

Keep track of your scores. By doing so, you will be able to gauge your progress and discover general weaknesses in particular sections. Give extra attention to the reviews that cover your areas of difficulty, as this will build your skills in those areas.

TExES 191 Generalist EC–6 Study Schedule

The following study schedule allows for thorough preparation for the TExES. The course of study here is seven weeks, but you can condense or expand the timeline to suit your personal schedule. It is vital that you adhere to a structured plan and set aside ample time each day to study. The more time you devote to studying, the more prepared and confident you will be on the day of the test.

Since the TExES 191 covers content areas in grades EC-6, you should review the state curricula for these grades (Texas Knowledge and Skills) available at *http://ritter. tea.state.tx.us/teks/*. It is also important to review the released examinations that students in grades 3-12 take to demonstrate mastery of the state curriculum. These tests are released after each administration, and can be used to review the content for the TExES examination. The released tests for grades 3 to 11 are available at *http://www. tea.state.tx.us/index3.aspx?id=44&menu_id3=793*.

Week	Study Schedule
1	**Take the diagnostic exam.** The scoring grid will indicate your strengths and weaknesses. Make sure you simulate real exam conditions when you take the test. Afterward, score it and review the explanations, especially for questions you answered incorrectly.
2	**Review the explanations for the questions you missed, and review the appropriate chapter sections.** Useful study techniques include highlighting key terms and information; taking notes as you review the book's sections; putting new terms and information on note cards to help retain the information.
3 and 4	**Reread all your note cards, refresh your understanding of the exam's competencies and skills, review your college textbooks, and read over class notes you've previously taken.** This is also the time to consider any other supplementary materials that your advisor or the Texas Education Agency suggests. Review the agency's website at *http://www.tea.state.tx.us/*. Take the first Practice Test.
5	**Begin to condense your notes and findings.** A structured list of important facts and concepts, based on your note cards and the book's competencies, will help you thoroughly review for the test. Review the answers and explanations for all missed questions.
6	**Have someone quiz you using the index cards you created.** Take the second Practice Test, adhering to the time limits and simulated test-day conditions.
7	**Review your areas of weakness using all study materials.** This is a good time to retake one or both of the practice tests.

About the Review Sections

The reviews in this book are designed to help you sharpen the basic skills needed to approach the TExES, as well as provide strategies for attacking the questions.

The TExES 191 is composed of five domains and 45 competencies. Each of the domains and its corresponding competencies are examined in separate chapters. The skills required for all five domains are extensively discussed to optimize your understanding of what the 191 Generalist EC–6 test covers.

Keep in mind that your schooling has taught you most of what you need to answer the questions on the test. The education classes you took should have provided you with the know-how to make important decisions about situations you will face as a teacher. Our review is designed to help you fit the information you have acquired into specific competency components. Reviewing your class notes and textbooks together with our competency reviews will give you an excellent foundation for passing the exam.

Scoring the TExES (191) Generalist EC–6

How Do I Score My Practice Test?

The passing rate for TExES 191 is generally done after the first administration of the test. At this writing, it has not been set yet; however, the passing rate is generally set between 70% and 80%. There are 125 scorable multiple-choice questions on this practice test. You must get 88 of those questions correct to score at the 70% and 100 questions to score at the 80%. Scores in these ranges suggests that you are developing an understanding of the content of the test covered in this book.

If you do not achieve a passing score on the practice test, review the detailed explanations for the questions you answered incorrectly. Note which types of questions you answered wrong, and re-examine the corresponding review. After further review, you may want to re-take the practice tests.

When and How Will I Receive My Score Report and What Will It Look Like?

The testing agency no longer sends test results via regular mail. As part of the registration process to take TExES examinations, students set up an account with the testing agency (ETS) in which they are assigned a username and password. This information will be used by you to login to view the results of the test.

Results of the paper-based examination are generally available within four weeks of the administration, and the results of the computer-based examination can be viewed within a week of the test.

The report you will receive will indicate whether you have passed the test. This report will also give you the following information:

- A total test scaled score that is reported on a scale of 100–300. The minimum passing score is a scaled score of 240. This score represents the minimum level of competency required to be an entry-level educator in this field in Texas public schools.

- Your performance in the major content domains of the test and in the specific competencies of the test. This information may be useful in identifying strengths and weaknesses and can be used in preparing for the test should you need to retake it.

- Information to help you interpret your results.

Test-Taking Tips

Although you may not be familiar with tests like the TExES, this book will help acquaint you with this type of exam and help alleviate your test-taking anxieties.

Listed below are ways to help you become accustomed to the TExES, some of which may be applied to other tests as well.

Tip 1. Become comfortable with the format of the TExES. When you are practicing, stay calm and pace yourself. After simulating the test only once, you will boost your chances of doing well, and you will be able to sit down for the actual TExES with much more confidence.

Tip 2. Read all of the possible answers. Just because you think you have found the correct response, do not automatically assume that it is the best answer. Read through each choice to be sure that you are not making a mistake by jumping to conclusions.

Tip 3. Use the process of elimination. Go through each answer to a question and eliminate as many of the answer choices as possible. By eliminating two answer choices, you have given yourself a better chance of getting the item correct since there will only be two choices left from which to make your guess. Do not leave an answer blank; it is better to guess than to not answer a question on the TExES test as there is no additional penalty for wrong answers.

Tip 4. Place a question mark in your answer booklet next to answers you guessed, then recheck them later if you have time.

Tip 5. Work quickly and steadily to avoid focusing on any one problem too long. Taking the practice test in this book will help you learn to budget your precious time.

Tip 6. Learn the directions and format of the test. Familiarizing yourself with the directions and format of the test will not only save time, but will also help you avoid anxiety (and the mistakes caused by getting anxious).

Tip 7. Be sure that the answer circle you are marking corresponds to the number of the question in the test booklet. Since the test is multiple-choice, it is graded by machine, and marking one wrong answer can throw off your answer key and your score. Be extremely careful.

The Day of the Test

Before the Test

On the day of the test, make sure to dress comfortably, so that you are not distracted by being too hot or too cold while taking the test. Plan to arrive at the test center early. This will allow you to collect your thoughts and relax before the test, and will also spare you the anguish that comes with being late.

You should check your TExES registration information to find out what time to arrive at the testing center. Also, return to your testing account and check your admission ticket 24 hours before the test in case there is a change. If there is a change, you will have to print out a new ticket.

Before you leave for the test center, make sure that you have your admission ticket and two forms of identification, one of which must contain a recent and recognizable photograph, your name, and signature (i.e., driver's license). All documents must be originals (no copies). You will not be admitted to the test center and you will forfeit your test fees if you do not have proper identification.

You must bring several sharpened No. 2 pencils with erasers, as none will be provided at the test center. If you would like, you may wear a watch to the test center. However, you may not wear one that makes noise, because it may disturb the other test takers. Dictionaries, textbooks, notebooks, calculators, briefcases, or packages will not be permitted. Do not bring cell phones, smart phones, PDAs and other electronic or photographic devices into the test center. Drinking, smoking, and eating are prohibited.

During the Test

Procedures will be followed to maintain test security. Once you enter the test center, follow all of the rules and instructions given by the test supervisor. If you do not, you risk being dismissed from the test and having your scores cancelled.

When all of the materials have been distributed, the test instructor will give you directions for filling out your answer sheet. Fill out this sheet carefully since this information will be printed on your score report.

Once the test begins, mark only one answer per question, completely erase unwanted answers and marks, and fill in answers darkly and neatly.

Can I Retake the Test?

If you don't do well on the TExES, don't panic! You can take it again, and in fact many candidates do. You can register to retake it at any subsequent test administration. To retake a test, submit a new registration along with the correct payment. It is recommended that you wait for your scores before reregistering. If you choose to register again for the same test before receiving your scores from a previous administration, you assume responsibility for test fees and any applicable late or emergency registration fees for both test dates.

After the Test

When you finish your test, hand in your materials and you will be dismissed. Then, go home and relax—you deserve it!

CHAPTER 1

English Language Arts and Reading

Competency 001: Oral Language

The teacher understands the importance of oral language, knows the developmental processes of oral language, and provides the students with varied opportunities to develop listening and speaking skills.

Language acquisition results from the combination of innate ability, imitation of what is said and heard, and multiple environmental influences. Children are said to be born with innate abilities and mechanisms to develop language. Noam Chomsky called this mechanism a Language Acquisition Device (LAD). According to Chomsky, humans possess an "internal grammar" or set of linguistic principles that are activated for all languages. Interestingly, the LAD is considered universal, as the LAD adapts depending on the language being learned. However, it should be noted that linguists have argued that language only emerges if this internal mechanism is triggered by stimuli from people in the child's environment.

Imitation is a learning strategy that young children frequently use to replicate someone's behaviors, actions, phrases, etc. In language acquisition, imitation provides young learners with the opportunity to begin producing language by observing and replicating their caregiver's phrases and words. Imitation decreases in effectiveness, however, as language learning becomes more complex. Children who are at the one-word stage of language acquisition use the strategy of imitation for language development. Due to memory limitations, infants appear to pay more attention to the ends of sentences or words. For example, a question such as, "Do you want to go out?" might receive a reply of "out." This reply probably means, "Yes, I want to go out."

After age two, imitation alone cannot meet the communication needs of children. It is at this point when they become creative rule makers. Toddlers begin testing language rules on their own as a way of trying to figure out how language operates. For example, imitation alone cannot explain idiosyncratic statements such as "I goed out yesterday." These nonstandard utterances show that the child is field-testing language rules. In this case, the child is testing the rule for the formation of the regular past tense and has applied it to an irregular verb. This type of overgeneralization characterizes the process of first language acquisition during most of the early childhood years. Direct language correction will not generally help in this case. Instead, parents and those around the child will present the standard version of the word, and the child will seem to ignore it until he or she is ready to internalize it. Parents and teachers should always be encouraged to address the communication needs of the child while modeling the standard version of the language. Moreover, appropriate modeling of the target language is a necessary task for teachers, especially when working with students for whom English is not their native language.

Language Is Learned in Social Settings

Participation in conversation provides children with the vocabulary and the format of conversations they need to begin developing oral language (Stewig and Jett-Simpson1995). Interestingly, parents do not always engage in direct language teaching; instead, parents assist in their children's language acquisition by communicating with the child and using the adult version of the language. As a result of this linguistic support, most children come to school with a strong vocabulary and language background. Conversely, some ethnic and linguistic groups might not follow the same pattern of linguistic interaction with their children. The expression "Children are to be seen, not heard" represents an example of how some groups view the appropriate interaction of children with adults. Children who are brought up in a society in which participation in adults' conversations is restricted might not have the same language development and most likely will begin school behind their classmates.

Children Are Concerned with Meaning

Children quickly understand that the main purpose of language is communication. Children begin to understand that language is used to generally have their needs met.

Young learners are not concerned with grammar. Because of this, direct error correction has little impact in the language development of early childhood children. They expect language to make sense. These children rely on sympathetic listeners to understand them. Therefore, modeling and not correction is always the best way to support language development in young children.

Language Components

All teacher candidates need to have a clear understanding of the basic components of any given language. These six components, which should be thought of as being interlocking pieces in a puzzle, are phonology, morphology, syntax, lexicon, semantics, and pragmatics. **Phonology** is the study of the sound system of a language. The basic units of sound are called **phonemes**. Graphemes or individual letters represent phonemes. For example, the word *through* has seven graphemes (i.e., letters) that represent only three sounds /th,r,u/. Teacher candidates should be able not only to differentiate these two terms, but they should also make their students aware of the difference between letters in a word and the sounds that the letters represent. **Morphology** is the study of the structure of words and word formations. **Morphemes** are the smallest representation of meaning. For example, the word *cars* is made up of two morphemes: the basic word or root word *car* and the plural morpheme *s*. Having an understanding of the morphology of a language will help students when they are required to decode printed information. **Syntax** entails the ways in which words are organized and arranged in a language. English has specific basic sentence structures that are referred to as *kernel sentences*. Examples of the four most common sentence structures in English can be found in Table 1-1.

Table 1-1 Types of Kernel Sentences

Noun	Intransitive Verb	Predicate Nominative
Katrina	was	a hurricane.
Katrina	was	destructive.
"Bear Mountain"	won	an Oscar.
Mark Cuban	gave	the Mavericks an incentive.

Lexicon refers to the vocabulary of a language. Because the meanings of words change based on context and its historical framework, vocabulary is said to be one of the most variable and rich components of a language. For example, the word *hot* can have several different meanings. Some of these include high temperature, fashionable, and lucky. In a few years, any of these more recent meanings might change or actually become obsolete.

Semantics refers to the way that meaning is conveyed in a language through the use of its vocabulary. The meaning of words is also based on culture as well as the context of the conversation taking place. Connotation and denotation are used in a language to convey meaning.

On the one hand, **connotation** refers to the implied meaning of words and ideas; therefore, speakers must have knowledge of the culture to understand an expression's implied meaning. Idiomatic expressions are one example of how its use implies meaning as a communication tool. Having this prior knowledge often presents a challenge to English language learners (ELLs) because they generally lack the familiarity with the American culture that native speakers have acquired. For instance, the common idiom "it's raining cats and dogs" may confuse ELLs who do not have such cultural knowledge and are therefore unfamiliar with this idiom. Thus, teachers need to teach idioms in a contextualized situation to provide this background knowledge that students lack. Teachers must also provide a description of the idiom, especially in regards to their intended meaning to allow students to fully understand their use.

Denotation refers to the literal meaning of words and ideas. For instance, a sign that reads "Dog Bites" might seem obvious because all dogs have the capability to bite. However, pragmatically, this phrase entails that people should go beyond the literal meaning of the phrase and understand that whoever posted such a sign meant that the dog is aggressive and might attack.

The *Amelia Bedelia* series written by Peggy Parish is one example of how the main character actually understands everything only literally (i.e., denotation). Her limited understanding creates many communication problems and comedic situations.

Pragmatics describes how context can affect the interpretation of communication. Pragmatics describes the hidden rules of communications understood by native speakers of the same language. Native speakers often call these rules "commonsense rules." However, these rules might be only common to native speakers. These rules are not immediately evident to ELLs. Thus, teachers should once again introduce these rules within context. Take, for example, a greeting exchange. In English, a person greets another person with a routine statement such as "How are you?" Pragmatically, the receiver in the conversation is expected to answer with a generic statement such as "Not bad," "I am OK," or "Fine." Once such an exchange of words is completed, the conversation is expected to end. However, ELLs and people who are new to the culture might misinterpret the routine question as a literal inquiry and try to answer it directly or provide more information than what the original person intended to hear.

Stages of Language Development

The process of first language acquisition is characterized by stages of development and maturation. Also, these stages are highly influenced by the learner's level and quality of exposure to the native language. Therefore, assigning a definite age for each of the language development stages is not possible. Linguistic milestones, however, can provide pointers to identify these stages and develop a working framework for readers. A description of these stages follows.

Babbling or Pre-Language Stage (0–6 months)

Children at this stage send and receive messages, and use reflexive crying to communicate with caregivers. They play vocally by producing multiple linguistic and nonlinguistic sounds (e.g., mmm, dada). Infants can identify the voices of parents and family members, and they are able to follow certain commands. They also begin understanding the intonation patterns used to convey anger or excitement and the patterns used to ask questions.

Holophrastic One-Word Stage (11–19 months)

Children at the one-word stage begin imitating inflections and facial expressions of adults. They recognize their name and follow simple instructions presented in contextualized situations. Children begin using adults as tools by pointing to objects and requesting assistance. They understand **word concepts** and use these to conceptualize complete ideas.

Two-Word Stage (13–24 months)

At the two-word stage, children begin producing rudimentary types of phrases. These constructions are characterized by a combination of two types of words—Pivot and Open words. **Pivot** refers to words that can be used to accomplish multiple functions, i.e., *no, up, all, see, more,* and *gone*. The **open** class contains words that are generally used to refer to one concept. Words like *home, milk, doggy, juice, pants,* and *shoe* are words that are used mostly to refer to one particular situation. Based on the vocabulary limitations of this stage, children use combinations of these two classes to create the subject and the predicate of the sentence. Some possible examples of utterances produced at this stage are "see baby," "see mommy," "no more," and "all gone."

Telegraphic Stage (18–27 months)

The telegraphic stage represents a higher degree of linguistic development in which the child goes beyond the two-word stage. Most of the words used at this stage are **content words** with high semantic value that can be used in multiple situations. Some examples of function words are nouns, adjectives, and verbs. At this stage children begin to use these content words in ways in which they have heard them being used. The use of **function words** such as prepositions and articles, however, is very limited at this stage because these do not convey as much information as content words. The typical sentence at this stage consists of subject, verb, object or adjective format. Some possible examples of utterances produced at this stage are "hello there," "milk all gone," and "that's not nice."

Ages Two to Three Years

At age two children have about 200 to 300 words in their linguistic repertoire and can generally produce short sentences. At this point, children begin using prepositions and pronouns with some level of inconsistency. The vocabulary of three-year-olds grows to about 900 to 1,000 words. Three-year-olds begin creating three- to four-word sentences. They are able to follow two-step commands and engage in short dialogues about familiar topics. In schools with programs for three-year-olds, children get exposed to informal and formal registers—variants of a language used for a particular purpose depending on the social setting. Children begin to request instead of demand, use courteous vocabulary, and begin following conversation formats.

Age Four

Four-year-olds generally have about 1,500 words in their speaking repertoire. They use more complex sentence structures, but their speech still contains pronunciation problems and overgeneralizations. Four year-olds are able to understand more than what they are able to verbalize. They can answer factual questions in contextualized situations, but have difficulties explaining the rationale for their answers.

Age Five

Five-year-olds have a vocabulary of about 2,100 words and a working knowledge of the grammar of the language. They may have problems dealing with compound sentences and sentences with embedded meaning. They are beginning to understand time concepts and use verbs accordingly. Most children at this stage have mastered the use of the progressive (-ing), regular past tense (-ed), and plurals (-s). Irregular verbs still constitute a challenge for five-year-olds. They are able to identify and produce specific sounds and blends (combinations of phonemes like in the word, *block*). The vocabulary continues to increase as children have more contact with peers and teachers in school.

Ages Six and Seven

Six- to seven-year-olds have a speaking vocabulary of about 2,100 words and a comprehension vocabulary of more than 20,000 words. Children use well-constructed sentences using all parts of speech. They still might have problems with certain words and structures, but their speech is fluent and clear. However, speakers at this age might still have problems with words containing sounds like /v/, /th/, /ch/, and /sh/. Some children will use the sound of the /w/ in place of the required /r/ and /l/ sounds. They are able to separate words into syllables and begin decoding written language. They are beginning to understand and address questions that call for reasons for an action. For example, they can explain their actions and answer questions such as "Why did you pick number five as the answer?" After age six, children continue to polish their language skills and add new and more sophisticated vocabulary.

Ages Eight to Twelve

The speaking repertoire of eight- to twelve-year-olds continues to grow and improve as their communication needs change from using language to have their needs met, to becoming language makers in academic settings. Eight-year-olds begin using relative pronoun clauses (i.e., The boy *that* you met yesterday is my friend). They also begin to use subordinated clauses that begin with *when, if,* and *because* (i.e., *If* you bother me, I am going to tell the teacher). At age nine, the use of the gerund has become common for speakers of this age (i.e., *Cheating* is bad). Children begin using more complex sentences, vocabulary, and verb construction. Their speech is more coherent through the use of connectors like *first, during, after,* and *finally*. At ages ten through twelve, students are able to make use of roots, prefixes, and suffixes to understand new words in the language. Also, their sentence structure is more complex.

Assessing the Speaking Ability

Intelligibility

A child's speaking ability is generally assessed informally in class as part of daily activities and conversations. First, teachers have to determine if the speech of the child is **intelligible** and can be understood by native speakers with minimum effort. Developmental issues, the use of dialectical variations, and speech disorders can cause communication or intelligibility problems in native speakers. To assess the speech of the child, teachers need an understanding of the developmental patterns in the process of language mastery, and use these patterns as a foundation for assessing a child's performance. Teachers should also develop an understanding of features from dialects spoken in the community to avoid confusion with features that contrast with Standard English. For example, speakers of **Ebonics**, a language variant used by some African-American children, and speakers of the **Boston dialect** drop the /r/ after a vowel. One example of this is in the statement "...park the car in Harvard yard" [Pahk the kah in Hahvud yahd]. In this case, the omission of post-vocalic /r/ cannot be identified as a pronunciation problem. Because of this, teachers need a working knowledge of the dialects used in the community in order to make accurate assessments of the children's speech.

The *International Dialects of English Archive* was founded in 1997 to provide the worldwide community with an opportunity to access samples of language produced by native English speakers all across the United States. One of the resources available in their site includes the archival of online audio samples of the various dialects used by people in all States. This resource can be used by teachers to identify ways in which these dialects may be used in their communities and to allow their students to listen to the various ways in which people in their own communities communicate orally. *http://web.ku.edu/~idea/northamerica/usa*

Language Interference

Teachers have to take into account how the first language of an ELL may interfere in the pronunciation of English. Phonologically, language interference can happen at the word or sentence level. The most noticeable form of language interference happens when students use the phonology of their first language to pronounce words in English. For example, most Spanish dialects do not use the /v/ sound; instead, they replace it with the /b/ sound. This feature creates semantic problems when native Spanish speakers pronounce the English word *vowel* as *bowel*, which can create an embarrassing situation for the speaker. Korean and Japanese speakers might also experience language interference when using the English /r/ sound because this sound is not present in their language. Chinese has both the /r/ and /l/ sounds; however, native Chinese speakers may experience problems with these two sounds when learning English. This is because they have the tendency to substitute the /r/ with the /l/ sound. This feature can create semantic problems when native Chinese, Korean, and Japanese speakers pronounce the English word *rice* as *lice*. A second type of interference can be caused by the application of incorrect **word stress** in English. For example, in Standard English most speakers will place the primary stress of the word *com.po.si.tion* on the second to last syllable, but never on the last syllable. However, Spanish speakers and speakers of Caribbean English might place the primary stress on the last syllable, resulting in nonstandard English pronunciation. Language interference can create communication problems and potentially embarrassing situations for ELLs. Thus, teachers have to become aware of conflicting language sounds and provide appropriate language support to ELLs.

Communication Style and Culture

Culture plays an important role in the way people communicate orally and in written form. In written and oral communication, English uses a linear rhetorical pattern that allows little flexibility to deviate from the topic. Other languages like Spanish, Russian, and Arabic allow for a more flexible progression to convey information. This latter flexibility is identified as a **curvilinear** style, because it allows speakers the option of deviating from the main topic without being penalized. This cultural and linguistic difference can create problems in assessing the speaking capabilities of children who are native speakers of languages other than English. Teachers have to be vigilant to determine how the first language (L1) and culture affect the performance of children in the second language (L2).

Speaking Checklist

Students' speaking abilities can also be assessed in the classroom with a structured checklist identifying specific features that teachers want to observe. Lapp et al. (2001) developed an instrument to assess the speaking ability called The Speaking Checklist. A summary of key elements is presented below.

The Speaking Checklist

1. Sticks to the topic
2. Builds support for the subject
3. Speaks clearly
4. Takes turns and waits to talk
5. Talks so others in the group can hear
6. Speaks smoothly
7. Uses courteous language
8. Presents in an organized and interesting way
9. Supports the topical thesis
10. Answers questions effectively
11. Is comfortable speaking publicly
12. Maintains listeners' interest
13. Volunteers to answer in class

The Texas Education Agency (TEA) has also developed an instrument to comply with the No Child Left Behind (NCLB) state accountability system called the Texas Observation Protocol (TOP). This instrument was designed to assess the language proficiency of ELLs in Texas (TEA, 2006a). This instrument contains a speaking component that assesses the speaking ability based on four levels of language proficiency: Beginning, Intermediate, Advanced, and Advanced High (TEA, 2006b). This instrument is also an observation tool that uses holistic scoring, administered by teachers in the bilingual or ESL classroom. A learner receiving a score that would qualify him/her at the Advanced High proficiency is, generally speaking, required to be reclassified as a fluent English speaker. A description of the Advanced High proficiency follows:

1. Student is able to participate in extended discussion in a variety of social and grade-appropriate academic topics.

2. Student is able to communicate effectively using abstract and concrete content-based vocabulary during classroom instruction.

3. Student is able to use complex English grammar structures and complex sentences at a level comparative to native speakers.

4. Student rarely makes linguistic errors that interfere with overall communication.

5. Student rarely uses pronunciation that interferes with overall communication.

Listening and Speaking

In any given language, meaning is created through socially shared conventions. During the first months of life, babies are active listeners. Long before they can respond orally, however, they communicate nonverbally by waving their arms, smiling, or wiggling. They are also capable of communicating their needs and wants through nonverbal communication, including body language and crying. Through listening, they develop the receptive language needed to begin communicating orally. Although listening is used extensively in communication, it does not receive much attention at school. While there is no well-defined model for teaching listening skills, some theorists link listening skills to reading skills. They feel that reading and listening both make use of similar language comprehension processes.

Listening and reading both require the use of skills in phonology, syntax, semantics, and knowledge of the structure of text, and both language skills seem to be controlled by the same set of cognitive processes. A number of studies suggest that the teaching of listening can be done by engaging in the kinds of activities that have been successful in developing reading, writing, and speaking proficiencies. For example, teachers can guide students' listening activities by setting a purpose for listening, providing questions before and after the listening activity, and encouraging children to forge links between the new information that was just heard and the knowledge already in place. In addition, children need to be coached in the use of appropriate volume and speed when they speak, and in the rules to participate in discussions. Students also need to follow the culturally defined rules for maintaining a polite conversation. In the American culture, such rules include staying on a topic and taking turns without interrupting speakers.

Communication Disorders

A communication disorder occurs when a person's speech interferes with his/her ability to convey messages during interactions with community members. The four classifications of language disorders include disorders in voice, fluency, articulation, and language processing (Piper, 2006).

Voice Disorders

Voice disorders are considered any type of distortion of the pitch, timbre, or volume of spoken communication. There are two types of voice disorders: phonation and resonance. **Phonation** disorder describes any kind of abnormality in the vibration of the vocal fold. For example, *hoarseness* or extreme breathiness can interfere with comprehension. **Resonance** disorder describes abnormalities created when sound passes through the vocal tract. The most typical example of resonance disorder occurs when the sound passing through the nasal cavity changes oral sounds to nasal, which is called *hyper-nasal sounds*. This type of disorder should not be confused with the nasal quality of Southern dialects like the Texas twang.

Fluency Disorders

Fluency disorders refer to any kind of condition that affects the child's ability to produce coherent and fluent communication. *Stuttering* and *cluttering* cause the most common types of fluency disorder. **Stuttering** is characterized by multiple false starts or the inability to produce the intended sounds. **Cluttering** occurs when children try to communicate in an excessively fast mode that makes comprehension difficult. Teachers have to be cautious when assessing ELLs who might experience temporary fluency dysfunction, such as hesitations, false starts, and repetition, which can be attributed to anxiety or confusion with the two languages. For instance, ELLs may stutter because they cannot find or might not know the appropriate word in English. Allowing students to code-switch from English to their first language and providing them more wait time can both be used as temporary remedies to stuttering. Additionally, children new to the language often use the intonation pattern and the speed of delivery of their native language. Thus, the delivery might become incomprehensible and be mistaken as a cluttering.

Articulation Problems

The most common articulation disorder is *lisping*. **Lisping** is a term used when children (or adults) produce the sound /s/, /sh/, /z/, and /ch/ with their tongue between the upper and lower teeth. Some other sounds that can present challenges to children are the /w/, /l/, and /r/ sounds. Children may have problems with specific sounds that can cause unintelligibility and the production of aesthetically displeasing sounds. Some of these problems might be developmental and will eventually be eliminated, while others might require speech therapy. Elmer Fudd and Sylvester the Cat, two popular cartoon characters, are well known for exhibiting these speech features (i.e., Sylvester's lisping and Elmer having difficulties with the /r/ sound like in "wabbit").

Language Processing Disorders

Language processing disorders are generally caused by a brain-based disturbance called aphasia. Three types of aphasia are known: receptive, expressive, and global. **Receptive aphasia**, or "sensory aphasia," results from a lesion to a region in the upper back part of the temporal lobe of the brain. Receptive aphasia creates problems with listening comprehension and retrieval of words from memory. People affected with this condition have the tendency of repeating formulaic phrases and producing unintelligible sequences of words or sounds. **Expressive aphasia** results from damage to the lower back part of the frontal lobe. This damage affects the speaking ability and causes specific problems with articulation and fluency. The speech produced is often very slow including multiple hesitations and problems with the suprasegmental features of language including intonation, rhythm, and stress. The sentences produced are generally very short and contain only the necessary features to convey the message. Their speech resembles the speech of children at the telegraphic stage of first language development. **Global aphasia** is also a brain-based disorder that affects both the receptive and expressive features of language. Children with this kind of severe impairment of articulation and fluency produce minimal speech and their comprehension is very limited. This type of language disorder is also known as "irreversible aphasia," which suggests that little can be done to help children suffering from this condition.

Activities to Promote Oral Communication

The best way to promote oral communication is to guide students into using language in meaningful situations. In classroom situations, teachers can organize activities to resemble real-life situations in order to promote communication among students. Some of these activities are described below.

Dramatic Play

Dramatic play using prompts is an ideal activity to develop communication. In dramatic play, students are given open opportunities to role-play by resembling real-life situations. Students may be given either a specific role to play, or they can improvise roles. For example, one child can play the role of a parent, another the role of a student in trouble, and a third student can play the role of a teacher.

Language Play

Language play involves the use of language in rhyme, alliteration, songs, and repeating patterns to amuse children. Tongue twisters are commonly used to practice pronunciation and language patterns. Through these activities, children acquire language knowledge in a relaxed and fun environment. Teachers can also use nursery rhymes, poems, and stories that contain rhyme to introduce these language features.

Show-and-Tell

In show-and-tell, children bring artifacts and personal items to class. Children show the object and are expected to describe its features to the class. In addition to the obvious benefit of oral communication, this kind of activity can be used to promote both home and cultural pride as well as multicultural awareness in one's classroom.

Puppet Show

Hand puppets, finger puppets, and string puppets can be used to promote communication and confidence among children. Puppet shows allow students to orally communicate using the puppet as a tool to convey information. The use of puppets is also an enjoyable and motivating activity for learners, especially young ones.

Pair Interview

Pair interview is an additional strategy that can be used to promote oral communication. In this strategy, children are paired to learn information from each other and then report their findings to the larger group. Depending on the children's age, the responses gathered during the pair interview can also be recorded in writing to be used later in the children's presentation. This strategy can be used throughout the year and for different classroom activities. The pair interview is also a recommended instructional strategy that can be used for the first day of class when students need to get to know each other.

Presentations

Preparing children to communicate what they think and know is common practice in classrooms. Depending on the children's age, the expectations surrounding the ways in which they share this information orally will vary. For instance, kindergarten teachers should not expect their students to deliver a 20-minute presentation. Instead, giving their students an opportunity to deliver presentations in a nonthreatening environment and activity (e.g., show-and-tell) can lead them to begin appreciating the art of public speaking from a very young age. As children enter elementary school, the expectations change considerably. For instance, elementary students are expected not only to use correct language when speaking, but to have accurate information when creating a presentation. To this end, students are expected to also find reliable information and sources when investigating a topic of interest or one assigned. Elementary students also learn that a topic of a presentation can be delivered to multiple and different audiences. In other words, students will need to be given opportunities to understand how one presentation can be modified to meet the needs of their audience. For example, children can be led to prepare a short presentation to inform other children at their school why recycling is important to the environment, and to ask them to start a recycling project in their classrooms. Then, these same students could be asked to revise their presentation to deliver it to community leaders so that they can receive the resources needed to start recycling projects in their communities. Regardless of the audience, students should be expected to create and deliver presentations in groups and individually.

Key Principles of the Competency

- Teach vocabulary words like preposition of places (under, over, between) to children to allow them to verbalize their position relative to objects, i.e., under the desk…

- Promote the development of listening skills by implementing listening activities as a routine in the daily schedule.

- Role-play using specific historical events to help students understand different points of view. For example, ask students to role-play soldiers from the South and the North during the Civil War.

- Present listening skills for various purposes and provide children with opportunities to engage in listening activities.

- Provide instruction and opportunities for children to evaluate the content and effectiveness of their own spoken messages.

- Select and use appropriate technologies to develop children's oral communication skills.

Competency 002: Phonological and Phonemic Awareness

The teacher understands phonological and phonemic awareness and employs a variety of approaches to help students develop phonological and phonemic awareness.

Importance of Phonological and Phonemic Awareness for Reading and Writing

Phonological and phonemic awareness constitute the foundation for the development of the metalinguistic awareness that children need to become successful language learners and effective readers. **Phonemic awareness** refers to a child's ability to understand that words have smaller components called sounds, and that these sounds together create syllables and words. Phonemic awareness is the basic linguistic principle required to develop an understanding of oral and written communication. Once children understand this principle, they begin discovering more sophisticated linguistic principles like phonological awareness. Children who have developed phonemic awareness are able to dissect a word into each phoneme, and put it back to re-create the word. The ability to manipulate spoken words has been linked to successful reading development.

Phonological Awareness

Phonological awareness is the ability to recognize and manipulate components of the sound system of a language. It includes the ability to segment words into smaller units like syllables and phonemes (sounds). Phonological awareness also encompasses the ability to identify and separate words within a sentence, identify stress in individual words, and identify the intonation pattern used in sentences.

Syllabication

Syllabication is an important component of phonological awareness. It refers to the ability to conceptualize and separate words into their basic pronunciation components, which are syllables. Syllables can be as simple as one vowel, or can be a combination of vowels and consonants. For example, the word *elegant* contains three syllables (el/e/gant), one of which is a vowel alone. Phonemes are the basic unit of a syllable, and syllables constitute the basic units for the pronunciation of the English language. Consequently, syllables influence the rhythm of the language, poetic meter, and word stress. Syllabication can be taught using the appropriate voice intonation in order to indicate the beginning and ending of a syllable. Teachers often use clapping to indicate syllable boundaries.

Phonemic Stress

Phonemic stress can be taught through the use of nursery rhymes, short poems, or stories like the traditional Humpty Dumpty character of Mother Goose nursery rhymes. The use of these rhythmic patterns in an enjoyable and relaxed environment introduces children to the sounds and music of language. Eventually, children will notice the ending of the words and how specific sounds relate to each other. Moreover, rhymes are particularly beneficial to ELLs as they begin to develop not only phonemic awareness and phonemic stress, but they can also learn chunks of language that they can use to participate in classroom conversations and communicate with peers and their teacher in the classroom.

Alliteration

Alliteration is a technique used to emphasize phonemes by using successive words that begin with the same consonant sound or letter. Tongue twisters are the best-known form of alliteration. Children can repeat tongue twisters for fun, and, at the same time, develop an awareness of the sound-symbol correspondence. In the following example, the /p/ sound is emphasized:

Peter **P**iper **p**icked a **p**eck of **p**ickled **p**eppers.

Word Stress

English has at least four levels of word stress but, for practical purposes, we only need to be concerned with the first two: main stress and secondary stress. Word stress can affect the ability to understand words and can also alter meaning. For example, the word *present* can have two meanings depending on how it is pronounced. With the stress on the first syllable (*présent*), it becomes a noun; but if the stress is placed on the last syllable (*presént*), it becomes a verb.

Intonation Patterns

The intonation pattern describes the pitch contour of a phrase or a sentence that is used to change the meaning of the sentence. In English, there are utterances that might appear to be identical but convey a different meaning. In the question below, the rising point at the verb *are* makes the utterance a question, while a slight change of intonation to the pronoun *you* changes the utterance to a reply to the question.

Question: How **are** you?

Reply: How are **you**?

Special Considerations when Teaching Phonemic and Phonological Awareness

- It is easier to break sentences into words, and break words into syllables than to break syllables into phonemes.

- Use a whole-to-the-parts approach to teach phonological awareness. Guide children to segment short sentences into words, and segment words into syllables first. Then, guide children to segment syllables into individual phonemes. Finally, reverse the process to re-create the word and eventually the whole sentence.

- Begin teaching phonemic awareness using short monosyllabic words. Introduce words with a consistent word structure like consonant-vowel-consonant, i.e., *bat* and *cat*, before introducing more difficult ones.

- Begin segmenting short words into phonemes. Once children understand this component of phonemic awareness, introduce syllabication.

- Teachers should introduce sounds in initial position, then sounds in final position, and finally (the most difficult ones) the phonemes in medial position.

- Teachers should introduce phoneme awareness first with simpler concepts like rhyming and initial phoneme identification, and then introduce blending and segmenting words into syllables.

- When teaching sound-symbol correspondence, introduce sounds that present the least chance for distortion. Sounds like the nasal /m/ and sibilant /s/ represent easier sounds for the child than the brief sounds created with stop sounds like /p/, /t/, and /k/.

Teaching Phonemic and Phonological Awareness

Teachers can promote phonemic and phonological knowledge through a variety of strategies. A list of these strategies follows:

- Teach the child to isolate phonemes. To follow a pattern from the simplest to the most difficult, begin with initial and final sounds first, and then add phonemes in the middle. Ask questions such as "What is the first sound of the word *boy*?"

- Guide children to blend sounds and come up with rhymes. Ask the child, "What word can you create when you blend the sounds *l* and *ake,* or *t* and *ake*."

- Introduce blending by guiding children to identify the word created when the following sounds are blended: /b/, /a/, and /t/.

- Guide children to identify a word like *tape* and then remove the onset and ask the child: "What word is left when we remove the first sound, *t*?" (Answer: *ape*.) Then ask students, "Is this a word?"

- Teach word segmentation by saying a word, and then guiding children to identify the sounds that they hear. Teachers can begin with simple monosyllabic words like *car* and then expand to more sophisticated words.

- Use onsets and rimes to teach the sound-symbol relationship. Guide children to create new words by substituting the first letter of monosyllabic words. For example, using the word *ring*, the child can replace the initial sounds to create additional words *sing*, *king*, and *spring*. An activity like this can emphasize phonemic awareness and also teach how word families can support vocabulary development.

- Teachers should lead children to segment or separate the sounds in words. Begin with words with consistent sound-symbol correspondence, like *bag* and *lag*, and later expand to words that contain clusters/blends as in the word *splash* and diagraphs as in the word *church*.

- Introduce minimal pairs, which are sets of words that differ in only one phoneme like *pail* and *bail*, to guide students to notice the difference. Teachers should pronounce both words and ask students if the words are the same or different. Initially, contrast words with initial consonant sounds as in *pat* and *bat*, and later expand to include more sophisticated contrasting pairs as in *bit* and *beet*.

- Say words and guide children to identify the number of sounds that they hear. Initially, avoid "stop" sounds because children might have difficulties perceiving the brief sound represented by these sounds.

- Guide children to recite nursery rhymes or children's songs and then guide them to repeat the rhyme or song, changing the initial word. For example, a simple Mother Goose rhyme like "Go to bed, Tom!" can be used to replace the parts of the rhyme. For example, students can repeat "Go to bed, Tom! Tired or not, Tom, Go to bed, Tom" (Anderson 2005). Students can then replace *Tom* with other names. Students can also replace the initial sound of each line to create standard and non-standard words. For example, guide children to substitute the initial sound of each major word to see how it sounds and to determine if the change created a word that they can recognize, i.e., So to Sed, Som, So to Sed, Som. In addition to teaching the phoneme system, children are guided to understand how phonemes can alter meaning.

Balanced Reading Program

The development of phonemic and phonological awareness is important for preparing students for formal reading instruction. However, a strong reading program must go beyond these components to incorporate a balanced reading program. The concept of a balanced reading program emerged as a result of the work of Catherine Snow, Susan Burns, and Peg Griffin (1998). The balanced reading program encompasses best teaching practices from two traditionally opposing reading instruction programs: the skills-based approach, which emphasizes phonics instruction, and the meaning-based approach, which promotes reading comprehension and enrichment. The researchers concluded that a balanced reading program, one that incorporates the best principles of phonics (skills-based) and whole language (meaning-based) instruction, can best address the reading needs of all children.

Key Principles of the Competency

- Helping students develop phonological and phonemic awareness must be a priority for teachers working with emerging readers.

- Teachers should plan instruction and adjust their teaching to meet the learning needs of all children.

- Using a variety of instructional approaches can best address the reading needs of all of the students in a class.

Competency 003: Alphabetic Principle

The teacher understands the importance of the alphabetic principle for reading English and provides instruction that helps students understand the relationship between spoken language and printed words.

The **alphabetic principle** has been described as the ability to connect letters with sounds, and to create words based on these associations. Children learning to read also must develop an understanding that letters and letter patterns represent the sounds of spoken English (TEA, 2002). Understanding the ways in which these sound-symbol relationships are created allows them to conceptualize that there are predictable connections between phonemes and graphemes.

How Is the Alphabetic Principle Learned?

Traditionally, children go through specific stages in the process of learning new words and mastering the alphabetic principle (Ehri, 1998). Preschoolers are exposed to components of the alphabetic principle through their environment. They can identify the logo of stores like Wal-Mart or Burger King by their design instead of by the specific letters contained in the logo. But because they are not connecting the letters and the sounds of the logo, this stage is generally considered a **pre-alphabetic phase** (U.S. Dept. of Education 2006). At home, children might also get exposed to the alphabet song, which most of them learn in a subconscious manner. Eventually, children engage in a **partial alphabetic phase** as they get exposed to alphabet block playing and concrete letter objects that are typical in early childhood programs. They begin connecting the shape of the letters with the sound that they represent. Children are also often exposed to children's literature and books in which the sound-symbol correspondence is carefully controlled. Children also begin connecting initial letter with the sound of the names of peers, like the **N** of Nancy and **A** of Alex.

A third phase of learning new words is identified as the **full alphabetic stage**. At this stage, children begin making connections between the letters, the sounds that they represent, and the actual meaning of the word. Children get very excited during this stage because they are beginning to "crack" the written code of the language. In the fourth and last stage of development, called the **consolidated alphabetic stage**, children begin conceptualizing that they can use components of words that they know to decode new words. They begin discovering how they can create new words with the use of onsets, rhymes, and other letter sequences. One of the main purposes of phonics instruction at this stage is to guide children into understanding the connection between the grapheme and phoneme and the sequence that they create to form words and sentences. This knowledge allows students the opportunity to expand the number of words that they recognize instantly (sight words), which prepares them for literacy.

Teaching the Grapheme-Phoneme Correspondence

The introduction of the grapheme-phoneme correspondence can be presented through games, songs, and other engaging activities; but eventually, the correspondence should be presented explicitly. Teachers have to bring the skills to the surface level and make students aware of the concepts and skills that they need to learn in order to become effective readers. Teachers should take into account the complexity of the language and the maturity level of the children when introducing children to the alphabetic principle. A list of considerations and strategies for teaching the grapheme-phoneme connection follows.

- The introduction of the letter-sound correspondence should be guided by the potential support of the children's efforts to become readers. That is, introduce the spelling of the letters that the child is most likely to encounter in text. For example the letters *m*, *a*, *t*, *s*, *p*, and *h* are used more frequently in writing than letters like *x*, *q*, or consonant diagraphs like *ght* or *gn*.

- It is also important to begin instruction in the grapho-phonemic relationship using sounds that present the least possible distortion or confusion with other sounds. Some of the sounds that are easier to perceive are the nasals /m/, /n/, the fricatives /f/, the sibilant /s/, and the English retroflex /r/.

- Teachers should postpone the introduction of less clear phonemes like the nasal /ng/, the distinction between the sibilants /s/ and /z/, the troublesome sounds in English like the voiced *th* in the word *them*, and the voiceless counterpart in words like *think*.

- Introduce words with one or two consonants and one short vowel sound such as in the words *on* and *car*. Later, long vowel sounds can be introduced.

- Next, add consonant blends like *try*, followed by digraphs like *th*, *sh*, and *ch* in words like *thanks*, *show*, and *chop*. Digraphs can lead students to recognize common words such as *this*, *she*, and *chair*. Introduce single consonants and consonant blends or clusters in separate lessons to avoid confusion.

- Avoid voiceless-stop sounds (/t/, /p/, /k/) at the beginning or middle of words because the short duration of these phonemes makes them difficult to perceive. Teachers should postpone the introduction of conflicting letter-sound correspondence of phonemes like the /b/ and /v/ or /i/ and /e/, or visually confusing graphemes like the *b* and *d* or *p* and *g*.

Types of Writing Systems

Several classifications exist for writing systems. Three of the most commonly known writing systems are pictographic, syllabic, and alphabetic writing. In a **pictographic writing system**, words, ideas, and concepts are represented with a visual or image. Pictographic writing was the first type of written language developed in the history of civilizations. In **syllabic writing systems**, syllables are depicted through the use of unique symbols. The **alphabetic writing system** uses the sounds of the language as a basic unit for writing. English uses an alphabetic writing system that is based upon phonetic signs. Theoretically, each symbol represents one unit of sound in this system. However, this principle works better with languages with consistent sound-symbol relationships. Many alphabetic languages like Spanish are more phonetically consistent than English. An analysis of the grapheme-phoneme correspondence of English follows.

The Grapheme-Phoneme Correspondence of English

The connection between graphemes and phonemes in English is not always consistent. English has 26 graphemes to represent 44 phonemes. The consonant system is more consistent than the vowel system. English has five letters to represent 12 vowel sounds, which makes decoding and pronunciation more challenging. This inconsistency is partially caused by the evolution of the English language and the influence of multiple languages in the development of modern English. Teachers need to be proactive by identifying these troublesome areas and organizing instruction to address these issues. Some of the potential areas of concern are explained below:

- Graphemes can represent multiple phonemes. For example, the grapheme *s* can represent multiple phonemes: car**s**-/**z**/, call**s**-/**z**/, sugar-/**sh**/, mi**ss**ion-/**sh**/, and walk**s**-/**s**/. This grapheme-phoneme inconsistency represents a challenge when attempting to use a phonic approach to teach reading.

- English has graphemes that represent a sound in some words and remain silent in other words. For example, the graphemes **s** and **l** become silent in the following examples without giving readers a reliable clue for this change: *island*, *calm*, and *palm*. (Some speakers will make an attempt to pronounce the /s/ and /l/ in these words.)

- English has multiple consonant diagraphs, which are two or more letters representing one sound. These consonant diagraphs are voiceless. This inconsistency presents a challenge to native English speakers as well as ELLs.

Table1-2 Consonant Diagraphs

Diagraphs	Examples
ch-	chair
gh-	ghost
gn-	gnat
kn-	know
-ght	thought
pn-	pneumonia
ps-	psychology
rh-	rhythm
wr-	write
sc-	scene

- English speakers use multiple contractions in daily communication. These can create listening comprehension problems for students and especially for ELLs. Teachers should introduce contractions together with the long version of the words to avoid confusion. Table 1-3 presents a few examples of the type of confusion that contractions can cause.

Table1-3 Contractions in English

Contractions	Regular Form	Possible Confusion
they're	they are	there and their
he's	he is	his
he'll	he will	hill, heel, heal
you're	you are	your

- English has multiple initial consonant clusters, which require students to be able to blend the sounds and at the same time recognize the sounds of individual phonemes. These sounds also represent a challenge for native Spanish speakers because Spanish does not have words that begin with particular letter sequences that exist in English. These types of clusters occur in medial positions and they are always preceded by the vowel *e*, such as in the words *espero*, *escapar*, and *estar*. Based on this feature, Latino children will place an e in front of English words containing the following clusters: *sp* (as in speak), *sc* (school), *st* (street), *spr* (spring), *scr* (scream), *str* (stream), *sm* (small), *sn* (snow), and *sl* (slate).

- Several words in English end in consonant clusters (e.g., *rant*, *cord*, *first*, and *card*). Both young native English-speaking children and ELLs may have difficulties blending clusters at the end of the words. For native Spanish speakers, these clusters represent a unique challenge because Spanish does not have words that end in consonant clusters. Based on this feature, Spanish-speaking children, and possibly most children in early childhood, may tend to simplify a final consonant cluster in English. For example, the word *board* might become *boar*.

Key Principles of the Competency

- Recognize that there will always be variation in students' alphabetic skills development, so plan accordingly.

- Take into consideration that not all languages are alphabetic and that some of your students may struggle when being asked to write in a way that is different from that which they are accustomed.

- The use of both formal and informal assessment tools and instruments can provide a more complete picture of a child's development than the use of only one type of tool.

Competency 004: Literacy Development and Practice

The teacher understands that literacy develops over time, progressing from emergent to proficient stages, and uses a variety of approaches to support the development of students' literacy.

Literacy development generally begins at home when parents read stories and create literacy opportunities for their children (Heath, 1983). Through such activities, they are helping their children to hear the similarities and differences in the sounds of words. As a result of linguistic stimulation, children begin to manipulate and understand sounds in spoken language, and eventually will practice this understanding by making up rhymes and new words on their own. When children are able to follow the written text together with the oral production, they begin to learn the names of the letters and the different sounds that each letter represents. Finally, children link the letters of the alphabet with the sounds of the words they speak. At this point children begin developing the phonemic and phonological awareness needed to become emergent readers.

Stages of Reading Development

A vast amount of research has been conducted on the stages of reading development. Three widely used labels for these stages include emergent readers, early readers, and fluent readers. It is important to note that researchers have concluded that these stages are considered to be cumulative (Chall 1983); that is, children need to develop the skills and knowledge in each of these stages to be later used in subsequent ones.

Emergent Readers

Emergent readers understand that print contains meaningful information. They imitate the reading process and display basic reading readiness skills like directionality movement (i.e., eye movement from top to bottom and from left to right). Emergent readers can participate in shared reading activities and are able to follow and match words with their pronunciation when teachers point to the words as they are read. Additionally, children at this stage:

- Use illustrations embedded in the texts to support comprehension.
- Listen and follow a story attentively and can easily develop an awareness of the story structure.

- Represent the main idea of a story through drawings and can retell major events in the story with or without illustrations.

- Use illustrations and prior experiences to make predictions and to support comprehension.

- Possess some degree of phonemic awareness.

- Are able to connect the initial letter of words with its representing phoneme.

Early Readers

Early readers have mastered reading readiness skills and are beginning to read simple text with some degree of success. They are also developing an internal list of high frequency words in print. Their reliance on picture clues has decreased now that they can get more information from print. Children at this stage also:

- Begin using the cuing system to confirm information in the text.

- Rely on grapho-phonemic information to sound out words as a decoding strategy.

- Show preference for certain stories.

- Begin noticing features from language and text like punctuation and capitalization, as well as the use of bold print and variation in format.

- Retell stories read to them with detail and accuracy.

- Engage in discussion of stories read and identify the main idea and story characters.

- Engage in self-correction when text does not make sense to them.

Newly Fluent Readers

Newly fluent readers can read with relative fluency and comprehension. They are able to use several cuing systems to obtain meaning from print (i.e., semantic, structural, visual, and grapho-phonemic cuing systems). They self-monitor their reading, and can identify and correct simple errors with minimum external support. They ask clarification questions to develop an understanding of the content. Newly fluent readers can also:

- Summarize the part of the story that they have read, and make inferences about the content.

- Handle more challenging vocabulary through the use of context clues.

- Begin using literary terms and grammar concepts.

- Enjoy reading from a variety of genres for information and for pleasure.

- Children at this stage are not totally independent readers but with practice and support from teachers, they soon become fluent and independent readers.

Literacy Development in School

As children enter school, formal reading instruction begins. How children should be taught to read is a subject that stirs up intense debate. Basically, it comes down to a discussion about starting points, and how to proceed with instruction. The two most common approaches used to teach reading in public schools are the skills-based approach, and the meaning-based approach. The skills-based approach is also called the bottom-up approach and the meaning-based is also known as the top-down approach.

Bottom-Up Approach (Skills-Based)

The **bottom-up approach** (Gough, 1972) proceeds from the specific to the general, or from the parts to the whole. This approach begins with phonemes and graphemes, and continues by expanding to the syllable, words, sentences, paragraphs, and then whole reading selections. The best representation of this approach is phonics instruction. **Phonics** is a method of teaching beginners to read and pronounce words by teaching them the phonetic value of letters, letter groups, and syllables. Because English has an alphabetic writing system, an understanding of the letter-sound relationship may prove helpful to the beginning reader. However, this view of reading instruction is that these relationships should be taught in isolation, in a highly sequenced manner, followed by reading words that represent the regularities of English in print. The children are asked to read decodable texts by sounding out words. Typically, this approach uses reading programs that offer stories with controlled vocabulary that are made up of letter-sound relationships and words with which children are already familiar. Thus, children might be asked to read a passage such as:

> The cat sat on a mat.
> The cat saw the rat in the pan.
> The rat saw the cat.
> The rat and the cat ran and ran.

Writing instruction follows in the same way. Children are asked to write decodable words, and fill in the blanks with decodable words in sentences in workbooks. This is based on the assumption that once the children progress past this initial reading instruction time frame, meaning will follow. Phonics instruction was widely used in the late 1960s and 1970s. Phonics is still being promoted today. The flaw in this kind of instruction is that many English words, including the highest frequency words, are not phonetically regular. Also, comprehension of text can be limited in phonics, because there is not a great deal to comprehend in texts such as "pig did a gig." Modern approaches to phonics instruction have made the stories more enjoyable and interesting. For example, the *Progressive Phonics Book* series, which is available through the Genki English Web site, uses computer sound technology, visuals, and more involving stories to engage the reader. The following is an example of this approach.

Don't Scowl at My Vowel

> I don't mind it if my dog
> Tries to **pat** me with his **paw**
> But I don't like it if my **cat**
> Tries to scratch me with her **claw**.

The assumption is that textual meaning will become apparent in time. Furthermore, it must be stressed that teaching phonics is not the same as teaching reading. Also, reading and spelling require much more than just phonics; spelling strategies and word-analysis skills are equally important. Nor does asking children to memorize phonics rules ensure application of those rules, and, even if that were true, the word the child is attempting to decode is frequently an exception to the stated rule. Teaching children to use phonics is different from teaching them about phonics. In summary, the skills-based approach begins reading instruction with a study of single letters, letter sounds, blends and digraphs, blends and digraph sounds, and vowels and vowel sounds in isolation, and in a highly sequenced manner. The children read and write decodable words, with a great emphasis on reading each word accurately, as opposed to reading to comprehend the text as a whole.

The Genki English Web site provides examples of strategies to use for phonics instruction. This site also provides free use of games, songs, and stories. The Genki English Web site can be accessed at *www. genkienglish.net/phonics.htm.*

Top-Down Approach (Meaning-Based)

Another approach to promoting literacy is the **top-down approach**. This approach begins with the whole and then proceeds to its individual parts. That is, the top-down approach begins with whole stories, paragraphs, sentences, words and then proceeds to the smallest units of syllables, graphemes, and phonemes. The approach that best represents this view is the **Whole Language Approach**. The Whole Language Approach grew out of the work of Dr. Kenneth Goodman, who was a leader in the development of the psycholinguistic perspective. This approach suggests that to derive meaning from text, readers rely more on the structure and meaning of language than on the graphic information from the text. Dr. Goodman and other researchers demonstrated that literacy development parallels language development. One of Dr. Goodman's contributions to the field was a process called **miscue analysis**, which is a process that begins with a child reading a selection orally, and an examiner noting variations of the oral reading from the printed text. Each variation from the text is called a miscue and is analyzed for type of variation. Previously, teacher candidates were urged to read and reread texts with young children until the child could read every word in the text perfectly. Goodman suggested, however, that only miscues that altered meaning needed to be corrected, while other, unimportant miscues could be ignored.

The Whole Language Approach stands in sharp contrast to the emphasis on phonics that is promoted in the skills-based approach to reading. The meaning-based approach to reading emphasizes comprehension and meaning in texts. Children focus on the wholeness of words, sentences, paragraphs, and entire books, and seek meaning through context. Whole-language advocates stress the importance of reading high-quality children's literature and extending the meaning of the literature through conversation, projects, and writing. Instead of fill-in-the-blank workbooks, children are encouraged to write journals, letters, and lists, and to participate in writing workshops. Word recognition skills, including phonics, are taught in the context of reading and writing, and are taught as those things relate to the text in hand. Children are taught the four cueing systems, and are taught to ask themselves, "Does it look right? Does it sound right? Does it make sense?" Children are taught that people read books to make meaning. Thus, the focus of this approach is on both comprehension and making connections.

Balanced Reading Program

Today, many classrooms are places where young children enjoy learning to read and write in a balanced reading instructional program. Research into best practices strongly suggests that the teaching of reading requires solid skill instruction, including several techniques for decoding unknown words. These techniques include but are not limited to, phonics instruction embedded in interesting and engaging reading and writing experiences with whole and **authentic literature-based** texts to facilitate the construction of meaning. In other words, this approach to instruction combines the best skill instruction and the whole language approach in order to teach both skills and meaning as well as to meet the reading needs of individual children. Some of the reading strategies used in a balanced literacy program include:

- Teacher directed/reading to students (read aloud)

- Shared reading, guided reading, and reading workshops

- Student-directed reading and independent reading

- Teacher directed writing, writing to/for students as part of the classroom routines, and process writing

- Shared writing as in language experience/interactive writing, writing workshops

- Student-directed writing and independent writing activities

Children's Literature

Genre is a particular type of literature that can be classified in multiple categories. Some of the most common genres used in elementary schools are science fiction, biography, and traditional literature, which encompasses folktales, fables, myths, epics, and legends. Classifications of genre are largely arbitrary and are based on conventions that apply a basic category to an author's writing. Classifications give the reader a general expectation of what sort of book is being chosen. Teachers today are expected to share a wide range of texts with children. The most common type of books for young children is picture books. **Picture books** are books in which the illustrations and the text work together to communicate the story. It is a very good idea to share picture books with children in several different formats. Sometimes, teachers simply read the book to the child without showing any of the pictures. The story is then discussed, and the children are asked if they would like the book to be reread, this time with the pictures being shared. Typically, this technique sparks a lively conversation about why the book with its illustrations is better than hearing the words alone.

Traditional literature comprises the stories that have their roots in the oral tradition of storytelling and have been handed down from generation to generation. This genre also includes the modern versions of these old stories. Teachers can read and share multiple versions of old stories, and then compare and contrast each version. It is also interesting to read a number of folktales and keep track of the elements that these old stories have in common and to guide children towards noticing where these old stories show up in their day-to-day lives. Children enjoy sharing what they notice. Some examples of folk literature are:

- Animal tales in which the characters are animals exhibiting human characteristics, e.g., *Anansi the Spider*.

- Fables in which the main characters are also animals and these present a moral, e.g., *The Tortoise and the Hare*.

- *The Pourquois Tales* comprise stories from around the world that explain how things were created.

- Every culture may have a different version of the way things were created, e.g., *How the Sea Was Created* and *The Legend of the Bluebonnet*.

- Wonder tales describe stories of enchantment in faraway lands. Traditionally, it presents the themes of good vs. evil, e.g., *Snow White*.

- Noodle head tales are stories of lovable fools. These stories include individuals that are not very bright, but manage to survive and often succeed, e.g., *Puss in Boots*.

- Cumulative tales represent stories in which the information is presented in a sequence and all the events in the sequence are repeated, e.g., *The Gingerbread Man* and *The Three Little Pigs*.

- Tall tales describe the story of legendary people or fictitious characters that manage to accomplish great things in life, e.g., *Paul Bunyan*, *John Henry*, and *Pecos Bill*.

- Ghost stories have traditionally been used to regulate the behavior of children. For example, the "Boogie Man" has been used in multiple cultures to scare children and encourage them to behave properly. In the Mexican culture, the "Boogie Man" is called "El Cucuy"; in the Puerto Rican culture, "El Cuco" or "El Coco."

Multicultural literature is a term used to describe literature other than traditional European stories. Traditionally, these are stories from countries throughout the world that are written by people from those countries. Original works of people from other countries are regularly used in American public schools. The term **authentic multicultural** has been used to describe literature written by members of a particular cultural group to represent their own historical development and culture. Some examples of literature that reflect the Latino experience are *The Gold Coin* by Alma Flor Ada, *Chato's Kitchen* by Gary Soto, *Hairs-Pelitos* by Sandra Cisneros, *Friends from the Other Side* by Gloria Anzaldua, *When I Was Puerto Rican* by Esmeralda Santiago, and *Tomas and the Library Lady* by Pat Mora.

Modern fantasy is a genre that presents make-believe stories that are the product of the author's imagination. Often, they are so beyond the realm of everyday life that the stories can't possibly be true. Extraordinary events take place within the covers of these books. Fantasy allows a child to move beyond the normal life in the classroom and speculate about a life that never was, and may never be. Fantasy is a genre that typically sparks intense discussions and provides ample opportunities to illuminate the author's craft for the child. The popular *Harry Potter* series by J. K. Rowling is a perfect example of both the genre and the debate generated by this type of fiction.

Historical fiction is fiction that is set in the past. This type of fiction allows children to live vicariously in times and places they cannot experience in any other way. This type of fiction often has real people and real events depicted, with fiction laced around them. Historical fiction informs the study of social studies. Examples include *Don't You Know There's a War On?* by James Stevenson (WWII), *Klara's New World* by Jeanette Winter (Swedish immigrant family), *A Horse Called Starfire* by Betty Boegehold (Native Americans' first encounter with the horse), and *Wagon Wheels* by Barbara Brenner (an African-American boy and family in 1870 Kansas).

Nonfiction books have the real world as their point of origin. These books help to expand the knowledge of children when they are studying a topic; however, these books need to be evaluated for accuracy, authenticity, and inclusion of the salient facts.

Nonfiction books can be used to support the teaching of content and to promote higher-level comprehension skills.

Biography is a genre that deals with the lives of real people. Autobiography is a genre that deals with the life of the author. These books invigorate the study of social studies because, through careful research, they often include information that transforms a name in a textbook into a person that one may like to get to know better.

Poetry is a genre that is difficult to define for children, except as "not prose." Poetry is the use of words to capture something: a sight, a feeling, or perhaps a sound. Poetry needs to be chosen carefully for a child, as poetry ought to elicit a response from the child—one that connects with the experience of the poem. All children need poetry in their lives. Poetry should be celebrated and enjoyed as part of the classroom experience, and a literacy-rich classroom will always include a collection of poetry to read, reread, savor, and enjoy. *The Owl and the Pussycat* by Edward Lear, Mother Goose rhymes, limericks, and haiku are all poems or types of poems that appeal to young children.

In summary, today there is an overwhelming variety of children's literature from which to choose. When selecting books for use in a classroom, a teacher has a number of issues to consider: Are the facts presented in the book accurate? Is the book aesthetically pleasing? Is the book engaging? Bear in mind that all children deserve to see positive images of children like themselves in the books they read, as illustrations can have a powerful influence on their perceptions of the world. Children also need to see positive images of children who are not like themselves, as who is or is not depicted in books can have a powerful influence on children's perception of the world. Teachers ought to provide children with literature that depicts an affirming, multicultural view, and the selection of books available should show many different kinds of protagonists. Both boys and girls, for example, should be depicted as able and strong.

To teach all components of all of the genres, teacher candidates should become aware of the terminology to analyze stories. They should also guide children to use the appropriate terms to describe different types of literature. This author taught elementary school after teaching for several years in high school and college, and quickly found that the term *fiction* was a foreign word for third graders. This author soon found out the magic word to refer to fiction for third graders was *make-believe*. Thus, teachers can introduce most of the terminology to study literature by using words to which students can relate. Once students understand the concept, teachers can introduce standard terminology to describe literature. Some of the concepts and terminology to describe literature follow:

- Information about the story including the author and illustrators, the publishing company, and even the International Standard Book Number (ISBN)

- Terminology to describe the characters of the story (the protagonist, the antagonist or villain, animals, humans)

- For older students, introduce the point of view of the author. A story's point of view can be first person (the author is one of the characters of the story and the narrator), the omniscient point of view (the narrator is an outsider who knows what the characters are thinking or feeling), or the limited point of view, or subjective consciousness (the narrator is not a character in the story). In the limited point of view, the narrator guides readers to see the story from a point of view of one of the characters.

- The narrator also conveys information that might seem unnatural coming from a character in the story.

- The setting refers to the geographical location and the general environment and historical circumstances of the story.

- The plot tells us what happens and the theme tells us why it happens. Some examples of themes are: problems of growing up and maturing, linguistic and cultural adjustment, love and friendship, family issues, and achieving one's identity.

- Literary style, which includes descriptions of the following:

  — Exposition: It is usually used to introduce the background information and to understand or introduce characters

  — Dialogue: Communication among the characters

  — Vocabulary: Word choice, use of concrete vs. abstract terminology (i.e., Is the vocabulary appropriate for the intended audience?)

  — Imagery: The use of words to create sensory impressions. It conveys sights, sounds, textures, smells, and tastes. Imagery includes the collection of images used to create an emotional response in the reader.

— Tone: The author's mood and manner of expression. It might be humorous, serious, satirical, passionate, sensitive, childlike, zealous, indifferent, poignant, or warm.

— Analysis of the story. It might be multicultural or traditional, or include possible stereotypes, sexism, religious issues, controversial elements, or words or ideas that might create controversy.

Key Principles of the Competency

- When students draw pictures and use invented spellings to write about them, we say that the child has developed the idea that print carries meaning.

- Discuss folktales from around the world and guide students to discuss common features and unique features (oral activities).

- When assessing the literal comprehension of students in the emergent stage of reading development, provide students with visual aids and ask them to explain what happened in the story.

- The invented spelling of emergent readers can be used to determine their ability to apply phonic skills.

- To teach the connection between spoken and written words to emergent readers, the teacher should use a big book and point to each word as she/he reads the story aloud.

- Use a story tree or story map containing parts of the story to teach critical analysis of literature. A story map contains the following parts:

  — Setting—Is it a real place or imaginary? Is the place important to the story line? Does the story take place in the past, present, or future?

  — Characters—Who is the principal character? Who are the good and bad characters?

  — Are the characters real or fictitious?

  — Plot—What is the main problem? What caused the problem?

  — Resolution—How did the story end? How did the problems get solved?

- To apply meta-cognitive skills and to enhance their comprehension, students should ask additional questions about the content and the story as a whole.

Fostering the Home-School Connection

Teacher candidates need to understand the impact that fostering the home-school connection can have on student learning. Teachers also must be aware that developing connections between home and school can positively impact the long-term achievement of the students in their classroom (Heath, 1983). Working with families and other professionals to promote student learning is therefore key when attempting to meet the needs of all students.

Ethnographic research conducted by Shirley Brice Heath demonstrated that home literacy and the expectations surrounding literacy opportunities and events can vary and differ from those provided at school (Heath, 1983). Teacher candidates must therefore work closely with parents to identify commonalities and differences in literacy practices, and build on both of these to establish a stronger home-school connection. When the experiences of parents and families are taken into account in the teaching and learning process, students and their families feel valued and welcome. Likewise, whenever parents can see that the child's literacy learning experiences at home are considered in school (e.g., when a child writes a poem about their family and this is shared in a poetry reading in class), these reinforce their work as "primary teachers." Many strategies exist to develop the home-school connection. Some of these include:

- Making parents and families feel welcome in your classroom and school by having an open door policy, whenever possible.

- Selecting reading (e.g., short stories) and display materials (e.g., banners) where the students and their families can see themselves portrayed in them allows them to feel that their cultural, linguistic, and ethnic background are all seen as resources in one's teaching.

- Creating a home-school journal in which the teacher and the families can share thoughts surrounding the child's development and progress in the classroom. The journal could be used as a formative assessment tool to have parents track their child's progress throughout the year.

- Display signs in an assigned area in your classroom in languages other than English (e.g., mural).

- Giving parents and families an opportunity to share their personal, cultural, and linguistic experiences in the classroom. Use these shared experiences not to simply give a "cultural diversity" focus in your classroom or lessons from time to time, but use them consistently to guide your practice.

- Providing parents with flexible meeting times to accommodate the parents' and families' schedules.

Teacher candidates must also ensure that parents and families see value in establishing such connections and the impact that their assistance is having on their child's learning. For instance, teachers should explain to parents that whenever they point to objects and labels in the grocery store, this simple activity could allow young children to begin developing the foundation for reading. As children grow older, teachers can provide parents with additional authentic tasks that can be used to integrate literacy with other content areas. Take for instance a unit on saving money. To complement the lesson, the teacher asks the parents to have the children make a grocery list. After writing the list, the child's task is to record the prices of the products they need to buy at the store. The latter will be an activity that will require both child and parent collaboration. Days after, the child will bring the grocery list to school and discuss ways in which their family can save in everyday items purchased at their home while reinforcing the skills taught in school.

Competency 005: Word Analysis and Decoding

The teacher understands the importance of word identification (including decoding, blending, structural analysis, sight word vocabulary, and contextual analysis) and provides many opportunities for students to practice and improve word identification skills.

Word analysis refers to the way that children approach a written word in order to decode and obtain meaning from it. Vocabulary building is a skill that needs to be practiced daily in the classroom. One of the goals of this is to assist children in becoming skillful in rapid word recognition. Research suggests that fluent word identification needs to be accomplished before a child can readily comprehend text. If a child needs to painstakingly analyze many words in a text, the memory and attention needed for comprehension are absorbed by word analysis, and the pleasure in a good story is lost. Typically, children who are beginning readers decode each word as they read it. Through repeated exposure to the same words, instant-recognition vocabulary grows. It is particularly important that developing readers learn to recognize those words that occur very frequently in print. These words are called sight words.

Dolch Words

In 1948, Edward W. Dolch identified 220 of the most frequently used words in the English language. He believed that if children were exposed to these words and learned to recognize them as sight words, they would become fluent readers. Some examples of Dolch words are *a, an, am, at, can, had, has, ran, the, after, but, got,* and *away*. The introduction of these sight words can expedite the decoding process and develop fluency among early readers.

Decoding Clues

In addition to working on placing sight words into readily available memory, there is sound research suggesting that students can use **context clues** to help identify unknown words. This body of research further suggests that instruction can help improve students' use of context clues. There are three main kinds of context clues: **semantic, syntactic, and structural**.

Semantic Clues

Semantic clues require a child to think about the meanings of words and what is already known about the topic being read. For example, when reading a story about hawks, teachers can help children to activate prior knowledge about the bird, and to develop an expectation that the selection may contain words associated with hawks, such as *predator, carnivorous, food chain*, and *wingspan*. This discussion might help a child gain a sense of what might be reasonable in a sentence. For ELLs who might not be familiar with the hawk, teachers need to identify equivalent species from their geographical area.

Syntactic Clues

The word order in a sentence might also provide clues to readers. For example, in the sentence, "Hawks are _____," the order of the words in the sentence indicates that the missing word must be an adjective. This open-ended sentence can lead students to words such as *carnivorous, predators,* or other descriptors for the bird. Furthermore, the illustrations in the book can often help with the identification of a word. A picture of a hawk eating prey can lead students to the words *predator* or *carnivorous*. Still, context clues are often not specific enough to allow students to predict the exact word. However, when context clues are combined with other clues such as phonics and structural clues, accurate word identification is usually possible.

Structural Clues

Another strategy to provide clues to readers is to pay attention to letter groups because there are many groups of letters that frequently occur within words, which are called morphemes. These specific clusters of letters can be taught. Common **derivational morphemes** in the form of prefixes, suffixes, and **inflectional endings** should be pointed out to students. An analysis of derivational and inflectional endings follows.

Most of the **derivational morphemes** come from foreign languages like Greek and Latin, and they represent relatively consistent meanings. For example, the meaning of the prefixes *pre, anti,* and *sub* is very consistent in English and in other languages; namely pre = before, anti = against, and sub = under. A large number of English prefixes are common to multiple Western languages such as Spanish, French, and German. See Table 1.4 for examples in English and Spanish. Derivational morphemes can change the syntactic classification of the word. That is, by adding a morpheme to a word, it can be changed from a verb to a noun or from an adjective to an adverb. Children who are guided to recognize derivational morphemes will have a definite advantage when decoding words.

Table 1-4 Examples of Common Prefixes in English and Spanish

Roots	Meaning	Words in English	Words in Spanish
bio	life	symbiosis	simbiosis
phobia (fobia)	fear of	xenophobia	xenofobia
phono (fono)	sound	phonetics	fonética
photo (foto)	light	photography	fotografía
geo	land, earth	geology	geología

Inflectional morphemes do not change the syntactic classification and typically follow derivational morphemes in a word. These are native of English and always function as suffixes. English has eight inflectional endings.

1. Short Plural **-s**, e.g., two *cars*, three *pens*

2. Long plural **-s**. Use long plurals after *ch, sh, s, z,* and *x*, e.g., *churches, washes, cases,* and *boxes*

3. Third person singular **-s**, e.g., Mary *walks* quickly.

4. Possessive **'s,** e.g., *Martha's* boy

5. Progressive **-ing**, e.g., She is *walking*. The gerund is not included in this group, i.e., **Walking** is good for your health.

6. Regular past tense **-ed**, e.g., He *worked* very hard.

7. Past participle **-en** or **-ed**, e.g., She has *beaten* the system, or It has been *ruined*.

8. Comparative and superlative **-er** (**better**) and **-est** (**best**), e.g., "Alex Rodríguez is **better** than Derek Jeter," or "He is the rich**est** player in the major leagues." Understanding the meaning of these morphemes can definitely enhance students' decoding and comprehension skills. The ability to rapidly and accurately associate sounds with a cluster of letters leads to more rapid and efficient word identification. As young readers build an increasing repertoire of words that they can recognize with little effort, they can use the words they know to help them recognize other, possibly related, words that are unfamiliar. The best practice for helping students gain skill in word-recognition is real reading and writing activities.

As children read and reread texts of their own choice, they have many opportunities to successfully decode a word, and realize that each time a letter combination such as *c-a-t* is found in the selection, it's read as *cat*. With each exposure to that word, the child reads the word more easily. A child who writes a sentence with that word is developing a greater sensitivity to meaning or context clues. The child attempting to spell that word is reviewing and applying what he knows about letter-sound associations.

Words That Can Create Comprehension Problems for Children

There are words that children can decode but they might have problems identifying the intended meaning. Some of these difficult words include homonyms and homophones. **Homonyms** are words that have the same sound and the same spelling but differ in meaning. Homonyms are common in the content areas and can create comprehension problems. The context will determine the meaning of the words. Examples of homonyms are presented in Table 1-5.

Table 1-5 Examples of Homonyms

Word	Meaning 1	Meaning 2
Club	A place to socialize	A wooden stick
Fine	To imply good or okay	A penalty
Bank	A place where money is stored	Margins of a river
Rock	A stone	Type of music

Homophones are words that sound the same but are spelled differently and have different meanings. Examples of homophones are *blew* and *blue*, *cents* and *sense*, *heir* and *air*, *wait* and *weight*, *hear* and *here*, *eight* and *ate*, *to*, *two*, and *too*, *there* and *their*, *deer* and *dear*, and *hair* and *hare*. **Homographs** are words that are spelled the same way but have more than one pronunciation and different meanings. For example, the word *bow* has two pronunciations, the first referring to the front part of a ship or the way that people bend to salute; the second referring to the decorative knot used in clothing. Consider the use of the word in the following sentence: The Japanese ambassador wore a red **bow**, stood on the **bow** of the ship and graciously **bowed** to the audience.

Compound words are created when two independent words are joined to create a new word. Often, knowing the meaning of the two words will guide students to understand the meaning of the compound word. For example, the compound word *birdhouse* is composed of the words *bird* and *house*. With this information, children can understand that the new word refers to a refuge or a house for birds. However, there are some examples of compound words in which the two words can create confusion among children. Examples of these deceptive compound words are *butterfly*, *nightmare*, and *brainstorm*.

Key Principles of the Competency

- Understands that many children develop word analysis and decoding skills in a predictable sequence

- Understands the importance of word recognition skills

- Knows a variety of formal and informal procedures for assessing children's word analysis

- Teaches the analysis of phonetically regular words in a simple-to-complex progression

---

- Teaches children to read passages using decodable texts as appropriate

- Teaches children to recognize high-frequency irregular words by selecting words that appear frequently in children's books

- Teaches children ways to identify vowel-sound combinations and multi-syllabic words

- Provides instruction in how to use structural cues to recognize compound words, as well as the base word, prefix, and suffix

- Teaches children to use knowledge of English word order

- Uses formal and informal assessments to plan and adjust instruction

Competency 006: Reading Fluency

The teacher understands the importance of fluency for reading comprehension and provides many opportunities for students to improve their reading fluency.

Reading fluency is the ability to decode words quickly and accurately in order to read text with the appropriate word stress, pitch, and intonation pattern (or prosody). Reading fluency requires automaticity of word recognition and reading with prosody to facilitate comprehension. **Automaticity** is the quick and accurate recognition of letters, words, and language conventions. Automaticity is achieved through continuous practice using texts written at the reading level of the child.

Fluency and Comprehension

Fluency is a prerequisite for language comprehension. Children struggling with fluency devote their time to mastering their language skills, which is an effort that takes away from the concentration that they should be placing on reading comprehension. When students read aloud in class, the main purpose of the activity is to develop fluency. If after reading aloud, teachers ask the child comprehension questions, the child will most likely have to read the same passage silently to be able to respond to the questions. Thus, teachers should separate these two activities—read silently for comprehension and read aloud to promote fluency.

What Is the Expectation?

Chapter 110.3 TEKS for English language arts and reading suggests that the typical child in first grade should be able to read about 60 words per minute (wpm) and the rate should increase by 10 words in each grade, i.e., second grade (70 wpm), third grade (80 wpm), and fourth grade (90 wpm). To determine the number of words per minute read, a simple formula is used; namely, words read in a minute, minus errors, equals words per minute (UT system/TEA, 2002). The expectation is that children in the first to fourth grade will be able to read independently with minimum difficulty, i.e., finding no more than 1 in 20 words difficult.

How Do We Teach Fluency?

. Teachers can use several strategies to promote reading fluency. Descriptions of these strategies follow.

Guided Oral Repeated Reading

Teachers can promote opportunities for **guided oral repeated reading** using text at the reading level of the child. Teachers, parents, and peers can provide support and feedback for these students. Allow the child to read the same story repeatedly to develop fluency.

Choral Reading

Reading "in group" is another activity used to promote reading fluency. This activity is ideal for ELLs and struggling readers because pronunciation and fluency problems will not be publicly noticed and they can use the model provided by fluent readers.

Pairing Students

Pairing proficient readers with ELLs or struggling readers can benefit both groups—the proficient child receives additional practice reading, and the ELLs and struggling readers are able to listen to fluent readers. ELLs and struggling readers can also read to their partners and receive input.

Interactive Computer Programs

Using interactive reading programs can provide individualized reading support for children. These computer programs often contain colorful pictures and interesting stories. The child should have the option of clicking on the words or pictures in order to have the selected word read aloud or to get animation of the word's meaning. The program can also read a story at normal speed while the child follows the highlighted words in a printed text.

Silent Sustained Reading

Guiding the child to read continuously for about 20 minutes a day can definitely improve reading fluency. This activity is also used to teach the child to read silently without moving his or her lips.

Readers' Theater

This activity has been used successfully to emphasize reading fluency. In this activity, a story is modified so that various characters have to read portions of the text. Students rehearse their reading part and then create a theater format to present the reading. Children enjoy this new approach and it improves reading fluency.

Developing Reading Fluency

Pointing to words while reading helps students see the letter-sound correspondence; however, this practice can also affect the development of reading fluency. Second graders should be guided to discontinue this practice. Continuous monitoring of reading fluency is required to insure children develop and maintain reading fluency when they are exposed to more challenging text. To be sure that students maintain reading fluency, teachers can conduct individual assessment using teacher-developed checklists or more standardized processes like running records.

Assessing Reading Fluency

A running record is an assessment strategy designed by Mary Clay (2002) to assess students' word identification skills and fluency in oral reading. As the teacher listens to a student read a page, the teacher uses a copy of the page to mark each word the child mispronounces. The teacher writes the incorrect word over the printed word, draws a line through each word the child skips, and draws an arrow under repeated words. In this activity teachers can identify the type of error made and can then provide additional support to individual learners.

Key Principles of the Competency

- Understands that fluency involves rate, accuracy, and intonation

- Understands how children's reading rate and fluency affect their comprehension

- Understands how children develop reading fluency

- Applies norms to identify and monitor children's fluency levels

- Selects and uses instructional strategies, materials, and activities to develop fluency

- Understands how to foster collaboration with families to promote reading fluency

---

Competency 007: Reading Comprehension

The teacher understands the importance of reading for understanding, knows the components and processes of comprehension, and teaches students strategies for improving their comprehension, including a variety of texts and contexts.

Helping students read for understanding is the central goal of reading instruction. Comprehension is a complex process involving the text, the reader, the situation, and the purpose for reading. There are a number of factors that come into play as a child attempts to comprehend a passage. First, students cannot understand texts if they cannot read the words. Thus, a teacher who is interested in improving students' comprehension skills needs to teach them to decode well. In addition, children need time during the school day to read texts that are easy for them to read, and also have time to discuss what has been read. Children need to read and reread easy texts often enough that decoding becomes rapid, easy, and accurate. It has been noted frequently in the literature that children who comprehend well have bigger vocabularies than children who struggle with reading. In part, this is true because their knowledge of vocabulary develops through contact with new words as they read text that is rich in new words. However, it has also been suggested that simply teaching vocabulary in isolation does not automatically enhance comprehension.

Background Knowledge

Reading comprehension can be affected by **prior knowledge**, and readers who possess rich prior knowledge about the topic of a reading often understand the reading better than classmates with less prior knowledge. A discrepancy between the schema intended by the author and the schema that the reader brings to the reading process can create confusion and comprehension problems. This is especially important for students from linguistically and culturally diverse backgrounds, who might not possess the cultural information to understand stories written for middle-class American students.

Guided Practice and Independent Practice

Through a gradual release of responsibility (Pearson & Gallagher, 1983) and careful and strategic scaffolding, teachers can guide students to practice and apply specific reading strategies in their independent reading. In guided practice, teachers provide various types of support and resources. Scaffolding learners with guided support means working within their zone of proximal development, or what the students can do with the assistance of a peer or adult (Vygotsky, 1978). In independent practice, students have opportunities to practice and apply the skills and strategies they learned during modeling and guided practice. In independent practice, students practice reading skills with text that is at their instructional and independent reading level. Teachers should reinforce reading strategies and skills on an ongoing basis through both guided and independent practice.

Pre-Reading Activities

Prior knowledge affects students' interest in what they read and what they want to read about. Generally, students like to read about topics that are familiar to them. This is an area in which the skill of the teacher can play a significant role. Teachers should identify interests in children and find appropriate stories to match their interests. A teacher can also make a previously unfamiliar topic seem familiar through **pre-reading activities** during which prior knowledge is activated, new prior knowledge is formed, and interest is stirred up. Teachers of ELLs often have to spend more time in pre-reading activities than the actual time devoted to reading the stories as they need to review unknown vocabulary, assess students' understanding of terminology and then build on this newly formed knowledge to increase students' interest in what is about to be read.

Setting the Purpose for Reading

Effective teachers clearly set up a purpose for reading and ask the students to predict what the purpose of the text being read is. By doing so both the teacher and the students can obtain and draw on students' prior knowledge about the topic. Making predictions about the upcoming text and then reading based on their predictions allows them to identify key points they need to pay attention to while reading. Children should be encouraged to generate questions about ideas in the text while reading. Successful teachers encourage children to also construct mental images representing ideas in the text, or to construct actual images from texts that lend themselves to this kind of activity.

Linking Prior Knowledge to New Knowledge

A successful teacher will help readers to process text containing new factual information through reading strategies, and to relate the new information to their prior knowledge. Questioning techniques is a simple but powerful mechanism to guide children to link current knowledge to new knowledge. Through questioning, teachers guide children to question the facts, the intent of the author, and also to check the answers through text verification. It is through conversation that children are able to compare their predictions and expectations about the content. It is also through these conversations that children see the need to revise their prior knowledge when compelling new ideas are encountered that conflict with prior knowledge. As part of these ongoing conversations, teachers will become alert to students who are applying the incorrect schema as they read, and will be able to encourage use of more appropriate knowledge. These conversations help children figure out the meanings of unfamiliar vocabulary words based on context clues, the opinions of others, and sometimes through the use of appropriate source materials such as glossaries, dictionaries, or an appropriate selection in another text. After reading activities, able teachers encourage children to revisit the text—to reread and make notes and paraphrase—in order to remember important points, interpret the text, evaluate its quality, and review important points. Children should also be encouraged to think about how ideas encountered in the text might be used in the future. As children gain competence, they enjoy showing what they know.

Story Grammar

Children should be encouraged to analyze stories using the story-grammar components of setting, characters, problems encountered by characters, attempts at a solution to the problem, successful solution, and ending. Teachers can use graphic organizers to present a visual clue of these components. Story frames can be modified to introduce various components of literature, as well as an assessment tool to check for comprehension.

As children's comprehension grows more sophisticated, they move from merely attempting to comprehend what is in the text to reading more critically. This means that they grow in an understanding that comprehension can go beyond the denotative components of the facts portrayed in text. With skillful instruction, children come to read not only what a text says, but also how the text portrays the subject matter. Students recognize the various ways in which every text is the unique creation of a unique author, and they also learn to compare and contrast the treatment of the same subject matter in a number of texts. For example, teachers can introduce the multiple versions of stories like *Cinderella* in order to discuss how stories can represent similar themes using unique settings and situations. To see different versions of the Cinderella story, visit *The Children Literature Web Guide* (Brown, 1997). Examples of variations on Cinderella are *Mufaro's Beautiful Daughters: An African Tale*, by John Steptoe; *Yeh-Shen, a Cinderella Tale from China*, by Ai-Ling Louie; and *The Egyptian Cinderella*, by Shirley Climo. Teachers can help students grow in comprehension through stages. In the beginning, teachers are usually happy if children are able to demonstrate their comprehension of what a text says in some authentic way.

The next stage is to have the children ponder what a text does—to describe an author's purpose, to recognize the elements of the text, and how the text was assembled. Finally, some children can attain the skill set needed to successfully engage in text interpretation, to be able to detect and articulate tone and persuasive elements, to discuss point of view, and to recognize bias. Over time, and with good instruction, children learn to infer unstated meanings based on social conventions, shared knowledge, shared experience, or shared values. They make sense of text by recognizing implications and drawing conclusions, and they move past the point of believing the content of a selection simply because it was in print.

Reflecting Reading—Bias in Traditional Stories

Certain traditional children's stories are filled with episodes of violence, sexism, and stereotypes. Fairy tales like *Cinderella* and *Snow White* portray women as weak creatures in need of support and rescuing. They also present old people as ugly and often as evil, e.g., the evil witch. Killing is also rampant in stories such as *Hansel and Gretel* where the main characters are left to die in the woods, and then are imprisoned by an "ugly and old witch" whom they kill eventually. Thievery and killing are also promoted in the story of *Jack and the Beanstalk*. In the original story the main character, Jack, steals from the "ugly" giant and kills him. Teachers should not ignore violence and bias in literature, and they should use these stories as a foundation to guide children to discuss and challenge bias and stereotypes.

Teachers can use traditional stories to examine controversial events in the stories. Teachers can lead children to discuss the actions of characters like Jack in *Jack and the Beanstalk* who steals the golden goose from the giant. Teachers can also introduce new stories and modern versions of traditional stories in which stereotypes and violence are challenged. For example, in Disney's version of the Chinese story of *Mulan*, the main character challenges the stereotypical role of women when she joins the Army disguised as a man in order to save the honor of the family and become a national heroine. In the *Paper Bag Princess*, the protagonist presents the idea that women do not always need to be saved by men or to marry a man who will protect them. In this story, the princess saves the prince from the dragon and eventually she decides not to marry him. Guiding children to examine themes and bias in literature can make them better readers and, more importantly, they can become reflective learners.

Monitoring Comprehension

Children need to be taught to monitor their own comprehension and to decide when they need to exert more effort, or to apply a strategy to make sense of a text. The goal of comprehension instruction is for the child to reach a level at which the application of strategies becomes automatic. In summary, comprehension is maximized when readers are fluent in all the processes of skilled reading—from the decoding of words to the articulation and easy application of the comprehension strategies used by good readers. Therefore, teachers need to teach predicting, questioning, seeking clarification, relating to background knowledge, constructing mental images, and summarizing. The teaching of comprehension strategies has to be conceived as a long-term developmental process, and the teaching of all reading strategies is more successful if they are taught and used by all of the teachers on a staff. In addition, teachers need to allow time for in-school reading, and recognize that good texts are comprehended on a deep level only through rereading and meaningful discussions.

Story retelling is a strategy used with young children to assess listening and reading comprehension. This strategy can also assess sentence structure knowledge, vocabulary, speaking ability, and knowledge about the structure of stories. An informal or more structured checklist can be used to assess a student's comprehension, sentence structure knowledge, and vocabulary development as they retell a story. Any checklist for listening comprehension should assess the ability of the child to (Lapp et al., 2001):

1. Retell the story with details

2. Show evidence of comprehension of the story line and plot, including the characters, setting, author's intention, and literal and implied meaning

3. Show evidence that the child understood major ideas and the ideas that support it

4. Bring background information to the selection

5. Analyze and make judgments based on facts

6. Retell the selection in sentences that make grammatical sense

7. Retell the story using sentences that include standard usage of verbs, adjectives, conjunctions, and compound sentences

8. Use a rich and meaningful vocabulary with minimal use of slang and colloquial expressions

9. Adapt spoken language for various audiences, purposes, and occasions

10. Listen for various purposes including critical listening to evaluate a speaker's message, and listening to enjoy and appreciate spoken language

Reading Strategies

Identifying strategies used by proficient readers can help teachers make skillful choices of activities that will maximize student learning. Anne Goudvis and Stephanie Harvey (2000) offer the following suggestions for useful activities.

Activating Prior Knowledge

Readers pay more attention when they can relate to the text. Readers naturally bring their prior knowledge and experience to reading, but they comprehend better when they think about the connections they make between the text, their lives, and the larger world. This strategy is especially important when teaching children from diverse cultural and linguistic backgrounds. Teachers need to explore the schemata necessary for children to understand the story and the background knowledge that children bring to the reading process. One of the strategies used to explore a child's background is the KWL chart. This is a chart that asks students to describe what they **K**now, **W**ant to know, **L**earned and still want to learn, or areas that the students did not understand that well. Because this is a class activity, children can benefit from what others already know, what others want to learn, and what areas were difficult for others.

Predicting or Asking Questions

Questioning is the strategy that keeps readers engaged. When readers ask questions, even before they read, they clarify understanding and forge ahead to make meaning. Asking questions is also at the heart of thoughtful reading. A variation of this strategy is to give students a true or false question about the content to be read. Once the students complete the questions, they then read to corroborate the answers.

Visualizing

Active readers create visual images based on the words they read in the text. These created pictures in turn enhance readers' understanding.

Drawing Inferences

Inferring is when the readers take what they know, garner clues from the text, and think ahead to make a judgment, discern a theme, or speculate about what is to come.

Determining Important Ideas

Thoughtful readers grasp essential ideas and important information when reading. Readers must differentiate between less important ideas and the key ideas that are central to the meaning of the text.

Synthesizing Information

Synthesizing information involves combining new information with existing knowledge to form an original idea or interpretation. Reviewing, sorting, and sifting important information can lead to new insights that change the way readers think.

Repairing Understanding

If confusion disrupts meaning, readers need to stop and clarify their understanding. Readers may use a variety of strategies to "fix" comprehension when meaning goes awry.

Confirming Predictions

As students read and after they have finished reading, they should confirm the predictions they originally made. There is no wrong answer. One can confirm negatively or positively. Determining if a prediction is correct is a goal.

Using Parts of a Book

Students should use the various parts of a book such as the charts, diagrams, indexes, and table of contents to improve their understanding of the reading content.

Reflecting

An important strategy is for students to think about, or reflect on, what they have just read. Reflection can be just thinking, or it can be more formal, such as a discussion or writing in a journal. While providing instruction in a subject area, the teacher needs to determine if the reading material is at the students' level of reading mastery. If not, the teacher needs to make accommodations either in the material itself or in the manner of presentation.

Assessing Comprehension

A frequent device for assessing comprehension is the use of oral or written questions. A question may be **convergent**, which indicates that only one answer is correct, or **divergent**, which indicates that more than one answer is correct. Most tests, however, include a combination of question types.

Another device for checking on comprehension is a **cloze test**, or a passage with omitted words the test-taker must supply. The test-maker must decide whether to require the test-taker to supply the exact word or to accept synonyms. Passing scores reflect which type of answer is acceptable. If assessing an understanding of meaning is the intent of the exercise, the teacher might accept synonyms and not demand the surface-level constructs, or the exact word.

The **speed** at which a student reads helps in determining the level of comprehension, up to a point. The faster that a student reads, the better that student comprehends, with some limitations. In general, the slow reader who must analyze each word does not comprehend as well as the fast reader. It is possible, however, to read too fast. Most students have had the experience of having to reread materials. For example, a student reading a chapter in preparation for a test might read more slowly than when reading a short story for pleasure or reading to get the main idea of a story.

Semantic mapping can also be used as a strategy to make direct connections between the vocabulary or words they are learning in the classroom and those that they may have seen, heard or learned priorly. The strategy generally works as follows:

1. The teacher puts a word or phrase representing the story in the middle of the board/paper/transparency. The teacher can have preselected categories related to the central word (3–5 categories).

2. The teacher asks students to brainstorm related words in each category. The teacher also introduces words related to the text.

3. Students can also look through the text to locate more words that may fit with the key word or phrase. Related words that may appear in future readings can be included also.

4. In discussing the words, students can also talk about their personal connections with the book.

   • Have some categories ready to add to the organizer. Preselect key words from the text and/or related to the concept to introduce to the semantic map.

> **Key Principles of this Competency**
>
> - Vocabulary can be taught both directly and indirectly.
>
> - A variety of techniques should be used in the classroom.
>
> - Students should be taught that some words have multiple meanings.
>
> - Semantic mapping can help students make explicit relationships between words (Nagy, 1988).
>
> - Building and activating schema or prior knowledge is necessary in students' literacy development.
>
> - Meaningful discussion of key concepts and words can show students the relationship and connections between words.
>
> - The four writing skills—speaking, listening, reading, and writing—should be thought of as interrelated components.
>
> - Key vocabulary learned extends to future lessons on related topics.

Competency 008: Reading, Research, and Inquiry Skills

The teacher understands the importance of research and inquiry skills to students' academic success and provides students with instruction that promotes their acquisition and effective use of those study skills in the content areas.

Transition from "Learning to Read" to "Reading to Learn"

Children from pre-K to second grade spend most of the language arts portion of their day trying to decode and make sense of written language. The main purpose of this stage is to read for pleasure. Traditionally, short stories with pictures that have a specific structure and predictable story line are used to guide the child in the process of "learning to read." However, in the upper elementary grades, the needs of the children go beyond decoding and reading for pleasure, and "reading to learn" becomes the main task. The "reading to learn" stage require students to decode written language, understand the content, and obtain vital information from the content. One important component of the process of "reading to learn" is to understand how text is organized in the content areas. Children need to identify key components of the organizational format and identify the type of information offered. Teachers have to guide children to notice and study the structure of text, including the table of contents, titles, subtitles, and headings.

Structure of Text

Students need to look closely at the structure of the text in order to comprehend it. To accomplish this task, skillful teachers guide the students through a picture, table, and graphic walk-through of the text while asking questions and pointing out useful text features to the students. Most texts have titles, subtitles, headings, glossaries, and bolded words. What techniques were used to make them stand out? Figuring out the structure of a text helps readers to read more efficiently. Children can anticipate what information will be revealed in a selection when they understand textual structure. Understanding the pattern of the text helps students organize ideas. Authors have a fairly short list of organizational patterns to choose from. The following are the most common patterns:

- Chronological order relates events in a temporal sequence from beginning to end

- Cause-and-effect relationships between described events, with the causal factors identified or implied

- Problem description, followed by solutions

- Comparisons and/or contrasts to describe ideas to readers

- Sequential materials, presented as a series of directions to be followed in a prescribed order

- Once children understand how information in the content areas is organized, they can become more efficient readers

Becoming More Efficient Readers

Students with strong comprehension skills and decoding ability are now ready to become more efficient readers by practicing the techniques of scanning and skimming to get content information. In **scanning**, children are guided to look for specific information in text. Children are taught to use headings, indices, boldface and italics to guide them to specific words or content. In **skimming**, students read major headings, table of contents, bold letters, graphic materials, and summary paragraphs to get the main idea of the content.

Study Skills

Students need to know how to study the information that has been presented to them in texts and other media. Graphic organizers help students to review material, and help them to see the relationships between one bit of information and another. For example, a Venn diagram helps students identify how things are alike and different. A Venn diagram can also be used to help students recognize how a single topic is treated in two readings, or how two books, animals, or ecosystems are alike and different. The student labels the two overlapping circles and lists items that are unique to each one in each respective circle. In the area in the center where there is an overlap, the student records the elements that the two items have in common.

Another skill students need to master is **note taking**. Unless a teacher wants to read passages directly out of an encyclopedia or other source material, he or she should take the time to actively teach note-taking techniques. Teachers should also think of an authentic task that requires students to accomplish higher level manipulation of the given information. First, help the children to formulate a researchable question. Second, have them highlight the words that might be used as key words in searching for information. Third, have students brainstorm in groups of other words to be used as key words. Next, ask then to list appropriate sources. Finally, as they skim articles, they can fill in the chart with little chunks of information.

Graphic Organizers

Graphic organizers help students improve organizational skills and provide a visual representation of facts and concepts and their relationships within an organized framework. The ability to organize information and ideas is fundamental to effective thinking. To increase reading comprehension among ELLs, allow students to share information about the story or passage. Through this activity, students can help each other using peer scaffolding and oral language interaction. Semantic mapping can be used before and after readings to organize materials in new ways by highlighting connections among ideas.

Think-Aloud

Think-alouds allow the teacher and students to problem solve together. The teacher poses a question to students and then, the teacher, group of students, or entire class responds at the same time. This strategy can be easily used to increase reading comprehension in the content areas. In modeling a think-aloud, the following steps are used (Wilhelm, 2001).

1. The teacher explains *what* the strategy is and what it is used for.

2. The teacher explains *why* the strategy is important for improving reading comprehension.

3. The teacher explains in what context to use the strategy: *when* to use the strategy.

4. The teacher models *how* to use the strategy using an authentic text. Modeling continues until the students begin to use prompts and strategies aloud.

5. The teacher guides student practice using *authentic* text. The teacher gradually releases responsibility for doing the think-aloud to students.

6. Students practice the strategy in pairs or independently. The teacher asks that students do a think-aloud in which they explain and articulate their thought processes for using the strategy.

Summarizing and Organizing Content

When children are guided to summarize and organize content, they are using basic reading comprehension and taking this content to a higher level of thinking including evaluation, analysis, and synthesis. By guiding children to go beyond the literal meaning and to reorganize content requires students to develop a deeper understanding of content. Guide students to reorganize content (study skills) by creating their own tables, charts, and graphs. For example, students can develop a chart containing the longest rivers of the world organized by regions and countries. When children are required to process and present information using a new structure, comprehension and knowledge of the content area increases and memory retention is enhanced.

Study Plans

To increase content comprehension, teachers might acquaint students with several study plans to help them read content materials. Many of these plans are well known and easily accessed, and the teacher and the students can simply select the plan(s) that works best for them within various subjects. Students may use **mnemonic devices**, or memory-related devices, to help them remember the steps in reading a chapter effectively.

SQ4R

Students often use plans like **SQ4R** when reading text in content areas. The acronym stands for **survey, question, read, reflect, recite, and review** (Tomas & Robinson 1972). An explanation of the different components of the SQ4R follows:

- **Survey:** During the **survey (S)** part, readers examine the headings, illustrations, bold letters, and major components of the text in order to develop predictions and generate **questions (Q)** about the topic.

- **Question:** The student may wish to devise some questions that the chapter will probably answer. Through these questions, students establish the purpose for reading and the questions serve as a reading guide. If the chapter has questions at the end, the student can also study these before reading the chapter.

- **Read (1R):** During the next stage, students read while looking for answers to the questions previously generated and/or those questions written by the publishers, which are usually located at the end of the section.

- **Write (2R):** Students monitor their comprehension as they write a summary of the story or text. Creating a summary allows students opportunities to internalize and make their own interpretation of the content.

- **Recite (3R):** The student attempts to answer orally, or in writing, the student-developed questions or the questions at the end of the chapter.

- **Review (4R):** Finally, students review the text to evaluate the accuracy of their answers and to show how much they learned about the content.

Reciprocal Teaching

Reciprocal teaching is an instructional activity designed for struggling readers in which the teacher engages students in a dialogue about specific portions of a text (Palinscar & Brown 1984). The main purpose of this activity is to guide children to construct meaning and to monitor reading comprehension. The dialogue is structured to elicit four components:

1. Summarizing the content of a passage

2. Asking a question about the main idea

3. Clarifying difficult parts of the content

4. Predicting what will come next

DRTA

The acronym **DRTA** stands for Directed Reading/Thinking Activity. This teacher-directed strategy helps students to establish a purpose for reading a story or reading expository writing from a content book (Reuzel & Cooter 1992). The teacher models the process of creating and correcting predictions as the story progresses to strengthen comprehension. DRTA has three main steps:

1. Sample the text to develop background: Children are guided to read the title, look at pictures or any kind of visual representations, and read some sample lines from the text to develop hypothesis about the content of the text.

2. Make predictions: Students make predictions based on a sample of the text.

3. Confirm or correct predictions: Children read the text and engage in follow-up activities to corroborate if the predictions were correct.

Reading Comprehension in the Content Areas

To assist children and especially ELLs in reading material that may be beyond their reading level, teachers can incorporate the following strategies.

- Record selected passages that students can listen to while reading along with the text. Teachers can use adult volunteers and fluent readers in the group to read to children unable to read it for themselves.

- Pair children off into a tutor/tutee arrangement or in a small group reading format. Teachers should pair children of different linguistic levels and degree of achievement to create a peer-support system.

- Introduce the technical vocabulary of the content areas prior to reading. Introduce elements such as connotation (implied meaning), denotation (literal meaning), and idioms in the way they are used in text. For example, the word *right* can have multiple meanings depending on the content area or the activity. In mathematics, *right* is an angle of 90 degrees, but in social studies *right* can be used to provide directions or to declare correctness.

- Teach content vocabulary through direct, concrete experiences as opposed to definitions. Definitions can lead to misinterpretations since additional words are required to define the term. Teaching vocabulary in a contextualized situation is particularly important for ELLs because they often rely on translations that do not always represent the intended concept. For example, in English, the word *bayou* is used extensively in Texas and Louisiana. However, *bayou* is very difficult to define for someone who has never seen one. What is the difference between a bayou, a creek, a swamp, or a marshland? How big is a bayou? If an adult has difficulty answering these questions, imagine how young children may struggle!

- Introduce instructional strategies for self-monitoring reading comprehension. In this kind of strategy, students read aloud a passage and then pause to question themselves about the meaning of the passage.

Strategies for Developing Critical-Thinking Skills

Critical-thinking skills include analysis, synthesis, and evaluation. Benjamin Bloom (1956) created taxonomy for categorizing levels of thinking processes typical in school children. The taxonomy presents a structure to categorize the levels of thinking required in order to ask and answer questions. These questions have traditionally been used to guide children from the basic recalling of information (**knowledge**) and understanding information (**comprehension**) to using higher order thinking skills such as analysis, synthesis, and evaluation. Recalling and understanding are important parts of reading comprehension; however, it is a teacher's responsibility to help children move from literal comprehension and explicit ideas to a more figurative comprehension and implicit ideas. Teachers have to guide children to analyze (**analysis**) the ideas presented in text and then to make inferences (**analysis**), to assess their inferences (**evaluation**), to draw conclusions about the ideas (**synthesis**), and perhaps to apply the ideas to new situations (**application**). Children who are able to go beyond the literal and explicit information in text develop a deeper understand of the content areas and are able to manipulate the content at higher levels of thinking.

Linguistic Accommodation Testing for ELLs and Special Education Students

The State of Texas provides for linguistic accommodation for ELLs and special education children taking the content portion of the TAKS examination in grades 3–8 and 10 in order to ensure that reading comprehension does not interfere in assessing content mastery. Based on specific recommendations from the Admission, Review, and Dismissal (ARD) and/or the Language Proficiency Assessment Committee (LPAC), districts can allow linguistic accommodations for special education and ELL students when taking the basic skills test (TAKS). A list of allowed linguistic accommodations follows (TEA, 2005).

1. Presenting the information in two languages side by side

2. Allowing the test administrator to read the questions or translate words, phrases, and sentences

3. Using dictionaries to find translations

4. Allowing the use of bilingual or English-language glossaries

5. Allowing the test administrator to present the information using simple language

6. Using visual and nonverbal communication to make content clear

7. Strategies like the linguistic accommodation testing (LAT) can be used to enhance reading comprehension of special populations in the content area.

Competency 009: Writing Conventions

The teacher understands the conventions of writing in English and provides instruction that helps students develop proficiency in applying written conventions.

The transition from oral language development to written communication requires students to develop an awareness of the following concepts (Peregoy, Boyle, & Cadiero-Kapplan, 2008):

1. Print carries meaning and it conveys a message.

2. Spoken words can be written and preserved.

3. English reading and writing follows a specific direction; that is, from left to right, and top to bottom.

4. Spoken language is composed of phonemes, and these sounds can be represented by specific letters of the alphabet (alphabetic principle).

5. As an alphabetic language, English has a sound-symbol correspondence but often it is inconsistent.

6. Spoken language can be used as a foundation for spelling (phonics).

Spoken and Written English

The productive skills of language—speaking and writing—are interconnected. A strong oral development can facilitate the development of written communication. However, because spoken language is generally more informal than written language, teachers need to be sure that students use formal language when writing.

English favors the use of active voice as opposed to passive voice in both oral and written communication. For example, the sentence *Katrina devastated the city of New Orleans* is stronger and more effective than a sentence using the passive voice such as *The city of New Orleans was devastated by Katrina*. To provide support in this area, guide students to work with a partner in converting passive sentences to active sentences; then guide them to discuss how these changes affect the tone and meaning of the sentences. If a student is having problems connecting sounds to written text, teachers can provide phonics instruction. Guiding students to "sound out" words as a foundation for spelling can improve written performance.

Developing Readiness for Writing

A visit to an early childhood classroom shows that children spend the bulk of the time singing, playing with blocks and puzzles, cutting figures with scissors, playing with clay, drawing, and painting. By looking at this picture, laypeople might question the value of instruction in early childhood. However, the reality is that children are doing intensive work on developing the fine motor skills needed to master pre-reading skills such as pencil grip, appropriate paper position, and the first strokes of representing the shapes of letters and words.

Spelling Stages

As children begin to name letters and read print, they also begin to write letters and words. Writing development seems to occur at about the same time as reading development—not afterward, as traditional reading readiness assumed. Whole language seeks to integrate the language arts rather than sequencing them. Just as change has marked educators' beliefs about reading instruction and the way that reading develops, change has also marked the methods and philosophies behind the teaching of writing in schools.

Drawing is the beginning of children's attempt to convey a message in written form. Teachers can use this interest to introduce writing skills by guiding them to add words to drawings to supplement the information. Initially, the children can dictate the story to teachers until they feel comfortable enough to write it on their own. The development of written communication generally follows a predictable sequence beginning with scribbling, then developing pseudo letters and invented words until conventional spelling is achieved. An analysis of the stages of spelling follows.

Scribbling

In this phase, children pretend that they are writing. Eventually, they develop letter-like symbols. This stage represents an awareness of the difference between writing and drawing to communicate. Scribbling is different from drawing because in scribbling, the child purposely scribbles from left to right and often also follows the top to bottom progression.

Pseudo Letters

In this phase, children attempt to create forms that resemble letters, but these forms cannot always be identified as such. They become aware that the alphabet contains characters of different shapes and attempt to reproduce these in a random way resulting in some form of invented spelling.

Random Letters

In this phase, children create individual letters from the alphabet in an attempt to create words. The letters are randomly selected with no clear connection with the phonemes that they are to represent. That is, children are not producing phonetic spelling at this stage. They write letter strings and often leave a space between strings, which suggest that they are beginning to understand word boundaries.

Invented Spelling

At this stage, children try to connect the sounds (phonemes) and the letters (graphemes) to create words resulting in nonstandard writing. A single letter or a series of letters, which represent the phonemes contained in the intended word, often represent this phonetic spelling. A child can write an *m* to represent the word mother and often they can point to the word. They can also use strings of letters, mostly consonants, to represent a word. For example, a kindergartner wrote the word *park* as *prk*, producing the three consonants and omitting the vowel. Because the phoneme-grapheme correspondence of vowels is not consistent, children generally have problems writing them.

Transitional Spelling

Eventually, children discontinue over-reliance on phonetic spelling and begin noticing visual clues and developing a knowledge of word structure. Sight word training becomes very important at this stage. Students begin producing more standard spelling and attempt self-correction. Writing samples might become difficult to read because students erase continuously in an attempt to self-correct. Some inflectional endings (plurals, comparative, superlative, past tense, and present progressive) may appear in writing samples. Students may continue having problems with words with double vowels, like *book* and *feed*, and words containing consonant diagraphs like ***through*** or ***eight***.

Conventional Spelling

At this stage, children spell most words using conventional spelling. They still may have problems with consonant digraphs, homonyms, contractions, compound words, as well as prefixes, suffixes, and more difficult letter combinations.

Writing Stages

In addition to the traditional spelling stages, students also go through specific stages of writing. Lapp et al. (2001) divided the process into three stages: emerging writers, early writers, and newly fluent writers. A summary of these stages follows (Lapp et al., 2001).

Characteristics of Emerging Writers

Students at the emerging stage of writing development are generally able to:

- Dictate an idea or a complete story

- Use initial sounds in their writing

- Use pictures, scribbles, symbols, letters, and/or known words to communicate a message

- Understand that writing symbolizes speech

Educational Implications

Read stories to children and ask them to retell the story while you record it. Then, read the story back to the child to emphasize the connection between speech and print. When children begin writing words or pseudo words, ask them to read it to you, and if necessary, provide conventional spelling as an alternative. Use the *Language Experience Approach* to guide children to connect spoken words with their written representations. That is, guide children to dictate words and sentences while you record them on the board. Read the words while pointing to them. Then, ask students to copy the sentences. The next day, review the sentences written and use them for additional language development. Introduce writing for functional tasks like labeling objects and places in the classroom, writing the plan of the day, taking notes, and listing names or things to remember.

Characteristics of Early Writers

Typically, children at the early stage of writing exhibit the following behaviors:

- Understand that a written message remains the same each time it is read

- Utilize their knowledge of sounds and letters as they progress through the stages of spelling development

- With modeling and assistance, incorporate feedback in revising and editing their own writing

- Begin to use conventional grammar, spelling, capitalization, and punctuation

Educational Implications

Guide children to read and reread the same information to establish a connection between letters and sounds. Identify specific words and divide them into syllables to establish a connection between the sounds within a syllable. Take expressions that are commonly used in children's literature and oral communication and guide them to hear word boundaries. For example, children at this stage might write the statement "Once upon a time" as "Oncesoponditim," which represents the way the expression is produced orally without appropriate word boundaries. Model the writing process using a LCD projection system or the traditional chalkboard. Think aloud while you are writing and ask for guidance from students, e.g., Do we need a comma here or a final period? Do we need a capital *A* in the word "american"? In the writing samples of children, use peer input for editing and guide students to conduct self-corrections. Instead of making direct error corrections, ask questions leading children to examine the grammaticality of the sentences and to make their own corrections.

Characteristics of Newly Fluent Writers

Newly fluent writers are generally able to:

- Use prewriting strategies to achieve their purposes

- Address a topic or write to a prompt creatively and independently

- Organize writing to include a beginning, a middle, and an end

- Consistently use conventional grammar, spelling, capitalization, and punctuation

- Revise and edit written work independently and/or collectively

- Produce many genres of writing

Educational Implications

Use prewriting activities to plan for writing using an outline that indicates the sequence of ideas. This activity is especially important for children whose native language does not require the use of the linear progression required in English writing. The outline will guide children to comply with this linear rhetorical pattern. Provide interesting writing prompts to children to guide their writing. You may use the prompt given on the TAKS released tests available online. Traditionally, the Texas Education Agency releases the tests used in its yearly examinations. For information on released TAKS tests, see the Texas Education Agency, Student Assessment Division, at *www.tea.state.tx.us/student. assessment/resources/release/taks/index.html.*

Continue using peer editing and encourage self-corrections. Guide students to produce different kinds of writing such as response to literature, journal writing, and persuasive writing (writing to convince someone or to argue a point).

Writing Expectations

Children in kindergarten through sixth grade are expected to progress through the stages of writing and develop conventional spelling and coherent compositions. The fourth-grade TAKS examinations require students to develop a coherent piece of writing free of major errors. It is also expected that children produce and refine compositions for general and specific audiences. Children are required to edit their work and the work of others based on clarity of ideas, coherence, and the conventions of writing.

Strategies for Using Writing Conventions

The main objective of writing is to put ideas in writing in a logical pattern. Once this is accomplished, students have to check for writing conventions—grammar, punctuation, and capitalization. Some of the strategies to introduce writing conventions are listed below.

Modeling

Modeling is one of the best tools to introduce effective writing. To model effective writing, teachers can introduce writing samples in which conventions are used appropriately. A variant of this activity is to present a writing sample to the whole class that contains typical errors in English conventions and to ask them to provide corrective feedback.

Sentence Builders

One of the typical problems found in the writing samples produced by children is the use of sentence fragments. To guide children to produce complete sentences, teachers can use a technique called "sentence builders." In this technique, the teacher provides students with a list of words by syntactic categories (articles, adjectives, nouns, verbs, and conjunctions) and guides children to produce sentences using each component. As a follow-up activity, children are asked to identify the subject and the predicate, and specifically the verb. They are also asked to read the sentence to see if it contains a complete idea.

Punctuation Exercises

To teach the importance of punctuation, teachers can use sentences in which commas or periods are necessary to deliver the intended ideas and guide students to use punctuation to clarify the intended message. For example, in the sentence *Mary, a student from Italy, requested bread, coffee and olive oil for breakfast*, it is not clear if Mary wants coffee mixed with olive oil or just coffee and also olive oil. In this case a comma is needed for clarification.

Identifying Common Grammar Problems

Assess students' writing to identify common problems across the group, and design lessons to address the identified problems. For example, if students are producing words like *bred* and *sale boat* in place of *bread* and *sailboat*, provide training in vowel digraph and compound words. A vowel digraph occurs when two vowels produce one sound, e.g., *ea* in beach. A consonant digraph is more than one consonant that produces only one sound, e.g., *th* in thought.

Connecting Discourse

Connecting discourse is a definite challenge to students in the early grades. Children generally produce choppy sentences without transition words or phrases to connect ideas or paragraphs. Most of these connectors are not used in daily speech unless students have had some speech training or an academic preparation in the area; thus, teachers need to teach connectors directly. When writing a composition, teachers can provide a list of possible sentence connectors to guide students to use them. Some of these include phrases such as "on the one hand," "moreover," and "furthermore," among others.

Dependent and Independent Clauses

Another way to minimize the use of choppy sentences in compositions is by guiding children to combine sentences in one of the following ways:

1. Use conjunctions such as *and, but, or, nor, or yet*. For example, *My car is beautiful, but it is getting old*. Notice that in the sentence, there are two independent clauses joined by a coordinate conjunction, *but*. A comma is required before the conjunction.

2. Join two complete sentences with a semicolon. For example, the sentence *Maricela is a highly intelligent student; she was the Valedictorian of the 2009 class*. Notice that lowercase is used after the semicolon.

3. Use dependent and independent clauses. For example, the sentence *Although Dora is my friend, she did not vote for me*. Notice that in this case, the use of a dependent linking word *although* at the beginning clause made the second clause necessary to complete the whole idea. The last statement makes sense by itself, but it becomes a more complete sentence when used together.

Strategies to Promote Written Communication

Reading to students can provide multiple benefits to children. It develops print awareness and understanding of the intonation pattern of the language. A discussion on the content of the story allows students opportunities to enhance comprehension and practice speaking. It also provides a model of fluent reading together with the appropriate intonation pattern of the language. Reading together can be enjoyable. Students laugh and talk about the story and the characters. Children can also be exposed to different kinds of writing (genre) like fiction, biography, and short stories. Finally, they are exposed to the story framework, which is the setting, characters, plot, climax, and resolution.

Dictated Materials—The Language Experience Approach

Children's individual or group-dictated stories, which can be written on experience charts, guide children to connect spoken language with its written representation. The teacher can record students' dictations or ask them to talk into any available voice-recording device. When the teacher is recording the stories, saying each word aloud while writing it down can be helpful to the students. Following the writing of the story, teachers read the story in a natural sounding tone of voice, pointing to each word as it is pronounced. To assist students in developing the knowledge of clauses and phrases, read the story placing a hand under each phrase as it is read. Students can also read the story in choral reading, by pairs, or individually.

Interactive Journals

As it was discussed earlier in the chapter, writing in journals provides students with opportunities to use language authentically in literary contexts. Teachers and students can have a designated time for journal writing to communicate on a daily basis. This gives students the freedom to use their own mechanics and invented spellings. Because the purpose of written journals is to communicate, teachers should not correct children's journal writing, but should write comments on content and provide encouragement and reassurance. Some of the key advantages of interactive journals for children and teachers are located in Table 1-6.

Table 1-6 Advantages of Interactive Journal Writing for Students and Teachers

Advantages for Students	Advantages for Teachers
• Students learn that written language communicates.	• Teachers learn about each child's interest, ideas, and everyday concerns.
• Students experience making choices about topics and develop a sense of ownership of the written product.	• Teachers interact and communicate on an individual basis with each child.
• Students develop their writing within meaningful context.	• Teachers model standard convention or writing in the context of authentic communication.
• Students develop a personal interaction with the teacher and with peers.	
• Students can use this safe environment to experiment with language.	

Using Routines as Literacy Events

Several routine activities can be modified to promote reading and writing development. Some of these activities are:

- Take attendance: Use a chart with students' names on it. In the morning, students get their card and move it to the chart showing that they are present. The names of the students can also be placed in alphabetical order, which uses indirect teaching to deal with that concept.

- The daily weather report: Use pictures and words representing the climatic conditions, i.e., cloudy, clear, raining. Students will move the cards to show the prevailing weather conditions for the day.

- Today's day: Students select the appropriate card to show the days of the week. Organize a calendar of events for the day or for the month. Review the plan of the day in the morning.

- Use notes to communicate with students. Praise them or discuss behavior in written form.

Competency 010: Development of Written Communication

The teacher understands that writing to communicate is a developmental process and provides instruction that promotes students' competence in written communication.

Writing is a developmental process that requires students to go through a series of steps to complete a written product. Some of these steps include brainstorming, semantic mapping, outlining, reading, and researching. Students must also know that they need to write for various audiences and purposes (e.g., expressive, informative, persuasive), and that they will be required to use their knowledge of text genres, structures (e.g., letter, poem, story, play), and strategies (e.g., peer conferences) for completing a written piece. Some of the steps that students must go through include drafting, editing, revising, proofreading, and publishing. Students should be aware, however, that writing is a recursive process; that is, there are always opportunities to continue improving what they are writing.

Children also need knowledge of English grammar and mechanics to revise their writing. It includes revising given texts in terms of sentence construction like revising run-on sentences and misplaced modifiers; revising subject-verb and pronoun-antecedent agreement; revising verb forms, pronouns, adverbs, adjectives, and plural and possessive nouns; and revising capitalization, punctuation, and spelling. Students also need to analyze and revise written work in relation to style, clarity, organization, intended audience, and purpose. This includes revising text prepared for a given audience or purpose, and improving organization and unity. Adding transition words and phrases, reordering sentences or paragraphs, deleting unnecessary information, and adding a topic sentence are other ways students can revise their work. Another strategy is to increase text clarity, precision, and effectiveness through word choices.

Dr. Donald Graves, a professor of education at the University of New Hampshire, developed an approach to writing instruction called **process writing** (1983). His notion was simple—teach children to write the way real writers write. What do writers do? They tend to write about what they want to write about. Then they may read about the subject, talk about the subject, take notes, or generally fool around with the topic before they compose. Then they may write a draft, knowing up-front that they are not done at this point. Writers may share the draft with others and end up writing all over it. They may also go over every sentence, thinking about word choice and looking for vague spots, or spots where the piece falls off the subject. Writers may then revise the draft again, share it again, revise it again, and so on, until they are satisfied with the product. Then they publish it. Often, writers receive feedback before and after the piece is published, which may lead to a new writing effort. Some writers save scraps of writing in a journal. They may save a turn of phrase, a comment overheard on a bus, a new word, good quotes, or an interesting topic.

Another aspect of process writing is celebration. Children are invited to share their work with the class. After young authors read their piece, classmates ought to offer affirmations and suggestions. Teachers should have children save each piece of paper generated in the writing process, and store them in a personal portfolio for review.

New Trends in Writing

In addition to process writing, there is a new trend emphasizing specific elements of the writing process. The best-known system is called the 6+1 Trait® Writing. This system, which was developed by the Northwest Regional Educational Laboratory (NREL), emphasizes seven elements of the writing process (2006). These elements are described below.

1. **Organization**—the internal structure of the sample

2. **Ideas**—how ideas are presented in the sample

3. **Voice**—the uniqueness of the author and how ideas are projected

4. **Word Choice**—the vocabulary used to convey meaning

5. **Sentence Fluency**—the flow of ideas and the use of connectors

6. **Conventions**—the use of capitalization, punctuation, and spelling

7. **Presentation**—how the final product looks in print

The Texas Education Agency developed a similar writing program emphasizing similar components:

1. **Focus and Coherence**—how the main idea is introduced and supported in the composition

2. **Organization**—the organization of ideas, including connectors

3. **Development of Ideas**—how the ideas are presented and supported in writing

4. **Voice**—the uniqueness of the author and how ideas are projected

5. **Conventions**—the use of capitalization, punctuation, and spelling

Both the 6+1 Trait Writing and the TAKS writing program guide children to demonstrate knowledge of writing traits. To assess their performance, both programs develop a four-point rubric for each of the writing traits.

Identifying the Characteristics of Modes of Writing

Writing serves many different functions. The main functions are to narrate, to describe, to explain, and to persuade. Students need to be aware of each of these functions. In any event, these four categories are neither exhaustive nor mutually exclusive. The **narrative** is a story or an account. It may recount an incident or a series of incidents. The account may be autobiographical to make a point. The narrative may be fiction or nonfiction.

The purpose of **descriptive** writing is to provide information about a person, place, or thing. Descriptive writing can be fiction or nonfiction. Description is a powerful tool in advertisement. Advertisements describe items using factual information, but the way the information is presented can become a persuasive type of writing for prospective buyers.

The purpose of **expository** writing is to explain and clarify ideas. Students are probably most familiar with this type of writing. While the expository essay may have narrative elements, the storytelling or recounting aspect is minor and subservient to the explanation element. Expository writing is typically found in many textbooks; for instance, a textbook on the history of Texas would likely be expository in nature.

The purpose of **persuasive** writing is to convince the reader of something. Persuasive writing fills current magazines and newspapers, and permeates the World Wide Web. The writer may be trying to push a political candidate, to convince someone to vote for a zoning ordinance, or even to promote a diet plan. Persuasive writing usually presents a point, provides evidence, which may be factual or anecdotal, and supports the point. The structure may be very formal, with counterpositions and counterarguments. Whatever the organizational pattern, the writer's intent is to persuade readers of the validity of some claim. Nearly all essays have some element of persuasion.

Authors choose their form of writing not necessarily just to tell a story but also to present an idea. Whether writers choose the narrative, descriptive, expository, or persuasive format, they have something on their minds that they want to convey to their readers.

Writing for a Variety of Audiences, Occasions, and Purposes

The writer must consider the audience, the occasion, and the purpose when choosing the writing mode. The writer's responsibility is to write clearly, honestly, and cleanly for the reader's sake and so the **audience** is very important. The teacher can designate an audience for students' writing. Knowing who will read their work, students can modify their writing to suit the intended readers. For instance, a fourth-grade teacher might suggest that the class take their compositions about a favorite animal to second graders and allow the younger children to read it. The writers soon will realize that they need to use manuscript and not cursive writing, to employ simple vocabulary, and to omit complex sentences when they write for their young audience.

The **occasion** also helps to determine the elements of writing. The language should fit the occasion. Students should keep in mind that particular words may have certain effects, such as evoking sympathy or raising questions about an opposing point of view. The students and teacher might try to determine the likely effect on an audience of a writer's choice of a particular word or words.

The **purpose** helps to determine the format (narrative, expository, descriptive, or persuasive) and the language of the writer. The students, for instance, might consider the appropriateness of written material for a specific purpose such as a business letter, a communication with residents of a retirement center, or a thank-you note to parents. The teacher and students might try to identify persuasive techniques used by a writer in a passage.

In selecting the mode of writing and the content, the writer might ask the following:

1. What would the audience need to know to believe you or to accept your position? Imagine someone you know (visualize her or him) listening to you declare your position or opinion and then saying, "Oh yeah? Prove it!" What evidence do you need to prove your idea to this skeptic?

2. With what might the audience disagree?

3. What common knowledge does the audience share with you?

4. What information do you need to share with the audience?

The teacher might wish to have the students practice selecting the mode and the language by adapting forms, organizational strategies, and styles for different audiences and purposes.

Types of Writing

Teachers need to encourage children to write for meaningful purposes. Meaningful writing can be easily incorporated as part of daily classroom activities and can enhance not only writing skills, but also content area mastery. Some of the types of writing that can be incorporated are functional writing and journal writing.

Functional Writing

Functional writing describes activities in which writing is used to achieve a specific purpose. For example, labeling areas and objects in the classroom is a meaningful and useful activity for all students, especially ELLs. Note taking or developing a grocery list or list of holiday gifts becomes a meaningful activity and will motivate children to write.

Journal Writing

Various types of journals can be used in elementary grades. Some of these include:

- **Personal journals** are used to record personal information and to encourage self-analysis of their experiences. This is a personal document and it is up to the child to make it available to others.

- **Dialogue journals** promote written communication among students and between the teacher and students. The main purpose is to communicate, not to teach writing skills. Teachers can model writing when they reply to children.

- **Reflective journals** are used to respond in writing to specific situations or problems. It is often shared with the teacher for input.

- **Learning logs** are commonly used in the content areas to record elements discussed in class. In these logs, students describe what they have learned and elements in which they have difficulties. Teachers read the document and act on the request for assistance.

Competency 011: Viewing and Representing

The teacher understands skills for interpreting, analyzing, evaluating, and producing visual images and messages in various media and provides students with opportunities to develop skills in this area.

According to the TEKS (1998), students in EC-6 grades need to develop the necessary skills to create and understand images and messages in a variety of media. The skills required by the students increase in complexity as they move from lower elementary grades to upper elementary. For instance, students in grades 1–3 are required to produce visual representations of the information they are learning in school or the tasks they are involved in (e.g., creating an image summarizing a story read). Students are also required to know how to discuss the visual representations they have created. In grades 4–6, students need to be able to understand, interpret, analyze, critique, and produce these visual representations as well as discuss their meaning or significance through the use of multiple media, including newsletters, charts, and electronic presentations, among others. Students are also required to understand the author's purpose and choice of various elements that were used by him/her to get their message across through the use of multiple media. The characteristics and functions of the various different types of media are explained below.

Types and Characteristics of Media

Media is considered to be any means used to convey information to others. There are at least three main types of media available. These include print, visual, and electronic media. **Print media** is what is used to disseminate information in print form such as that found in newspapers, magazines, and direct mail. Print media is static; that is, once it is published, the information cannot be changed. **Visual media** incorporates the use of visual imagery to either complement or supplement the message being carried. Visual media can also stand by itself. For example, photographs and paintings can convey meaning without the need of including texts. Moreover, visual media is also an integral part of print media to illustrate messages. As such, visual media can take many forms, including photography, film, and even cartoons. Visual media can be either static (e.g., still photograph) or dynamic as seen in movies or videos. In addition to incorporating print and visual imagery, **electronic media** requires the use of an external device such as a television, computer, or personal assistant device to display the information and images being presented. Electronic media is used in many different fields including journalism, fine arts, commerce, education, and communications. A primary type of electronic media that encompasses different electronic tools is the Internet, where one can find blogs, email, Web sites, etc.

Technology changes at a rapid pace, and teachers must keep this in mind when working with students. In fact, many of the tools that are used for presenting information are improved and refined every day. For instance, the process for creating photographs has evolved from creating these on plates and then film to now being created digitally.

In this information era, beginning teachers should also understand that there is a vast array of possibilities to create and display information by making use of existing types of media. In fact, as the need for using and sharing massive amounts of information with others becomes necessary, some of these types of media will take precedence over others. Take, for instance, the use of electronic media such as the use of online sources. The use of online information has become so pervasive in today's society that static types of media such as print media is now being channeled electronically (e.g., newspapers). Also, the use of online resources and Web sites has become a staple activity. As such, students expect those around them to know how to use the tools and to use them appropriately. Students are also looking to have opportunities for using and producing different types of products through the use of various types of media.

Representing Messages and Meanings through Media

Charts, tables, graphs, pictures, and print and nonprint media are examples of materials used to solely present or summarize information and/or to complement the message being conveyed. For instance, a chart can be used to summarize large amounts of information without the need to use extensive written explanations. Students should understand that visual representations are important and that the purpose for using them is to present information and to facilitate the communication of the message. Visual images should also be used to make information more understandable. A graphic can expand a concept, serve as an illustration, support points, summarize data, organize facts, add a dimension to the content (such as a cartoon adding humor), compare information, demonstrate change over time, or furnish additional information. Through graphics, the reader can interpret, predict, and even apply information with some careful observation. Actively questioning students as they create visual images (e.g., asking them what they are trying to convey or how they think someone will interpret their image) as well as providing ongoing feedback may allow students to specifically focus on and clarify the information that is being presented and that can be derived in such graphic formats.

Understanding How Students May Interpret and Evaluate Visual Images

It is important for teachers to realize that even a graphic that appears uncomplicated may challenge a reader's interpretive skills. Many inferences may be necessary for even the simplest visual aid or graphic. Many students may initially skip over graphics, or may just notice their presence without interpreting them. Likewise, students may only focus on the graphic aspects being presented in such visual media but not focus on the complementary or written explanations. Even students who have some training in the use of graphic information may not be able to transfer that knowledge to other content areas, or may have trouble going from print to graphic and then back to print. In either case, students may not have been taught how to use multiple representations of information. Teachers can help students use multiple representations of information by using open-book and guided reading. A teacher can also demonstrate how to use a chart or graph through the use of electronic tools including overhead projectors and interactive whiteboards. Examples of presentations and steps toward creating an effective presentation can be shared with the students. Resources and software that would be useful as "mentor texts" (Dorfman & Cappelli, 2007) can give students representative examples of how to best select images to use in parallel with the text (e.g., consideration of how the image parallels or complements the text).

Visual design can be thought of as containing its own grammar (Kress & van Leeuwen, 2001). Teachers can help students to understand and apply the elements of such visual grammar by teaching its component parts (Wysocki, Johnson-Eilola, Selfe, & Sirc, 2004):

- **Visual impact:** the ways in which the overall visual design appeals to the reader (e.g., through detail, layout, use of color).

- **Visual coherence:** the ways in which the design of the piece creates a sense of unity and wholeness (e.g., by use of shapes, line, imagery).

- **Visual salience:** using design features to generate a certain effect (e.g., through varying size, colors, clip art, etc.)

- **Organization:** the layout of the page to create a unique pattern, especially one that is understandable to the reader (e.g., through consideration of how the different aspects of the layout might be arranged).

Of course, these features of visual literacy overlap and can be used flexibly to guide students towards creating an awareness of the visual literacy that parallel and differ from the features of print literacy.

Modeling how to read, complement, and interpret visual images should be done by teachers whenever students are required to create visual images as part of their work in the classroom. Pictures and other graphics can arouse interest and stimulate thinking. Additionally, graphics can add clarity, prevent misunderstandings, show step-by-step developments, exhibit the status of things, events, and processes, and demonstrate comparisons and contrasts (Vacca and Vacca 1989).

Integrating Technology for Producing Communications

Teachers should provide students with opportunities to use state-of-the-art technology and tools to not only motivate children to read, write, and monitor their writing, but to create various kinds of communications products with a variety of media. For instance, one could assume that the goal for using **word processor** software is to simply record written information. Interestingly, with the advances in technology, such software has improved their features to even offer writers assistance with the actual editing of their documents. Other uses for this type of software include creating semantic maps, tables, charts, and graphs. Writing-related elements like spell check, definitions of terms, thesaurus, and even suggestions for sentence constructions are commonly available in programs like Microsoft Word. The real function of a spell checker is not only to identify misspelled words, but also to free students from the pressure of getting spelling right, at least at the drafting stage. Students should be encouraged to put their ideas in writing without stopping to check for spelling. Once they finish the content of the writing, they can take care of other important elements like spelling. Students should, however, be aware that there may be cases in which the spell checker may be ineffective. Therefore, children should be guided to pay attention to corrections and to learn from them.

Teachers have to teach children how to use and take advantage of programs available for communicating and creating electronic products in their classrooms. Some of these products include creating a classroom newsletter, a multimedia presentation, and a video response to a group project. Students should be aware that they must keep their audience and purpose for creating such products in mind whenever they are creating their pieces. Students should also make sure that the language being used is appropriate and understandable for their audience.

Competency 012: Assessment of Developing Literacy

Teachers understand the basic principles of literacy assessment and use a variety of assessments to guide literacy instruction.

Knowledge and Use of Literacy Assessment

There are two main types of assessment: formal and informal. Both have a place in the classroom, particularly in the literacy classroom. The effective teacher understands the importance of ongoing assessment as an instructional tool and uses both informal and formal assessment measures to understand students' learning in his/her classroom. There is never an occasion to group children permanently on the basis of one assessment, either formal or informal. Any grouping of students should come about after the consideration of several assessments, and the grouping should be flexible enough to consider individual differences among the students in each group.

Informal Assessments

Teachers can learn valuable information by simply observing their students at work. Many school districts use a type of inventory/report card to inform adults at home about the progress that children are making. Experienced teachers usually develop, through trial and error, their own means of assessing the skills of students in their classes. Almost every book on teaching reading and writing contains its own informal tests. Teachers can also develop their own informal reading assessment. The purpose of these assessments is to collect meaningful information about what students can and cannot do. A **running record** is a way to assess students' word identification skills and fluency in oral reading. In a running record, the teacher uses a copy of the page to mark each word the child mispronounces as the teacher listens to a student read a page. The teacher writes the incorrect word over the printed word, draws a line through each word the child skips, and draws an arrow under repeated words.

Reading Levels

Reading specialists have identified three reading proficiency levels—independent, instructional, and frustration. If the student reads 95% of the words correctly, the book is at the child's **independent level**. If the student reads 90% to 94% of the words correctly, the book is at the child's **instructional level**, which means the child can perform satisfactorily with help from the teacher. If the student reads 89% or fewer words correctly, the book is probably at the child's **frustration level**. These reading levels are determined based on the ability of children to answer comprehension questions after reading passages. Reading levels are generally assessed through reading informal reading inventories.

Informal Reading Inventories

Informal reading inventories are informal assessment instruments designed to identify the reading levels of children. Most basal reader books contain some type of informal reading inventory. These are graded (by reading levels) passages that include **comprehension questions**. Teachers begin with a passage at the reading level of the child and continue increasing the complexity until the child is not able to respond to the comprehension questions.

Asking a child to **retell a story** is another type of informal assessment. The ability to retell a story is an informal type of assessment that is useful to the teacher, parent, and eventually, the child. Informal assessment measures can also include observations, journals, written drafts, and conversations.

The teacher may also make **observations** during individual or group work. Usually, the teacher makes a **checklist** of competencies, skills, or requirements, and then uses the list to check off the ones a student or group displays. A teacher wishing to emphasize interviewing skills could devise a checklist that includes personal appearance, mannerisms, confidence, and addressing the questions asked. A teacher who wants to emphasize careful listening might observe a discussion with a checklist that includes paying attention, not interrupting, summarizing the ideas of other members of the group, and asking questions about others.

Checklists give teachers the potential for capturing behaviors that cannot be accurately measured with a paper-and-pencil test, such as following the correct sequence of steps in a science experiment, or including all-important elements in a speech in class. One characteristic of a checklist that is both an advantage and a disadvantage is its structure, which provides consistency but inflexibility. However, an open-ended comment section at the end of a checklist can help overcome this disadvantage.

Anecdotal records are helpful in some instances, such as capturing the process a group of students uses to solve a problem. These anecdotal records can be useful when giving feedback to the group. Students can also be taught to write explanations of the procedures they use for their projects or science experiments. One advantage of an anecdotal record is that it can include all relevant information. Disadvantages include the amount of time necessary to complete the record and the difficulty in assigning a grade. If the anecdotal record is used solely for feedback, no grade is necessary.

Portfolios are collections of students' best work. They can be used in any subject area in which the teacher wants students to take more responsibility for planning, carrying out, and organizing their own learning. Like a portfolio created by an artist, model, or performer, a student portfolio provides a succinct picture of the child's achievements over a certain period. Portfolios may contain essays or articles written on paper, videotapes, multimedia presentations on computer disks, or a combination of these. Language arts teachers often use portfolios as a means of collecting the best samples of student writing over an entire year. An important consideration when working with portfolios is that teachers should provide, or assist students in developing, guidelines for what materials should go in their portfolios because it would be unrealistic to include every piece of work in one portfolio. Using portfolios requires that the students devise a means of evaluating their own work. A portfolio should not be a scrapbook for collecting handouts or work done by other individuals, but it can certainly include work by a group in which the student was a participant.

Some advantages that portfolios have over testing are that they provide a clear picture of students' progress, they are not affected by one inferior test grade, and they help develop students' self-assessment skills. One disadvantage of portfolios is the amount of time required to teach students how to develop meaningful portfolios. However, the time is well spent if students learn valuable skills. Another concern is the amount of time teachers must spend to assess portfolios. However, as students become more proficient at self-assessment, the teacher can spend more time in coaching and advising students throughout the development of their portfolios. Another concern is that parents may not understand how the teacher will grade the portfolios. The effective teacher devises a system that the students and parents understand before work on the portfolios begins.

Miscue Analysis

Miscue analysis is an assessment procedure to assess oral reading. Miscues refer to any deviation from text made during oral reading. Here is the procedure for its implementation:

1. Select reading material a little bit above the current reading level of the child. The complete story should be about 500 words in length.

2. Provide a copy of the selection to the child.

3. Get a copy of the selection that is triple spaced to allow room to write comments.

4. Record the reading.

5. Provide instructions to the child, and tell the student that you cannot help him/her during the reading.

6. Ask questions about the story.

7. Let the reader listen to the recording and then analyze it.

8. Look for consistent miscues and pay special attention to initial and final clusters/blends and digraphs.

Running Records

Running records is a form of ongoing assessment designed to identify early reading difficulties in children. The teacher evaluates the reading performance of individual children based on checklists. Through informal observations and through the use of inventories (formal and informal), teachers should be able to determine the **learning styles** of their students. Student learning styles play an important role in determining classroom structure.

Formal Assessments

Formal measures may include teacher-made tests, district exams, and standardized tests. Both formative and summative evaluations are part of effective instruction. **Formative evaluation** occurs during the process of learning when the teacher or the students monitor progress while it is still possible to modify instruction. **Summative evaluation** occurs at the end of a specific time or course of study. Usually, a summative evaluation applies a single grade or score to represent a student's performance.

The effective teacher uses a variety of formal assessment techniques. Teacher-made instruments are ideally developed at the same time as the planning of goals and outcomes, rather than at the last minute after the completion of the lessons. Carefully planned objectives and assessment instruments serve as lesson development guides for the teacher. Paper-and-pencil tests are the most common method for evaluating student progress.

Criterion-Referenced Tests

In **criterion-referenced tests (CRTs)**, the teacher attempts to measure each student against uniform objectives or criteria. CRTs allow the possibility that all students can score 100 percent on the test because they understand the concepts being tested. Teacher-made tests should be criterion-referenced because the teacher should develop them to measure the achievement of predetermined outcomes for the course. If teachers have properly prepared lessons based on the outcomes and, if students have mastered the outcomes, then scores on CRTs should be high. In this type of test, students are not in competition with each other for a high score, and there is no limit to the number of students who can score well. Some commercially developed tests are criterion-referenced; however, most are norm-referenced.

The **Texas Assessment of Knowledge and Skills** (TAKS) is a basic skills test for children in grades 3 to 12. This criterion-referenced test assesses the implementation and the mastery of the Texas Essential Knowledge and Skills (TEKS)—the Texas state curriculum.

Norm-Referenced Tests

The purpose of a norm-referenced test (NRT) is to compare the performance of groups of students. This type of test is competitive because a limited number of students can score well. A plot of NRT scores resembles a bell-shaped curve, with most scores clustering around the center, and a few scores at each end. The midpoint is the average of test data; and, therefore, half of the population will score above average and half below average. The bell-shaped curve is a mathematical description of the results of tossing coins. As such, it represents the chance or normal distribution of skills, knowledge, or events across the general population. A survey of the height of sixth-grade boys will result in an average height, with half the boys being above average height and half below. There will also be a very small number with heights far above average and a very small number with heights far below average; but most heights will cluster around the average. A percentile score (not to be confused with a percentage) is a way of reporting a student's NRT score. The percentile score indicates the percentage of the population whose scores fall at or below the student's score. For example, a group score at the eightieth percentile means that the group scored as well as or better than 80 percent of the students who took the test. A student with a score at the fiftieth percentile has an average score. Percentile scores rank students from highest to lowest. By themselves, percentile scores do not indicate how well the student has mastered the content objectives. Raw scores indicate how many questions the student answered correctly and are, therefore, useful in computing a percentage score.

The Texas Education Agency (TEA) has a comprehensive list of approved norm-reference tests that districts can choose from to assess achievement of students in the state. This list includes the California Achievement Test (CAT), Stanford Achievement Test, and the Iowa Test of Basic Skills (ITBS), among others.

Performance-Based Assessment

Some states and districts are moving toward performance-based tests, which assess students on how well they perform certain tasks. Students must use higher-level thinking skills to apply, analyze, synthesize, and evaluate ideas and data. For example, a content-based performance-based assessment might require students to read a problem, design and carry out a laboratory experiment, and then write summaries of their findings. The performance-based assessment would evaluate both the processes students used and the output they produced. An English performance-based test might ask students to first read a selection of literature and then write a critical analysis. A mathematics performance-based test might state a general problem, require students to invent one or more methods of solving the problem, use one of the methods to arrive at a solution, and write the solution and an explanation of the processes they used. Performance-based assessments allow students to be creative in solutions to problems or questions, and it requires them to use higher-level skills. During these assessments, students work on content-related problems and use skills that are useful in various contexts. There are weaknesses in this approach, however. This type of assessment can be time consuming. Performance-based assessments often require multiple resources, which can be expensive. Teachers must receive training in applying the test. Nonetheless, many schools consider performance-based testing to be a more authentic measure of student achievement than traditional tests.

Classroom Tests

Teachers must consider fundamental professional and technical factors when constructing effective classroom tests. One of the first factors to recognize is that test construction is as creative, challenging, and important as any aspect of teaching. The planning and background that contribute to effective teaching are incomplete unless evaluation of student performance provides accurate feedback to the teacher and the student about the learning process.

Good tests are the product of careful planning, creative thinking, hard work, and technical knowledge about the various methods of measuring student knowledge and performance. Classroom tests that accomplish their purpose are the result of the development of a pool of items and refinement of those items based on feedback and constant revision. It is through this process that evaluation of students becomes valid and reliable. Tests serve as a valuable instructional aid because they help determine student progress and also provide feedback to teachers regarding their own effectiveness. Student misunderstandings and problems that the tests reveal can help the teacher understand areas of special concern in providing instruction. This information also becomes the basis for the remediation of students and the revision of teaching procedures. Consequently, the construction, administration, and proper scoring of classroom tests are among the most important activities in teaching.

Authentic Assessments

Paper-and-pencil tests and essay tests are not the only methods of assessment. Other assessments include projects, observations, checklists, anecdotal records, portfolios, self-assessments, and peer assessments. Although these types of assessments often take more time and effort to plan and administer, they can often provide a more authentic measurement of student progress.

Essay Tests

There are advantages and disadvantages to essay tests. Advantages of essay questions include the possibility for students to be creative in their answers, the opportunity for students to explain their responses, and the potential to test for higher-level thinking skills. Disadvantages of essay questions include the time students need to formulate meaningful responses, and the time teachers need to evaluate the essays. In addition, language difficulties can make essay tests extremely difficult for some students, including ELLs. Consistency in evaluating essays can also be a problem for some teachers, but an outline of the acceptable answers—a scoring rubric—can help a teacher avoid inconsistency. Teachers who write specific questions and know what they are looking for are more likely to be consistent in grading. Also, if there are several essay questions, the effective teacher grades all student responses to the first question, then moves on to all responses to the second, and so on.

Using Rubrics for Assessment

A **rubric** is a checklist with assigned point values. To construct a rubric, a teacher uses the lesson objectives. Students should receive an explanation of the rubric *before* starting to work on their writing assignment, and they can use the rubric as a guideline while they are preparing their writing assignment. The teacher can use the rubric to evaluate the completed assignment. Then teachers can provide clear, well-planned instructions and guidelines for activities; they can significantly decrease student frustration. Rubrics can provide this valuable guidance. When teachers model what they expect and state clear objectives or goals for each assignment, students perform better. Accordingly, there should be a clear and obvious link between the assignment's goals and the students' achievement.

Scoring Compositions

Holistic scoring is used to evaluate the composition and writing performance of students in Texas. The whole writing sample is scored based on a pre-established criterion contained in a rubric. The writing rubric used to score the performance on TAKS is based on four levels. Students need to score at level three or four to pass the test.

Ongoing Assessment

Ongoing assessment provides teachers with updated information about the progress and challenges that children are facing in writing. This information can then be easily incorporated in daily instruction.

Assessing English Language Learners

The Texas English Language Proficiency Assessment System (TELPAS) was designed to comply with the accountability system required in the No Child Left Behind (NCLB) Act (TEA, 2006b). The legislation requires that ELLs are assessed yearly in all language skills—listening, speaking, reading, and writing. Students begin taking TELPAS in kindergarten and only stop participating when they are exited from the program. This system is composed of two testing components: the Reading Proficiency Tests in English (RPTE) and the Texas Observation Protocols (TOP). Both assessment instruments were especially developed for ELLs. The RPTE is an assessment that measures reading skills of ELLs. These skills are: word meaning, supporting idea, summarization, analyzing, and evaluating. RPTE is given in a booklet in a multiple-choice format.

The TOP is an assessment that measures four language skills through classroom observation and daily interactions. It is graded holistically. Both assessments are broken down into four levels: beginning, intermediate, advanced, and advanced high. Listening, speaking, reading, and writing are assessed with the TOP in kindergarten to second grade. In grades 3 and up, the TOP assesses listening, speaking, and writing; reading is assessed with the RPTE. To assess the writing component for ELLs in grades 2 through 12, at least five writing samples a year are collected and assessed holistically to comply with the four language levels mentioned earlier—beginning, intermediate, advanced, or advanced high level. ELLs stop taking the RPTE when they reach the advanced high level of the combined TOP and RPTE scores.

Diversity in the Classroom

The effective teacher appreciates human diversity. An empowered instructor recognizes how diversity in the classroom creates an environment in which everyone accepts and celebrates both the diversity and the uniqueness of individuals. In that environment, the teacher and the students view race, ethnicity, religion, national origin, learning style, and gender of learners as strengths that foster learning with and from each other.

Key Principles of this Competency

- Formal and informal assessments must be used in the classroom as the mechanism to improve the instruction and the learning of all students.

- Teachers must know how to analyze and interpret the information gathered through informal and formal means.

- Test results should be used in conjunction with other types of assessment to improve the instruction and literacy development of students.

- Students' native languages as well as cultural background should be taken into consideration when teaching and assessing children.

- The multiple uses of criterion-referenced, norm-referenced, performance-based, classroom, and authentic assessments are essential to giving the child, the teacher, and the parents a complete picture of the child's progress and learning.

References

Bloom, B. S. 1956. *Taxonomy of educational objectives: The classification of educational goals: Handbook I, cognitive domain*. New York: Toronto: Longmans, Green.

Brown, D. K. 1997. The children's literature web guide. *http://www.ucalgary.ca/~dkbrown/cinderella.html* (accessed August 27, 2009).

Browning Schulman, M. and C. D. Payne. 2000. *Guided reading: Making it work*. New York: Scholastic, Inc.

Chall, J. S. 1983. *Stages of reading development,* New York: McGraw-Hill.

Clay, M. M. 2002. *An observation survey of early literacy achievement*. 2nd ed. Portsmouth, NH: Heinemann.

Dorfman, L. R., and R. Cappelli. 2007. *Mentor texts: Teaching writing through children's literature, K–6*. Portland, ME: Stenhouse Publishers.

Ehri, L. 1998. Grapheme-phoneme knowledge is essential for learning to read words in English. In *Word Recognition in Beginning Literacy*, eds. J. Metsala and L. Ehri, 3–40, Mahwah, NJ: Erlbaum.

Goudvis, A. and S. Harvey. 2000. *Strategies that work*. Portland, ME: Stenhouse Publishers.

Gough, P. B. 1972. One second of reading. In *Theoretical Models and Processes of Reading*, 3rd ed., eds. H. Singer, & R. B. Ruddell, 661–686. Newark, Delaware: International Reading Association.

Graves, D. H. 1983. *Writing: Teachers and children at work*. Portsmouth, NH: Heinemann Educational Books.

Heath, S. B. 1983. *Ways with words: Language, life and work in communities and classrooms*. Cambridge: Cambridge University Press.

Kress, G. & T. J. Van Leeuwen. 2001. *Multimodal Discourse: The modes and media of contemporary communication.* London, England: Oxford University Press.

Lapp, D., D. Fisher, J. Flood, and A. Cabello. 2001. An integrated approach to the teaching and assessment of language arts. In *Literacy assessment of second language learners.* eds. S. Rollins Hurley and J. Villamil Tinajero. 1–24. Boston, MA: Allyn and Bacon.

Northwest Regional Education Laboratory. 2006. 6+1 Trait Writing. *http://www.thetraits. org/about.php* (accessed August 27, 2009).

Palinscar, A. S. & Brown, A. L. 1984. Reciprocal teaching of comprehension-fostering and comprehension-monitoring activities. *Cognition and Instruction* (1): 117–175.

Peregoy, S. F., O. F. Boyle, and K. Cadiero-Kapplan. 2008. *Reading, Writing and Learning in ESL: A Resource Book for K-12 Teachers*. 5th. ed. New York: Pearson.

Piper, T. 2006. *Language and learning: The home school year.* 4th ed. Columbus, Ohio: Merrill Prentice Hall.

Reuzel, R. D., and R. Cooter. 1992. *Teaching children to read: From basals to books.* New York: Macmillan Publishing Co.

Snow, C. E., M. S. Burns, and P. Griffin. 1998. *Preventing reading difficulties in young children.* Washington, DC: National Academy Press.

Stewig, J. W. and Jett-Simpson. 1995. *Language arts in the early childhood classroom.* Belmont, CA: Wadsworth.

TAKS. 2005. Chapter 110. 3 English Language arts and reading. Subchapter A. Elementary. Texas Education Code, §28.002.

TEA. 2002. Guidelines for Examining Phonics and Word Recognition Programs. *Texas Reading Initiative. http://www.tea.state.tx.us/reading/products/products.html* (accessed August 27, 2009).

TEA. 2005. *Linguistically Accommodated Testing (LAT) Supplement to the TAKS and SDAA II. Test Administrator Manuals. http://www.tea.state.tx.us/student.assessment/*

admin/rpte/LAT_TA_supp.pdf#xml=http://www.tea.state.tx.us/cgi/texis/webinator/ search/xml.txt?query=Linguistic+accommodations&db=db&id=f8b138c3acf474d6 (accessed July 21, 2009).

TEA. 2006. Texas Observation Protocol (TOP). Rater Manual Grades K–12. *Texas English Language Proficiency Assessment System (TELPAS)*. Austin, TX: Texas Education.

TEA. 2006. *Texas English Language Proficiency Assessment System (TELPAS)*. *http:// www.tea.state.tx.us/student.assessment/resources/guides/coormanual* (accessed July 21, 2009).

Tomas, E., and H. Robinson. 1972. *Improving reading in every class: A source book for teachers*. Boston: Allyn and Bacon.

U.S. Department of Education. 2006. A closer look at the five essential components of effective reading instruction. *http://www.tea.state.tx.us/reading/readingfirst/reading-first.html* (accessed August 23, 2009).

Vacca, R. T., and J. A. Vacca. 1989. *Content area reading*. Glenview, IL: Scott Foresman.

Wysocki, A. F., J. Johnson-Eilola, C. L. Selfe, and G. Sirc. 2004. *Writing new media: Theory and applications for expanding the teaching of composition*. Logan, UT: Utah State University Press.

Mathematics

The teacher understands how students learn mathematical skills and uses that knowledge to plan, organize, and implement instruction and assess learning.

In 2000, the National Council of Teachers of Mathematics (NCTM) published the *Principles and Standards for School Mathematics*. The national organization's goals include the development and improvement of mathematics education. In the NCTM publication, the association identified six principles and ten standards that children in K-12 ought to master. The document guides states and district curricula development and specifies the mathematics content knowledge students should develop.

Principles of Mathematics

The NCTM (2000) identified six principles that should guide mathematics instruction. These include: equity, curriculum, teaching, learning, assessment, and technology. These are defined as follows:

- **Equity**—Excellence in mathematics education requires equity: high expectations and strong support for all students.

- **Curriculum**—A curriculum must be coherent, focused on important mathematics, and well-articulated concepts across the grades.

- **Teaching**—Effective mathematics teaching requires understanding of what students know and need to learn and then challenging and supporting students to learn it well.

- **Learning**—Students must learn mathematics with understanding, actively building new knowledge from experience and previous knowledge.

- **Assessment**—Assessment should support the learning of important mathematics concepts, and furnish useful information to both teachers and students.

- **Technology**—Technology is essential in teaching and learning mathematics; it influences the teaching of mathematics and enhances students' learning.

Standards for Mathematics

The Content Standards describe the five strands of content that students should learn; and the Process Standards highlight ways of acquiring and applying content knowledge.

Content Standards

1. *Number and Operations.* This standard deals with understanding numbers, developing meanings of operations, and computing fluently.

2. *Algebra.* Algebraic symbols and procedures for working with them are a towering mathematical accomplishment in the history of mathematics, and are critical in mathematical work. Algebra is best learned as a set of concepts and techniques tied to the representation of quantitative relations and as a style of mathematical thinking for formalizing patterns, functions, and generalizations.

3. *Geometry.* Geometry has long been regarded as the place in high school where students learn to prove geometric theorems. The Geometry standard takes a broader view of the power of geometry by calling on students to analyze characteristics of geometric shapes and make mathematical arguments about the geometric relationship, as well as to use visualization, spatial reasoning, and geometric modeling to solve problems.

4. *Measurement.* The study of measurement is crucial in the school mathematics curriculum because of its practicality and pervasiveness in so many aspects of life. The Measurement standard includes understanding the attributes, units, systems, and processes of measurement as well as applying the techniques, tools, and formulas to determine measurements.

5. *Data Analysis and Probability.* Students must formulate questions and collect, organize, and display relevant data to answer key questions. Additionally, it emphasizes learning appropriate statistical methods to analyze data, making inferences and predictions based on data, and understanding and using the basic concepts of probability.

Process Standards

1. *Problem Solving.* Students require frequent opportunities to formulate, grapple with, and solve complex problems that involve a significant amount of effort. Students are able to acquire ways of thinking, habits of persistence and curiosity, and confidence in unfamiliar situations that serve them well outside the mathematics classroom.

2. *Reasoning and Proof.* Mathematical reasoning and proof offer powerful ways of developing and expressing insights. Students are able to identify patterns, structure, or regularities in both real-world and mathematical situations. They make and investigate mathematical conjectures; and develop and evaluate mathematical arguments and proofs, which are ways reasoning and providing justification.

3. *Communication.* Mathematical communication is a way of sharing ideas and clarifying understanding. Through communication, ideas become objects of reflection, refinement, discussion, and amendment.

4. *Connections.* Mathematics is an integrated field of study. When students connect mathematical ideas, their understanding is deeper and more lasting, and they come to view mathematics as a coherent whole.

5. *Representations.* Mathematical ideas can be represented in a variety of ways: pictures, concrete materials, tables, graphs, number and letter symbols, spreadsheet displays, and so on.

Texas Mathematics Standards

Standard 1—Number Concepts:

The mathematics teacher understands and uses numbers, number systems and their structure, operations and algorithms, quantitative reasoning, and technology appropriate to teach the statewide curriculum (Texas Essential Knowledge and Skills [TEKS]) in order to prepare students to use mathematics (TEA, 2009a).

Standard 2—Patterns and Algebra:

The mathematics teacher understands and uses patterns, relations, functions, algebraic reasoning, analysis, and technology appropriate to teach the statewide curriculum (Texas Essential Knowledge and Skills [TEKS]) in order to prepare students to use mathematics.

Standard 3—Geometry and Measurement:

The mathematics teacher understands and uses geometry, spatial reasoning, measurement concepts and principles, and technology appropriate to teach the statewide curriculum (Texas Essential Knowledge and Skills [TEKS]) in order to prepare students to use mathematics.

Standard 4—Probability and Statistics:

The mathematics teacher understands and uses probability and statistics, their applications, and technology appropriate to teach the statewide curriculum (Texas Essential Knowledge and Skills [TEKS]) in order to prepare students to use mathematics.

Standard 5—Mathematical Processes:

The mathematics teacher understands and uses mathematical processes to reason mathematically, to solve mathematical problems, to make mathematical connections within and outside of mathematics, and to communicate mathematically.

Standard 6—Mathematical Perspectives:

The mathematics teacher understands the historical development of mathematical ideas, the interrelationship between society and mathematics, the structure of mathematics, and the evolving nature of mathematics and mathematical knowledge.

Standard 7—Mathematical Learning and Instruction:

The mathematics teacher understands how children learn and develop mathematical skills, procedures, and concepts, knows typical errors students make, and uses this knowledge to plan, organize, and implement instruction; to meet curriculum goals; and to teach all students to understand and use mathematics.

Standard 8—Mathematical Assessment:

The mathematics teacher understands assessment and uses a variety of formal and informal assessment techniques appropriate to the learner on an ongoing basis to monitor and guide instruction and to evaluate and report student progress.

Standard 9—Professional Development:

The mathematics teacher understands mathematics teaching as a profession, knows the value and rewards of being a reflective practitioner, and realizes the importance of making a lifelong commitment to professional growth and development.

Mathematics and English Language Learners

Contrary to popular belief, mathematics is not a universal language. It is a language with special nomenclature and unique concepts. Even the way that people perform mathematical processes is often different. For example, in Mexico and the Dominican Republic the processes used for division differ from the process used in the United States. In Mexico the problem is set up in a similar fashion but most of the steps are done mentally, as opposed to the American way, where students write every single step as part of the process. For example, in the problem, 11 divided by 2, children in Mexico are taught to multiply 5 by 2 and get 10, but they do not write the 10 under the 11; they do it mentally and write the remainder below the 11. In the Dominican Republic, children do not use the traditional division bracket used in the United States and Mexico; instead, they use a bracket similar to an elongated **L**, and they place the *divisor* inside the bracket and the *dividend* outside. Thus children from Mexico and the Dominican Republic might experience confusion when asked to perform division the "American way."

Table 2–1 illustrates the three different processes used to perform division.

The use of Arabic numbers does not present problems for English language learners (ELLs). The real challenge is to comprehend the explanation of the process in a language that ELLs have not yet mastered. Providing examples of mathematics process and modeling while describing them can definitely improve comprehension. Students who enjoy *inductive teaching*—learning through examples—will definitely benefit from this approach. However, children who enjoy the *deductive approach*—learning step by step—might experience comprehension problems.

Table 2–1 Processes of Division

American	Mexican	Dominican
$2\overline{)11}^{5}$ -10 $1R$	$2\overline{)11}^{5}$ $1R$	11 5 -10 2 $1R$ 10

The Nomenclature of Mathematics

In addition to the obvious English communication problems, English learners face a number of challenges with the technical vocabulary or the nomenclature of mathematics for at least three reasons. First, the mathematics classroom tends to abound in assumptions concerning students' prior knowledge of specialized terms such as *denominator, subtraction, minuend, divisor, subtrahend*, and others. Second, the terms that have one meaning in one subject domain can assume an entirely different meaning in the vocabulary of mathematics; these terms include *quarter, column, product, rational, even, and table*. Finally, the vocabulary tends to encompass a variety of homophones (words pronounced in the same way but have different meanings) and can be troublesome for English learners who are unaccustomed to the new language. The **Table 2–2** lists various mathematic terms and structures that may be confusing for all students.

Table 2–2 Terminology of Mathematics

Terminology	Generic Meaning	Mathematical Meaning
Even	Equal amount, same level	Numbers divisible by 2
Faces	Front of human head	Surface of a geometric solid
Plane	Flat surface, aircraft, or without adornment	A two-dimensional surface
Mean	Not nice, or to express a particular message	Arithmetic average of a set of values
Right	Correct, proper, or a direction	Forming a 90° right angle
Sum/Some	A small amount	Answer to addition problem
Volume	Loudness of sounds	Quantity of Liquid

(continued)

Unfamiliar Structures
Technical terms (e.g., equation, exponents, inequalities, quotient)
Varied degrees of focus on problem solving versus computation and notation.
Use of Passive Voice for most problem solving questions and statements.
Use of various mathematical symbols unfamiliar to ELLs (e.g., π, \$, <, =, $\pm$, and $\neq$).
Multiple words or phrases indicating the same operations (e.g., fractional parts, divide, separate, equivalent parts, etc.)
"If . . . then . . ." problem statements that are unclear.
Cultural specific examples in word problems drawn from unfamiliar situations.
Focus on problem solving using culturally bias strategies or context unfamiliar to ELLs.
Multiple words with similar meanings (e.g., mean mode, median, and range).
New information that does not fit with prior knowledge of subject matter (e.g., time, temperature, money, measurement, use of manipulative in the classroom).

Developmentally Appropriate Instruction

Children develop a basic understanding of numbers as early as two years of age or even at a younger age. Infants and toddlers understand the concepts of "one" or "more," usually within the context of food. Rote counting or the verbal repetition of numbers begins at around the age of 2–3 years. This rote memorization can be used as a foundation for building understanding of number concepts of combining, separating, and naming amounts using concrete objects as soon as language develops. In their effort to develop the idea of amount, children must first know the language of number words (Fuson & Hall, 1983). Sometimes children appear to be counting when, in fact, they are naming the objects. For example, when a child has eight red blocks and begins to count out loud, "One, two, three, four, five, six, seven, eight," pointing to each block as he/she goes, and then says, "Eight," we need to ask questions. "How do you know" or "show me eight" will tell us whether the child recognizes that the entire set makes up "eight-ness" or that the last block is named "Eight." They need to understand that the idea of amount is inclusive of all the previously counted blocks, not just the name of the last block.

Children should be encouraged to think about numbers and the quantity of objects in meaningful situations. For example, children may be asked to hold up five crayons or hand out five crayons to each student. Kamii (2000) states that to deepen quantification knowledge students should compare sets in real life situations rather than just count out objects. It is important for children to use movable objects, moving to larger quantities, in order to create their own internal mental relationships while interacting with various types of objects (Pepper & Hunting, 1998).

In making the move from quantification to computation, it is helpful to pose an addition question using concrete objects. Using a context for the objects helps children to make their own sense and helps them to develop their own autonomy about the operation of addition. For example, a simple addition problem can be introduced by putting beads on a string and asking children to add or subtract the various colors to create a necklace or bracelet. Many times children will prefer to "use paper and pencil" instead of objects, so they can externalize their own ideas and use drawings instead. This is probably why children do not choose to use counters to solve word problems (Kamii, 2000).

Several materials or concrete objects can be used to help children demonstrate the mathematics of the problems. It is important to distinguish between discrete models, such as counters, and continuous models, such as number lines that children might choose for solving problems. Personal algorithms can grow directly from meaningful experiences acting out problems, whether through direct modeling or counting until the mathematics concepts make sense to the child.

Cognitive Development and Mathematics

The cognitive development of children in Pre-K through grade 6 represents a special challenge when attempting to learn the symbolic and abstract representation used in mathematics. Children are expected to learn an entire organized discipline, usually represented in symbolic form. They may learn to deal with symbols well enough to perform arithmetic operations. However, having learned arithmetic procedures is not sufficient for real understanding of the concepts that symbolic manipulations represent. It is not guaranteed that children will be able to use those concepts to solve problems.

Learning mathematics requires that children create and recreate mathematics relationships in their own mind. Children need direct and concrete interaction with mathematic ideas; these ideas are not accessible from abstractions and symbols. Continuous interaction between a child's mind and concrete experiences in the real world are necessary to learn concepts in math.

As a developmental biologist, Jean Piaget (1896–1980) observed and recorded the intellectual abilities of infants, children and adolescents. His stages of intellectual development were related to brain growth and led him to conclude that the thinking and reasoning of children was dominated by preoperational thought—a pattern of thinking that is egocentric, centered, irreversibly and nontransformational (Piaget & Inhelder, 1969). His theory concerned the growth of intelligence, the emergence and acquisition of schemata-schemes of a child using "developmental stages" to explain how children acquire new information. Piaget divided schemes that children use into four main stages, these include:

- Sensorimotor stage (birth–2 years)

- Preoperational stage (years 2–7)

- Concrete Operational stage (years 7–11)

- Formal Operational stage (years 11–adult)

The importance of these stages of development as conceptualized by Piaget is the recognition that the child's ability to integrate symbolic referents (objects or experiences) and to interpret the mathematical concept. Children about six years old (first graders in the Preoperational stage) tend to fix their attention on a single aspect of a relationship. For example, if two rows of the same number of coins are lined up, one-to-one, equally spaced, and children are asked if the number of coins in the two rows are the same, they are likely to judge the two to be equal. When the appearance of one of the rows is changed, either by spreading the coins out further or stacking them, the child is more likely to judge them as being unequal. Their response is not based on logical reasoning but on their own perception.

According to Piaget, the Preoperational stage of development includes the following processes: symbolic functioning, centration, intuitive thought, egocentrism, and inability to conserve. Children in the Concrete Operational stage exhibit the developmental processes of: decentering, reversibility, conservation, serialization, classification, and elimination of egocentrism. The Formal Operational stage of cognitive development begins around eleven years of age (puberty) and continues into adulthood. The characteristics of this stage focus on the ability to use symbols and think abstractly.

Sperry Smith (2008) reports that children in the Preoperational stage experience problems with at least two perceptual concepts—centration and conservation.

- **Centration**—Characterized by a child focusing only on one aspect of a situation or problem. For example, take two 5" × 8" cards and roll each into a tube, rolling one the short way and the other the long way. Tape them to make cylindrical containers. Fill each tube with beans to compare how much each holds. A preschool child might judge the quantity of beans in the tall cylinder to be more than the shorter based on their perception of tall and short.

- **Conservation**—Understanding that quantity, length, or number of items is unrelated to the arrangement or appearance of the object or items. This limitation can affect children's ability to measure volume and to understand the value of money. For example, children may think a nickel is worth more than a dime because the coin is larger, or that five nickels are more than a quarter.

During the Concrete Operational stage of cognitive development—second to seventh grades—children experience rapid growth in cognitive development. This stage is characterized by the ability to think logically about concrete objects or relationships. Some of the characteristics of children at this stage are as follows:

- **Decentering**—Where the child can take into account multiple aspects of a problem to solve it. Can form conclusion based on reason rather than perception;

- **Reversibility**—Where the child understands that the objects can be changed, then returned to their original state. Can determine that $4 + 4 = 8$ and $8 - 4 = 4$; the original quantity.

- **Conservation**—Where the child understands that quantity, length, or number of items is unrelated to the arrangement or appearance of the object. Can discern that if water is transferred to a pitcher it will conserve the quantity and be equal to the other filled cup.

- **Seriation**—Where the child is able to arrange objects in an order according to size, shape, or any other attribute. Can arrange geometric forms by shape, size, color, and thickness of the form.

- **Classification**—Where the child can name and identify sets of objects according to appearance, size, or other characteristic. Can arrange objects based on characteristics.

- **Elimination of Egocentrism**—Where the child is able to view things from another's perspective. Can retell a story from another child's perspective.

Since Piaget completed his work, contemporary researchers (often referred to as neo-Piagetian and post-Piagetian researchers) found that Piaget had underestimated the abilities of children in the preschool and early elementary years. Even before the second or early third grade, some students develop more sophisticated thinking and reasoning skill, especially if they have had adequate instruction and opportunities to interact with adults and competent peers (Vygotsky, 1986). Children's intellectual development appears to proceed continuously, and their cognitive development is influenced by their culture and by instruction (Santrock, 2003). This relates to cognitively guided instruction (CGI) (Carpenter, Fennema, Franke, Levi, & Empson, 1999; Flavell, 1985; Kamii, 2000). The CGI model depends heavily on a well-developed structure of how children learn a given topic and on the ability of the teacher to assess the knowledge of each child and provide appropriate experiences. Kamii's work and CGI's researchers connect their respective research to understanding how children learn mathematic concepts and how to recognize different strategies young children use when they execute operations.

Mathematics in Real-Life Situations

Mathematical concepts are an integral part of our daily life. Children should be encouraged to pay attention to daily activities and identify the mathematical principles used to perform the activity or the task. A simple visit to the local supermarket requires some level of mathematical development to communicate effectively. For instance, reading product labels requires an understanding of weights and measurements. It also requires knowledge of the standard and metric systems and the value of money. Without this kind of knowledge, it would be practically impossible to make intelligent decisions.

Consider the following situation:

A consumer is trying to decide between two products—a kilogram of coffee for $3.99 or 2 pounds of the same coffee for $3.99. What item represents the best value?

In order to make this decision, the consumer must have an understanding of the *standard* and *metric* systems of measurement. Most consumers in the United States will probably go with 2 pounds because they are familiar with the *standard* system of measurement. However, this option is not the best value for the money because 1 kilogram is equivalent to 2.2 pounds. Parents can present this kind of problem to children and ask them to help in the decision-making process. When mathematics is used in real-life situations, it becomes more meaningful and easier to internalize.

Manipulatives in Mathematics

Children can benefit from group instruction and the use of concrete objects and manipulatives. Manipulatives can be use to provide "hands-on-learning" for kindergarten to high school students. Manipulatives enhance student understanding, enable students to have conversations that are grounded in a common model, and help students recognize and correct their own misconceptions in concept attainment. Manipulatives are an excellent way for students to develop self-verbalizing learning strategies. As they use the senses of sight, touch, and hearing, students should be encouraged to talk their way through each problem, either with peers or to themselves. Physical materials can model the situation and illuminate some of the aspects of the processes of various operations, such as multiplication and division. It is important that the concept is first understood by the student and that the manipulative is appropriate for the concept in order for the materials to be used in ways that make sense. Rather, it is important that students develop relationships that are mental abstractions about the mathematics being represented by the physical materials and then develop a corresponding symbolic representation. Teachers have to ask good questions and listen to students explain their thinking to know whether they have abstracted the idea from the physical models.

Games are highly motivational for children in pre-kindergarten through grade 6. A simple game using dice can be used to teach counting, place value, and probability. Color tiles, unifix cubes, two-color counters, and pattern blocks can be used to teach sequencing, patterns, odd and even numbers, probability, and statistics. Children learn best when they can manipulate materials to check their understanding and link what they are learning to real-life situations. For example, they learn about fractions initially outside the school. Often they hear adults use fractions in various conversations:

- You can have half of my cookie.

- The dishwasher is less than half full.

- I need to buy two and a half yards of ribbon.

- My gas tank is half full.

- It is a quarter past three.

- Do you have any quarter-inch plywood?

- The recipe calls for two-thirds of a cup of Rice Krispies.

- May I have half a pound of sliced turkey?

Numbers and fractions represent a challenge to elementary students. From their experiences, a number of ideas about fractions take shape informally in children's minds. They may have heard of one-half, one-fourth, and one-third of a unit—but not two-thirds or three-fourths. Therefore, their understanding may be incomplete and confused. Children think of "half" as any part of a whole, rather than one of two equal parts, and refer to one-half being larger than another. For example, they may say, "My half is bigger than yours." Additionally, they may not understand relationships, such as three-fourths of an inch is one-fourth less than one inch. Classroom instruction should build on children's previous experiences and focus within the context of real life before moving to the symbolic representations. Fractions may be taught using fraction kits, where students cut and label the pieces to relate the fractional notation to the concrete pieces and compare the sizes of fractional parts. They are able to see that $\frac{1}{4}$, for example, is larger than one-sixteenth, and they can measure to prove that two of the $\frac{1}{8}$ pieces are equivalent to $\frac{1}{4}$. Table 2–3 presents an analysis of fractions.

Table 2–3 Equivalent Fractions

One Whole = $\frac{1}{1}$							
One-half = $\frac{1}{2}$				One-half = $\frac{1}{2}$			
One-fourth = $\frac{1}{4}$		One-fourth = $\frac{1}{4}$		One-fourth = $\frac{1}{4}$		One-fourth = $\frac{1}{4}$	
One-eighth = $\frac{1}{8}$	$\frac{1}{8}$	$\frac{1}{8}$	$\frac{1}{8}$	$\frac{1}{8}$	$\frac{1}{8}$	$\frac{1}{8}$	$\frac{1}{8}$
$\frac{1}{16}$ $\frac{1}{16}$	$\frac{1}{16}$ $\frac{1}{16}$	$\frac{1}{16}$ $\frac{1}{16}$	$\frac{1}{16}$ $\frac{1}{16}$	$\frac{1}{16}$ $\frac{1}{16}$	$\frac{1}{16}$ $\frac{1}{16}$	$\frac{1}{16}$ $\frac{1}{16}$	$\frac{1}{16}$ $\frac{1}{16}$

Use of Technology

As rapidly as technology is changing and improving, educators are having difficulty keeping up with those advances and how to use technology to improve instruction. Clearly changes need to be made in how schools acquire access to these new advances. These changes must be equitably implemented so that students who live in poverty have the same access to technology and challenging mathematics as their affluent peers. The newest advancements in hand-held computers present educators with both opportunities and responsibilities. The primary opportunity is that of allowing access to challenging mathematics for every student, regardless of the student's past mastery of arithmetic or rote skills.

Digital videos provide opportunities for students to evaluate their own explanations of problem solutions. Students may present their videos and discuss similarities and differences in approaches to solving problems. These may be uploaded onto a website to allow for online discussions using discussion board tools, blogs, and various communication tools with other students. Students can develop effective presentations, online resources, wikis, and other projects for sharing with learners around the world. Additional digital presentation tools may help students to develop effective presentations that communicate mathematic ideas. Programs such as PowerPoint and HyperStudio allow students to integrate graphics, digital images and video, and text into their presentations.

Learning Environment

The *Professional Standards for Teaching Mathematics* (NCTM, 2007) presents six standards for the teaching of mathematics, organized under four categories: tasks, discourse, environment, and analysis. These are crucial in shaping what goes on in mathematics classrooms. These four strands are integrated and interdependent, and they include the following:

- TASKS are the projects, questions, problems, constructions, applications, and exercises in which students engage.

- DISCOURSE refers to the way of representing, thinking, talking, and agreeing and disagreeing that teachers and students use to engage in these tasks.

- ENVIRONMENT represents the setting for learning.

- ANALYSIS is the systematic reflection in which teachers engage.

The teacher of mathematics should create a learning environment that fosters the development of each student's mathematical ability, by doing the following:

- provide and structure the time necessary to explore sound mathematics and grapple with significant ideas and problems;

- use the physical space and materials in ways that facilitate the learning of mathematics;

- provide a context that encourages the development of mathematical skill and proficiency;

- Respect and value students' ideas, ways of thinking, and mathematical dispositions.

Included in the *Professional Standards for Teaching Mathematics* are five major shifts in the environment of mathematics classrooms from current practice to teaching for the empowerment of students. These major shift areas include:

- Classrooms as mathematical communities—away from classrooms as simply a collection of individuals;

- Logic and mathematical evidence as verification—away from the teacher as the sole authority for right answers;

- Mathematical reasoning—away from merely memorizing procedures;

- Problem solving—away from an emphasis on mechanistic answer-finding;

- Connecting mathematics, its ideas, and its applications—away from mathematics as a body of isolated concepts and procedures.

Strengthening Mathematical Concepts Using Manipulatives and a Variety of Tools

In addition to the manipulative used in mathematics, the typical classroom contains a variety of instructional materials (See Table 2–4) to support children in the learning process. Teachers should be encouraged to use these to make mathematics more engaging and meaningful to children.

The Texas Essential Knowledge and Skills (TEKS)

The Texas Essential Knowledge and Skills (TEKS) is the state's required curriculum. The implementation of TEKS for Mathematics requires a well-balanced curriculum beginning in Kindergarten and continuing through grade 12 (See: TAC, Chapter 111— *The provisions of §111.11 adopted to be effective September 1, 1998, 22 TexReg 7623.*).

Table 2–4 Materials used in the Mathematics Classroom

Types of Manipulatives and Instructional Materials					
Grades K-1	**Grade 2**	**Grade 3**	**Grade 4**	**Grade 5**	**Grades 6**
Beads, string, sewing cards	Blocks	Base Ten Blocks	Geometric Solids	Cuisenaire Rods	Cuisenaire Rods
Snap Cubes, straws	Cubes	Tangrams	Geoboards	Virtual manipulative	Virtual manipulative
Color Tiles	Chips	Pattern Blocks	calculators	Calculators	Calculators
Two-color counters	Measuring cups	Playing Cards	Protractors	Graduated cylinders	Attribute Logic Block
Macaroni, beans, cereal, candy, raisins, crackers	Attribute Shapes	Scales: customary & metric	Tangrams	Timers	Algebra tiles
Buttons, sticks, stones, shells	Money Models	Magnetic numbers, chalk boards	Pentominoes	Metric Beaker Set for Volume	Video games
Paper Clips	Number lines	Spinners, dice	Graphing paper	Metric Trundle Wheel	Math software games
Toothpicks	Dominoes	Calendar	Fraction Kit	Fraction tower cubes	iPods
Legos	Unifix cubes	Fractional Shapes	Platform scale	Connecting cubes	Balance Metric weight set
Egg cartons	Clock faces	Games	Customary Weight set	Board games	Computer/Internet
Teddy Bear counters	Ruler, yard stick, metric stick	Measuring tape	Metric weight set	Fraction tiles	Smart boards
Board games	Balance scales	0–99 Charts	Graphing boards	Geoboards	Digital cameras, camcorders
Pictographs	Linear Graphs	Bar Graphs	Scatter plot graphs	Pie charts & graphs	Computer templates

Pre-kindergarten content has been aligned with the TEKS and may be found at the Texas Education Agency, Pre-kindergarten Curriculum Guidelines (1999a) online at: *www.tea.state.tx.us/curriculum/early/prekguide.html*

Both the TEKS and the Pre-kindergarten Curriculum Guidelines incorporate the principles and standards of the NCTM, which provide early experiences and exploration of number concepts using concrete objects to learn about one-to-one correspondence. In the first and second grade, students continue exploring number concepts and begin learning basic computation skills. In third through the fifth grades, they continue developing number concepts to include multiplication, division, fraction and decimal representations, geometric principles, and algebraic reasoning. Table 2–5 presents the focal points from Pre-kindergarten through grade 6.

Table 2–5 Mathematics Curriculum:
Number Concepts Strand for Pre-K–Grade 6

Grade Level	Numbers and Operations
Pre-K	1. Exploration of concrete models and materials, begins to arrange sets of concrete objects in one-to-one correspondence, count by ones to 10 or higher, by fives or higher, and combine, separate, and name "how many" concrete objects. 2. Begin to recognize and describe the concept of zero (meaning there are none), to identify first and last in a series, to compare the numbers of concrete objects using language (e.g., "same" or "equal," "one more," "more than," or "less than").
Kindergarten	1. Uses whole number concepts to describe how many objects are in a set (through 20) using verbal and symbolic descriptions, uses sets of concrete objects to represent quantities given in verbal or written form (through 20), uses one-to-one correspondence and language such as more than, same number as, or two less than to describe relative sizes of sets of concrete objects, and names the ordinal positions in a sequence such as first, second, third, etc. 2. Begins to demonstrate part of and whole with real objects. 3. Sorts to explore numbers, uses patterns, and able to model and create addition and subtraction problems in real situations with concrete objects.
First	1. Ability to create sets of tens and ones using concrete objects to describe, compare, and order whole numbers, reads and writes numbers to 99 to describe sets of concrete objects, compares and orders whole numbers up to 99 (less than, greater than, or equal to) using sets of concrete objects and pictorial models. 2. Separates a whole into two, three, or four equal parts and use appropriate language to describe the parts such as three out of four equal parts. 3. Models and creates addition and subtraction problem situations with concrete objects and writes corresponding number sentences. 4. Identifies individual coins by name and value and describes relationships among them.
Second	1. Uses concrete models of hundreds, tens, and ones to represent a given whole number (up to 999) in various ways. Begins to use place value to read, write, and describe the value of whole numbers to 999, uses models to compare and order whole numbers to 999, and records the comparisons using numbers and symbols ($<, =, >$). 2. Uses concrete models to represent and name fractional parts of a whole object (with denominators of 12 or less). 3. Models addition and subtraction of two-digit numbers with objects, pictures, words, and numbers, solve problems with and without regrouping, and is able to recall and apply basic addition and subtraction facts (to 18). 4. Determines the value of a collection of coins up to one dollar and describes how the cent symbol, dollar symbol, and the decimal point are used to name the value of a collection of coins.

Grade Level	Numbers and Operations
Third	1. Uses place value to read, write (in symbols and words), and describes the value of whole numbers and compares and orders whole numbers through 9,999.
	2. Uses fraction names and symbols to describe fractional parts of whole objects or sets of objects and compares fractional parts of whole objects or sets of objects in a problem situation using concrete models
	3. Selects addition or subtraction and uses the operation to solve problems involving whole numbers through 999. Uses problem-solving strategies, able to use rounding and compatible numbers to estimate solutions to addition and subtraction problems.
	4. Applies multiplication facts through 12 by using concrete models and objects (up to two digits times one digit), uses models to solve division problems, and uses number sentences to record the solutions. Identifies patterns in related multiplication and division sentences (fact families).
Fourth	1. Uses place value to read, write, compare, and order: whole numbers through 999,999,999 and decimals involving tenths and hundredths, including money, using concrete objects and pictorial models.
	2. Uses concrete objects and pictorial models to generate equivalent fractions.
	3. Uses multiplication to solve problems (no more than two digits, times two digits) and uses division to solve problems (no more than one-digit divisors and three-digit dividends).
	4. Uses strategies, including rounding and compatible numbers to estimate solutions to addition, subtraction, multiplication, and division problems.
Fifth	1. Uses place value to read, write, compare, and order whole numbers through 999,999,999,999 and decimals through the thousandths place.
	2. Identifies common factors of a set of whole numbers, uses multiplication to solve problems involving whole numbers (no more than three digits times two digits) and uses division to solve problems involving whole numbers (no more than two-digit divisors and three-digit dividends), including solutions with a remainder.
Sixth	1. Compares and orders non-negative rational numbers, generates equivalent forms of rational numbers including whole numbers, fractions, and decimals, uses integers to represent real-life situations.
	2. Able to write prime factorizations using exponents, identifies factors of a positive integer, common factors, and the greatest common factor of a set of positive integers.

Analysis of Teaching and Learning

The teacher of mathematics should engage in ongoing analysis of teaching and learning by doing the following:

- observing, listening to, and gathering other information about students to assess what they are learning;

- examining effects of the task, discourse, and learning environment on students' mathematical knowledge, skills, and dispositions; in order to ensure that every student is learning sound and significant mathematics and is developing a positive disposition toward mathematics;

- challenge and extend students' ideas;

- adapt or change activities while teaching;

- make plans, both short- and long-range;

- describe and comment on each student's learning to parents and administrators, as well as to the students themselves.

Making Connections With the Real World

The U.S. Department of Labor (2008–09) developed a list of the top professions that require a strong knowledge in mathematics. Some of the most prominent jobs are accountants and auditors, computer programmers, computer scientists, computer engineers and system analysts, economists and marketing research analysts, managers, mathematicians, operations research analysts, statisticians, and financial planners.

The preceding list is useful for emphasizing the importance of mathematics in our lives; however, most children in early childhood might not be aware of, and cannot relate to, these kinds of jobs. The best way to link mathematics to real jobs or activities is to guide students to develop a list of jobs available in their community. For example, a unit about community helpers will yield a large list of occupations, such as *nurses, physicians, sanitary workers, home builders, landscapers, plumbers, carpet, and tiles installers,* among others. Teachers can assign readings about these professions and invite community sources to describe and demonstrate how they use mathematics in their profession. The interactive and concrete approach can easily present the need for mathematics in our daily lives.

One of the key challenges in promoting interest in mathematics is to convince children that mathematics plays an important role in their lives. Based on this assumption, teachers need to introduce mathematics concepts in a problem-solving format using real-life situations. Some examples for PK through grade 4 follow:

- Purchase inexpensive items in the dollar store and set up a "classroom store" where the students can go to purchase items using play money. Children can earn money as part of the classroom management program, which can reward students with play money for good behavior.

- Organize cooking activities at home or in school using recipes requiring specific units of measurement; this activity can also be linked to science and particularly to chemistry.

- Guide students to identify the most appropriate measuring system to compute the size of objects and the area of spaces in the classroom or school.

- Plan a field trip where students have to estimate the cost of the trip. Children have to use computations skills to determine the cost of the activity.

- Plan a road trip using *mapquest.com* or any other program to calculate distance from one place to the other. Then use the distance to calculate travel time and gas expenses based on mileage.

Using Thematic Units

Thematic instruction is the organization of curriculum content based on themes or topics. Thematic instruction integrates basic disciplines like reading, math, music, art, and science with the exploration of broad subjects like *American Indians*, *Six Flags over Texas*, *State symbols*, *river systems in Texas*, *the rain forest*, *recycling resources*, and so on. The selection of the theme can be done schoolwide, by grade, or by individual teacher.

Thematic planning provides opportunities for the students to hear similar information in various instructional segments and from a variety of sources. Additionally, it allows students opportunities to apply cognitive processes and creativity through content-area instruction based on real-life situations.

Planning and Organization of Thematic Units

There are several important elements that teachers must consider when planning thematic units. The basic steps are as follows (Fredericks, Blake-Kline, and Kristo, 1997).

Selecting the Theme

Identify a theme, taking into account the interest to children, relevance of the topic, and the connection to the state curriculum. The theme should be broad enough to allow the integration of content areas. For example, a topic like "our solar system" is broad enough to cover every content area in the curriculum. However, a topic like "goldfish" might be too limited in scope to allow the easy integration of subjects.

Designing the Integrated Curriculum The state curriculum (TEKS) should be the guiding force in the organization of the integrated curriculum. Once this connection is established, teachers must identify the main principles or generalization about the theme. Using the generalizations, teachers need to identify the key objectives to involve each content area and the materials needed to implement instruction.

Gathering Materials for the Unit Gathering materials for the unit can be challenging for first-year teachers. They should request input from veteran teachers and from the school librarian. Some of the key considerations when selecting materials are as follows:

- The materials should focus on the same set of generalizations/principles and each of the content areas.

- Materials should include narratives, expositions, drama, poems, and a variety of materials and resources books, magazines, newspapers, movies, Internet materials, videotapes, and audiotapes.

- Materials should also represent a range of thinking abilities and literacy development, including materials written in a language other than English.

- Materials should represent the home as well as the school culture and language of the students.

Designing Instruction

Thematic instruction minimizes the artificial boundaries created through traditional course scheduling. The fixed course scheduling for the content areas can now be combined into larger segments where multiple content areas are delivered in an integrated manner. When designing instruction for children in the early grades, teachers must take into account the developmental characteristics of the children to keep them focus and engaged.

Arranging Thematic Materials and Activities

Traditionally, thematic units are organized into three main segments—introduction to the unit, presentation of the content, and a closing activity. The opening activity is designed to motivate children and to get them interested in the theme. Children are exposed to the goals and the steps in the presentation of the theme. The presentation of the content is done through various coordinated lessons and activities. The closing activity is designed to review and pull together the concepts learned and to celebrate the mastery of the content.

Types of Questioning Strategies

It should be clear for all teachers to use questions that do not have simple yes/no answers. Questions should focus students' thinking, require them to think critically, and help them to "clarify or justify their ideas orally and in writing." Good questions "elicit language and challenge each student's thinking" (NCTM, 2000, p. 35). Teachers need to model these questioning strategies. See the following chart with the NCTM proposed five types of questions strategies teacher should use.

Table 2–6 Questioning Strategies for Mathematics Discourse

The NCTM Professional Standards propose five types of questions that teachers should ask to elicit justification and reasoning, in the following:

Category 1—Questions that help students learn how to make learning math meaningful.

"Do you agree? Disagree with the correct answer?"

"Does anyone use a different strategy to get the correct answer, explain it?"

Category 2—Questions that help students to become self-reliant and determine whether something is mathematically correct.

"Does that make sense?"

"Tell me what makes this a reasonable solution to the task?"

Category 3—Questions that help students learn to reason mathematically.

"What have you tried that has worked or not worked?"

"How could you explain this in your own words?"

Category 4—Questions that help students learn to solve problems.

"What would happen if...?"

"What would happen if not...?"

"What pattern do you see, and how would you explain your answer?"

Category 5—Questions that relate to helping students connect mathematics, its ideas, and its applications.

"Have we solved a problem that is similar to this one?"

"Can you write another problem like this one?"

Source: Charles Al. Dana Center, Mathematics TEKS Toolkit. UT-Austin. Available online at: *http://www.utdanacenter.org/mathtoolkit/support/questioning.php*.

Using Formal and Informal Assessment

The Texas Assessment of Knowledge and Skills (TAKS) is the state assessment for reading, math, writing, science, and social studies. The TAKS test evaluates student learning based on the state-required curriculum, the Texas Essential Knowledge and Skills. TAKS replaced the Texas Assessment of Academic Skills (TAAS) in 2003. It is a "high-stakes" testing system that provides accountability for districts, schools, administrators, teachers, and students. By law, Texas students must pass the TAKS test to be promoted at certain grade levels and graduate from high school.

In 2007, the TEA introduced TAKS (Accommodated), TAKS-M, and TAKS-Alt to assess students receiving special education services. This accommodation is determined by an Admission Review and Dismissal (ARD) committee and based on each individual student's instructional needs.

Competency 014: Number Concepts and Operations

The teacher understands concepts related to numbers, operations and algorithms, and the properties of numbers.

Number Concepts and Algorithms

One of the key challenges in mathematics education is the teaching of technical vocabulary and concepts. Teachers as well as students need to have an understanding of the key terms used in mathematics to communicate effectively in the classroom. An **algorithm** is an established and well-defined step-by-step problem solving method used to achieve a desired mathematical result. A summary of key mathematical terms and concepts follows.

Integers

An integer is a whole number that includes all positive and negative numbers, including zero. This may be represented on a number line that extends in both directions from 0. You might have –45, –450,000, 0, 234, or 78,306. Integers do not include decimals or fractions. The set of integers: {..., –6, –5, –4, –3, –2, –1, 0, 1, 2, 3, 4, 5, 6...}

You can represent many real-life situations with integers.

Natural Numbers

A natural number is a positive integer or a non-negative integer. There is a small difference because non-negative integers also include "0." A list of positive integers would only include whole numbers, but not zero. Natural numbers include 1, 2, 3, 4, 5 ... ∞ (Note: ∞ is the symbol for infinity). They are all whole numbers. Natural numbers do not include negative numbers, fractions, or decimals.

Rational Numbers

A number that can be expressed as a ratio or quotient of two non-zero integers is known as a rational number. Rational numbers can be expressed as common fractions or decimals, such as $\frac{3}{5}$ or 0.6. Finite decimals, repeating decimals, mixed numbers, and whole numbers are all rational numbers. Non-repeating decimals cannot be expressed in this way, and are said to be irrational.

Irrational Numbers

An irrational number is a number that cannot be represented as an exact ratio of two integers. The decimal form of the number never terminates and never repeats. Examples: The square root of 2 ($\sqrt{2}$) or Pi (π).

Real Numbers

A real number describes any number that is positive, negative, or zero and is used to measure continuous quantities. A real number also includes numbers, which have decimal representations, even those with infinite decimal sequences (e.g., Pi (π)).

Exponential Notation

Exponential notation is a symbolic way of showing how many times a number or variable is used as a factor. In the notation 5^3, the exponent 3 shows that 5 is a factor used three times; that is calculated in the following way: $5^3 = 5 \times 5 \times 5 = 125$.

Scientific Notation

Scientific notation is a form of writing a number as the product of a power of 10 and a decimal number greater than or equal to 1 and less than 10.

Example $2,400,000 = 2.4 \times 10^6$, $240.2 = 2.402 \times 10^2$, $0.0024 = 2.4 \times 10^{-3}$

Absolute Value

The absolute value is the number's distance from zero on the number line. This action ignores the + or − sign of a number. $|x|$ is the graphic used to describe the action of absolute value. Example: $|-5| = 5$ or $|5| = 5$.

Expanded Form

The expanded form of an algebraic expression is the equivalent expression without parentheses, for example the expanded form of $(a+b)^2$ is $a^2 + 2ab + b^2$. A way to write numbers that shows the place value of each digit, for example: 263 = 200 + 60 + 3 or 263 which is equal to 2 hundreds, 6 tens, and 3 ones.

Expanded Notation

Expanded notation is showing place value by multiplying each digit in a number by the appropriate power of 10.

Example $523 = 5 \times 100 + 2 \times 10 + 3 \times 1$ or $5 \times 10^2 + 2 \times 10^1 + 3 \times 10^0$

Estimating

Estimating is generally done by rounding the numbers to the nearest decimal place required for accuracy. For example, a sum 23 + 35 can be solved easily by rounding 23 to **20** and 35 to **40** to obtain the estimation 20 + 40 = 60.

Place Values

Place Values are the basic foundation for understanding mathematic computation. A simple number like 1984 can be explained based on the positions of the numbers in the value scale. See the example in table 2-7.

Table 2–7 Place Value

Thousand	Hundred	Ten	One
1000	900	80	4
1	9	8	4

Fractions, Decimals, and Percentages

A **fraction** is a number that represents part of a whole, part of a set, or a quotient in the form a/b which can be read as a divided by b.

Finding Equivalent Fractions or Simplification of Fractions

To identify an equivalent fraction, follow these steps using the example $\frac{2}{4}$:

- Find a number that can be divided evenly into the numerator and the denominator. For example, in the fraction $\frac{2}{4}$, the number 2 can be divided evenly into (2) and (4).

- Divide the numerator and denominator by 2 and get the result: $\frac{2}{4} = \frac{1}{2}$.

Adding and Subtracting Homogeneous Fractions

When adding or subtracting fractions with the same denominator (homogeneous fractions), add or subtract the numerators—the denominator remains the same, for example:
$\frac{2}{5} + \frac{1}{5} = \frac{3}{5}; \frac{7}{9} - \frac{5}{9} = \frac{2}{9}$.

Changing Improper Fractions to Mixed Numbers

To change an improper fraction, like $\frac{5}{2}$, to a mixed number, divide the numerator by the denominator and represent the remainder as a fraction, for example: $2\frac{1}{2}$.

$$\frac{5}{2} = \frac{4+1}{2} = \frac{2 \times 2 + 1}{2} = 2\frac{1}{2}$$

Adding and Subtracting Mixed Numbers

To add and subtract mixed numbers, see the examples and follow the rule provided.

$$2\frac{5}{10} \qquad 7\frac{9}{12}$$

$$+1\frac{4}{10} \qquad -5\frac{4}{12}$$

$$3\frac{9}{10} \qquad 2\frac{5}{12}$$

Add or subtract the fractions, then add or subtract the whole numbers. "Borrow" from the whole numbers if necessary to complete the operation as needed.

Changing Mixed Numbers to Fractions

To change a mixed number, multiply the denominator by the whole number; then add the result to the numerator to obtain the new numerator.

$$2\frac{3}{4} = \frac{2\times4+3}{4} = \frac{8+3}{4} = \frac{11}{4}$$

Adding Fractions with Different Denominators

To work with these kinds of fractions, it is necessary to *rename fractions* using a *common denominator*. For example, to rename the fractions $\frac{1}{2}$ and $\frac{2}{3}$, it is necessary to find a common denominator between them. In this case the lowest common denominator is 6, because both of the original denominators are factors of 6. That is, $\frac{1}{2}$ can be written as $\frac{3}{6}$, and $\frac{2}{3}$ can be written as $\frac{4}{6}$. $\frac{3}{6}$ and $\frac{4}{6}$ now can be added: $\frac{7}{6}$.

Multiplying Fractions

Multiplying fractions involves multiplying the numerator together and the denominators together (horizontally), then simplifying the product.

$$\frac{2}{3}\times\frac{3}{4} = \frac{6}{12} = \frac{6\times1}{6\times2} = \frac{1}{2}$$

If the numbers to be multiplied are mixed fractions, first rewrite them as "improper" fractions like $\dfrac{6}{2}$ and then proceed to multiply as described earlier.

Dividing Fractions

To perform this operation, invert the second fraction (the one doing the dividing) and multiply the numbers as described earlier. In the case of $\dfrac{1}{5}$ divided by $\dfrac{3}{8}$, follow these steps: Invert the second fraction $\dfrac{3}{8}$ to $\dfrac{8}{3}$. Proceed to multiply.

$$\frac{1}{5} \div \frac{3}{8} = \frac{1}{5} \times \frac{8}{3} = \frac{8}{15}$$

Decimal Numbers

Decimal numbers are fractional numbers that are written using base ten. A mixed decimal number has a whole number part as well, for example: 0.28 is a decimal number and 3.9 is a mixed decimal number.

Adding and Subtracting Decimals

Decimal numbers are fractions whose denominators are powers of 10 (i.e., 10, 100, 1000, and so forth). For example: 0.098 is equivalent to $\dfrac{98}{1000}$. To add or subtract decimal numbers, arrange them vertically, aligning decimal points then add or subtract as for whole numbers. See the following example.

$$\begin{array}{r} 23.5 \\ +\,20.4 \\ \hline 43.9 \end{array}$$ The decimal point remains in the same location.

Multiplying Decimals

Multiplication of decimals does not require aligning decimal points; the numbers can be arranged vertically, with right *justification*. The numbers can then be multiplied as if they were whole numbers. The numbers of digits to the right of the decimal point in the product should be equal to the sum of the number of digits to the right of the decimal point in the two factors.

$$1.25 \times 0.6 = 0.750$$

Count the number to the right of the decimal and place it accordingly.

Dividing Decimals

Division of decimals is done like traditional whole number division. The number of digits to the right of the decimal point in the **divisor** is how far the decimal point in the answer (quotient) should be moved to the right.

$$0.3\overline{)1.44} = 3\overline{)14.4} = 4.8$$

Percent

Percent is another way of expressing a fractional number. Percent always expresses a fractional number in terms of $\frac{1}{100}$ or 0.01's. Percents use the "%" symbol (e.g., 40 parts out of 100 is 40%).

$$100\% = \frac{100}{100} = 1.0$$

$$25\% = \frac{25}{100} = 0.25$$

As shown in these examples, a percent is easily converted to a common fraction or a decimal fraction. To convert a decimal to a common fraction, place the percent in the numerator and use 100 as the denominator (simplify as necessary). To convert a percent to a decimal fraction, divide the percent by 100, or move the decimal point two places to the left.

$$25\% = \frac{25}{100} = \frac{1}{4} \text{ and } 25\% = 0.25$$

To convert a *common fraction to a percent*, follow this procedure: 1) Carry out the division of the numerator by the denominator of the fraction, and 2) round the result to the hundredths decimal place. To convert the decimal to a percentage, move the decimal point two places to the right (adding 0's as placeholders, if needed) and round as necessary.

$$\frac{1}{4} = 1 \div 4 = \frac{25}{100} = 0.25 = 25\%$$

$$\frac{2}{7} = 2 \div 7 = 0.286 \approx 29\%$$

If you wish to find the *percentage* of a known quantity, change the percent to a common fraction or a decimal fraction, and multiply the fraction times the quantity. The percentage is expressed in the same units as the known quantity. For example, to find 25% of 360 books, change 25% to 0.25 and multiply times 360, as follows: $0.25 \times 360 = 90$. The result is 90 books. (*Note*: The known quantity is the base, the percent is the rate, and the result is the percentage.)

Number Theory

Teacher candidates have to have a solid command of basic number theory. Some of the elements required for elements covered in the EC-6 curricula are discussed next:

Prime Factorization

You can use exponents to write the prime factorization of a number. Every composite number can be written as a product of prime numbers. This is called the prime factorization of the number. When a factor is repeated in a prime factorization, express the repeated factor using an exponent. A factor tree can also help you find the prime factorization of a composite number. It does not matter which factor pair you start with, as long as you continue factoring until you have only prime numbers. See example from 6th grade TAKS Exam study guide (TEA, 2009b) available online at: *http://ritter.tea.state.tx.us/student.assessment/resources/guides/study/G6MathE-SG.pdf*

What is the prime factorization of 48 using exponents?

- $48 = 3 \times 16$

- $48 = 3 \times 2 \times 8$

- $48 = 3 \times 2 \times 2 \times 4$

- $48 = 3 \times 2 \times 2 \times 2 \times 2$

The prime factorization of 48 is 3×2^4.

The exponent 4 shows how many times the base number 2 is used as a factor. The factor 3 is used only once. It has an exponent of 1. Exponents of 1 do not need to be written because they are implied. Prime factorizations are usually written in order from least to greatest base number. The prime factorization of 48 can also be written $2^4 \times 3$.

Greatest Common Divisor (GCD)

The greatest common divisor (GCD) of two or more non-zero integers is the largest positive integer that divides into the numbers without producing a remainder. This is useful for simplifying fractions into their lowest terms, for example: GCD (42, 56) = 14.

$$\frac{42}{56} = \frac{3 \times 14}{4 \times 14} = \frac{3}{4}.$$

Although 42 and 56 are divisible by larger numbers (21 and 28, respectively), the largest number, which is a factor of both 42 and 56, is 14.

Common Multiple

A common multiple is a whole number that is a multiple of two or more given numbers, for example: The common multiples of 2, 3, and 4 are 12, 24, 36, 48 . . .

Composite Number

A number greater than zero which is divisible by at least one other number besides **one (1) and itself** resulting in an integer (i.e., it has at least 3 factors). For example: 9 is a composite number because it has three factors: 1, 3, and 9

Basic Operations

Some of the basic operations covered in the EC-6 Curricula are discussed below.

Addition

Addition is the mathematical operation of combining two or more numbers into a sum. Addition in mathematics refers to the process of combining two or more digits into one number. In addition of whole numbers, the key element is to align the numbers based on place value—ones, tens, hundreds, thousands, and so forth. Following the alignment, proceed to add beginning with the ones—in a right to left progression.

$$
\begin{array}{r}
25 \\
+32 \\
\hline
57
\end{array}
$$

Step 1: Add the numbers in the ones place ($5 + 2 = 7$).
Step 2: Add the numbers in the tens place ($2 + 3 = 5$).

Subtraction

Subtraction is the process/operation of removing objects from a larger group, or finding parts of a whole. It is the opposite of addition and/or finding parts of a whole. Subtraction is indicated by the minus sign (−). When a number is subtracted from another number, the resulting number is smaller than the minuend. The minuend is the quantity from which the subtrahend is deducted in subtraction. The difference is the result of the subtraction, as in the following:

From a group of 25 cars, 20 were sold. How many are left?

The child might know the operation but may not understand that the word "left" in the problem calls for subtraction. Teachers need to develop a list of key words linked to each of the four basic operations.

See the following operation.

$$
\begin{array}{r}
25 \\
- 20 \\
\hline
05
\end{array}
$$

(minuend)
(subtrahend)
(remainder or difference)

Step 1: Beginning with the ones, subtract the bottom numbers from the top numbers.

Step 2: Subtract the tens using the same process to get the results.

Like addition, subtraction is a process in which children must see their learning task as one of making sense of whatever they are studying. It is not appropriate to teach children how to do a procedure without teaching them how to reason. Students should not be expected to do things by rote or be made to say things they do not honestly understand.

Additionally, the complexity of the language can create problems for all children, especially for ELLs. For example, some common phrases used in forming subtraction word problems include: 1) How many are left or left over? 2) How many more are needed? 3) How many less or fewer? 4) How many more than? 5) How many would you have if a half were subtracted? Words and phrases used for explaining subtraction include: *Minus, take away, decrease, reduce, deduct, remove, less than,* and *how many do you need to take away to get* a certain number.

Children need to make sense of the procedure. The most obvious message to a child is that addition and subtraction require that you follow the "rules." Teaching "what to do" in mathematics is a widespread practice in the classroom. However, it is important to understand that teaching procedures and teaching procedures in relation to their meaning are two very different approaches to teaching mathematics. When students do not have the broader understanding, they may lack the cognitive flexibility to deal with situations that may differ (even slightly) regarding the format of the problem/question from the particular situation learned. Have children describe their thinking processes and explain why their answers make sense. When children understand why, their understanding and skills can be applied more easily to new tasks.

Multiplication

Multiplication is a mathematical operation of combining groups of equal amounts; and may be described as repeated addition and/or the inverse of division. Traditionally, multiplication requires students to memorize the multiplication facts and develop computation facility. After memorizing all the "times tables," children learn to multiply with paper and pencil, first practicing with one-digit multipliers (24 × 5 = ___) and progressing to two-digit and three-digit multipliers, etc. Word problems provide a way for children to being applying the concepts of multiplication in various situations. Example of the steps in the process, include the following example:

$$
\begin{array}{r}
95 \\
\times\ 7 \\
\hline
665
\end{array}
$$

95   (factor)

× 7   (factor)

665   (product)

Step 1: Multiply 7 × 5 = 35.

Step 2: Since the number has more than one digit (i.e., 3 tens and 5 ones), place the 3 at the top of the tens column and the 5 in the ones column.

Step 3:   Multiply the digit in the tens place (9) $7 \times 9 = 63$.

Step 4:   Add the 63 to the 3 placed in the tens place; this equals 66.

Step 5:   Place the 66 on the left of the ones to obtain the final result is 665.

Teachers should link multiplication to real-world contexts. Having children explore with groups of objects helps children link the idea of multiplication as repeated addition. Children need to interact with the concept of multiplication pictorially by drawing sets of objects, symbolically by writing the multiplication sentences ($4 \times 6 = 24$), and verbally by reading the sentences (4 sets of 6 equals 24; 4 groups of 6 equals 24; and/or 4 times 6 equals 24). Children need opportunities to see mathematics in their daily lives, not as existing in the classrooms or on the pages of their textbooks.

Division

Division is a mathematical operation involving two numbers that tells how many groups there are or how many are in each group. The symbol for division is ÷ or /.

$$\frac{7 \text{ R2}}{8 \overline{)\ 58}}$$

Step 1:   Place the divisor outside the bracket on the left-hand side and the dividend inside the bracket.

Step 2:   Examine the first digit of the dividend. If this is smaller than the divisor, then take both numbers of the dividend.

Step 3:   Identify how many times the divisor (8) can fit into the dividend (58).

Step 4:   Place the result on top of the bracket (i.e., 7).

Step 5:   Multiply the quotient (7) with the divisor (8)–56.

Step6:   Subtract 56 from 58 to identify a possible remainder.

Step 7:   Place the remainder on the quotient (i.e., R2).

Counting Techniques for Solving Problems

Students use counting techniques to solve mathematic problems. Some of the techniques are presented next.

- Use networks, traceable paths, tree diagrams, Venn diagrams, and other pictorial representations to find the number of outcomes in a problem situation. Example: In a motel there are 4 different elevators that go from Joan's room to the pool and 3 different doors to the pool area. Use a tree diagram to show how many different ways Joan can get from her room to the pool.

- Use the fundamental counting principle to find the number of outcomes in a problem situation. Example: You are getting dressed one morning when you realize that you have far too many choices. You have 6 shirts to choose from, 4 pairs of jeans, and 3 pairs of shoes. Ignoring color coordination, construct a tree diagram or other pictorial representation to show how many different outfits you could assemble.

- Use combinatorial reasoning to solve problems. Example: You know that your locker combination contains the numbers 2, 4, 6, and 8, but you have forgotten the order in which they occur. What is the maximum number of combinations you need to try before your locker opens?

- Use counting techniques to solve probability problems. Example: In the last example, what is the probability that your locker opens with the first combination you try?

- Use simulations to solve counting and probability problems. Example: A panel of 12 jurors was selected from a large pool that was 70% male and 30% female. The jury turned out to be 11 men and 1 woman. Suspecting gender bias, the defense attorneys asked how likely is it that this situation, or worse, would occur purely by chance. Simulate this situation using a random number generator to select 12 numbers, letting 0, 1, and 2 represent women and 3, 4, 5, 6, 7, 8, and 9 represent men. Note the number of times that 11 or 12 men are chosen.

Order of Operations

Students may first learn the distributive property when they are learning order of operations. The distributive property is expressed in math terms as the following equation: $a(b + c) = ab + ac$. You can read this as the product of a and $(b + c)$ is equal to the sum of **a times b and a times c**. When you're looking at an equation like this, you can see that the multiplication part distributes evenly to all the numbers within the parentheses. It would be incorrect to multiply ab and just add c, or to multiply ac and add b. The distributive property reminds us that everything within the parentheses needs to be multiplied by the outside number.

In mathematics, we encounter many problems in which the solution involves a series of calculations. An arithmetic expression is evaluated by following these ordered steps: (1) simplify within grouping symbols such as parentheses or brackets, starting with the innermost; (2) apply exponents—powers and roots; (3) perform all multiplications and divisions in order from left to right; (4) perform all additions and subtractions in order from left to right.

For example: What is the correct answer to $3 + 2 \times 6 = n$?

Should we go "left to right" and just do the + first and get 30, or do we do the multiplication first and get 15? In order to avoid confusion and get the correct answer, mathematicians decided long ago that all calculations should be done in the same order. You may have learned the order of operations as being: ***Please Excuse My Dear Aunt Sally!*** The words in this sentence stand for *Parentheses, Exponentiation, Multiplication, Division, Addition*, and *Subtraction (PEMDAS)*. So what is the correct answer for our problem? The order of operations would say that in the absence of parentheses, you would multiply 2×6 first, and then add 3. **So, the answer would be 15**. If you were to add $3 + 2 = 5$, then multiply 5×6 that would be 30, a very different answer!

Front-End Estimation

Estimation is used to make an approximation that is still close enough to be useful. When using front-end estimation, use the leading or the left-most digit to make an estimate, for example: Estimate the sum of 594, 32, and 221.

An initial estimate would be $600 + 0 + 200 = 800$.

Rounding Numbers

Rounding may be used to estimate a sum, difference, or product and to make mental approximations. This is done by rounding all the numbers first to nearest ten or hundred and then performing the operation. The rules for rounding are:

- If the digit is 0, 1, 2, 3, or 4, round down.
- If the digit is 5, 6, 7, 8, or 9, round up.

For example, in addition, add in this way by rounding up or down: 532 + 385 + 57 = 500 + 400 + 60 = 960. The result is less precise, but easier to perform mentally in most cases. This example is sometimes referred to **front-end estimation** using the leading, or left-most digit to make an estimate quickly and easily.

Rounding may also be used to reduce the number of digits in a number. The term **"digit"** in mathematics is a number symbol (e.g, 1, 2, or 3) used in numerals to represent numbers (these are real numbers or integers) in positional numeral systems. In this case, the purpose for rounding is to have fewer digits in the answer when dividing numbers with remainders. For example, if we are dividing a 20 cm long wire into 3 equal pieces, we would divide 20 by 3 to get the length of each piece. This example would be calculated in the following manner:

$$\frac{20}{3} = 6.6666666666666666\ldots$$

The 6 repeats an infinite number of times. This is known as a **repeating decimal**. Typically, we would **round** the answer based on the required number of decimal places. By "decimal places" we refer to the number of digits to the **right** of the decimal point. Usually rounding to the tenths or hundredths place is sufficient. We could **round** the answer (6.666...) to the nearest hundredths place. In our example, 6.666 . . . , the next digit in the thousandths place is 6, so we would round up, giving 6.67 as the desired answer.

Repeating Decimal

A decimal in which one or more digits repeat infinitely, for example: 0.3333...or 0.3 (with line over the 3) and 5.27272 . . . or 5.$\overline{27}$.

Competency 015: Patterns and Algebra

The teacher understands concepts related to patterns, relations, functions, and algebraic reasoning.

Numbers and their Properties

Numbers have basic properties that can help simplify mathematics problem solving and reasoning skills. Some of these are:

Commutative Property

The order of the **addends** or **factors** do not change the result.

$$a + b = b + a \quad \text{and} \quad a \times b = b \times a$$

Addition: $6 + 8 = 14$ is the same as $8 + 6 = 14$

Multiplication: $5 \times 8 = 40$ is the same as $8 \times 5 = 40$

Associative Property of Multiplication and Addition

The order of the addends or product will not change the sum or the product.

$$(a + b) + c = a + (b + c) \quad \text{and} \ (a \times b) \times c = a \times (b \times c)$$

Addition: $(2 + 3) + 5 = 10, 2 + (3 + 5) = 10$

Multiplication: $(2 \times 3) \times 5 = 30, 2 \times (3 \times 5) = 30$

Property of Zero

The sum of a number and zero is the number itself, and the product of a number and zero is zero.

Addition: $8 + 0 = 8$

Multiplication: $8 \times 0 = 0$

Distributive Property

You can add and then multiply or multiply then add.

$$a(b + c) = (a \times b) + (a \times c)$$

$$8(5 + 2) = (8 \times 5) + (8 \times 2) = 56$$

Linear and Nonlinear Functional Relationships

Many functions can be represented by pairs of numbers. When the graph of those pairs results in points lying on a straight line, a function it is said to be linear. When not on a line, the function is nonlinear.

A real-valued function for a real variable is a rule that assigns to each real number x in a specified set of numbers, called the domain of f, a single real number $f(x)$. The variable x is called the independent variable. If $y = f(x)$ we call y the dependent variable. A function can be specified in the following ways: 1) numerically by the means of a table, 2) algebraically by means of a formula, or 3) graphically by means of a graph. A **numerical specified function** is listed in Table 2–8:

Table 2–8 Numerical Specified Function

x	0	1	2	3
$f(x)$	3.01	−1.03	2.22	0.01

Then, $f(0)$ is the value of the function when $x = 0$. From the table, we may have the following values: $f(0) = 3.01$ and $f(1) = -1.03$

An algebraically specified function: Suppose you had function f specified by $f(x) = 3x^2 - 4x + 1$. Then:

$f(x) = 3x^2 - 4x + 1$ (Substitute 2 for x) $f(2) = 3(2)^2 - 4(2) + 1$

The answer: $f(2) = 12 - 8 + 1$, this would $= 5$

$f(-1) = 3(-1)^2 - 4(-1) + 1$ (Substitute −1 for x) $= 3 + 4 + 1$, this would $= 8$

A **linear function** is one whose graph is a straight line (that is why it is called "linear"). A linear function is one of the most fundamental and important relationship concepts as a foundation for advanced mathematics. A linear function is one which always satisfies the following: $f(x + y) = f(x) + f(y)$ and $f(\alpha x) = \alpha f(x)$. In this definition, x and y are input variables and α is a constant.

For example: Consider the function $f(x) = 2x$. Assuming there are two input values ($x = a + b$), the function now becomes $f(x) = f(a + b) = 2(a + b) = 2a + 2b$. We see that if we substitute ($x = a$ and then $x = b$) we obtain $f(a) = 2a$ and $f(b) = 2b$ where we see that $f(a + b) = f(a) + f(b)$ and satisfies the first rule. Checking the second constraint we have $f(\alpha x) = 2\alpha x$ which is equivalent to $\alpha f(x) = \alpha 2x$ due to the associative/commutative properties of multiplication.

A non-linear function is one that does not satisfy the constraints stated previously. For example, the function $f(x) = x^2$ is non-linear because $f(a + b) = (a + b)^2 = a^2 + 2b + b^2$ is not equal to $f(a) + f(b) = a^2 + b^2$.

We will revisit the concept of linear and non-linear functions in the proceeding sections.

Function

Functions can be used to understand how one quantity varies in relation to (is a function of) changes in the second quantity. For example, there is a functional relationship between the price per pound of a particular type of meat and the total amount paid for ten pounds of that type of meat. You can see that values of one variable determine the values of another.

Patterns

A pattern can be a design (geometric) or sequence (numeric or algebraic) that is predictable because some aspect of it repeats. Examples: Numeric pattern that adds increments of 3's: 4, 7, 10, 13... Algebraic pattern that adds one to the multiple: x, x2, x3, ... An example is when students are asked to identify patterns using fact families, as in the following:

Example from TAKS Objective 2

(3.6) (C) identify patterns in related multiplication and division sentences (fact families) such as $2 \times 3 = 6, 3 \times 2 = 6, 6 \div 2 = 3, 6 \div 3 = 2$.

This student expectation lists only one fact family: *such as* $2 \times 3 = 6$, $3 \times 2 = 6, 6 \div 2 = 3, 6 \div 3 = 2$

However, there are many other fact families students may use to identify patterns in multiplication and division sentences.

Source: Grade 3 TAKS Mathematics Information Booklet, p. 11

Algebraic Pattern

An algebraic pattern is a set of numbers and/or variables in a specific order that form a pattern. An example would be a chart showing the distance in feet if Max travels on his bicycle a different number of seconds. Given the chart below, what is one way to find the number of feet Max travels on his bicycle in 1 second?

# of seconds	6	8	9
# of feet	90	120	135

First, students need to be able to understand the algebraic pattern presented in the chart and how the numbers are listed. Students should divide the number of feet by the number of seconds to find the correct answer. However, in this problem the answer 15 does not answer the test question. Students need to be able to tell which operation they used to derive the answer to the question.

Algebraic Expression

An algebraic expression is a mathematical phrase that is written using one or more variables and constants, but which does not contain a relation symbol (e.g., $5y + 8$).

A *variable* or an unknown is a letter that stands for a number in an algebraic expression.

Coefficients are the numbers that precede the variable to give the quantity of the variable in the expression. Algebraic expressions are comprised of terms, or groupings of variables and numbers. An algebraic expression with one term is called a *monomial*; with two terms, a *binomial*; with three terms, a *trinomial*; with more than one term, a *polynomial*.

For example, $2ab - cd$ is a binomial algebraic expression with variables a, b, c, and d, and terms $2ab$ and $(-cd)$. 2 is the coefficient of ab and -1 is the coefficient of cd. $x^2 + 3y - 1$ is a trinomial algebraic expression using the variables x and y, and terms x^2, $3y$, and (-1); $z(x - 1) + uv - wy - 2$ is a polynomial with variables z, x, u, v, w, and y, and terms $z(x - 1)$, uv, $(-wy)$, and (-2).

Operations with algebraic expressions are governed by various rules and conventions.

- In **addition and subtraction**, *only like algebraic terms (same exponent) can be added or subtracted* to produce a simpler expressions. For example, $2x^3$ and $3x^3$ can be added together to get $5x^3$, because the terms are *like* terms; they both have a base of x^3. You cannot add, say, $7m^3$ and $6m^2$ because they are *unlike* bases. (*Note*: To *evaluate* an algebraic expression means to simplify it using conventional rules.)

- When **multiplying exponential terms** together, the constant terms are multiplied, but the *exponents of terms with the same variable bases are added together*, which is somewhat counterintuitive. For example, $4w^2$ multiplied by $8w^3$ gives $32w^5$ (not $32w^6$, as one might guess).

- When like algebraic terms are **divided**, exponents are subtracted. For example, $\dfrac{2x^7}{5x^3}$ becomes $\dfrac{2x^{7-3}}{5} = \dfrac{2x^4}{5}$.

Multiplication of Binomials

In algebra, it is frequently necessary to multiply two *binomials*. Binomials are algebraic expressions of two terms. The FOIL method is one way to multiply binomials. FOIL stands for "first, outer, inner, last": Multiply the first terms in the parentheses, then the outermost terms, then the innermost terms, then the last terms, and then add the products together. For example, to multiply $(x + 3)$ and $(2x - 5)$ you multiply x by $2x$ (the first terms), x by -5 (outer terms), 3 by $2x$ (inner terms), and 3 by 5 (last terms). The four products ($2x^2$, $-5x$, $6x$, and -15) add up to $2x^2 + x - 15$. If the polynomials to be multiplied have more than two terms (*trinomials*, for instance), make sure that *each* term of the first polynomial is multiplied by *each* term of the second. The opposite of polynomial multiplication is factoring. Factoring a polynomial means rewriting it as the product of factors (often two binomials). The trinomial $x^2 - 11x + 28$, for instance, can be factored into $(x - 4)(x - 7)$. (You can check this by "FOILing" the binomials.) When attempting to factor polynomials, it is sometimes necessary to factor out any factor that might be common to all terms first. The two terms in $5x^2 - 10$, for example, both contain the factor 5. This means that the expression can be rewritten as $5(x^2 - 2)$.

Algebraic Relationship

To express the relationship between two or more numbers using an algebraic expression. The algebraic relationship which represents 2, 4, 6, 8... is $2n$ (where $n = 1, 2, 3, ...$) and the algebraic relationship which represents 4, 7, 10, 13, ... is $3n + 1$ (where $n = 1, 2, 3, ...$).

Algebraic Solution

An algebraic solution is the process of solving a mathematical problem using the principles of algebra.

Performing Operations with Negative and Positive Numbers

When performing operations on negative and positive numbers, the key component is to pay attention to the sign—the positive or negative value. Rules for multiplication and division are the same—two positives and two negatives make a positive, and mixing negative with positive makes a negative. See the following examples.

- negative $\times$ negative = positive ($-6 \times -5 = 30$)

- positive $\times$ positive = positive ($6 \times 5 = 30$)

- positive $\times$ negative = negative ($6 \times -5 = -30$)

Graphs and Symbolic Representations

A graph is an image or chart representation used to show a numerical relationship. On the TExES, teacher candidates are required to study graphs, charts, and tables and answer questions based on the information presented. A **table** is a systematic or orderly list of values, usually in rows and columns. They are often organized from a function or relationship. Four kinds of **graphs** are generally used in grades PK to grade 6—pictorial, bar, pie, and line.

Pictorial graphs are the most concrete representation of information. They represent a transition from the real object graphs to symbolic graphs (Sperry Smith, 2008). These are usually used to introduce children to graphing in PK through grade 1. For example, the teacher can use pictures of pizzas and hot dogs to represent the number of children that prefer one food over the other.

Bar graphs are used to represent two elements of a **single** subject. For example, the bar graph that follows presents the number of books read by a group of students. This graph presents in a concrete fashion that child E was the top reader with 5 books, while child A is the one with the lowest number of books read.

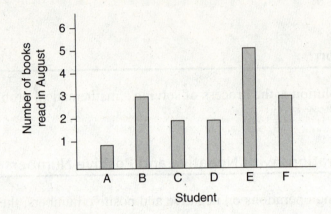

Line graphs present information in a similar fashion as the bar graphs, but it uses points and lines. This type of representation is more abstract for children and is therefore more challenging for them. A line graph tracks one or more subjects. One element is usually a time period over which the other element increases, decreases, or remains static. The following line graph depicts U.S. immigration statistics from 1820 to 2000.

Immigration to the US, 1820–2006

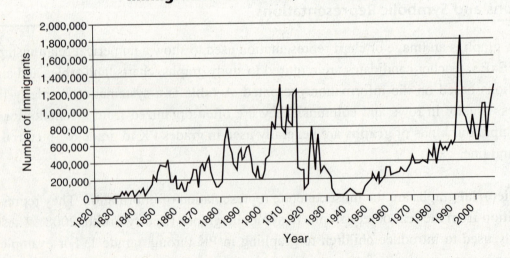

Pie charts are used to help visualize relationships based on percentages of a subject. The figure is divided based on the percentages out of a possible 100%. This graph appears to be easy to read, which is deceptive. It requires an understanding of percentages, which makes it inappropriate for children in the early grades. A pie graph representing food preferences follows.

Food Preferences

Identifying Patterns using Concrete Models

Kindergarten students begin to use concrete models to construct, describe, extend, and determine what comes next in repeating patterns. In order to identify and construct repeating patterns, students must be able to identify the attributes of the objects in the pattern. Therefore, students sorting objects by their attributes, before they begin constructing their own patterns. Students construct patterns with two (AB, AAB, ABB) or three (ABC) elements. As students become more familiar with the structure of patterns they are able to begin to think about how two patterns are similar and different.

By Grade 5, students continue their work from Grades 3 and 4 by examining, representing, and describing situations in which the rate of change is constant. Students move from using concrete models, to figures and numbers. They create tables and graphs to represent the relationship between two variables in a variety of contexts and are able to describe the rules for each situation. For example, consider the perimeters of a set of rectangles made from rows of tiles with three tiles in each row: If the value of one variable (the number of rows of three tiles) is known, the corresponding value of the other variable (the perimeter of the rectangle) can be calculated. Students express these rules in words and then in symbolic notation.

Throughout their work, students use tables, graphs, and equations and between those representations and the situation they represent. Their work with symbolic notation is closely related to the context in which they are working. By moving back and forth between the contexts, their own ways of describing general rules in words, and symbolic notation, students learn how this notation can carry mathematical meaning.

Linear and Nonlinear Functions

As stated previously, a **linear function** is one whose graph is a straight line. An equation whose graph is a straight line is called a linear function. A linear function has an equation that can be written in the form of $y = mx + b$. A linear function has a constant rate of increase or decrease. The constant rate of change is the slope of the line and is represented by m in the equation. It can be written in this form:

$f(x) = mx + b$ (function form)   Example: $f(x) = 3x - 1$ $(m = 3, b = -1)$.

$y = mx + b$ (Equation form)   Example: $y = 3x - 1$

Here is a partial table of values of the linear function $f(x) = 3x - 1$.

x	−4	−3	−2	−1	0	1	2	3
y	−13	−10	−7	−4	−1	2	5	8

The linear equation has $m = 3$ (slope), $b = -1$ (y-intercept). You will notice that $x = 0$ gives $y = -1$, the value of b. Numerically, b is the value of y when $x = 0$. On the graph, the corresponding point $(0,-1)$ is the point where the graph crosses the y-axis, and we say that $b = -1$ is the y-intercept of the graph. The role of m in the equation $y = mx + b$ means that the value of y increases by $m = 3$ for every increase of 1 in x. This is caused by the term $3x$ in the formula.

On the graph, the value of y increases by exactly 3 for every increase of 1 in x, the graph is a straight line rising by 3 for every 1 we go to the right. We say that we have a **rise** of 3 units for each **run** of 1 unit. Similarly, we have a rise of 6 for a run of 2, a rise of 9 for a run of 3, and so on. Thus we see that $m = 3$ is a measure of the steepness of the line; we call m the **slope of the line**. Geometrically, the graph rises by m units for every 1 unit move to the right; m is the slope of the line.

Non-linear functions are not linear and have an exact solution. An example is $x^2 + x - 1 = 0$. This may be written as $f(x) = C$, where $f(x) = x^2 + x$ and $C = 1$. Though nonlinear, this simple example may be solved exactly using a quadratic formula and is very well understood. To determine whether the function is linear or nonlinear, see the following examples:

$y = 4x$	$y = x^2 + x - 2$	$y = 7/x$
Linear, $y = 4x$ can be written as $y = mx + b$	Nonlinear, $y = x^2 + x - 2$ cannot be written as $y = mx + b$	Nonlinear, $y = 7/x$ cannot be written as $y = mx + b$

Problem Solving Situations into Equations Involving Variables

The role of operations in problem solving involves developing critical thinking and rational powers. The uses of operations in problem solving include: applications, study of patterns and relationships, translation of word problems with a variety of structures and situations into symbolic representations using equations, and the selection of problem solving strategies.

Proportional Reasoning

Proportional reasoning is important in preparing students for algebra. Students in 5th grade begin to use a ratio chart to solve proportion problems. Proportions present a challenge for students because proportions are difficult for students to grasp because two values are related in a certain way that may be solved using multiplication. Students can be influenced by the context, so it is important to expose students to various examples, as in the following types of problems:

1. The office copier uses 5 reams of paper every 2 weeks. At the end of 6 weeks, how many reams of paper will the office copier use within this period of time?

2. Each table in the restaurant has a vase with three long stem roses. The restaurant has fifteen tables; how many flowers are there altogether?

3. The soccer coach orders new soccer balls for the team. She orders 3 out of 4 soccer balls in the school colors. If she orders 36 soccer balls, how many of these will be painted in the school colors?

Linear Function—Data Sets

A mathematical **linear function** refers to a first-degree polynomial function of one variable. In analytic geometry, the term *linear function* is sometimes used to mean a first-degree polynomial function of one variable. These functions are called "linear" because they are precisely the functions whose graph in the Cartesian coordinate plane is a straight line. Such a function can be written as $f(x) = mx + b$ (called slope-intercept form), where m and b are real constants and x is a real variable. The constant m is often called the slope or gradient, while b is the y-intercept, which gives the point of intersection between the graph of the function and the y-axis. Changing m makes the line steeper or shallower, while changing b moves the line up or down.

Examples of functions whose graph is a line include the following:

- $f_1(x) = 2x + 1$

- $f_2(x) = \dfrac{x}{2} + 1$

- $f_3(x) = \dfrac{x}{2} - 1$.

The graphs of these are shown below:

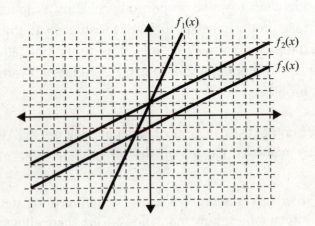

Variables, Equations and Inequalities

Equations

An equation is a mathematical sentence stating that two expressions are equal. Many mathematical expressions include letters called variables. Variables are classified as either free or bound. For a given combination of values for the free variables, an expression may be evaluated, although for some combinations of values of the free variables, the value of the expression may be undefined. Thus an expression represents a function whose inputs are the values assigned the free variables and whose output is the resulting value of the expression.

For example, the expression $\frac{x}{y}$ evaluated for $x = 10$, $y = 5$, will give 2; but is undefined for $y = 0$.

The evaluation of an expression is dependent on the definition of the mathematical operators and on the system of values that is its context. See Formal Semantics and Interpretation (logic) for the study of this question in logic.

Two expressions are said to be equivalent if, for each combination of values for the free variables, they have the same output, i.e., they represent the same function. Example:

The expression $\sum_{n=1}^{3} (2nx)$ has free variable x, bound variable n, constants 1, 2, and 3, two occurrences of an implicit multiplication operator, and a summation operator. The expression is equivalent with the simpler expression $12x$. The value for $x = 3$ is 36.

The '+' and '−' (addition and subtraction) symbols have their usual meanings. Division can be expressed either with the '/' or with a horizontal dash, i.e., $x / 2$ or $\frac{x}{2}$ are perfectly valid. Also, for multiplication one can use the symbols $\times$ or a "·" (dot), or else simply omit it (multiplication is implicit); so: $\times x2$ or $2x$ or $\times 2$ or $x \cdot 2$ are all acceptable (please notice in the first example above how the "times" symbol resembles an "x" and also how the "·" symbol resembles a decimal point, so to avoid confusion it's best to use one of the later two forms).

An **expression** must be well-formed. That is, the operators must have the correct number of inputs, in the correct places. The expression 2 + 3 is well formed; the expression * 2 + is not, at least, not in the usual notation of arithmetic.

Algebraic Inequality

An algebraic inequality is a statement that is written using one or more variables and constants that shows a greater than or less than relationship. Example: $2x + 8 > 24$.

Solving an algebraic inequality means finding all of its solutions. A "solution" of an inequality is a number which when substituted for the variable (for example: x) makes the inequality a true statement. An algebraic inequality is defined as a statement that is written using one or more variables and constants that shows a greater than or less than relationship. As in the case of solving equations, there are certain manipulations of the inequality, which do not change the solution. Consider the algebraic inequality in the following example: $2x + 8 > 24$.

Here is a list of possible manipulations:

1. Adding/subtracting the same number on both sides: $2x + 8 > 24$ has the same solution as the inequality $2x > 16$. (The second inequality was obtained from the first one by subtracting 8 on both sides.

2. Switching sides and changing the orientation of the inequality sign: $2x + 8 > 24$ has the same solution as $24 < 2x + 8$ (We merely switch sides and turned the ">" into a "<")

Last, the operation which is at the source of all the trouble with inequalities:

3a. Multiplying/dividing by the same POSITIVE number on both sides.

3b. Multiplying/dividing by the same NEGATIVE number on both sides AND changing the orientation of the inequality sign.

This does not seem too difficult. The inequality $2x \leq 6$ has the same solution as the inequality $x \leq 3$. (We divided by +2 on both sides). The inequality $-2x > 4$ has the same solutions as the inequality $x < -2$. (We divided by (−2) on both sides and switched ">" to "<").

The inequality $x^2 > x$ does not have the same solutions as the inequality $x > 1$. (We were planning on dividing both sides by x, but this is not possible, because we do not know whether x will be positive or negative). In fact, it is easy to check that $x = -2$, that solves the first inequality, but does not solve the second inequality.

Consider the inequality: $2x + 8 > 24$

The basic strategy for inequalities and equations is the same: isolate x on one side. Following this strategy, let's move $+8$ to the right side. We accomplish this by subtracting 8 on both sides (Rule 1) to obtain $(2x + 8) - 8 > 24 - 8$, after simplifying we obtain $2x > 16$. Once we divide by $+2$ on both sides (Rule 3a), we have succeeded in isolating x on the left: $2x/2 > 16/2$, or simplified, $x > 8$. All real numbers greater than 8 solve the inequality. We say that the "set of solutions'" of the inequality consists of all real numbers greater than 8.

An algebraic inequality is an algebraic statement about the relative size of one or more variables and/or constants. Inequalities are used to determine the relationship between these values. Example: Taking x as a variable and saying, "*x is less than 5*," may be written as $x < 5$.

Competency 016: Geometry and Measurement

The teacher understands concepts and principles of geometry and measurement.

Geometry and measurement are significant strands of mathematics. In the elementary classroom, children's experience in geometry should provide for the development of the concepts of direction, shape, size, symmetry, congruence, and similarity in using two-dimensional and three-dimensional shapes. Experiences for children should begin with exploring, playing, and building with shapes using familiar objects and a wide variety of concrete materials. Children must use these experiences to develop appropriate vocabulary and build on their understanding. Middle school students use formal generalizations to understand geometric relationships.

Concepts and skills in the measurement strand of mathematics deal with making comparisons between what is being measured and the standard for measurement. Children need first-hand experiences with measuring activities that require them to practice the skill. Additionally, children should be aware that measurement is never exact, but is actually an estimation. However, it is important that children learn to practice making estimates. Measuring gives children practical applications to apply their computation skills. It also provides a way to link geometric concepts to number concepts.

The van Hiele Theory

Although the van Hiele theory (van Hiele, 1986) has been recognized for its role in describing the levels of thinking associated with the learning of geometry, it has also been developed as a general theory of mathematics education. In 1988, Fuys, Gedds, and Tischler interpreted much of that work. The van Hiele theory is a stage theory, set out in levels. The theory does not stop at the description of "levels of thinking," but provides a foundation for understanding the movement between these levels, and the role of the teacher in assisting with this progression. The theory goes beyond the concerns of Piaget, who did not address the question of how students may be encouraged to progress from level to level. The van Hiele theory, in addition to describing levels of thinking, offers an important addition. This is the notion of *stages of learning* as means by which the learner may be assisted to use higher level thinking skills. Five such stages are specified in Table 2–11 (van Hiele, 1986):

Principles and Properties of Geometry

A fundamental concept of geometry is the notion of a *point*. A point is a specific location, taking up no space, having no area, and frequently represented by a dot. A point is considered to have no dimensions. In other words, it has neither length nor breadth nor depth.

Through any two points there is exactly one straight line; straight lines are two-dimensional. Planes (think of flat surfaces without edges) are two-dimensional, meaning they have infinite length and breadth but no depth. From these foundational ideas you can move to some other important geometric terms and ideas.

- A segment is any portion of a line between two points on that line. It has a definite start and a definite end. The notation for a segment extending from point A to point B is $\overline{AB}$.

- A ray is like a line segment, except it extends forever in one direction. The notation for a ray originating at point X (an *endpoint*) through point Y is $\overrightarrow{XY}$.

Table 2–11 van Hiele's Levels of Geometric Thinking

What the teacher needs to know	What the learner can do
van Hiele's Level 0—Visualization Learners develop a mental picture of each shape; therefore, teachers need to provide a multitude of good physical examples and nonexamples for exploration.	**Learner able to:** • Select a specific shape from a set of shapes; • Able to sort and match shapes; • Identify shapes in the environment; • Point out a baseball diamond, etc.
van Hiele's Levels 1—Analysis Learners begin to talk and notice the properties of the shapes. Teachers can focus on the various components of the geometric shape.	**Learner able to:** • Predict a shape's final form after just seeing only a part of it; • Able to list several attributes of each shape; • Can subdivide a shape into parts, describe the various pieces, and create a shape from parts.
van Hiele's Levels 2—Informal Deduction Students stop relying on visualization, they now use relationships to make a conclusion. Focus on the first two levels for students in K-8.	**Learner able to:** • Recognize that squares belong in both the rectangle and rhombus category; • Use "if" statements describing the shape; • Able to divide a rectangle into two congruent triangles; • Able to identify parallelograms based on the criteria regarding opposite equal angles.
van Hiele's Levels 3—Formal Deduction Focus on higher levels of geometry; using various theorems to teach how two triangles are congruent (e.g., side-angle-side theorem).	**Learner able to:** • Able to make deductions and to support those deductions; • Able to do high school level geometry including construction of their own proofs involving quadrilaterals drawn on a sphere.
van Hiele's Levels 4—Rigor Associated with college level geometry.	**Learner able to:** • Able to compare different geometries at the proof level.

Formulas for Lengths, Perimeters, Area, and Volume

Finding the Perimeter

The *perimeter* of a two-dimensional (flat) shape or object is the distance around the object (think of a fence, for example). Perimeter is measured in linear units (e.g., inches, feet, and meters). See the chart for the formulas used to find perimeter:

Perimeter of a Square	$P = 4s$
Perimeter of a Rectangle	$P = 2l + 2w$ or $P = 2(l + w)$

The **perimeter of a square** is found by multiplying four times the measure of a side of the square. This relationship is commonly given by the formula $P = 4s$, where s is the measure of a side of the square. For example, if a square has $s = 5$ feet, then the perimeter of the square is given by $P = 4(5 \text{ feet}) = 20$ feet.

The **perimeter of a rectangle** is found by adding twice the length of the rectangle to twice the width of the rectangle. This relationship is commonly given by the formula:

$P = 2l + 2w$, where l is the measure of the length and w is the measure of the width. For example, if a rectangle has $l = 10$ m and $w = 5$ m, then the perimeter of the rectangle is given by $P = 2(10 \text{ m}) + 2(5 \text{ m}) = 30$ m.

The **perimeter of a triangle** is found by adding the measures of the three sides of the triangle. This relationship can be represented by $P = s_1 + s_2 + s_3$, where s_1, s_2, and s_3 are the measures of the sides of the triangle. For example, if a triangle has three sides measuring 3 inches, 4 inches, and 5 inches, then the perimeter of the triangle is given by $P = 3 \text{ inches} + 4 \text{ inches} + 5 \text{ inches} = 12$ inches.

Finding the Area

The **area of a rectangle** is found by multiplying the measure of the length of the rectangle by the measure of the width of the triangle. This relationship is commonly given by $A = l \times w$, where l is the measure of the length and w is the measure of the width. For example, if a rectangle has $l = 10$ m and $w = 5$ m, then the area of the rectangle is given by $A = 10 \text{ m} \times 5 \text{ m} = 50 \text{ m}^2$.

The **area of a square** is found by *squaring the measure* of the side of the square. This relationship is commonly given by $A = s^2$, where s is the measure of a side. For example, if a square has $s = 5$ ft, then the area of the square is given by $A = (5 \text{ ft})^2 = 25 \text{ ft}^2$.

Volume

Volume refers to how much space is inside of three-dimensional, closed containers. It is useful to think of volume as how many cubic units could fit into a solid. If the container is a rectangular solid, multiplying width, length, and height together computes the volume.

If all six faces (sides) of a rectangular solid are squares, then the object is a cube.

Cube

A **cube** is a three-dimensional solid figure. This figure has 6 faces, 12 edges, and 8 vertices. The number of faces, edges and faces can be identified visually, or through the application of the following formula:

Formula for the figure: $F + V = E + 2$

- **Vertex**: A vertex is the union of two segments or point of intersection of two sides of a polygon.

- **Faces:** Each of the plain regions of a geometric body is a face.

- **Edge:** An edge is a line segment where two faces of a three-dimensional figure meet.

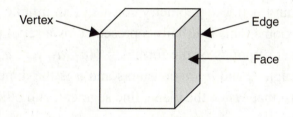

Using Triangles to Explore Geometric Relationships

Sufficient evidence for congruence between two triangles can be shown through the following comparisons:

- **SAS** (Side-Angle-Side): If two pairs of sides of two triangles are equal in length, and the included angles are equal in measurement, then the triangles are congruent.

- **SSS** (Side-Side-Side): If three pairs of sides of two triangles are equal in length, then the triangles are congruent.

- **ASA** (Angle-Side-Angle): If two pairs of angles of two triangles are equal in measurement, and the included sides are equal in length, then the triangles are congruent.

- **AAS** (Angle-Angle-Side): If two pairs of angles of two triangles are equal in measurement and a pair of *corresponding* sides equal in length, then the triangles are congruent.

Points, Lines, Angles, Lengths, and Distances

Points

Points are most often considered within the framework of Euclidean geometry, where they are one of the fundamental objects. Euclid originally defined the point vaguely, as "that which has no part." In two-dimensional Euclidean space, a point is represented by an ordered pair, *(x, y)*, of numbers, where the first number conventionally represents the horizontal and is often denoted by **x,** and the second number conventionally represents the vertical and is often denoted by **y**. This idea is easily generalized to three-dimensional Euclidean space, where a point is represented by an ordered triplet, *(x, y, z)*, with the additional third number representing depth and often denoted by *z*.

Many constructs within Euclidean geometry consist of an infinite collection of points that conform to certain axioms. This is usually represented by a set of points. As an example, a line is an infinite set of points of the form $L = \{(a_1, a_2, \ldots, a_n) [a_1 c_1 + a_2 c_2 + \ldots a_n c_n = d\}$, where c_1 through c_n and d are constants and n is the dimension of the space. Similar constructions exist that define the plane, line segment, and other related concepts.

In addition to defining points and constructs related to points, Euclid also postulated a key idea about points. He claimed that any two points can be connected by a straight line, this is easily confirmed under modern expansions of Euclidean geometry, and had grave consequences at the time of its introduction, allowing the construction of almost all the geometric concepts of the time. However, Euclid's axiomatization of points was neither complete nor definitive, as he occasionally assumed facts that didn't follow directly from his axioms, such as the ordering of points on the line or the existence of specific points, but in spite of this, modern expansions of the system have since removed these assumptions.

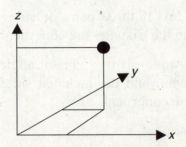

Angles

When two rays (or lines) share an endpoint, an *angle* is formed. Typically, a *degree* is the unit of measure of the angle created. If a circle is divided into 360 even slices, each slice has an angle measure of 1 degree.

- If an angle has exactly 90 degrees it is called a ***right*** **angle**.

- Angles of less than 90 degrees are ***acute*** **angles**.

- Angles greater than 90 degrees but less than 180 degrees are ***obtuse*** **angles**.

- If two angles have the same size (regardless of how long their rays might be drawn), they are *congruent*. Congruence is shown this way: $\angle m \cong \angle n$ (read "angle *m* is congruent to angle *n*").

Angle Measure

Angles are often measured in degrees. A circle has a measure of 360°, a half-circle 180°, a quarter-circle 90°, and so forth. If the measures of two angles are the same, then the angles are said to be congruent as stated earlier. Three types of angles are commonly identified—right, acute, and obtuse.

- Right angles measure 90°.

- Acute angles measure less than 90°.

- Obtuse angles measures more than 90° but less than 180°.

In addition to the traditional type of angles, combinations of two angles are classified as complementary and supplementary.

- Supplementary angles add up to 180°.

- Complementary angles add up to 90°.

Vertical (Opposite) Angles

If two lines intersect, they form two pairs of equal angles. The measures of vertical angles are equivalent; that is, vertical angles are congruent.

Parallel and Perpendicular Lines

Parallel lines

Parallel and *perpendicular* are important concepts in geometry. Consider the two parallel lines that follow, and the third line (a *transversal*), which crosses them. Note that among the many individual angles created, there are only two angle measures: (30° noted in the figure) and 150° (180° − 30°).

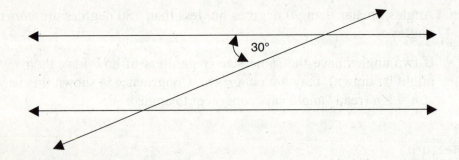

Perpendicular lines

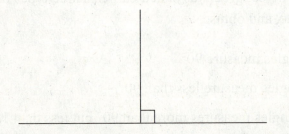

Two- and Three-Dimensional Figures

Circle

Finding the circumference of a circle, you would use the following formula:

C = 2πr or C = πd (pi is the ratio of a circle's circumference to its diameter).

The value of π is the same for all circles; approximately 3.14159. The approximation 3.14 is adequate for most calculations. In the formula the *d represents the diameter and the r stands for the radius* of the circle.

Diameter and Radius

The *diameter* of a circle is a straight line segment that goes from one edge of a circle to the other side, passing through the center. The *radius* of a circle is half of its diameter (from the center to an edge). A *chord* is any segment that goes from one spot on a circle to any other spot (all diameters are chords, but not all chords are diameters).

Triangles

Properties of Triangles

The sum of the measures of the angles of a triangle is 180°. Triangles are three-sided polygons. There are three types of triangles—isosceles, equilateral, and scalene.

- An **isosceles** triangle is a polygon with two equal sides and two equal angles.

- If the measures of all sides of the triangle are equal, then the triangle is called an **equilateral** triangle (this means all angles will be equal).

- A **scalene** triangle is a polygon with three unequal sides.

Problem: Find the measures of the angles of a right triangle if one of the angles measures 30°.

Solution: Since the triangle is a right triangle, a second angle of the triangle measures 90°. We know the sum of the measures of a triangle is 180°, so that $90° + 30° + x° = 180°$. Solving for $x°$, we get $x° = 60°$. The measures of the angles of the triangle are 90°, 60° and 30°.

Formulas for Basic Polygons

Area of a square	$A = s^2$
Area of a rectangle	$A = lw$ or $A = bh$
Area of a triangle	$A = \frac{1}{2} bh$ or $A = bh/2$
Area of a trapezoid	$A = \frac{1}{2}(b_1 + b_2)h$ or $A = \dfrac{(b_1 + b_2)h}{2}$
Area of a circle	$A = \pi r^2$
s = side, l = length, w = width, b = base, h = height, π = pi	

Polygons

A polygon is a many-sided plane figure bounded by a finite number of straight lines or a closed figure on a circle bounded by arcs. These figures are described based on the number of sides. Some of the most common are the following:

- Three-sided polygons are *triangles*.
- Four-sided polygons are *quadrilaterals*.
- Five-sided polygons are *pentagons*.
- Six-sided polygons are *hexagons*.
- Eight-sided polygons are *octagons*.

If two polygons (or any figures) have exactly the same size and shape, they are *congruent*. If they are the same shape, but different sizes, they are *similar*.

The following are formulas for finding the areas of basic polygons (formally defined as closed, coplanar geometric figures with three or more straight sides). Abbreviations used are as follows: *A* stands for area, *l* stands for length, *w* stands for width, *h* stands for height, and *b* stands for length of the base.

Triangle (a three-sided polygon): $A = \dfrac{b \times h}{2}$

(Note that, as shown in the figure that follows, the height of a triangle is not necessarily the same as the length of any of its sides.)

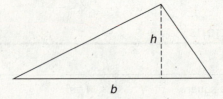

Rectangle (a four-sided polygon with four right angles): $A = l \times w$

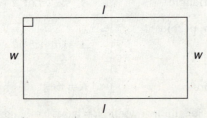

Parallelogram (a four-sided polygon with two pairs of parallel sides): $A = l \times h$ (Note that, as with triangles, and as shown in the figure below, the height of a parallelogram is not necessarily the same as the length of its sides.)

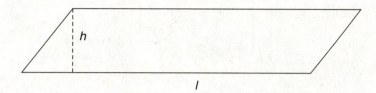

Circle The area of a circle can be found by squaring the length of its radius, then multiplying that product by π. The formula is given as $A = \pi r^2$ (pi is the ratio of a circle's circumference to its diameter).

The value of π is the same for all circles; approximately 3.14159. (The approximation 3.14 is adequate for most calculations.) The approximate area of the circle shown below can be found by squaring 6 (giving 36), then multiplying 36 by 3.14, giving an area of about 113 square units.

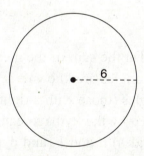

Here are several commonly used **volume formulas**:

The volume of a rectangular solid is equal to the product of its length, width, and height; $A = l \times w \times h$. (A rectangular solid can be thought of as a box, wherein all intersecting edges form right angles.)

A prism is a polyhedron—a three-dimensional solid consisting of a collection of polygons—with two congruent, parallel faces (called bases) and whose lateral (side) faces are parallelograms. The volume of a prism can be found by multiplying the area of the prism's base by its height. The volume of the triangular prism shown hereafter is 60 cubic units. (The area of the triangular base is 10 square units, and the height is 6 units.)

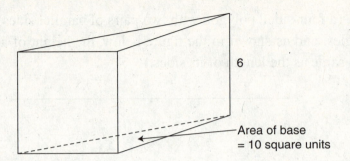

Area of base
= 10 square units

A cylinder is like a prism in that it has parallel faces, but its rounded "side" is smooth. The formula for finding the volume of a cylinder is the same as the formula for finding the volume of a prism: the area of the cylinder's base is multiplied by the height. The volume of the cylinder in the following figure is approximately 628 cubic units ($5 \times 5 \times \pi \times 8$).

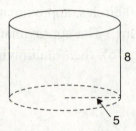

A property of all triangles is that the sum of the measures of the three angles is 180°. If, therefore, the measures of two angles are known, the third can be deduced using addition, then subtraction. Right triangles (those with a right angle) have several special properties. A chief property is described by the Pythagorean theorem, which states that in any right triangle with legs (shorter sides) a and b, and hypotenuse (the longest side) c, the sum of the squares of the sides will be equal to the square of the hypotenuse ($a^2 + b^2 = c^2$). Note that in the following right triangle, $3^2 + 4^2 = 5^2$.

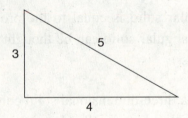

Symmetry

Symmetry—The correspondence in size, form, and arrangement of parts on opposite sides of a plane, line, or point. For example, a figure that has line symmetry has two halves that coincide if folded along its line of symmetry.

Lines of Symmetry

Polygons may have lines of symmetry, which can be thought of as imaginary fold lines that produce two congruent, mirror-image figures. Squares have four lines of symmetry, and non-square rectangles have two, as shown in the following figures. Circles have an infinite number of lines of symmetry.

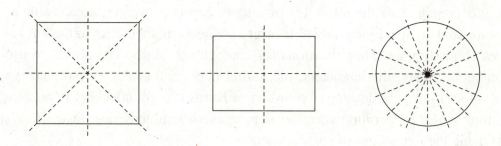

Tessellations

The arrangement of polygons that forms a grid is called a tessellation; however, other shapes may also tessellate. A tessellation is a pattern formed by the repetition of a single unit or shape that, when repeated, fills the plane with no gaps and no overlaps. Familiar examples of tessellations are the patterns formed by paving stones or bricks, and cross-sections of beehives. (See Math Forum at: *http://mathforum.org/geometry/rugs/symmetry/grids.html.*

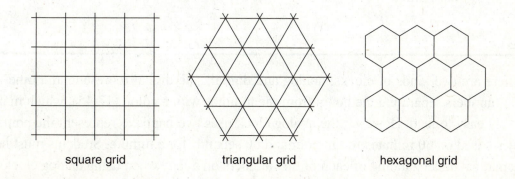

square grid   triangular grid   hexagonal grid

Grids

Grids are usually based on regular polygons: squares, equilateral triangles, and hexagons. Or they can be based on rectangles, parallelograms, and rhomboids.

Concepts of Measurement

Concepts and skills in the Measurement strand of the math curriculum all deal with making comparisons between what is being measured and some suitable standard of measure. Measurement offers opportunities for interdisciplinary learning in social studies, geography, science, art and music. Key to the development of skills in measurement is allowing for various types of measurement activities. Children need firsthand practice with measuring and making estimates in measurement. The principles of measurement involve understanding of the attributes of length, capacity, weight, area, volume, time, temperature, and angles. Being able to measure connects mathematics to the environment and gives children practical applications for computation skills. The ability to use measurement tools: rulers, thermometers, measuring cups, and scales to estimate is necessary skills for children to develop. According to Burns (2000), concepts in measurement include four stages in learning when developing classroom activities. Instruction should progress using the four stages of measurement.

Concepts in Measurement Include Four Stages in Learning

1. Comparing objects by matching—ordering items based on size

2. Comparing a variety of objects for measuring—using body parts, blocks, cubes, etc.

3. Comparing objects using standard units—using standard and metric systems

4. Comparing using suitable units for specific measurements—choosing standard units

Time

There are two kinds of clocks: analog and digital. The digital represents the time using Arabic numbers separating the hours from the minutes with a colon (12:45), which makes it relatively easy to read. However, the analog clock uses two hands to represent the hours and minutes based on 60 minutes for an hour and 60 seconds for a minute. Students must have a mathematical understanding of each of the numbers on a face when using analog clocks.

Time

1 year = 365 days

1 year = 12 months

1 year = 52 weeks

1 week = 7 days

1 day = 24 hours

1 hour = 60 minutes

1 minute = 60 seconds

Temperature

Temperature is measured using a thermometer, which is filled with mercury (a liquid metallic element that expands with heat). The **Fahrenheit** scale is used in the U.S., whereas the **Celsius** scale is used in countries throughout the world. The Celsius scale is specifically useful in scientific experimentation. Water boils at 212°F or 100°C, and freezes at 32°F or 0°C.

Money

Teaching the concept of money involves the understanding of base ten. Children learn how to relate each denomination to pennies and understand the relationship between the other coins. Use real currency to introduce this concept. Children begin by observing the various coins and their attributes. They learn to associate the value for each of the coins and make equivalences. Suggest that students begin by counting out a bag of coins and then trade out the various coins for larger denominations, for example 5 pennies for one nickel, etc.

Translations, Rotations, and Reflections

Translation (also called a slide)—In geometry a translation simply means moving. Every translation has a direction and distance. This is known as a transformation that moves a geometric figure by sliding. Each of the points of the geometric figure moves the same distance in the same direction. This may be shown on a graph by moving the figure without rotating or reflecting it.

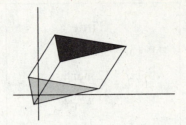

Rotation (also called a turn)—In geometry this is known as a transformation that means a rotation or to turn the shape around. Each rotation has a center and an angle for movement around a given number of degrees.

Reflection (also called a flip)—This is known as a transformation that means to reflect an object or to make the figure/object appear to be backwards or flipped. It produces the mirror image of a geometric figure.

Conversions Within and Between Measurement Systems

Units of Measurement

TEKS require that students in kindergarten through grade 6 become familiar with and apply knowledge of measurement using both U.S. Customary (standard) and metric systems. Table 2–12 provides a comparison of these two units of measurement.

Customary Units

- Linear measurement: Customary units of length include inches, feet, yards, and miles.

- Measurement of mass: Customary units of weight include ounces, pounds, and tons.

- Volume measurement: Customary units of capacity include teaspoons, tablespoons, cups, pints, quarts, and gallons.

Metric Units

- Linear measurement: Metric units of length include millimeters, centimeters, meters, and kilometers. The centimeter is the basic metric unit of length, at least for short distances. There are about 2.5 centimeters to 1 inch. The kilometer is a metric unit of length used for longer distances. It takes more than 1.5 kilometers to make a mile.

- Measurement of mass: Metric units of weight include grams and kilograms. The gram is the basic metric unit of mass (which for many purposes is the same as *weight*). A large paper clip weighs about 1 gram. It takes about 28 grams to make 1 ounce.

- Volume measurement: Metric units of capacity include milliliters and liters. The liter is the basic metric unit of volume. A liter is slightly larger than a quart, so it takes more than four liters to make a gallon.

Table 2–12 The Customary and Metric Systems

Customary System	Metric System
Linear 12 inches (in.) = 1 foot (ft.) 3 feet (ft.) = 1 yard (yd.) 1,760 yards (yds.) = 1 mile (mi.) 5,280 feet (ft.) = 1 mile (mi.)	**Linear** 10 millimeters (mm) = 1 centimeter (cm) 100 centimeters (cm) = 1 meter (m) 1000 meters (m) = 1 kilometer (km)
Capacity and Volume 1 gallon (gal.) = 4 quarts (qt.) 1 gallon (gal.) = 128 fluid ounces 1 quart (qt.) = 2 pints (pt.) 1 pint (pt.) = 2 cups (C.) 1 pint (pt.) = 16 fluid ounces (oz.) 1 cup (C.) = 8 fluid ounces (oz.)	**Capacity and Volume** 1 liter (L) = 1000 milliliters (ml) 1 liter (L) = 1.0556 quarts (qt.)
Mass and Weight 1 ton = 2000 pounds (lbs.) 1 pound (lb.) = 16 ounces (oz.)	**Mass and Weight** 1 kilogram (kg) = 1000 grams (g) 1 gram (g) = 1000 milligrams (mg)

Logical Reasoning

The development of logical reasoning is closely related to children's language development. Elementary mathematics instruction should help students learn to organize ideas, understand what they are studying, and explain their thinking as they solve problems. Activities should provide students with opportunities to make generalizations and conclusions, to justify them with logical arguments, and to be able to communicate their reasoning to others. Mathematics is a way of thinking, rather than a body of facts. This is an important distinction for children to understand. Critical thinking and logical reasoning aid students in clarifying their thought processes and may apply this skill in all curriculum areas.

In the early grades through grade 3, logical thinking should be introduced using an informal approach. There should be many opportunities for children to explore, manipulate, and experience concrete objects to identify their attributes, to make comparisons, to classify by their characteristics and to make generalization about their properties. The use of words such as *all, some, if, then,* or *not* helps children gain knowledge with the language used in logic. In upper elementary grades, students should be provided with learning activities involving deductive and inductive reasoning.

Deductive Reasoning

This requires moving from the assumption to conclusion. Deductive reasoning is reasoning from the general to the specific, and it is supported by deductive logic. Students use this type of reasoning in daily life, for example: "It is raining so I need to take my umbrella to school." Note that conclusions reached via deductive reasoning are only sound if the original assumptions are actually true.

Inductive Reasoning

This involves examining particular instances to come to some general assumptions. This type of reasoning is informal and intuitive. When thinking inductively, students make hypotheses, extend thought patterns, use analogies, and make reasonable conclusions from examining what appears to be a large enough body of evidence. Students use this type of reasoning regularly in life situations, for example: If I do my homework all this week, I think my mother will take me to the concert on Saturday. With *inductive* reasoning, a general rule is inferred from specific observations (which may be limited). Moving from the statement, "All fish that I have ever seen have fins" (specific but limited observations) to "All fish have fins" (a general proposition) is an example of inductive reasoning. Conclusions arrived using inductive reasoning are not always necessarily true.

Axiomatic Structure

An axiom is a mathematical rule. This basic assumption about a system allows theorems to be developed. For example, the system could be the points and lines in the plane. Then an axiom would be that given any two distinct points in the plane, there is a unique line through them.

Apply Reasoning Skills

Reasoning skills include drawing conclusions using the principles of similarity, congruence, parallelism, and perpendicularity; and using inductive and deductive reasoning. Geometric figures are *similar* if they have the exact same shapes, even if they do not have the same sizes. In transformational geometry, two figures are said to be similar if and only if a similarity transformation maps one figure onto the other. In the figure that follows, triangles A and B are similar.

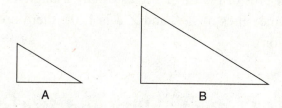

Corresponding angles of similar figures have the same measure, and the lengths of corresponding sides are proportional.

In the following figure, rectangles A and B are congruent.

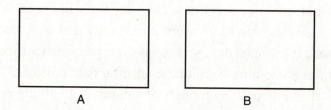

The corresponding sides are proportional, meaning that figures are *congruent* if they have the same shape *and* size (Congruent figures are also similar.)

Straight lines within the same plane that have no points in common (that is, they never cross) are parallel lines. Note that the term *parallel* is used to describe the relationship between two coplanar lines that do not intersect. Lines that are not coplanar—although they never cross—are not considered to be parallel. Coplanar lines crossing at right angles (90°) are perpendicular.

An example of how logical reasoning can be used to solve a geometry problem is given hereafter. (In this case *deductive* reasoning is used to find the measure of ∠ *J*.)

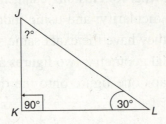

The sum of the measures of the three angles of any triangle is 180° (a general proposition). The sum of the measures of ∠ *K* and ∠ *L* is 120°, therefore the measure of ∠ *J* is 60° (a specific proposition).

Competency 017: Probability and Statistics

The teacher understands concepts related to probability and statistics and their applications.

Statistics is the science or study of data. Statistical methods are used to describe, analyze, evaluate, and interpret information. The information is then used for predicting, drawing inferences, and making decisions. Data analysis involves both probability and statistics. Probability gives a way to measure uncertainty and is essential for understanding statistical methods. It explains data sets to give a type of generalized statistic, to make a prediction, or to infer something beyond the specific data collected. Probability is used to create experimental and theoretical models of situations involving probabilities.

There is some general agreement with regard to six underlying facts about the learning and teaching of data analysis. These include the following:

Research on Teaching Data Analysis

1. Problem solving approach to teaching is consistent with how learners develop data analysis knowledge. (Lajoie, Jacobs, & Lavigne, 1995)

2. Concept knowledge must be developed first before developing procedural knowledge. This can then be further developed using problem solving, for

example understanding the concept of sample before gathering data to analy-sis a problem/situation. (Horvath & Lehrer, 1998)

3. Concepts and procedures are interdependent. (Konold & Higgins, 2003)

4. Statistical representations can become more sophisticated using technology and as students have more experiences with data. (Friel, S.N., Curcio, F.R., & Bright, G. W. (2001))

5. Data organization can be improved by using technology tools. (Konold, 2002; Lehrer & Romberg, 1996)

6. Teachers must sequence instruction based on developmental age-appropri-ate situations and so students may examine certain types of situations before other types. For example, students should study situations in which all out-comes are equally likely before studying situations in which all outcomes are **not equally likely.** (Horvath & Lehrer, 1998)

Probability

Learning probability and statistics provides real applications of arithmetic. When basic computation skills are used in context, students have the opportunity to see the advantages and limitations of their calculations. Most arithmetic is done with a degree of uncertainty, for example estimating costs, making calculations of needed building materi-als, approximating estimated time of arrival (ETA) on trips, and estimating time for bak-ing or cooking food.

A set of data can be describe by its range, mean, median, and/or mode.

The **range** of a set of data is the difference between the greatest and the least numbers in the data set. Subtract to find the difference.

The **mean** of a set of data is the average of the data values. To find the mean, add all the data values and then divide this sum by the number of values in the set.

The **median** of a set of data is the middle value of all the numbers. To find the middle value, list the numbers in order from the least to greatest or from greatest to least. Cross out one value on each end of the list until you reach the middle. If there are two values in the middle, find the number halfway between the two values by adding them together and dividing their sum by 2.

The **mode** is the value (or values) that appear in a set of data more frequently than any other value. If all the values in a set of data appear the same number of times, the set does not have a mode.

Studying probability and statistics should involve real problems and/or simulations. A theoretical or abstract approach is not appropriate for students in elementary mathematics. The approach should be based on experiments that draw on children's experience and interests. Children's intuition needs to be challenged. Once they understand or can say what "should happen" in a situation, then they may be able to conduct experiments to test their predictions. Basic to probability and statistics are the following steps:

1. Data Collections

2. Sampling

3. Organizing and Representing Data

4. Interpreting Data

5. Assigning Probabilities

6. Making Inferences

Probability is a way of describing how likely it is a particular outcome will occur. A random event occurs when a selection is made without looking. A fraction can be used to describe the results of a probability experiment in this way: 1) the numerator of the fraction is the number of favorable outcomes for the experiment. 2) The denominator of the fraction is the number of all the possible outcomes for the experiment.

Gabrielle is randomly choosing a marble from a bag containing three marbles—1 red marble, 1 blue marble, and 1 green marble. What is the probability that she will choose a green marble on a single pull?

• There is 1 green marble in the bag. There is 1 favorable outcome.

• There are $1 + 1 + 1 = 3$ marbles in the bag. There are 3 possible outcomes.

$$\text{Probability of choosing a green marble} = \frac{\text{Number of favorable outcomes}}{\text{Total number of possible outcomes}} = \frac{1}{3}$$

The probability that Gabrielle will choose a green marble on a single pull is $\frac{1}{3}$, or 1 out of 3.

Students need to demonstrate an understanding of probability and statistics and be able to do the following: 1) use experimental and theoretical probability to make predictions; and 2) use statistical representations to analyze data. A **sample space** is the set of all possible outcomes of an experiment. For example, if you flip a coin, it will land either heads or tails. Students learn to list all the possible outcomes: heads or tails. Sample spaces may also be listed on a chart or tree diagram.

Permutations—All possible arrangements of a given number of items in which the order of the items makes a difference, for example the different ways that a set of four books can be placed on a shelf.

Jones, Langral, Thornton, and Mogill (1999) have developed a four-stage framework that attempts to explain the learning process for probability. Learners begin at the subjective level, at which they are easily swayed by personal experiences when making probabilistic statements. At the second level, transitional learners begin to recognize the importance of organizing information. The third level involves students becoming informal quantitative thinkers. Finally, students work at the purely numerical level in which they understand the nuances of numerical argument and use sophisticated procedures to determine numerical facts.

Students should learn to read graphs, making quick visual summaries as well as further interpretations and comparisons of data through finding means, medians, and modes. Students use tables, line graphs, bar graphs, circle graphs, line plots, and pictographs to organize and display data. This is a helpful strategy used in problem solving. A **line plot** represents a set of data by showing how often a piece of data appears in that set. It consists of a number line that indicates the values of the data set. An X is placed above the corresponding number each time that value appears in the data set, for example the wheights of 10 twelve-year-old girls were measured and recorded. A line plot is used to record the data from a chart. Then, students may make comparisons of the range of height, find the tallest or shortest girl, and interpret the data found.

In real-world problems, students may sample a part of a population. Students need to learn the difference between random and nonrandom samples and the importance this difference makes in statistical studies, for example to determine the percentage of people who are left-handed. Students would not poll famous athletes as a random sampling.

For students to fully understand data analysis, all frameworks and researchers agree that student should generate their own data. They should work with simulations that model real situations. They should use dice, spinners, two-color counters, and coins. As students begin to understand how to gather their own data, they need to be consciously aware of any graphical representations they might choose to use, recognizing the difference between discrete and continuous situations. Finally, technology is a highly useful tool in data analysis and in making sense of the data.

Competency 018: Mathematical Processes

The teacher understands mathematical processes and knows how to reason mathematically, solve mathematical problems, and make mathematical connections within and outside of mathematics.

The National Council of Teachers of Mathematics (NCTM) and the Texas Essential Knowledge and Skills (TEKS) have emphasized the importance of teaching mathematical reasoning for children from kindergarten through grade 12. TEKS requires children to explore mathematical reasoning as early as kindergarten. This requirement presents a challenge for teachers since the ability to perform operations involving logical reasoning requires some level of cognitive maturity and the ability to think abstractly. From kindergarten to grade 2, children must understand the principles and patterns of the number system and the symbols used to represent numbers. Principles of measurement and basic geometry are also introduced early in the process. In grades 1 and 2, children begin using quantitative reasoning and basic algorithms for addition and subtraction. Beginning in grade 3 and continuing throughout elementary school, students continue improving their basic knowledge of the number system and the abstraction of mathematical reasoning. Children begin exploring basic algebraic, geometric, and spatial reasoning. They also master multiplication facts and division. Word problems and mathematical reasoning are heavily emphasized in third-grade preparation for TEKS, which is offered in grades 3 to 12.

Logical Reasoning

Teachers must create opportunities to motivate children to engage in exploratory mathematics to develop logical thinking. For the early grades this exploration can be done in *learning centers*, where children have the opportunity to work with blocks, shapes, and other manipulatives. Learning centers are designed to exposure children to manipulatives, which are used to teach mathematical concepts in an indirect fashion through student-selected activities.

In addition to exposure to mathematics concepts in learning centers, teachers use instructional strategies to apply mathematics concepts in real-life situations. For example, a role-play activity involving ordering food in a restaurant may be simulated in the classroom. A group of children can be given a budget to order food in a restaurant. This type of activity may guide children to understand basic mathematical concepts, including calculating sums of money, giving change, understanding percentages to determine an appropriate gratuity or sales tax, and the use of mathematics in daily life.

Logical reasoning is thinking of something in a way that makes sense. Thinking about mathematics problems involves logical reasoning. You can use logical reasoning to find patterns in a set of data. You can then use those patterns to draw conclusions about the data that can be used to solve problems. Finding patterns involves identifying characteristics that numbers or objects have in common. Look for the pattern in different ways. A sequence of geometric objects may have some property in common. For example, they may all be quadrilaterals or all have right angles.

Problem Solving Strategies

Solving problems involves more than just numerical computation; logical reasoning and careful planning also play important roles. Various methods used to solve word problems; strategies may include, but are not limited to: acting it out, drawing a picture or graph, using logical reasoning, looking for a pattern, using a process of elimination, creating an organized chart or list, solving a simpler but related problem, using trial and error (guess and check), working backwards, writing an equation. Here are some of the steps using in solving problems.

> ### Steps to follow when solving problems:
>
> **Understand the problem**
> Organize the information you are given and identify the question. You may be given extraneous information that is not needed to solve the problem.
>
> **Choose a strategy and/or make a plan**
> After you have organized the information, decide how to use this information to find an answer. Think about the math concepts that apply to the situation. Identify the order in which you will find new information and carry out your strategy.
>
> **Carry out the plan**
> After you have chosen a problem-solving strategy, use the strategy to work out the problem. Go step-by-step through your plan, writing down important information at each step.
>
> **Check your answer**
> Check your answer to see if it makes sense. Does it answer the question? Is it stated in the correct units? Is it reasonable? You can estimate the solution and then compare the estimate to your answer. They should be approximately equal.

Developmental Considerations

Children in Pre-K through kindergarten might have problems understanding basic number systems and how numbers are presented symbolically. They might have difficulties dealing with measurement activities that require them to master the principle of *conservation*. They might think that an apple split in half is more than a single apple, or a soda drink in a tall and narrow glass might be more than the same liquid poured in a shorter and wider glass. These cognitive and reasoning limitations tend to disappear as children develop. By first grade, the principle of conservation is generally acquired.

Mathematics instruction in kindergarten through grade 6 involves not only knowing mathematical processes but also being able to determine when a given process is required.

Children must develop the ability to reason through word problems and understand the type of answer required. Most third graders can do addition, subtraction, multiplication, and even division. However, they might have difficulties with word problems and problem-solving activities that require them to identify the appropriate mathematical process. They might also have problems understanding questions involving multiple steps and deciding on the appropriate answer. The word problem that follows represents an example.

Joe can place a maximum of 5 apples in a paper sack. If he needs to put 32 apples in sacks, how many sacks does he need?

In this example, most students will know that the problem calls for division—32 divided by 5—which will yield the expected number of 6.4. Some students will provide 6.4 as the answer, but the real question is: "How many sacks does Joe need?" Children will have to reason that paper sacks cannot be divided; thus the answer cannot be 6.4 but 7 paper sacks.

Mathematical reasoning is crucial for understanding and using mathematics. This type of contextual or situational reasoning is certainly important, and questions such as the preceding one have a solid place in the curriculum and on state tests. Logical reasoning is the foundation for understanding mathematics and its use in life.

Historical Development of Mathematics

Every culture has developed some form of functional mathematics concept. In most cases, accomplishments of these civilizations have been transmitted to and enhanced by other groups. This transmission of knowledge and its cumulative effects have resulted in the creation of the modern-day mathematics used around the world. Some of the key civilizations that impacted the development of mathematics in the Western world are discussed in the following sections.

Egyptians and Babylonians

The first mathematicians that impacted the development of modern-day mathematics were from the ancient civilizations of Babylon and Egypt around the third millennium BCE. The ancient Egyptians wrote numbers using hieroglyphs to represents the numbers 1, 10, 100, 1,000, 10,000, and 1,000,000. They used numbers into the millions for practical purposes like managing resources and for building large-scale public structures like temples and pyramids.

The Babylonians made great advances in science, math, and specifically in astronomy. They also developed tables for multiplication, division, and square and cube roots. One of the greatest accomplishments of Babylonian civilization was the development of a number system with a base of 60. This number system constituted the foundation for the advanced mathematics evolution that followed the Egyptians and Babylonians.

Greeks

The Greeks built on the accomplishments of the Egyptians and Babylonians and further developed the field of mathematics. Most historians believe that the formal study of mathematics as a discipline began with the Athenian Greek school of Thales and Pythagoras. Some authorities identify Thales and Pythagoras as the founders of Greek mathematics. Thales (640–550 BCE) was a merchant who traveled extensively and became acquainted with Egyptian mathematics. Some of his contributions include the following: a circle is bisected by the diameter, angles at the base of an isosceles triangle are equal, and a semicircle creates a right angle. Pythagoras, his former pupil, followed Thales's ideas and eventually became one of the leading figures of Greek mathematics. Pythagoras taught that there is a basic relationship between harmony and mathematics. He developed the Pythagorean Theorem. It was after the early Athenian Greeks that the Alexandrian Greeks emerged as the leaders in the study of science and mathematics. Around 300 BCE, Ptolemy founded the university at Alexandria in Egypt, which became the center of learning for the Western world.

This institution became the leading force in the study of mathematics, contributing multiple discoveries and some of the greatest thinkers of the time. Two of the leading figures that emerged during this period were Archimedes and Euclid.

Archimedes calculated the distances of the planets from the Earth and constructed a spherical planetarium imitating the motions of the sun, moon, and six then known planets. He also made multiple discoveries with scientific and military applications. Euclid was one of the most influential Greek mathematicians in the world. He is believed to have learned geometry from the students of Plato. He is famous for providing a complete record of the mathematics accomplishments of Ancient Greece. He wrote several books on the elements of geometry. His mathematics knowledge has served as the standard mathematics textbook for over two thousand years.

The Greeks also discovered that real numbers could not accurately express all mathematical values. Based on this need, they developed the concept of irrational numbers. An irrational number cannot be expressed as a fraction. In decimal form, numbers do not repeat in a pattern or terminate; they continue to infinity. Some examples of irrational numbers are as follows:

$$\pi = 3.141592654\ldots \text{ and } \sqrt{2} = 1.14121356\ldots$$

Hindus

Around the fifth century CE, the Hindus developed a system of mathematics that allowed for astronomical calculations. They developed a technique of computation, which later influenced the development of modern-day algebra.

Arab Contributions

The Arabs were the first civilization to solve sophisticated algebraic equations currently used in science and engineering, for example quadratic equations. They also developed and perfected geometric algebra. Arab mathematicians used the work of the Greeks in geometry and improved the development of the field. They founded *non-Euclidian* geometry and made advances in trigonometry. The greatest contributions of the Arabs were the development of the numeric system, which resulted in the spread of the cumulative knowledge of mathematics to the world.

The Concept of the Zero

Some historians believe that the concept of zero used today originated in India around 650 CE. Others suggest that it was perfected from the work of Greek astronomers. However, all seem to agree that eventually, the Arabs used the concept of the zero to develop the current system of enumeration used in the world. The concept of zero was also developed separately by the Mayans in 700 CE; however, there is no evidence to suggest that the Mayan concept of zero impacted the development of mathematics beyond the Maya empire in Central America. The zero that we know today came from the Hindu tradition.

The Number System

The number system used in modern days is described as an Hindu-Arabic numeration system. It uses numbers from 1 to 9 and the zero. Historians seem to agree that the Hindus contributed to the development of the base-10 digit system and the Arabs perfected it and spread it through the world.

The cumulative knowledge the Babylonians, Egyptians, and Greeks was translated from Greek into Arabic. At the same time, the mathematic accomplishments of the Hindus were also translated into Arabic. The collective knowledge of these civilizations and the improvement and innovations developed in the Arab world became the mathematics of Western Europe and, over a period of several hundred years of further development, became the mathematics of the world.

Contributions from Other Civilizations

Other civilizations, like the Mayans and the Aztecs, made significant progress in mathematics. The Mayan civilization around 700 BCE developed an elaborate calendar and the mathematical concept of zero. The Mayans also had highly advanced knowledge of astronomy, engineering, and the arts.

The Aztec civilization flourished around 1325 BCE. The Aztecs were also skilled builders and engineers, accomplished astronomers, and mathematicians. Like the Egyptians, they used mathematic principles for functional purposes like engineering to build pyramids, palaces, plazas, and canals.

There are other places in the world that developed significant accomplishments in mathematics. China, Japan, and several kingdoms from Africa are examples of civilizations that made sizeable progress in mathematics; however, their accomplishments did not have a direct impact on the development of mathematics in the Western world. For a detailed analysis of the historical development of mathematics and the contribution of various civilizations, see the "History of Mathematics" website, maintained by David E. Joyce of Clark University in Worcester, Massachusetts. (*http://aleph0.clarku. edu/~djoyce/mathhist/*)

Developments of Mathematics Education in the U.S.

In the last half century, the American education system has made important changes in the teaching of mathematics. Some of the key changes are listed below.

1950s to 1960s

- Significant changes in content of elementary mathematics programs
- New content added
- Standard content taught at earlier grade levels

1970s

- Slowing down of content changes
- Attention and focus on "system of delivery" of content

Late 1970s, early 1980s

- Back to basics movement
- Heavy emphasis on drill and practice

Late 1980s

- Increased emphasis on teaching concepts and problem solving

1990s

- Increased use of computers and calculators for computation
- Increased emphasis on estimation, problem solving, and higher-level thinking
- Release of *Professional Standards for Teaching Mathematics* (1991)

2000s

- Increased emphasis on assessment, equity, technology, learning, teaching and curriculum standards
- Use of literature and cultural connections with mathematics and its implication in teaching
- Increased emphasis on research-based instructional strategies

References

Burns, M. 2000. *About teaching mathematics: A K-8 resource.* Sausalito, CA: Math Solutions Publications.

Carpenter, T.M., E. Fennema, M. L. Franke, L. Levi, and S. B. Empson. 1999.

Children's mathematics: Cognitively guided instruction. Portsmouth, NH: Heinemann.

Fredericks, A. D., B. Blake-Kline, and J. V. Kristo. 1997. *Teaching the integrated language arts: Process and practice.* New York: Longman.

Friel, S.N., F. R. Curcio, and G. W. Bright. 2001. Making sense of graphs: Critical factors influencing comprehension and instructional implication. *Journal of Research in Mathematics Education*, 32(2), 124–158.

Flavell, J.H. 1985. *Cognitive development.* 2nd ed. Upper Saddle River, NJ: Prentice Hall.

Fuson, K. 1988. *Children's counting and concepts of numbers.* New York: Springer.

Fuson, K. C., and J. W. Hall. 1983. The acquisition of early number word meanings: A conceptual analysis and review. In *The development of mathematical thinking,* ed. H. P. Ginsburg, pp. 49–107. Orlando, FL: Academic Press.

Fuys, D., D. Gedds, and R. Tischler. 1988. The van Hiele model of thinking in geometry among adolescent. *Journal of Research in Mathematics Education Monograph #3.* Reston, VA: NCTM.

Horvath, J.K. & R. Lehrer. 1998. A model-based perspective on the development of children's understanding of chance and uncertainty. In *Reflections on statistics: Learning teaching, and assessment in grades K-12,* ed. S.P. Lajoie, pp. 121–148. Mahwah, NJ: Lawrence Erlbaum Associates.

Jones, G.A., C. W. Langrall, C. A. Thorton, and A. T. Mogill. 1999. Student's probabilistic thinking in instruction. *Journal for Research in Mathematics Education*, 30(5), 487–519.

Kamii, C. 2000. *Young children reinvent arithmetic: Implications of Piaget's theory.* New York: Teacher College Press.

Konold, C. 2002. Teaching concepts rather than conventions. *New England Journal of Mathematics Education, 34(2),* 69–81.

Konold, C. and T. Higgins. 2003. Reasoning about data. In *A research companion to principles and standards for school mathematics,* eds. J. Kilpatrick, W.G. Martin, and D.E. Schifter, Reston, VA: NCTM.

Lejoie, S.P., V. R. Jacobs, and N. C. Lavigne. 1995. Empowering children in the use of statistics. *Journal of Mathematics Behavior, 14(4),* 401–425.

Lehrer, R. and T. Romberg. 1996. Exploring children's data modeling. *Cognition and Instruction, 14(1),* 69–108.

National Council of Teachers of Mathematics 2007. *Professional standards for teaching mathematics. http://toolkitforchange.org/toolkit/view.php?obj=1039&menu=i* (accessed August 20, 2009)

National Council of Teachers of Mathematics 2000. *Principles and standards for school mathematics.* Reston, VA: NCTM.

Pepper, C. and R. P. Hunting. 1998. Preschooler's counting and sharing. Journal for *Research in Mathematics Education, 29(2),* 14–183.

Piaget, J. and B. Inhelder. 1969. *The psychology of the child.* New York: Basic Books.

Santrock, J.W. 2003. *Children,* 7th ed. Boston, PA: McGraw-Hill.

Sperry Smith, S. 2008. *Early childhood mathematics,* 4th ed. Boston, MA: Allyn and Bacon.

Texas Education Agency. 2009a. Texas Essential Knowledge and Skills. Texas Administrative Code (TAC), Title 19, Part II Chapter. Texas Essential Knowledge and Skills for Mathematics.

Texas Education Agency. 2009b. TAKS Exam study guide available online at *http://ritter. tea.state.tx.us/student.assessment/resources/guides/study/G6MathE-SG.pdf*

U. S. Department of Labor 2008–09. Bureau of Labor Statistics, U.S. Department of Labor Occupational Outlook Handbook, 2008–09 edition, Bulletin 2700. Superintendent of Documents, U.S. Government Printing Office, Washington, DC: Author. *http://www.bls.gov/OCO/* (accessed August 1, 2009)

van Hiele, P.M. 1986. *Structure and Insight.* Orlando, FL: Academic Press.

Vygotsky, L. S. 1986. *Thought and language* (new rev.ed.) Cambridge, MA: MIT Press

Social Studies

Competency 019: Social Science Instruction

The teacher uses social science knowledge and skills to plan, organize, and implement instruction and assess learning.

Social Studies Curricula

Social studies is an umbrella term used to encompass the disciplines of history, geography, civics and government, economics, and psychology. All five components are intertwined with the standards or strands shown in Figure 3-1, which were developed by the National Council for the Teaching of Social Studies in 1997 (NCTSS 2006). The Texas Education Agency (TEA) used these strands and curriculum standards as a foundation to develop the state social studies curriculum for kindergarten through grade 12.

Texas Essential Knowledge and Skills (TEKS) in Social Studies

The Texas Essential Knowledge and Skills (TEKS) is the state curriculum for kindergarten to grade 12. The TEKS organizes the social studies content inductively, from the known to the unknown. In this vertical alignment, children begin learning about the self in kindergarten and expand their knowledge with each successive grade, eventually encompassing the community, the state, the nation, and the world. A summary of the key components of the social studies curriculum covered in kindergarten through grade 6 follows.

Kindergarten—Child, Home, Family, and Classroom

- The child as an individual

- Home and families

- State and national heritage

- Patriotic holidays and the contribution of historical characters

Figure 3-1. Social Studies Strands

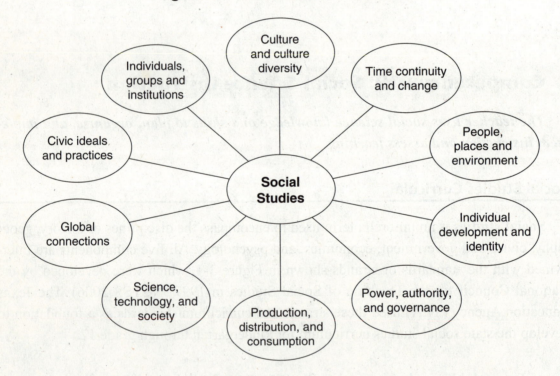

Grade 1—Child's Relationship to the Classroom, School, and Community

- The concept of chronology developed by distinguishing among past, present, and future

- Anthems and mottoes of Texas and the United States

Grade 2—Local Community

- Impact of significant individuals and events in the history of the community, state, and nation

- Concepts of time and chronology by measuring calendar time by days, weeks, months, and years

- Relationship between the physical environment and human activities

- Functions of government and services that it provides

Grade 3—How Individuals Change Their Communities and the World

- Past and present heroes and their contributions

- People who overcame obstacles

- Economic, cultural, and scientific contributions made by individuals

Grade 4—History of Texas

- History of Texas from its beginning to the present

- Events and individuals of the nineteenth and twentieth centuries

- Human activity and physical features of regions in Texas and the Western Hemisphere

- Native Americans in Texas and the Western Hemisphere

- European exploration and colonization

- Types of Native American governments

- Characteristics of Spanish and Mexican colonial governments

Grade 5—United States History

- History of the United States from its early beginnings to the present

- Major events and significant individuals of the late 19th and 20th centuries including contributions of famous inventors and scientists

- Regions of the United States that result from physical features and human activity

- Characteristics and benefits of the free enterprise system

- Roots of representative government

- Important ideas in the Declaration of Independence

- Meaning of the Pledge of Allegiance

- Fundamental rights guaranteed in the Bill of Rights

- Customs and celebrations of various racial, ethnic, and religious groups in the nation

Grade 6—People and Places of the Contemporary World

- People and places of the contemporary world

- Societies from the following regions in the world: Europe, Russia and the Eurasian republics, North America, Middle America, South America, Southwest Asia-North Africa, Sub-Saharan Africa, South Asia, East Asia, Southeast Asia, Australia, and the Pacific Realm

- Influence of individuals and groups from various cultures on selected historical and contemporary events

- Different ways of organizing economic and governmental systems

Using Maps and Globes

Symbolic representation can pose challenges for children in kindergarten through grade 4, and even students in fifth and sixth grades. Maps and globes are tools for representing space symbolically. In the early grades, the main purpose for using globes is to familiarize children with the basic roundness of the earth and to begin developing a global perspective. It can also be used to study the proportion of land and water. In kindergarten through third grade, teachers should use a simplified 12-inch globe. Generally, this type of globe uses no more than three colors to represent land elevation and no more than two to represent water depth. For this age group, the globe should include only the largest rivers, cities, and oceans. In grades 4 through 6, students can use a 16-inch globe containing additional details. Generally, seven colors are used to represent land elevation and three colors to represent water depth.

Activities for Students in Kindergarten through Grade 6

Teaching map concepts in kindergarten through grade 4 should include the following activities:

- Stress that the globe is a very small representation of the earth.

- Show children how land areas and water bodies are represented on the globe.

- Identify major land and water bodies.

- Show the location of the North Pole and the concept of the Northern Hemisphere, where most of the world's land is located.

- Show the location of the South Pole and the concept of the Southern Hemisphere, where most of the world's water is located.

- Show the relationship and location of the earth in the solar system.

- Use the globe to find the continent, the country, the state, and the city where the children live.

- Encourage children to explore the globe to find places by themselves.

- Compare the size of the continents represented on a globe with their representation on a Mercator projection—the flat representation.

Teaching map concepts in fifth and sixth grade should include the following activities:

- Create and interpret maps.

- Use maps and globes to pose and answer questions.

- Locate major historical and contemporary societies on maps and globes.

- Use maps to solve real-life problems, i.e., using road maps to plan a route to a specific destination.

Latitude and Longitude—Developmental Considerations

The concepts of latitude and longitude are generally covered in fourth grade and up. However, even fourth graders may have difficulty understanding the mathematics involved in the grid system. Children might get confused with these concepts:

- The sizes of the meridians of longitude and the parallels of latitude on a globe and Mercator projection look different.

- The meridians of longitude have a consistent size, but the parallels of latitude vary in size, becoming smaller as they move away from the equator.

They might have problems conceptualizing and separating the Western Hemisphere and the Eastern Hemisphere, or the Northern and Southern hemispheres. Teachers should use concrete materials like a pumpkin to represent these concepts.

Using Technology Information in Social Studies

Research in social studies involves the use of systematic inquiry. Engaging children in inquiry involves the ability to acquire information from various resources. Inquiry involves the ability to design and conduct investigations, which requires students to develop an understanding of key information in social studies content.

To gather content information, students should become familiar with the various resources used in social sciences research. Those resources include primary and secondary sources, encyclopedias, almanacs, atlases, government documents, artifacts, and oral histories. Students are expected to apply critical-thinking skills to organize and use information acquired from a variety of sources including electronic technology. Information about social studies is available from the Internet; however, students need to evaluate the scholarship of the many sources available and use only those known to be reliable. In addition to sources available electronically, students can use commercially developed programs like *Oregon Trails* and *Where in the World is Carmen San Diego?* These kinds of interactive programs can expose students to problem-solving skills and social studies content in a fun and supportive environment.

Integration of Social Studies

As mentioned earlier, the teaching of social studies by definition implies integration of content from five disciplines: history, geography, civics and government, economics, and psychology. However, teachers can go beyond this integration and add components from other content areas. The use of a literature-based approach is an ideal way to integrate social studies with language arts. Through the use of authentic multicultural literature, teachers can expose children to quality reading and the cultures of the many ethnic and linguistic groups living in the United States.

The use of thematic units can also help teachers to integrate the content areas. In this approach, a teacher or teachers select a theme and organize content area instruction around it. Thematic instruction can be done in a self-contained classroom or in a departmental format in which several teachers teach the content.

Thematic instruction is ideal for English language learners (ELLs) because the use of a common theme in multiple content areas makes content more cognitively accessible for them. For example, in a unit on the *solar system*, the names of the planets and the terminology used to describe the system can be introduced and repeated in several subjects through the duration of the unit. The presentation and repetition of content in different subjects and conditions allow students the opportunity to develop English vocabulary while learning content.

Graphic Representations of Historical Information

Information in social studies can be presented in a visual form through the use of graphs and charts to make content accessible to all children, including ELLs.

Graphs

The most commonly used graphs are the pictorial graph, the bar graph, the pie or circle graph, and the line graph. The pictorial graph is the most concrete type of graph because it uses a picture of the object being represented. Bar graphs are more concrete than pie graphs. Although the pie graph appears to be simple enough for children in the elementary grades, students need to understand the concept of percentages to correctly interpret the meaning of this type of graph, and the concept of percentages is not acquired until late in the elementary grades. At first, teachers can use real-life situations to guide students in the construction of graphs. For example, teachers can create a simple graph showing information about students in the classroom, like the number of boys and girls in the classroom or their color or food preferences. Figure 3-2 shows the results of a poll on the favorite foods of first-grade boys and girls.

Figure 3-2—Food Preferences for Children

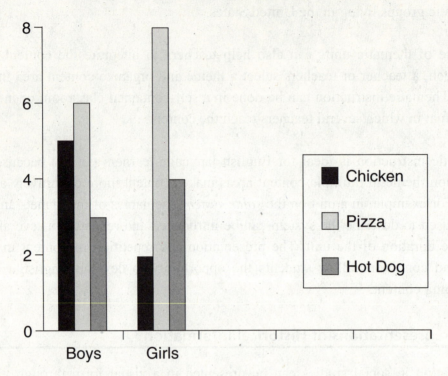

Figure 3-3—Pie Graph—Methods of Transportation

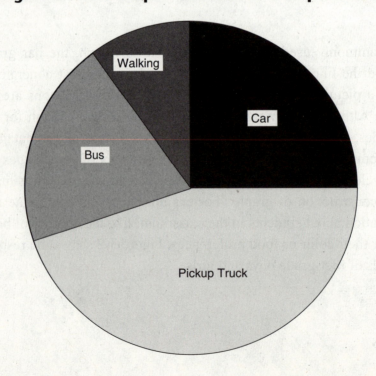

Teachers can use more sophisticated graphs like the pie to represent research information. For example, children can take 5 to 10 minutes a day to observe the types of transportation used by people in the neighborhood and prepare a graph similar to the one presented in Figure 3-3. Teachers can use this information to guide children to make inferences about the information contained in the graph. Why are so many people using pickup trucks as a mode of transportation? Why are only a small number of people walking?

Charts

Charts can be used to record information and present ideas in a concise way. Charts are ideal for promoting concept formation in a concrete fashion. **Data retrieval charts** are used to gather and keep track of data gathered from research, observation, or experimentation. The chart is constructed to allow the easy comparison of two or more sets of data. For example, students could use the chart shown in Table 3-1 to record information about the foods of the ethnic groups represented in their classroom.

Table 3-1. Data Retrieval Chart—Ethnic Foods

Ethnic Group	Breakfast	Dinner	Special Days
Mexican American	Tortilla/eggs	Enchiladas/rice	Tamales/menudo
Puerto Rican	Bread/eggs	Pinto beans/rice	Roasted Pork/rice
African American	Grits/eggs	Collard greens/meat	Glazed smoked ham
Italian American	Frittata (omelet)	Spaghetti/meatballs	Special lasagna

Narrative charts are used to show events in a sequence. For example, students can develop charts showing the steps in making their favorite dishes. A narrative chart can also be used to present a time line of historical events. An example of a simple time line is one that shows a child's personal history. Because children in kindergarten through grade 2 might have problems conceptualizing time, initial exposure to time lines should begin with things that they did yesterday, things that they are doing today, and things that will be done tomorrow. Starting in third grade, children can begin introducing more challenging components, like the ones listed in Figure 3-4.

Figure 3-4 A Time Line—My History

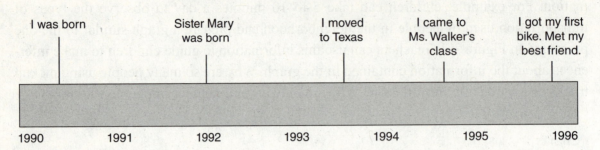

A tabulation or classification chart provides orderly columnar display of information for comparison. For example, Table 3-2 compares data from the 2000 United States census.

Table 3-2 Tabulation or Classification Chart—
U.S. and Texas Populations by Group

Ethnic Group Population	Percentage of U.S. Population	Percentage of Texas Population
Caucasian	75.1%	71%
African American	12.3%	11.5%
Asian American	3.8%	0.6%
Hispanic	12.5%	32.0%
Native American	0.1%	0.6%
Total Population	281,421,906	20,851,820

Using developmentally appropriate vocabulary, teachers can guide students to recall or infer data from the chart.

A **pedigree chart** shows the origin and development of something. Examples are a person's family, the pedigree line of a purebred dog, and the development of a political party. Figure 3-5 presents a pedigree chart.

Figure 3-5 A Pedigree Chart—My Family Tree

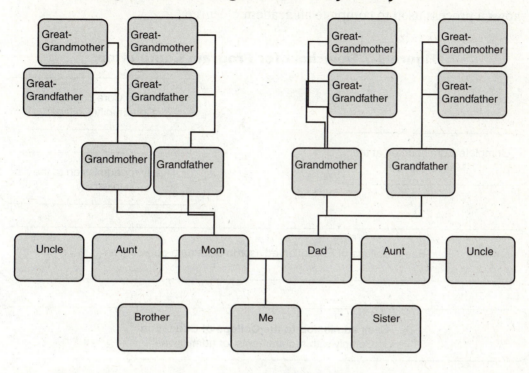

An organizational chart shows the structure of an organization, like a school or business. Figure 3-6 is a chart showing the typical organization of an elementary school

Figure 3-6 Organizational Chart—Elementary School

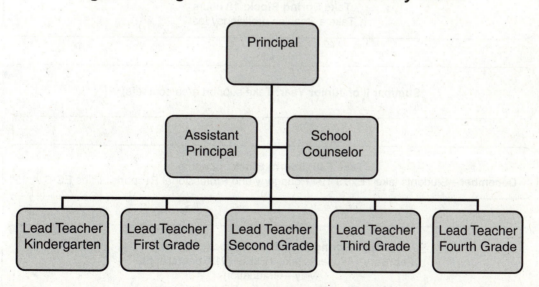

A **flowchart** shows a process involving changes at certain points—for example, Table 3-7 shows a process used to complete an academic degree.

Figure 3-7 Flowchart for Program Completion

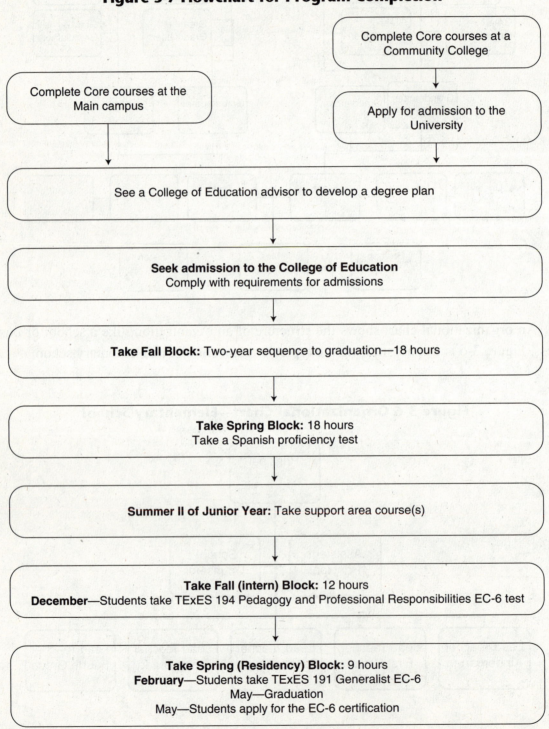

Addressing the Needs of English Language Learners

English language learners can find social studies instruction quite challenging; thus, teachers need to modify instruction to make the content comprehensible for this group. Some textbooks have been written with ELLs in mind. These books use numerous visual and graphic representations to make the content cognitively accessible to children learning English. For example, *Adventure Tales of America*, written by Jody Potts (1994), is an American history book that uses cartoons and illustrations to explain complex concepts like the processes of electing the president and making a bill into law. It also uses concrete time lines to represent the historical development of the nation. The illustrations give ELLs the fundamental meanings of important concepts from which teachers can develop lessons.

Other books integrate language instruction with content to deliver both components in a contextualized format. One example is the ESL series titled *Avenues*, published by Hampton Brown (Schifini et al. 2004). This set of books presents ESL lessons in conjunction with content from other disciplines. The integration of content and language is one of the most effective strategies to promote content area mastery and language development.

Cognates and Suffixes

English and most Western languages have been heavily influenced by the Greek and Roman civilizations. The association has resulted in the creation of multiple cognates—words that are similar in two languages. Most of the sophisticated English words in the content areas and especially in social studies are cognates of Spanish and other Western languages. Teachers can use these similarities to expand the vocabulary of students and enhance content area comprehension. Table 3-3 presents examples of the connection between English and Spanish words (Rosado and Salazar 2002–2003).

Table 3-3. Common Greek and Latin Roots and Affixes

Roots/Affixes	Meaning	English/Spanish Cognates
Phobia Xeno	Fear of Foreigners or strangers	Xenophobia/Xenofobia
Phono Logy(ia)	Sound Study of	Phonology/Fonología
Photo Graphy	Light Graph, form	Photography/Fotografía
Homo Sapiens	Same, Man Able to Think	*Homo sapiens/homo sapiens*
Demo Cracy	People Government	Democracy/Democracia

Instructional Techniques to Support ELLs

Teachers need to implement a variety of activities to teach the state curriculum to ELLs at the grade level and complexity required of native English speakers. Scaffolding was originally used to describe the way in which adults support children in their efforts to communicate in the native language (L1). The same concept can be used to facilitate language and content development for ELLs. The term *scaffolding* alludes to the provisional structure used to provide support during the construction of a building. This support is eliminated when the structure is complete. Following this analogy, ELLs receive language support to make content cognitively accessible to them until they achieve mastery in the second language (L2); once that mastery is accomplished, the language support is eliminated.

Graphic organizers are visuals used to show relationships. These are the most common graphic organizers:

- A **semantic web** or **tree diagram** shows the relationship between main ideas and subordinated components.

- A **time line** presents a visual summary of chronological events and is ideal for showing historical events or events in a sequence.

- A **flowchart** shows cause-and-effect relationships and can be used to show steps in a process, like the process for admission to a school or program.

- A **Venn diagram** uses circles to compare common and unique elements of two or three distinct components, such as properties of numbers, elements of stories, or events or civilizations (like the Maya, Inca, and Aztec shown in Figure 3-8).

The **SQ4R** is a study strategy in which the learner is engaged in the entire reading process. The acronym stands for **survey**, **question**, **read**, **reflect**, **recite**, and **review**. During the **survey** part, readers examine the headings and major components of the text to develop predictions 'and generate questions. Through these **questions**, students establish the purpose for reading. As they **read**, students look for answers to the questions they generated. They monitor their comprehension as they **reflect**, write a summary, and **recite** the content they learned. Finally, they **review** to evaluate how much they learned about the content.

Figure 3-8. Venn Diagram—Three Civilizations

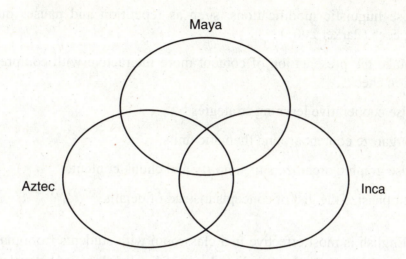

Strategies to Integrate Language Arts and Social Studies

Sheltered English

Sheltered English is an instructional approach designed to make content comprehensible for ELLs (Echevarria, Vogt, and Short 2000). In the program, children are "sheltered" from the pressure of competing with native English learners. To deliver comprehensible input, content instruction is linguistically simplified through contextualized instruction, visual aids, hands-on activities, and body language. Some strategies teachers can use to modify language to make it comprehensible are listed here:

- Control the length and complexity of the sentences. Children respond better to short, simple sentences.

- Introduce technical vocabulary before beginning the lesson.

- Use repetition, restatement, and paraphrasing to clarify concepts.

- Control the speed of delivery, and use a different type of intonation to emphasize important concepts.

- Supplement oral presentations with diagrams, graphic organizers, and manipulatives to make content easier to understand.

- Help students use drawings and graphic organizers to visualize word problems and experiments, and as tools for communication.

- Guide students in using role-play to represent important concepts.

- Use linguistic modifications, such as repetition and pauses during speech (Parker 2001).

- Make the presentation of content more interactive with comprehension checks.

- Use cooperative learning strategies.

- Organize content around thematic units.

- Use graphic organizers to simplify and chunk content.

- Emphasize the gist of concepts instead of details.

Sheltered English is most effective in a classroom with students from many language groups who are at least at the intermediate level of English language development (Schifini 1985).

Academic Vocabulary in Social Studies

Academic vocabulary is the vocabulary needed to understand the concepts of school. In other words, it is the vocabulary of teaching and learning. Marzano and Pickering (2005) emphasize the importance of teaching academic vocabulary to English language learners and recommend a six-step systematic approach that includes direct instruction as well as practice and reinforcement. The steps to teach academic vocabulary are presented next.

- The teacher provides a description, explanation, or example of the new term.

- Students restate the description, example, or explanation in their own words.

- Students create a representation of the word by drawing a picture, symbol, or graphic of the word.

- Students periodically participate in activities that help to add to their knowledge of terms.

- Students discuss terms with one another.

- Students participate in games and activities that reinforce the new term.

Cooperative learning is a teaching strategy designed to create a low-anxiety learning environment in which students work together in small groups to achieve instructional goals. As a result of this instructional arrangement, students with different levels of ability or language development work collaboratively to support each other to ensure that each member masters the objectives of the lesson. This approach can easily be used to deliver content and language instruction. Traditionally, the strategy is delivered in specific steps (Arends 1998):

1. **Present Goals**—The teacher goes over the objectives of the lesson and provides the motivation.

2. **Present Information**—The teacher presents information to students either verbally or with text.

3. **Organize Students into Learning Teams**—The teacher explains to students how to form learning teams and helps groups make an efficient transition.

4. **Assist Teamwork and Study**—The teacher assists learning teams as they do their work.

5. **Test Students on the Content**—The teacher tests students' knowledge of learning materials as each group presents the results of their work.

6. **Provide Recognition**—The teacher finds ways to recognize both individual and group efforts and achievements.

To emphasize the cooperative nature of the strategy, specific methods were developed to enrich the lessons. These specialized methods are described in the sections that follow.

Student Teams Achievement Division (STAD)

1. The teacher presents new academic information to students.

2. Students are divided into four- or five-member learning teams.

3. Team members master the content and then help each other learn the material through tutoring, quizzing one another, or carrying on team discussions.

4. Each student receives an improvement score that helps show the growth he or she has made.

5. Daily or weekly quizzes are given to assess mastery.

6. Each week, through newsletters or a short ceremony, groups and individual students are recognized for showing the most improvement (Slavin 1986).

Group Investigation

1. Students select a subtopic within a general area.

2. The teacher divides the class into small groups, each composed of two to six students. Group composition should be ethnically and academically heterogeneous.

3. The students and the teacher plan specific learning procedures, tasks, and goals.

4. Students carry out the plan using various sources. The teacher monitors the process and offers assistance as needed.

5. The students analyze and evaluate information and plan how they can summarize it in an interesting fashion for possible display or presentation to the class as a whole.

6. The students present their final product.

7. The teacher conducts individual or group evaluation (Thelen 1981).

Think-Pair-Share

This activity was developed as a result of the wait-time research. Wait-time research suggests that pausing for a few seconds to allow children to reflect on the question can improve the quality of the response and the overall performance of children (Rowe 1986).

1. **Think**—The teacher poses a question and asks students to spend a minute thinking alone about the answer. No talking or walking is allowed.

2. **Pair**—Students pair off and discuss what they have been thinking about, sharing possible answers or information.

3. **Share**—Students share their answers with the whole class. The teacher goes around the classroom from pair to pair until a fourth or a half of the class has a chance to report (Lyman 1981).

Numbered Heads Together

This activity was designed to involve more students in the review of materials covered in class.

1. **Number**—The teacher divides the students into teams with three to five members each and assigns a number to each member.

2. **Question**—The teacher asks a question.

3. **Heads Together**—Students put their heads together to figure out the answer and to be sure everyone knows the answer.

4. **Answer**—The teacher calls a number, and students from each group with that number raise their hands and provide the answer (Kagan 1985).

Competency 020: History

The teacher understands and applies knowledge of significant historical events and developments, multiple historical interpretations and ideas, and relationships between the past, the present, and the future as defined by the Texas Essential Knowledge and Skills (TEKS).

World History

The World History Encyclopedia divides the history of the world into five periods: the Ancient World, the Middle Ages, the Age of Discovery, Revolution and Industry, and the Modern World (Ganeri, Martell, and Williams 1999). A summary and time line of key events in each period is presented here.

The Ancient World (4 Million Years Ago to 500 CE)[1]

Study of the ancient world focuses on the development of the first humans, the first farmers, and the first civilizations. It emphasizes the history of the ancient civilizations of Mesopotamia, Sumer, Assyria, Babylon, Egypt, the Indus Valley, megalith Europe,

---

1   The terms "Before Common Era (BCE)" and "Common Era (CE)" are being used in place of the traditional "Before Christ (BC) and Anno Domini (AD) to identify historical periods. These terms are more inclusive and eliminate religious references.

ancient China, Phoenicia, ancient America, ancient Greece, the Celts, the Romans, and empires in Africa and India.

Time Line of the Ancient World

4000 BCE	*Homo sapiens* appear in various regions in the world
3500 BCE	The Sumerians of Mesopotamia invent writing and the wheel
3100 BCE	Egypt becomes unified
2800 BCE	Building begins in Stonehenge, England
2500 BCE	Indus civilization flourishes in India
1600–1100 BCE	Mycenaean control of Greece
1200–400 BCE	Olmecs civilization flourishes in western Mexico
1000–612 BCE	New Assyrian Empire flourishes
753 BCE	Foundation of Rome
605–562 BCE	King Nebuchadnezzar rebuilds the city Babylon
476–431 BCE	Golden age of Athens
336–323 BCE	Alexander the Great rules the world
27 BCE to 14 CE	Augustus rules as the first Roman emperor
476 CE	Western Roman Empire falls

The Middle Ages (500–1400 CE)

This period includes the Byzantine civilization, the rise of Islam, civilizations of the Americas, the Vikings, the feudal system, the Crusades, Genghis Khan and China, the African kingdoms, and the Hundred Years' War.

Time Line for the Middle Ages (CE)

500	Eastern Roman (Byzantine Empire) at its peak
600	Teotihuacán civilization flourishes in Mexico
600	Rise of Islam
700	Mayan civilization at its height in Central America
700	Feudal system begins in Europe; peasants serve a lord in exchange for protection

711	Moors invade Spain
750	Abbasid dynasty is founded; Arab Empire at its peak
800	Charlemagne crowned emperor of the Holy Roman Empire
900	Rise of Toltec civilization in Mexico
1000	Vikings land in North America
1095	Muslim Turks take Jerusalem and ban Christian pilgrims from the city
1096–1270	Crusades try to rescue Jerusalem from the Muslims
1215	Genghis Khan and the Mongols invade China
1271	Marco Polo travels to China from Italy
1300	Renaissance begins in Europe
1325	Aztecs established Tenochtitlán near modern day Mexico City
1368	Foundation of the Ming dynasty in China
1453	Fall of the eastern Roman Empire (Constantinople)
1454	Gutenberg invents the printing machine
1500	Inca Empire at its peak in Peru

Age of Discovery (1400–1700)

This period includes the Renaissance, the development of the Aztec and Inca civilizations, voyages of discovery from Spain and Portugal, African empires, the Reformation, the Ottoman Empire, and the Ming dynasty in the slave trade.

Time Line for the Age of Discovery

1441	Portuguese begin slave trade from Africa to Europe
1448	Portuguese explorers reach the southern part of Africa
1492	Columbus sails from Spain to America
1492	Spain becomes unified and expels the Moors
1497	Portuguese reach India
1517	Martin Luther begins the religious Reformation in Europe
1520	Suleiman rules the Ottoman Empire
1522	Magellan travels around the world

1535	Spain completes the conquest of the Aztecs in Mexico and the Incas in Peru
1543	Copernicus suggests that the sun is the center of the universe, not the earth
1571	Europeans defeat the Muslim Ottomans in the battle of Lepanto
1588	England defeats the Spanish Armada and becomes the greatest naval power in the world
1607	England begins the colonization of North America
1609	Galileo uses a new invention, the telescope, to study the universe
1618	Thirty Years' War begins

Revolution and Industry (1700–1900)

This period includes the Russian Empire, the Manchu dynasty in China, the period of Enlightenment in Europe, the growth of Austria and Prussia, the birth of the United States, the French Revolution, the Napoleonic era, the Industrial Revolution, the British Empire, the American Civil War, and the unification of Italy and Germany.

Time Line for the Age of Revolution and Industry

1644	The Manchu overthrow the Ming dynasty of China
1682–1725	Peter the Great rules Russia
1740	Frederick the Great becomes king of Prussia—Domination of Europe
1756–63	Seven Years' War ensues, with France, Austria, and Russia clashing against Prussia and England
1768	James Cook visits regions in the Pacific
1776	America declares independence from England
1789	French Revolution begins with the fall of the Bastille in Paris
1791	As part of the Enlightenment period, Thomas Paine publishes *The Rights of Man.*
1804	Napoleon declares himself emperor of France, beginning the Napoleonic Era
1808	Wars for independence begin in Spanish America
1837–1901	British Empire at its peak under Queen Victoria
1848	Year of revolution in all Europe
1861–65	American Civil War
1869	Union Pacific Railroad links the East and West coasts of the United States

The Modern World (1900–Present)

This period includes the struggle for equal rights for women, World War I, the Russian Revolution, the Great Depression, the rise of fascism, revolution in China, World War II, Israel versus Palestine, the Cold War, the space race, the Korean and Vietnam wars, and globalization.

Time Line for the Modern World

1914	World War I begins when Austria declares war on Serbia and Germany on Russia
1917	Russian Revolution starts when the Bolsheviks, led by Lenin, seize power from Czar Nicholas II.
1918	World War I ends; Europe is in ruins, and Germany is heavily punished
1929	Great Depression begins in the United States.
1933	Adolf Hitler achieves power in Germany
1936–39	Spanish Civil War brings Francisco Franco to power
1939	World War II begins when Germany invaded Poland and Czechoslovakia
1941	United States enters World War II
1945	Germany surrenders to the Allied Forces, and Japan surrenders after the United States detonates two atomic bombs in Hiroshima and Nagasaki
1947	Pakistan and India obtain independence from Great Britain
1948–49	State of Israel is founded in Palestine, and the Arabs declare war
1949	Communist Mao Zedong (Tse-tung) gains control of China
1959	Cuban Revolution
1960	Many countries in Africa gain independence
1965–72	America participates in the Vietnam War
1969	Neil Armstrong lands on the moon
1990	Germany is reunited
1991	Soviet Union collapses, and the Cold War ends
1994	Free elections in South Africa and the end of apartheid
2001	9/11 terrorist attack in New York City and Washington, D.C.

2001	War in Afghanistan against the Taliban
2003	War in Iraq
2009	Barack Obama becomes the 44th President of the United States.

For details about these historical periods, go to these websites: Kidipede—History for Kids (*www.historyforkids.org*) and Ancient Mesoamerican Civilizations, created and maintained by Kevin L. Callahan of the University of Minnesota, Department of Anthropology (*www.angelfire.com/ca/humanorigins*).

The Industrial Revolution and Modern Technology

The Industrial Revolution began in England in the mid-eighteenth century. Inventions that made mining of fossil fuel (charcoal) easier provided the energy needed to expand and promote industrial development. Improvement on the steam engine and industrial machines led to the mass production of goods and a better distribution system. The economic growth motivated people to leave the rural areas and move to the cities. The following time line highlights inventions that supported the industrial revolution and modern life:

Time Line for Industrial and Technological Development

1769	Richard Arkwright patents the spinning machine powered by a waterwheel
1810	A German, Frederick Koenig, invents an improved printing press
1831	An American, Cyrus H. McCormick, invents the reaper
1836	Samuel Colt invents the first revolver
1837–1938	Samuel Morse invents the telegraph and Morse code
1846	Ascanio Sobrero, an Italian chemist, invents nitroglycerin
1856	Louis Pasteur invents the process of pasteurization
1858	Jean Lenoir invents an internal combustion engine
1866	Albert Nobel invents dynamite
1876	Alexander Graham Bell patents the telephone
1885	Gottlieb Daimler invents the first gas engine motorcycle
1900	Ferdinand Von Zeppelin invents a hot air balloon called the zeppelin
1903	The Wright brothers invent the first gas-powered airplane

1905	Albert Einstein publishes the theory of relativity: $E = mc^2$
1914	Henry Ford introduces the assembly line and begins building the first American cars
1928	Biologist Alexander Fleming discovers penicillin
1930	Vannevar Bush at the Massachusetts Institute of Technology in Boston invents the analog computer
1940	Peter Goldmark invents modern color television
1946	The atomic bomb is invented
1952	The hydrogen bomb is invented
1955	The antibiotic tetracycline is invented
1959	Jack Kilby and Robert Noyce invent the microchip
1969	The predecessor of the Internet, called the ARPAnet, is invented
1971	Ray Tomlinson invents Internet-based e-mail
1985	Microsoft invents the Windows program
1988	Digital cellular phones are invented
1990	Tim Berners-Lee created the Internet protocol HTTP and the World Wide Web language HTML

Ancient Civilizations of the Americas

Among the most developed ancient civilizations in the Americas were the Mayas, Toltecs, Olmecs, Aztecs, and Incas.

Mayas

One of the earliest civilizations of Mesoamerica was the Mayan, from regions of Mexico's Yucatán Peninsula, Guatemala, and Honduras. The Mayas developed a highly integrated society with elaborate religious observances for which they built stone and mortar pyramids. The center of the Maya civilization was the city of Chichén Itzá and its religious centers, where human victims were sacrificed. The Mayas developed an elaborate calendar, a system of writing, and the mathematical concept of zero. They also had highly advanced knowledge of astronomy, engineering, and art. By the time the Spanish conquerors arrived, most of the Mayan religious centers had been abandoned and the civilization was in decline.

Zapotecs, Olmecs, and Toltecs

Farther north in Mexico, three highly sophisticated civilizations emerged: the Olmecs, Zapotecs, Teotihuacán, and Toltecs. Beginning with the Olmecs, who flourished around 1200 BCE and followed by the Toltecs and Zapotecs, these groups developed highly sophisticated civilizations. They had already begun to use a ceremonial calendar and had built stone pyramids on which they performed religious observances. Teotihuacán is the best-known example of religious ceremonial sites built by these civilizations. They developed a partly alphabetic writing system and left codices describing their history, religion, and daily events.

Aztecs

The Aztec civilization achieved the highest degree of development in Mexico. They had a centralized government headed by a king and supported by a large army. The Aztecs were also skilled builders and engineers, accomplished astronomers and mathematicians. They built the famous city of Tenochtitlan, with many pyramids, palaces, plazas, and canals. At the peak of their civilization, the Aztecs had a population of about five million. For information about the civilizations that emerged in Mexico, go to the Web site titled "Teotihuacán: The City of the Gods," hosted by Arizona State University, at *http://archaeology.la.asu.edu/teo/intro/intrteo.htm* and the National Indian Education Association website at *www.xmission.com/~amauta/index.htm*.

Incas—Children of the Sun

The Inca civilization covered the modern countries of Ecuador, Peru, and central Chile. Although they were not as advanced in mathematics and the sciences as the Mayans and Aztecs, the Incas had a well-developed political system. They also built a monumental road system to unify the empire. Their civilization was at its peak when the Spanish conquerors arrived in Cuzco, the capital of the empire.

Mound Builders in North America

In North America, two major groups, known as the Woodland and Mississippian peoples, lived in the Great Lakes and Mississippi area. These people built burial mounds dated as early as 500 CE. The Mississippian people built flat-topped mounds as foundations for wooden temples dating from 500 CE. The chiefs and the priests of these groups lived in residences built on the top of the mounds, while the rest of the population lived in houses below. These mound-building civilizations declined gradually and disappeared by the fourteenth century.

Inhabitants of the South and Southwest

In the southwestern United States and northern Mexico, two ancient cultures developed: the Anasazi and the Hohokam. The Anasazi developed adobe architecture consisting of individual apartments, storage areas, and a central plaza. They worked the land extensively, had a highly developed system of irrigation, and made cloth and baskets. The Hohokam built separate stone and timber houses around a central plaza. Neither group developed a written language. Drought and attacks from rival tribes contributed to the decline of these civilizations. Historians believe that the Anasazi built the cliff dwellings at Mesa Verde, Colorado, during the fourteenth and fifteenth centuries to protect themselves from these attacks.

Pueblo Indians

There is evidence to suggest that the Anasazi settled along the Rio Grande and intermarried with the local population, leading to the emergence of the Pueblo people. The Pueblo culture continued and improved on the architectural tradition and farming techniques of their predecessors. They were able to produce drought-resistant corn and squash, which became the foundation of their diet. The Pueblo Indians managed to survive the Spanish conquest and colonization period.

Iroquois

The Iroquois inhabited the area of Ontario, Canada, and Upstate New York for at least 4,500 years before the arrival of Europeans. They hunted and fished, but farming became the main economic activity for the group. The Iroquois had a matrilineal line of descent, with women doing most of the farming to support the community. They developed the Iroquois Confederation to discourage war among the groups and to provide for a common defense.

American History

Colonization

In 1565, the Spaniards established the first successful European settlement in North America near the current city of Jacksonville, Florida. Following the Spaniards, the English attempted to establish a permanent colony on Roanoke, an island off the coast of North Carolina. This colony eventually disappeared. Further north, the Dutch settled colonies in the region of present-day New York and New Jersey. Following the Dutch, numerous private companies received royal charters, or patents, permitting them to begin the colonization process in North America. Three of the first and most successful companies were the Plymouth Company, the Massachusetts Bay Company, and the London Company. The London Company was the first to exercise this patent.

The English Colonies

Thirteen colonies were established on the Atlantic coastline. Three types of colonies developed based on three types of charters: corporate colonies, royal colonies, and proprietary colonies. These were divided in three geographical regions: the New England Colonies, the Middle Colonies, and the Southern Colonies. The New England Colonies consisted of: Massachusetts, Connecticut, Rhode Island, and New Hampshire. The economy of the New England colonies was based on farming and very small industries such as fishing, lumber, and crafts. The Middle Colonies consisted of: New York, New Jersey, Delaware, Maryland, and Pennsylvania. The economy of the Middle Colonies was based on farming, shipping, fishing, and trading. The Southern Colonies were: Virginia, North Carolina, South Carolina, and Georgia. The economy of the Southern Colonies was based on the crops of tobacco, rice, indigo, and cotton plantations. Plantations produced agricultural crops in large scale and exploited workers as well as the environment.

Virginia (1607)

The London Company established the first English colony in Jamestown, Virginia. The leader of the colony was Captain John Smith. Natives of the area captured Smith and sentenced him to death. Pocahontas, daughter of the tribe's chief, intervened and saved his live. Contrary to popular belief, John Smith did not marry Pocahontas; instead, Pocahontas married John Rolfe, a tobacco farmer from the same colony.

Massachusetts (1620)

The Puritans, who fled England to avoid religious persecution, founded Plymouth. The group obtained a patent from the London Virginia Company. Before arriving at their destination, they wrote the Mayflower Compact, a document containing rules to guide life in the community. This compact established the first type of government in North America.

New Hampshire (1623)

Two groups founded the colony of New Hampshire. The first group was led by Captain John Mason, who established a fishing village in 1623. In 1638, a group led by John Wheelwright founded a second settlement called Exeter. That colony began as a proprietorship but eventually became a royal colony.

New Jersey (1623)

The Dutch founded the New Jersey colony in 1623. After taking over the Dutch territory between Virginia and New England in 1664, King George II of England gave these possessions to his brother, the Duke of York. The duke then gave the territory as a proprietary grant to Sir George Carteret and Lord Berkeley. In 1702, New Jersey became an English colony.

New York (1624)

The area of New York was part of New Amsterdam, a possession of the Dutch government. In 1674, the British took control of the territory, and in 1685 New York officially became a royal colony.

Maryland (1633)

In 1632, King Charles I granted a Maryland Charter to Lord Baltimore (George Calvert). In 1633, the colony was established as a refuge for freemen, especially Catholics.

Rhode Island (1636)

Roger Williams founded the Rhode Island colony in 1636, and in 1638 Anne Hutchinson settled an additional part of the colony. Both Williams and Hutchinson had been banned from Massachusetts for their religious and political views and were looking for sanctuary. The colony was initially a corporation and eventually became a royal colony.

Connecticut (1636)

As early as 1633, Dutch traders had established a permanent settlement near Hartford. After the decline of the Dutch influence in the area, Thomas Hooker established the colony of Connecticut. Hooker and his followers were also seeking religious freedom after being expelled from Massachusetts. In 1662, Connecticut obtained a Royal Charter under the leadership of John Winthrop Jr.

Delaware (1638)

The Dutch and Swedish initially settled this colony. With the decline of the Dutch influence in the area, the English took control. In 1682, Delaware was awarded to William Penn.

North Carolina (1653)

By 1653, Virginia colonists began moving south and settling in the North Carolina region. In 1691, the region was officially recognized as a colony, and Charles I granted a royal charter in 1729.

South Carolina (1663)

In 1663, King Charles II created the colony of Carolina by granting the territory, of what is now the region of present-day North Carolina, South Carolina, and Georgia, to loyal supporters. It began as a proprietary colony and became a royal colony in 1719. Sir John Yeamans, a plantation owner from Barbados, founded the city of Charleston in 1670.

Pennsylvania (1682)

As early as 1647, Swedish, Dutch, and English settlers tried to establish permanent settlements in Delaware. In 1681, a large territory, which included Pennsylvania, was granted to William Penn. Penn was a member of a religion persecuted in England, the Quakers. He made Pennsylvania a safe haven for Quakers, and a large number of German

Quakers settled in the colony. In 1683, the first group of settlers arrived in Pennsylvania and formed Germantown near Philadelphia.

Georgia (1732)

This colony was founded with two main purposes: to establish a buffer zone from the Spanish settlement south of the colony and to provide a safe haven for poor people.

Table 3-4 summarizes the key historical characters and events of the colonies.

Table 3-4 The Thirteen American Colonies

Colony	Year Established	Colonizer	Historical Features/ Characters
Virginia	1607	London Company	Captain John Smith, John Rolfe, and Pocahontas
Massachusetts	1620	Puritans with a patent from the London Virginia Company	Puritans, Mayflower, Mayflower Compact, John Smith
New Hampshire	1623	Proprietary colony	Captain John Mason, John Wheelwright
New Jersey	1623	Dutch possession, then a proprietorship	Duke of York
New York	1624	Dutch possession, then a proprietorship	Purchase of the island of Manhattan, Duke of York
Maryland	1633	Proprietorship	George Calvert (Lord Baltimore), the colony served as a refuge for persecuted Catholics
Rhode Island	1636	Corporate colony	Roger Williams and Anne Hutchinson
Connecticut	1636	Corporate colony	Thomas Hooker and John Winthrop
Delaware	1638	Corporate colony	First, under the Dutch, Swedish, and finally under British control. William Penn
North Carolina	1653	Proprietorship	King Charles II
South Carolina	1663	Proprietorship, then a charter colony	King Charles II, Sir John Yeamans
Pennsylvania	1682	Proprietorship	William Penn and Quakers
Georgia	1732	Charter colony	James Edward Oglethorpe

Representative Government in Colonial America

Colonists brought with them their tradition of hard work, individual freedom, and representative government. They believed in the right to elect the people who would represent them in important issues such as taxes. The Virginia House of Burgesses was the first colonial assembly of elected representatives from the Virginia settlement. It was established in Jamestown to represent the colonists in the state of Virginia in the lawmaking process.

The Mayflower Compact was drawn and signed by the Pilgrims aboard the Mayflower. They pledged to consult one another to make decisions and to act by the will of the majority. It is one of the earliest agreements to establish a political body and to give that political body the power to act for the good of the colony.

Indentured Servants

The indentured servant system was used to bring workers to the New World. In practice, the indentured servant would sell him- or herself to an agent or ship captain before leaving England. In turn, the contract would be sold to a buyer in the colonies to recover the cost of passage. Criminals and people in debt could also be sold for life or until they paid their debts. In some cases, at the end of the service, servants remained as salaried workers, or in the best situations, the servants were given a piece of land for their services. This system of provisional servitude was not applied to Africans; instead, permanent slavery was instituted.

The Enlightenment—The Age of Reason

The Enlightenment refers to a period during the seventeenth and eighteenth centuries when people began questioning religious dogmas and emphasizing scientific reasoning and knowledge. The result of this quest for knowledge was the development of modern chemistry and biology. People also began questioning governments and started searching for individual freedom. The search for freedom led countries to seek independence and fight tyranny. For example, the quest for freedom led to the American War of Independence and the French Revolution. The American Revolution motivated the Spanish colonies to seek independence. Some of the leading thinkers of this period were Jean-Jacques Rousseau, John Locke, Charles Montesquieu, Voltaire, and Francis Bacon. The ideas of the Enlightenment quickly reached the British colonies. Many of the leaders responsible for the writing of the Constitution were familiar with the leading thinkers of the movement, and framed the Constitution protecting the natural rights of the individual and limiting the power of the government.

American Revolution

The main reasons for the War of Independence were economic in nature. England, as well as other European nations, had established the *mercantilism system* to exploit the colonies. This system had three main principles:

1. The wealth of the nation is measured in terms of commodities accrued, especially gold and silver.

2. Economic activities can increase the power and control of the national government.

3. The colonies existed for the benefit of the mother country.

England used the system of mercantilism quite effectively in the thirteen colonies, but after more than a century of British rule, the colonies were primed for independence, and war with England became inevitable.

Another reason for the rebellion was the cost of the French and Indian War. This war, which was the North American portion of the Seven Years' War, emptied the British coffers, and the British Crown needed a quick way to recover financially. The taxation system that followed the French and Indian War was unbearable for the colonies. The colonies responded with civil disobedience and by boycotting the government of King George. In response to civil disobedience, the British sent troops to Boston, where the groups clashed and several colonists were killed. The event was called the Boston Massacre. One of the best-known boycotts was the Boston Tea Party, in which the colonists dumped tea in the Boston harbor to protest against taxation. All these events and the repression that followed led to the American War of Independence.

Continental Congress

Following the events in Massachusetts, representatives of the colonies met in Philadelphia to discuss the political and economic situation in the colonies. No clear solutions were reached at this congress. Once the hostilities started, the Second Continental Congress met to discuss preparations for war. George Washington was elected commander of the American forces, and war was declared against the British. The congress named a committee, led by Thomas Jefferson, to prepare the Declaration of Independence, which was officially signed on July 4, 1776.

The Declaration of Independence

The Declaration of Independence pronounced the colonies free and independent states. It consists of a preamble, or introduction, followed by three main parts. The first part stresses natural unalienable rights and liberties that belong to all people from birth. The second part consists of a list of specific grievances and injustices committed by Britain. The third part announces the colonies as the United States of America. This document provided the foundation to establish equal rights for all people.

Revolution

The American Revolution began in Massachusetts in the outskirts of the towns of Concord and Lexington. In 1775, while the colonists were preparing for war, hundreds of British soldiers marched against them. Paul Revere warned the colonists of British troop movements, and minutemen took up arms to face the enemy. At Concord, the British were repelled and forced back to Boston. On their way back, American sharpshooters ambushed and killed hundreds of British soldiers. Following this initial victory for the colonists, the battle of Bunker Hill was fought near Boston. In this battle, the British lost large numbers of soldiers but managed to defeat the colonial troops. Later, in Long Island, the British won another decisive victory over the Americans. The French joined the war in support of the Americans, in retaliation for their defeat at the hands of the British in the Seven Years' War. Eventually, with the support of the French, the American troops defeated the British forces in Yorktown, Virginia, in 1781. The Treaty of Paris, officially signed in 1783, ended the war and gave independence to the new nation. For additional details about the American Revolution, go to the web page of HistoryCentral.com at *www. multied.com/Revolt/index.html*.

Articles of Confederation

During the Revolutionary War, the Second Continental Congress ran the government. After independence, the Articles of Confederation defined a new form of government. The new government was composed of representatives from thirteen independent states with limited power. The Congress could not declare war or raise an army. They could ask the states for money or for soldiers, but it was up to the states to agree to provide them.

Under this type of government, each state printed its own money and imposed taxes on imports from the other states.

On the positive side, the new government provided for a common citizenship—citizens of the United States. It organized a uniform system of weights and measurements and the postal service. It also became responsible for issues related to Native Americans living within the borders of the new nation. The confederation served as the official government of the young republic until 1789, when the states ratified the Constitution.

United States Constitution

After six years under the Articles of Confederation, the leaders of the nation realized that the American government needed revision to bolster its strength. To accomplish this goal, a constitutional convention was held in Philadelphia in 1787. The leaders of this initiative were George Washington, James Madison, Benjamin Franklin, and Alexander Hamilton. From this convention, a new form of government emerged. The Constitution was officially ratified in 1788, and in 1789 George Washington was selected to be the first president of the United States. The republic defined by the Constitution was composed of three branches, the executive, judicial, and legislative, and a system of checks and balances to regulate each branch.

To learn more about historical American documents, go to "A Chronology of U.S. Historical Documents," a website created and maintained by the University of Oklahoma Law Center, at *www.law.ou.edu/hist*.

Policies of the New Nation

Monroe Doctrine

In 1823, President Monroe made clear to European countries that the United States was not going to permit the establishment of colonies in the Western Hemisphere. Monroe also banned European countries from attacking the new American republics that were just becoming established in the early nineteenth century. Nor was the U.S. to become involved in European affairs. This concept of "America for Americans" is known as the Monroe Doctrine.

Manifest Destiny

In 1844, President James K. Polk declared to the world that the United States would eventually become a world power and expand to its natural borders. Some of the borders mentioned were the Pacific to the west and Mexico to the south. Eventually, Polk's expectations became a reality as a result of the war between Mexico and the United States from 1846 to 1848.

Slavery in the United States

The Dutch brought the first African slaves to Virginia in 1619 to work on plantations. From 1640 to 1680, large numbers of slaves were brought to the Americas. With the invention of Eli Whitney's cotton gin, cotton became the economic mainstay of the South, and the demand for labor increased the slave trade. From 1798 to 1808, more than 200,000 African slaves were brought to America, mostly to the southern region.

Beginning in 1774, the North began regulating and eventually prohibiting slavery. By 1804, New York and New Jersey had passed gradual emancipation laws. Meanwhile, the slave trade in the South grew to meet the economic needs of the area. Eventually, the issue of slavery, along with other economic and ideological differences between the regions, resulted in the American Civil War. In 1862, Abraham Lincoln issued the *Emancipation Proclamation*, granting freedom to slaves in the South. After the war, the Thirteenth Amendment to the Constitution officially abolished slavery. Additionally, in 1866 the Fourteenth Amendment gave African Americans full citizenship, and the Fifteenth Amendment granted voting rights to black men.

Civil War

With the expansion of the United States came additional problems for the young nation. One problem that divided the nation was the issue of slavery. By the 1800s, slavery had been virtually abolished in the North. The northern states' reasons for turning against slavery were primarily economic: the North had become more urban and industrialized than the South, and northern states received large numbers of immigrants who provided the necessary labor. Southern states remained mostly rural and received few immigrants, making slavery the foundation of their economy. With the nation's expansion westward and the addition of new states, the question of slavery became a contentious issue. Any new state would affect the balance between the free and slave states.

The issue of slavery became the main topic of the presidential election of 1860. The candidates were clearly aligned either in favor of or against slavery. The southern Democrats backed a strong proslavery candidate, John C. Breckinridge of Kentucky, while the new Republican Party selected a strong antislavery candidate in the figure of Abraham Lincoln. The election of Abraham Lincoln resulted in the secession of the southern states from the union, the creation of the Confederacy, and the start of the American Civil War. The southern states created the Confederate States of America and selected Jefferson Davis as president.

Battle of Gettysburg

Several battles were fought in this war, but none was as memorable as the Battle of Gettysburg. Fought in 1863, this battle was the most disastrous event of the war and perhaps in the history of the United States. In this battle, more than 50,000 soldiers from the North and the South lost their lives. In a speech delivered on the battlefield in November 1863, President Lincoln eulogized the fallen Union soldiers in a speech known as the *Gettysburg Address*. After five years of fighting and the loss of thousands of lives and millions of dollars in property, in 1865 the commander of the Confederate army, General Robert E. Lee, surrendered to General Ulysses S. Grant, commander of the Union forces.

Reconstruction Era (1865–1877)

Because the war was fought primarily in the South, that area was practically destroyed. Therefore, the physical reconstruction of the country focused on the South. However, the emotional reconstruction and the reconstruction of American unity had to be done nationwide, and admission of rebel states back into the Union was not automatically granted. The Reconstruction period was characterized by hatred and violence. Because Lincoln was assassinated in 1865, shortly after the end of the war, leadership of the reconstruction effort fell on the shoulders of Andrew Johnson, a southerner who was disliked by the North as well as the South. Eventually, he was impeached and almost removed from power.

A major obstacle to the reunification of the nation resulted from the black codes. These very restrictive laws were passed by southern legislatures to control former slaves. Some black codes restricted free assembly, while others restricted the types of jobs that they could do. In 1867, the U.S. Congress, still composed entirely of northerners, passed legislation to eliminate the black codes. Additionally, Congress required southern states to ratify the Fourteenth Amendment of the Constitution prior to being allowed back into the Union. The Fourteenth Amendment gave citizenship to blacks. Finally, in 1870, the last two states (Texas and Florida) were allowed back in the Union.

Ku Klux Klan

The Ku Klux Klan was one of various secret societies established during Reconstruction to continue the implementation of the black codes and to terrorize African Americans. Members of the group warned blacks not to vote or exercise individual freedoms. The Klan divided the South based on color lines. More subtle legislation was passed in the South to control the progress of African Americans. These new laws were known as Jim Crow laws. Racial separation characterized life in the South and other parts of the nation for most of the twentieth century.

Economic Development

After the reunification of the country, energy was redirected to the economic development and growth of the nation. New inventions, together with the development of the railroad, paved the way to economic recovery. The reconstruction that followed the war also played a vital role in the development of the United States as a solid economic and industrial nation.

Civil Rights Movement

Civil rights are legal and political rights of the people who live in a particular country. In the United States, the Constitution and the Bill of Rights guarantee civil rights to American citizens and residents. The first 10 amendments to the U.S. Constitution are known as the Bill of Rights. Following these initial amendments and as a result of the American Civil War, three additional amendments were added. The Thirteenth, Fourteenth, and Fifteenth Amendments to the Constitution were passed during the Reconstruction era. The 13th Amendment freed all the slaves without compensation to slave owners. The 14th Amendment declared that all persons born in the U.S. were citizens (except Native Americans), that all citizens were entitled to equal rights, and that their rights were protected by due process. The 15th Amendment granted black men the right to vote.

The civil rights movement sought equality for African Americans. Even after the 13th, 14th, and 15th Amendments were added to the Constitution, blacks were denied full civil rights. Discrimination existed throughout the nation. Jim Crow laws enforced strict separation in the South. They were also kept from voting by poll taxes and literacy tests. In the North many qualified African Americans were not able to find good jobs. Segregation rules restricted blacks to separate facilities in public places such as theaters, restaurants, buses, restrooms, and schools. Discrimination also affected other minorities such as Latinos and Native Americans. In 1896, *Plessy v. Ferguson* legalized segregation, allowing "separate but equal facilities" for black and white students.

Several historic events marked the beginning of what is today known as the Civil Rights Movement. In 1947, Jackie Robinson became the first African American to play baseball on a major league team. In 1948, President Truman ordered the integration of the armed forces and introduced civil rights legislation in Congress. The National Association for the Advancement of Colored People (NAACP) challenged the laws of segregation with the *Brown v. Board of Education of Topeka* case, and in 1954 the Supreme Court ruled that racial segregation in public schools was unconstitutional.

Another important event in the civil rights movement era was the Montgomery Bus Boycott. In December 1955, Rosa Parks, a well-known activist and respected citizen of Montgomery, Alabama, refused to give up her seat on the bus to a white man as Alabama's Jim Crow laws required. She was consequently arrested and sent to jail. Her actions prompted local community leaders of the NAACP to form a new organization called the Montgomery Improvement Association.

The association chose a young Baptist minister, Dr. Martin Luther King Jr., to lead the organization and to direct a boycott of the Montgomery bus company. The boycott began in December 1956 and ended about a year later when the U.S. Supreme Court ruled segregation on buses unconstitutional. This victory gained national attention and Dr. King became one of the most prominent figures of the civil rights movement. He founded the Southern Christian Leadership Conference (SCLC) with other African American leaders. The SCLC favored nonviolent forms of protest such as sit-ins, boycotts, and protest marches. His famous *I Have a Dream* speech took place during the march in Washington in support of the Civil Rights Act of 1964. The eloquent speech and orderly demonstration gained more supporters for the cause. He was assassinated in 1968 in Memphis, Tennessee, but his work resulted in the official Civil Rights Act in 1964.

President John F. Kennedy proposed new civil rights laws as well as programs to help the millions of Americans living in poverty. After his assassination in Dallas in 1963, President Lyndon B. Johnson urged Congress to pass the laws in honor of Kennedy persuading the majority of Democrats and some Republicans. The Civil Rights Act passed in 1964 prohibited segregation in all public facilities and discrimination in education and employment.

The Mexican American Civil Rights Movement

During the 1960s Mexican Americans were engaged in the struggle for human rights. As part of the process, the Mexican-American leaders initiated a movement called the Chicano Movement. This movement was cultural as well as political (Rosales Castañeda n.d.). It embraced four main goals: the restoration of land grants, the farm workers' rights, education, and political rights (Mendoza, 2001). The movement also sought to rescue the cultural and linguistic identity of Mexican Americans.

Activist Reies Tijerina initiated the Chicano Movement in New Mexico with the *land grant movement,* which sought to recover the land taken from the Mexican Americans as a result of the Guadalupe Hidalgo Treaty of 1848 and the eventual annexation of the American Southwest. In Colorado, Rodolfo "Corky" Gonzales founded the *Crusade for Justice* as a platform for the political movement (Mendoza, 2001). He also defined the movement through his epic poem "Yo Soy Joaquín/I am Joaquin." In this poem he provided a historical development of Mexican-American identity and described their struggles in the United States.

As part of the effort to support the rights of farm workers, human rights leaders Cesar Chávez and Dolores Huertas founded the United Farm Workers (UFW) union. Through the UFW they fought for better working conditions and fair compensation for agricultural workers.

In Texas, the movement focused its attention on the educational and political rights of Mexican Americans. In Crystal City, students took a leadership role organizing Mexican-American voters and joining the political process. As part of this process, Mexican American Student Organization (MAYO), under the leadership of José Ángel Gutiérrez and Mario Compean founded the Raza Unida Party (RUP) in 1970. Through the RUP, they sought to bring greater economic, social, and political autonomy to Mexican Americans (Acosta, n.d.). As a result of this movement, the RUP nominated candidates for mayor, city councils, and school boards in three South Texas cities—Crystal City, Cotulla, and Carrizo. In these communities, the RUP won fifteen seats. This political awakening of the Mexican-American voters in Texas paved the way for better schools and programs for Mexican American and minority children in general.

Women's Rights

While the 19th Amendment to the Constitution guaranteed women the right to vote in 1920, women remained subject of discrimination. The civil rights movement provided the impetus for the women's movement of the 60s. The women's movement attained better employment and professional opportunities for women. The Equal Pay Act of 1963 and the Civil Rights Act of 1964 prohibited discrimination based on gender. In 1966, Betty Friedan, author of *The Feminine Mystique*, and other leaders founded the National Organization for Women (NOW). This organization adopted the activist approach used by the African-American leaders of the civil rights movement. The Equal Rights Amendment of 1972 guarantees women's equal rights.

Temperance Movement—Prohibition

The temperance movement sought to prohibit alcohol consumption in the United States. This movement began in the 1830s, and by 1855 thirteen states had enacted legislation to prohibit the use of alcohol. In 1919 the U.S. Constitution was amended to prohibit alcohol consumption at the national level; this marked the adoption of the 18th Amendment (Cardinale, 2007). However, the prohibition was never fully enforced. Battles between law enforcements agents, like Eliot Ness, and organized crime characterized the prohibition era. Leaders of organized crime, like Al Capone, made millions selling alcohol. After 14 years of prohibition and unsuccessful attempts to enforce the law, it was finally repealed in 1933 with the 21st Amendment.

Conflicts and Wars

Spanish American War of 1898

The war between Spain and the United States made the United States a world power. As a result of this war, the United States established its power and influence in the Caribbean Sea and Pacific Ocean. Cuba became an independent nation, and the United States gained control of the Philippines, Guam, and Puerto Rico. Eventually, the Philippines became an independent nation, while Puerto Rico and Guam remained U.S. territories. Eventually, the people from Guam and Puerto Rico became American citizens.

World War I

The first global war began in Europe and involved two alliances: the Allies and the Central Powers. The Allies were England, France, Russia, and Italy. The Central Powers were Germany, the Austria-Hungary Empire, Turkey, and Bulgaria. Initially, the Americans remained neutral and benefited extensively from trading with the Allies. America's neutrality was challenged, however, when the Germans developed a new weapon, the submarine, and used it successfully to destroy Allied ships. In 1915, the Germans sank a British liner, the *Lusitania*, killing more than 1,100 passengers, including 128 Americans. Additionally, American cargo ships were sunk, which forced President Wilson to ask Congress to declare war against Germany and the Central Powers. The influx of fresh American forces fostered the Allies' victory in 1918.

With the Treaty of Versailles, the war officially ended. In this treaty, the Central Powers were severely punished and forced to pay for the war. Additionally, the Austria-Hungary Empire was dismembered and new countries created. The punitive conditions of the Treaty of Versailles created the resentment of the Germans that eventually led to the second global confrontation, World War II.

The Bolshevik Revolution in Russia

In 1917, the Communists, led by Vladimir Lenin, took over the government in Russia. As a result of this revolution, Russia underwent a period of governmental reconstruction to incorporate the communist philosophy in the nation. With a new government in power, Russia withdrew from World War I.

The Great Depression

After World War I, the United States enjoyed a period of prosperity, the golden 1920s. But it all came to an abrupt end on October 29, 1929, when the stock market crashed, initiating a ten-year period that we now call the Great Depression. During the Depression, millions of people lost their capital and jobs. Between 1933 and 1937, President Franklin D. Roosevelt implemented a series of government-sponsored programs, called the New Deal, designed to revitalize the economy and alleviate poverty and despair caused by the Depression.

World War II

The emergence of totalitarian countries like Russia, Germany, and Italy created instability in Europe and eventually led to war. Communist Russia, under the leadership of Stalin, became a threat to European countries. Italy was a fascist, belligerent state where individual liberties were ignored. Germany, under the leadership of Adolf Hitler, was ready to avenge the humiliating treatment it suffered as a result of World War I. In the Pacific, Japan was building an empire that had already conquered parts of China. All these conditions promoted the creation of military alliances that eventually led to World War II. Germany, Italy, and Japan created the Axis powers, and Russia, France, and England became the Allies. The war started with the German invasion of Poland in 1939. Two days later, France and England declared war against Germany. Hitler conquered most of Europe in a relatively short time. France was occupied, and England was brought close to submission. The United States supported the Allies with supplies and weapons but did not send troops. Although it remained neutral for the first few years of the war, the United States joined the Allies when Japan attacked its naval base in Pearl Harbor, Hawaii, in 1941.

D-Day

With Hitler in full control of Europe, the United States joined England and representatives of the French government to plan and execute the invasion of Europe in 1944. On June 6, General Dwight D. Eisenhower, together with a quarter of a million Allied soldiers, crossed the English Channel into France and launched one of the largest offensives against the German occupying forces. This large attack on Germany was known as D-Day. As a result of the collective effort of the Allies, France was freed from German occupation. With the combined forces of England, Russia, Canada, and the United States, Hitler and the Axis forces were finally defeated.

Yalta Conference

The Allies met in Yalta, Russia, to discuss the terms of the treaty to end the war. In this meeting, the leaders of the Allied forces—Winston Churchill, Joseph Stalin, and Franklin D. Roosevelt—met to discuss peace. Under the terms of peace agreed to at Yalta, Germany was to be divided into four sections, each controlled by an Allied country—Britain, France, Russia, and the United States. The Germans were to pay the Russians for war reparations in money and labor. Poland was divided, and the Russians received control of one section (later they took full control of the nation). Finally, plans were set to organize the United Nations to prevent future conflicts in the world.

Hiroshima and Nagasaki

The United States was fighting the war on two fronts, and the Japanese appeared to be invincible. The best available option seemed to be the atomic bomb. By the order of President Harry Truman, the United States dropped two atomic bombs on the cities of Hiroshima and Nagasaki. The death and destruction caused by these two bombs forced the Japanese government to surrender in 1945, which officially ended WWII.

Marshall Plan

The Marshall Plan was a U.S.-supported program to rebuild the economic infrastructure in Europe. The United States provided money and machinery for the reconstruction of the continent.

The Holocaust and Creation of Israel

During World War II, Hitler devised a "master plan" to exterminate the Jewish population. Germany placed European Jews in concentration camps and systematically killed millions. This act of genocide is known today as the Holocaust. At the end of the war, under the leadership of the Great Britain, the United States, and the United Nations, the state of Israel was created in Palestine. On that same day, the Arab Liberation Army (ALA) was created to fight the Jewish state. This liberation movement has resulted in several wars between Israel and the Arabs. Today, this war has expanded to include Europe and the United States, with many terrorist attacks committed during the new century.

Truman Doctrine

In response to the threat of the Soviets, Harry Truman issued a proclamation warning communist countries that the United States will help any nation in danger of falling under communist control. This declaration was called the Truman Doctrine. As a result of this doctrine, the United States became involved in two major military conflicts: the Korean War and the Vietnam War.

Cold War

As a result of the Yalta agreement, Russia became the most powerful country in the region. After taking over Poland and East Berlin, and building the Berlin Wall, a new war emerged between the Soviet Union and the United States—the Cold War. Although war was never formally declared between the two nations, confrontations occurred from 1945 to 1991. In 1963, the two nations were on the verge of nuclear war after Premier Nikita Khrushchev ordered the deployment of nuclear missiles to Cuba. An intense negotiation between Premier Khrushchev and President Kennedy avoided war between the two countries. This most intense confrontation of the Cold War was called the Cuban Missile Crisis.

The Cold War finally ended with the fall of the Soviet Union under the leadership of Mikhail Gorbachev. The fall of the Soviet empire resulted in the reunification of Germany and the creation of multiple smaller countries in Russia that gained independence.

War on Terrorism

In 2001, terrorists from abroad attacked American soil. The attacks on the twin towers of the World Trade Center in New York and the Pentagon in Arlington, Virginia, on September 11 killed more than 3,000 people. As a result of the attacks, the United States declared war on terrorism and attacked the Taliban regime in Afghanistan. American forces succeeded in conquering the country but failed to capture Saudi Arabian militant Osama bin Laden, the mastermind of the 9/11 attacks. The search for weapons of mass destruction led the United States into war with Iraq. Currently, the United States is still fighting to stabilize the region.

History of Texas

Before European Colonization

Several Native American groups inhabited the territory known today as Texas. The three groups living in the coastal plains—the Coahuiltecans, Karankawas, and Caddos—were food gatherers, fishermen, and farmers. When the Spanish arrived in Texas, they made initial contact with these groups. The name Texas came as a result of contact with the Caddos. Attempting to communicate to the Spaniards that they were not hostile, some Caddos identified themselves with the word *taysha*, which in their language meant "friend" or "ally" (Fry n.d.). When the Spaniards heard the word *taysha*, they thought the Caddos were identifying the name of the region. From that exchange, the name Texas and the state motto, "Friendship," emerged. A fourth group, the Jumanos, lived in the mountains and basins of West Texas. The information about this group is limited because they virtually disappeared before the Spaniards arrived in the area. The last two groups are the Comanches and the Apaches. These two groups coexisted with Europeans and resisted the colonization efforts. After they domesticated horses, previously introduced by the Spanish, the Comanches and Apaches became fearless warriors and successful buffalo hunters. The domestication of the horse allowed the development of the culture of the buffalo. When buffalo were later annihilated in the area, these two groups became practically extinct. Table 3-5 presents a summary of Native American groups from Texas.

European Colonization

Cabeza de Vaca

The Spanish exploration of the territory today known as Texas began in 1528, when Cabeza de Vaca and three companions landed in the territory. The four Spaniards made contact with the Caddo in the southeastern part of the state, near modern-day Houston. In his account of the meeting, de Vaca described the Caddo as a very sophisticated Native American group. From there, de Vaca continued exploring the region of modern-day New Mexico and Arizona (Sheppard n.d.). No other significant events happened in the region until 1541, when Francisco Vázquez de Coronado explored Texas.

Francisco Vázquez de Coronado

In response to reports of the mythical Seven Cities of Cibola, Coronado led an expedition of almost a thousand men in search of the golden cities. The expedition left Mexico City and explored the southwestern United States and northern Texas. In 1542, Coronado returned to Mexico empty handed. For the next 140 years, the Texas region remained isolated, and no other attempts were made to colonize it.

Table 3-5. Native American Groups from Texas

Regions	Native Group
Coastal plains, flatland	**Coahuiltecan** (Rio Grande Valley) **Economic Activity:** Food gatherers and hunters—roots, beans of the mesquite tree, rabbit, birds, and deer **Features:** Lived in family groups
	Karankawa (Southeastern Texas) **Economic Activity:** Fishing and food gathering **Features:** Lived as nomads and used canoes for fishing
	Caddo (East Texas, Piney Woods) **Economic Activity:** Farming—squash, pumpkins, tobacco, and corn (good food supply) **Features:** Built villages and lived in groups
Central plains, flatland, and hills	**Apache** (Central and western Texas) **Economic Activity:** Farming and hunting **Features:** Lived as nomads, built portable housing called tepees, domesticated horses, and hunted bison
Great Plains, flatland, and hills	**Comanche** **Economic Activity:** Hunters **Features:** Lived as nomads and built portable housing; also domesticated the horse and hunted the buffalo
Mountains and basins	**Jumano** (West Texas) **Economic Activity:** Farming and hunting **Features:** Mostly sedentary and built homes of adobe

Juán de Oñate

In 1595, Oñate received permission from King Philip II of Spain to colonize New Mexico. In 1598, he founded the first European settlement west of the Mississippi in New Mexico.

First Mission in Texas

In 1682, the Spanish established the first permanent settlement in Texas—the mission of Ysleta del Sur near the present-day city of El Paso. After this mission, no serious efforts were made to colonize the area until the French began to threaten the Spanish hegemony in East Texas.

French Influence in Texas

In 1682, Robert de la Salle established a French settlement in Fort Saint Louis in East Texas. A few years later, the Spaniards expelled the French and established a series of missions in East Texas to control the French threat in the region

San Antonio

In 1718, the Spanish established a mission and a fort—San Antonio de Valero and Fort San Antonio de Bexar—near what is now the city of San Antonio. These settlements were established to provide protection and support to the settlements in East Texas.

Mexican Independence

During the first part of the nineteenth century, the Spanish empire began crumbling. Mexico obtained its independence in 1821 and took control of the colony of Texas.

Anglo-American Presence in Texas

In 1820, Moses Austin received permission from the Spanish government to bring Anglo-American families to settle in Texas. This agreement was voided when Mexico took control of the territory. Later, Austin's son, Stephen, negotiated with the Mexican government and obtained a similar agreement to allow Anglo-Americans to settle in Texas. By 1835, the settlers were the majority in the region, which antagonized the Mexican government and resulted in war

Texas War for Independence

Conflicts between Texans and the Mexican government started as early as 1830. The colonists felt that the government was not providing adequate support and protection to Texas. Initially, they wanted to negotiate with the new president, Santa Anna, and sent Stephen Austin to Mexico City to represent the colony. The Mexican government was not willing to negotiate and jailed Austin for a year.

First Battle in Gonzales

The town of Gonzales had a cannon to protect the colonists from the Indians. By order of the government, Mexican soldiers came to take the cannon from the colonists in October 1835. The Texans refused to relinquish their weapon and fired the cannon against the Mexican soldiers. With this incident in Gonzales, the war for Texas independence began.

Sam Houston

A delegation of Texans traveled to Washington, D.C., to secure support from the U.S. government. Sam Houston, a former governor of Tennessee, volunteered to fight for Texas and eventually became the commander-in-chief of the Texas army.

The Alamo and Goliad

The first meaningful battle of the Texas war for independence took place near the present-day city of San Antonio in a small mission and fort known as the Alamo. When the war began, fewer than 200 men, led by Colonel William Travis, protected the Alamo. Eventually, additional historical characters like James Bowie and Davy Crockett joined Travis in defending the fort. In 1836, General Antonio López de Santa Anna and the Mexican army took the fort and killed all its defenders, including Texans of Mexican ancestry. Following this victory, Santa Anna continued marching against the rebels and took the city of Goliad, where more than 300 rebels were killed. These two battles provided the patriotic emotion that resulted in the creation of an army and eventually led to victory against Mexico.

Texas Declaration of Independence

A few days before the Battle of the Alamo, a group of Texans met at Washington-on-the-Brazos to issue a declaration of independence and to form the new government. An interim government for the republic of Texas was established, with David G. Burnet as president and Lorenzo de Zavala as vice president.

Battle of San Jacinto

While the colonists were fighting the Mexican army at the Alamo and in Goliad, General Sam Houston was strengthening the army of the new republic. The Texan army continued retreating ahead of the Mexican forces until they reached the San Jacinto River, near the city of Houston. In a battle that lasted less than twenty minutes, Houston's troops defeated the Mexican army and captured General Santa Anna. Texas President Burnet and Mexican President Santa Anna signed the Treaty of Velasco, with Santa Anna agreeing to withdraw his troops from Texas in exchange for safe conduct back to Mexico, where he would lobby for recognition of Texas independence. Santa Anna's commitment never materialized, and the Mexican government refused to recognize Texas as an independent republic. Nevertheless, Sam Houston became the president of the new republic, and from 1836 to 1845, Texas functioned as an independent nation. However, the Mexican government still considered it one of its rebellious provinces that it could one day reclaim (Barker & Pohl, 2009).

Republic Period

Despite the economic hardship typical of new nations, Texas managed to remain independent for ten years and was recognized by several nations in the world, including the United States. However, unable to secure its borders and reverse its financial situation, the new nation sought the support of the United States.

Texas Joins the United States

In 1845, Texas became the twenty-eighth state of the American union. Immediately, the U.S. government sent troops to the Rio Grande (which Mexicans considered their territory) to secure the Texas border. The ensuing clashes between Mexican and U.S. forces resulted in Congress declaring war in May 1846.

Mexican-American War

Between 1846 and 1848, Mexico and the United States waged a war that ended with a decisive victory and tremendous land acquisitions for the United States. As a result of the Treaty of Guadalupe Hidalgo, Mexico withdrew its claim over Texas and established the Rio Grande, or Rio Bravo, as it is known in Mexico, as the official border between the two countries. Mexico also ceded California and the territory known today as the American Southwest to the United States. Figure 3-9 presents a timeline of important events in Texas from 1528 to 1861.

Confederacy Period (1861–65)

At the onset of the American Civil War, Texas left the union and joined the Confederacy as a proslavery state. After five years of war, the Confederate army, led by General Robert E. Lee, surrendered to General Ulysses S. Grant, the leader of the Union forces.

Figure 3-9. Texas Time Line from 1528 to 1861

1528	1541	1682	1682	1690	1718	1820
Cabeza de Vaca lands in Texas	Coronado explores Texas	Mission founded in El Paso	La Salle (French) lands in Texas	First mission in East Texas San Francisco de los Tejas	Mission and fort founded in San Antonio	Austin arrives in San Antonio

1861	1848	1846	1845	1836	1835	1833
Texas secedes from the union	Treaty of Guadalupe Hidalgo	Mexican-American war begins	Texas becomes the 28th state in the union	Battle of San Jacinto, Texas declares independence	Battle of Gonzales marks beginning of Texas revolution	Santa Anna becomes president of Mexico

After the war, the Union forces occupied the South for a period of 12 years (1865–1877). This era was called the Reconstruction Period.

Reconstruction Period

During Reconstruction, Texas was briefly under occupation by U.S. troops. Texas was allowed to rejoin the union in 1870. The Ku Klux Klan became very active at this time, terrorizing African Americans in Texas and the southern states.

Economic Development after Reconstruction

After Reconstruction, the Texas economy flourished, largely based on the growth of the cattle industry. Barbed wire was introduced in 1880, and ranchers began using scientific cattle breeding to increase production and improve the quality of meat.

Oil in Texas

In 1901, oil was discovered in the Spindletop Oil Field near Beaumont. The development of the oil industry made Texas the leading producer of oil in the United States. As a result of this boom, cities like Houston and Dallas became large urban and industrial centers.

World Wars and Beyond

As a result of World War I, Texas emerged as a leading military training center. Several military bases were established in the state, bringing economic growth. The rapid development of the aircraft industry and highly technological businesses led to rapid industrialization in the state. By World War II, Texas was a leading state in the defense industry. The modern economy of Texas still relies on agriculture, ranching, and oil production, but new high-technology industries are rapidly becoming the top economic forces in the state.

Six Flags over Texas

The phrase "Six flags over Texas" describes the different countries that have exerted control in Texas from 1519, when the first European exploration of the region by Cortés took place, to the present:

- Spain (1519–1821)
- France (1685–1690)
- Mexico (1821–1836)
- Republic of Texas (1836–1845)
- United States (1845–1861)
- Texas in the Confederacy (1861–1865)
- Back to the American union (1870–present)

State Facts and Symbols

Texas has adopted the following symbols to represent the state:

- State flower   Bluebonnet
- State bird   Mockingbird
- State tree   Pecan
- State motto   Friendship

- Border states   Oklahoma, Louisiana, Arkansas, and New Mexico
- State song   "Texas, Our Texas," by William J. Marsh and Gladys Yoakum Wright

Texas, our Texas! All hail the mighty State!
Texas, our Texas! So wonderful so great!
Boldest and grandest, withstanding ev'ry test;
O Empire wide and glorious, you stand supremely blest.

[Refrain]
God bless you Texas! And keep you brave and strong,
That you may grow in power and worth,
thro'out the ages long.

Key Principles of the Competency

- The Enlightenment period of European history (eighteenth century) helped to restore religious unity that had been disrupted by the Protestant Reformation.

- The America Revolution influenced political development in Latin America by demonstrating that it was possible to overthrow European colonial rule.

- The introduction of horses and firearms had a great impact on the colonization of the American plains and the West.

- Early civilizations in Asia and Africa were located near river valleys. Some of these civilizations were Egypt, Mesopotamia, and Persia (Iran). This location provided access to fresh water for crop growing and for human consumption.

- The civil rights movement of the 1960s addressed issues that were major topics during the Reconstruction era following the Civil War—individual and human rights.

- Louis Pasteur's germ theory of diseases was one of the most important breakthroughs of nineteenth-century Europe.

- Every culture has a way to explain the formation of the earth and develops a way to adapt to the physical environment.

- In 1492, Columbus claimed America for Spain. Following that, they established colonies in the Caribbean. In 1519, Spain initiated the colonization of Mexico. Presidios and missions were established to protect the colony and to convert the natives to Christianity.

- In 1598, Juan de Oñate founded the first European settlement west of the Mississippi in New Mexico.

- The first Spanish missions in Texas were established to strengthen the control of Spain in the area and to reduce the threat of the French: San Francisco de los Tejas (1690) in East Texas and Fort San Antonio and the Alamo (1718).

Competency 021: Geography and Culture

The teacher understands and applies knowledge of geographic relationships involving people, places, and environments in Texas, the United States, and the world; and also understands and applies knowledge of cultural development, adaptation, diversity, and interactions among science, technology, and society as defined by the Texas Essential Knowledge and Skills (TEKS).

Geography

Geography is the study of the earth's surface, the organisms that populate it, and their interaction within the ecosystem. Geography can be divided into two main areas: physical geography and cultural geography. *Physical geography* refers to the physical characteristics of the surface of the earth and how those features affect life. *Cultural geography* deals with the interaction of humans with their environment and how that interaction produces changes. Humans can alter the physical environment of the earth, but the physical environment can also shape humans and their culture. For example, the Incas built the capital of their empire, Cuzco, in the Andes Mountains in what is now Peru. This city has an altitude of 11,152 feet above sea level, where oxygen is scarce and agriculture is a challenge. However, the Incas managed to live and flourish under these conditions. They carved the land for agriculture and built roads and cities. In turn, the environment changed the Incas, who had to evolve to tolerate the low levels of oxygen. Studies conducted on the Indians from Peru suggest that people of the Andes developed genetic adaptations for high-altitude living (Discovery Channel, 2004 March 10). By adapting to the conditions of their environment, inhabitants of the area not only survived but also flourished in less-than-ideal conditions.

Locating Places and Regions on a Map

There are two categories of maps: reference maps and thematic maps. *Reference maps* show the locations of places, boundaries of countries, states, counties, and towns. Atlases or road maps are examples of reference maps. *Thematic maps* show a particular topic such as population density or distribution of world religions, and physical, social, economic, political, agricultural, or economic features. A *physical map* shows the topography of the earth including land features and elevations. A *political map* shows how a country is organized. An *economic map* shows the important resources of a country or region. A *historical map* is used to show historical events including places of the past. *Population maps* are used to show where people live in a particular region.

A globe is a scale model of the Earth shaped like a sphere. Because a globe resembles the actual shape of the Earth it shows sizes and shapes more accurately than a Mercator projection map (a flat representation of the Earth). However, the cylindrical shape and portability of Mercator projections makes them more useful than globes.

The Grid System

A grid system is a network of horizontal and vertical lines used to locate points on a map or a chart by means of coordinates. This grid shows the location of places. Latitude and longitude lines form divisions in this grid system that consist of geometrical coordinates used in designating the location of places on the surface of the earth on a globe or map. The lines measure distances in degrees.

Latitude lines are horizontal lines that run parallel around the earth measuring the distance north and south of the equator. The equator is identified as the 0 degree line of latitude, and it divides the earth into the Northern and the Southern hemispheres. The United States is located in the Northern Hemisphere, while Brazil is located in the Southern Hemisphere. Longitude lines are vertical lines that run north and south going east and west. The 0 degree line of longitude is known as the prime meridian. It goes through Greenwich, England, and it divides the Earth into the Eastern and Western hemispheres. The United States is in the Western Hemisphere and Japan in the Eastern Hemisphere.

Geographic Symbols

A compass rose is a design printed on a chart or map for reference. It shows the orientation of a map on Earth and shows the four cardinal directions (north, south, east, and west). A compass rose may also show in-between directions such as northeast or northwest. Symbols are used for a map to contain a large amount of information that can be easily understood. Common symbols used on a map include dots, stars, and small pictures to represent cities or places. Some maps use different colors to represent features such as elevations and divisions. These symbols and colors are defined in the map's key, or legend. A map scale shows the distance between two places in the world. The scale to which a map is drawn represents the ratio of the distance between two points on the earth and the distance between the two corresponding points on the map.

Time Zones

Time zones are established based on the lines of longitude, or meridians. These lines run from north to south. The prime meridian, or the meridian at 0 degrees, has been set in Greenwich, England. On the other side of the globe is the International Date Line. The prime meridian divides the earth into the Western and Eastern hemispheres. Following the sunlight as it travels along the rotating earth, the time decreases moving from east to west. When people travel from China (east) to the United States (west), they save a day; that is, they might spend a day traveling but still arrive on the same calendar day.

The United States has six time zones of one hour difference each—Eastern, Central, Mountain, Pacific, Alaska, and Hawaii. Figure 3-10 represents the six time zones in the United States with a key city for each zone. For more information about time zones, go to the website provided by the National Institute of Standards and Technology (an agency of the U.S. Department of Commerce) and the U.S. Naval Observatory at *www.time.gov/about.html*.

Figure 3-10 Times Zones in the United States

West ← ——————————————————————————— → East

Hawaii	Alaska	Pacific	Mountain	Central	Eastern
1:00 PM	2:00 PM	3:00 PM	4:00 PM	5:00 PM	6:00 PM
Honolulu	Anchorage	Los Angeles	Phoenix	Dallas	New York City

Regions of the World

A world region is an area of the world that shares similar, unifying cultural or physical characteristics that are different from those of surrounding areas. The physical features refer to topographic characteristics like elevation, rivers, and mountains. The cultural features include all the features that distinguish different groups of people, for example: language, religion, government, economics, food, architecture, shared values, and family life.

Geographers have divided the world into ten regions: North America, Central and South America, Europe, Central Eurasia, the Middle East, North Africa, Sub-Saharan Africa, South Asia, East Asia, and Australasia. These divisions are based on physical and cultural similarities. North America consists of Canada, the United States, and Mexico. It is the third largest continent, and it is located between the Arctic Circle and the Tropic of Cancer. The Europeans colonized the North American region. Table 3-6 presents an overview of the world regions by physical and cultural features.

Table 3-6 World Regions

World Region	Physical Features	Cultural Features
North America	• Consists of Canada, the United States, and Mexico. • The United States is the fourth largest country in the world. • Oil is an important resource in the U.S. • Most of the U.S. has a humid-continental or humid-subtropical climate • Most of Canada has a subarctic or tundra climate. • Over 75% of Canadians live along the Southern border. • The areas of greatest concentration of population in the U.S. are along the East Coast and California. • The climate of Mexico ranges from humid tropical and subtropical to desert and highland. • Mexico has rich mineral resources including oil.	• Europeans colonized this region. • Languages spoken are predominantly English, Spanish, and French. • Most people hold Christian beliefs.

(continued)

World Region	Physical Features	Cultural Features
Central and South America	• Includes the countries of Central America, the Caribbean islands, and South America. • The majority of this continuous mass of land is south of the Equator. • South America extends from Point Gallinas in Colombia to Cape Horn. • Part of South America lies closer to the South Pole than any other land mass of this size. • Venezuela is one of the world's leading exporters of oil. • Most of Eastern Central America and equatorial South America have a humid tropical climate.	• Most people speak Spanish, but many other languages are spoken: Portuguese, French, Dutch, English, and several Native American languages and dialects. • Christian beliefs, the Roman Catholic religion is predominant. • Architecture, law, religion, traditions, and language are strongly influenced by Europe's colonial rule of this region. • The many ethnic groups in this region are separated by geographical barriers such as the Andes and the Amazon.
Europe	• Western section of the Eurasian continent • Shares a mountain chain, the Alps. • Most of Europe has a temperate climate. • Europe's irregular coastline has many harbors that are important manufacturing and trade centers. • The rivers of Europe are important resources for trade, water, and hydroelectricity. • European population growth rates are the smallest in the world.	• Shares a common history in the Roman Empire and later the Catholic Church and Latin language. • English is the most spoken language in Europe, German and French are also widespread. • Cultural diffusion or shared cultural traits spread throughout Europe. • Ninety percent of all adults ages 15–24 speak a second language and some countries are considered multilingual. • Europeans practice many different religions. • Roman Catholicism is the predominant religion of many European countries. • Most of Northern and Central Europe is Protestant. • Jews live in many parts of Western Europe.
Central Eurasia	• Central Asia and Eastern Europe • United around one continuous mass of land located in the idle of the continent. • Little access to the sea • The borders of Eastern European countries have changed many times. • From WWII to the late 1980s, the Soviet Union controlled Eastern Europe and introduced communism to the region.	• Conquered at different times by the Persians, Mongolians, Tartars, the French, the Germans, and the Russians. • Slavic languages are predominant. • Most people in the Eastern part of the region follow the Eastern Orthodox church, people in the Northern area are mostly Roman Catholic.

World Region	Physical Features	Cultural Features
Middle East	• Consists of the area of southwest Asia and North Africa. • Access to sea water • The majority of the land is desert. • Rich in oil	• While the majority of people follow the religion of Islam there are also groups that follow Christianity, and Judaism. • The religion defines the law in many places. • The most ancient of human civilizations. Egyptians, Assyrians, Babylonians, Persians, Greeks, and Romans have left their mark in this region. • This region has been the fighting ground for many religious battles.
North-Africa	• Part of the African continent • Includes Egypt, Libya, Tunisia, Algeria, and Morocco • Extensive coastline • The Sahara desert and the Nile river are two important physical features of this area • Rich in oil • Egypt is undergoing rapid growth and urbanization, and industrialization	• The majority of people follow the religion of Islam. • People speak Arabic predominantly. • Religious issues influence the politics of this area.
Sub-Saharan Africa	• Consists of Africa south of the Sahara • Most of the area is a savanna • Has abundant rain • Extensive coastline • Fertile land • Most people live in the forest zone and the dry savannas • Agriculture is the predominant activity in West Africa • Livestock is the predominant economic activity in the northern area	• Cultural diversity reflects indigenous, Arab, and European influences. • Majority follows tribal beliefs, Christianity, or a combination of both. • Most people speak native African or European languages. • Over 500 ethnic groups live in this region.
South Asia	• Consists of a large Indian peninsula that extends into the Indian Ocean. • Abundant rainfall • Strong seasonal winds called monsoons • Rice is an important crop. • One of the most populated regions in the world. • The world's highest mountains are located in the northern area of this region. • Many major manufacturing and trade centers are located along the coast.	• People in South Asia speak many languages. • Predominant beliefs are of Eastern origins such as Buddhism and Hinduism. • Many South Asians are farmers who live in small villages. • Many cultural influences • Through the efforts of Mohandas Gandhi the region gained its independence from Britain in 1947.

(continued)

World Region	Physical Features	Cultural Features
East Asia	• Consists of China, Korea, Taiwan, and Japan. • It is the most densely populated region in the world. • Large expanse of coastline.	• Buddhism and Taoism are predominant religions. • Confucian philosophy • People speak Chinese, Japanese, Korean, Mongolian, and many other languages. • Chinese Script or characters influence many of the writing systems of these languages. • Culturally, China has had a major influence in this region.
Australasia	• It is composed of the Australian continent and surrounding islands. • South of the equator	• English is the predominant language of most of the nations in this region • Population is a large Christian majority.

Regions of the United States

The concept of regions facilitates the examination of geography by providing a convenient and manageable unit for studying the earth's human and natural environment. The continental United States can be divided into eight broad geographic divisions:

- **Laurentian Highlands** are part of the Canadian Shield that extends into the northern United States and the Great Lakes area. This area has a hard winter, and agriculture is very limited.

- **Atlantic–Gulf Coastal Plains** are the coastal regions of the eastern and southern states. It includes New York City in the North, the Mid-Atlantic states to Florida in the South, and all the way west to Texas on the Gulf Coast.

- **Appalachian Highlands** covers the Appalachian Mountains, the Adirondack Mountains, and New England—the states of Connecticut, Maine, Massachusetts, New Hampshire, Rhode Island, and Vermont.

- **Interior Plains and the Great Plains** covers the interior part of the United States. Included in this area are the states west of the Appalachians, south of the Great Lakes, and as far west as Montana, Wyoming, Colorado, New Mexico, and northwestern Texas. Most of the nation's wheat, corn, and feed crops are grown in this area.

- **Interior Highlands** is also part of the interior continental United States. This area includes the Ozark Mountains and the states of Missouri, Arkansas, Kentucky, and part of Oklahoma and Kansas.

- **Rocky Mountain System** is in the western United States and Canada extending from British Colombia to Montana, Utah, Colorado, and New Mexico. The mountain range is called the **Continental Divide**, because it separates the eastward-flowing rivers from the westward-flowing rivers. The waters that flow eastward empty into the Atlantic Ocean, and those that flow westward empty into the Pacific Ocean.

- **Intermontane Plateaus** is a large region that includes the Pacific Northwest, the Colorado Plateau, and the basins of the southwestern United States. This area covers the states of Washington, Oregon, Idaho, part of Utah, New Mexico, and Arizona. It also covers the areas of the Grand Canyon and Death Valley.

- **Pacific Mountain System** covers the west coast of the United States. This area extends from the Cascade Mountains in the north down the entire west coast through the states of Washington, Oregon, and California.

Texas Regions and Economic Activity

Texas is the second-largest state in the United States, behind only Alaska. Covering 268,601 square miles, the state contains five geographic regions within its boundaries. Table 3-7 lists the regions and the key cities and main economic activities of each.

Largest Rivers in the World

These are the three largest rivers in the world:

- The Nile (North and East Africa) is the longest river in the world. It originates in Lake Victoria in Uganda and ends in the Mediterranean Sea.

- The Amazon (South America) is the second-largest and the widest river in the world. It originates in Peru, and its mouth is at the Atlantic Ocean off the cost of Brazil.

- The Chang Jiang or Yangtze (China) is the third-largest river in the world. Its source is the Tibetan Plateau, and its mouth is the East China Sea.

For information about the world's largest rivers, go to the Social Studies for Kids website at *www.socialstudiesforkids.com/articles/geography/longestriverstable.htm*.

Table 3-7. Regions and Economic Activity in Texas

Region	Key Cities	Main Economic Activities	Key Statistics
Coastal plains, flatland	Dallas, Houston, San Antonio, Austin, Corpus Christi, Laredo	Lumber—East Texas (Piney Woods) Oil—Refineries in Houston Farming—Rice, oranges, cotton, wheat, milo Ranching—Cattle in Kingsville Shipping—Houston	Population—High: 1 of 3 Texans Rainfall—High Distinguishing Mark—Hurricanes
Central plains, flatland and hills	Fort Worth, Arlington, San Angelo, Abilene	Ranching—Cattle, wool (mohair), sheep Farming—Grains	Population—High Rainfall—Medium Distinguishing Marks—Tornadoes, northerlies (cold winds), hailstorms; large ranches
Great Plains Flatland and hill country	Midland, Odessa, Lubbock, Amarillo, Texas Panhandle	Ranching—Cattle, sheep Minerals—Graphite Oil—Odessa and Midland Farming—Wheat	Population—Average Rainfall—Medium Distinguishing Marks—Snowstorms, dust storms, windmills, use of aquifers
Mountains and basins, Rocky Mountains, Davis, Chisos, and Guadalupe, Chihuahuan Desert	El Paso	Ranching—Limited large ranches Mexico-U.S. border economy based on trading of goods produced by the industries established in Mexico—Maquiladoras.	Population—Low Rainfall—Low; hard rain wears out the rocks and land Distinguishing Mark—Big Bend National Park

Rivers in the United States

These are the largest and most important rivers in the United States:

- The Mississippi is the longest river in the United States and the fourteenth longest in the world. It begins in Minnesota and ends in the Gulf of Mexico.

- The Ohio River begins near Pittsburgh and runs southwest, ending in the Mississippi River on the Illinois and Missouri borders.

- The Rio Grande begins in the San Juan Mountains of southern Colorado and ends in the Gulf of Mexico. The river is the official border between the United States and Mexico, where it is known as the Rio Bravo.

- The Colorado River begins in the Rocky Mountains and ends in California.

- The Missouri River begins in the Rocky Mountains, flowing north first and then generally southeast across the central United States, ending at the Mississippi River, just to the north of St. Louis, Missouri.

- For information about rivers in the United States, visit WorldAtlas. com. To view the most significant rivers of the continental United States, visit *www.worldatlas.com/webimage/countrys/namerica/ usstates/artwork/rivers/uslayout.htm.*

Mountains in the World

With notable exception of the peak known as K2, which is part of the Karakoram Range, the tallest mountains in the world are located in the Himalayas, ranging across the countries of China, Pakistan, Nepal, and Tibet. Table 3-8 lists the top ten tallest mountains. Compared with the world's tallest peaks, the United States' mountains are small. The highest mountain is Mt. McKinley in Alaska. In fact, the state of Alaska has the 16 highest peaks in the United States. A list of the mountains with 16,000 feet or above is presented in Table 3-9. For additional information about the world's mountains, go to the Infoplease.com Web site at *www.infoplease.com/ipa/A0001771.html.*

Deforestation

Deforestation can increase soil erosion and in some instances can lead to tragedies like the mudslides that occurred in 2006 in the Philippines, where thousands of people were buried alive. The rate of soil erosion is most likely to exceed the rate of soil formation in areas like Brazil, where people have cut forests to clear land for farming.

Table 3-8. Tallest Mountains in the World

Mountain	Location	Height (in feet)
Everest	Nepal/Tibet	29,035
K2	Pakistan/China	28,250
Kanchenjunga	India/Nepal	28,169
Lhotse I	Nepal/Tibet	27,940
Makalu I	Nepal/Tibet	27,766
Cho Oyu	Nepal/Tibet	26,906
Dhaulagiri	Nepal	26,795
Manaslu I	Nepal	26,781
Nanga Parbat	Pakistan	26,660
Annapurna	Nepal	26,545

Table 3-9. Tallest Mountains in the United States

Mountain	Location	Height (in feet)
Mt. McKinley	Alaska	20,320
Mt. St. Elias	Alaska	18,008
Mt. Foraker	Alaska	17,400
Mt. Bona	Alaska	16,500
Mt. Blackburn	Alaska	16,390
Mt. Sanford	Alaska	16,237

Deposition

Deposition is the process of carrying soil from one place to another, usually by means of water or wind. This process is responsible for the creation of beaches, sand dunes found in desert areas, and landforms created by glaciers.

Map Skills by Grade—Scope and Sequence

In addition to the basic knowledge required in the Texas Essential Knowledge and Skills (TEKS), each student in kindergarten through grade 6 needs to acquire the following specific geography skills and concepts:

Kindergarten

- Understands and uses terms related to location, direction, and distance (up, down, left, right, here, near, far).

- Recognizes a globe as a model of the earth.

- Recognizes and uses terms that express relative size and shape (big, little, large, small, round, square).

- Identifies school and local community by name.

- Recognizes and uses models and symbols to represent real things.

- Identifies bodies of water—oceans, seas, lakes, rivers, ponds, and bayous (TEKS).

- Identifies landforms—plains, mountains, deserts, hills, and canyons (TEKS).

- Identifies natural resources—water, soil, trees, metals, and fish (TEKS).

Grade 1

- Makes and uses simple classroom maps to locate objects.

- Knows geographical location of home in relation to school and neighborhood.

- Knows the layout of the school campus.

- Identifies state and nation by name.

- Follows and gives verbal directions (here, there, left, right, below, above).

- Distinguishes between land and water symbols on globes and maps.

- Relates locations on maps and globes to locations on the earth.

- Observes, describes, and builds simple models and maps of the local environment.

- Knows the four cardinal points (TEKS).

- Identifies the physical characteristics of places—precipitation, body of water, landforms, types of vegetation, and climate (TEKS).

Grade 2

- Makes and uses simple maps of the school and neighborhood.

- Interprets map symbols using a legend.

- Knows and uses cardinal directions.

- Locates community, state, and nation on maps and globes.

- Identifies local landforms.

- Differentiates between maps and globes.

- Locates other neighborhoods studied on maps.

- Knows the continents of the world (TEKS).

- Identifies important landmarks—Statue of Liberty and others (TEKS).

- Identifies natural resources (TEKS).

- Identifies aspects of the physical environment, from organisms to communities (TEKS).

Grade 3

- Uses distance, directions, scale, and map symbols.

- Compares own community with other communities.

- Compares urban and rural environments.

- Uses charts to record and present information (TEKS).

- Understands climate and the elements that influence climate like wind velocity, precipitation, and proximity to bodies of water.

- Uses the compass rose as a means of orientation on a map of the earth (TEKS).

- Uses graphs (TEKS).

- Uses graphic organizers and diagrams to arrange items in meaningful way (TEKS).

- Understands that landforms change through the processes of erosion and deposition (TEKS).

- Understands that regions are areas of the earth's surface (TEKS).

- Uses scale to represent distances (TEKS).

- Uses time lines to chronologically list events.

Grade 4

- Interprets pictures, graphs, charts, and tables.

- Works with distance, directions, scale, and map symbols.

- Relates similarities and differences between maps and globes.

- Uses maps of different scales and themes.

- Recognizes the common characteristics of the map grid system.

- Compares and contrasts regions on a state, national, or world basis.

- Understands the concepts of adaptation and modification, such as changing the landscape to meet survival needs and building to adjust to a new environment (TEKS).

- Identifies elements that affect the climate (TEKS).

- Uses a compass rose to find true directions.

- Indentifies key explorers and their achievements (TEKS).

- Identifies geographic factors that affect the settlement and development of places.

- Understands the connection between climate and vegetation on earth.

- Identifies global divisions, like the prime meridian, the equator, the Northern and Southern hemispheres, and the Eastern and Western hemispheres (TEKS).

Grade 5

- Uses geographic tools to collect, analyze, and interpret data (TEKS).

- Applies geographic tools such as grid systems, legends, symbols, scales, and compass roses to construct and interpret maps (TEKS).

- Translates geographic data into a variety of formats such as graphs and maps (TEKS).

- Understands the concept of regions and can describe a variety of regions in the U.S. that result from patterns of human activity such as political, population, and economic regions or from physical characteristics such as landform, climate, and vegetation regions (TEKS).

- Locates the 50 states on a map and identifies regions made up by groups of states such as New England and the Great Plains (TEKS).

- Understands and describes location and patterns of settlement as well as their distribution (TEKS).

- Analyzes the location of cities in the United States including capital cities (TEKS).

- Understands how people adapt and modify their environment in order to meet basic human needs (TEKS).

- Analyzes the consequences of human modification of the environment in the United States (TEKS).

Grade 6

- Uses maps, globes, graphs, charts, models, and databases to answer geographic questions.

- Creates maps, graphs, models, and databases (TEKS).

- Poses and answers questions about geographic distributions and patterns from selected world regions and countries (TEKS).

- Compares selected world regions and countries using data from maps, graphs, charts, databases, and models (TEKS).

- Understands the characteristics and relative locations of major historical and contemporary societies (TEKS).

- Locates major historical and contemporary societies on maps and globes (TEKS).

- Identifies and explains geographic factors affecting patterns of population in places and regions (TEKS).

- Understands how geographic factors influence the economic development, political relationships, and policies of societies (TEKS).

- Understands the impact of physical processes on patterns in the environment (TEKS).

- Understands the impact of interactions between people and the physical environment on the development of places and regions (TEKS).

Cultural Diffusion

The term *cultural diffusion* describes the exchange or transmission of cultural information and lifestyles from people around the world. For example, most people in the world use cotton, a fabric developed in India, and silk, developed in China. Chicken and pigs were originally domesticated in Asia, but by the process of cultural diffusion, these animals are common today in most countries in the world. Many countries are predominantly Christian today, but Christianity was born in the Middle East, a place where most people are Muslim. The Romans facilitated the cultural diffusion of Christianity around the ancient world. Travelers visiting Morocco, a Muslim country in North Africa, may be surprised to hear Puerto Rican salsa and Jamaican reggae music being played in local nightclubs. The popularity of Latin and Caribbean rhythms in a predominantly Muslim country is an example of the powerful effect of cultural diffusion.

Competency 022: Economics

The teacher understands the concepts and processes of government and the responsibilities of citizenship; knows how people organize economic systems to produce, distribute, and consume goods and services; and applies social science skills to information, ideas, and issues related to government and economics.

Basic Principles of Economy

Economics is a social science that analyzes the principles that regulate the production, distribution, and consumption of resources in society. It emphasizes how these principles operate within the economic choices of individuals, households, businesses, and governments. Economics can be divided into two main areas: macroeconomics and microeconomics. *Macroeconomics* is the study of the economy at the world, regional, state, and local levels. Some of the topics include reasons and ways to control inflation, causes of unemployment, and economic growth in general. *Microeconomics* deals with specific issues related to the decision-making process at the household, firm, or industry levels.

Theory of Supply and Demand

This theory states that prices vary based on balance between the availability of a product or service at a certain price (supply) and the desire of potential purchasers to pay that price (demand). This balance of supply and demand can occur naturally or be created artificially. An example of an artificially created balance is the intentional destruction of a surplus of a given product on the world market to maintain the price level. Another way is to control the production and availability of the product to create a scarcity of a product. For instance, the Organization of Petroleum Exporting Countries (OPEC) often reduces its production of oil to cause an increase in price.

Goods and Services

The use of machines increases the availability of goods and services to the population. This kind of production can decrease the cost of producing the goods and consequently its price. For example, as a result of the division of labor and the use of assembly lines developed by Eli Whitney in 1799, production costs of manufactured goods decreased and productivity increased. Mass production that came as a result of the Industrial Revolution made contemporary families and children more likely to become consumers rather than producers. However, before the Industrial Revolution, especially in colonial America, children were used to produce goods and contribute to the group.

Free Enterprise

Free enterprise is an economic and political doctrine of the capitalist system. The concept is based on the premise that the economy can regulate itself in a freely competitive market through the relationship of supply and demand, and with minimum governmental intervention. One of the main benefits of the system of free enterprise is the competition among businesses that results in a greater choice and better prices for consumers. The system of free enterprise has led to globalization. *Globalization* can be defined as a continuous increase of cross-border financial, economic, and social activities. It implies some level of economic interdependence among individuals, financial entities, and nations. As a result of globalization, trade barriers have been eliminated and tariffs imposed on imported products have been largely discontinued. In a global market, it is difficult to determine the origins of products. For example, Toyota from Japan and Ford from the United States joined forces to build cars using parts and labor from Mexico.

The concept of *economic interdependence* describes a positive, close connection between producers and consumers of goods and services within a nation or across nations. This economic interdependence has guided nations to establish large markets of free trade zones like the European Union (EU) trade agreement and the North American Free Trade Agreement (NAFTA) for Canada, Mexico, and the United States. The European Union went a step further; in 2002 they adopted a common currency for the Union—the Euro. As a result of this alliance, the Euro is today one of the strongest currencies in the world.

Money and Banking

Under the presidency of Woodrow Wilson, the Federal Reserve System was established. The main purpose of this institution is to keep the banking industry strong to ensure a supply of currency. The Federal Reserve is run by the Federal Reserve Board of Governors, a seven-member body appointed to a four-year term, with the option of being reappointed to a maximum of fourteen-year terms. Alan Greenspan served as chairman of the Federal Reserve Board from 1987 to 2006. He finished an unexpired term and then served for a full fourteen-year term for a total of eighteen and a half years. The current chair is Ben S. Bernanke. His term will expire in January 2010. At this writing, President Obama is studying the option of extending his term or naming a new chairman. The main function of the Federal Reserve Bank is to promote fiscal stability and economic growth in the nation and to regulate inflation and deflation. The Board of Governors controls the flow of money and sets the interest rate that banks use to lend money. They increase the interest rate to control inflation and lower the interest rate when business slows down.

Inflation and Deflation

Inflation reduces the purchasing power of money, which technically affects the value of the currency. Countries generally devalue their currency to keep up with inflation. Deflation is the opposite of inflation: the purchasing power of money increases, thereby lowering the prices of goods and services. In a period of deflation, consumers benefit but industry suffers. The Federal Reserve controls the flow of money and keeps a healthy balance between inflation and deflation.

American Federal Income Tax System

In 1913, the Sixteenth Amendment of the U.S. Constitution allowed the imposition of direct taxation of citizens. This direct taxation is known as the federal income tax.

Interdependence of State, National, and World Economies

The economy of Texas is based primarily on telecommunications, software, financial services, business products and services, semiconductors, biotechnology, and oil and coal. Agriculture and ranching are still viable economic activities, but they are no longer carrying the economy. A large percentage of these products are exported to members of NAFTA—Mexico and Canada—and to the world markets. According to the Texas Economic Update, if Texas were a nation, it would rank as the eighth-largest economy in the world (Strayhorn 2004).

The Texas economy relies heavily on exports of goods and services. From 2002 through 2005, Texas was ranked as the number one state in terms of export revenues (BIDC 2006). Without its exports, the Texas economy could not sustain its growth. Because of the interdependence of state and global economies, political turmoil and economic problems in the world can have a direct impact on the Texas economy. For example, because part of the economy of Texas is based on petroleum, the decisions of OPEC have a direct impact on the state's economy.

Competency 023: Government and Citizenship

The teacher understands and applies knowledge of concepts of government, democracy, and citizenship, including ways that individuals and groups achieve their goals through political systems.

Forms of Government

The U.S. Department of State identifies 26 forms of governments in the world (CIA, n.d).

Some of best-known forms of government listed are communism, socialism, democracy, monarchy, and oligarchy. A description of these types of government follows:

1. **Communism** is a system in which the state controls economic activity in the nation. The state rejects free enterprise and capitalism; consequently, private ownership is discouraged and often prohibited. Usually the nation is ruled through a one-party system. In theory communism believes that the country

should not have social classes, as a way to avoid the oppressor–oppressed dichotomy that exists in the world.

2. **Socialism** is a system of government in which the central government controls the production and distribution of goods, services, and labor in the nation. The goal is to promote an equitable distribution of resources among the people. In theory, the working class should take over and administer collectively the resources for their benefit and the benefit of the national as a whole.

3. **Democracy** is a form of government in which the majority rules. In practice it becomes a representative democracy, in which the people elect candidates to represent them in the government.

4. **Monarchy** is a system in which a king or queen leads the nation. The monarch can have supreme powers and become dictator, or he/she can have limited or ceremonial powers limited by a parliament or a constitution.

There are three main broad classifications for these forms of government based on the number of people in power—government by one person, a group, or by many people:

Rule by One

In this form of government, one person becomes the supreme leader of the nation. Some of the terminology and concepts linked to this type of government are:

- **Autocracy**: Ruler has unlimited power, uses power in an arbitrary manner.

- **Monarchy**: Ruled by a king or queen who holds complete control over the subjects. Ruler sometimes claims birth and divine rights.

- **Dictatorship**: The ruler holds absolute power to make laws and to command the army.

Ruled by a Few

In this system, a group of influential people takes control of the government. Traditionally, they appoint one of their own to function as the supreme leader of the government. Some examples of this type of government are:

- **Theocracy**: Ruled by a group of religious leaders, e.g., the Taliban in Afghanistan.

- **Aristocracy**: A group of nobles controls the economy and the government.

- **Oligarchy**: A small group of powerful and wealthy people rule the nation with the support of the military.

- **Military**: A committee of military officers or a *junta* becomes the rulers of the nation.

Rule by Many

In this type of government, the citizens of the nation, technically, become the government. In practice, the citizens elect members to represent them and become the government. Some examples of this type of government are:

- **Democracy**: The citizens of the nation directly or through elected members make important decisions, and become part of the government.

- **Constitutional Democracy**: It is a democratic form of government regulated by a constitution.

- **Parliamentarian Monarchy**: The monarch shares the power with the parliament. Often, the powers of the monarch are ceremonial in nature, like in Great Britain.

- **Federal Republic**: A constitutional government in which the powers of the central government are restricted to create semi-autonomous bodies (states or provinces) with certain degrees of self-governing powers, e.g., the United States.

The American Government

The governmental system of the United States has been identified as a federal republic and constitutional representative democracy. It is a federal republic because the U.S. government is limited by law; in this case, the government is limited by the Constitution. It is a constitutional representative democracy because the citizens elect senators and representatives to represent them in Congress.

The Constitution is the supreme law of the nation. It contains a description of the government and the rights and responsibilities of its citizens. The document can be amended with the approval of two-thirds of the House and the Senate and the ratification of individual state legislatures. Amendments to the U.S. Constitution have made it more democratic than the original document. The first ten amendments to the Constitution are known as the Bill of Rights.

Executive Branch

The executive branch of the U.S. government is composed of a president and a vice president elected every four years by electoral votes. The president is the commander-in-chief of the armed forces. He or she appoints cabinet members, nominates judges to the federal court system, grants pardons, recommends legislation, and has the power to veto legislation.

Judicial Branch

The judicial branch is composed of a federal court system that includes the Supreme Court and a system of lower courts—district courts, appeals courts, bankruptcy courts, and special federal courts. Federal judges are nominated by the president of the United States and confirmed by the Senate. All federal judges are appointed for life. The Supreme Court is composed of nine judges, and their ruling is considered final. Some of the major responsibilities of this body are to interpret the Constitution, resolve conflicts among states, and interpret laws and treaties.

Legislative Branch

The legislative branch is composed of the Congress, which is divided in two parts—the Senate and the House of Representatives. The Senate comprises two senators from each state, while the composition of the House is based on the population of each state. The Congress makes the laws of the nation, collects taxes, coins money and regulates its value, can declare war, controls appropriations, can impeach public officials, regulates the jurisdictions of federal courts, and can override presidential vetoes.

System of Checks and Balances

The U.S. Constitution provides for a system of checks and balances among the three branches of the government. In this type of system, individual branches check the others to be sure that no one assumes full control of the central government. The legislative branch can check the executive branch by passing laws over presidential veto (by a two-thirds majority in both houses). This branch exerts control over the judicial branch by refusing to confirm the president's judges. The executive can check the legislative branch by the use of the veto and the judicial branch by appointing federal judges. The judicial branch can check the other two branches through the process of judicial review, which can declare legislation unconstitutional or illegal.

Judicial Review Process—*Marbury v. Madison*

A dispute that occurred as the Thomas Jefferson administration came into power fundamentally altered the system of checks and balances of the American government. In this case, the judicial branch confirmed its power to review and assess the constitutionality of the legislation passed by Congress and signed by the president. This process is now called the judicial review.

Bill of Rights

After the U.S. Constitution was enacted in 1783, the founders felt that additional measures were necessary to preserve basic human rights. The first ten amendments to the U.S. Constitution came to be the Bill of Rights. A summary of the first ten amendments follows:

First Amendment—separation of church and state; freedom of religion, speech and press; and the right to peaceful assembly

Second Amendment—rights to keep and bear arms

Third Amendment—made it illegal to force people to offer quarters to soldiers in time of peace

Fourth Amendment—rights to privacy and unreasonable searches or seizures

Fifth Amendment—rights of due process, protection against self-incrimination, and protection from being indicted for the same crime twice (double jeopardy)

Sixth Amendment—rights to speedy public trial by an impartial jury and to counsel for ones defense

Seventh Amendment—right to sue people

Eighth Amendment—protection against cruel and unusual punishment

Ninth Amendment—enumeration of specific rights in the Constitution cannot be taken as a way to deny other rights retained by the people

Tenth Amendment—rights not delegated to the federal government by the Constitution are reserved to the states or to the people

Power Sharing Between State and Federal Governments

One of the most significant principles of the U.S Constitution is the concept of power sharing between the federal and state governments. Some of the powers reserved to the federal and state governments follow.

Powers Reserved for the Federal Government

- Regulate interstate and foreign commerce
- Print money and regulate its value
- Establish the laws for regulation of immigration and naturalization
- Regulate admission of new states
- Declare war and ratify peace treaties
- Establish a system of weights and measures
- Raise and maintain armed forces
- Conduct relations with foreign nations

Powers Reserved for State Governments

- Conduct and monitor local, state, and federal elections
- Provide for local government
- Ratify proposed amendments to the Constitution
- Regulate intrastate commerce
- Provide education for its citizens
- Establish direct taxes like sales and state taxes
- Regulate and maintain police power over public health and safety
- Maintain control of state borders

In addition to the powers reserved to the states, the Tenth Amendment of the U.S. Constitution provides additional powers to the state. In this amendment, the powers not specifically delegated to the federal government are reserved for the states.

Local and State Governments

Most states in the United States follow the type of government established in the U.S. Constitution. State governments generally have three branches—executive, legislative, and judicial. The main difference is that the executive branch is led by a governor and the judicial branch is composed of a state court system subordinate to the federal court system. The city government is generally headed by a mayor or city manager with the support of a city council.

Citizenship

The development of civic ideas and practices is a lifelong process that begins in school by observing patriotic holidays, learning about the contribution of historical characters, and pledging allegiance to the American and Texas flags each day. In first grade, encouraging good citizenship continues with the introduction of the American anthem and the mottoes of Texas and the United States. Civic education and the principles of democracy are infused through active participation in community activities. To promote civic responsibility, students can get involved in discussions about issues that affect the community. Teachers guide students to suggest possible solutions to community problems, while students are guided to listen and analyze contributions. Through this exchange, students are guided to practice principles of democracy and to value individual contributions to solve community problems.

In grades K–6 students will become familiar with the meaning and importance of national holidays observed during the year. Holidays with historic significance observed during the year are Memorial Day, Labor Day, Columbus Day, Independence Day, Veteran's Day, and Martin Luther King Jr. Day. Memorial Day honors members of the military who died in war. Labor Day recognizes the importance of workers and labor unions. Columbus Day commemorates the arrival of Christopher Columbus to the Americas. Independence Day commemorates the adoption of the Declaration of Independence. Martin Luther King Jr. Day honors the leader of the civil rights movement. Veteran's Day celebrates all those who have served in our country's armed forces.

Children as early as prekindergarten can be guided to develop civic responsibility. Teachers can promote this sense of responsibility by involving students in real-life situations in which they take civic responsibility. For example, teachers can make children aware of how producing trash can affect the environment. As part of this process, students can be guided to examine the amount of trash that they produce daily and explore ways to reduce it. Promoting a sense of responsibility to the well-being of everyone constitutes the main principle for developing responsible citizenship.

American Symbols

American Patriotic Symbols

Patriotic symbols are visible signs of national pride. The U.S. National Flag, the Pledge of Allegiance, the Statue of Liberty, the Liberty Bell, and the White House are important examples of patriotic symbols.

- The United States of America National Flag has 50 stars represent the 50 states of the Union. The color red represents hardiness and valor, the white symbolizes purity and innocence and the blue symbolizes vigilance, perseverance, and justice. The Congress approved a new flag with 13 red and white alternating horizontal stripes and 13 stars representing the original colonies in 1777. A star and stripe were added to the flag each time a state entered the union. The Congress set the number of stripes at thirteen in 1818 and approved to continue to add a star for each new state.

- The Pledge of Allegiance is a declaration of patriotism. It was first published in 1892 in *The Youth's Companion* was believed to be written by the magazine's editor, Francis Bellamy. The original purpose was for the pledge was to be used by school children in activities to celebrate the 400th anniversary of the discovery of America. The Pledge was widely used in morning school routines for many years and received official recognition by Congress on 1942. The phrase "under God" was added in 1954 and a law indicating the proper behavior to adopt when reciting the pledge, which includes standing straight, removing hats or any other headgear, and placing the right hand over the heart.

- The Star-Spangled Banner is the national anthem of the United States. It was originally a poem written by Francis Scott Key during the Battle of Baltimore in the War of 1812 against the British. In 1931, it was made the official national anthem of the United States.

- The Statue of Liberty was a gift of friendship from the people of France to the people of the United States commemorating the United States' 100th anniversary. It is a universal symbol of freedom, democracy, and international friendship.

- The Liberty Bell is a symbol of freedom and liberty. The Pennsylvania Assembly ordered the Liberty Bell to commemorate the 50th anniversary of Pennsylvania's original constitution, the William Penn's Charter of Privileges. It is traditionally believed that it was rung to summon the people of Philadelphia to hear the Declaration of Independence. It became an icon when the abolitionists adopted it as a symbol of freedom. The abolitionists changed its name from The State House Bell to the Liberty Bell.

- The White House was originally planned by President George Washington in 1791 and was completed in 1800 when its first resident, President John Adams, moved in with his wife, Abigail. It was originally called the President's House. President Theodore Roosevelt christened it with the name The White House in 1901, and for over 200 years it has been the home of the U.S. Presidents and their families. It is recognized as a symbol of the Presidency of the United States throughout the world.

- The Great Seal of the United States consists of a bald eagle holding an olive branch and a bundle of arrows. The olive branch represents peace and the arrows represent military strength. The eagle holds a scroll in its beak with the nation's motto: "*E Pluribus Unum*" which means "Out of many, one."

For additional information about symbols of the United States go to *http://govdocs. evergreen.edu/symbols.html*, a website created and maintained by Evergreen State College in Olympia, Washington, or *http://www.ushistory.org*, a website created and hosted by the Independence Hall Association in Philadelphia.

References

Acosta, T. P. 2009. Raza Unida Party. *The Handbook of Texas Online. Texas State Historical Association.* http://www.tshaonline.org/handbook/online/articles/RR/war1.html (accessed August 28, 2009).

Arends, R. 1998. *Learning to Teach*. 4th ed. Boston: McGraw-Hill.

Barker, E. C. and J. W. Pohl. 2009. Texas Revolution. *The Handbook of Texas Online. Texas State Historical Association.* http://www.tshaonline.org/handbook/online/articles/TT/qdt1.html (accessed August 24, 2009).

Business and Industry Data Center (BIDC). 2006. Overview of the Texas Economy. *Office of the Governor, Economic Development and Tourism.* http://governor.state.tx.us/ecodev/business_research/texas_economy/ (accessed October 1, 2009).

CIA World Fact Book. Central Asia: Russia. *https://www.cia.gov/library/publications/the-world-factbook/geos/rs.html* (accessed October 1, 2009).

CIA World Fact Book. Nations: Forms of Government. *HistoryGuy.com. http://www.historyguy.com/nations/government_types.html* (accessed August 27, 2009).

Echevarria, J., M. Vogt, and D. Short. 2000. *Making content comprehensible for English language learners: The SIOP model*. Needham Heights, MA: Allyn and Bacon.

Fry, P. L. "Origin of Name." *The Handbook of Texas Online. Texas State Historical Association. http://www.tshaonline.org/handbook/online/articles/TT/pft4.html* (accessed August 24, 2009).

Ganeri, A., H. M. Martell, and B. Williams. 1999. *The World History Encyclopedia*. Bath, UK: Parragon.

Kagan, S. 1985. *Cooperative learning resources for teachers*. Riverside, CA: Spencer Kagan.

Kerr, A. 2006. Temperance and prohibition. History Department, Ohio State University. *http://prohibition.osu.edu/* (accessed October 1, 2009).

Lyman, F. T. 1981. The responsive classroom discussion: The inclusion of all students. In *Mainstreaming Digest,* ed. A. S. Anderson, 109–113. College Park: University of Maryland Press.

Marzano, R., and D. Pickering. 2005. *Building academic vocabulary: Teacher's manual.* Alexandria, VA: ASCD.

Mayell, H. 2004. Three high-altitude peoples, three adaptations to thin air. *National Geographic. http://news.nationalgeographic.com/news/2004/02/0224_040225_evolution. html* (accessed October 1, 2009).

Mendoza, V. 2001. Video review of *Chicano! History of the Mexican American Civil Rights Movement. The Journal for MultiMedia History,* Volume 3. *www.albany.edu/ jmmh/vol3/chicano/chicano.html* (accessed August 28, 2009).

National Council for the Teaching of Social Studies (NCTSS) 2006. Expectations of Excellence: Curriculum Standards for Social Studies—Executive Summary. *www. socialstudies.org/standards/execsummary* (accessed October 1, 2009).

Parker, W. C. 2001. *Social Studies in Elementary Education.* 11th ed. Columbus, OH: Merrill Prentice-Hall.

Potts, J. 1994. *Adventure Tales of America.* Dallas, TX: Signal Media.

Rosado, L., and D. Salazar. 2002–2003. La Conexión: The English/Spanish connection. *National Forum of Applied Educational Research Journal* 15(4): 51–66.

Rosales Castañeda, O. 2006. *The Chicano Movement in Washington State* HistoryLink.org (accessed October 21, 2009) *1967-2006.*

Rowe, M. B. 1986. *Wait Times: Slowing Down May Be a Way of Speeding Up. Journal of Teacher Education,* 37, 43–50.

Schifini, A. 1985. *Sheltered English: Content area instruction for limited English proficiency students.* Los Angeles County Office of Education.

Schifini, A., H. García, D. J. Short, E. E. García, J. Villamil Tinajero, E. Hamayan, and L. Kratky. 2004. *Avenues: Success in language, literacy and content.* Carmel, CA: Hampton-Brown.

Seattle Civil Rights and Labor History Project. 2006. *http://depts.washington.edu/civilr/Chicanomovement_part1.htm* (accessed August 28, 2009).

Sheppard, D. E. *Cabeza de Vaca in North America.* Floridahistory.com. 23 *http://www.floridahistory.com/cabeza.html* (accessed August 23, 2009).

Slavin, R. 1986. *Student Learning: An Overview and Practical Guide.* Washington, DC: Professional Library National Education Association.

Strayhorn, C. K. 2004, Fall. "The Rebound is Here." *Texas Economic Update.* Window on State Government. *http://www.window.state.tx.us/ecodata/teufall04/* (accessed August 24, 2009).

CHAPTER 4

Science

The National Science Teachers Association (NSTA) supports the idea that scientific inquiry should be a basic component of the curriculum in every grade in American schools (NSTA 2002). A position paper of the organization published in 2002 emphasizes the importance of offering students early experience in problem solving and scientific thinking. The report suggests that children learn science best under the following conditions:

- Students are actively involved in firsthand exploration of scientific concepts.

- Instruction is related and built on the abilities and experiences of the learners.

- Instruction is organized thematically.

- Mathematics and communication skills are integrated.

The report also indicates that curriculum should emphasize the contributions of people from a variety of cultures. Finally, the NSTA (2002) states that science education can be successful if teachers receive adequate professional development and school administrators show a genuine interest in science education.

Competency 024: Safe and Proper Laboratory Processes

The science teacher manages classroom, field, and laboratory activities to ensure the safety of all students and the ethical care and treatment of organisms and specimens.

Classroom and Laboratory Health and Safety

Teachers must create a safe environment for children involved in scientific inquiry. Here are some of the principles and practices that teachers can follow to reduce risks and protect children:

- Require students to use appropriate personal protective gear, like goggles, laboratory coats, and gloves.

- Use appropriate procedures for cleaning and disposing of materials.

- Adhere to appropriate disciplinary procedures to avoid accidents; for example, do not allow children to play with water or other lab materials.

- Substitute less hazardous equivalent materials when possible; for example, use cleaning products instead of chemicals in their pure form.

- Use polyethylene or metal containers in place of glass.

- Advise children to avoid tasting or ingesting substances or materials.

- Label containers appropriately to avoid confusion.

- Control the use of sharp objects that can puncture the skin.

- Supervise the use of living organisms and the cleaning of instruments.

- Avoid experimenting with human cells and bodily fluids.

- Share the responsibility for the safety of the students with the whole group; that is, students should motivate each other to follow safety procedures.

- Make provisions for the movement and handling of equipment and materials for students with special needs.

- Prepare, review, and send home an age-appropriate safety contract requiring parent/guardian signature.

- Organize all materials to be used in class by placing them in separate bins for a member of each student group to pick up for use for the lab activity and for returning materials after the lab activity.

- Prepare and practice an emergency plan with students should an accident occur.

- Clearly label and demonstrate the use of safety equipment with students, such as the eyewash station and fire blanket.

- Document all accidents, regardless of how minor, and have another teacher sign as witness if possible.

- Clearly write and read to students the safety precautions for the laboratory before beginning the activity.

- Place posters around the room emphasizing the safety rules of the classroom and laboratory.

- Keep all chemicals and glassware in locked cabinets.

- Maintain regular inventory of all laboratory materials and chemicals.

- Store acids and other caustic chemicals in cabinets close to the floor in case they fall when retrieving for use.

- If using an open flame, such as lit candles, students must tie long hair back and tape or roll up loose sleeves to avoid contact with the fire.

The use of dangerous chemical substances in the elementary classroom is limited in scope. Many laboratory chemicals can be substituted with household products. However, care needs to be taken even when handling household chemicals. It is important to demonstrate safe laboratory procedures for the classroom because household products are still chemicals and pose some level of risk to students. Safety management of chemicals in the classroom requires teachers to have knowledge of those chemicals and their properties. For example, teachers need to be aware that a simple tool like a mercury thermometer can break and pose a danger to children. In general, maintaining safety requires teachers to take the following steps:

- Assess the relative danger of each chemical used in the classroom.

- Label and store chemicals appropriately.

- Implement safety procedures for the use and handling of materials and equipment.

- Follow appropriate procedures for cleaning containers and disposing of chemicals.

Proper Laboratory Procedures and Precision

Scientific experimentation cannot rely solely on our senses to record information. We need to extend what can be observed with our senses by using scientific instruments such as balances, microscopes, beakers, and graduated cylinders to make precise observations and measurements. Science requires the use of standard measuring devices to be sure that the information is clear, accurate, and able to be replicated in experimental settings. The United States uses a combination of the English system of measurement (standard) and the metric system. In fact, the United States is the only technologically developed country in the world that uses the English system for business transactions and for day-to-day activities. However, for international business, engineering, and natural sciences, all countries use a more standardized, precise system of weights and measurement, the metric system. The English system uses pounds, gallons, and inches for measurement, while the metric system uses kilos, liters, and meters. The metric system uses a system of fractions and multiples of units that are related to each other by powers of 10, allowing conversion and comparison of measures simply by shifting a decimal point, and avoiding the lengthy arithmetical operations required by the English system. The TEKS requires the teaching of both the metric and the English systems; however, all scientific data are to be reported using the metric system.

Competency 025: Scientific Inquiry

The teacher understands the history and nature of science, process, and role of scientific inquiry, and the role of inquiry in science instruction.

Planning and Implementing Scientific Inquiry

Scientific inquiry is promoted through students engaging in hands-on activities and experimentation. From their experiences conducting scientific experiments, students acquire information firsthand and develop problem-solving skills. Children in grades EC-6 are inquisitive and want to understand the environment around them. Teachers can use this interest to provide students with opportunities to use electronic and printed sources to find answers to their questions and to expand their knowledge about the topic. It is important for children to develop inquiry skills. This can only be accomplished by allowing them to experience science for themselves in hands-on investigations. By doing so, students develop important science inquiry and thinking skills (Table 4-1).

Table 4-1. Science Thinking Skills (FOSS, 2000)

- **Observing:** Using the senses to get information
- **Communicating:** Talking, drawing, and acting
- **Comparing:** Pairing and one-to-one correspondence
- **Organizing:** Grouping, seriating, and sequencing
- **Relating:** Cause-and-effect and classification
- **Inferring:** Super-ordinate/subordinate classification, if/then reasoning, and developing scientific laws
- **Applying:** Developing strategic plans and inventing

The model of inquiry that best supports science learning is a model known as the *learning cycle*, consisting of three phases: *exploration*, *concept invention*, and *application* (Lawson, Abraham, and Renner 1989; Marek and Cavallo 1997). Over time the learning cycle was extended with the addition of two new phases becoming what is known as the 5-E model (Bybee 1989). What follows is some history on the development of inquiry-based teaching via the learning cycle and 5-E model.

The original three-phase learning cycle model developed by Robert Karplus in the early 1960s was based upon the following theoretical foundation:

1. Science must be taught in a way that is *consistent with the nature of science*. Science is discovery and investigation, and that means science must be taught as an active process—as something we *do*. The children need to have the opportunity to experience the true nature of science by doing science exploration for themselves through direct experiences and hands-on investigations.

2. Science teaching must be focused on promoting the main purpose of education, namely, to promote the development in our students the *ability to think*—to be critical and independent thinkers. Science must be taught in a way that promotes the students use of independent, critical, and higher-level

thinking abilities (e.g., logic). Promoting this purpose of education is best accomplished by *not* giving or telling students the "answers" or information (e.g., as in giving a lecture); but instead by first giving students hands-on, direct experiences in which they use logic and reasoning to find "answers" or explanations for themselves; further discussion and teacher guidance can follow the students' direct experiences.

3. Science must be taught in a way that *matches how students learn,* described as the mental functioning model by Piaget (1964). How individuals learn is through mentally experiencing the following three-phase mental process. We first *assimilate* or "take in" information with our senses from our environment and what we are experiencing in our environment. During assimilation, we may have a sense of "disequilibrium," which is confusion or "cognitive conflict" as we try to make sense of our experiences. When in disequilibrium, we need to go back and *assimilate* more information—make more observations and gather more data, for example. When we have assimilated enough information and made sense of the information we have gathered, our minds experience *accommodation.* That is the "aha!" moment, the point when we ultimately feel "cognitive relief"—we figured it out, or what we have observed/experienced now makes sense! Third, our minds take that newly accommodated information and we *organize* it into our mental structures. That is, we connect the new idea or what we have just figured out/made sense of to what we already know, what we experience in everyday life, and/or to new, related concepts.

The three phases of learning described by Piaget, assimilation-accommodation-organization, *match* the original learning cycle's three phases: Exploration-Concept Invention-Application. The logic in developing the learning cycle in these three phases was that, given what we know about how children (people) *learn*, we should be *teaching* in a sequence or way that matches this learning pattern. To do so, teachers should first provide children with an *Exploration* phase in which students can assimilate information using their senses. The students may or may not experience disequilibrium, but, as teachers, we should guide them (not tell them!) through the sense-making process. We should then carry out a discussion in the *Concept Invention* phase in which students share their observations and findings. With careful questioning, teachers guide students to review their data/observations toward helping them reach the "aha!" moment or accommodation. The summarizing statement the students are to write, post on the board, and/or state aloud to others in this phase represents their accommodation or understanding of the concept. The teacher then helps students organize the new concept by guiding them through *Applica-*

tion of the concept in new contexts, in which students can connect the concept with what they observe in everyday life, or what they already know, for example.

Furthermore, by teaching via the learning cycle, we are teaching in a way that is consistent with the nature of science—as an active, hands-on process characterized by investigation and discovery—and we are teaching in a way that supports the purpose of education, that is, we are promoting children's development of higher level thinking abilities. The learning cycle and its origins and theory base is more fully described in a book by Marek and Cavallo (1997) titled *The Learning Cycle: Elementary School Science and Beyond.*

Over time, science educators added some additional phases to the learning cycle, namely, the *Engage* phase, with the idea that teachers need to do something that will gain the students' attention before beginning the exploration phase. Engage can be a demonstration (without explanation) or simply posing a question, challenge, or problem. So the original learning cycle model's first phase, *Exploration*, became two phases, *Engage* and *Explore*. Though identical, the *Concept Invention* phase's name was changed to *Explain* and *Application* phase had the name changed to *Elaborate,* to sustain the alliteration. Assessment or the measurement of learning in the original three-phase model was to take place throughout the learning cycle. However, science educators at the time preferred to have assessment articulated as an additional phase, which again to keep the "E" pattern, was termed *Evaluate.* So the three-phase **learning cycle** model was expanded into a **5-E Model**: *Engage, Explore, Explain, Elaborate, Evaluate.*

The two models are basically the same and grew out of the same underlying philosophy and theoretical foundation. However, the three phases more closely follow the model of learning—assimilation, accommodation and organization—as first described by Piaget; whereas the 5-E incorporates two additional essentials of classroom teaching, namely gaining students focus and attention, and measuring student learning.

Most importantly, in both models, the learning cycle and 5-E, students are *not told* the science concept or information before beginning the inquiry, but must discover the concept themselves through hands-on investigation, observation, and collection of data. In using the *Engage* phase (from 5-E) the students' learning experience begins with the teacher posing one or more questions, giving an interesting demonstration, or providing a laboratory guide; but in all of these, this phase captures their curiosity and motivates them to learn. Whether or not an *Engage* phase is used, students next (or first) experience an *Exploration* phase—and it must be a student-centered hands-on activity, investigation, or experiment. In the *Exploration* phase, students make observations and gather data on a science idea or topic area. In this phase, students can determine the experimental design or it can be pre-determined by the teacher. The main aspect, however, is that students are doing the lab activity themselves, and have not been told the expected outcome beforehand. For example, students may grow plants in the light and in the dark, and make observations, draw and/or take photos, and measure the plants grown under the two differing conditions over a period of time. All other variables are controlled (soil, water, air); only the light received by the plants is different, which is the variable.

After the observations have been made and data has been gathered by students, the teacher begins the next instructional phase called *Concept Invention*, or in the 5-E model, the *Explain* phase. In this phase the students present and share data with their classmates in a teacher-guided discussion of findings. The teacher uses questions to guide students' thinking and encourages the use of logic and reasoning as they interpret their data. For example, students may post the photos or drawings of plants grown in the dark and in the light, make line graphs of plant height over time, or share qualitative information about how the plant appeared after grown under the two conditions (e.g., plants in the light were green, whereas plants in the dark were yellow and pale). At the end of this phase, the students construct an overall statement that summarizes their data and observations, which is the central science *concept*. The science vocabulary is then linked to the concept students "invented."

Next the teacher helps students through the *Application* (from the learning cycle) or *Elaborate* (from the 5-E model) in which students use the new concept they learned as it is applied in new contexts. For example, students can create new questions to investigate or hypotheses to test based on what they just learned (the concept) and develop a way to answer their questions or test their hypotheses (e.g., what color of light is best for plants to grow?). They can also go to the Internet to learn more about the concept they just invented. In this phase the teacher can engage students in additional hands-on laboratories, readings, discussions, field trips, and/or writing activities that extend and expand upon the concept. These models of inquiry science teaching and learning are endorsed by NSTA (NSTA, 1998, 2003).

The diagram in Figure 4-1 shows the inquiry-based learning cycle model as it corresponds to the 5-E model of science teaching. The template shown in Table 4-2 explains each phase of the learning cycle as it relates to the 5-E Model for structuring inquiry-based science teaching for all students.

Figure 4-1. The Learning Cycle and 5-E Model

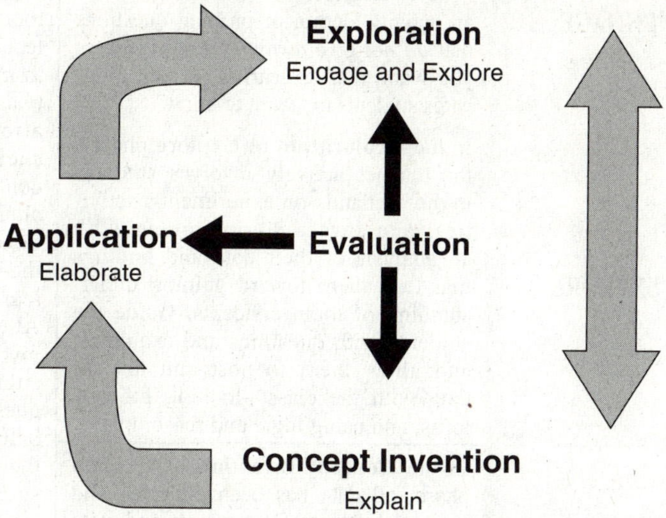

Exploration
Engage and Explore

Application
Elaborate

Evaluation

Concept Invention
Explain

Interpreting Findings in Science Inquiry

In planning and conducting experiments, teachers should guide children to develop an appropriate procedure for testing hypotheses, including the use of instruments that can yield measurable data. Even at the early stages of scientific experimentation, the procedure must be clear and tangible enough to allow replication by other students or scientists. Help students understand the concept of controlling variables and testing only one variable at a time. Students need to learn to be precise in the collection of data and measurements. Ensure the use of the metric system in obtaining all measurement data.

Allowing students to gather their own data and observations for interpretation promotes their critical and logical thinking abilities. It also gives them experience with using appropriate tools, resources, and technology of science that will lead to accurate organization and analysis of data. The students will be able to experience and practice science skills by verifying their findings, basing findings on evidence, and analyzing sources of error. Having students collect and report their own data also brings the teacher opportunities to discuss scientific ethics with students.

Table 4-2. Description of the Phases of the Learning Cycle and 5-E Model

Learning Cycle Phases	5-E Model Phases	Explanation of the Phases	
EXPLORATION PHASE	**ENGAGE**	In beginning of the Learning Cycle's **Exploration** phase and/or in the 5-E Model's **Engage**, the teacher begins with an activity, demo, or probing questions that *do not give away the main concept* you want them to learn—but that motivates students to "want to know."	In both, **Evaluation** of student learning during the learning cycle and the 5-E model's **Evaluate** phase, the teacher uses authentic ways to measure learning in each phase. This authentic evaluation means the teacher checks and measures students learning using various alternative as well as traditional methods throughout the various phases of the learning cycle/5-E model. Alternative evaluation may involve simple techniques such as asking students questions to respond to verbally or in writing, asking them to draw their understandings, reviewing their journals, checking charts and graphs and mathematical calculations and measurements, reviewing their concept statements, assessing their verbal statements, administering a laboratory practical, and requiring oral and/or visual presentations. The use of more traditional methods includes the administration of short tests or quizzes. In both models, the teacher measures learning *throughout* to gauge students' learning and make adjustments in instruction as needed.
	EXPLORE	In the **Exploration** or **Explore** phases, the teacher actively involves students in direct, hands-on experiments, activities, and investigations; along with an analysis of their data and findings that lead them toward gaining understanding of main concepts. Guide the students with questions and examples, and allow them to post and discuss data with the class—looking for patterns, and using logic and reasoning.	
CONCEPT INVENTION PHASE	**EXPLAIN**	In the **Concept Invention** or **Explain** phase, all data has been collected and now students are to construct and state for themselves the main concept that they have drawn from their exploration and analysis of observations and data. The teacher guides students with questions but does not "tell" students the concept—they invent it from their findings. After the students have stated the concept and/or posted it on the board, the teacher may supply the scientific terminology or labels for the concept and further explain what the students have found.	
APPLICATION PHASE	**ELABORATE**	The **Application** or **Elaborate** phase takes the concept students have constructed in this learning cycle and uses it in different contexts. In this phase the teacher works to expand and enhance students' understanding of the main concept(s) by applying it to real-world contexts and experiences, using mathematical calculations, additional but related experiments, further discussion on the topic, interactive lectures, computer research and/or simulations, readings, journal writing, and/or *any* teaching methods that will help students gain a more deep and interconnected understanding of the concept, creating a foundation in the learners minds for future, more complex science and mathematics learning.	

In explaining data collection procedures and display of findings to English language learners, the teacher needs to demonstrate and provide a model of what the end results should look like. In using inquiry, students work in groups, which is particularly helpful for second language learners as they interpret and exchange ideas about data and scientific reasoning.

When students complete their experiments, teachers need to engage them in the process of analyzing their own, and other groups' data for similarities, differences, and variations including error. This occurs in the concept invention or "explain" phase of the learning cycle and 5-E model, and again in any application or "elaborate" activities in which data has been collected. After data has been collected from students' explorations, they display their data in charts and graphs, for example, and communicate their observations and, ultimately, concept statements to the class by posting them on the board and/or through an oral presentation. The data helps them develop conclusions and form new research questions or hypotheses as they evaluate their findings, setting the foundation for new explorations. Students should be able to present pertinent data using graphic representations, and communicate their findings in written and oral forms to others.

In using scientific inquiry as in the learning cycle and 5-E model, scientific vocabulary is introduced *after* students have had hands-on experiences in the (engage and) exploration phase *and* have used their observations and data to construct meaning from their experiences in the *concept invention* or "explain" phase. Once students have had the hands-on direct experience with the concept, and have stated the meaning of their observations, the scientific vocabulary or terms that label the concept can be introduced by the teacher. In the application or elaborate phase, the teacher and students use the new vocabulary in extended experimentation, discussion, readings, writing, and other learning activities. Introducing terms after students have directly experienced the science inquiry and constructed meaning from their experiences by making a concept statement is especially important for second language learners in facilitating the development of understanding of science concepts. For all students, but especially for second language learners, this helps them understand concepts when terms are later *re-introduced*. By giving students the experience—something they *do*—and then allowing them to form meaning from their experience in ways that make sense to them, then when the term that labels what they learned is introduced, they are able to link it to prior knowledge and learning experiences in their minds. The terms are now able to build their background knowledge, which is critical for second language learners to understand the language of science. Making a connection between the hands-on activities and scientific vocabulary is beneficial to all students but especially to English language learners (ELLs), who can link the actions with the appropriate concept and vocabulary words without engaging in translations.

Promoting Logical Thinking and Scientific Reasoning

Interpreting results is one of the most challenging phases of scientific inquiry for children in EC-6. Students can easily discuss the observable results but might have difficulty interpreting their meaning. Teachers have to use developmentally appropriate practices to guide students to make extrapolations and infer information from the data, which involves the teachers' use of questioning, as addressed later in Competency 028.

Scientific Tools and Equipment for Gathering and Storing Data

Various tools or instruments are used in scientific experimentation in kindergarten through grade 6. The classroom can be equipped with measuring devices like graduated cylinders, beakers, scales, dishes, thermometers, meter sticks, and micrometers. They might also have anatomical models showing the body systems. Teachers need to learn to use these tools and equipment properly in order to help their students know how to use them and to collect accurate data in their inquiry investigations.

The TEKS requires students to gather information using specific equipment and tools. Examples of the tools required in kindergarten through grade 6 are presented in Table 4-3 (TEA 2006).

History and Nature of Science, Diversity, and Equity in Science

The history and nature of science provides an important framework for student learning. By learning the history of science, students will come to understand that science is changing and dynamic rather than fixed and tentative. They will understand that their own conceptions and understandings of science can change in light of new experimental observations and evidence. Therefore, it is important to use the history and nature of science as a tool to promote students' learning. For example, the students can learn about the earth-centered model of the solar system that prevailed for hundreds of years before Copernicus, and then Galileo supported a new model, which is now the accepted view of a sun-centered model of the solar system. With better tools developed through time and the extension of findings through observations and experiments, our scientific knowledge constantly shifts and changes.

Table 4-3. Tools and Equipment Required in the TEKS

Tools and Equipment	Kindergarten	1st	2nd	3rd	4th	5th	6th
Nonstandard measurements	√	√	√				
Hand lenses	√	√	√	√	√	√	√
Computers	√	√	√	√	√	√	√
Balances	√	√	√	√	√	√	√
Cups and bowls	√	√	√	√	√	√	√
Thermometers		√	√	√	√	√	√
Clocks			√	√	√	√	√
Meter sticks			√	√	√	√	√
Microscopes				√	√	√	√
Safety goggles				√	√	√	√
Magnets				√	√	√	√
Compasses				√	√	√	√
Timing devices					√	√	√
Calculators					√	√	√
Sound recorders					√	√	√
Hot plates						√	√
Burners						√	√
Beakers						√	√
Graduated cylinders						√	√
Flasks (Erlenmeyer and Florence)						√	√
Test tubes and holders						√	√

Science for all has long been the theme of science education's guiding documents such as Project 2061, a long-term initiative of the American Association for the Advancement of Science created in 1989, and the National Science Education Standards, published by the National Research Council in 1996. *Science for all* means that teachers need to help their students abandon stereotypes they may hold of science and scientists. For example, that science is a male-dominated profession. Teachers should help students to more appropriately view science as a field for males and females and for all cultures and ethnicities. To accomplish this goal, teachers need to be aware of their own potential, often not intentional, bias toward science and scientists that may be exclusionary. Posters of scientists displayed in the room should represent male and female scientists of diverse ethnicities and cultures, as well as of many different fields of science, such as environmental science, veterinary medicine, geology, engineering, and architecture, as well as the more traditionally represented physics and chemistry. Likewise, discussions of science and scientific discovery should include contributions from a diverse range of scientists. In giving examples to students, it is important to alternate between the use of "he" and "she," and to use and or vary examples to be more gender neutral and meaningful to a variety of ethnicities. In laboratory activities it is important that all group members have the opportunity to handle the materials and perform the experiment, and that the same students are not delegated to note taking. Varying laboratory responsibilities can be accomplished by assigning each group member roles to perform when they are conducting a laboratory activity, such as materials collector, record keeper, reporter, and lab facilitator, and then rotating these roles from one laboratory activity to the next to ensure all have an opportunity to work in the various roles.

Competency 026: Impact on Daily Life/Environment

The teacher understands how science impacts the daily lives of students and interacts with and influences personal and societal decisions.

Science in Daily Life

Students need to be aware of how science is present and plays a role in their daily lives. The functioning of their bodies, the natural environment that is around them, and their everyday use of electrical appliances, bicycles, computers, and cell phones are examples of biological and physical science in their lives. However, students tend to keep the science they learn in school separate from the science they experience in everyday life! It is important that teachers help students connect the science they are learning in school to the world around them to broaden their understandings and promote the usefulness, value, and applicability of science. In the learning cycle and 5-E models, the best time to help students make these connections is in the application/elaboration phase. After students have experienced a hands-on lab activity and constructed an understanding of the concept, the teacher should help them relate that new concept to their everyday lives and see how the concept works in differing contexts. Connecting newly learned concepts to the students' life experiences makes the learning more meaningful for students and helps them retain understanding of the concept for later use. Relating science to what students already know and experience in life helps bridge the disconnections between "school science" and science they observe and experience in everyday life.

Science has brought society many advantages that have served to increase the health and longevity of humans, and to improve the quality of life for all. However, there may be consequences, often unforeseen, to scientific discovery and invention that impacts society and the natural environment, as well as the habitats and survival of the living organisms that share this planet. To better understand these issues, students need to gain scientific knowledge and evidence of what is known. Armed with appropriate background knowledge, students will be in the position to weigh the pros and cons of various scientific discoveries and debate issues that prevail in our global community. Students should be apprised of issues such as global warming, for example, but before taking a position on the topic, they must be prepared with accurate scientific information on the topic. When students are given opportunities to use scientific concepts as support for sound logic and reasoning to debate or evaluate a scientific issue, they are operating at a high cognitive level important to their intellectual development. Equally important is student awareness of the ethical, personal, societal, and economic implications of science, from both positive and negative perspectives. Students need to realize the trade-offs often present in scientific discovery and experimentation, for example, laboratory testing on animals. Many new and important discoveries have improved the quality of life at the cost of animals' lives. In order to best understand the complexity of how science interfaces with personal and societal issues, students need to be engaged in electronic and library research on impactful science topics and in discussion with peers and experts in the science fields. Topics such as cloning, global warming, alternative and fossil fuels, and acid rain are just a few additional topics tied to ethical, personal, societal, and economic concerns. It is important that students fully understand the scientific knowledge that underlies all such complex issues, and can formulate decisions based on this knowledge.

Energy as a source of fuel and electricity is a major issue threatening the economic, environmental, and personal status of living in the U.S. and global society. It is important to know about fossil fuels, their origin, how they are obtained, and how they are used for energy consumption. In addition, it is important to know that fossil fuels are nonrenewable and will one day be expended. Therefore, science must continue to develop and improve upon alternative sources of energy such as wind, hydroelectric, and geothermal. Teachers must be knowledgeable about these other sources of energy and be able to guide students toward understanding how these alternative, renewable energy sources are used and how they impact our society's energy needs.

A significant impact of science on daily life relates to student fitness and health. Childhood obesity is a serious problem in the U.S., and teachers can play an important role in educating children on the negative health issues associated with poor nutrition and a lack of exercise. Students need to learn about factors that impact physical and psychological health and about how to make good choices on such factors, including nutrition, hygiene, physical exercise, smoking, drugs and alcohol. Understanding human biology, therefore, is important for students to realize how obesity and other factors such as substance use/abuse affect their physical and mental health. The topics of heart disease, diabetes, and cancer should be included in the curriculum as ways to help students understand the detrimental effects of unhealthy life choices.

Competency 027: Unifying Concepts and Processes in Science

The teacher knows and understands the unifying concepts and processes that are common to all sciences.

Explanatory Framework across Science Disciplines

Science is a way of knowing, a process—it is a systematic way of looking at the world and how it works. This competency focuses on how science uses a regular, consistent method of collecting and reporting data about scientific phenomena. Science is a way of organizing observations and then seeking patterns and regularity in order to make sense of the world. In science we organize evidence, create models, and explain observations in a logical form. We make predictions and hypotheses and test our predictions and hypotheses through controlled experimentation, meaning all variables of the experiment remain constant except for the variable being tested. We repeat experiments multiple times and seek constancy in our findings in form and/or function. We seek patterns and consistency in our observations and data in order to construct explanations and make new predictions.

Science embraces a broad spectrum of subject matter, such as life science, physical science, and earth science, all of which is interrelated. For example, in studying the ecosystem, teachers must understand the biological aspects (e.g., the living organism) and how they interact, as in predator-prey relationships and symbiotic relationships (e.g., parasitism, commensalism), as well as the chemical aspects of the ecosystem (e.g., nitrogen cycle), the geologic or earth science aspects (e.g., the landscape, the water, and the climate) and the physics aspects (e.g., energy transfer, motion). Ecosystems, for example, regardless of location on earth, share unifying components and characteristics, and teachers must understand this unity. In life science, there is unity of what makes organisms "living"—they all must carry on life functions and are composed of one or more cells. These are the criteria that unify life forms and classify something like a virus, for example, as non-living (it does not carry on the life functions and is not composed of cells).

All scientific observations can be described by their characteristics or "properties." These properties organize the observations according to commonalities, or classification. Observed properties and patterns are centered on space, time, energy, and matter.

Scientific Models

Models are representations of the natural world and universe in order to help better understand how something appears, its form and/or its function. For example, we may make models of the solar system, cells, or an atom to help us better explain its form and function and interactivity with other structures. Such models can be helpful to us in understanding the actual concept the model represents, and scientists often make models for this purpose. However, it is important to understand that, though it represents the actual science phenomena or concept and provides explanatory power, it is not the same as the actual science concept and is limited. Models in science may be physical, as in a physical model of a cell; conceptual, as in a concept map or an analogy; and/or mathematical as in a formula showing relationships, such as $d = m/v$ (formula for density).

Competency 028: Theory and Practice of Teaching Science

The teacher has theoretical and practical knowledge about teaching science and about how students learn science.

Developmentally Appropriate Practices

Children's processing of scientific inquiry can begin as early as age three or four. However, teachers must be aware of the stages of cognitive, social, and emotional development of children to appropriately introduce children to science concepts. For example, observing and experimenting with water and colors can easily be done by three- or four-year-olds, but using microscopes to observe and analyze animal or vegetable cells might be more appropriate for children in third and fourth grades. Students in EC-6 need direct experiences in order to understand concepts. According to Piaget (1964), children are transitioning through stages of development that require direct involvement to make sense of their experience. The model of teaching described earlier, the learning cycle and 5-E model, are based upon promoting the intellectual development of children. Thus, these models of teaching were designed to be consistent with the nature of science—and importantly, to match how children naturally learn (Marek and Cavallo, 1997; Renner and Marek, 1990). It is important that teachers understand the theory and research that underlie such models, as well as know how to use these models in teaching.

Misconceptions or alternative conceptions are a pervasive problem in science teaching and learning. Children tend to view the world from their own perspectives and draw conclusions based on their limited experiences. Once misconceptions are established in learners' minds, they are difficult to change. Therefore, teaching needs to allow children the opportunity for direct experience and collecting evidence. The learning cycle has been established as a teaching model that promotes conceptual change, helps students resolve misconceptions, and leads to more scientifically accurate understandings (Sandoval 1995).

Teachers need to begin lessons with direct, concrete activities giving students experience with objects. After concept understandings are established in learners, then teachers can move them from the concrete to more abstract reasoning. For example, in learning the concept of density, it is important that students have objects to touch, feel, weigh (take the mass of) and measure first, as in the exploration phase of the learning cycle. From direct experience with the objects, students should construct the concept that "a certain amount of matter (mass) is packed into a given amount of space (volume)." The term that labels this concept is "density." As application, teachers help students develop their abstract-thinking abilities by having them solve problems using the formula for density, $d=m/v$. Teachers need to select instruction appropriately such that concrete experiences are used first, leading the students to later use abstract reasoning. Teachers need to select learning experiences that will promote the students scientific knowledge, skills, and use of inquiry. Further, the students are able to use the prior knowledge they have formed about density to learn more extended, related concepts such as buoyancy. This example demonstrates the instructional knowledge and skills teachers need to have to prepare the best possible science learning experiences for students. The learning cycle or 5-E model are consistent with the goals of this competency.

The use of good questions by the teacher is critical to promoting logical thinking and scientific reasoning among students. Good questioning causes students to reflect upon the logic of their data and observations with confidence and also identify possible misinformation or misunderstanding of important concepts. Students learn to effectively use scientific argumentation and respond to challenges to their findings in order to support their conclusions. Teachers use questioning to reveal student learning and assess their progress in forming sound scientific frameworks of understanding. Questioning is the hallmark of science inquiry and should be used throughout inquiry instruction. In the learning cycle/5-E model, questioning must be designed to lead students toward being able to state the concept, so it is especially critical in the concept invention or "explain" phase.

Teachers can guide students at various levels of development to observe events; and through questioning, teachers can help students develop high-order thinking skills. For example, a teacher can lead children to make predictions while conducting experiments with objects that float or sink in water. By asking students to predict and explain why an object might sink or float, the teacher is leading students to analyze the properties of the object and the water to make an evaluative decision; that is, the children are using analysis and evaluation to complete that simple task. The following guide will help teachers best promote and elevate logical thinking abilities among students.

1. **USE KEY QUESTIONING TERMS AIMED AT THE FULL RANGE OF THE COGNITIVE DOMAIN** (Bloom & Krathwohl, 1956; Anderson & Krathwohl, 2001).

LEVEL 1: Knowledge

Recall of factual information

Examples   *List* the five Kingdoms.

                  Label the parts of the cell in the diagram provided.

                  Write the formula for density.

LEVEL 2: Comprehension

Communicate an idea in a different form

Examples   *Explain* heat transfer through conduction.

Restate what a habitat is in your own words.

Submit a definition of photosynthesis in your own words.

LEVEL 3: Application

Use what is known to find new solutions or apply in new situations

Examples   *Relate* the concept of convection to lake turn over.

Utilize your understanding of burning to explain why sand works to put out a fire.

Making use of the clothes you are wearing, how can you stay afloat for several hours?

LEVEL 4: Analysis

Break things and ideas down into component parts and find their unique characteristics

Examples   *Examine* blueprints of the electrical circuitry of your school building and explain how it works to bring electricity to your laboratory station.

Study the diagram of human digestion and *reason* what the organ marked #7 might be and explain its function.

Using the given laboratory materials, *deduce* the identities of the substances labeled "A," "B," and "C."

LEVEL 5: Synthesis

Use what is known to think creatively and divergently; make something new or original; pattern ideas or things in a new way

Examples   *Create* a burglar alarm system for the classroom.

Build a telescope for classroom use.

Develop a plan for cleaning the pollutants in the Trinity River.

LEVEL 6: Evaluation

Use what is known to make judgments and ratings; accept or reject ideas; determine the worthiness of an idea or thing

Examples   *Decide* whether or not you agree with the production of more nuclear power plants and provide justification for your decision.

Make a ruling you would give to car manufacturers on global warming and provide support for your ruling.

Rank the top five greatest discoveries in scientific history and *explain* why you have chosen those discoveries and ranked them in that particular order.

2. **AVOID YES/NO QUESTIONS (UNLESS PART OF A GAME) AND QUESTIONS WITH OBVIOUS ANSWERS.**

Examples   Showing a picture of a cell
Not so good

Is this a cell?
Better

What is this structure and how do you know?
(Students watching a chemical reaction in which the solution turns blue)
Not so good

Did it turn blue?
Better

What happened? What did you observe? Why did this happen?

3. **USE QUESTIONS BEGINNING WITH THE WORDS *WHY*, *HOW*, *WHAT*, *WHERE*, AND *WHEN* THAT PROBE STUDENTS' THINKING.**

Examples   How do you know?

Why do you think that?

Where did you see a change?

What is your explanation for this observation?

When did you notice the change occur?

What do you think?

Competency 029: Assessments in Science Learning

The teacher knows the varied and appropriate assessments and assessment practices for monitoring science learning in laboratory, field, and classroom settings.

Measuring Student Learning

Teaching cannot occur without student *learning*, and in order to determine that learning is occurring, student progress needs to be assessed on a regular basis. Assessment of learning should occur on some scale, large or small, every class day, and as students move through the learning of concepts, as in the learning cycle and 5-E models. Measuring learning as it is occurring is "authentic assessment" and allows teachers to adjust the instruction according to student learning and potential difficulties in learning. Alternative assessment methods, in addition to the more traditional testing formats (e.g., multiple-choice) should be used to obtain a full picture of what students know and do not know or can and cannot do. Alternative assessments include techniques such as verbal reports, laboratory practical exams, story writing, developing advertisements or brochures, constructing a concept map, writing essays, creating drawings or models, and developing a play or skit. In each assessment, the concepts to be learned are represented in alternative ways—yet clearly communicate what students have learned and understand.

It is essential that teachers monitor and assess students' understanding of concepts and skills on a regular, consistent basis and use this information to adjust instruction. The results of frequent informal and formal/traditional and alternative assessments should be used as a tool for planning subsequent instruction. Teachers must communicate progress to students so they can learn to self-monitor their own learning and understand what is needed to achieve learning goals.

Assessing the Science Curriculum

As part of the accountability system, Texas has a very comprehensive assessment system to measure the state uniform curriculum—the Texas Essential Knowledge and

Skills (TEKS). In this system, students take the Texas Assessment of Knowledge and Skills (TAKS) test in grades 3 through 12. However, the science component of TEKS is assessed only in grades 5, 8, and 10. The fifth-grade science test is available in Spanish; thus, Spanish-speaking ELLs can take the test in Spanish. In addition to the required science TAKS examinations, students are assessed through teacher- and district-developed tests in kindergarten through grade 12.

Competency 030: Physical Science

The teacher understands forces and motion and their relationships.

Universal forces include gravity, electricity, and magnetism, which are important to understanding this competency.

Magnetism and Gravity

Magnetism is the force of attraction or repulsion between objects that results from the positive and negative ionic charges of the objects. Usually, the objects are metals, such as iron, nickel, and cobalt. Magnets have two poles that have opposing charges or forces: north (+) and south (−). When the north pole of a magnet is placed close to the north pole of a second magnet, repulsion occurs. When poles of different kinds (north and south) are placed close, they attract one another. The strength of the forces depends on the size and the proximity of the magnets. The charged area around a magnet is called a magnetic field. The Earth is like a large magnet, with opposing forces—the north pole and south pole, and the magnetic field of attraction of Earth that we know as gravity is like that of a magnet. Without gravity, all objects on Earth, including the atmosphere, would not be held onto its surface. Planets and other celestial objects that are more massive than Earth, such as Jupiter, have stronger gravitational forces, and those that are less massive and/or dense, such as our moon, have weaker gravitational forces.

Force and Motion

Force is defined as the action of moving an object by pulling or pushing it. Force can cause an object to move at a constant speed or to accelerate. When force is applied over a distance, work is done. **Work** is the product of the force acting in the direction of movement and causing displacement. **Energy** is defined as the ability to do work; when a tow truck uses force to pull a car and move it to a different location, energy is used and work is accomplished. Newton's laws of motion are important to understand in fulfilling this competency. Newton's first law is that an object at rest will remain at rest unless acted upon by an (unbalanced) force, and an object in motion will continue to stay in motion with the same speed and in the same direction unless acted upon by an (unbalanced) outside force. This first law is also called *inertia*. Newton's second law is that acceleration is produced when a force acts on mass and the greater the mass of the object being accelerated, the greater the amount of force needed to accelerate that object. Newton's third law of motion is that for every action there is an equal and opposite reaction (see *http://teachertech.rice.edu/Participants/louviere/Newton/*).

Force and motion, as well as changes in motion, may be measured through hands-on activities in which variables such as time, speed, distance, and direction can be recorded and graphed, and teachers need to know how to do so. For example, teachers can have students experience and record what happens when an object with higher mass (such as a large marble or ball bearing), collides with an object with less mass (e.g., a small marble or ball bearing). Teachers should also know what happens when the rate of speed is high when the objects collide compared to when the rate of speed is low. The game of pool or billiards is a good example. When forces are unbalanced, it may cause the object to change its motion or position.

Relationships between Force and Motion: Machines, Space, and Geologic Processes

A machine is something that makes work easier. Machines can be as simple as a wedge or a screw or as sophisticated as a computer or gas engine. A **simple machine** has few or no moving parts and can change the size and direction of a force. A screw, hammer, wedge, and incline plane are examples of simple machines. Simple machines are part of our daily activities. For example, children playing on a seesaw are using a simple machine called a **lever**. Thus, teachers and their students should know the practical use of these simple machines in everyday life. A **complex machine** is two or more simple machines working together to facilitate work. Some of the complex machines used in daily activities are a wheelbarrow, a can opener, and a bicycle.

Force and motion is what keeps the sun, Earth, moon, and planets in their orbits and explains the structure and changes of the universe. On Earth, force and motion are found in all geologic processes, explaining phenomena such as tides and tsunamis.

Competency 031: Physical Science

The teacher understands the physical and chemical properties of and changes in matter.

Matter

Matter is anything that takes up space and has mass. The **mass** of a body is the amount of matter in an object or thing, and **volume** describes the amount of space that matter takes up. Mass is also the property of a body that causes it to have weight. **Weight** is the amount of gravitational force exerted over an object. It is important not to confuse mass and weight. What students are measuring on their balances in the laboratory is an object's *mass*. Weight changes as an object goes from one level of gravitational force to another, for example, from Earth to the Moon, because the amount of "pull" on that object is different; but the mass of the object—how much matter or material is in the object—does not change unless we do something to actually take away or add matter to that object.

There are 112 basic kinds of matter, called **elements**, which are organized into the **periodic table**. An element is composed of microscopic components called **atoms**. Atoms are made up of particles called **electrons**, **neutrons**, and **protons**. The mass of the atom is located mostly in the nucleus, which is made up of protons and neutrons. The electron contains little mass and follows an orbit around the nucleus. **Molecules** are two or more atoms bonded together in a chemical bond. The atoms of a molecule can be more than one of the same *kind* of atom, as in the naturally occurring oxygen molecule, O_2, or a molecule can be two or more different atoms as in carbon dioxide, CO_2, ammonia, NH_3, and glucose, $C_6H_{12}O_6$. **Compounds** are when you have two or more *different* kinds of atoms in the molecule and you have a given amount of that substance. In other words, compounds consist of matter composed of atoms that are chemically combined with one another in molecules in definite weight proportions. An example of a compound is water; water is oxygen and hydrogen combined in the ratio of two hydrogen molecules to one molecule of oxygen H_2O. So, you can also call it *one* H_2O a molecule.

Properties of Matter

Matter has physical, thermal, electrical, and chemical properties. These properties are dependent upon the molecular composition of the matter.

Physical Properties

The physical properties of matter are the way matter looks and feels. It includes qualities like color, density, hardness, and conductivity. **Color** represents how matter is reflected or perceived by the human eye. **Density** is the mass that is contained in a unit of volume of a given substance. **Hardness** represents the resistance to penetration offered by a given substance. **Conductivity** is the ability of substances to transmit thermal or electric current.

Thermal Properties

Matter is sensitive to temperature changes. Heat and cold produce changes in the physical properties of matter; however, the chemical properties remain unchanged. For example, when water is exposed to cold temperature (release of heat), it changes from liquid to solid; and when water is exposed to heat, it changes from solid to liquid. With continued heat, the water changes from liquid to gas (water vapor). Water vapor can be cooled again and turned back into liquid. However, through all these states, water retains its chemical properties—two molecules of hydrogen and one molecule of oxygen or H_2O.

Electrical Properties

Matter can be classified as a conductor or nonconductor of electricity. Conductive matter allows the transfer of electric current or heat from one point to another. Metals are usually good conductors, while wood and rocks are examples of nonconductive matter.

Chemical Properties

The chemical properties of one type of matter (element) can react with the chemical properties of other types of matter. In general, elements from the same groups will not react with each other, while elements from different groups may. The more separated the groups, the more likely they will cause a chemical reaction when brought together. A type of matter can be chemically altered to become a different type of matter; for example, a metal trash can will rust if it is left out in the rain.

States of Matter

Matter can exist in four distinct states: solid, liquid, gas, and plasma. Most people are familiar with the basic states of matter, but they might not be familiar with the fourth one, plasma. Plasmas are formed at extremely high temperatures when electrons are stripped from neutral atoms (University of California 2006). Stars are predominantly composed of plasmas. Solids have mass, occupy a define amount of space or *volume* or have a definite shape, and are more dense than liquids. Liquids have mass, occupy a definite volume, do not have a definite shape, but instead take the shape of their container. Gases have mass, do not have a definite volume, have no definite shape but take the shape of their container, and are the least dense of the three states of matter. Plasma has no definite shape or volume, and is a substance that cannot be classified as a solid, liquid, or gas. When substances change from one state of matter to another, such as ice melting, it is a physical change, and not a chemical change.

Mixtures and Solutions

Mixtures are combinations of two or more substances, where each substance is distinct from the other, that is, made up of two or more types of molecules and not chemically combined. The two substances in the mixture may or may not be evenly distributed, so there are no definite amounts or weight proportions. Mixtures may be *heterogeneous*, which means an uneven distribution of the substances in the mixture throughout. A mixture may be *homogeneous,* which means the components are evenly distributed throughout. Examples of mixtures include milk, which is a heterogeneous mixture of water and butterfat particles. The components of a mixture can be separated physically. For example, milk producers and manufacturers remove the butterfat from whole milk to make skim milk.

Solutions are *mixtures* that are *homogeneous*, which means that the components are distributed evenly and there is an even concentration throughout. The solute is the substance in the smaller amount that dissolves and that you add into the substance that is in the larger amount—the solvent. Water is a common solvent. Solids, liquids, and gases can be solutes. Examples of solutions are seawater and ammonia. Seawater is made up of water and salt, and ammonia is made up of ammonia gas and water. In these examples, the salt and the ammonia (NH_3) are the solutes; water is the solvent.

Physical and Chemical Changes in Matter

A **physical change** is a change in a substance that does not change what that substance is made of. Examples of physical changes are melting ice (boiling water), tearing paper, chopping wood, writing with chalk and mixing sugar and water together. In the mixing of sugar with water, or salt with water, even though the sugar or salt may not be visible to the naked eye in the water, it is still there and still has the same composition—that is, the molecules that make up the sugar or salt and water are still the same as when you mixed them. You can evaporate the water and you will recover your sugar or salt crystals.

A **chemical change** is when the substances that were combined are no longer the same molecules—they have changed to new substances. For example, burning wood, mixing baking soda and vinegar, or a rusting nail, which is when the iron of the nail (Fe) combines with oxygen (in the presence of water) to form a new substance—that is, a new molecule is formed, iron oxide Fe_2O_3.

Physical changes can be reversed, whereas chemical changes generally cannot be reversed. Evidence of a chemical change include that the combination of the substances gives off a gas (bubbles are observed), it changes color (not always a chemical change, but may be if the other evidences are also present), gives off heat and becomes warmer, or absorbs heat and becomes colder (temperature change), and forms a precipitate (a solid substance). When heat is given off in a chemical change, it is an **exothermic** reaction; and when heat is absorbed in a chemical change (the combination becomes colder), it is an **endothermic** reaction. Everyday examples of exothermic reactions are firewood burning or the use of a hand warmer that many mountain climbers and snow skiers use, and examples of endothermic reactions are a cold pack used in sports injuries or the combination of baking soda and vinegar (try it with a thermometer in the vinegar during the reaction and see!).

Chemical Reactions in Everyday Life

Chemical reactions occur in everyday life and are an essential part of our physical and biological world. The burning of gasoline in automobiles is a chemical change—and burning of any kind for that matter. Burning is the combination of oxygen from the atmosphere with substances containing the carbon atom. The proper temperature has to be reached in order to begin this exothermic reaction, but once started, the chemical reaction can continue until the oxygen is used up or is prevented from entering into the reaction. So since gasoline is a fossil fuel (a once living organism), it contains carbon. When we provide the energy it needs to begin the reaction, called activation energy, as long as oxygen is present, the carbon substance will burn. Burning is a chemical reaction because the carbon and oxygen combine to form new substances such as carbon monoxide (CO) and carbon dioxide (CO_2). The same reaction occurs in burning wood, candles, and even in cell respiration—the oxygen we breathe and carry through our bloodstream is combined in our cells with carbon-containing glucose molecules in a type of "controlled" burning. Our bodies give off heat from this reaction, which is why we are able to maintain a fairly high temperature of about 98.6 degrees Fahrenheit. Other examples of chemical reactions in everyday life include chemical batteries, the digestion of food, and cooking/baking. Moreover, the process of photosynthesis, where plants use sunlight to convert carbon dioxide gas and water into food for the plant known as glucose (a simple sugar), is also an important chemical reaction responsible for providing food for and sustaining all life on Earth.

Competency 032: Physical Science

The teacher understands energy and interactions between matter and energy.

Principles of Energy

Energy is available in many forms, including heat, light, solar radiation, chemical, electrical, magnetic, sound, and mechanical energy. It exists in three states: potential, kinetic, and activation energies. An object possessing energy because of its ability to move has **kinetic energy**. The energy that an object has as the result of its position or condition is called **potential energy**. The energy necessary to transfer or convert potential energy into kinetic energy is called **activation energy**. All three states of energy can be transformed from one to the other. A vehicle parked in a garage has potential energy. When the driver starts the engine using the chemical energy stored in the battery and the fuel, potential energy becomes activation energy. Once the vehicle is moving, the energy changes to kinetic energy.

Heat and Temperature

Heat is a form of energy. Temperature is the measure of heat. The most common device used to measure temperature is the thermometer. Thermometers are made of heat-sensitive substances—mercury and alcohol—that expand when heated.

Heat and Light

The most common form of energy comes from the sun. Solar energy provides heat and light for animals and plants. Through **photosynthesis**, plants capture radiant energy from the sun and transform it into **chemical energy** in the form of glucose. This chemical energy is stored in the leaves, stems, and fruits of plants. Humans and animals consume the plants or fruits and get the energy they need for survival. This energy source is transformed again to create kinetic energy and body heat. **Kinetic energy** is used for movement and to do work, while **heat** is a required element for all warm-blooded animals, like humans. Cold-blooded animals also require heat, but rather than making it themselves through the transformation of plant sugar, they use solar energy to heat their body. Energy transformation constitutes the foundation and the driving force of an ecosystem. In addition to heat and solar radiation, energy is available in the forms of electricity and magnetism.

Heat Transfer

The transfer of heat is accomplished in three ways: conduction, radiation, and convection. **Conduction** is the process of transferring heat or electricity through a substance. It occurs when two objects of differing temperatures are placed in contact with each other and heat flows from the hotter object to the cooler object. For example, in the cooling system of a car, heat from the engine is transferred to the liquid coolant. When the coolant passes through the radiator, the heat transfers from the coolant to the radiator, and eventually, out of the car. This heat transfer system preserves the engine and allows it to continue working.

Radiation describes the energy that travels at high speed in space in the form of light or through the decay of radioactive elements. Radiation is part of our modern life. It exists in simple states as the energy emitted by microwaves, cellular phones, and sunshine or as potentially dangerous energy as X-ray machines and nuclear weapons. The radiation used in medicine, nuclear power, and nuclear weapons has enough energy to cause permanent damage and death.

Convection describes the flow of heat through the movement of matter from a hot region to a cool region. In its most basic form, the concept of convection is that warmer air rises and colder air sinks. The colder air contracts and so is denser, thus it sinks; the warmer air is expanded, or more spread out, and so is less dense and rises. Thus, convection occurs when the heating and circulation of a substance changes the density of the substance. A good example is the heating of air over land near coastal areas coupled with the influx of cooler sea breezes offshore. The heated air inland expands and thus decreases in density, causing the cooler, more dense air to rush in to achieve equilibrium. A more common example of convection is the process of heating water on a stove. In this case, heat is transferred from the stove element to the bottom of the pot to the water. Heat is transferred from the hot water at the bottom to the cooler water at the top by convection. At the same time, the cooler, denser water at the top sinks to the bottom, where it is subsequently heated. This circulation creates the movement typical of boiling water. Convection currents created by the combining or colliding of cold and warm air masses is one factor responsible for storms and circular rotation of the air in tornados and hurricanes. Ocean currents are also caused by the collision of cold water and warm water masses in the oceans (Cavallo 2001).

Electricity and Magnetism

When you arrange an energy source, such as a battery, a wire, and a light bulb (or motor, or bell, or any electrical device) such that all *metal* parts are touching (metal is a good "conductor" of energy) in a circle—the bulb will light (the motor will run, the bell will ring, and so on). What has been created by arranging the items in this circle is known as an "electric circuit." The energy from the battery or other energy source is able to "flow" or be transferred through the metal wires and parts of the circuit. A **closed circuit** is when all metal parts are touching and the electrical charge is able to continue to be transferred through the circuit. A light switch or other "on button" closes the circuit and allows the electricity to flow. An **open circuit** is when there is a break someplace in the flow of electricity through the circuit. A switch or "off button" opens the circuit and stops the electricity flow. When you ring a door bell, you are closing the circuit or allowing all metal parts to touch and send electricity through it to make the bell ring; when you let go of the doorbell button, the circuit is open, and so the flow of electricity stops and so does the bell's ringing.

Lightning is a form of *static* electricity which means it is not "flowing" or being transferred in the way it is through a metal wire, but is caused by friction, much the same as walking across a carpet in socks and getting a shock when a metal doorknob is touched. In both kinds of electricity, the electrons in the atoms of the substance, which are negatively charged, are pulled away from their atom's nucleus, giving the object, or cloud, a negative charge. The negative charge is quickly attracted to a positive charge—in the case of lightning, that positive charge could be something (or someone!) on the ground. The positive charge quickly jumps toward the negative charge and the negative charge quickly jumps toward the positive charge, and a flash of lighting and clap of thunder is heard; or in the case of the doorknob, a spark and a snap sound. Electric circuits are just a way to channel the electricity and the opposing charges through a conductor such as metal wires to allow us to use the energy to do work and to transform the energy into different forms such as sound (a radio), light (light bulbs), mechanical (machinery), and/or heat energy.

Light Energy

Light energy, and all energy for that matter, travels in waves and in a straight-line path. The electromagnetic spectrum shows the different wavelengths and frequencies of energy, including the small portion that is visible light. The electromagnetic spectrum includes, for example, micro-waves, x-rays, radio waves, infrared radiation, visible light waves, and ultraviolet radiation, all of which have different wavelengths and frequencies that distinguish one type of wave from another (see *http://imagine.gsfc.nasa.gov/docs/science/know_l1/emspectrum.html*).

Visible light is the wavelength of light we can see, which our eyes see as white light. However, this white light is composed of a host of other wavelengths of light that our eyes cannot always distinguish, which we know as the visible light spectrum, or a rainbow. The colors of white light include red, orange, yellow, green, blue, indigo, and violet (although some sources now eliminate indigo as separate from violet), or ROYGBIV. When light, again, traveling in a straight line, hits an object or substance and is *bent*, it is called **refraction**. The bending of light waves may result in the colors of light in the spectrum becoming visible, as when we see a rainbow in the sky (the water molecules in the air bend the light) or when light travels through cut glass such as with a prism. **Reflection** is when light waves bounce back, as when looking in a mirror. The principles of reflection and refraction are used in periscopes and telescopes in order to be able to see objects we may otherwise not be able to see. They are often popular in magic shows when objects are said to "disappear." In actuality, the light of the object has been refracted or reflected to a place away from our eyes so that we can no longer see it.

Refraction is also used to our advantage through concave and convex lenses. Concave or convex lenses work such that when light passes through it changes the focal point. The eye contains a lens, but when light passing through the eye cannot properly focus on the "screen" known as the retina, the object being viewed may be blurred. Concave or convex lenses are used in eyeglasses to adjust and correct the focal point. These lenses are also used in cameras, microscopes, and telescopes. A spoon is an example of both a concave and a convex lens—if you look into the concave side, you will see yourself upside down. If you look into the convex side of the spoon, you will see yourself right side up. This is due to refraction (and reflection) of light. For more on this topic, see *http://camillasenior.homestead.com/optics4.html*.

Sound Energy

Sound also travels in waves. Sounds are caused by vibrations, such as a guitar string (or a rubber band), or banging on a drum or cymbal. Sound has a certain wavelength, frequency, pitch, and amplitude (loudness). Sound waves must travel through a medium, which may be solid, liquid, or gas. Sound travels best through solids because there are more molecules (particles) to vibrate, and least well through gases.

The types of sound waves are longitudinal and transverse. **Longitudinal waves** move parallel to the direction the wave moves, and **transverse waves** move perpendicular to the direction of the wave. For more information and animations on sound waves, see *www. glenbrook.k12.il.us/gbssci/Phys/Class/waves/u10l1c.html.*

Competency 033: Physical Science

The teacher understands energy transformations and the conservation of matter and energy.

Electricity

Electricity is the flow of electrons or electric power or charge. The basic unit of charge is based on the positive charge of the proton and the negative charge of the electron. Energy occurs naturally in the atmosphere through light. However, it is not feasible to capture that type of energy. The electricity that we use comes from secondary sources because it is produced from the conversion of primary (natural) sources of energy like fossil fuels that are **nonrenewable** (natural gas, coal, and oil) and nuclear, and **renewable** resources such as wind and solar energy. All sources of energy are used to produce a common result—to turn a turbine that generates electricity (see *www.sce. com/kids/science/producing.html*). Electricity that is generated can then be sent through wires for human use, and can be transformed into other forms of energy, including sound, light, heat, and force.

Conservation of Energy

The main principle of energy conservation states that energy can change form but cannot totally disappear. For example, the chemical energy stored in a car battery is used to start the engine, which in turn is used to recharge the battery. Another example of energy conservation is placing merchandise on shelves. Energy was used to do the work (placing merchandise on a shelf) and it was stored as potential energy. Potential energy in turn can be converted to kinetic energy when the merchandise is pushed back to the floor. In this case, work was recovered completely, but often the recovered energy is less than the energy used to do the work. This loss of energy can be caused by friction or any kind of resistance encountered in the process of doing the work. For example, as a vehicle's tires roll across the pavement, doing the work of moving forward, they encounter friction. This friction causes heat energy to be released, as well as kinetic energy.

In essence, energy cannot be created or destroyed, only changed in form. Likewise, matter cannot be created or destroyed, only changed in form. Thus, energy from the sun is changed, for example, to chemical energy when plants use the energy to make glucose in photosynthesis. The energy from the sun is stored in the chemical bonds of the glucose molecule and will be released for use by the organism—the plant itself, or any organism that eats the plant and its glucose—when the molecule's chemical bonds are "broken" by oxygen in cell respiration and/or stored in another chemical form known as ATP. Likewise, electrical energy comes from burning, or breaking the bond of carbon-based molecules as in fossil fuels. This electricity generated is then transformed to another form by first capturing and sending that electrical energy through metal wires originating at the power generating plant, and sending it in a complete, closed circuit to homes, businesses, and industries. There the electrical energy may be transformed to sound, heat, light, and/or mechanical energy. In all cases, the energy is not lost, it is changed in form.

It is important to conserve matter and energy generated from fossil fuels as these are non-renewable sources and will one day be expended. It is also important to continue exploring alternative, renewable forms of energy and electricity generation to meet our society's energy demands and maintain our Earth's clean air and water supplies.

Key Principles of the Physical Science Competencies 030–033

- To help students develop higher-order thinking skills, teachers need to guide students to analyze research data and make extrapolations or inferences based on data analysis.

- Matter is anything that has mass and takes up space.

- Mass is the amount of matter something contains.

- Volume refers to the amount of space taken up by an object.

- The states of matter are solid, gas, liquid, and plasma.

- There are 112 basic kinds of matter called elements.

- Elements are made up of atoms. An atom is the smallest part of matter.

- A compound is a kind of matter made up of two or more elements. A chemical formula describes the kinds of elements present in a compound. The chemical formula of water is H_2O because it has two molecules of hydrogen and one molecule of oxygen.

- Physical properties of matter are the characteristics that can be seen or measured without changing the material.

- Chemical properties of matter are the characteristics that can only be seen when the material changes and new materials are formed; for example, wood burns and turns into ashes. A chemical property of wood is its ability to burn.

- Water boils at 212 degrees Fahrenheit or 100 degrees Celsius, and it freezes at 32 degrees Fahrenheit or 0 degrees Celsius.

- Mass is the amount of matter or material of an object.

- Weight is the amount of gravitational force exerted over an object.

- When measuring dry chemicals on a balance scale, teachers should follow these steps: (1) Place and weigh a watch glass or dish, (2) place the dry chemical inside the watch glass or dish, and (3) subtract the weight of the glass or dish from the total to obtain the real weight of the chemical.

- Energy and matter may be changed from one form to another but are not lost.

- Heat is transferred by conduction, convection, and radiation.

- Electric circuits may be open or closed.

- Potential energy is stored energy; kinetic energy is energy in motion or actively being used. Activation energy is the energy it takes to change potential energy into kinetic energy.

- Light travels in waves and in a straight line; light may be refracted or bent and/or reflected.

- Sound is caused by vibrations.

Competency 034: Life Science

The teacher understands the structure and function of living things.

Structure and Function

All living things carry on life functions, such as, respiration, nutrition, response, circulation, growth, excretion, regulation, and reproduction, all of which characterize them as *living* as opposed to nonliving. In addition, all living things are composed of the basic unit of life known as *cells*. Organisms, as well as individual cells of an organism and single-celled organisms, carry on these life functions using specialized structures. For example, earthworms carry on respiration through their moist skin; plants excrete gases from tiny pores on the underside of leaves called stomata; a single-celled Amoeba ingests food by use of a "false foot" or pseudopodia; and insects respond to chemical attractants called pheromones of the opposite-sex insect for mating.

Animal and Plant Cells

Animal and plant cells are similar in appearance. Animal cells contain mitochondria, small round or rod-shaped bodies found in the cytoplasm of most cells. The main function of mitochondria is to produce the enzymes for the metabolic conversion of food to energy. This process consumes oxygen and is termed **aerobic respiration**.

Plants cells also contain mitochondria, which allow plants to carry on respiration where they use oxygen and excrete carbon dioxide and water just like animals. However, plants also have specialized organelles called chloroplasts that are used for taking in sunlight and using this energy to convert another gas, carbon dioxide, and water taken in from the roots to make glucose—a simple sugar that is the food for the plant. Chloroplasts contain chlorophyll, which is used in this process of converting light into chemical energy. This process is called **photosynthesis**. Photosynthesis is the process by which chlorophyll-containing organisms convert light energy to chemical energy.

Cell System

The cell is the basic unit of living organisms and the simplest living unit of life. Living organisms are composed of cells that have the following common characteristics:

- Have a membrane that regulates the flow of nutrients and water that enter and exit the cell

- Contain the genetic material (DNA) that allows for reproduction

- Require a supply of energy

- Contain basic chemicals to make metabolic decisions for survival

- Reproduce and are the result of reproduction

Eukaryotic and Prokaryotic Cells

There are two kinds of cells—prokaryotic and eukaryotic. **Prokaryotic cells** are the simplest and most primitive type of cells. They do not contain the structures typical of eukaryotic cells. Prokaryotic cells lack a nucleus and instead have one strand of deoxyribonucleic acid (DNA). Some prokaryotic cells have external whip like flagella for locomotion or a hairlike system for adhesion. Prokaryotic cells come in three shapes: cocci (round), bacilli (rods), and spirilla or spirochetes (helical cells). Bacteria (also called Monera) are prokaryotic cells. For more information and animated illustrations of prokaryotic cells see *www.cellsalive.com/cells/bactcell.htm*.

Eukaryotic cells evolved from prokaryotic cells and in the process became structurally and biochemically more complex. The key distinction between the two cell types is that only eukaryotic cells contain many structures, or organelles, separated from other cytoplasm components by a membrane. The organelles within eukaryotic cells are the nucleus, mitochondria, chloroplasts, and Golgi apparatus. The nucleus contains the deoxyribonucleic acid (DNA) information. The mitochondria have their own membrane and contain some DNA information and proteins. They generate the energy for the cell. The chloroplast is a component that exists in plants only, allowing them to trap sunlight as energy for the process of photosynthesis. The Golgi apparatus secretes substances needed for the cell's survival. For information and animations on eukaryotic cells, see *www.cellsalive.com/cells/3dcell.htm*.

Classifications of Living Things

Living things are divided into five groups, or **kingdoms**: Monera (bacteria), Protista (protozoans), Fungi, Plantae (plants), and Animalia (animals).

Monera consists of unicellular organisms. It is the only group of living organisms made of prokaryotic cells—the cells with a primitive organization system. Some examples of this organism are bacteria, blue-green algae, and spirochetes.

Protista contains a type of eukaryotic cell with a more complex organization system. This kingdom includes diverse, mostly unicellular organisms that live in aquatic habitats, in both freshwater and saltwater. They are not animals or plants but unique organisms. Some examples of Protista are protozoans and algae of various types. The Amoeba, Paramecium, and Euglena are in the Protista Kingdom.

Fungi are multicellular organisms with a sophisticated organization system—that is, containing eukaryotic cells. Fungi exist in a variety of forms and shapes. Because they do not have chlorophyll, they cannot produce food through photosynthesis. Fungi obtain energy, carbon, and water from digesting dead materials. Some examples of these types of organisms are mushrooms, mold, mildews, and yeast.

Plants are multicellular organisms with a sophisticated organization system. In addition to more familiar plants, moss and ferns also fall under this category. Plant cells have chloroplasts, a component that allows them to trap sunlight as energy for the process of photosynthesis. In photosynthesis plants use carbon dioxide from the atmospheric environment and as the by-product of this process, supply the oxygen needed for the survival of animals.

Animals are also multicellular with multiple forms and shapes, and with specialized senses and organs. The Animalia kingdom is composed of organisms like sponges, worms, insects, fish, amphibians, reptiles, birds, and mammals. Animals are the most sophisticated type of living organisms and represent the highest levels of evolution. Animals live in all kinds of habitats, and they are as simple as flies or as sophisticated as humans.

For additional information about living things, go to the website of the Behavioral Sciences Department of Palomar College, San Marcos, California, at *http://anthro.palomar.edu/animal/default.htm*.

Life Cycles

Life traditionally begins with a seed or a fertilized egg, which goes through metamorphosis until the organism is fully formed. The development and growth of organisms can take days, months, or years, but eventually they all go through similar stages: creation, maturation, reproduction, and death. Some organisms, like insects, go through a short cycle, reproducing once and then dying. Others, like vertebrates, spend more time in the reproductive stage. Some examples of living organisms and the changes that they go through are presented in Table 4-4.

Table 4-4. Life Cycles of Common Organisms

Organism	Stage 1	Stage 2	Stage 3	Stage 4	Stage 5
Darkling Beetle	Egg (fertilized by male sperm)	Larva—called "mealworm" though not a true worm	Pupa—mealworm curls up into a pupated or sleeplike state	Darkling Beetle	Reproduction—organisms lay eggs Death of the adult
Butterfly	Egg (fertilized by male sperm)	Larva—called caterpillar	Pupa—caterpillar forms a cocoon or chrysalis	Butterfly	Reproduction—organisms lay eggs Death of the adult
Frog	Egg (fertilized by male sperm)	Embryo	Tadpole	Frog	Reproduction—organism lays eggs Death of the adult
Human	Egg (fertilized by male sperm)	Embryo/Fetus	Child through adolescent	Human adult	Reproduction—organisms have live birth of offspring Death of the adult
Trees	Seed with embryo or "baby plant" inside (egg or ovule inside of flower, ovary fertilized by male sperm, nuclei inside of pollen grains)	Sprout	Growing plant	Mature tree	Reproduction—Tree produces flowers with new seeds that are dispersed Death of the adult

Some of the most spectacular metamorphoses (changes from one stage of life to another) are experienced by insects, amphibians, and humans. Insects, like the Darkling Beetle and the butterfly, go through drastic changes in a period of weeks. Frogs go through similar transmutations that allow them to move from an aquatic environment to land. Humans, on the other hand, begin life as microscopic beings and after nine months develop into a six- to nine-pound physically functional individual. The National Science Education Standards (NSES) and the TEKS emphasize that during the elementary school grades, students should be exposed to the concept of life cycles for plants and animals, including humans.

Life Cycle of Plants

The life cycle of plants generally begins with seeds. Mature plants produce the seeds, which are transported through various means: wind, water, hitchhiking on animals, or ingested as food and released as droppings or waste. For the seeds to germinate, they need air, the right amount of heat or proper temperature specific for that seed, and water. They do not need light to *germinate* or initially sprout, but do need light to grow since they need to carry on photosynthesis for their source of food, and to mature into an adult plant that can reproduce new seeds. Growing plants also need the right kind of soil, sufficient water, and heat/light from the sun. As part of the growth process, plants develop a root system for support and to extract the water and minerals they need from the soil. It is important to understand that fertilizers are *not* food for the plant—they only provide vitamins and minerals for the plant to help it remain healthy. The only food the plant has is what it makes for itself through photosynthesis.

Through the process of **photosynthesis**, a plant containing chlorophyll captures energy from the sun and converts it into chemical energy. Part of the chemical energy is used for the plant's own survival, and the rest is stored in the stem and leaves. As part of the growth process, some plants produce flowers, which are pollinated by insects or through the wind. That is, the pollen, which contains sperm nuclei, is transferred from the male part of the flower, the stamen, to the female part of the flower, the pistil. Once pollination occurs, the sperm leaves the pollen and travels to the ovules or eggs inside the ovary of the pistil and fertilizes the ovules. The fertilized ovules become the seeds. The ovary swells to become the fruit, and the flower itself dies because it has now served its purpose. The fruits contain, carry, and protect the seeds until they are dispersed to a place where they can sprout, and the cycle of the plant continues.

For information on how this process can be presented to children in the elementary school grades, visit the following site: "The Life Cycle of Plants," at *www.cast.org/teachingeverystudent*. For additional information about photosynthesis, visit the following site: "Exploring Photosynthesis," at *www.botany.uwc.ac.za/ecotree/photosynthesis/photosyn-*

thesis1.htm. An inquiry-based curriculum on the life cycle of plants can also be found in the NSTA publication, *Science and Children* by Cavallo (2005) titled, *Cycling Through Plants.*

Life Cycle of Animals

Many animals come from eggs. For some animals, the egg grows inside the female animal and is fertilized by the male, for others such as most fish species, the eggs are fertilized by the male after they have been expelled from the female's body. When fertilized internally, the fertilized egg may be laid externally from the female as in many insects, reptiles, and birds, or it may remain in the body of the female until birth. The egg has an outer lining to protect the animal growing inside. Bird eggs have hard shells, while the eggs of amphibians, like the turtle, have hard but flexible coverings. With the appropriate care and heat, an egg will hatch. After hatching, in some species, the parents protect and feed the newborn until it can survive on its own; in other species, the eggs are left on their own to survive. On reaching adulthood, females begin laying eggs, and the cycle of life continues. Mammals are also conceived through egg fertilization, but the resulting embryo is kept inside the mother until it is mature enough for life outside the womb.

Needs of Living Organisms

Living organisms like plants and animals need to have ideal conditions for their survival. They need nutrients, the appropriate temperature, and a balanced ecosystem to survive and reproduce. A healthy ecosystem must contain an appropriate system for energy exchange or a food chain. The right combination of herbivorous and carnivorous animals is necessary for a healthy ecosystem. The food chain generally begins with the primary source of energy, the sun. The sun provides the energy for plants; plants in turn are consumed by animals; and animals are consumed by other animals. These animals die and serve as food sources for fungi and plants. When this balance is disrupted either by the removal of organisms or the introduction of nonnative species, the ecosystem is affected, forcing animals and plants to adapt or else die. Thus, the common basic needs of all living organisms for survival are: *air, water, food,* and *shelter.*

Body Structure and Function

Cells are the basic unit of all living organisms. Within cells there are specialized organelles that carry on all of the life functions at a microscopic/chemical level. For example, the mitochondria carries on cell respiration, and ribosomes assemble proteins for use both inside the cell and out. Teachers should know the parts of the cell, called organelles, and their functions, particularly, the nucleus, mitochondria, chloroplasts (plants only), ribosomes, Golgi, endoplasmic reticulum, vacuoles, and cell membranes. An explanation of organelles may be found at *www.cellsalive.com/cells/3dcell.htm*.

Moving outward from the *cell*, it is important to know that cells communicate with one another on a chemical level and work together to perform specific functions. The shape of these groups of cells and activity levels differ according to their particular function in the body; for example, muscle cells are long and narrow so they may better respond to stimuli and contract. Groups of cells with similar functions are called *tissues*. Tissues are organized together to perform a specific life function. A complex system of tissues working together to carry on one of the body's life functions is an *organ*. A group of different organs working together to support and help carry out a life function and keep the organism alive is called an *organ system*. Examples of systems include the digestive system, the respiratory system, the immune system, the muscular system, the skeletal system, the nervous system, and the circulatory system. Organ systems are organized into an *organism*. The order of organization is as follows:

Cells → Tissues → Organs → Systems → Organ Systems → Organism

For more information on the structure and function of organisms, see *www.palmbeach. k12.fl.us/MULTICULTURAL/ESOLCurriculumDocs/Secondary/SciOrganism.pdf* .

Systems of the Human Body

Musculoskeletal System

The human skeleton consists of more than 200 bones held together by connective tissues called ligaments. Movements are effected by contractions of the *skeletal muscles*, and skeletal muscles are arranged in pairs, such as the biceps and triceps of the upper arm. When one of the pair contracts, it causes a certain movement of the bones; in the meantime the opposing muscle relaxes. When the opposing pair of muscle contracts, a different movement of the bones occurs, and the original muscle of the pair relaxes. For example, when the biceps (the muscle on top of the upper arm) contracts, the arm bends upwards; when the opposing muscle of the pair, the triceps, contract, the arm extends. Skeletal muscles are attached to bones with specialized connective tissue called tendons.

The specialized connective tissue that attaches bones to other bones is called ligaments. The soft spongy tissue on the ends of bones is called cartilage. Muscular contractions are controlled by the nervous system.

In addition to skeletal muscle, the body also has muscles that are not part of the musculoskeletal system, thus not attached to bones. One such muscle type is called *smooth muscle*. Smooth muscle forms the inner linings of our digestive system and is controlled involuntarily by our autonomic (automatic) nervous system. A third type of muscle is *cardiac muscle*, which is the muscle of the heart, and is also controlled by our autonomic nervous system.

Nervous System

The nervous system has two main divisions: the somatic and automatic. The somatic allows the voluntary control of skeletal muscles, and the automatic, or involuntary, controls cardiac and glandular functions. **Voluntary movement** is caused by nerve impulses sent from the brain through the spinal cord to nerves to connecting skeletal muscles. **Involuntary movement** occurs in direct response to outside stimulus. Involuntary responses are called reflexes. For example, when an object presents danger to the eye, the body responds automatically by blinking or retracting away from the object.

Circulatory System

The circulatory system follows a cyclical process in which the heart pumps blood through the right chambers of the heart and through the lungs, where it acquires oxygen. From there it is pumped back into the left chambers of the heart, where it is pumped into the main artery (aorta), which then sends the oxygenated blood to the rest of the body using a system of veins and capillaries. Through the capillaries, the blood distributes the oxygen and nutrients to tissues, absorbing from them carbon dioxide, a metabolic waste product. Finally, the blood completes the circuit by passing through small veins, which join to form increasingly larger vessels. Eventually, the blood reaches the largest veins, which return it to the right side of the heart to complete and restart the process.

Immune System

The main function of the body's immune system is to defend itself against foreign proteins and infectious organisms. The system recognizes organisms that are not normally in the body and develops the antibodies needed to control and destroy the invaders. When the body is attacked by infectious organisms, it develops what we know as a fever. Fever is the body's way of fighting invading molecules. The raised temperature of a fever will kill some bacteria. The major components of the immune system are the thymus, lymph system, bone marrow, white blood cells, antibodies, and hormones.

Respiratory System

Respiration is carried out by the expansion and contraction of the lungs. In the lungs, oxygen enters tiny capillaries, where it combines with **hemoglobin** in the red blood cells and is carried to the tissues through the circulatory system. At the same time, carbon dioxide passes through capillaries into the air contained within the lungs.

Animals inhale oxygen from the environment and exhale carbon dioxide. Carbon dioxide is used by plants in the process of photosynthesis, which produces the oxygen that animals use again for survival.

Digestive and Excretory Systems

The energy required for sustenance of the human body is supplied through the chemical energy stored in food. To obtain the energy from food, it has to be fragmented and digested. Digestion begins at the moment that food is placed in the mouth and makes contact with saliva. Fragmented and partially digested food passes down the esophagus to the stomach, where the process is continued by the gastric and intestinal juices. Thereafter, the mixture of food and secretions makes its way down the small intestine, where the nutrients are extracted and absorbed into the bloodstream. The unused portion of the food goes to the large intestine and eventually is excreted from the body through defecation. For a detailed analysis of each component of the body system go to the Human Anatomy Online website at *www.innerbody.com/htm/body.html*.

Reproductive System

Students in the upper elementary grades (5 and 6) should know some basic biological facts about human reproduction. They should know that the body matures and develops in order for child-bearing to occur. The menstrual cycle should be understood by students, including what occurs in ovulation to prepare the egg cell, namely, the process of meiosis. In males, the process of meiosis occurs to produce the sperm cell. Students should know that these specialized cells, called gametes (egg and sperm), unite to form a fertilized egg, which grows and develops in distinct stages to produce new offspring.

Competency 035: Life Science

The teacher understands reproduction and the mechanisms of heredity.

Reproduction

An organism may consist of only one cell, or it may comprise many billions of cells of various dimensions. For example, cells are complete organisms, such as the unicellular bacteria; others, such as muscle cells, are parts of multicellular organisms. All cells have an internal substance called cytoplasm—a clear gelatinous fluid—enclosed within a membrane. Each cell contains the genetic material containing the information for the formation of organisms. Cells are composed primarily of water and the elements oxygen, hydrogen, carbon, and nitrogen.

Growth in most organisms is caused by nuclear cell division (**mitosis**.) In mitosis the chromosomes (containing DNA which is the genetic material of the cell or blueprint) first replicate—in humans the 46 chromosomes in the cell double. The cell then divides through a series of steps resulting in 2 new cells that each has the original 46 chromosomes, or the exact copy of the original. Through mitosis, new cells are made, for example, to form a scar after an injury, new bone cells, muscle cells, blood cells, and any cell that is needed by the body throughout life and growth.

However, in single-celled organisms, mitosis is the cell's form of reproduction—making exact copies of the DNA in each of the two "daughter" cells, and is often called binary fission. This type of reproduction is also called **asexual reproduction** because only one organism (the single cell) is involved and there is no exchange of genetic material or DNA. Thus, the two offspring cells, or daughter cells, are identical to the original or parent cell.

In humans and many other organisms, particularly mammals, another form of cell division occurs only in the reproductive organs (in most called the female ovaries and male testicles) where the DNA is replicated/copied; however, the cell divides *twice* in a process called **meiosis**. Meiosis is how sperm and egg cells are formed through a series of steps. The original cell in the female ovary or male testicle first duplicates (replicates) its 46 chromosomes (containing the genetic blueprint material, DNA) and then divides *twice,* the result is four cells with half the number of chromosomes, or 23 chromosomes each. In forming the egg cell, only one is a viable egg that can be fertilized and the remaining three are polar bodies that eventually dissolve. In the male, all four sperm cells that were formed by meiosis of the original cell are viable and capable of fertilizing the egg. The process is similar in other organisms; however, the number of chromosomes may be different, depending on the particular species—a similar process even occurs in plants, where the flower is the reproductive organ—the ovules are the egg cells, and the pollen contains the sperm. This form of reproduction is known as **sexual reproduction**, because it requires the combination of DNA between two organisms of the same species (male, female). The fertilization of the egg by sperm cells occurs through copulation in vertebrates, and for fish and some amphibians it occurs through cross-fertilization. Cross-fertilization occurs outside the body; the female lays the eggs (ovum), and the males spray them with sperm to fertilize them.

Plant Reproduction

The reproduction of plants can also be divided into asexual and sexual mechanisms. Asexual reproduction of plants takes place by cutting portions of the plant and replanting them. Sexual reproduction involves seeds produced by female and male plants, which are then cross-pollinated with help from insects or other animals. As mentioned, the flower is the reproductive organ of the plant. The flower consists of several parts that are the male and female reproductive organs. Some flowers may have only the male part, and likewise, some flowers contain only the female part of the same species of plant/tree. So there actually can be a "male" tree and a "female" tree for example. In the flower, the male reproductive organ is the stamen, which is divided into filament and anther. The filament simply holds up the anther, and the anther contains the pollen and in the pollen are the sperm nuclei. Flowers may also contain the female reproductive organ, or pistil, which consists of the ovary, style, and stigma. The ovary contains the egg cells, which in the flower are called ovules. The style is the tube above the ovary, and the stigma is the top of the style which has a sticky substance. The pollen needs to either be manually placed on the stigma, or blown there by the wind, or what usually happens, it needs to stick to the body of a bee or butterfly (who are actually in search of sugary nectar in the flower and not the pollen). When the pollen sticks to the body of the insect, it may then be transferred from the anther (male part) to the stigma (female part). In essence, the sperm nuclei then travel down the style until it reaches the ovules, where fertilization occurs. The fertilized egg then becomes the seed. The ovary of the flower may swell and become the fruit (as in a peach or apple). This process helps protect the seeds and also helps with seed dispersal (animals eat the fruit, the seed has a seed coat that protects it and is indigestible, the animals excretes the seed, unharmed, in its fecal matter). Seed germination—where the seed sprouts into a plant—requires the appropriate quantity of air, water, and heat.

Hereditary Material

Deoxyribonucleic acid or *DNA* is the hereditary material of living organisms. DNA has as its smallest complete component what is called a nucleotide. A single nucleotide consists of the sugar deoxyribose, a phosphate molecule, and a nitrogen base molecule. There are four nitrogen bases that are paired in the double-helix structure of DNA. These nitrogen bases are adenine, thymine, guanine, and cytosine. In DNA, adenine always pairs with a nucleotide having thymine as its nitrogen base (A-T); and guanine always pairs with a nucleotide having cytosine as its nitrogen base (G-C), and vice versa (T-A; C-G)

In bacteria, also called monera or prokaryotic cells, DNA is in a single strand. In more complex organisms including protista, fungi, animals and plants, all eukaryotic cells, the DNA is arranged in *chromosomes*, and these chromosomes with its DNA are located in the nucleus (though there is new evidence of DNA in other cell organelles, particularly the mitochondria). The number of chromosomes in the cells of organisms varies from one species to another—but it is the same for all members of that species. Along the strands of DNA that exist inside of chromosomes, there are certain locations that direct specific functions of cells, including hereditary traits, called *genes*. Certain genes give the cell directions, in the developing embryo for example, for the expression of traits such as eye color, hair color, and leg shape and size. In already developed organisms, as the human adult, other genes (sections of DNA) direct the production of substances and control specific activities and functions. The production of insulin in pancreatic cells, for example, is controlled by certain genes in the chromosomes in the cells of the organ known as the pancreas. In inheritance and cell functions, traits can be controlled or determined by more than one gene, located on the same, or even on different chromosomes. Likewise, there may be several traits influenced by one single gene.

As discussed earlier, the fertilized egg that eventually grows into the organism that then goes through its respective life cycle to adult contains half the number of chromosomes from the female egg (mother) and half the number of chromosomes from the male sperm (father). In the human, there are 23 chromosomes in the egg and 23 in the sperm, so the fertilized egg and, therefore, the offspring (baby) has 46 chromosomes—which is the normal number for all cells in all organisms of the human species. The 23 chromosomes of the egg have an exact pair or match in the sperm. That matching chromosome contains genes with DNA that direct the same traits. So along the length of chromosome number 20, for example, in the egg cell, you will find it controls the same traits that are along the length of chromosome number 20 in the male sperm. However, the 23 chromosomes in the egg contain the specific qualities or characteristics of the mother; whereas, the 23 chromosomes in the sperm contain the specific qualities or characters of the father. Though more than one chromosome controls eye color—we will use one chromosome as an example. In one of the egg cell's chromosomes, there is a gene that controls eye color, and in the egg this eye color could be "blue." In the same number chromosome in the same location in the sperm cell, there will also be a gene for eye color, but the characteristic of that eye color may instead be "brown." So traits are located on the same number chromosome whether that chromosome originated from the egg or the sperm; however, the quality or characteristic may differ (that is, the pigment color that section of DNA or gene directs the cell to make). The gene for eye color and other traits that are the paired chromosomes in the same location are called *alleles*. When the egg is fertilized, the directions coded in the DNA alleles are set. In many alleles, one of the traits directed by the gene on one chromosome is **dominant**, and the other is **recessive**. The dominant trait is the one that typically "shows" or is *expressed* in the offspring. In the case of eye color, brown is usually dominant over blue eye color, so if one of the alleles is for "blue" eyes and the other allele from the other parent is for "brown" eyes, the offspring will show the dominant trait and have brown eyes. Again, it must be cautioned that many genes may direct eye color especially in an organism as complex as humans, but it is simply used as an example here. In addition, it is important to note that **environmental factors** play an important role in the expression (showing up) of traits in the offspring as they grow and develop. Sometimes environmental stressors, for example, can cause a genetic change in an organism that otherwise may not have been expressed, such as certain food allergies or intolerances.

For more genetics information and activities go to *www.kidsturncentral.com/links/geneticslinks.htm*

Competency 036: Life Science

The teacher understands adaptations of organisms and theory of evolution.

Adaptations and Change over Time

Genetics plays an important role in the ability of organisms to be able to survive and thrive in their environment and, ultimately, produce new offspring where they can pass on similar genetic material, like that which allowed *them* to survive and thrive, and maybe survive and thrive even better. Some inherited traits, called *adaptations,* allow the organisms to best survive in their environment and others do not, and may even lead to their demise (and those prevent the prospect of future offspring). Adaptations do not suddenly arise or develop in the lifetime of organisms. They occur gradually in the species over time. For example, if a certain deer-like animal thousands of years ago was particularly fast—that is, it was born with stronger muscle tissue than most, and a better bone and muscle physical structure—perhaps it was better able to run away from predators and survive. Therefore, this deer-like animal was able to survive long enough for it to have offspring with similar genetic material. At the same time, those deer-like animals that were not born with the same muscular and structural soundness as this one were killed as prey before they could reproduce. The animal that was best adapted to its environment (needing to run from predators) was the first deer-like animal. In time, those animals that are best suited in this, as well as in other ways, are the organisms who survive, as do their offspring. Those not well adapted perish. It is also the case that the organism that survives will breed with another that also has better adapted characteristics, and was also able to survive in the natural environment. A change or **mutation** in the genetic material, that is, the genes that direct the development of a trait, may give rise to a new characteristic that either is or is not better suited for the environment. In the case that it is better suited, the organism will survive and produce offspring with this same mutation. Over the years, mutations that are better suited to the environment may make the organism appear quite different than it did hundreds, thousands, and millions of years earlier. If the environment itself changes, however, organisms that were able to survive under the previous conditions (climate, water supply, vegetation, landscape) may be unable to survive in the new environmental conditions. Thus, a catastrophic event, such as perhaps a large asteroid striking the earth, could change the environmental conditions and either lead to the extinction of organisms, or the survival of organisms that would not have survived under the conditions before the strike. Likewise, selective breeding, which is human selection of which organisms breed with another, and thus, control of the genetic material that is passed onto offspring, also effects the change over time of organisms. The combination of genetics, adaptations, changes over time, mutations, selective breeding, and environmental conditions/changes contribute to the concept known as evolution.

Competency 037: Life Science

The teacher understands the relationships between organisms and the environment.

Ecology

Ecology studies the relationship of organisms with their physical environment. The physical environment includes light, heat, solar radiation, moisture, wind, oxygen, carbon dioxide, nutrients, water, and the atmosphere. The biological environment describes living and nonliving organisms in the ecosystem. There are three main components of an ecosystem:

- **Producers** are green plants that produce oxygen and store chemical energy for consumers.

- **Consumers** are animals, both herbivores and carnivores. The herbivores take the chemical energy from plants, and carnivores take the energy from other animals or directly from plants.

- **Decomposers**, like fungi and bacteria, are in charge of cleaning up the environment by decomposing and freeing dead matter for recycling back into the ecosystem.

Maintaining a Healthy Balance

A successful ecosystem requires a healthy balance among producers, consumers, and decomposers. This balance relies on natural ways to control populations of living organisms and is maintained mostly through competition and predation.

Competition

When a shared resource is scarce, organisms must compete to survive. The competition, which occurs between animals as well as between plants, ensures the survival of the fittest and the preservation of the system.

Predation

Predation is the consumption of one living organism, plant or animal, by another. It is a direct way to control population and promote natural selection by eliminating weak organisms from the population. As a consequence of predation, predators and prey evolve to survive. If an organism cannot evolve to meet challenges from the environment, it perishes.

Adaptation for Survival

Changes in the environment force living organisms to modify their ways and even develop new physical features for survival. For example, over thousands of years, the anteater species and its offspring were able to survive better if they had a long snout to be able to reach for ants, and frogs developed a long, sticky tongue to catch flies. Adaptation for animals, plants, and even humans is a matter of life and death. Changes in the food chain of animals often force them to change their behaviors and adapt to new conditions.

For example, because their habitats are destroyed when land is developed by humans, raccoons and opossums have learned to coexist with humans and to get new sources of food. Bears have managed to successfully adapt to colder climates by hibernating during the winter and living on the fat they accumulate during the rest of the year. Other animals, like the chameleon or the fox, have developed camouflage to hide from predators. Humans are not exempt from the need to adapt to new situations. For example, humans have had to adapt and use tools to produce, preserve, and trade the food supplies they needed to sustain them. All these examples represent ways in which organisms adapt to deal with challenges in their ecosystem.

Key Principles of the Life Science Competencies 034–037

- When working with animals, teachers are ethically responsible for their well-being. Teachers need to provide an adequate environment for the survival and development of animals under their care.

- By observing the development of frogs and butterflies, students directly acquire information on the life cycles. Students can also observe how organisms adapt to their environment.

- Fungi obtain energy, carbon, and water from dead material. Fungi do not have chlorophyll, so they cannot produce food through photosynthesis.

- Chromosomes contain the genetic code, or DNA.

- Mitosis describes the process of a cell splitting to create two identical cells.

- Meiosis is the process of cells dividing to produce the egg and sperm cells, each with half the number of chromosomes as the parent cell so they are ready to restore the normal number of the species upon fertilization.

- Photosynthesis is the process of capturing, storing, and converting solar energy. It is also the source of oxygen in the atmosphere.

- Insects have three main parts: head, thorax, and abdomen.

- Humans have several body systems, including the musculoskeletal, nervous, circulatory, immune, respiratory, and digestive/excretory systems.

- Adaptations are features or characteristics of an organism that best help it survive in its environment.

- Organisms in the environment depend upon one another for survival and are inextricably linked in the ecosystem.

Competency 038: Earth and Space Science

The teacher understands the structure and function of earth systems.

Structure and Composition of the Earth (Geology)

Landform Characteristics

The formation of deserts, mountains, rivers, oceans, and other landforms can be described in terms of geological processes. Mountains are formed by colliding plates. For example, the Appalachian Mountains in the United States were formed 250 million years ago when the tectonic plate carrying the continent of Africa collided with the plate carrying the North American continent (Badder et. al. 2000). Rivers and natural lakes form at low elevations where rainfall collects and eventually runs down to the sea. The sediment gathered by the rivers in turn accumulates at river mouths to create deltas. These are both constructive and destructive processes that form the earth. Constructive processes include those that build mountains, such as the gradual (over millions of years) collision and crushing together of the earth's tectonic plates. Destructive processes include weathering and erosion—the wearing down of mountains and rock by forces such as water, wind, and ice. For more information on these processes, go to *www.edu.pe.ca/southernkings/face.htm.*

Layers of the Earth

The average circumference of the Earth at the equator is 25,902 miles, and its radius is about 3,959 miles. The Earth is divided into three main parts:

- The **crust** is the outer portion of the Earth where we live. The thickness of the crust varies from about 3 miles to 40 miles, depending on the location. It contains various types of soil, metals, and rocks. The crust is broken down into several floating tectonic plates. Movements of these plates cause earthquakes and changes in landforms.

- The **mantle** is the thickest layer of the Earth located right below the crust. It is composed mostly of rocks and metals. The heat in the mantle is so intense that rocks and metals melt, creating magma and the resulting lava that reaches the surface.

- The **core** is the inner part of the Earth. It is composed of a solid **inner core** and an **outer core** that is mostly liquid. The inner core is made of solid iron and nickel. Despite temperatures in the inner core that resemble the heat on the surface of the sun, this portion of the Earth remains solid because of the intense pressure there.

- For more information about the layers of the earth, go to the following website: *http://scign.jpl.nasa.gov/learn/plate1.htm.*

Continental Drift

In 1915, the German scientist Alfred Weneger proposed that all the continents were previously one large continent but then broke apart and drifted through the ocean floor to their present locations. This theory was called the Continental Drift, and it was the origin of today's concept of plate tectonics.

Tectonic Plates

Based on the theory of plate tectonics, the surface of the Earth is fragmented into large plates. These plates are in continuous motion, floating on the liquid mantel and always changing in size and position. The edges of these plates, where they move against each other, are sites of intense geologic activity, which results in earthquakes, volcanoes, and the creation of mountains. The generator for the movement of the continents/Earth's plates is the mid-Atlantic ridge—a huge volcanic mountain range on the floor of the Atlantic Ocean that is continuously erupting and pushing the plates apart in opposite directions from each other. For more information go to *pubs.usgs.gov/gip/dynamic/understanding.html#anchor5567033*.

Forces That Change the Surface of the Earth

Three main forces and processes change the surface of the Earth: weathering, geological movements, and the creation of glaciers.

Weathering

Weathering is the process of breaking down rock, soils, and minerals through natural, chemical, and biological processes. Two of the most common examples of physical weathering are exfoliation and freeze thaw.

- **Exfoliation** occurs in places like the desert when the soil is exposed first to high temperatures, which cause it to expand, and then to cold temperatures, which make the soil contract. The stress of these changes causes the outer layers of rock to peel off.

- **Freeze-thaw** breaks down rock when water gets into rock joints or cracks and then freezes and expands, breaking the rock. A similar process occurs when water containing salt crystals gets into the rock. Once the water evaporates, the crystals expand and break the rock. This process is called salt-crystal growth.

Weathering can be caused by chemical reactions. Two of the most common examples of chemical weathering are acid formation and hydration. Acid is formed under various conditions. For example, sulfur and rain are combined to create acid rain, which can weather and change the chemical composition of rock. Hydration occurs when the minerals in rock absorb water and expand sometimes changing the chemical composition of the rock. For example, through the process of hydration, a mineral like anhydrite can be changed into a different mineral, namely gypsum.

Erosion

After weathering, a second process called erosion can take place. **Erosion** is the movement of sediment from one location to the other through the use of water, wind, ice, or gravity. The Grand Canyon was created by the processes of weathering and erosion. The water movement (erosion) is responsible for the canyon being so deep, and the weathering process is responsible for its width (Badder et al. 2000).

Earthquakes and Geologic Faults

The movement of the Earth's plates has forced rock layers to fold, creating mountains, hills, and valleys. This movement causes **faults** in the Earth's crust, breaking rocks and reshaping the environment. When forces within the Earth cause rocks to break and move around geologic faults, earthquakes occur. A fault is a deep crack that marks the boundary between two plates. The San Andreas fault in central California is a well-known origin of earthquakes in the area. The epicenter of an earthquake is the point on the surface where the quake is the strongest. The **Richter scale** is used to measure the amount of energy released by the earthquake. The severity of an earthquake runs from 0 to 9 on the Richter scale. Small tremors occur constantly, but every few months, a major earthquake occurs somewhere in the world. Scientists are researching ways to predict earthquakes, but their predictions are not always accurate.

Volcanoes

Volcanoes are formed by the constant motion of tectonic plates. This movement creates pressure that forces magma from the mantel to escape to the surface, creating an explosion of lava, fire, and ash. The pressure of the magma and gases creates a monticule, or a small cone, that eventually grows to form a mountain-like volcano. Volcanic activity can create earthquakes, and the fiery lava can cause destruction.

Gravity

Gravity is the force of attraction that exists between objects. Gravity keeps the Earth in its orbit by establishing a balance between the attraction of the sun and the speed at which the Earth travels around it. However, gravity is also responsible for many of the Earth's forces that change the land. For example, when ice melts on the tops of mountains, it is because of gravity that the water will form streams and rivers that flow down the mountain, eventually making its way to the lowest point. Some of the main functions of gravity are listed here:

- Keeping the Earth's atmosphere, oceans, and inhabitants from drifting into space

- Pulling the rain to the rivers and eventually to the sea

- Guiding the development and growth of plants

- Affecting the way that our bones and muscles function

For information about the Earth and space, go to the official website of the National Aeronautics and Space Administration (NASA) at *www.nasa.gov/home/index. html?skipIntro=1*. This site includes special sections for children, students from kindergarten through grade 12, and teachers.

Surface Water and Groundwater

Surface water is the water in streams, lakes and rivers, and all water that is on the surface of the land. Ground water is water that seeps beneath the surface of the land and forms an underground "river" of water. The groundwater seeps into the soil until it reaches an impermeable layer of rock. The water stays on top of this layer and is a source of drinking water. This water may be tapped into via aquifers and wells. For more information, see *http://ga.water.usgs.gov/edu/earthgw.html*.

The Earth's Atmosphere

The Earth is surrounded by a large mass of gas called the atmosphere. Roughly 348 miles thick, this gas mass supports life on the Earth and separates it from space. Among the many functions of the atmosphere are these:

- Absorbing energy from the sun to sustain life

- Recycling water and other chemicals needed for life

- Maintaining the climate, working with electric and magnetic forces

- Serving as a vacuum that protects life

The atmosphere is composed of 78 percent nitrogen, 21 percent oxygen, and 1 percent argon. In addition to these gases, the atmosphere contains water, greenhouse gases like ozone, and carbon dioxide. The Earth's atmosphere has five layers. The layer closest to the Earth is called the troposphere, and the weather we experience occurs in this layer. For more information on the atmosphere, go to *www.windows.ucar.edu/tour/link=/earth/ Atmosphere/layers.html&fr=t%20t*.

Natural and Human Influences on Earth Systems

It is important to understand that many natural processes on Earth can change its systems. For example, earthquakes and volcanoes can be destructive and change the structure and composition of the landscape. Tsunamis, an enormous wall of water that crashes into shorelines caused by earthquakes under bodies of water such as oceans, can create a dramatic change in that shoreline. However, human influences may also change Earth systems. The destruction of the rainforests, called deforestation can change the structure and composition of the land, and on a larger scale, affect the balance of atmospheric gases including carbon dioxide and oxygen levels. Carbon dioxide emissions from factories, automobiles, and airplanes, as examples, may play a role in changing the atmospheric composition as well. Carbon dioxide, called a "greenhouse gas" tends to trap heat energy and result in an overall warming of the atmosphere, which has an impact on climate and plant growth that in turn affects all living organisms on Earth. There are many natural and human influences that contribute to the increase of greenhouse gases in the atmosphere producing what is known as "global warming." Other greenhouse gases include methane (CH_4) and ozone, which is the molecule O_3, that when at the surface of the Earth are components of smog.

It is important to distinguish global warming and the ozone that is in smog from the destruction of the ozone layer (hole in the ozone layer) which is a different phenomenon. Ozone forms a layer at the top of the atmosphere that blocks harmful ultraviolet rays from the sun from reaching the Earth's surface ("good ozone"). The "hole" in the ozone layer means there is a destruction of this ozone layer, and now harmful ultraviolet radiation is reaching Earth's surface where this hole is present. Chlorofluorocarbons, which are found in aerosols, contribute to the destruction of the ozone layer. For more information on greenhouse gases and ozone, go to *http://hvo.wr.usgs. gov/volcanowatch/2005/05_07_28.html*.

Competency 039: Earth and Space Science

The teacher understands cycles in Earth systems.

Rock Types

The hard, solid part of the Earth's surface is called rock. Rocks are made of one or more minerals. Rocks like granite, marble, and limestone are extensively used in the construction industry. They can be used in floors, buildings, dams, highways, or the making of cement. Rocks are classified by the way they are formed. Here are descriptions of the three types of rock:

- **Igneous** rocks are crystalline solids that form directly from the cooling of magma or lava. The composition of the magma determines the composition of the rock. **Granite** is one of the most common types of igneous rocks and is created from magma (inside the Earth). Once magma reaches the Earth's surface, it is called lava. Lava that has cooled forms a rock with a glassy look, called **obsidian**.

- **Sedimentary** rocks are called secondary rocks because they are often the result of the accumulation of small pieces broken off from preexisting rocks and then pressed into a new form. There are three types of sedimentary rocks:

  ○ **Clastic** sedimentary rocks are made when pieces of rock, mineral, and organic material fuse together. These are classified as conglomerates, sandstone, and shale.

  ○ **Chemical** sedimentary rocks are formed when water rich in minerals evaporates, leaving the minerals behind. Some common examples are gypsum, rock salt, and some limestone.

  ○ **Organic** sedimentary rocks are made from the remains of plants and animals. For example, coal is formed when dead plants are squeezed together. Another example is a form of limestone rock composed of the remains of organisms that lived in the ocean.

- **Metamorphic** rocks are also secondary rocks formed from igneous, sedimentary, or other types of metamorphic rock. When hot magma or lava comes in contact with rocks or when buried rocks are exposed to pressure and high temperatures, the result is metamorphic rocks. For example, exposing limestone to high temperatures creates marble. The most common metamorphic rocks are slate, gneiss,

and marble. For more information, go to *http://jersey.uoregon.edu/*
~mstrick/AskGeoMan/geoQuerry13.html.

Rock Cycle

The formation of rock follows a cyclical process. For instance, rocks can be formed when magma or lava cools down, creating igneous rocks. Igneous rocks exposed to weathering can break into sediment, which can be compacted and cemented to form sedimentary rocks. Sedimentary rocks are exposed to heat and pressure to create metamorphic rocks. Finally, metamorphic rocks can melt and become magma and lava again (Badder et al. 2000). An illustration of the rock cycle and forces causing the changes in rock can be found at *www.classzone.com/books/earth_science/terc/content/investigations/ es0602/es0602page02.cfm*.

Minerals

Minerals are the most common form of solid material found in the Earth's crust. Even soil contains bits of minerals that have broken away from rock. To be considered a mineral, a substance must be found in nature and must never have been a part of any living organism. Minerals can be as soft as talc or as hard as emeralds and diamonds. Dug from the Earth, minerals are used to make various products:

- **Jewelry**—Gemstones such as amethysts, opals, diamonds, emeralds, topazes, and garnets are examples of minerals commonly used to create jewelry. Gold and silver are another type of mineral that can be used to create jewelry.

- **Construction**—Gypsum boards (drywall) are made of a mineral of the same name—gypsum. The windows in homes are made from another mineral, quartz.

- **Personal Use**—Talc is the softest mineral and it is commonly applied to the body in powder form.

Water Cycle

The hydrologic cycle describes a series of movements of water above, on, and below the surface of the Earth. This cycle consists of four distinct stages: storage, evaporation, precipitation, and runoff. It is the means by which the sun's energy is used to transport, through the atmosphere, stored water from the rivers and oceans to land masses. The heat of the sun evaporates the water and takes it to the atmosphere from which, through condensation, it falls as precipitation. As precipitation falls, water is filtrated back to underground water deposits called aquifers, or it runs off into storage in lakes, ponds, and oceans.

Tides

The word *tides* is used to describe the alternating rise and fall in sea level with respect to the land, produced by the gravitational attraction of the moon and the sun. Additional factors such as the configuration of the coastline, depth of the water, the topography of the ocean floor, and other hydrographic and meteorological influences may play an important role in altering the range, interval, and times of the arrival of the tides.

Nutrient Cycles

Nutrient cycles include the carbon and nitrogen cycle. The **carbon cycle** is the capture of carbon from carbon dioxide in the atmosphere by plants to make glucose. When this glucose is used as food for the plant or other organisms, it is digested, then by respiration, broken apart again into carbon dioxide and returned back to the atmosphere. The process continues in a life sustaining process. More information on the carbon cycle can be found at *www.ucar.edu/learn/1_4_2_15t.htm*.

For the **nitrogen cycle** it is important to recognize that most of the air we breathe is nitrogen, but it is not useful to us in that form, so it is exhaled. Lightning causes nitrogen in the air to combine with oxygen. Certain bacteria that live on the roots of certain plants, called nitrogen-fixing bacteria, are able to take nitrogen in this combined form with oxygen and make it available for use by plants. The plants can incorporate the nitrogen into their plant structure, and when eaten by animals and other organisms, this nitrogen becomes available for use. The nitrogen returns to the soil when the plant or other living organism dies and decays, releasing nitrogen gas back into the atmosphere. Nitrogen is important to all living things because it is a major component of DNA, RNA, and amino acids, which are the building blocks of proteins. A good animation of the nitrogen cycle is found at *www.classzone.com/books/ml_science_share/vis_sim/em05_pg20_nitrogen/ em05_pg20_nitrogen.html*, and further explanation is located at *http://eo.ucar.edu/kids/ green/cycles7.htm*.

Competency 040: Earth and Space Science

The teacher understands the role of energy in weather and climate.

Weather

The elements of weather include interactions between wind, water (precipitation), wind speed and direction, air pressure, humidity, and temperature. Wind is caused by air masses that have different amounts of heat (temperatures), where there may be a warm air mass that is moving toward a cold air mass for example. Air pressure is related to both the amount of water in the air mass and its temperature (heat content), in that warm air has higher pressure than cold air—warm, high pressure air masses move toward cold, low pressure air masses. One simple rule is that energy always moves from *warmer to colder*. So, if you open a window on a hot summer day when your air conditioning is on, the cold does *not go out*—the warm air comes in. The same is true on a larger scale with warm and cold air masses.

Humidity is a measure of the percentage of water that is in the air. Dew point is the temperature at which the air needs to be for the water to condense out of the air in liquid form as precipitation; or it may be observed as "dew." In other words, air has a certain amount of water vapor (water in the gas state) in it (the percent is measured as humidity). That water vapor will turn to liquid water as temperatures drop overnight, in which we observe dew, or when a cold front moves in that lowers the temperature, which can result in a rain or snow storm. For resources and information on weather, go to the National Weather Service education website at *www.nws.noaa.gov/os/edures.shtml*.

Wind is measured by an instrument called an *anemometer*. Air pressure is measured by a *barometer*; *rain gauges* and other instruments measure precipitation. Temperature is measured by a *thermometer*. Relative humidity is measured by a *psychrometer*. For more information on these instruments, see *http://schoolscience.rice.edu/duker/winstruments.html*.

Climate

Weather is the conditions of the atmosphere at a given, relatively short period of time. Climate, however, is the weather conditions in an area on a continuous, seasonal basis. The climate is more complex and can be measured by the average variety of weather conditions, such as temperature and precipitation, that occur seasonally in that geographic region of the world over a long period of time. More information, including the contrast between weather and climate, can be found at *www.nasa.gov/mission_pages/noaa-n/climate/climate_weather.html.*

Predicting Weather

Weather can be predicted by tracking weather patterns using maps and charts. These maps have special symbols that indicate, for example, warm and cold air masses, air pressure, and relative humidity in a region. By knowing how air behaves, such as cold air goes down and warm air rises, warmer air always moves toward colder air, and high pressure always moves outward toward lower pressure, we can track the weather and make predictions. Clouds are also an indication of the type of weather occurring in an area. For a summary of predicting weather as well as a description of cloud types, see *www.ussartf.org/predicting_weather.htm.*

Interpreting weather maps is an important skill for weather prediction. The symbols and their meanings can be found at *http://eo.ucar.edu/webweather/forecasttips.html.*

The Earth's Surface and Position as a Factor in Weather and Climate

The Earth's surface is primarily water, and bodies of water affect the weather and climate of an area. Water has a high specific heat, which means that it takes longer to take in heat and longer to release the heat it has absorbed than any other material on Earth. Therefore, coastal areas tend to be warmer than areas inland or away from water, because the water moderates the temperature, even if the locations are at the same latitude. In the U.S., for example, areas in the middle of the country will have greater extreme differences in the cold temperatures in the winter and warm temperatures in the summer compared to a location at the same latitude near the ocean.

Large lakes, such as the Great Lakes also create a situation called "lake effect" in the winter—the air over the lake is relatively warm, and so can carry water vapor (evaporation). As soon as that air carrying water moves over land, however, it rapidly cools and releases its water (precipitation) in the form of snow over the land. Mountains and other landforms also have an effect on the weather. When air holding water hits a mountain side, it is forced upward which makes the air cool and therefore rain (or snow) on that side of the mountain. This is typically the western side of the mountain in the U.S. as in the mountain ranges of the Rocky Mountains. Once the precipitation is gone from that air mass and the air mass crosses the mountain to the other side, it drops back down and warms, but now it is dry air and so may result in an arid region or desert. The Gobi Desert of the U.S. is a result of this phenomenon.

On a much larger scale, the tilt of the Earth itself—as a planet—is responsible for weather and climate. The Earth is on a 23° tilt on its axis in space. This tilt means the Earth's North Pole is pointed *away* from the sun when it is in one location in its orbit (path around the sun), and *toward* the sun when it is in the opposite orbital location. This tilt of the Earth results in the seasons, with extreme changes being in locations closer to the North and South poles. See more information on this topic at *www.windows.ucar.edu/ tour/link=/earth/climate/cli_seasons.html.*

Competency 041: Earth and Space Science

The teacher understands the characteristics of the solar system and the universe.

Properties and Characteristics of Objects in the Sky

Galaxies

Galaxies are large collections of stars, hydrogen, dust particles, and other gases. The universe is made of countless galaxies. The solar system that includes Earth is part of a galaxy called the Milky Way.

Stars

Stars like the sun are composed of large masses of hydrogen pulled together by gravity. The hydrogen, with strong gravitational pressure, creates fusion inside the star, turning the hydrogen into helium. The liberation of energy created by this process causes solar radiation, which makes the sun glow with visible light, as well as forms of radiation not visible to the human eye.

The Earth-Sun-Moon System

Movements of Planet Earth

Earth performs two kinds of movement: rotation and revolution. **Rotation** describes the spinning of Earth on its axis. Earth takes approximately 24 hours to make a complete (360°) rotation, which creates day and night.

While Earth is rotating on its axis, it is also following an orbit around the sun. This movement is called **revolution**. It takes a year, or 365¼ days, for Earth to complete one revolution. The tilt of Earth as it moves around the sun and its curvature create **climate zones** and seasons. The zones immediately north and south of the equator are called the tropics—Cancer (north) and Capricorn (south). The Arctic Circle (North Pole) and Antarctic Circle (South Pole) are the area surrounding Earth's axis points. Latitude lines are imaginary horizontal lines around the Earth, and longitude lines are likewise vertical lines around the Earth from the North to the South Poles. These lines form a grid that helps us locate positions on Earth according to the locations specific latitude and longitude.

Phases of the Moon

During each lunar orbit around Earth (about 28 days), the moon appears to go through several stages based on the portion of the moon visible from Earth. The moon does not have its own source of light but reflects the light from the sun. The shape of the moon varies from a full moon, when Earth is between the sun and the moon, to a new moon, when the moon is located between the sun and Earth. A description of the major stages of the moon follows:

- **New Moon**—The moon is not visible to Earth because the side of the moon facing Earth is not being lit by the sun.

- **Crescent Moon**—At this stage between the half moon and the new moon, the shape of the moon is often compared to a banana.

- **Half Moon, or First Quarter**—During this stage, half of the moon is visible.

- **Gibbous Moon**—In this stage, about three quarters of the moon is visible.

- **Full Moon**—The whole moon is visible from Earth.

The term **blue moon** describes the appearance of two full moons in a single calendar month. The expression "once in a blue moon" represents an event that is not very frequent.

Components of Our Solar System

Solar System

The sun is the center of our solar system, which is composed of nine planets, many satellites that orbit the planets, and a large number of smaller bodies like comets and asteroids. Short definitions of these terms follow:

- Planets are large bodies orbiting the sun.

- Dwarf planets are small bodies orbiting the sun. For further distinction between planets and dwarf planets, see *www.windows.ucar.edu/ tour/link=/our_solar_system/dwarf_planets/dwarf_planets.html*.

- Satellites are moons orbiting the planets. Our planet has one moon whereas other planets may have no moons (Mercury, Venus), or many moons (Jupiter, Saturn).

- Asteroids are small dense objects or rocks orbiting our star, the sun. The Asteroid Belt of our own solar system is located between Mars and Jupiter. Some theorize that the asteroids could be the remains of an exploded planet.

- Meteoroids are fragments of rock in space, most originating from the debris left behind by comets that burn up/vaporize upon entering Earth's atmosphere due to friction from the air molecules.

- Comets are small icy objects traveling through space in an elongated, elliptical orbit around the sun.

Planets

The objects in our solar system revolve around our star, which we call the sun. The **inner** solar system contains the planets Mercury, Venus, Earth, and Mars, in this order. The **outer** solar system comprises the planets Jupiter, Saturn, Uranus, and Neptune, and a number of dwarf planets, including Pluto, Ceres, Eris and others, with likely more yet to be found (see Table 4-5). More information about our solar system can be found at *http:// starchild.gsfc.nasa.gov/docs/StarChild/StarChild.html*.

Table 4-5. Planets and Dwarf Planets of our Solar System

Inner Planets	Mercury Venus Earth Mars
Outer Planets	Jupiter Saturn Uranus Neptune
Dwarf Planets	Pluto Ceres Eris Haumea Makemake

┌─ **Key Principles of the Earth Science Competencies 038–041** ─┐

- Our solar system is part of the Milky Way, one of many galaxies in the universe.

- Minerals and rocks are commonly used in our daily life.

- The movement of tectonic plates creates intense geologic activity that results in earthquakes and volcanic activity.

- The Earth's atmosphere protects and preserves life

- The water cycles are the movement and distribution of water within the Earth's atmosphere.

- The tilt of the Earth causes the seasons, and not the distance it is in its orbit away from the sun.

- Human activities as well as natural processes impact the landscape and processes on Earth.

- Weather is the interaction of many factors, including air temperature, air pressure, and humidity. Weather is the conditions in the atmosphere at a given location and time.

- The solar system consists of the sun, inner planets, outer planets, dwarf planets, satellites, asteroids, comets and meteoroids.

└──┘

References

American Association for the Advancement of Science. 1989. *Science for All Americans: A Project 2061 Report on Literacy Goals in Science, Mathematics, and Technology.* Washington, DC.

Anderson, L. W., D. R. Krathwohl, et al. Eds. 2001. *A Taxonomy for Learning, Teaching, and Assessing: A Revision of Bloom's Taxonomy of Educational Objectives.* Boston, MA: Allyn & Bacon (Pearson Education Group)

Badder, W., D. Peck, L. J. Bethel, C. Sumner, V. Fu, and C. Valentino. 2000. *Discovery works.* (Texas ed.). Boston: Houghton Mifflin.

Bloom, B. S. and D. R. Krathwohl. 1956. *Taxonomy of Educational Objectives: The Classification of Educational Goals, by a committee of college and university examiners. Handbook I: Cognitive Domain.* NY, NY: Longmans, Green

Bybee, R., Buchwald, C.E., Crissman, S. Heil, D., Kuerbis, P., Matsumoto, C. & McInerney 1989. *Science and Technology Education for Elementary Years: Frameworks for Curriculum and Instruction.* Washington, DC: The National Center for Improving Science Education.

Cavallo, A.M.L. 2005. Cycling through plants. *Science and Children, 4,* 22–27.

Cavallo, A.M.L. 2001. Convection connections: Integrated learning cycle investigations that explore convection—the science behind wind and waves. *Science and Children, 38,* 20–25.

Full Option Science System (FOSS). 2000. Lawrence Hall of Science, University of California, Berkeley, CA.

Lawson, A.E., M.R. Abraham, and J. W. Renner. 1989. *A theory of instruction: Using the learning cycle to teach science concepts and thinking skills.* NARST Monograph No. 1.

Marek, E. A., & Cavallo, A. M. L. (1997). *The Learning Cycle: Elementary School Science and Beyond* (Rev. ed.). Portsmouth, NH: Heinemann.

National Science Teachers Association. 2003. *Standards for Science Teacher Preparation: Skills of Teaching* (Revised Version). Washington, DC: National Science Teachers Association.

National Science Teachers Association (NSTA). 2002. Elementary school science. Position paper. Retrieved September 22, 2009, from *www.nsta.org/positionstatement&psid=8/.*

National Science Teachers Association. 1998. *Standards for Science Teacher Preparation: Skills of Teaching.* Washington, DC: National Science Teachers Association.

National Research Council. 1996 *National Science Education Standards.* Washington, D.C.: National Academy Press.

Piaget, J. 1964. Cognitive development in children: Piaget, development and learning. *Journal of Research in Science Teaching,* 2, 176–80.

Renner, J. W., and Marek, E. A. 1990. An educational theory base for science teaching. *Journal of Research in Science Teaching.* 27(3): 241–46.

Sandoval, J. S. 1995. Teaching in subject matter areas: Science. *Annual Review of Psychology,* 46, 355–74.

Texas Education Agency (TEA). 2006. Prekinder curriculum guide-lines. Retrieved September 22, 2009, from *www.tea.state.tx.us/curriculum/early/prekguide.html#4.*

_____. 2006. Texas Essential Knowledge and Skills. *www.tea.state.tx.us/teks/.*

University of California, Lawrence Livermore National Laboratory. 2006. Plasma: The fourth state of matter. Retrieved September 18, 2009, from *http://FusEdWeb.llnl.gov/CPEP/.*

Fine Arts and Music

Competency 042: Visual Arts

The teacher understands concepts, processes, and skills involved in the creation, appreciation, and evaluation of art and uses this knowledge to plan and implement effective art instruction.

Fine Arts or Visual Arts?

The term **fine arts** is an umbrella term used to describe artworks that appeal to people's aesthetic perceptions. The fine arts include music, theater, sculpture, painting, printmaking, and other traditional forms of art. However, the fine arts exclude applied arts or craftwork like basket-weaving, ceramics, and textiles. To include more forms of artistic expression and to encompass these other forms of aesthetic expression, the term **visual arts** was coined. The term visual arts refers to artistic expression such as sculpture, painting, and printmaking, but it also includes less familiar forms of art like textiles, basket weaving, ceramics, metalworking—blacksmithing and jewelry-making, and more modern art forms like photography and filmmaking. The term *visual arts* is a more inclusive term and a better descriptor for the arts produced and appreciated in modern society.

Children's Artistic Development

Young children's earliest experiences with the visual arts are much more scientific than artistic in nature. A child making marks by moving a crayon or marker across a surface is concentrating on the sensory experience rather than on self-expression or symbolism. The child is most interested in the texture of the surface, the colors that appear, and the shapes that emerge. It is not until age three or four that the child may notice a similarity between an actual object and a mark that has been made. At this point, the child artist begins to realize that the colors and shapes being applied can symbolize people, objects, and events in reality.

Children of all cultures may experiment in their drawings with variations of the *mandala,* a circle intersected by lines, and the *tadpole person,* a circle representing a human head with lines protruding to represent arms and legs. Around age five, children move into drawing individual symbols to represent people and objects. A house, for example, may be consistently represented as a square with a triangle on top, regardless of the appearance of the house in reality. The use of symbolized drawings continues through the early elementary years, when children typically become enamored with repeating a particular theme in their drawings. A scene with a house, a tree, and hills in the background, or one with a spaceship, a planet surrounded by rings and a quarter moon may be repeated many, many times with little variation as the child artist works toward his/her own ideas of perfection. As children move into the middle and later elementary years, they strive increasingly to achieve photographic realism in their artwork. The frustration they may experience at this point will convince some children that they do not have artistic abilities and make them very reluctant to engage in art activities.

Goals in Art Education

The overall goals of art education include developing children's aesthetic perception, providing experiences with many art forms, and facilitating reflections on and discussions of observations and responses to art. Art education provides opportunities for children to develop and extend their own artistic abilities, and exposes children to characteristics and objects of art. Art education empowers children to analyze diverse forms of the visual arts using informed judgments. Because of these important benefits and life skills, art education is an important component of the Texas Essential Knowledge and Skills from grades K–12.

Texas Essential Knowledge and Skills

The state curriculum for fine arts and visual arts is organized around four main strands—**perception, creative expression, historical/cultural heritage,** and **critical evaluation**. A summary of the key elements required for children in grades K–6 is presented in Table 5.1 (TEA 2006). Traditionally, these curriculum components are delivered by an art teacher in collaboration with EC-6 teachers. EC-6 teachers should know and understand the visual art curriculum components and be able to integrate them meaningfully throughout their grade-level curriculum.

Art Techniques and Materials

While painting and drawing are familiar activities to most elementary teachers, other techniques and materials used in the visual arts curriculum may be less known. Some of these activities are:

1. **Printmaking:** This is the artistic process of making a print in which color (paint or ink) is applied to an object; the object is then pressed onto a surface. When the object is lifted, a print is left on the surface.

2. **Ceramic:** The use of clay to create ceramics is one of the oldest forms of art. Figurines, tiles, and tableware are made by applying high heat to fresh clay and then cooling the object until it becomes solid.

3. **Textiles**: The textile arts are those that use plant, animal, or synthetic fibers to construct practical or decorative objects, including stitchery, weaving, dying and printing, lace making, knitting, crocheting, and embroidery.

4. **Basket weaving:** This ancient art uses unspun fibers (pine straw, animal hair, hide, grasses, thread, or wood) to create baskets or other forms for artistic or utilitarian purposes.

5. **Metalworking:** The traditional metalworking is the artistic process of working with metals to produce individual pieces, assemblies, or structures, including jewelry.

6. **Photography and filmmaking:** This relatively modern art creates still or moving pictures by recording radiation on a sensitive medium, such as a photographic film or an electronic sensor.

7. **Sculpture:** A sculpture is a three-dimensional artwork made by shaping or combining hard material such as marble, rock, glass, wood, or metal. Some sculptures are created directly by carving in a solid material; others are assembled, built together and fired, welded, molded, or cast.

8. **Computer-generated art:** This relatively new form of art is created through the manipulation of pixels, either through drawing and painting software or through electronic images stored in the computer. The computer screen serves as the canvas and colored light is the medium.

The Art Classroom

Whether art experiences happen in the art room or the regular classroom, the room should allow for individual seating arrangements as well as small-group and large-group arrangements. There should be areas for the teacher to lecture and display students' work, space for learning centers, areas for drawing, painting, printmaking, creating computer graphics, modeling, and assembling crafts. There should be both natural and artificial lighting in the room. Materials should be stored in cabinets, with access controlled by the teachers. Safety guidelines are critical, and following them is mandatory for students. Ease of cleanup is a requirement; therefore, sinks and surfaces must have durable, cleanable finishes

Visual Arts Activities for K–6

Throughout the elementary grades, students engage in a variety of art activities such as drawing, painting, designing, constructing, crafts, sculpting, weaving, and finger painting. In grades 3 and 4, students continue perfecting the skills from K through 2 and begin working with new techniques like printmaking, sponge painting, graphics, film animation, and environmental design. In grades 5 and 6, students develop their art from personal experience and direct observation and are expected to demonstrate technical skills.

The elementary curriculum encourages the integration of visual art in the regular classroom, as well as specialized activities in the art room. Appropriate art activities should first of all focus on the self-expression of young artists. While the developing fine motor and perceptual skills of young children may lead to art products that have little resemblance to reality, it is important that children are encouraged to experiment, explore, and express their own ideas through their own efforts. Teacher-made models, pre-cut outlines and templates that standardize art products are not appropriate for elementary age children.

Table 5.1 Visual Arts Strands for K–6 in Texas

Grade	Perceptions	Creative Expressions	Historical/ Cultural	Critical Evaluation
Kindergarten	Identify colors, textures, and forms in the environment	Create artwork using a variety of colors, forms, and line	Share ideas about personal artworks and show respect for different opinions	Express ideas about personal artworks, and the artworks of peers or professional artists
1	Identify art elements such as color, texture, form, and line with emphasis on nature and human-made environments	Invent images that combine color, form, and line, and organize forms to create designs	Demonstrate a basic understanding of art history. Select artwork that show families and groups	Make informed judgment about their personal artworks and the work of peers
2	Continue using color, texture, form, line, space, and art principles, like emphasis, patterns, and rhythm to create artworks	Produce drawings, paintings, prints, constructions, and modeled forms using a variety of art materials	Develop respect for the tradition and contributions in the art of diverse groups	Define reasons for preferences in artworks
3	Continue emphasizing art principles such as emphasis, patterns, rhythm, balance, proportion, and unity in artworks	Express ideas through original artworks using a variety of media. Develop compositions using design skills; and produce drawings, print constructions, and ceramics	Compare artworks from different cultures and link it to different kinds of jobs in everyday life	Apply simple criteria to identify main ideas in original artworks
4	Communicate ideas about self, family, school, and community using sensory knowledge and experiences	Invent ways to produce artworks and to explore photographic imagery using a variety of media and materials	Compare artworks from various groups; identify the role of art in American society	Interpret ideas and moods in original artwork
5	Develop and organize ideas from the environment	Express ideas through original artworks, using a variety of media with appropriate skill	Demonstrate an understanding of art history and culture as records of human achievement	Make informed judgments about personal artworks and artworks of others
6	Develop and organize ideas from the environment	Express ideas through original artworks, using a variety of media with appropriate skill	Demonstrate an understanding of art history and culture as records of human achievement	Make informed judgments about personal artworks and the artworks of others

Art materials for the elementary art program include scissors, wet and dry brushes, fabrics, wrapping papers, film, computers, clay, glue, construction paper, crayons, beads, and multiple household items that can be used to create art. Safety is a primary concern during art activities, and toxic substances or potentially dangerous tools should not be allowed in the classroom. While elementary children enjoy variety in the materials they use in their art projects, teachers should recognize that the introduction of new materials leads children to explore the properties of those materials rather than to engage in creative expression. A regular rotation of familiar materials in classroom art projects is most likely to encourage artistic engagement.

Assessment in the visual arts is, of course, based on the individual child's attitudes and dispositions toward engagement in both art production and art appreciation activities. Does the child engage in art production activities willingly and enthusiastically? Is the child willing to try new materials and techniques? Does the child express original ideas in his or her artwork? Does he or she carefully consider the art products of others and discuss the elements and principles of art exhibited? These are questions to be carefully considered by both the EC-6 teacher and the arts specialist during the assessment process.

By relating art production in the elementary curriculum to art products created by artists from other historical eras and cultures, children are introduced to art appreciation and the basic elements and principles of art. An analysis of the elements and principles of arts follow.

Elements and Principles of Art

Art is a way of communicating and expressing ideas, emotions, and experiences. In order to communicate their own ideas and to understand the communications of other artists, children must have knowledge of and be able to use the elements of art. The elements and principles of art are used by artists to create paintings, drawings, and/or designs; they are the basic principles of design.

Elements of Art

The elements of art are the individual components that combine to create artwork—line, shape, space, value, color, and texture (Wallace, 2006). Most works of art have some small aspect of each element. A description of each element follows.

1. **Line** refers to marks from a pen or brush used to highlight a specific part of a painting or a structure. More subtle lines can also be used to accomplish the opposite effect.

2. **Shape** represents a self-contained, defined area of a two- or three-dimensional area creating a form. There are two basic types of shapes: geometric and organic. The term *geometric shapes* refers to squares, triangles, circles, and rectangles. *Organic shapes* describes more natural-looking shapes like leaves, animals, and clouds.

3. **Space** describes the emptiness around or within objects. Space can be used to create perspective, to create objects or people in different planes, and to create a sense of depth. Positive space is the main area or object of focus in an artwork. Smaller objects in a painting seem farther away, while larger objects will appear to be closer.

4. **Value** refers to the darkness or lightness of an artwork. Values are commonly used to create the two-dimensional quality of artwork. Values also indicate the source of light in a work and provide a three-dimensional view of figures by suggesting shadows. Values can also represent the mood of the artist and the artwork. Darker values are used to represent sadness, mystery, or formality, while lighter values usually represent contentment and relaxation.

5. **Color** represents reflected light and the way it bounces off objects. There are three primary colors (red, yellow, blue); three secondary colors (green, orange, violet); and an unlimited amount of tertiary colors, which are colors that fall between the primary and secondary colors, and compound colors. Compound colors are colors containing a mixture of the three primary colors. There also warm colors (such as yellow, orange, and red) and cool colors (such as blue, green, and purple). Artists use all these color combinations to create the environment of the painting.

6. **Texture** describes the surface quality of a figure or shape. A shape can appear to be rough, smooth, soft, hard, or glossy. Texture can be physical (felt with the hand, e.g., a buildup of paint) or visual (giving the illusion of texture, e.g., the paint gives the impression of texture, but the surface remains smooth and flat).

Principles of Art

The principles of art describe the guidelines that artists follow to create art and to deliver their intended message. Artists use the elements of art to communicate the principles in their creations. The principles of art include emphasis, balance, rhythm, contrast, movement, and harmony (Wallace 2006). A description of these components follows.

1. **Emphasis** is the technique of making one part of a work standout from the rest of the artwork. It guides viewers to pay attention to specific details or components of the artwork. Often the lines and texture lead viewers to the target feature. Lines in paintings and sculpture can point or lead to the focus of attention. By making texture different in one area from the rest of the artwork, the artist can also make the target area stand out.

2. **Balance** refers to the positioning of objects in such a way that none of them overpower the other components of the artwork. Size, space, color, shape, and lighting can be used to create balance. A large shape, for example, that is close to the center can be balanced by a smaller shape that is close to the edge. A large light-toned shape can be balanced by a small dark-toned shape. There are two main kinds of balance: symmetrical and asymmetrical. Symmetrical balance occurs when two halves of a figure coincide creating a mirror image. The line of symmetry is the line that divides the figure in two. The easiest way to identify symmetric figures is to fold the figure in half, and if these two halves are identical, then we can say that the figure is symmetrical. Asymmetrical balance occurs when two sides of an artwork are different. For example, the artwork of the American flag—horizontal lines of different sizes, a smaller rectangle in the upper left corner with stars—makes it asymmetrical.

3. **Rhythm** describes the type of patterns used in the artwork. For example, placing a repetition of objects evenly spaced presents a regular type of rhythm. Elements increasing or decreasing in size in an artwork presents a progressive rhythm.

4. **Contrast** is used to create interest through the combination of elements. Contrast is used to break the monotony or repetitious pattern in a work of art. Rembrandt's paintings are well-known for using value (lightness and darkness) to create contrast. He also used lighter values to highlight portions of the paintings.

5. **Movement** refers to the way that artists produce the appearance of motion. In painting, artists use the element of line to simulate the movement of wind or water. This technique leads viewers to perceive the effects of motion and action through the artwork.

6. **Harmony** is used to represent a sense of completeness in the artwork. It shows the unity of the artwork. For example, texture and color can be combined to provide a sense of balance and harmony.

While the elements and principles of art provide the foundations of artwork in all media and styles, they also have application in other disciplines and in contemporary occupations. **Line**, **shape**, **space**, and **balance** are terms with parallel meanings in the field of mathematics, while **texture** and **color** are also basic objects in science observations. Similarly, **rhythm** and **harmony** are used to describe synonymous concepts in both art and music. Mathematical concepts such as symmetry, angle, distance, and convergence are illustrated in artwork and must be explicitly understood by artists. Similarly, artists regularly explore science concepts related to light, water, and temperature in their work. Engagement in art also requires artists, whether adults or children, to think critically and to problem-solve. Artists must carefully consider how to communicate emotions and ideas in their work, how to convey change and movement, and how to use symbolism. Artists of all ages must also learn to evaluate their own efforts and the work of others.

While art at its most basic is self-expression, the skills and dispositions required of artists have application in other fields and occupations. Architects and interior designers, for example, draw upon the elements and principles of art, as well as other technical skills, to create aesthetically pleasing designs for buildings, landscaping, and interior spaces. Commercial artists may use their abilities in advertising, animation of comics or cartoons, or illustrating print media.

Identifying Characteristics of Style in Works of Art

A **style** is an artist's manner of expression. When a group of artists during a specific period (which can last a few months, years, or decades) have a common style, it is called an **art movement**. Art movements are found predominantly in Western cultures and occur in both visual art and architecture.

There are eight main historical periods, with various artistic styles and art movements within each. Although some periods have only one or two unique art styles, the twentieth century has produced 36 unique styles. Descriptions of some of the best-known styles throughout history follow (Witcombe 1995).

The **Prehistoric** period is characterized by paintings that represent the daily activities of a group of people. The best-known representation of this type of art is the Caves of Altamira, in modern Spain. The Paleolithic peoples of Europe produced small, stylized stone carvings of women as symbols of fertility. These small statues have been found most often in modern France, Italy, and Austria.

The **Ancient** period produced a large number of masterpieces from varied civilizations, such as the Sumerians, Babylonians, Assyrians, Egyptians, Greeks, and Romans. These civilizations skillfully carved even the hardest rocks, such as granite and basalt, into narratives of battles and historical records. Egyptian statues, like their architectural monuments the pyramids, were often of colossal size in order to exalt the power of the society's leaders and gods. The art of ancient Greece has its roots in the Minoan civilization on the island of Crete, which flourished from about 2500 to 1400 BCE. The palace at Knossos held characteristic wall paintings revealing a civilization enamored with games, leisure, and the beauty of the sea.

The mainland of the Greeks of the **Classical** period, about 1,000 years later than the ancient period, was fascinated by physical beauty. Fashioned in the human image, with a universal ideal of perfection and guided by a master plan, the Greeks recreated their Olympian gods in their idealized and gracefully proportioned sculptures, architecture, and paintings. In the **Hellenistic** period (330–30 BCE), the populace, fascinated by physical beauty, appreciated these various objects of art for their beauty alone. The culture of Rome excelled in engineering and building, skills intended to efficiently organize a vast empire and provide an aesthetic environment for private and public use. The Romans built temples, roads, bathing complexes, civic buildings, palaces, and aqueducts. One of the greatest of their artistic and engineering accomplishments was the massive-domed temple of all the gods called the Pantheon, which is today one of the most perfectly preserved of all buildings from the classical period.

The **Medieval** period (500–1400 CE) also produced large numbers of artistic masterpieces. The Romanesque style of art and architecture was preeminent from about 800 to 1200 CE. By then many local styles, including the decorative arts of the Byzantine Empire, the Near East, and the German and Celtic tribes, were contributing to European culture. Common features of Romanesque churches are round arches, vaulted ceilings, and heavy walls that are ornately decorated—primarily with symbolic figures of Christianity. Realism had become less important than the message. The Gothic architecture flourished during this period with the creation of magnificent ribbed vaulting and pointed roofs. The cathedrals in this style are some of the purest expressions of an age. They combine a continued search for engineering and structural improvement with stylistic features that convey a relentless verticality, a reach toward heaven, and the unbridled adoration of God.

Soaring and roomy, the construction of the Gothic cathedrals employed such elements as flying buttresses (structure to reinforce a wall) and pointed arches and vaults; a number of sculptures and stained-glass windows that were, for the worshippers, visual encyclopedias of Christian teachings and stories.

Renaissance (14th to 16th century) artists developed new forms and revived classical styles and values, with the belief in the importance of the human experience on Earth and realism. Great sculptors approached true human characterization and realism as they revived elements of Greek architecture. Like the painters of the period, Renaissance architects took a scientific, ordered approach and emphasized perspective and the calculated composition of figures in space. Art became more emotional and dramatic, and because of this, the use of color and movement increased, compositions were more vigorous, and references to classical iconography and the pleasures of an idyllic golden age increased. Typical examples of this emotional, dramatic art are Michelangelo's magnificent Sistine Chapel frescoes and his powerful sculptures of David and Moses; Leonardo da Vinci's *Mona Lisa*; Raphael's *School of Athens* fresco; and the increasingly dramatic and colorful works of the Venetian and northern Italian masters Titian, Correggio, Giorgione, and Bellini.

Baroque style emerged in the 17th century in Europe. The baroque style used exaggerated motion, and elaborate and detailed artwork. The movement produced drama, tension, exuberance, and grandeur in sculpture, painting, literature, and music.

Rococo art characterizes the art of the early eighteenth century. Artists of the Rococo era turned the agitated drama of the baroque style into light, pastel-toned, swirling compositions that seem placed in an idyllic land of a golden age.

Nineteenth-century art was characterized by three elements—romanticism and idealism, realism, and impressionism. In the first half of the nineteenth century, landscape painting in England reached a zenith with the works of John Constable and Joseph Mallord William Turner. Turner's awe-inspiring landscapes form a bridge between the spirit of romanticism and the expressionistic brushwork and realism of the Barbizon School in France, whose chief painters were Charles Daubigny and Jean-Baptiste-Camille Corot. Beginning with Barbizon, the French painters of the nineteenth century concentrated increasingly on the reporter-like depiction of everyday life and the natural environment in a free, painterly (gesture and brushwork) style.

Realism rejected traditional means of composing a picture, academic methods of figure modeling and color relations, and accurate and exact rendering of people and objects in favor of an art that emphasized quickly observed and sketched moments from life, the relation of shapes and forms and colors, the effects of light, and the act of painting itself. The realist pioneers were Gustave Courbet (*The Stone Breakers, A Burial at Ormans*), Jean-François Millet (*The Sower, The Angelus*), and Honoré Daumier (*The Third-Class Carriage*).

Impressionism began with Edouard Manet in France in the 1860s. French artists continually blurred the boundaries of realism and abstraction. They used light and color to capture the impression of images as opposed to the real "real image." The landscapes and everyday-life paintings of impressionist artists like Claude Monet, Camille Pissarro, Auguste Renoir, Alfred Sisley, and Edgar Degas gave way to the more experimental arrangements of form and color of the great postimpressionists: Paul Gauguin, Vincent van Gogh, Georges Seurat, and Henri de Toulouse-Lautrec. Auguste Rodin produced powerful sculptures with the freedom of impressionist style.

Twentieth-century art provided new avenues for artistic expressions:

Surrealism is one of the new trends in painting that emerged in the 20th century. Inspired by the psychoanalytic writings of Sigmund Freud and Carl Jung, artists made the subconscious and the metaphysical important elements in their work. The influence of psychology is especially evident in the work of the surrealist artist Salvador Dali. Salvador Dali created non-realistic paintings as revealed in dreams, free of conscious controls of reason and conventions.

Cubism and abstract paintings of Pablo Picasso also emerged during the twentieth century. This new type of art represents the most direct call for the total destruction of realistic depiction. Artists challenged common realistic conventions to create new representations of reality or imagination. Cubism is the most important and influential movement of European paintings and sculptures in the early 20th century.

Muralists and social realists between WWI and WWII created art that was physically interesting and whose subjects were accessible to the average person. John Sloan, George Bellows, Edward Hopper, Thomas Hart Benton, Grant Wood, and John Stuart Curry were among those who celebrated the American scene in paintings, frequently in murals for public buildings, and through widely available fine prints. The great Mexican muralists, who usually concentrated on political themes—Diego Rivera, José Clemente Orozco, and David Siqueiros—brought their work to the public both in Mexico and in the United States.

Photorealism also emerged as a new form of art in which paintings resemble photos, lifelike—often portraits, still lifes, and landscapes.

Graffiti is a new and controversial type of art form that emerged in inner cities in America. The controversial nature of this new form of art is caused by the way that the expression is conducted. Traditionally, spray painting and using brushes, the artists create the work on the surface of private and public buildings with or without the approval of the owners. For some people, graffiti is a nuisance while for others, it becomes a liberating response to the pressure of modern-day living.

Art in Other Cultures

The progression of art in **China** is divided into periods according to the ruling dynasty and the development of technology. The earliest Chinese art products were made from pottery, jade, and, eventually, bronze. Porcelain art forms were introduced in early imperial China and were refined to the extent that in English the word *china* came to mean high-quality porcelain. Buddhism arrived in China in the first century BCE[1] and strongly influenced artists throughout the country. Calligraphy and painting were popular art forms at this time, with artists working primarily on silk until paper was invented. While classical sculpture was the dominant art form of the Tang dynasty, landscape painting, almost Impressionistic in its portrayal of distance, was dominant during the Song dynasty. Color painting and printing were emphasized during the Ming dynasty and reached their peaks during the Qing dynasty when painters known as **Individualists** began to use free brushwork to express their ideas more openly. Beginning in the 19th century, Chinese artists were increasingly influenced by Western ideas and techniques. In the early 20th century, **social realism** was the dominant theme of Chinese artists. During the Cultural Revolution of the mid-20th century, art schools were closed and exhibitions were prohibited. Following the Cultural Revolution, however, art exchanges were established with other countries and artists began to experiment with various themes and methods. Of particular note is

---

[1] The terms "Before Common Era (BCE)" and "Common Era (CE)" are being used in place of the traditional "Before Christ (BC)" and "anno Domini (AD)" to identify historical periods. The new terms are more inclusive and eliminate religious references.

artist Wang Yani, a child prodigy whose work since 1975 has exemplified *xieyi hua,* a freehand style.

Traditional **African** art was generally intended to both please the viewer and to uphold moral values. Because traditional African art was based in religious and ethical meanings, the human figure was the primary subject. African art was most often created and exhibited or used in ritual contexts that dealt with important moral and spiritual concerns (Ray, 1997).

Native American, or American Indian, art encompasses a broad variety of media and techniques including pottery, woodcarving, weaving, stitchery, painting, beadwork, and jewelry-making. Art forms and symbols vary considerably across Native American tribes. Tribal artisans relied on available natural resources to determine the media in which they worked. Generally, art was used to beautify everyday objects and to create objects of spiritual significance.

For a comprehensive analysis of the history of art visit *http://witcombe.sbc.eduARTH Links.html.*

Integration of the Arts in the Content Areas

The arts can be easily integrated with other academic content areas. In reading, children draw to represent the main idea of a story. Later in writing, they begin adding words to their drawings. Art appreciation activities also provide an appropriate context for children to notice and discuss details in a painting. Through observation and description, children practice new vocabulary and use descriptive language. Scientific principles like light, color, and texture can be easily introduced through artwork. Likewise, art concepts of space, proportion, and balance can be introduced through mathematics. Artworks in all media provide meaningful contexts for the discussion of culture and history.

Evaluating Works of Art

To judge the quality of a work of visual art, students should be given basic criteria for evaluation. The main principle of the criteria can be derived through questions similar to the ones presented below:

- What is the purpose of the artist? Does the work achieve the purpose?

- Has the artist spoken with a unique voice, regardless of style, or could this artwork just as easily be the work of someone else?

- Is the style appropriate to the expressed purpose of the work?

- Is the work memorable and distinctive?

- Was it created to meet social or cultural needs?

- Has the artist used the elements and principles of art effectively?

After answering such questions, a student might be able to determine the specific timeframe of the painting and the style in which it was painted.

When addressing these questions, students should be able to describe a work of art using terms such as line, color, value, shape, balance, texture, repetition, rhythm, and shape. They should be able to discuss some of the major periods in the history of the visual arts. It is important that students be able to confront a work and judge its aesthetic merits, regardless of their ability to recognize it from memory.

Competency 043: Music

The teacher understands the concepts, processes, and skills involved in the creation, appreciation, and evaluation of music, and uses that knowledge to plan and implement effective and engaging music instruction.

The goal of music education is to develop independent musicians through the use of conceptual teaching of musical skills. It is expected that music teachers be literate in music similar to how an English teacher is literate in language. Teachers of music should be able to teach children how to sing in tune, keep a steady beat, listen to different styles of music appropriately, and perform music expressively. Teachers should also learn and use music terminology and the elements of music. They should also learn the appropriate methodology to integrate music in the content areas, and apply the legal and ethical principles of music education.

Elements of Music

Essential to the understanding of music are the key elements upon which all music is based—rhythm, melody, harmony, form, and expression. **Rhythm** is the varied lengths of sounds and silences in relation to the underlying beat. Usually children (K–3) confuse beat and rhythm and try to make them the same thing. Beat is the pulse that is felt in the music and rhythm is typically called the melodic rhythm or word rhythm found in the song. Audiate[2] the song *Happy Birthday*; the beat is the underlying pulse and the melodic rhythm is the words to the song. Now audiate *The Star-Spangled Banner*; the beat may or may not be faster or slower (the speed of the underlying pulse of music is called tempo). The beginning of *The Star-Spangled Banner* has the same melodic rhythm as the beginning of *Happy Birthday*. *Happy Birthday* begins with "Happy birthday to you" and has the same melodic rhythm as "Oh say can you see." After this beginning the two songs do not have the same melodic rhythm. Melodic rhythm is identified using musical notation (the writing of music), which includes various types of notes and rests (see Figure 5-1).

Figure 5-1. Notes and Rests

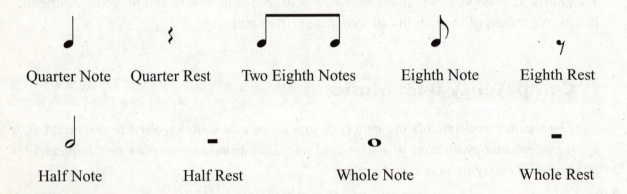

| Quarter Note | Quarter Rest | Two Eighth Notes | Eighth Note | Eighth Rest |

| Half Note | Half Rest | Whole Note | Whole Rest |

Melody is the succession of sounds and silences that may move upward, downward, or stay the same. The "tune" or the singable part of the song is the melody. A **musical staff** (see Figure 5-2), consisting of five parallel lines and four spaces, is needed to read a musical tune. The pitches are represented by symbols called notes placed on the staff. There are seven letters found in the musical alphabet (A, B, C, D, E, F, G). The **clef signs** at the beginning of the song determine the pitch level, either higher or lower. Typically, the **treble clef** is the singing range of women and the right hand on the piano; and the **bass clef** is the singing range of men and the left hand on the piano (see Figure 5-3).

---

[2] Audiation is to hear music inside one's head.

Figure 5-2. Musical Staff

Five Lines—a line going through the note head

Four Spaces—a note head between two lines

Figure 5-3. Musical Staff with Clefs and Notes

Treble Clef

Bass Clef

Harmony is usually the accompaniment or supportive sounds to a melody. These accompaniments are typically played by a pitched instrument, such as a piano, guitar, or autoharp. Another way to produce harmony is through the use of singing rounds, such as *Row, Row, Row Your Boat.*

Form is the structure or design of the music. A phrase, which is a musical line that contains groups of pitches, is similar to a sentence in language. Several musical phrases make up a song just like several sentences make up a paragraph. These phrases can define a song. Musical forms are analogous to mathematical patterns. Common forms in elementary music are binary (AB), ternary (ABA), theme and variation (A A1 A2 A3 A4 etc.), and rondo (ABACA).

Expression consists of dynamics and timbre. Dynamics is a term used by musicians to represent the louds and softs in music. Typically, younger children (K–2) confuse dynamics with pitch level or melodic direction. The word "up" in music is usually associated with pitch level (the music moves up or goes higher) whereas, in the home if children are asked to turn up the music or television, the word "up" is associated with a dynamic level (louder). Dynamics are expressed using the Italian language (see Table 5-2).

Table 5-2. Dynamics

Italian Term	Dynamic Level
Piano	Soft
Mezzo piano	Medium soft
Mezzo forte	Medium loud
Forte	Loud

Timbre is defined as tone color in music. This tone color refers to the quality of sound that distinguishes one voice or instrument from another. Kindergarten children distinguish between the four human voices—speaking, whispering, calling, and singing; whereas, first- and second-grade students can identify the timbre of classroom instruments (woods, metals, and skins). Students in grades 2–6 can identify the timbre of singing voices (soprano, alto, tenor, baritone, bass) and orchestral instruments (strings, woodwinds, brass, percussion, and keyboard).

Curriculum Requirements

Texas has developed the Texas Essential Knowledge and Skills (TEKS) for music into four basic strands—**perception, creative expression/performance, historical and cultural heritage,** and **critical evaluation** (see Table 5-3). Teachers of music are expected to have their students develop and master each strand within the prescribed state curricula.

Table 5-3 Music Education Strands for K–6
(Texas Education Agency, 2006)

Grade Levels	Perception	Creative Expression/ Performance	Historical/ Cultural Heritage	Critical Evaluation
K–2	Identify the difference between the voices, timbre of voices, and instruments. Use basic music terminology to explain sounds and performances. Identify musical forms (AB, ABA).	Perform a varied repertoire of music from diverse cultures. Read and write music notation. Create rhythmic and melodic patterns.	Sing songs and play musical games from diverse cultures. Identify relationships between music and other subjects. Identify music from various periods of history and culture.	Distinguish between musical concepts (e.g., higher/lower, louder/softer) in musical performances. Show appropriate audience behavior during live performances.
3–4	Categorize voices, orchestral instruments, and instruments of various cultures. Use standard terminology in explaining music. Identify musical forms (AB, ABA, and rondo).	Perform a varied repertoire of music from diverse cultures. Read and write music notation. Create patterns and simple accompaniments. Identify and interpret music symbols.	Identify excerpts of music representing diverse genres, styles, periods, and cultures. Perform music and movement from diverse cultures and American and Texas heritage.	Define and apply basic criteria in evaluating musical performances. Practice concert etiquette as a participant and exhibit audience etiquette during live performances.
5–6	Distinguish among a variety of musical timbres. Use standard terminology in explaining music. Identify a variety of musical forms.	Perform independently and musically accurate a varied repertoire of music representing styles from diverse cultures. Read, write, create, and arrange music within specified guidelines.	Describe music representing diverse styles, periods, and cultures. Describe various music-related vocations. Perform music representative of diverse cultures, including American and Texas heritage. Relate the other fine arts to music.	Apply and identify criteria for evaluating performances. Evaluate the quality and effectiveness of music and musical performances. Exhibit concert etiquette as an informed, actively involved listener during varied live performances.

Music in the Classroom

Elementary music teachers in Texas typically use two approaches to teach students music, Orff Schulwerk and Kodály.

Orff Schulwerk Method

Orff Schulwerk[3] is a "learning by doing" approach to teaching music. It is based on what is most natural to children: singing, moving, chanting, creating, improvising, and playing instruments. In an Orff classroom every child participates and experiences all aspects of music in a noncompetitive atmosphere. Orff Schulwerk begins with speech because Carl Orff, the creator of Orff Schulwerk, believed that speech is tied to rhythm and rhythm is the strongest musical element. These speech rhythms are transferred to the body in the form of body percussion (snap, clap, patchen[4], and stamping). Special Orff instruments are used to accompany the songs or rhymes. These instruments (unpitched and barred) allow students to be creative, which leads to improvisation and, later, composition.

Unpitched rhythm instruments (e.g., wood block, triangle, claves, drums, finger cymbals, etc.) and melodic instruments or barred instruments (xylophones, metallophones, and glockenspiels) make up the Orff ensemble. Usually, the unpitched instruments play rhythmic figures and add a nice contrast to the Orff ensemble.

The barred instruments are unique to Orff Schulwerk and can be found in classrooms all over the world. "The xylophone and metallophone are similar to traditional xylophones and vibes, but are small and have removable bars" (Lange 2005, p. 9). The easy removal of bars enables children to have greater success during the instrumental experience. "There are three sizes of xylophones and metallophones: bass, alto, and soprano. The bars on the xylophone are made of wood; the bars on the metallophone are made of metal and have a ringing timbre that is important in the ensemble because of the contrast in sound with xylophones" (Lange 2005, p. 9). The glockenspiels are smaller (alto and soprano only) and have removable metal bars, similar to the xylophone and metallophone.

The Orff instruments are typically played in elementary music classes. The classroom music teacher does not teach traditional band and orchestral instruments. Usually, study of these instruments begins in middle school with a specialized band or orchestra teacher.

---

[3] Schulwerk means "school work" in German.
[4] Patchen is German for patting legs.

However, the elementary music teacher first introduces these band and orchestral instruments during listening lessons. Learning the names and aural identification of band and orchestral instruments may aid in the selection of playing one of these instruments later in their musical career.

The American Orff Schulwerk Association (AOSA) offers several educational opportunities to teachers around the country. There are six Orff chapters in Texas that offer workshops on several Saturdays throughout the school year and AOSA sponsors a national conference yearly. Also, there are two-week certification courses, offered for graduate credit, at numerous universities around the country. These teacher training courses are divided into three levels, and it is recommended that they be taken over three consecutive summers (American Orff Schulwerk Association 2009).

The Kodály Method

The **Kodály Method** developed out of Zoltán Kodály's principles as a step-by-step process for Hungarian teachers. This teaching technique is rooted in Hungarian culture, nevertheless can be adapted to other cultures and is used by some Texas music teachers. The main goals of the Kodály Method are to instill the love of music into all children; to have children achieve music literacy; start music education in early childhood; teach music sequentially; use quality folk songs; and cultivate the singing voice. The 3 Ps (preparation, presentation, and practice) is vital to the teaching process in Kodály. These 3 Ps are similar to the whole-part-whole approach in which the teacher prepares a concept, teaches the concept, and then through repetition and review masters that concept. The tools used in Kodály are solfege (*do, re, mi, fa, sol, la, ti, do*), hand signs (to present a visualization in space of the high-low relationships of the pitches being sung), and rhythm syllables (quarter note = ta, two eighth notes = ti ti, etc.). Other tools include musical flash cards, stick notation (the music notation without the note head) and musical ladders that show the melodic direction of the music.

One primary goal of Kodály is to teach music literacy and singing is the vehicle to achieve this goal. Singing is as important to the current Kodály teacher as it was to Zoltán Kodály himself. Kodály believed that music was "meant to develop one's entire being—personality, intellect, and emotions" (Organization of American Kodály Educators 2009) and used folk songs as his basis of teaching music.

There are professional development opportunities offered in Kodály that are similar to Orff Schulwerk. The Organization of American Kodály Educators (OAKE) has chapters around the country with one large chapter in Texas. Chapters offer Saturday workshops and the OAKE offers national conferences and teacher education programs to further the education of the music teacher (Organization of American Kodály Educators, 2009).

Singing and Repertoire

For young children to learn to sing well they must sing songs that will not strain the undeveloped vocal chords by singing too high or too low. Typically, the classroom teacher sings too low for children and as a result children strain their voices or do not sing along with the teacher. The best singing range for students in K–2 is from D–A (see Figure 5-4). Students in grades 3–6 can sing a little higher, usually from D–D (see Figure 5-5). Children in K–6 have a breathy tone quality and should not be asked to sing louder or project their voice. If a louder sound is necessary, add more children. If an adult asks children to sing louder, children will typically yell instead of sing and therefore damage their voice.

Figure 5-4. Singing Range of Students in K–2

Figure 5-5. Singing Range of Students in 3–6

When selecting music for students in K–6, make sure that most of the pitches fall within the desired range listed above. Avoid songs that are too low, which will cause strain and harm to the voice. There are several music collections from around the world that are appropriate for children. When choosing this music try to choose recordings that are as authentic to the culture as possible.

Singing patriotic songs is an important component in the Texas music curriculum. There are national patriotic songs, such as *The Star-Spangled Banner, America, America the Beautiful,* and *God Bless America.* Explaining the historical significance behind each song is one of the TEKS standards for music. For example, *The Star-Spangled Banner* was written during the War of 1812 when Francis Scott Key wrote the poem. He was detained on a British ship in the harbor, while the British bombed Fort McHenry in Baltimore, Maryland. Key wrote the poem on an envelope early the next morning when he saw the American flag still flying on the Fort (Star-Spangled Banner n.d.). The poem was later set to a tune written by John Stafford Smith and approved by Congress as the National Anthem on March 3, 1931.

Music has the power to heal wounds and patriotic songs typically help in nationalistic healing. Since September 11, 2001, the singing of *God Bless America,* which can be heard regularly at Major League Baseball games, has played an important part in American culture. For younger students (K–2) *America (My Country 'Tis of Thee)* is an appropriate patriotic song that allows for discussion of American history. Another patriotic song appropriate for middle- to upper-elementary students (grades 3–6) to teach history and culture is *America the Beautiful.* The text of this song was written by an American educator, Katharine Lee Bates, and describes the landscape of the country.

Texas has an amazing history that can be taught in music class through song. *Texas, Our Texas* was adopted in 1929 by the Texas Legislature as the Texas state song. It was modified once in 1959 when Alaska became a state and therefore the wording in the song needed to be changed from "largest" state to "boldest" state in the third line of the song (Texas State Libraries and Archives 2009). Other Texas songs that should be taught in elementary school are *Deep in the Heart of Texas, The Yellow Rose of Texas,* and several others that discuss the history and culture of Texas.

Music from diverse cultures is not only one of the TEKS standards for music but is popular in Texas schools. For example, Tejano and Mariachi are prevalent in several districts throughout the state. **Tejano** music dates back to 1690 when Spain settled the area that is now known as Texas. The music developed over the centuries with new settlers from different parts of the world, thus combining several ethnic backgrounds, Mexican, German, Czech, and Cuban. The featured instrument is the accordion and the Tejano orchestra has been influenced by Mexican, Cuban, German, and Czech brass bands. In addition to the instrumentation, the roots of Tejano include various dance styles, which adds to its diversity and cultural heritage (The Roots of Tejano and Conjunto Music 2009).

Mariachi is a group of musicians that is Mexican in heritage. The instrumentation consists of violins, trumpets, a Spanish guitar, and a guitarrón (a large deep-bodied six-stringed acoustic bass from Mexico). Typically, several of the band members will sing along while playing an instrument. Usually, the group all dress in the same attire with silver studded charro outfits and wide brimmed hats. The size of the group varies from three to fifteen members. Mariachi has become popular in Texas schools, where the band director teaches and leads the group.

Listening

Teaching elementary-aged students how to listen to music and what to listen for in music is important for musical understanding. If students are not taught what to listen for in a piece of music, they will typically begin talking and the music therefore becomes background noise. Preparation of a listening lesson should consist of historical background of the music (e.g., time period and composer biography) followed by information of the music itself (e.g., main theme, instrumentation, musical form, dynamics, etc.). This preparation prior to listening to the music allows for the students to be actively engaged while listening and should ensure greater concert etiquette. Students in grades K–6 are expected to demonstrate appropriate concert etiquette. Whispering, talking, and turning around in a seat are unacceptable in most classical concert settings. MENC: The National Association for Music Education has developed "The Ten Rules of Concert Etiquette" for students and parents. (Editor's note: A former title for the group was the Music Educators National Conference, hence the MENC.) These rules are reproducible for distribution so inappropriate behavior at concerts does not occur. Other inappropriate behaviors, in addition to the three listed above, are the use of dangling jewelry, watch alarms, and chewing gum loudly (National Association for Music Educators 2009). Teaching students the expectations at a concert will benefit everyone involved, performers and audience members alike.

Copyright Law

The Copyright Law of the United States is quite complicated and changes regularly, especially with the technological advances in our society. In order to remain current, it is suggested that before any music is copied, reproduced, performed, or sold that the law be read. If possible, consult an expert. Currently, the copyright protection consists of the following:

- Works created after 1/1/1978—Life of the longest surviving author plus 70 years

- Earliest possible public domain date is 1/1/2048

- Works registered between 1/1/1923 and 1/1/1978—95 years from the date copyright was secured

- Works registered before 1/1/1923—Copyright protection for 75 years has expired and these words are in public domain (Public Domain Information Project 2009).

There was an amendment to the Copyright Protection Law in 1998 called the **Sonny Bono Copyright Term Extension Act**, which states that works registered before January 1, 1978, are now extended from 75 years to 95 years. That means that no new musical works will enter public domain until January 1, 2019 (Public Domain Information Project 2009).

Music that is **public domain**, which means that the music does not have an author or the song has exceeded the copyright protection, can be used without securing permission. Songs, such as cowboy songs or folk songs, can be reproduced without obtaining permission; however, the difficulty with public domain is that the original source must be located to make sure the date is correct, it has an unknown author, and that the music has entered public domain. Just because everyone knows a song does not mean that is it in public domain. For example, *Happy Birthday* was written by two women in Kentucky, who were kindergarten teachers, and is highly controversial with regard to the copyright law. It was registered for copyright in the 1930s and then when the Sonny Bono Copyright Term Extension Act was implemented, the copyright for *Happy Birthday* was extended until approximately 2030. With this extension it is illegal to publicly perform *Happy Birthday* without paying the appropriate royalties. That is why restaurant employees no longer sing *Happy Birthday* to its customers.

It is imperative that the copyright law be followed when teaching, distributing, and performing music. The song *Texas, Our Texas* cannot be copied or distributed without permission from Southern Music Company in San Antonio, who owns the copyright (Texas State Libraries and Archives 2009). Remember, copying music is illegal and the fines for copyright infringement are large and enforced.

Evaluation

Evaluation is subjective and evaluating musical performances is no different. The way to add objectivity to evaluating music is to use **performance evaluations** (rubrics). A well-written rubric gives students positive feedback to improve their performance, and allows the teacher to measure many students performing at the same time. Rubrics identify critical components to be assessed, and communicate acceptable levels of student performance or expected behavior. Any rubrics used should be simple enough to allow the students opportunities for self-assessment.

The RubiStar, a website from the University of Kansas, provides opportunities for teachers to create their own rubric. This interactive site lets you choose from a list of music assessment components. Included are rubrics for judging classical concert etiquette, a general rubric for elementary standards and benchmarks, and a rubric for judging instrumental musical performance and music composition. Teachers select the area to be measured and the system provides a description of the levels of performance or the expected behavior. The system also allows the option to customize the rubric. See an example of a customized version to assess classical concert etiquette for elementary education students.

Table 5.4 Sample Rubric for Elementary Education Students

Measuring Component	Levels of Performance		
Category	**Best Behavior**	**Needs Improvement**	**Unacceptable**
Entering hall or auditorium	Stands quietly outside the door, then follows usher quietly to assigned seat	Talks in soft voice while waiting and while being seated	Talks in a loud voice while waiting and while being seated
Attention	Listens politely to the music. Has an interested expression almost all the time	Does not appear to be listening or interested, but keeps hands and feet to himself or herself.	Distracts others by talking, moving, rattling things, playing with toys, etc. during the actual performance
Showing appreciation	Claps at an appropriate volume at the end of all musical selections	Does not clap for all selections or claps at the wrong time	Claps too loudly, drawing audience attention, or whistles and screams while clapping

Using these types of rubrics gives elementary grade students the opportunity to develop criteria for evaluating their behavior during musical performance, actual musical performances, and for evaluating music when they become adults and consumers of music.

References

American Orff Schulwerk Association (AOSA). *http://www.aosa.org/index.html* (accessed July 6, 2009).

Lange, D. M. 2005. *Together in harmony: Combining Orff Schulwerk and music learning Theory.* Chicago: GIA Publications.

National Association of Music Educators (MENC). *http://www.menc.org/resources/view/rules-for-concert-etiquette* (accessed July 26, 2009).

Organization of American Kodály Educators (OAKE). *https://www.oake.org/default.aspx* (accessed July 6, 2009).

Public Domain Information Project. *http://www.pdinfo.com/index.php* (accessed June 26, 2009).

Ray, B. C. 1997. *African art: Aesthetics and meaning. http://www2.lib.virginia.edu/artsandmedia/artmuseum/africanart/index.html* (accessed June 26, 2009).

Shirrmacher, R., and J. E. Fox. 2009. *Art and creative development for young children.* 6th ed. Upper Saddle River, NJ: Cengage Learning.

Star-Spangled Banner. *http://encarta.msn.com/encyclopedia_761575047/Star-Spangled_Banner.html* (accessed June 11, 2009).

Texas State Libraries and Archives. *http://www.tsl.state.tx.us/ref/abouttx/statesong.html* (accessed June 11, 2009).

Texas Education Agency. 2006. Texas Knowledge and Skills. *http://www.tea.state.tx.us/teks/* (accessed July 31, 2009).

The Roots of Tejano and Conjunto Music. *http://www.lib.utexas.edu/benson/border/arhoolie2/raices.html* (accessed July 2, 2009).

Wallace, L. 2006. Utah Education Network (UEN). *http://www.uen.org/* (accessed July 31, 2009).

Witcombe, C. L. 1995. *Art history*. Sweet Briar College, VA. *http://witcombe.sbc.edu/ARTHLinks.html (accessed July 31, 2009).*

Health and Physical Education

Competency 044: Health

The teacher uses knowledge of the concepts and purposes of health education to plan and implement effective and engaging health instruction.

Enhancing Wellness

In today's world, the leading causes of illness, disease, and death are not infectious by nature, but rather lifestyle related. Heart disease, obesity, and cancer are all influenced by and result from people's chosen behaviors. The key to achieving good health is taking responsibility for your daily actions and creating a proactive lifestyle. Recognizing that you make daily choices that impact your total well-being will enable individuals to experience high-level wellness and avoid disease throughout life.

The benefits of a consistent program of diet and exercise are many and varied. Improvements in cardiac output, maximum oxygen intake, mood stabilization, and enhancing the blood's ability to carry oxygen are just a few of these benefits. Another aspect of health education is the awareness and avoidance of risks that are present in our everyday lives. Some risk factors include being overweight, smoking, using drugs, having unprotected sex, inactivity, and excessive unmanaged stress. Education is the key to minimizing the presence of these risk factors.

Body Systems

The body has a system of interrelated subsystems working together to keep the body functioning properly. Cells are the building blocks of the human body, and tissues are groups of similar cells working together to perform a specific job. An organ consists of many kinds of tissues working together for a larger purpose, and a group of organs working together is called an organ system. There are several organ systems in the human body.

Circulatory System. The heart pumps blood in the circulatory system. The blood passes through the right chambers of the heart and through the lungs, where it acquires oxygen, and back into the left chambers of the heart where it is pumped into the aorta, which branches into increasingly smaller arteries throughout the body. Beyond that, blood passes through tiny, thin-walled structures called capillaries. In the capillaries, the blood gives up oxygen and nutrients to tissues and absorbs metabolic waste products containing carbon dioxide. Finally, blood completes the circuit by passing through small veins, joining to form increasingly larger vessels until it reaches the largest veins, which return it back to the right side of the heart.

Respiratory System. Respiration results from the expansion and contraction of the lungs for gas exchange in the body. In the lungs, oxygen enters tiny capillaries, where it combines with hemoglobin in the red blood cells and is carried to the body's tissues. At the same time, carbon dioxide passes through capillaries into the air contained within the lungs. Inhaling draws air that is higher in oxygen and lower in carbon dioxide into the lungs; exhaling forces air that is high in carbon dioxide and low in oxygen from the lungs.

Digestive System. Food provides the energy required for sustenance of the human body. After the fragmenting of food by chewing and mixing with saliva, digestion begins. Chewed food passes down the esophagus into the stomach, where gastric and intestinal juices continue the digestion process. Thereafter, the mixture of food and secretions makes its way down the alimentary canal using peristalsis (the rhythmic contraction of the smooth muscle of the gastrointestinal tract). The smallest units of food are ultimately absorbed into the blood stream and transported throughout the rest of the body for utilization.

Immune System. The body defends itself against foreign proteins and infectious microorganisms by means of a complex immune system. The immune system is composed of a dual system that depends on recognizing a portion of the surface pattern of the invader and the generation of lymphocytes and antibody molecules to destroy invading molecules.

Skeletal System. The human skeletal system consists of more than 200 bones held together by connective tissues called ligaments. The bones are attached to the skeletal muscles; contractions of these skeletal muscles affect movements.

Nervous System. The nervous system controls muscular contractions. The nervous system has two divisions: the somatic, which allows voluntary control over skeletal muscle, and the autonomic, or involuntary, which controls cardiac and glandular functions. Nerve impulses carried by cranial or spinal cord nerves that connect the brain to skeletal muscles cause voluntary movement. Involuntary movement, or reflex movement, occurs in direct response to outside stimulus. Various nerve terminals, called receptors, constantly send impulses to the central nervous system. Each type of receptor routes nerve impulses to specialized areas of the brain for processing.

Diet and Exercise

Statistics show that Americans get fatter every year. Even though countless books and magazine articles are available on the subject of weight control, often the only place a student gets reliable information about diet is in the classroom. The unfortunate reality is that people who are overweight on average do not live as long as those who are not. Being overweight has been isolated as a risk factor in various types of cancer, heart disease, gall bladder problems, and kidney disease. Chronic diseases such as diabetes and high blood pressure are also aggravated by, or caused by, being overweight. Conversely, being underweight presents a great many dangers to health as well. Our society often places too much emphasis on losing weight and being thin. Women are especially prone to measuring their self-worth by the numbers they read on the bathroom scale. Young girls are especially susceptible to these messages and eating disorders can result.

According to the National Institute of Mental Health (2009) ideal weight and a good body fat ratio should be the goals when trying to lose weight. A correlation may exist between body fat and high cholesterol. Diet and exercise is the key to maintaining a good body fat ratio. Exercise helps keep the ratio low, improves cholesterol levels, and prevents heart disease. In order to lose weight, calories burned must exceed calories consumed.

Metabolism is a set of chemical processes that occur in the body to keep it functioning, growing, responding to the environment, and maintaining life balance. Basal Metabolic Rate (BMR) is the pace at which the body burns the vast majority of calories efficiently at rest. Adjustments in the BMR are slow, occur over time, and are dependent upon the demands put upon the body physically (i.e., exercise) and calorie consumption. If calorie intake is restricted too much, the body goes into starvation mode and operates by burning fewer calories in order to conserve energy. Just a 250 calorie drop a day combined with a 250 calorie burn will result in a loss of one pound a week. Crash diets, which bring about rapid weight loss, are not only unhealthy but also ineffective. Slower weight loss is more lasting. Aerobic exercise is a major component to successful weight loss. Exercise speeds up metabolism and causes the body to burn calories efficiently. Timing of exercise may also enhance the benefits. Exercise before meals speeds up metabolism and helps suppress appetite. Through education, people will be better able to realize that maintaining a healthy weight is crucial to a healthy life and should be a constant consideration.

Along with exercise, a healthy diet is vital to good health, learning, academic achievement, and longevity. The elements of good nutrition, the role of vitamins, elimination of risk factors, and strategies to control weight are all part of a healthy lifestyle. In the spring of 2005, the U.S. Department of Health and Human Services changed the food pyramid to guide Americans to improve their eating habits (U.S. Department of Health and Human Services, 2006). As shown in Figure 6-1, the food pyramid has six divisions reminding us of what kind of foods need to be proportioned in our diet. The climbing figure reminds us all to be active.

Figure 6-1. USDA Food Pyramid

Source: U.S. Department of Agriculture, *Steps to a Healthier You, www.mypyramid.gov.*

The food groups indicated on the pyramid (left to right) are as follows:

1. Grains (e.g., bread, cereal, rice, and pasta); 6–11 daily servings

2. Vegetables; 3–5 daily servings

3. Fruits; 2–4 daily servings

4. Oils; use sparingly

5. Milk (yogurt and cheese); 2–3 daily servings

6. Meat and Beans; 2–3 daily servings

Nutrients are divided into two main groups: macro-nutrients (carbohydrates, proteins, and fats) and micro-nutrients (vitamins and minerals). Most foods contain a combination of the two groups. Complex carbohydrates (e.g., vegetables, fruits, whole grain breads, and cereals) are the preferred energy source for the body and should comprise up to one-half of the diet. These foods provide fiber, which helps digestion, reduces constipation, and reduces the risk of colon cancer. Proteins (e.g., milk, eggs, meat, fish, and beans) are one of our most essential nutrients because the body uses it to build and repair itself in more ways than any other food. Fats (e.g., olive and canola oils) are important to the body for regulating blood pressure, forming cell structures, transporting vitamins, and triggering immune system responses. Vitamins are essential given they perform highly specific metabolic processes in the cells and aid with many other functions such as growth and maintenance of the body. Minerals (e.g., calcium, iron, potassium, and zinc) help build strong bones and teeth, aid in muscle function, and help the nervous system transmit messages. Keeping a balance of nutrients consistently in the body combined with hydration will keep systems functioning appropriately and minimize overall health risk. A world of nutrition information is available to teachers at the Dietary Guidelines for Americans, published by the United States Department of Health and Human Services (2006).

Stress Management

Stress is the product of any change, either negative or positive. Multiple components and situations can cause stress. Some of these are:

• Environmental factors such as noise, air pollution, and crowding

• Physiological factors such as sickness and physical injuries

• Psychological factors such as self-deprecating thoughts and negative self-image

In addition to the normal stressors that everyone experiences, some students may be living in dysfunctional families, some may be dealing with substance abuse and addictions, and some may be experiencing sexual abuse.

People have numerous sources of stress in their lives, and it is important that students and teachers learn acceptable ways to cope with stress. The first step is to recognize the role that stress plays in our daily lives. A teacher might lead a class through a brainstorming activity to help the students become aware of the various sources of stress affecting them. Next, the teacher could identify positive ways of coping with stress, including positive self-talk, physical exercise, proper nutrition, adequate sleep, balanced activities, time management techniques, good study habits, and relaxation exercises.

Students facing stress often experience a wide range of emotions. They may be sad, frustrated, or afraid. Effective teachers realize that students' emotions play a significant role in students' classroom performance and achievement. Thus, they should seek to create a classroom environment supportive of students' emotional needs. They should have appropriate empathy and compassion for the emotional conflicts facing students, as well as a realistic awareness that students need to attain crucial academic and social skills that will give them some control over their environment as they become increasingly independent individuals and, eventually, productive citizens.

The state curriculum for health (Texas Essential Knowledge and Skills) has incorporated objectives and standards to prepare school-age children to face the multiple physical, environmental, and emotional challenges that children face in the United States. Health education teachers and teachers in general are required to teach these health objectives in formal health classes through the integration of health components in the general curricula. Knowledge of the state health curriculum is required for all teachers in the state. An analysis of the health curriculum mandates in Texas follows.

Curriculum Requirements for Health

The Texas Essential Knowledge and Skills (TEKS) contain all the curriculum components in the area of Health. Health education teachers are expected to implement the prescribed state curriculum (Texas Administrative Code 2009a). In conjunction with the national initiative, The Texas Essential Knowledge and Skills provides for the teaching of developmentally appropriate content and strategies for health education to children in grades K–12. Some of the key components of the TEKS require children to develop an understanding of their body, proper nutrition practices, and safety procedures, and to use reliable information to make personal health decisions. Some of the topics introduced in grades K–6 are:

1. Identify and consume healthy food choices

2. Strategies to avoid health and safety risks

3. Strategies for protection against sexual predators

4. Role of media and Internet influencing health decisions

5. Assertive behaviors and strategies to deal with risky situations

6. Gang prevention programs

7. Drugs and alcohol prevention programs

8. Knowledge of the human body

9. Safety procedures in school and the community

Some of the key skills and activities required in the state K–6 curriculum are listed below.

Kindergarten

Children should be able to:

1. Identify types of foods that help the body grow such as healthy breakfast foods and snacks

2. Identify the purpose of protective equipment such as a seat belt and a bicycle helmet

3. Identify how to get help from a parent and/or trusted adult when made to feel uncomfortable or unsafe by another person/adult

4. Demonstrate procedures for responding to emergencies including dialing 911

5. Demonstrate how to seek the help of parents/guardians and other trusted adults in making decisions and solving problems

First Grade

Children should be able to:

1. Name safe play environments

2. Explain the harmful effects of, and how to avoid, alcohol, tobacco, and other drugs

3. Identify and practice safety rules during play

4. Identify common illnesses and diseases and their symptoms

5. Name various members of his/her family who help him/her to promote and practice healthy habits

Second Grade

Children should be able to:

1. Describe and demonstrate personal health habits such as brushing and flossing teeth and exercise

2. Identify the major organs of the body such as the heart, lungs, and brain and describe their primary functions

3. Apply practices to control spread of germs in daily life such as hand washing and skin care

4. Demonstrate refusal skills

5. Identify various media that provide health information

Third Grade

Children should be able to:

1. Describe ways to improve personal fitness

2. Identify types of nutrients

3. Explain the body's defense systems and how they fight disease

4. Relate how protecting the environment promotes individual and community health

5. Describe how the media can influence knowledge and healthy behaviors

Fourth Grade

Children should be able to:

1. Identify information on menus and food labels

2. Explain how to develop a home-safety and emergency response plan such as fire safety

3. Explain how sleep affects academic performance

4. Identify the importance of taking personal responsibility for developing and maintaining a personal health plan such as fitness, nutrition, stress management, and personal safety

5. Identify ways to avoid drugs and list alternatives for the use of drugs and other substances

Fifth Grade

1. Apply information from the food guide pyramid to make healthy food choices

2. Calculate the relationship between caloric intake and energy expenditure

3. Explain strategies for avoiding violence, gangs, weapons, and drugs

4. Explain the impact of neglect and abuse

5. Assess the role of assertiveness, refusal skills, and peer pressure on decision making and problem solving

Sixth Grade

1. Analyze healthy and unhealthy dietary practices

2. Explain the consequences of sexual activity and the benefits of abstinence;

3. Seek the input of parents and other trusted adults in problem solving and goal setting;

4. Make healthy choices from among environmental alternatives such as leaving a smoke-filled room or selecting healthy snacks from vending machines;

5. Describe chemical dependency and addiction to tobacco, alcohol, and other drugs and substances. (Texas Administrative Code 2009a)

Human Growth and Development

A teacher does not have to be an expert in anatomy and physiology to see the physical changes that accompany students' growth and maturity. The preschool child has trouble grasping pencils and crayons in a manner that facilitates handwriting; however, even most two-year-olds can grasp crayons sufficiently to make marks on papers and thus enjoy the creative excitement of art. Physiological changes play a significant role in the development of children as they increase their control of bodily movements and refine their motor skills. Their ability to engage in simple to complex classroom and playground activities increases as they develop. Teachers must adjust and adapt classroom and playground activities to be developmentally appropriate for students' various skill levels.

Girls, on average, reach maturational milestones before boys. Physical changes may cause embarrassment to both females and males when they draw unwelcome attention. These changes almost always create some discomfort as adolescents find the body they were familiar and comfortable with to be quite different, sometimes seemingly overnight. To facilitate this transition, teachers need to make children aware that these changes are part of their natural development.

Many major factors relate to and are necessary to build both social and emotional health. It is critically important for teachers to develop a basic understanding of the principles of human development and its multiple dimensions (e.g., physical, mental, emotional, and social). Additionally, teachers must appreciate a dynamic and interactive view of human development. This approach to understanding human development is one that recognizes that human beings do not develop in a vacuum. People exist in an environment that, friendly or unfriendly, supportive or non-supportive, evokes and provokes reactions from individuals. Moreover, human development is not a one-way street with the environment doing all the driving. People also act in certain ways to shape and form their environment.

A constant interaction occurs between people and their environments. Thus, effective teachers must be sensitive to and knowledgeable of both personal characteristics of students (internal factors) and characteristics of their environment. Internal factors, beyond the general characteristics that humans share as they grow and mature, also include students' personality characteristics, their self-concept and sense of self-esteem, their self-discipline and self-control, their ability to cope with stress, and their general outlook on life (attitude).

Empowerment has many components, one of which is self-concept. A good definition of self-concept is what we think and believe to be true about ourselves, not what we think about others and not what they think about us. Related to self-concept is self-efficacy. Simply stated, self-efficacy is the confidence you have in your ability to cope with life's challenges. Self-efficacy refers to your sense of control over life or over your responses to life. Experts say that ideas about self-efficacy get established by the time children reach age four. Because of this early establishment of either a feeling of control or no control, classroom teachers may find that even primary grade students believe that they have no control over their lives, that it makes no difference what they do or how they act. Therefore, it is all the more important that teachers attempt to help students achieve coping skills and a sense of self-efficacy.

Substance Use and Abuse

Drug and alcohol problems can affect anyone, regardless of age, sex, race, marital status, place of residence, income level, or lifestyle. However, there are certain identifiable risk factors for substance abuse. These factors include individual, familial, social, and cultural characteristics.

Some of the personal characteristics that have been linked to substance abuse are: aggressiveness, emotional problems, inability to cope with stress, and low self-esteem. Feelings of failure and a fragile ego can also contribute to this problem. The presence of physical disabilities, physical or mental health problems, or learning disabilities can add to the student's vulnerability to substance abuse. In many ways, students who are at-risk for academic problems are also susceptible to substance abuse problems.

Associated with substance abuse among youth are several family characteristics. First, and perhaps most important, is the alcohol or other drug dependency of a parent or both parents. This characteristic might relate to another significant factor: parental abuse and neglect of children. Antisocial and/or mentally ill parents are also factors that put children at risk for drug and/or alcohol abuse. Other conditions like family unemployment or underemployment, and parents with little education or who are socially isolated can also become risk factors. Single parents without family or other support, family instability, a high level of marital and family conflict or violence, and parental absenteeism due to separation, divorce, or death can also increase children's vulnerability to substance abuse. Finally, other important factors to consider are the lack of family rituals, inadequate parenting, little child-to-parent interaction, and frequent family moves. These factors describe children without affiliation or a sense of identity with their families or the community. Any of these family factors could lead to a substance abuse problem in a student.

Living in an economically depressed area with high unemployment, inadequate housing, a high crime rate, and a prevalence of illegal drug use are social characteristics that can put an individual at risk for substance abuse. Cultural risk factors include minority status involving racial discrimination, differing generational levels of assimilation, low levels of education, and low achievement expectations from society at large. All the recognized risk factors are only indicators of the potential for substance abuse. They are not necessarily predictive of an individual's proclivity to drug or alcohol abuse. Some children who are exposed to very adverse conditions grow up to be healthy, productive, and well-functioning adults. Yet, knowing the risk factors, teachers are better able to identify children vulnerable to substance abuse and develop prevention education strategies. If teachers recognize these risk factors in some of their students, there are certain things that teachers can do to increase the chances that the child will resist the lures of illegal and dangerous alcohol and drug abuse.

Sometimes it can be difficult to tell if someone is using illegal drugs or alcohol. Usually, people who abuse drugs or alcohol (including young people) go to great lengths to keep their behavior a secret. They deny and/or try to hide the problem. However, certain warning signs can indicate that someone is using drugs or drinking too much alcohol: (1) Lying to teachers and family members, (2) Avoiding people who are longtime friends or associates, (3) Having slurred speech, (4) Complaining of headaches, nausea, or dizziness, (5) Having difficulty staying awake in class, and (6) bloodshot, glazed over, and/or squinting eyes. These examples are insufficient to confirm a substance abuse problem, but in combination and when displayed consistently over time, they are strong indicators. Teachers should record their observations and keep written reports of the behavioral changes they witness. Moreover, they should report their suspicions to the appropriate school authorities.

Violence and Abuse

Child abuse is a common problem in the United States. According to the American Academy of Pediatrics, more than 2.5 million cases of child abuse and neglect are reported annually in the nation (Shelov, & Remer, 2009). Half of these cases involves neglect while the other half involves physical and sexual abuse. Despite all the media attention given to child abuse and neglect, many teachers still believe that it cannot happen to one of their students. They may think, "This is a nice neighborhood," or "Most of these students have both a mother and a father living at home." However, abuse and neglect may happen to children, possibly even to one of your students. Abused children typically show signs of over stimulation—being "wired," unruly, and/or belligerent. By contrast, the behaviors of neglected children point to under stimulation—all they want is to be left alone and typically they are unsociable, sedate, and/or withdrawn. The child learns this behavior at home during periods of neglect. The neglect may change the child's behaviors from almost flat (registering no emotion) to anger. Although poor attention, tears, violence, and apathetic behavior may be indicators of either abuse or neglect, neglected children usually have feelings of hopelessness and cannot adequately control their thoughts and emotions. Students either become obsessed by the neglect or refuse to acknowledge that the neglect is really happening.

One of the most obvious visible signs of child abuse is red swelling or bruising caused by being hit. The appearance of marks on a child may be proof of child abuse, and the teacher must report the evidence immediately. Visible signs are also one way teachers can separate real abuse cases from unfounded ones. While marks from the hand, fist, or belt are usually recognizable, other marks in geometric shapes (i.e., eating utensils, paddles, coat hangers, or extension cords) can signify child abuse as well.

In addition to the physical marks, victims of child abuse and neglect can also exhibit nontraditional behaviors. The most common documented characteristics include: (1) frequent illness; (2) hyperactivity disorders; (3) depression; (4) bowel or bladder control problems; (5) impulsivity, aggressiveness, or defiance; and (6) academic difficulties. Neglect is more common than abuse but receives much less attention largely because it does not show easily observable manifestations.

Teachers hope they will never have to manage a disclosure of any kind of maltreatment of a child, although such revelations are the responsibility of these trusted adults and student advocates. Following the disclosure of abuse from a child, it is important for teachers to respond in a calm manner and thank/support the child for bringing this important matter to their attention. Teachers should not question the child about the details; rather gather information and follow-up with administrators, counselors, and/or nurses. The best course of action is to make an immediate referral or report of these suspicions.

Teachers in Texas are required by law to report any suspicion of child abuse or neglect to the Department of Human Services. Thus, they must be vigilant for possible symptoms or indications of child abuse. Failure to file a report of suspicion of child abuse or neglect has consequences, and it can result in legal action against the teacher. After the report, the teacher should realize that the child may feel that the educator has exposed the child's private life. While accepting the child's feeling of betrayal, the teacher can explain that the report was necessary and assure the child of protection against reprisals for telling about the abuse. Sometimes the child benefits from just knowing that others do care about his or her well-being.

Safety and Accident Prevention

Peer counseling, peer mediation, and peer leadership programs have demonstrated little effectiveness for reducing violence, encouraging safety in schools, and preventing accidents. In addition, restricting promotion to succeeding grades for violent students have shown to have negative effects on achievement, attendance, and behavior toward school. Research shows that the most successful programs are those that are multifaceted and linked to a variety of services. Characteristics of such programs include: (1) early start and long-term commitment; (2) strong collaborative leadership that enforces explicit disciplinary policies; (3) ongoing staff development; (4) parental involvement and parental education (e.g., home visits); and (5) role-modeling activities designed to be culturally relevant.

School Violence

School violence is a prevalent feature in most American schools. Some of the elements that contribute to school violence are: (1) overcrowding, (2) poor design and use of school space, (3) lack of disciplinary procedures, (4) student alienation, (5) multicultural insensitivity, (6) rejection of at-risk students by teachers and peers, and (7) anger or resentment at school routines. On the other hand, factors contributing to school safety include (1) a positive school climate and atmosphere, (2) clear and high performance expectations for all students, (3) practices and values that promote inclusion, (4) bonding of the students to the school, (5) high levels of student participation and parental involvement in school activities, and (6) opportunities to acquire academic skills and develop socially. Effective teachers need to be alert to the signs of potentially violent behavior, acknowledging that signs can easily be misinterpreted and misunderstood. Warning signs should be used to get help for children, not to exclude, punish, or isolate them. Some of the imminent warning signs of school violence are: (1) serious physical fighting with peers or family members; (2) serious destruction of property; (3) rage for seemingly minor reasons; (4) detailed threats of lethal violence; (5) possession and/or use of firearms and weapons; and (6) other self-injurious behaviors or threats of suicide. Teachers have to become vigilant to these signs of violence and notify the appropriate authorities of these behaviors. Violence prevention strategies at school range from adding social skills training to the curriculum to installing metal detectors at the entrances to buildings. Schools should teach all students procedures in conflict resolution and anger management, and should explain the school's rules, expectations, and disciplinary policies.

Mental and Emotional Health

Mental and emotional disorders present various emotional and physical signs. Depression can manifest itself in an overall lack of interest in activities, constant crying, or talk of suicide. Anxiety or obsessive thoughts are another indication of a possible mental or emotional disorder. Physical signs include a disruption in eating or sleeping patterns, headaches, nausea and stomach pain, or diarrhea. The teacher needs to consider these signs as a cause for serious concerns and treatment.

Psychotic disorders, such as schizophrenia, are serious emotional disorders. These disorders are rare in young children and difficult to diagnose, although one of the warning signs for psychotic disorders is that the student experiences a complete break from the reality of his or her surroundings. Schizophrenics may have difficulty expressing themselves, resulting in unusual speech patterns or even muteness. Schizophrenics, who are more likely to be boys than girls, may also exhibit facial expressions that are either markedly absent of emotion or overly active.

Infantile Autism

Infantile autism is another serious emotional disorder that appears in early childhood. Characteristics include withdrawn behavior and delayed or absent language and communication skills. Symptoms of autism can appear in children between four and eighteen months of age. Autistic children will usually distance themselves from others and may be unable to experience empathy. In addition, they often cannot distinguish or appreciate humor. Autistic children may have a preoccupation with particular objects or may perform particular activities repeatedly. While autistic children can range in all levels of intelligence, some children may have particular skills in focused areas, such as music or math. Diagnosis might inaccurately determine mental retardation, hearing/auditory impairment, or brain damage. Treatment for autistic children may involve therapy, drugs, or residential living. However, only five percent of autistic children ever become socially well-adjusted adults. Many of these high-functioning autistics are placed in the regular classroom, some with personal aides to facilitate their success.

Eating Disorders

Eating disorders are not due to a failure of will or behavior; rather, they are real, treatable medical illnesses in which certain maladaptive patterns of eating take on a life of their own (National Institute of Mental Health, 2009). The main types of eating disorders are anorexia nervosa (lack of desire or interest in food which results in starvation of the body) and bulimia nervosa (episodes of secretive excessive eating followed by inappropriate methods of weight control such as self-induced vomiting). A third type of problem that exhibits a total lack of control for eating is compulsive overeating or binge-eating disorder. Many professionals have suggested this condition as a formal disorder in today's world although it has not yet been approved as a formal psychiatric diagnosis. Eating disorders frequently develop during adolescence or early adulthood, but some reports indicate their onset can occur during childhood or later in adulthood. Treatments for eating disorders are complex and most often requires professional help (e.g., psychotherapy, support groups, and/or hospitalization).

Healthy Interpersonal Relationships

The social domain of health is manifested in our ability to practice good social skills and maintain comfortable relationships with others. Socially healthy people are effective at communicating respect for others, being tolerant and patient, and accepting differences without compromising relationships. Successful teachers are able to listen intently and recognize the needs and issues of others. Ultimately, effective educators recognize ways they enrich and are enriched by their relationships and use these skills to role-model appropriate behaviors.

To become effective communicators, students need a variety of learning opportunities to practice interpersonal skills in a variety of situations they are likely to encounter (e.g., communicating empathy, resisting peer-pressure, managing conflicts, and asking for help). As a result of practicing such methods, a natural link is established for students to express their healthy intentions when the correct situation/environment arises. Educators should constantly look for ways in which to practice assertive communication including stating a position, offering a reason that makes sense or is healthy, and acknowledging other's feelings.

Health Care Information

The *Surgeon General's Report* on Health Promotion and Disease Prevention was first released in 1979 creating a public health revolution that emphasized disease prevention and taking personal responsibility for one's health. In 1990, the United States Department of Health and Human Services published *Promoting Health/Preventing Disease: Objec-*

tives for the Nation, which outlined specific objectives for meeting those goals identified in the earlier *Surgeon General's Report*. These objectives led to the development of *Healthy People 2000*, a document that aimed to reduce preventable death and disability and enhance the quality of life for American society. Today, *Healthy People 2010* (n.d.) is setting the disease prevention agenda for the United States using science, technology, and education. Administrators, teachers, and health professionals have to become familiar with the policy of the federal government and incorporate its principles in schools.

Health Care Professionals

School health services typically include a set of policies and programs that assess and protect the health of students. Specifically, the school nurse leads this collaborative effort to direct patient care, screen and diagnose symptoms, promote health counseling services, participate in health promotion and disease prevention, and maintain relationships with allied health professionals and community health service providers. School administrators have the legal responsibility for the safety of all students and for the supervision of the health services program offered in school. Regrettably, many school districts have assigned these tasks to untrained teachers and/or staff, which lead to dangerous practices for the students, teachers, and school district.

Like other states, Texas has a legislative mandate requiring all children to be immunized against certain communicable diseases (e.g., polio, diphtheria, measles, mumps, rubella, chicken pox, and hepatitis) prior to enrolling in public school. All policies governing communicable diseases should be available to teachers and school employees to promote collaboration and risk reduction. Teachers should always be proactive in obtaining information when a child who suffers from a communicable disease can safely return to school. In addition to any formal instruction in health, other teachers should integrate the content areas (e.g., social studies, science, art, and music) to health-related issues. Examples of topics that can be integrated easily into other content areas are:

1. the effects of pollution on health and occupational-related disease (e.g., "black lung" disease)

2. the health care options available to people in different parts of the world and in different economic circumstances

3. differentiation between communicable and noncommunicable diseases

4. the importance of washing hands frequently

Older children should be able to explain the transmission and prevention of communicable diseases, and all children should learn which diseases cannot be transmitted through casual contact.

Students as young as kindergartners and first graders can learn how to recognize advertisements that might lead them to unhealthy behavior (e.g., for candy or sugar-laden cereal). By third or fourth grade, children should be able to demonstrate that they are able to make health-related decisions regarding advertisements in various media. Teachers can encourage students to: (1) avoid alcohol, tobacco, stimulants, and narcotics; (2) get plenty of sleep and exercise; (3) eat a well-balanced diet; (4) receive the proper immunizations; and (5) avoid sharing toothbrushes, combs, hats, beverages, and food with others.

External Influences

The school is a community agency that cannot function appropriately in isolation. With that said, the range of problems associated with students does not only result from school, but also parents/family, neighborhoods, and larger community influences (e.g., consumerism, media, and environment). All those who advocate for students must realize that the complexity of today's health and social problems require all community stakeholders to take responsibility for the current situation and work together with the schools to improve the health of students. An important step to confronting these challenges is the need for local districts to establish a school health advisory council that includes members from all segments of the community (e.g., school personnel, medical professionals, non-profit organizations, and the business sector). Such committees work to increase visibility of initiatives, increase the quantity and quality of health-promotion efforts, and reduce duplication of services.

First Aid

First aid is the immediate, temporary care of an injured or ill person. Occasionally, during physical education classes or during school hours, injuries and illnesses occur. Therefore, a basic knowledge of first aid is important for physical education teachers and other instructors. However, a teacher should not attempt first aid if the procedures are unclear. A course in first aid is important for the classroom teacher, and they are readily available from the local American Red Cross.

The following are some common injuries and a brief description of their emergency treatments:

1. **Bone Fracture**: A fracture is a break in a bone. Fractures can be simple, multiple (many breaks in the bone), or compound (a break in the bone and the skin).

   Treatment: Immobilize, use ice to control swelling, and seek medical aid. In the case of a compound fracture, it is important to stop the bleeding.

2. **Traumatic Shock**: Traumatic shock is the severe compression of circulation caused by injury or illness. Symptoms include cool sweaty skin and a rapid weak pulse.

   Treatment: Minimize heat loss and elevate the legs without disturbing the rest of the body. Seek medical help.

3. **Sprain Injury**: A sprain is an injury to a joint caused by the joint being moved too far or away from its range of motion. Both ligaments and tendons can be injured in a sprain. Ligaments join bone to bone, and tendons join muscle to bone.

   Treatment: Guide the victim to rest, apply ice to the injury, and compression. The use of the acronym RICE—rest, ice, compression, and elevation—provides an easy way to remember the appropriate treatment for sprains.

4. **Strain Muscle**: A strain is a muscle injury caused by overwork.

   Treatment: Use ice to lessen the swelling and rest. Applying some heat after icing can be beneficial although opinion on the value of heat varies.

5. **Dislocation of a Joint**: In this type of injury, the bone becomes out of place at the joint. As a result, ligaments can be severely stretched and/or torn.

   Treatment: Immobilize and seek medical help. Some people advocate "popping" the dislocation back into place, but this can be risky for both the injured person and for the person giving the first aid (liability). Therefore, allow the medical professionals to put the joint back in place.

6. **Heat Exhaustion**: The symptoms of heat exhaustion include cold and sweaty skin, nausea, dizziness, and paleness. Heat exhaustion is not as severe as heat stroke.

   Treatment: Increase water intake, replace salt, and get out of the heat.

7. **Heat Stroke**: The symptoms of heat stroke include high fever, dry skin, and possible unconsciousness.

   Treatment: Attempt to cool off the body gradually, get into the shade, and seek medical attention immediately.

8. **Heart Attack**: The symptoms of heart attack include shortness of breath, pain in the left arm, pain in the chest, nausea, and sweating.

   Treatment: Elevate the head and chest, give cardiopulmonary resuscitation if indicated, and seek medical assistance. In the heart stops, apply resuscitation techniques. Resuscitation is a first-aid technique that provides artificial circulation and respiration. Remember the ABCs: A is for "airway," B is for "breathing," and C is for "circulation." Check the airway to make sure it is open, and check breathing and circulation.

9. **Seizures**: The cause of seizures is often epilepsy.

   Treatment: Clear the area around the victim to avoid injury during the seizure. Do not place anything in the victim's mouth; seek medical help after the seizure if necessary.

Competency 045: Physical Education

The teacher uses knowledge of the concepts, principles, skills, and practices of physical education to plan and implement effective and engaging physical education instruction.

Principles of Physical Education and Physical Activity

In 1986, the National Association for Sport and Physical Education (NASPE) appointed a committee to develop a working definition of the characteristics that physically educated people ought to exhibit (National Association for Sport and Physical Education 2009). As a result of this initiative, NASPE introduced the following definition. A physically educated person is someone who:

1. has learned skills necessary to perform a variety of physical activities

2. knows the implications of and the benefits from involvement in physical activity

3. participates regularly in physical activity and is physically fit; and values physical activity and its contribution to a healthy lifestyle

With this definition in mind, NASPE developed the National Standards for Physical Education:

Standard 1: Demonstrates competency in motor skills and movement patterns needed to perform a variety of physical activities.

Standard 2: Demonstrates understanding of movement concepts, principles, strategies, and tactics as they apply to the learning and performance of physical activities.

Standard 3: Participates regularly in physical activity.

Standard 4: Achieves and maintains a health-enhancing level of physical fitness.

Standard 5: Exhibits responsible personal and social behavior that respects self and others in physical activity settings.

Standard 6: Values physical activity for health, enjoyment, challenge, self-expression, and/or social interaction.

In order to help students achieve these standards, physical education teachers must have an understanding of the human body, and how physical activity can impact it. Knowledge of anatomy and physiology can guide teachers in the selection and implementation of games and physical activities appropriate for development. Anatomy describes the structure, position, and size of various body parts and organs. Because our bones adapt to fill a specific need, exercise is of great benefit to the skeletal system. Bones that anchor strong muscles thicken to withstand the stress put on it. Weight-bearing bones can develop heavy mineral deposits while supporting the body. Because joints help provide flexibility and ease of movement, it is important to know how each joint moves. Types of joints are ball and socket (e.g., shoulder and hip), hinge (e.g., elbow and knee), pivot (e.g., head of the spine), gliding (e.g., carpal (wrist) and tarsal (ankle) bones), angular (e.g., wrist and ankle joints), partially movable (e.g., vertebrae), and immovable (e.g., bones of the adult cranium).

Muscles are the active movers in the body. In order to properly teach any physical education activity, the functions and physiology of the muscles must be understood. Because muscles move by shortening or contracting, proper form should be taught so the student can get the most out of an activity. It is also important to know the location of each muscle. This knowledge will help in teaching proper form while participating in physical education activities. Understanding the concept of antagonistic muscles, along with the related information concerning flexors and extensors, is also vital to the physical educator. Imagine trying to teach the proper form of throwing a ball if you do not understand the mechanics involved. Knowledge of anatomy and physiology is also necessary to teach proper techniques used in calisthenics as well as all physical activities. Without this knowledge, exercise itself can cause harm to the body.

Exploration of movement activities through fun activities constitutes the main focus of the physical education curriculum in the early grades. However, the curriculum can provide for more organized activities like yoga or low impact aerobic exercise. Aerobic exercise involves both muscle contractions and movement of the body. Aerobic exercise requires large amounts of oxygen and when done regularly, will condition the cardiovascular system. Some aerobic exercises are especially suited to developing aerobic training benefits, with a minimum of skill and time involved. Examples of good aerobic activities are walking, running, swimming, and bicycling. These activities are especially good in the development of fitness because all of them can be done alone and with a minimum of special equipment. In order to be considered true aerobic conditioning, an activity must require a great deal of oxygen for the body to utilize, it must be continuous and rhythmic, it must exercise major muscle groups and burn fat as an energy source, and it must last for at least 20 minutes in an individual's target heart rate range. Children can participate in low impact aerobics training but parents and teachers must monitor their performance. Children will probably try to keep up with adults, and initially they may not have the strength, flexibility, and/or skill to keep pace. This could lead to undue fatigue, needless muscle soreness, and/or injury.

Benefits of an Active Lifestyle

The axiom "Use it or lose it" certainly holds true for the human body. Our bodies thrive on physical activity, which is any bodily movement produced by skeletal muscles and resulting in energy expenditure. Physical fitness enables a person to meet the physical demands of work and leisure comfortably. A person with a high level of physical fitness can enjoy a better quality of life and minimize the development of life-threatening diseases. Unfortunately, Americans tend to be relatively inactive.

Lack of activity can cause many problems, including weak muscles and heart, poor circulation, shortness of breath, obesity, coronary artery disease, hypertension, type II diabetes, osteoporosis, and certain types of cancer. Overall, mortality rates from all causes are lower in physically active people than in sedentary people. In addition, physical activity can help people manage mild-to-moderate depression, control anxiety, and prevent weakening of the skeletal system. By increasing physical activity, a person may improve heart function and circulation, respiratory function, and overall strength and endurance. All of these lead to improved vigor and vitality. Exercise also lowers the risk of heart disease by strengthening the heart muscle, lowering pulse and blood pressure, and lowering the concentration of fat in both the body and the blood. It can also improve appearance, increase range of motion, and lessen the risk of back problems associated with weak muscles, weak bones, and osteoporosis. Every person should engage in regular physical activity and reduce sedentary activities to promote health, psychological well-being, and a healthy body weight. On most days of the week, children should engage in at least 60 minutes of physical activity. Proper hydration is also important during physical activity. To help prevent dehydration during prolonged physical activity or when it is hot, people should consume water regularly during the activity and drink several glasses afterwards.

Evaluating and Monitoring Fitness Levels

One of the primary reasons for the teaching of physical education is to instill a willingness to exercise and encourage students to make good decisions about their health. Therefore, the evaluation of student performance and progress is becoming increasingly important and has, therefore, become an essential responsibility of the physical education teacher. In 2007, the Texas state legislature passed a law that all students from grades 3–12 will be measured once a year on the Fitnessgram (2009). The Fitnessgram is not a test of athletic ability, rather a health-related fitness assessment that uses criterion-referenced standards to measure physical health (i.e., muscular fitness, aerobic fitness, and flexibility). With regular physical activity all students should be able to achieve a score on the Fitnessgram that will place them within or above the Healthy Fitness Zone on all Fitnessgram test items. The idea is that all students should learn to assess their own level of fitness, interpret assessment results, plan personal programs, and motivate themselves to remain active throughout their lives.

The assessment plan for an elementary physical education program determines the degree to which students reach the identified goals. These critical objectives or "performance indicators" ensure that the teacher is focusing activities on skill development and improved performance during movement games and activities. To obtain good body management skills is to acquire, expand, and integrate elements of motor control. This is done through wide experiences in movement, based on a creative and exploratory approach. It is important that children not only manage their body with an ease of movement, but also realize that good posture and body mechanics are important parts of their movement process and patterns. In other words, a child with good motor control is a child who is confident and graceful. This is important not just for playing games and sports, but also for safety. Children without these skills are more prone to accidents and injury. It is the physical educator's responsibility to identify and halt movement patterns that are incorrect, demonstrate proper forms of movement, and assist learners to perform the desired movement pattern.

Development of Motor Skills

Physical changes play a significant role in the development of children as they gradually gain control of the movements and functions of their bodies. As they develop physically, children refine their motor skills, enabling them to engage in increasingly complex movement lessons and/or activities. For teachers to be able to identify patterns of physical development, they must first assess the level at which students can control specific movement patterns and then create educational activities that are developmentally appropriate for their students' physical abilities.

Children between the ages of three and four have already mastered standing and walking. At this stage, children are developing gross motor skills, including the ability to hop on one foot and balance, climb stairs without support, kick a ball, throw overhand, catch a ball that has bounced, move forward and backward, and ride a tricycle. Children between the ages of three and four are also developing fine motor skills, such as using scissors, drawing single shapes, and copying shapes like capital letters. By age four or five, when most children enter school, they are developing the gross motor ability to do somersaults, use a swing, climb, and skip. These skills require a multitude of movement patterns with increasing coordination. In addition, children at this age can begin to dress themselves using zippers, buttons, and possibly tying their shoes. They can also eat independently using utensils. Children at this age are increasingly capable of copying shapes, including letters and numbers. They can cut and paste and draw a person with a head, body, arms, and legs. These fine motor skills develop quickly in children of this age. By age six, children can bounce a ball, skate, ride a bike, skip with both feet, and dress themselves independently. As the student develops year by year, the physical skills (both fine and gross motor) become increasingly complex and involve more muscles and more coordination. By age nine, children can complete a model kit, learn to sew, and cook simple recipes. By age ten, children can catch a fly ball and participate in all elements of a softball game.

Recognizing the basic milestones that most children will achieve by a certain age (i.e., Texas Essential Knowledge and Skills [TEKS]) will assist teachers in making decisions about academic lessons and tasks. In addition, teachers may be able to identify children who may not be reaching their developmental milestones with the rest of the class. In short, the physical ability of students to engage in simple to complex activities in school gradually increases as they develop. Physical Educators must adjust and adapt classroom and playground activities to be developmentally appropriate for the specific skill levels of students.

During play activities, a child engages in meaningful movement patterns that utilize large muscle groups in the body. Movement education is the process by which a child is helped to develop competency in those general movement patterns. It has been defined as learning to move and moving to learn. Movement competency requires the student to manage his or her body through space, time, and direction with the ability to accomplish basic and specialized physical tasks and traverse various obstacles. Basic movement skills are necessary for a child's daily living, whereas specialized skills are required to perform sports and other complex activities that have very clear techniques. Of course, basic skills must be mastered before the child can develop specialized ones.

Perceptual motor competency is another consideration in teaching body management. Perceptual motor concepts that are relevant to physical education include those that give attention to balance, coordination, lateral movement, directional movement, awareness of space, and knowledge of one's own body. Basic skills can be divided into three categories, locomotor, non-locomotor, and manipulative skills. A more complex movement pattern might include skills from each category. **Locomotor skills** describe the type of movement children have to master in order to travel or move within a given space. These include walking, running, leaping, jumping, hopping, galloping, sliding, and skipping. **Non-locomotor skills** are used to control the body in relation to the force of gravity. These are typically done while in a stationary position (i.e., kneeling or standing). Some of these activities include: pushing, pulling, bending, stretching, twisting, turning, swinging, shaking, bouncing, rising, and falling. **Manipulative skills** are used when a child handles, moves, or plays with an object. Most manipulative skills involve using the hands and feet, but other parts of the body may be used as well. Hand-eye and foot-eye coordination are improved when manipulating objects. Throwing, batting, kicking, and catching are important skills to be developed using balls and beanbags. Starting a child at a less challenging level and progressing to a more difficult activity is an effective method for teaching manipulative activities. Most activities begin with individual practice and evolve to partner activities. When teaching throwing and catching for example, the teacher should emphasize skill performance, principles of opposition, weight transfer, eye focus, and follow through. Some attention should be given to targets when throwing because students need to be able to catch and throw to different areas and levels. For detailed information on physical education activities for K–6 children, visit the PE Central website at *www.pecentral.org*.

Promoting Physical Fitness

Children in early childhood are not concerned with physical fitness; instead, they are interested in having fun. Based on this premise, a physical education program for this age group should reflect this interest. The child who is actively involved in fun physical activities will get the same benefits as children in a highly structured physical fitness program. To that end, it is important for K–6 physical educators to understand that programming activities that focus on the enjoyment of moving their bodies is much more important than being groomed for success at a specific event or sport.

Movement education enables the child to make choices of activity and the method they wish to employ. Teachers can structure learning situations so the child can be challenged to develop his or her own means of movement. The child becomes the center of learning and is encouraged to be creative in carrying out the movement experience. In this method of teaching, the child is encouraged to be creative and progress according to his/her abilities. The teacher is not the center of learning, but offers suggestions and stimulates the learning environment through guided discovery. Student-centered learning works especially well when there is a wide disparity of motor abilities. If the teacher sets standards that are too high for the less talented students, they may become discouraged and lose motivation. On the other hand, if the teacher sets standards that are too low, the more talented students will become bored and also lose interest. Providing an array of options for learners is the best way to facilitate movement games and activities. This way, learners can identify which option or challenges are most appropriate and perform up to their developmental level with little assistance and/or cues from the teacher. Movement education attempts to develop the children's awareness not only of what they are doing but how they are doing it. Each child is encouraged to succeed in his or her own way according to his or her own capacity. If children succeed at developing basic skills in elementary school, they will have a much better chance at acquiring the specialized skills required for sports, events, and specific activities later on in the secondary school setting.

To teach a basic or specialized movement skill to a variety of learners, the instructor must present and use explanation, demonstration, and drill. Other students can do demonstrations, provided the teacher monitors the demonstration and gives cues for proper form. Drills are excellent to teach specific skills but can become tedious unless they are done in a creative manner. Using game simulations to practice skills is also an effective method to maintain interest during a practice session. Teachers must remember to use observation and feedback when teaching a skill or activity. Of course, positive feedback is much more conducive to skill acquisition than negative feedback. The typical "old school" intimidation tactics of physical education coaches will not work for children at this age. Appropriate feedback means correcting with suggestions to improve. For example, if a student playing kickball continually misses the ball or kicks the ball out of play, he or she is aware that something is not right. The teacher should indicate what the problem is and tell the student how to be successful when kicking the ball into the play area.

Many physical education professionals have advocated for the Teaching Games for Understanding model as a sound philosophy regarding movement games education. It is a socio-constructivist teaching and learning approach to physical education that emphasizes the learners' engagement in the construction of knowledge, skills, and experience. This student-centered model is built upon critical thinking, problem-solving, observation, and debriefing the experience for specific learning outcomes (i.e., teamwork, sportsmanship, and skill performance). Strategies of this model can be implemented across a variety of physical education curriculum including adventure education, cooperative learning, fitness education, tactical games, and sports education.

Curriculum Requirements for Physical Education

The Texas Essential Knowledge and Skills (TEKS) comprises all the curriculum components in the area of Physical Education. Physical Education teachers are expected to implement the prescribed state curriculum (Texas Administrative Code, 2009b). In conjunction with the national initiative, The Texas Essential Knowledge and Skills (TEKS) requires children to demonstrate knowledge and skills for movement that provide the foundation for enjoyment, continued social development through physical activity, and access to a physically active lifestyle. All children are expected to develop muscular strength and endurance of the arms, shoulders, abdomen, back, and legs. They are also expected to become aware of how the muscles, bones, heart, and lungs function in relation to physical activity. The activities and skills for children in K–6 are designed to keep children active, to develop the fitness necessary for appropriate physical development, and to maintain a healthy body and mind. Some of the key skills and activities required in the state K–6 curriculum are listed below (Texas Administrative Code, 2009b).

Kindergarten

Children should be able to:

1. Play with other children within boundaries during games and activities

2. Develop muscular strength and endurance of the arms, shoulders, abdomen, back, and legs such as hanging, hopping, and jumping

3. Demonstrate knowledge of a variety of relationships such as under, over, behind, next to, through, right, left, up, down, forward, backward, and in front of

4. Roll sideways (right or left) without hesitating

5. Toss a ball and catch it before it bounces twice

First Grade

Children should be able to:

1. Demonstrate proper foot patterns in hopping, jumping, skipping, leaping, galloping, and sliding

2. Demonstrate the ability to work with a partner such as leading and following

3. Clap in time to a simple rhythmic beat; create and imitate movement in response to selected rhythms; jump a long rope; and demonstrate on cue key elements in overhand throw, underhand throw, and catch

4. Demonstrate proper foot patterns in hopping, jumping, skipping, leaping, galloping, and sliding

5. Demonstrate control in balancing and traveling activities

Second Grade

Children should be able to:

1. Demonstrate skills of chasing, fleeing, and dodging to avoid or catch others

2. Demonstrate mature forms of walking, hopping, and skipping

3. Demonstrate a variety of relationships in dynamic movement situations such as under, over, behind, next to, through, right, left, up, or down

4. Demonstrate simple stunts that exhibit personal agility such as jumping with one and two foot takeoffs and landing with good control

5. Demonstrate on cue key elements of hand dribble, foot dribble, kick and strike such as striking a balloon or ball with a hand

Third Grade

Children should be able to:

1. Demonstrate mature forms in jogging, running, and leaping

2. Demonstrate control and appropriate form such as curled position and protection of neck in rolling activities

3. Transfer their bodies on and off equipment with good body control such as boxes, benches, stacked mats, horizontal bar, and balance beam

4. Clap echoes in a variety of one measure rhythmical patterns

5. Demonstrate key elements in manipulative skills such as underhand throw, overhand throw, catch, and kick

Fourth Grade

Children should be able to:

1. Change speed during straight, curved, and zigzag pathways

2. Catch a football pass on the run

3. Jump and land for height and distance absorbing force such as bending knees and swinging arms;

4. Perform basic folk dance steps such as schottische (German folk dance), and step-together-step

5. Demonstrate key elements in manipulative skills such as volleying, hand dribble, foot dribble, and punt, also, striking with a body part, racquet, or bat

Fifth Grade

1. Demonstrate smooth combinations of fundamental locomotor skills such as running and dodging and hop-step-jump

2. Demonstrate the ability to contrast a partner's movement

3. Identify common phases such as preparation, movement, follow through, or recovery in a variety of movement skills such as a tennis serve, handstand, and free throw

4. Self-monitor the heart rate during exercise

5. Identify potentially dangerous exercises and their adverse effects on the body

Sixth Grade

1. Use relationships, levels, speed, direction, and pathways effectively in complex group and individual physical activities such as crouching low for volleyball digs, stretching high during lay-ups, positioning for a soccer pass, or passing ahead of a receiver

2. Move in time to complex rhythmical patterns such as 3/4 time or 6/8 time

3. Hand and foot dribble while preventing an opponent from stealing the ball

4. Practice in ways that are appropriate for learning skills such as whole/part/whole; shorter practice distributed over time is better than one long session; or practicing is best in game-like conditions

5. Modify games/activities to improve the game/activity

Managing Instruction

Managing a large class of kids in a loud gymnasium or outdoor learning environment is no easy task. Therefore, a major goal of the physical education teacher is to have all students listen to directions prior to activity. The instructions should be short, to the point, and as clear as possible. A teacher who talks longer than 20 seconds during any single instructional period will soon find the class beginning to lose interest. This leads to an environment difficult to manage. For this reason, teachers should alternate short instructional episodes (including one or two points of focus) with longer periods of activity. Minimizing instructional content will reduce both student frustration and difficult situations to manage. Most students and teachers enjoy a learning environment that is organized, efficient, and allows a maximum amount of class time to be devoted to learning skills.

Management behavior routines must be enforced regularly by the instructor (especially early on); otherwise, the environment will always be chaotic and difficult to manage. Effective physical educators identify a consistent keyword to use with learners that commences a new activity (i.e., "Begin" or "Ready Go"). This implies encouraging youngsters to listen to the entire set of instructions before preparing for the next exercise. Since the keyword is not given until all directions have been issued, students cannot begin until they hear the selected keyword. Similarly, a consistent signal should be established for stopping an activity (i.e., "Freeze" or "Clap once… Clap twice… Clap three times…"). Whatever the signal, it must be practiced everyday so learners come to know the signal and it becomes second nature. Using an audio signal (i.e., whistle blast) and a visual signal (i.e., raising the hand overhead) may also be effective, since some youngsters may not hear the audio signal if they are engrossed in loud activity. Whereas a loud audio signal may be used to stop a class, a voice command should always be used to start the class. If children do not respond to these signals, the procedure must be practiced. Remember, if a teacher settles for less than full attention, students will fulfill those expectations of being chaotic and unmanageable.

Physical education teachers should also know how to divide students into teachable groups quickly. Simple games can be used to accomplish this such as "Back to Back" or "Foot to Foot" in which individuals get back to back (or foot to foot, etc.) with a partner as fast as possible. Students without a partner are instructed to go to the center of the teaching area (marked by a cone or spot) to immediately find someone else without a partner. If students are staying near a friend, teachers can tell the class to move throughout space using a locomotor skill and then find a different partner each time the body part is called. If arranging students in groups larger than two people, Whistle Mixer works effectively. When the whistle is blown a certain number of times, students form groups corresponding to the number of whistle blows and sit down to signify that they have the correct number of people in their group.

Physical education teachers need to use a consistent approach for dealing with undesirable behavior. "Time-Out" is generally used to deal with inappropriate behavior. The time-out approach moves youngsters out of the class setting and places them into a designated area when they misbehave. Being placed in the time-out area does not imply that the student is a "bad person," but rather that he/she has forgotten to follow the rules. When placing students in time-out, teachers should communicate to children that they are loved individuals, but their misbehavior is unacceptable, hence, the reason they are in time-out.

To minimize incidence of undesirable behavior, teachers are encouraged to develop a set of expectations and rules for the class. The plan's expectations should be no more than five items, posted in the teaching area for easy reference. The rules should be discussed regularly so children clearly understand what are the expected behaviors and consequences. A set of consequences might be as follows: First misbehavior—the student is warned quietly on a personal basis to avoid embarrassment. Sometimes, students are unaware that they are bothering others and a gentle reminder is all that is needed to refocus the behavior. Second misbehavior—the student is told to go to a designated time-out spot. The student must stay there until ready to reenter the activity and demonstrate the desired behavior. It is acceptable for the student to go to the area for a short period and almost immediately return to the activity since the assumption is that they have agreed to stop misbehaving. Third misbehavior—the student goes to time-out for a longer period or the remainder of the period. In addition to negative consequences, teachers are also asked to identify positive consequences. The reward system is used to reward those students that follow the rules and comply with instructions, and as a way to motivate others to exhibit appropriate behavior

Adaptive Physical Education

The Americans with Disabilities Act (2009) requires the placement of students in the least restrictive environment. For most "handicapped children," the least restrictive environment is the regular classroom, which includes participation in physical education activities. The challenge in teaching physical education to handicapped children is tailoring activities to fit each child. For example, blind or partially sighted students can participate in dance, and some gymnastic and tumbling activities. These students can also participate in some other activities with modifications. A beeper ball together with verbal cues can be used for T-ball or even for softball. If a beeper is not available, the teacher can put the student in position and assist in aiming and cueing when to hit the ball. For students using assistive devices like walkers or crutches, they can be allowed to hit the ball from a seated position and use the crutch to bat. If the child is unable to run, allow a substitute runner. Many games and activities can be modified for the handicapped child. Sometimes all it takes is a little ingenuity to change activities so handicapped students can enjoy participating.

References

Americans with Disability Act. 2009. Information and technical assistance on the Americans with Disabilities Act. *www.usdoj.gov/crt/ada/adahom1.htm* (accessed July 16, 2009).

Fitnessgram. 2009. Activity and fitness assessment and personal physical activity management. *www.fitnessgram.net/home* (accessed on June 29, 2009).

Healthy People 2010. Healthy People Website. *www.healthypeople.gov/* (accessed July 16, 2009).

National Association for Sport and Physical Education. 2009. Physical activity guidelines published by the national association for sport and physical education. *www.aahperd.org/NASPE/template.cfm?template=ns_index.html* (accessed July 2, 2009).

National Institute of Mental Health. 2009. Eating disorders: Facts about eating disorders and the search for solutions. *www.nimh.nih.gov/Publicat/eatingdisorders.cfm* (accessed June 21, 2009).

PE Central. 2009. The premier website for health and physical education. *www.pecentral.org* (accessed May 27, 2009).

Shelov, S., and T. Remer. 2009. Caring for baby and young child: Birth to age 5. American Academy of Pediatrics. *www.aap.org/publiced/BK0_ChildAbuse.htm* (accessed July 8, 2009).

Texas Administrative Code. 2009a. Title 19, Part II Chapter 115. Texas Essential Knowledge and Skills for Health Education. *www.tea.state.tx.us/rules/tac/chapter115/index.html* (accessed May 22, 2009).

Texas Administrative Code. 2009b. Title 19, Part II Chapter 116. Texas Essential Knowledge and Skills for Physical Education. *www.tea.state.tx.us/rules/tac/chapter116/index.html* (accessed May 22, 2009).

U.S. Department of Agriculture. 2009. My food pyramid: Steps to a healthier you. *www. mypyramid.gov* (accessed June 7, 2009).

U.S. Department of Health and Human Services. 2006. Dietary Guidelines for Americans. *www.health.gov/DietaryGuidelines/* (accessed June 29, 2009).

Diagnostic Test

TExES 191 Generalist EC-6

ANSWER SHEET DIAGNOSTIC TEST

1. Ⓐ Ⓑ Ⓒ Ⓓ
2. Ⓐ Ⓑ Ⓒ Ⓓ
3. Ⓐ Ⓑ Ⓒ Ⓓ
4. Ⓐ Ⓑ Ⓒ Ⓓ
5. Ⓐ Ⓑ Ⓒ Ⓓ
6. Ⓐ Ⓑ Ⓒ Ⓓ
7. Ⓐ Ⓑ Ⓒ Ⓓ
8. Ⓐ Ⓑ Ⓒ Ⓓ
9. Ⓐ Ⓑ Ⓒ Ⓓ
10. Ⓐ Ⓑ Ⓒ Ⓓ
11. Ⓐ Ⓑ Ⓒ Ⓓ
12. Ⓐ Ⓑ Ⓒ Ⓓ
13. Ⓐ Ⓑ Ⓒ Ⓓ
14. Ⓐ Ⓑ Ⓒ Ⓓ
15. Ⓐ Ⓑ Ⓒ Ⓓ
16. Ⓐ Ⓑ Ⓒ Ⓓ
17. Ⓐ Ⓑ Ⓒ Ⓓ

18. Ⓐ Ⓑ Ⓒ Ⓓ
19. Ⓐ Ⓑ Ⓒ Ⓓ
20. Ⓐ Ⓑ Ⓒ Ⓓ
21. Ⓐ Ⓑ Ⓒ Ⓓ
22. Ⓐ Ⓑ Ⓒ Ⓓ
23. Ⓐ Ⓑ Ⓒ Ⓓ
24. Ⓐ Ⓑ Ⓒ Ⓓ
25. Ⓐ Ⓑ Ⓒ Ⓓ
26. Ⓐ Ⓑ Ⓒ Ⓓ
27. Ⓐ Ⓑ Ⓒ Ⓓ
28. Ⓐ Ⓑ Ⓒ Ⓓ
29. Ⓐ Ⓑ Ⓒ Ⓓ
30. Ⓐ Ⓑ Ⓒ Ⓓ
31. Ⓐ Ⓑ Ⓒ Ⓓ
32. Ⓐ Ⓑ Ⓒ Ⓓ
33. Ⓐ Ⓑ Ⓒ Ⓓ
34. Ⓐ Ⓑ Ⓒ Ⓓ

35. Ⓐ Ⓑ Ⓒ Ⓓ
36. Ⓐ Ⓑ Ⓒ Ⓓ
37. Ⓐ Ⓑ Ⓒ Ⓓ
38. Ⓐ Ⓑ Ⓒ Ⓓ
39. Ⓐ Ⓑ Ⓒ Ⓓ
40. Ⓐ Ⓑ Ⓒ Ⓓ
41. Ⓐ Ⓑ Ⓒ Ⓓ
42. Ⓐ Ⓑ Ⓒ Ⓓ
43. Ⓐ Ⓑ Ⓒ Ⓓ
44. Ⓐ Ⓑ Ⓒ Ⓓ
45. Ⓐ Ⓑ Ⓒ Ⓓ
46. Ⓐ Ⓑ Ⓒ Ⓓ
47. Ⓐ Ⓑ Ⓒ Ⓓ
48. Ⓐ Ⓑ Ⓒ Ⓓ
49. Ⓐ Ⓑ Ⓒ Ⓓ
50. Ⓐ Ⓑ Ⓒ Ⓓ

DIAGNOSTIC TEST

1. The use of thematic planning is ideal for English language learners (ELLs) because in this curriculum arrangement students are exposed to

    A. cultural features through the use of concrete objects in real-life situations.

    B. the same information in all content areas.

    C. instruction in highly contextualized situations.

    D. concepts and vocabulary related to the themes in various content areas.

2. The main purpose of using semantic mapping in social studies is to

    A. teach geography concepts to ELLs.

    B. identify critical features of a given concept.

    C. ish connections between concepts in two languages.

    D. present a graphic representation of a process.

3. The Spaniards Francisco Pizarro and Hernán Cortés conquered, respectively, which of the following two civilizations?

    A. Mayan and Aztec

    B. Inca and Aztec

    C. Toltec and Olmec

    D. Taino and Quechua

4. The earliest European colonization efforts in North America began with the founding of

    A. Virginia and Massachusetts.

    B. Texas and New Mexico.

    C. Saint Augustine and Roanoke.

    D. New York and New Jersey.

5. The Earth, spherical in shape, is artificially divided into 24 time zones to account for its rotation around the axis and its varying exposure to the sun. What is the degree of separation among these time zones?

   A. 10°

   B. 20°

   C. 30°

   D. 15°

6. The tallest mountains in the world are part of the

   A. Andes Range.

   B. Himalayas Range.

   C. Karakoram Range.

   D. Kunlun Range.

7. The United States has 50 states and at least four territories. Based on these figures, what is the maximum number of senators that can serve in the U.S. Senate?

   A. 50

   B. 100

   C. 54

   D. 435

8. A census of the population in the U.S. is conducted every 10 years. Based on census results, identify the agency or entity that can be affected by population changes.

   A. House of Representatives

   B. U.S. Senate

   C. Justices of the Supreme Court

   D. The Executive Branch

9. Identify the syntactic structure that represents the following sentence—*Mary gave me a dollar*.

   A. noun, intransitive verb, predicative nominative

   B. noun, intransitive verb, predicative adjective

   C. noun, transitive verb, indirect object, direct object

   D. noun, transitive verb, direct object

10. **Scenario:** Joe is a third grader having difficulties with American idioms. He often gets confused with expressions like "keep an eye on the baby" and "keep your nose clean." Joe is having problems dealing with

    A. academic English.

    B. denotative language.

    C. connotative language.

    D. metaphors and similes.

11. **Scenario:** Mr. Figueroa introduced a cooperative learning activity for fourth graders wherein the students were to identify the syntactic classification for selected words. Accent marks were used to indicate the appropriate pronunciation of a word and also to give a clue for its meaning. The students were also to write a sentence with each of the words assigned.

Word	Word Classification	Example of Sentence
Example: in•sert´	Verb	I insert a key to open my door.
sub•ject´		
sub´•ject		
in´•sert		
con´•vert		
con•vert´		

In addition to promoting vocabulary development, what is the main phonological component presented through this activity?

    A. The use of sight words for decoding

    B. The importance of using accents to guide pronunciation of words in English

    C. The semantic value of word stress

    D. The importance of contrasting similar words to help in their spelling

12. The key feature of a balanced reading program is that it uses

   A.   a balance between the receptive and productive skills of the language.

   B.   a balance between theory and application of reading concepts.

   C.   phonics instruction as the primary method to teach English reading.

   D.   the best practices from the skill-based and the meaning-based approaches.

13. Identify the rationale for the popularity of onset and rime to teach spelling skills in English.

   A.   It is used to compensate for the grapheme-phoneme inconsistency of English.

   B.   It is used to teach words as sight words.

   C.   It is the best approach to teach words with multiple syllables.

   D.   It is the best approach to teach the spelling pattern for prefixes and suffixes.

14. What is the main reason for introducing the letter-sound correspondence of the *m, b, t, p,* and *s* prior to the letters like the *x* or *q*?

   A.   Children might have more interest in the first set of sounds.

   B.   The first set of graphemes occurs more frequently in reading.

   C.   Children have muscular control and can pronounce nasal sounds.

   D.   The last set of graphemes can create language interference.

15. During the pre-reading stage of the shared book experience, teachers can increase interest in the story by

   A.   encouraging students to make predictions based on the title and the pictures.

   B.   encouraging students to draw a picture representing the main idea of the story.

   C.   encouraging students to draw pictures representing the characters of the story.

   D.   introducing students to the author's biography and other books written by the author.

16. During the first reading of the shared book experience, the teacher reads the whole story in an enthusiastic and dramatic manner. The main purpose of this activity is

   A.   to make the content understood by children so they can enjoy it and corroborate their earlier predictions about it.

   B.   to introduce decoding skills and the main idea.

   C.   to introduce unknown vocabulary and decoding skills to the children.

   D.   to review the parts of the book, check for comprehension, and practice the use of contextual clues.

17. What is the main purpose of exposing third-grade Spanish-speaking children learning English as a second language to common prefixes that are used in both Spanish and English?

    A. To present the idea that English has been influenced by other languages

    B. To present the idea that English has many foreign words

    C. To present the idea that elements from Spanish can transfer to English

    D. To present the idea that English is not a difficult language

18. The word "predestined" is composed of

    A. one inflectional morpheme and one derivational morpheme.

    B. one derivational morpheme, the root of the word, and two inflectional morphemes.

    C. two inflectional morphemes and the root of the word.

    D. one derivational morpheme, the root, and one inflectional morpheme.

19. Silent sustained reading (SSR) is designed to promote

    A. reading fluency.

    B. reading comprehension.

    C. word analysis.

    D. decoding skills.

20. The main purpose of an intergenerational literacy initiative is to

    A. improve the literacy development of adults and the community.

    B. use children as a reason to involve parents in school activities.

    C. promote literacy among children by using the support of parents and other family members.

    D. begin in preschool and continue through high school.

21. Kindergarten students can identify the main idea of a story by

    A. drawing a picture representing the story.

    B. writing a short paragraph summarizing the story

    C. verbalizing the main points of the story and writing a chronology of events in the story.

    D. developing a detailed analysis of the story line.

22. Reciprocal teaching is a technique used with struggling readers and is designed to

    A. promote reading fluency.

    B. promote reading comprehension in the content areas.

    C. establish an environment where students can practice oral language skills.

    D. introduce cooperative learning activities.

23. When planning for the accommodations to be used when assessing special education students, the first element teachers should consider is

    A. the cost associated with the proposed accommodations.

    B. the legality of the proposed adaptations.

    C. the feasibility of time and resources available for such accommodations.

    D. the type of disability the child has.

24. What is the key advantage of using interactive writing journals for emerging writers?

    A. Students can communicate silently in class.

    B. Students learn that writing can be used for communication.

    C. Students can correct each other's writing samples.

    D. Students can learn about personal information from teachers and peers.

25. Connectors are used in writing to create cohesive and coherent compositions. Connections like "on the contrary," "conversely," and "on the other hand" are commonly used in compositions addressing

    A. opinion.

    B. sequencing.

    C. contrast.

    D. results.

26. English writing samples from Spanish-dominant ELLs may contain which key feature?

    A. The stories are simple in content and written in a linear fashion.

    B. The stories might have complex sentence patterns and sophisticated words from Spanish.

    C. The stories might be perceived as disjointed and lacking a logical sequence.

    D. The stories might switch from Spanish to English within the same sentence.

27. Effective writing requires students to tailor compositions to their audience or to the purpose of an occasion. The writing portion of the TAKS test uses which of the following to achieve this purpose?

    A. A multiple-choice test

    B. Specific instructions to guide children in the writing sample

    C. Writing prompts

    D. A series of questions to guide the development of the writing sample

28. Miscue analysis was developed by John Goodman to assess

    A. the performance of children in silent sustained reading.

    B. the performance of children in their development of writing.

    C. the performance of children in their ability to speak.

    D. the performance of children in oral reading.

29. Informal reading inventories are designed to

    A. assess the literacy development of children in kindergarten through the sixth grade.

    B. identify the reading level of children.

    C. assess informally the performance of students in middle school and high school.

    D. determine the level of complexity of reading passages.

30. Identify the statement that best represents the real value of manipulatives to teach mathematics.

    A. Manipulatives are more appropriate for students at the preoperational stage of cognitive development.

    B. The use of manipulatives should be restricted to children in kindergarten to fourth grade.

    C. The use of manipulatives is more appropriate for teaching computation skills and geometry.

    D. Manipulatives can be used to teach mathematics in grades Pre-K to high school.

31. Multiply $\frac{3}{4}$ by $\frac{2}{3}$. Show your answer in simplified (reduced) form.

    A. $\frac{5}{7}$

    B. $\frac{5}{12}$

    C. $\frac{1}{2}$

    D. $\frac{6}{12}$

32. Divide 6.2 by 0.05.

    A. 124

    B. 1.24

    C. 12.4

    D. 0.124

Use the figure below to answer the following question.

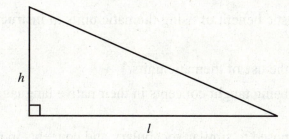

33. Which formula can be used to find the area of the triangle?

    A. $A = \dfrac{(l \times h)}{2}$

    B. $A = \dfrac{(l + h)}{2}$

    C. $A = 2(l + h)$

    D. $A = 2(l \times h)$

Use the figure below to answer the following question.

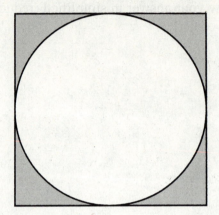

34. What is the approximate area of the shaded region, given that

    1. the radius of the circle is 6 units
    2. the square inscribes the circle

    A. 106 square units

    B. 31 square units

    C. 77 square units

    D. 125 square units

35. What is the linguistic benefit of using thematic units in instructing English language learners (ELLs)?

    A. ELLs enjoy the use of thematic units.

    B. ELLs enjoy being taught concepts in their native language (L1) and in English (L2).

    C. ELLs are exposed to similar vocabulary and concepts in multiple formats.

    D. ELLs learn about mathematics and other content areas concurrently.

36. The concept of zero evolved in India but was also developed, disconnectedly, by the

    A. Babylonians.

    B. Mayans

    C. Arabs.

    D. Romans.

37. Which of the following is a complementary color pair?

    A. Blue and green

    B. Red and green

    C. Yellow and red

    D. Purple and red

38. Flying buttresses, pointed arches, and stained glass windows are characteristic of which historic style of architecture?

    A. Romanesque

    B. Renaissance

    C. Byzantine

    D. Gothic

39. Some of the musical instruments typically introduced in K–4 are

    A. tambourine, triangle, and sticks.

    B. flute, clarinet, and trumpet.

    C. violin, guitar, and guitarrón.

    D. bongos, piano, and harp.

40. Identify the most appropriate first step to take in helping a child experiencing heat exhaustion.

    A. Get the child out of the heat and initiate CPR.

    B. Get the child to a shaded area and give him/her water to drink.

    C. Get the child out of the heat and seek medical attention immediately.

    D. Get the child to a shaded area and pour ice water on top of the child.

41. Activities that develop gross motor–visual skills almost always involve the use of a

    A. ball.

    B. balance beam.

    C. trampoline.

    D. exercise mat.

42. For an aerobic workout to be effective, exercise should be performed at an individual's targeted heart rate for a minimum of

    A. 10 minutes.

    B. 20 minutes.

    C. 45 minutes.

    D. 5 minutes.

43. The most appropriate and safest way to provide exercise for kindergarten and first-grade students is through

    A. jogging and walking.

    B. contact sports.

    C. games that require endurance.

    D. games that require physical activity.

44. Identify the test designed to measure flexibility in children.

    A. Pull-up test

    B. Sit-and-reach test

    C. Grip strength test

    D. Push-up test

45. **Scenario:** Ms. Pachuta uses a fish tank filled with water to teach students how to make predictions about the ability of objects to float or sink. Students have fun with this activity, but they don't really know the scientific principle demonstrated in it, which can be best described as

    A. the mass and amount of matter in an object.

    B. the concept of density and its relation to mass and volume.

    C. the properties of matter.

    D. the concept of weight and its connection with gravitational forces.

46. What is the role of evaporation and condensation in the water cycle?

    A. They recycle and redistribute the water in an ecosystem.

    B. They keep the ecosystem clean of pollutants.

    C. They provide water for vegetation and animals.

    D. They change water from liquid to vapor.

47. The capability of predatory animals to develop new physical traits to improve their ability to capture prey represents an example of

    A. intelligent creation.

    B. adaptation.

    C. metamorphosis.

    D. reproduction.

48. **Scenario:** Ms. Salinas used the following statement to teach the position of the planets (even the newly designated "dwarf planet," Pluto) with regard to the sun:

My	very	elegant	mother	just	served
Mercury	Venus	Earth	Mars	Jupiter	Saturn

us	nutritious	pizza.
Uranus	Neptune	Pluto

    Identify the statment below that best characterizes the use of mnemonic devices to teach content.

    A. Some students can analyze the structure of the sentence and remember information about the space.

    B. For some students this device can lead to application of concepts and the use of higher-order thinking skills.

    C. For some students this activity might lack purpose, while for others it might be an effective way to remember facts.

    D. Students should definitely reject this approach, because it emphasizes rote memorization.

49. Use the information in Question 48 to answer the following question: How many planets have a year that is shorter than that of Earth?

    A. 4

    B. 8

    C. 2

    D. 1

50. **Scenario:** Ms. Cena asked her students to bring their raincoats outside to observe the clouds. Once outside, her students observed cumulus clouds. Based on their observation, what kind of weather were they experiencing that day?

    A. A sunny day

    B. A cloudy day

    C. A rainy day

    D. A snowy day

ANSWER KEY – DIAGNOSTIC TEST

Question	Answer	Competency
1	D	004
2	B	004
3	B	020
4	C	020
5	D	041
6	B	038
7	B	023
8	A	023
9	C	005
10	C	007
11	C	005
12	D	004
13	A	005
14	B	005
15	A	007
16	A	007
17	C	005
18	D	005
19	B	007
20	C	004
21	A	009
22	B	007
23	D	008
24	B	009
25	C	009

Question	Answer	Competency
26	C	010
27	C	010
28	D	006
29	B	007
30	D	013
31	C	014
32	A	014
33	A	016
34	B	016
35	C	013
36	B	015
37	B	042
38	D	042
39	A	043
40	B	044
41	A	045
42	B	044
43	D	045
44	B	044
45	B	031
46	A	039
47	B	036
48	C	028
49	C	041
50	A	040

Detailed Explanations for Diagnostic Test

1. **D**

   Concepts and vocabulary are introduced through the thematic unit. Through repeated exposure to content, ELLs have a better chance to internalize the concepts and vocabulary contained in it. Choice A is incorrect because it fails to describe the full benefit of thematic instruction. Cultural exposure can occur in any instructional setting. Choice B is incorrect because, in thematic instruction, students do not get the same content in all areas. The only element that is common to all classes is the theme. Choice C is incorrect because instruction delivered in highly contextualized situations is not restricted to thematic instruction. **Competency 004**

2. **B**

   Semantic mapping is a visual representation of interconnected characteristics or features of a given concept. This interrelatedness can be represented with words or symbols. For example, the concept of *landscape* can be linked to pictures of lakes, rivers, mountains, grass, trees, and other images that represent possible attributes of the concept. This word mapping can be linked to geography (A); however, the intended meaning of the word goes beyond geography. People can use semantic mapping to contrast concepts in L1 and L2 (C), but the process was not designed to accomplish only that. Choice D describes a possible type of mapping, but does not represent the specific type of mapping required in the question—semantic. **Competency 004**

3. **B**

   Francisco Pizarro conquered the Incas of Peru, and Hernán Cortés conquered the Aztecs of Mexico. Choice A is incorrect because the Maya had virtually disappeared before the arrival of the Spaniards to America. Choice C is incorrect because these Mesoamerican groups, the Toltec and Olmec, disappeared before the Spanish colonization. Choice D is incorrect because the Tainos were from the Caribbean, an area that was under Spanish control before the intervention of Cortés and Pizarro. Additionally, the word *Quechua* refers to the language spoken by the Incas and other groups in the Andes Mountains. **Competency 020**

4. **C**

   The Spaniards established St. Augustine, the first permanent European colony in North America, in 1565 near what is today Jacksonville, Florida. Subsequent to this, the English made an attempt to establish a colony off the coast of North Carolina—Roanoke. Choice A is incorrect because Virginia, Massachusetts, and all the American colonies were established in the seventeenth century. Choice B is incorrect because New Mexico was established a few years later, in 1598, to become the first European colony west of the Mississippi. The first mission in Texas was established more than one hundred years later, in 1682. Choice D is incorrect because the Dutch did not begin bringing families to the area of New York and New Jersey until 1624. **Competency 020**

5.   **D**

The Earth, a sphere, has 365 degrees, and its rotation around its axis takes 24 hours. This rotation creates day and night. The correct choice is 15 degrees, which is calculated by dividing 365 degrees by 24 hours of day/night. Choices A, B, and C are incorrect based on the previous explanation. **Competency 041**

6.   **B**

With the exception of peak K2, the top 10 mountain peaks are all part of the Himalayas Range. Choice A is incorrect, because, despite the fact that the Andes Range contains several high mountains, none of them ranks within the top 50 in the world. Choice C is incorrect because only three of the top 20 mountains in the world are part of the Karakoram Range. Choice D is incorrect because only one mountain from the Kunlun Range ranks within the first 25. **Competency 038**

7.   **B**

The U.S. Constitution provides for two senators to represent each of the 50 states, for a total of 100. Territories are not represented in the U.S. Senate. Choices A and C are incorrect based on the previous explanation. Choice D is incorrect because it represents the current number of members of the U.S. House of Representatives. **Competency 023**

8.   **A**

The number of members of the House of Representative is adjusted to reflect a proportion of the total U.S. population; thus, every time there is a census, the number can change. Choices B, C, and D are incorrect because population changes do not affect the composition of the Senate, Supreme Court, or the Executive Branch. **Competency 023**

9.   **C**

The sentence contains a noun (Mary), a transtive verb (gave), an indirect object (me), and a direct object (dollar). The key clue to answering this question correctly is found within the type of verb used in the sentence—a transitive verb. Transitive verbs by definition can take objects. To determine if the sentence contains a direct object or an indirect object, we ask the following two questions: Mary gave what?—the answer is the direct object—a dollar. The second question is, Mary gave it to whom?—the answer is *me*—the indirect object. Choices A and B are incorrect because both contain intransitive verbs. Choice D is incorrect because it does not contain an indirect object. **Competency 005**

10. **C**

Idiomatic expressions rely on culture referents and connotative, or implied, meanings. That is why ELLs experience difficulties understanding them. Choice A is incorrect because idioms are regarded not as academic English expressions but as a part of social language. Choice B is incorrect because denotative language refers to the literal meaning of the words, and obviously idioms have implied meaning. Choice D is incorrect because idioms do not necessarily incorporate direct (metaphors) or indirect comparisons (similes). **Competency 007**

11. **C**

The words presented in this activity show the importance of word stress and how it can alter the meaning and the syntactic classification of words. Choice A is incorrect because the words mentioned are typical of the type taught as sight words. Choice B is incorrect because written accents are not traditionally used to teach English pronunciation. However, teachers of ELLs often use accent marks to help students identify the primary stress in words. Choice D is incorrect because both sets of words are spelled identically. The activity presented emphasizes the importance of word stress to differentiate word meaning. **Competency 005**

12. **D**

A balanced reading program combines phonics instruction, a skill-based approach, to teach decoding skills, and a meaning-based approach (a whole language strategy) to teach reading. Choice A is incorrect because the main thrust of a balanced reading program is not directly related to the listening and reading (receptive) and the speaking and writing (productive) components of language. It makes sense to establish a balance between theory and application, but there is no direct connection with the concept of a balanced reading program (B). Choice C is incorrect because a balanced approach uses not only phonics skills but also whole-language strategies. **Competency 004**

13. **A**

The use of onset and rime is used to compensate for the phoneme–grapheme inconsistency of English. Through the use of rime, children can learn to recognize and spell multiple words. Choice B is incorrect because the use of onset and rime can contribute to the ability to recognize words, but it does not constitute the main reason for their use. Choice C is incorrect because traditionally, onset and rime is not used to deal with polysyllabic words. Choice D is incorrect because prefixes generally represent morphemes, while the onsets generally do not. Prefixes and suffixes are generally introduced using structural analysis. **Competency 005**

14. **B**

Teachers generally introduce the letters that can help the most in decoding written language. The first set of letters occurs more frequently in written text than the second set. Choice A is incorrect because there is no evidence to suggest that children might be more inclined to prefer one set of letters over the other. Choice C is incorrect because only the phoneme /m/ is a nasal sound. Choice D is incorrect because there is no evidence to suggest that the sounds of the graphemes x and q can create language interference. **Competency 005**

15. **A**

By guiding children to notice the title, major headings, and pictorial clues, they can make predictions about the story. Approaching the story content in this way can increase a child's interest in reading because they want to corroborate their predictions with the actual content of what they read. Choices B, C, and D are incorrect because they describe activities typical of the post-reading stage, not the pre-reading stage. **Competency 007**

16. **A**

The first reading is designed to communicate the content of the story and by doing so, children will determine if their predictions were accurate. Choice B is incorrect because activities involving decoding strategies that determine the main idea are usually addressed after the initial activity. Choices C and D are incorrect because the parts of the book and the vocabulary of the story are usually introduced prior to reading the story. **Competency 007**

17. **C**

Affixes common to Spanish and English generally create words with similar spellings and meanings—cognates. Since these words are so similar, children can transfer this knowledge to the second language. Choices A and B are incorrect because the topic of the influence of foreign language on English might not be that relevant or even developmentally appropriate for third-grade ELLs. Choice D is incorrect because the complexity of a new language cannot be eliminated by emphasizing only prefixes and suffixes. **Competency 005**

18. **D**

The word *predestined* contains three morpheme-units of meaning. The first morpheme is a derivational morpheme—*pre*—the root word—*destin*(y), and the inflectional ending—*ed*. **Competency 005**

19. **B**

Silent reading is designed primarily to improve vocabulary development and reading comprehension. It can also improve reading fluency, but reading fluency is best promoted through reading orally; thus, choice A is not the best answer. Choices C and D are incorrect because the primary goal of SSR is not to guide children to conduct word analysis or to practice decoding skills. These skills obviously happen during the reading process as a by-product of SSR. **Competency 007**

20. **C**

Intergenerational literacy programs are designed to involve parents and family members in the education of their children. Choice A is incorrect because the literacy development of adults and the community is not the only or the primary purpose of an intergenerational literacy program. Children are the most important component in this process. Involving parents is an important component of the program, but it is not the purpose of the program. Traditionally, intergenerational literacy initiatives are designed for the early grades, and successful programs can impact the child for life; however, the program traditionally does not go beyond the elementary grades. Thus, choice D is incorrect. **Competency 004**

21. **A**

Since students cannot write effectively in kindergarten, drawing becomes an alternate means to express their understanding of the story. Choices B and C are incorrect because children at this level of literacy development cannot write well.

Choice D is also incorrect because children in kindergarten might not have the cognitive maturity to develop a detailed analysis of the story line. They are generally able to present the gist of the story and identify meaningful events. **Competency 009**

22. **B**

Reciprocal teaching engages the teacher and students in a dialogue designed to guide children in reading comprehension (e.g., summarizing the content, generating questions, clarifying, and predicting). Choice A is incorrect because reciprocal teaching is not a technique to promote reading fluency. Choices C and D are incorrect because the primary goal of reciprocal teaching is not related to cooperative learning per se or the development of oral communication. **Competency 007**

23. **D**

The ARD committee will determine the types of accommodations based on the disability of the child. Choices A and C are incorrect because teachers are not generally responsible for dealing with adaptation costs or the feasibility of resources required by the ARD committee. Choice B is incorrect because it is the responsibility of the ARD committee and school administrators to deal with the legality of testing accommodations. **Competency 008**

24. **B**

Students begin using writing for meaningful communication when they want to get information from teachers and peers. Choice A is incorrect because journal writing was not designed as a classroom management activity. Choice C is incorrect because error correction is not generally encouraged in journal writing. Teachers and more advanced students provide input through modeling. Choice D is incorrect because learning personal information about teachers and peers is not the primary goal of journal writing. **Competency 009**

25. **C**

The connectors are guided to compare and contrast ideas and to identify the preference of the author. Choices A, B, and D are incorrect because the connectors presented do not call for opinions, sequencing, or results. **Competency 009**

26. **C**

The English writing samples of ELLs from a Spanish background often follow a curvilinear progression and might include multiple stories embedded within the narrative. This deviation from the linear progression expected in English writing creates the impression that the story is disjointed and lacks coherence. Based on the previous explanation, choice A is incorrect—children might not produce compositions following a linear progression. The compositions of children might contain complex sentences and an occasional use of Anglicized words or even Spanish words, but these features do not represent the main characteristics of English compositions of Latino children. Based on this explanation, choices B and D are incorrect. **Competency 010**

27. **C**

The TAKS provides a prompt to guide children to produce the writing sample. In responding to the prompt, students have to address the audience, purpose, and occasion implied in it. Choice A is incorrect because the multiple-choice portion of the test addresses primarily writing conventions. Choice B is incorrect because, in the instructions given to children, there is no indication that they must address a purpose of a specific audience. Choice D is incorrect because the instructions do not contain specific questions to guide the writing. **Competency 010**

28. **D**

Miscue analysis was designed to assess how well children read aloud. Choice A is incorrect because during silent reading miscues cannot be identified. Choice B is incorrect because miscue analysis was designed to understand the reading process, not the development of writing. Choice C is incorrect because miscue analysis was not designed to assess the oral performance of children speaking but of reading aloud. **Competency 006**

29. **B**

Choice B is correct. Informal reading inventories allow teachers to administer a series of comprehension tests to identify reading levels among children. Choice A is incorrect because the statement is too generic in nature and does not address the issue of reading levels. Choice C is incorrect because the statement is also generic in nature. Additionally, the use of informal reading inventories is not restricted to students in middle school and high school. Choice D is incorrect because the reading complexity of passages is assessed through a specific system, like the Fry Readability formula. **Competency 007**

30. **D**

Manipulatives can be used to simplify the teaching of mathematics in all grade levels—Pre-K to high school. Choices A and B are incorrect because the use of manipulatives does not have to be restricted to early childhood (prekindergarten through fourth grade). Choice C is incorrect because manipulatives can be used to teach concepts including computation skills and geometry but its use is not limited to these two components. **Competency 013**

31. **C**

The useful, traditional approach to multiplying simple fractions (those between 0 and 1) is to first multiply the numerators together and then to multiply the denominators together to find the product. In this case, $\frac{3}{4} \times \frac{2}{3} = \frac{6}{12}$. That fraction is then shown in simplest form, $\frac{1}{2}$. Based on the explanation, choices A, B, and D are incorrect. **Competency 014**

32. **A**

The traditional whole number division algorithm (method) is helpful when dividing decimals longhand. The work can be set up like this:

$$0.05\overline{)6.2}$$

Dividing (while temporarily ignoring the zeros and decimal points) gives

$$
\begin{array}{r}
124 \\
0.05\overline{)6.20} \\
\underline{5} \\
12 \\
\underline{10} \\
20 \\
\underline{20} \\
0
\end{array}
$$

Next, you count the number of digits to the right of the decimal point in the divisor (two). **Two**, then, is the number of places that you shift the "inside" decimal point to the right, and then "up" into the answer:

$$0.05\overline{)6.2}^{\,124} \longrightarrow 0.05\overline{)6.20}^{\,124}$$

Because the answer is a whole number, the decimal point does not have to be shown. **Competency 014**

33. **A**

The area of any rectangle is equal to the measure of its length times the measure of its width (or to say it differently, the measure of its base times the measure of its height). A right triangle can be seen as half of a rectangle (sliced diagonally). Choice A represents, in effect, a rectangle's area cut in half (i.e., divided by 2). Based on this explanation, choices B, C, and D are incorrect. **Competency 016**

34. **B**

First, it is helpful to view the shaded area as the area of the square minus the area of the circle. With that in mind, you simply need to find the area of each simple figure, and then subtract one from the other. You know that the radius of the circle is 6 units in length. That tells you that the diameter of the circle is 12 units. Because the circle is inscribed in the square (meaning that the circle fits inside of the square touching in as many places as possible), you see that the sides of the square are each 12 units in length. Knowing that, you compute that the area of the square is 144 square units (12 × 12). Using the formula for finding the area of a circle (πr^2), and using 3.14 for π, you get approximately 113 square units. (3.14 × 6 × 6). Then, you subtract 113 (the area of the circle) from 144 (the area of the square) for the answer of 31. Based on the explanation given, choices A, C, and D are incorrect. **Competency 016**

35. **C**

In thematic instruction, the same concepts and vocabulary are presented in multiple lessons. This repetition can reinforce vocabulary and concepts and can improve comprehension of the content. Choice A is incorrect because it does not provide specific reasons for the linguistic benefit. Choice B is incorrect because there is no guarantee that thematic instruction is delivered in L1 and L2. Choice D is incorrect because learning mathematics and other content areas does not have a clear linguistic connection. **Competency 013**

36. **B**

The Mayans developed the concept of the zero around 700 CE. However, there is no evidence to suggest that its discovery has any connection with the development of the same concept in India. Choice A is incorrect because there is no evidence to suggest that the Babylonians developed the concept of the zero as part of their numeric system based on 60. Choice C is incorrect because most historians agree that the Arabs used information from the Hindus to develop our modern numeric system, which includes the zero. Choice D is incorrect because there is no evidence to suggest that the Romans developed the concept of the zero as part of their numeric system. **Competency 015**

37. **B**

Red, yellow, and blue are the primary colors. Their respective complements are green, purple, and orange. Based on this explanation, choices A, C, and D are incorrect. **Competency 042**

38. **D**

The flying buttress was a device invented specifically to support the high vaults of Gothic churches. Flying buttresses, pointed arches, and stained glass windows appear together only on Gothic style buildings, most of which were built between 1150 and 1500. Choice A is incorrect because buildings of the Romanesque period (c. 1050–1150) usually employ wall buttresses and rounded arches, with only a few having pointed arches. Choices B and C are also incorrect because Byzantine and Renaissance buildings are often characterized by domes and rounded arches. **Competency 042**

39. **A**

Rhythm instruments like the tambourine, triangle, and sticks are commonly used to allow children opportunities to explore musical sounds. Choices B, C, and D are instruments traditionally taught in middle school. **Competency 043**

40. **B**

Heat exhaustion is not as severe as heat stroke. Getting the child to a shaded area and providing him/her with water should take care of the problem. Choice A is incorrect; heat exhaustion does not require CPR. Choice C is the appropriate action for a heat stroke victim. Choice D is incorrect because pouring ice water on a hot body can do more harm than good. **Competency 044**

41. **A**

Gross motor-visual skills involve movement of the body's large muscles as visual information is processed. A ball is always used to perfect these skills. In some cases a bat or racquet will also aid in developing these skills. Choices B, C, and D are incorrect because they address motor skills, but fail to include a visual component in the activity. **Competency 045**

42. **B**

Cardiovascular exercise for a minimum of 20 minutes per session, as part of an exercise program, will have positive physical effects when combined with a proper nutritional diet. Choice C (45 minutes) is an effective time period when performing slower-paced activities like weightlifting. Choice B (20 minutes) is the correct time for an aerobic workout. Choice D (5 minutes) is more appropriate for a warm-up or stretching exercise. **Competency 044**

43. **D**

Games involving physical activity are the best way to exercise children in kindergarten and first grade. Choice A is incorrect because, traditionally, jogging might be inappropriate for children at this early age. Choices B and C are incorrect because contact sports and sports that require endurance are not developmentally appropriate for kindergarten and first grade students. **Competency 045**

44. **B**

The sit-and-reach test measures the flexibility of the child. Choices A, C, and D are incorrect because they measure muscular strength and endurance. **Competency 044**

45. **B**

Density is the amount of mass that is contained per unit of volume of a given substance. A combination of the density and the weight (pull of gravity) of an object determines whether it will sink or float. Choice A is incorrect because mass is a measurement of the amount of matter something contains, and mass by itself does not fully explain why the objects sink or float. Choice C is incorrect because it does not provide a specific scientific explanation of the experiment. Choice D is incorrect because weight by itself does not fully explain the forces acting on the objects. **Competency 031**

46. **A**

The heat from the sun changes water into water vapor, which rises to the atmosphere until it reaches cool air. Upon contact with cool air, it changes into small droplets of water, forming clouds. Once the clouds are saturated, precipitation occurs. We say that the system redistributes the water because large amounts of the liquid resulting from the process comes from the ocean and other bodies of water. Rain will fall miles away from the source from which it originated. Choice B is not accurate since the function of the system is not necessarily cleaning the environment; however, pollutants might be washed away as a result of rain. Choice C provides a plausible answer; however, it does not address the main question. Choice D is incorrect because it describes the evaporation system but does not address condensation. **Competency 039**

47. **B**

Organisms develop new features to cope with needs and demands of the environment. For example, predatory animals might develop stronger legs to run faster in order to catch prey. Potential prey, in turn, might develop stronger claws to dig holes for escaping from predators. Choice A is incorrect because "intelligent creation" refers to the creation of the universe by a supreme being—God. Choice C is incorrect because it describes primarily physical changes that organisms go through in the process of maturation. For example, frogs go through a series of metamorphoses before reaching maturity. Choice D is incorrect because there is no direct connection between developing new physical features and reproduction. **Competency 036**

48. **C**

Depending on people's learning modalities, mnemonic devices might be an ideal way to remember facts. However, for others, it might be a waste of instructional time. (A) is incorrect, because it goes beyond the planets; with this activity, students can learn about the positions of the planets only. (B) is incorrect because mnemonic devices are traditionally used for remembering facts, but not necessarily to engage in higher-order thinking skills. (D) is incorrect because rejecting the approach is too drastic, and some students can benefit from it. **Competency 028**

49. **C**

The movement of rotation around the sun constitutes a year, and the closer the planet is to the Sun, the shorter the year. Based on this, only Mercury and Venus have a year shorter than that of the Earth. **Competency 041**

50. **A**

Cumulus clouds are formed during sunny summer days. Choices B and C are incorrect because cumulonimbus clouds cover the sky during cloudy and rainy days. Choice D is incorrect because nimbostratus clouds indicate the possibility of snow. **Competency 040**

Practice Test 1

TExES 191 Generalist EC-6

ANSWER SHEET PRACTICE TEST 1

1. Ⓐ Ⓑ Ⓒ Ⓓ
2. Ⓐ Ⓑ Ⓒ Ⓓ
3. Ⓐ Ⓑ Ⓒ Ⓓ
4. Ⓐ Ⓑ Ⓒ Ⓓ
5. Ⓐ Ⓑ Ⓒ Ⓓ
6. Ⓐ Ⓑ Ⓒ Ⓓ
7. Ⓐ Ⓑ Ⓒ Ⓓ
8. Ⓐ Ⓑ Ⓒ Ⓓ
9. Ⓐ Ⓑ Ⓒ Ⓓ
10. Ⓐ Ⓑ Ⓒ Ⓓ
11. Ⓐ Ⓑ Ⓒ Ⓓ
12. Ⓐ Ⓑ Ⓒ Ⓓ
13. Ⓐ Ⓑ Ⓒ Ⓓ
14. Ⓐ Ⓑ Ⓒ Ⓓ
15. Ⓐ Ⓑ Ⓒ Ⓓ
16. Ⓐ Ⓑ Ⓒ Ⓓ
17. Ⓐ Ⓑ Ⓒ Ⓓ
18. Ⓐ Ⓑ Ⓒ Ⓓ
19. Ⓐ Ⓑ Ⓒ Ⓓ
20. Ⓐ Ⓑ Ⓒ Ⓓ
21. Ⓐ Ⓑ Ⓒ Ⓓ
22. Ⓐ Ⓑ Ⓒ Ⓓ
23. Ⓐ Ⓑ Ⓒ Ⓓ

24. Ⓐ Ⓑ Ⓒ Ⓓ
25. Ⓐ Ⓑ Ⓒ Ⓓ
26. Ⓐ Ⓑ Ⓒ Ⓓ
27. Ⓐ Ⓑ Ⓒ Ⓓ
28. Ⓐ Ⓑ Ⓒ Ⓓ
29. Ⓐ Ⓑ Ⓒ Ⓓ
30. Ⓐ Ⓑ Ⓒ Ⓓ
31. Ⓐ Ⓑ Ⓒ Ⓓ
32. Ⓐ Ⓑ Ⓒ Ⓓ
33. Ⓐ Ⓑ Ⓒ Ⓓ
34. Ⓐ Ⓑ Ⓒ Ⓓ
35. Ⓐ Ⓑ Ⓒ Ⓓ
36. Ⓐ Ⓑ Ⓒ Ⓓ
37. Ⓐ Ⓑ Ⓒ Ⓓ
38. Ⓐ Ⓑ Ⓒ Ⓓ
39. Ⓐ Ⓑ Ⓒ Ⓓ
40. Ⓐ Ⓑ Ⓒ Ⓓ
41. Ⓐ Ⓑ Ⓒ Ⓓ
42. Ⓐ Ⓑ Ⓒ Ⓓ
43. Ⓐ Ⓑ Ⓒ Ⓓ
44. Ⓐ Ⓑ Ⓒ Ⓓ
45. Ⓐ Ⓑ Ⓒ Ⓓ
46. Ⓐ Ⓑ Ⓒ Ⓓ

47. Ⓐ Ⓑ Ⓒ Ⓓ
48. Ⓐ Ⓑ Ⓒ Ⓓ
49. Ⓐ Ⓑ Ⓒ Ⓓ
50. Ⓐ Ⓑ Ⓒ Ⓓ
51. Ⓐ Ⓑ Ⓒ Ⓓ
52. Ⓐ Ⓑ Ⓒ Ⓓ
53. Ⓐ Ⓑ Ⓒ Ⓓ
54. Ⓐ Ⓑ Ⓒ Ⓓ
55. Ⓐ Ⓑ Ⓒ Ⓓ
56. Ⓐ Ⓑ Ⓒ Ⓓ
57. Ⓐ Ⓑ Ⓒ Ⓓ
58. Ⓐ Ⓑ Ⓒ Ⓓ
59. Ⓐ Ⓑ Ⓒ Ⓓ
60. Ⓐ Ⓑ Ⓒ Ⓓ
61. Ⓐ Ⓑ Ⓒ Ⓓ
62. Ⓐ Ⓑ Ⓒ Ⓓ
63. Ⓐ Ⓑ Ⓒ Ⓓ
64. Ⓐ Ⓑ Ⓒ Ⓓ
65. Ⓐ Ⓑ Ⓒ Ⓓ
66. Ⓐ Ⓑ Ⓒ Ⓓ
67. Ⓐ Ⓑ Ⓒ Ⓓ
68. Ⓐ Ⓑ Ⓒ Ⓓ
69. Ⓐ Ⓑ Ⓒ Ⓓ

70. (A) (B) (C) (D)
71. (A) (B) (C) (D)
72. (A) (B) (C) (D)
73. (A) (B) (C) (D)
74. (A) (B) (C) (D)
75. (A) (B) (C) (D)
76. (A) (B) (C) (D)
77. (A) (B) (C) (D)
78. (A) (B) (C) (D)
79. (A) (B) (C) (D)
80. (A) (B) (C) (D)
81. (A) (B) (C) (D)
82. (A) (B) (C) (D)
83. (A) (B) (C) (D)
84. (A) (B) (C) (D)
85. (A) (B) (C) (D)
86. (A) (B) (C) (D)
87. (A) (B) (C) (D)
88. (A) (B) (C) (D)
89. (A) (B) (C) (D)
90. (A) (B) (C) (D)
91. (A) (B) (C) (D)
92. (A) (B) (C) (D)
93. (A) (B) (C) (D)

94. (A) (B) (C) (D)
95. (A) (B) (C) (D)
96. (A) (B) (C) (D)
97. (A) (B) (C) (D)
98. (A) (B) (C) (D)
99. (A) (B) (C) (D)
100. (A) (B) (C) (D)
101. (A) (B) (C) (D)
102. (A) (B) (C) (D)
103. (A) (B) (C) (D)
104. (A) (B) (C) (D)
105. (A) (B) (C) (D)
106. (A) (B) (C) (D)
107. (A) (B) (C) (D)
108. (A) (B) (C) (D)
109. (A) (B) (C) (D)
110. (A) (B) (C) (D)
111. (A) (B) (C) (D)
112. (A) (B) (C) (D)
113. (A) (B) (C) (D)
114. (A) (B) (C) (D)
115. (A) (B) (C) (D)
116. (A) (B) (C) (D)
117. (A) (B) (C) (D)

118. (A) (B) (C) (D)
119. (A) (B) (C) (D)
120. (A) (B) (C) (D)
121. (A) (B) (C) (D)
122. (A) (B) (C) (D)
123. (A) (B) (C) (D)
124. (A) (B) (C) (D)
125. (A) (B) (C) (D)
126. (A) (B) (C) (D)
127. (A) (B) (C) (D)
128. (A) (B) (C) (D)
129. (A) (B) (C) (D)
130. (A) (B) (C) (D)
131. (A) (B) (C) (D)
132. (A) (B) (C) (D)
133. (A) (B) (C) (D)
134. (A) (B) (C) (D)
135. (A) (B) (C) (D)
136. (A) (B) (C) (D)
137. (A) (B) (C) (D)
138. (A) (B) (C) (D)
139. (A) (B) (C) (D)
140. (A) (B) (C) (D)

1. Identify the number of syllables and the number of phonemes present in the word *thought*.

    A.   Two syllables and three phonemes

    B.   One syllable and three phonemes

    C.   Three syllables and six phonemes

    D.   Two syllables and three phonemes

2. All of the following are characteristics of emergent readers EXCEPT:

    A.   Use illustrations in the texts they are reading to aid in their comprehension

    B.   Develop awareness of the story structure

    C.   Represent the stories read through the use of visual images and drawings

    D.   Engage in self correction when text does not make sense to them

3. When teaching English to ELLs of Spanish background, Ms. Rico introduced a list of Greek and Latin prefixes common to Spanish and English. She explained the spelling patterns and the meaning of each of the prefixes. She presented examples of words that contain the prefixes, and led students to decode these based on the meaning of the prefixes. What decoding strategy is Ms. Rico using?

    A.   Contextual

    B.   Structural

    C.   Pictorial

    D.   Syntactic

4. Perform the indicated operation: $(-36) - 11$.

    A.   47

    B.   25

    C.   −47

    D.   −25

5. Simplify: $6 \cdot 2 + 3 \div 3$.

A. 18

B. 5

C. 10

D. 13

6. If a can weighs 14 oz., how many cans would you need to have a ton? (Round your answer to the nearest ones place and pick the best answer.)

A. 2,285

B. 2,286

C. 2,287

D. 2,300

7. Which of the following is LEAST likely to lead to illness and disease?

A. Stress

B. Hydration

C. Dietary sugar

D. Isolation

8. To apply the concept of time zones, students need to have a clear understanding of

A. the International Date Line.

B. the Earth's yearly revolution.

C. the concept of the meridians of longitude.

D. the concept of the parallels of latitude.

9. Mr. Chapman is a third-grade teacher who is working at a school that is implementing a balanced reading program. He will use all of the following reading strategies in his classroom EXCEPT

A. reading to students (read aloud).

B. implementing shared reading, guided reading, and reading workshops.

C. having students engage in independent reading.

D. having students independently decode words in reading and writing.

10. Identify the statement that best describes the country of Iraq.

   A.   It is a linguistically and ethnically homogeneous Muslim nation.

   B.   It is a Muslim nation with multiple ethnic groups within its borders.

   C.   It is located in Southeast Asia.

   D.   It is a province of Pakistan.

11. The Mayflower Compact was one of the earliest agreements to

   A.   establish a political body and to give that political body the power to act for the good of the colony.

   B.   establish rules for farming and trading.

   C.   establish a plan to implement plantation systems.

   D.   establish a policy for settlement.

Use the information in this scenario to answer the next three questions.

Scenario: Mr. Jetter organized a lesson to introduce sixth-grade students to the concept of marine habitats. As a focus activity he presented two 25-gallon aquariums. Aquarium A has a variety of aquatic plants, 10 snails, and 25 unique varieties of small fishes. Aquarium B contains a variety of aquatic plants, three snails, and five small fish of the same variety. To implement the lesson, he organized the students in groups of five. Once the groups were formed, students were asked to discuss the appropriateness of the combination of aquatic plants and number of animals. The ultimate goal is to predict the success of the habitats, including successful breeding among animals.

12. What is the main science objective of Mr. Jetter's lesson?

   A.   Guide students to communicate with peers.

   B.   Promote scientific inquiry and problem-solving skills using scientific data.

   C.   Work in cooperative groups.

   D.   Keep students engaged and interested in the scientific concepts presented in class.

13. After a lengthy discussion, students agreed that Aquarium B had a better chance to establish and maintain a successful habitat. What information led students to arrive at this conclusion?

    A.   The size of the aquarium

    B.   The ratio of plants to animals

    C.   The number of plants

    D.   The number of fish

14. Students also agreed that Aquarium B has a better chance of successful breeding among the fish. What information did students use to arrive at this conclusion?

    A.   The ratio of plants to fish

    B.   The number of fish in each tank

    C.   The size of the tanks

    D.   The types of fishes in each tank

15. By second grade, students are generally guided to discontinue the practice of pointing to the words being read. What is the rationale for this change of strategy?

    A.   Students get tired of pointing to the words while reading.

    B.   Students find this practice annoying and typical of younger children.

    C.   This practice can interfere with the development of reading fluency.

    D.   This practice is archaic and does not seem to help in the reading process.

16. Vocabulary development is a key predictor of success in reading. Identify a strategy that parents can use with preschool children to promote vocabulary development in a fun and relaxed environment.

    A.   Use flash cards and concrete objects to introduce vocabulary words.

    B.   Play a game in which the parent and the child teach each other a new word every day.

    C.   Play games in which children have to name antonyms and synonyms.

    D.   Ask children to memorize a list of vocabulary words every day.

17. Characteristics of emergent writers include the following EXCEPT

    A. dictating of an idea or a complete story.

    B. using initial sounds in their writing.

    C. using pictures and scribbles.

    D. using conventional spelling in their writing.

18. What causes earthquakes?

    A. Thermal activity in the core

    B. The movement of continental plates

    C. The melting of rocks and minerals

    D. The movement or rotation of Earth

19. A two-year-old child using a crayon to scribble on manila paper is focusing on

    A. expressing his thoughts and ideas.

    B. drawing personal symbols that represent objects in the environment.

    C. the texture of the paper and the color and shape of the marks being made.

    D. repeating themes to achieve photographic realism.

20. What song has the same rhythm as *Happy Birthday*?

    A. *America*

    B. *The Star-Spangled Banner*

    C. *Take Me Out to the Ballgame*

    D. *America the Beautiful*

21. Based on the Individuals with Disabilities Education Act (IDEA), children with crutches or any other types of assistive devices should

    A. not be allowed to participate in physical education activities.

    B. be allowed to participate like any other student.

    C. be provided with appropriate modification for participation in physical education activities.

    D. be provided with a special physical education class designed for them.

22. The Virginia House of Burgesses was established in Jamestown to

    A. function as the official body of the U.S. government.

    B. regulate trading among colonies.

    C. function as a form of representative government.

    D. regulate the establishments of religions.

23. A globe is a scale model of the Earth shaped like a sphere. A globe shows sizes and shapes more accurately than

    A. a compass rose.

    B. a Mercator projection map.

    C. a map scale.

    D. a thematic map.

24. Two paper bags are each filled with four blue marbles and four red marbles. What is the probability of selecting a blue marble from the first bag and a blue marble from the second bag?

    A. $\dfrac{1}{4}$

    B. $\dfrac{2}{16}$

    C. $\dfrac{1}{2}$

    D. $\dfrac{4}{8}$

25. Running records, teacher observations, and speaking checklists are examples of what type of assessment?

    A. Teacher-developed assessment instruments

    B. Informal literacy assessment

    C. Formal literacy assessment

    D. Objective literacy instruments

26. Identify the statement that best represents the rationale for the implementation of initial reading instruction in the student's native language.

    A. Reading skills are transferable from L1 to L2.

    B. Reading skills are identical in L1 and L2.

    C. Reading skills are confusing for English language learners (ELLs).

    D. Reading skills affect the cognitive process in bilingual students.

27. How many lines of symmetry do all non-square rectangles have?

    A. 0

    B. 2

    C. 4

    D. 8

28. One of the best known models of scientific inquiry is the 5-E model. In this model, students go through five steps: *engage, explore, explain, elaborate,* and *evaluate*. What is the main purpose of the "*explore*" component of the process?

    A. To guide students begin experimenting and gathering data about a scientific concept.

    B. To increase interest in the scientific principle studied

    C. To guide students present and share data with their classmates

    D. To capture the curiosity of the students

29. Identify the most appropriate strategy(ies) to meet the needs of children at the emerging stage of writing development.

    A. Identify errors in the writing sample and guide children to self-correct.

    B. Provide a prompt and guide children to write a composition based on it.

    C. Read stories and ask children to retell the story while you write it down.

    D. Allow the child to read for at least 30 minutes every day.

30. In which grade should pupils' experiences in critically evaluating their own art and the art of others begin?

    A. Kindergarten

    B. First grade

    C. Second grade

    D. Third grade

31. Xylophones, metallophones, and glockenspiels are instruments associated with what classroom musical approach?

    A. Orff

    B. Kodály

    C. Mariachi

    D. Tejano

32. The most appropriate exercises for kindergarten and first-grade students are

    A. jogging and walking.

    B. contact sports.

    C. games that require endurance.

    D. fun games that require physical activity.

33. Germaine, a fourth-grade student, notices that the shape of South America is similar to the shape of Africa. To demonstrate this, he cut out the South American map, placed it next to the map of Africa, and found an almost perfect match. He was amazed by his discovery and asked the teacher if Africa was once part of South America. What type of theory or scientific principle can the teacher introduce to make Germaine's discovery a teachable moment?

    A. Theory of evolution of the species

    B. Theory of intelligent design

    C. Theory of transcontinental migration

    D. Theory of plate tectonics

34. Luke's mother has commented that her two-year-old is constructing sentences with only two or three words at a time. For instance, she says that Luke responds by saying, "no more play" and "mommy milk more." She suggests that he has heard his brothers use phrases like these. Luke uses these two phrases frequently. Based on the information above, in which stage of language acquisition is Luke at this point?

    A. Babbling stage

    B. Holophrastic stage

    C. Two word stage

    D. Telegraphic stage

35. Mr. Obama uses monosyllabic words to present the concept of onset and rimes. Identify the pair of words that best represents this concept.

    A. want-ed—walk-ed
    B. very—berry
    C. think-ing—eat-ing
    D. s-ank—b-ank

36. Newly fluent readers can read with relative fluency and comprehension. Which cuing system is NOT one they would use to obtain meaning from print?

    A. Semantic cuing systems
    B. Structural cuing systems
    C. Visual cuing systems
    D. Punctuation cuing systems

37. Simplify to a single term in scientific notation: $(2 \cdot 10)^3 \cdot (6 \cdot 10^4)$.

    A. $0.12 \cdot 10^7$
    B. $12 \cdot 10^7$
    C. $48 \cdot 10^7$
    D. $4.8 \cdot 10^8$

38. Identify the mathematical properties involved in the following problem: $(6 + 2) + 5 = 6 + (2 + 5)$.

    A. Distributive property
    B. Associative property of addition
    C. Property of zero
    D. Associative property of multiplication

39. Identify the statement that best describes the relationship between the eight social studies strands and the TEKS in the implementation of the Texas curriculum.

    A. There is no connection between the TEKS and the social studies strands.
    B. The social studies strands have been used as a foundation for the development of the state curriculum.
    C. The strands apply to programs at the university level and the TEKS applies to K–12 curricula.
    D. The strands apply to programs at the high school level; while the TEKS applies to all grade levels.

40. In what grade does the state curriculum officially introduce children to Texas history?

    A. Prekindergarten

    B. First grade

    C. Third grade

    D. Fourth grade

41. To make the science curriculum cognitively accessible to English language learners in grades K–2, teachers use thematic units and incorporate

    A. techniques from various foreign language methods.

    B. scientific exploration and hands-on activities.

    C. a variety of instructional strategies and sophisticated scientific tools.

    D. the use of chemicals and human specimens used by scientists.

42. Probably as a response to the war in Iraq and Afghanistan, the Organization of Petroleum Exporting Countries (OPEC) cut the production of oil. As a result of this action, the cost of gasoline increased to almost $3.00 per gallon in 2005. What is the economic principle or statement that is best represented by this situation?

    A. During war, the prices of fossil fuels increase.

    B. The American economy is dependent on foreign oil.

    C. The law of supply and demand determines the prices of goods and services.

    D. OPEC was boycotting the United States.

43. In the problem, $5 + 6 \times \dfrac{3}{2}$, what is the first operation which should be performed according to the order of operations?

    A. Exponent

    B. Multiply

    C. Subtract

    D. Add

44. Which answer about your metabolism is FALSE?

    A. More total calories are expended during rest (Basal Metabolic Rate) than exercise.

    B. "Fasting" (not eating for long periods of time) speeds up your metabolism.

    C. Exercise stimulates your metabolism.

    D. Adjustments in metabolism are slow and take place over long periods of time.

45. Why might children in prekindergarten and kindergarten have problems understanding how the Earth is represented in globes and flat representations?

    A. They might not be developmentally ready to understand symbolic representations.

    B. They might pay more attention to the colors and features of globes and maps than the concepts being taught.

    C. They might not be interested in maps and globes.

    D. They might have problems recognizing the Earth's features presented on the 12-inch globe representation.

46. Which of the following words can be used as a good example for homonyms?

    A. to – tube

    B. club – club

    C. to – toe

    D. to – two

47. Which of the following sets of symptoms best describes heat stroke?

    A. Cool, moist, pale skin

    B. Red, hot, dry skin, unconsciousness

    C. Nausea and dizziness

    D. Headache and excessive sweating

48. The state curriculum for fine arts and for visual arts is organized around the following four strands:

    A. art production, art appreciation, art advocacy, and art evaluation.

    B. sensory awareness, creativity, art production, and crafts.

    C. perception, creative expression, historical/cultural heritage, and critical evaluation.

    D. creative expression, art appreciation, art evaluation, and cultural crafts.

Use the information in this scenario to answer the next two questions.

Scenario: Corals are invertebrates that generally live in a symbiotic relationship with algae. Some of them build reefs, others do not. Most of them filter water to obtain nutrients for survival.

49. Based on this description, corals belong to which of the following kingdoms?

    A. Monera

    B. Animal

    C. Plant

    D. Fungi

50. The term *symbiotic* in this case means that corals

    A. are parasites attached to algae.

    B. share the same environment with algae.

    C. exchange services with other organisms.

    D. are living organisms.

51. Newspapers and magazines have traditionally been considered what type of media?

    A. Electric media

    B. Visual media

    C. Print media

    D. Electronic media

52. Mrs. Thompson has requested that their students create a PowerPoint presentation on the history of visual media. Before working on such a presentation, students need to pick a topic to create their presentation. Which of the following would be the most appropriate topic for such a presentation?

    A. The evolution of billboards on the highway

    B. Using Twitter in school

    C. The internet is a superhighway

    D. You email me, I email you

Use the following figure to answer the question that follows. Assume that point *C* is the center of the circle. Angles *xyz* and *xCz* intercept minor arc *xz*. The measure of angle *xyz* is 40°.

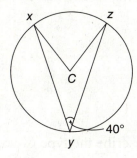

53. What is the measure of major arc *xyz*?

    A. 140°

    B. 280°

    C. 160°

    D. 320°

54. What is the primary disadvantage of using written essay to assess the performance of English language learners (ELLs)?

    A. Scoring rubrics are often unavailable or unfamiliar to students in general.

    B. Students can be creative in formulating their answers.

    C. Language difficulties can make it difficult to assess competence.

    D. Students can conceptualize and deliver information in unique ways.

55. Which statement best describes an example of the Language Experience Approach?

    A. The teacher records a student's story saying each word aloud while writing it down.

    B. The students participate in writing down a shared experience by taking turns writing.

    C. Students read a story orally while the teacher helps as needed with decoding.

    D. The teacher models writing while orally thinking aloud about her own experiences.

56. Mrs. Cameron plans to buy carpeting for her living room floor. The room is a rectangle measuring 14 feet by 20 feet. She wants no carpet seams on her floor even if that means that some carpeting will go to waste. The carpeting she wants comes in 16-foot-wide rolls. What is the minimum amount of carpeting that will have to be wasted if Mrs. Cameron insists upon her no-seams requirement?

    A. 40 ft^2

    B. 60 ft^2

    C. 80 ft^2

    D. 100 ft^2

57. The technical term used to describe the type of vocabulary needed to understand social studies concepts is known as

    A. teaching vocabulary.

    B. learning vocabulary.

    C. academic vocabulary.

    D. social vocabulary.

58. Why are Indian tribes from the Central and Great Plains of Texas better known than their counterparts from the Coastal Plains?

    A. They had a more advanced civilization.

    B. They were sedentary and built better ceremonial sites and permanent structures.

    C. They domesticated the horse, which made them better hunters and warriors.

    D. They had an abundance of food sources and were stronger.

59. Two coins are tossed at the same time. What is the probability that only one head is obtained in each of the tosses?

    A.   0.25

    B.   0.75

    C.   0.5

    D.   0.1

60. Identify the steps that best describe the writing process.

    A.   Develop an outline of the intended writing project, complete an initial draft, and edit for content.

    B.   Complete an initial draft, revise for the accuracy of the content, and publish.

    C.   Brainstorm for ideas, develop an outline, complete an initial draft, edit, and publish.

    D.   Write an initial draft, share it with peers, review it for grammaticality, and publish.

61. The process by which physical movements develop and become specialized for motor performance depends primarily upon

    A.   socioeconomic status.

    B.   natural talent.

    C.   daily practice.

    D.   a supportive environment.

62. Mrs. Morris presented a lesson to her fifth graders about the early development of major science concepts. She discussed how people in Europe thought that the Earth was the center of the universe at a given time in history, and how first physicians bled the patients to try to cure them. Other than the historical value of the lesson, what is the educational purpose of this lesson?

    A.   To develop an understanding of the evolution of science concepts and knowledge

    B.   To develop an understanding of the lack of knowledge people had during the Middle Ages

    C.   To identify a reason why people died so young during that time frame

    D.   To identify a reason for the lack of development of European countries in the present time

63. Identify the order of the products that have supported the Texas economy through its history.

    A.   Petroleum, cotton, oranges, and cattle

    B.   Cattle, corn, petroleum, and education

    C.   Cotton, cattle, petroleum, and computers and electronics

    D.   Cattle, petroleum, beef, venison, and poultry

64. A card is drawn from a deck of cards, what is the probability that the card is a queen or a black four?

    A. $\dfrac{6}{52}$

    B. $\dfrac{8}{52}$

    C. $\dfrac{25}{52}$

    D. $\dfrac{12}{52}$

65. In a group of people, there are 18 blondes, 17 brunettes, and 5 red heads. What is the probability of selecting a red head from the group?

    A. $\dfrac{1}{10}$

    B. $\dfrac{1}{8}$

    C. $\dfrac{1}{12}$

    D. $\dfrac{1}{7}$

Answer the two questions that follow based on the scenario below.

Scenario: Mr. Mackey has seven ELLs in his class who are having difficulties pronouncing English words containing the letters *sh* and *ch*. To support these students, he organizes small-group instruction to address their specific needs. He introduces pronunciation and vocabulary concepts through a chart. The chart is color-coded to guide students in the pronunciation of phonemes; i.e., he uses blue for the /sh/, green for /ch/, brown for /k/. Every week, he adds new words to the chart until he is satisfied that students have mastered the grapheme-phoneme correspondence. The chart for this week is shown below.

1. sh—/sh/ blue	2. ch—/ch/ green	3. ch—/k/ brown	4. ch—/sh/ green	5. s—/sh/ blue	6. t—/sh/ blue
shower	church	Christmas	chef	sure	caution
short	chart	chemistry	Chevron	sugar	contribution
shell	choice	chrome	Chevrolet	mission	communication

66. Based on the information provided in the chart, what is the primary reason for the confusion that ELLs experience with these two phonemes?

    A. They cannot distinguish the difference between the two phonemes.

    B. They cannot pronounce either of the two phonemes.

    C. They might not be interested in learning these differences.

    D. The grapheme-phoneme correspondence is inconsistent.

67. What might be the advantages of using the chart to teach pronunciation?

    A. The chart provides examples of the graphophonemic consistency of English.

    B. The students become aware of the words that follow grapheme-phoneme correspondence and those that do not.

    C. The chart can be used to teach the intonation pattern of the language.

    D. Children get exposed to vocabulary words and develop graphophonemic awareness.

68. What is the approximate volume of the following cylinder?

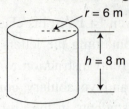

$r = 6\,m$

$h = 8\,m$

A. 904 m³

B. 301 m³

C. 151 m³

D. 452 m³

69. Mr. Rovira guides five-year-old children in the recitation of the following utterance: "Round the rugged rock the ragged rascal ran." Children have fun with this activity and try to say it without errors. What literary technique is he using?

A. Alliteration

B. Tongue twister

C. Nursery rhyme

D. Memorization drills

70. Which of the following sets of numbers is not an integer followed by its square?

A. –8, 64

B. 8, 64

C. 6, 32

D. –9, 81

71. Which of the following is equivalent to $17(64 + 8^2) - 4^3$?

A. $64(17 + 82) - 46$

B. 64×34

C. 64×33

D. $17(128) - 12$

72. Jamie rolls a pair of dice hoping to get an odd number. What is the probability that the sum of the dice will show an odd number?

    A.   0.625
    B.   0.75
    C.   0.25
    D.   0.5

73. The Sumerians, Akkadians, Babylonians, and Assyrians were some of the civilizations that flourished in Mesopotamia—the land between the rivers. What rivers are being alluded to in this statement?

    A.   Nile and Amazon
    B.   Tigris and Euphrates
    C.   Nile and Indus
    D.   Volga and Danube

74. Identify the statement that best describes the connection between reading and writing.

    A.   The development of reading and writing skills is sequential.
    B.   The development of reading and writing skills are interrelated and developed concurrently
    C.   The development of reading and writing skills is controlled by the structure of the language.
    D.   The development of reading and writing skills is controlled by the age of exposure to the language and the type of strategies used to teach them.

75. In the early grades, mathematic and spatial reasoning are introduced in learning centers through the use of manipulatives. What is the main advantage of using learning centers to introduce mathematics and spatial reasoning?

    A.   Children explore and learn reasoning skills indirectly using concrete objects in informal settings.
    B.   Children can play and enjoy the benefits of manipulatives.
    C.   Children are taught mathematics concepts deductively using manipulatives and other concrete objects in an informal format.
    D.   Children are exposed to the state curriculum in a highly structured learning environment.

76. In her first-grade class, Ms. Swanson wants to present the fact that scientists can be male or female, and can come from all ethnic and racial groups, and countries in the world. What might be the best strategy to accomplish that goal?

   A. Bring a female scientist to talk to the class

   B. Tell the students that scientists come from different countries, racial and ethnic groups, and cultures

   C. Read and discuss the biography of male and female scientists from different racial and ethnic groups

   D. Bring in posters of male and female scientists

77. Mike is a four-year-old monolingual, Spanish-speaking child. His parents read Spanish books to him every day. As a result of their effort, Mike has mastered directionality in reading and basic decoding skills. He can also decode words by linking two syllables. Based on his literacy growth, what might be the next logical step for the parents to promote his growth?

   A. Stop reading to him to encourage self-sufficiency.

   B. Continue reading to him and introduce comprehension strategies.

   C. Continue challenging the child by introducing books for advanced first graders.

   D. Stop teaching Spanish reading and introduce English only.

78. The use of hot plates and burners are initially allowed in

   A. second grade.

   B. third grade.

   C. fifth grade.

   D. sixth grade.

79. Charts, tables, and graphs are commonly used in language arts to

   A. summarize information.

   B. entertain the audience.

   C. present detailed explanations of a topic covered in class.

   D. contradict information presented orally.

80. The United States is probably the only industrialized country in the world that uses the English system of measurement in daily life. What is the rationale for using the metric system in scientific research and engineering?

    A. The metric system is widely used in the world.

    B. The English system is an archaic and outdated system used mostly in business.

    C. The metric system is more precise than the English system.

    D. The English system allows for the easy computation of measurements.

81. Identify the modern-day country that encompasses most of the territory of ancient Mesopotamia.

    A. Iran

    B. Pakistan

    C. Kuwait

    D. Iraq

82. George placed a metal spoon on an open flame and the spoon became so hot that it burned his hands. What scientific principle represents this type of energy transfer?

    A. Radiation

    B. Conduction

    C. Convection

    D. Kinetics

83. After devouring its prey, a crocodile opens its mouth to allow a bird to remove and eat the pieces of meat wedged between the teeth. Once the pieces of meat are removed, the bird flies away. What kind of relationship does this scenario create?

    A. Commensalism

    B. Parasitism

    C. Predator-prey

    D. Symbiotic

84. In which grade are the *principles of art* introduced?

    A. Kindergarten

    B. Second grade

    C. Fourth grade

    D. Sixth grade

85. In a science class for sixth graders, Ms. Anderson posted a list of controversial scientific issues including global warming, searching for oil in natural reserves, and genetically engineered food. She asked students to take a position or a stand on one of the issues, and to come to class ready to defend their position. What is the educational benefit of this kind of assignment?

   A. Students are guided to learn to use the computer and search engines to gather data.

   B. Students have to become familiar with the terminology and information to defend their position.

   C. Students are able to contribute good information about the values of these discussions.

   D. Students gather the information to have an intelligent conversation with peers and teachers.

86. Mr. Ojeda supports his students' learning of writing by reading aloud examples of stories in which the author's uniqueness is portrayed and projected. This models which writing trait BEST for students?

   A. Organization

   B. Voice

   C. Sentence fluency

   D. Conventions

87. The U.S. Constitution was designed so that no single branch of the government—executive, judicial, or legislative—could exert full control over the other two. This unique feature of the Constitution is known as

   A. judicial review.

   B. the pocket veto.

   C. checks and balances.

   D. habeas corpus.

88. The main purpose of an interactive/dialogue journal is to provide children with opportunities to

   A. practice speaking and writing skills.

   B. communicate freely in a written form.

   C. receive corrective feedback from peers.

   D. practice listening, speaking, reading, and writing.

89. How can teachers minimize the danger of working with chemicals in their pure form?

    A.   Avoid the use of chemicals in the classroom.

    B.   Substitute pure chemicals with household items containing a diluted version of the chemical.

    C.   Substitute the chemical with water, soda, or other less dangerous substances available in the school.

    D.   Avoid experiments in which dangerous chemicals are used.

90. Stacy went to the store to purchase a loaf of bread. She originally thought she had only $9.55 in nickels in her purse. She then discovered she had 10 extra nickels in her pocket. How many nickels did she originally have in her purse?

    A.   161

    B.   173

    C.   192

    D.   191

91. Which of these numbers/number representations are irrational numbers?

    A. π

    B. $\sqrt{2}$

    C. $e \approx 2.71821818...$

    D.   All of the above

92. Alternative assessment, such as verbal reports, laboratory practical exams, story writing, developing advertisements or brochures, constructing a concept map, creating drawings or models, developing a play or skit, can provide a better view of the students' performance in science. Why are these assessment practices effective?

    A.   They are student-centered, ongoing, and collected as part of daily instruction.

    B.   They are summative in nature and collected using instruments approved by the state.

    C.   They are easy to collect and analyze.

    D.   They emphasize student weaknesses and should promote self-monitoring.

93. What are Venn diagrams commonly used for in reading instruction?

    A. Compare similarities and differences between two stories.

    B. Identify the parts of a story.

    C. Identify key attributes of a given concept.

    D. Guide children to identify the main idea and supporting details.

94. A rubric to rate the writing skills of children in first grade should not place heavy emphasis on the mastery of spelling because

    A. the use of phonemic and invented spelling is part of specific stages of writing development in children.

    B. the use of standard spelling is not important in the development of compositions.

    C. spelling addresses visual memory and should not be given great value.

    D. the development of standard spelling requires students to use structural and phonics rules effectively.

95. An example of a prime number is

    A. 9

    B. 682

    C. 49

    D. 67

96. The most advanced pre-Columbian civilizations of Mesoamerica were the

    A. Aztecs and Incas.

    B. Maya and Aztecs.

    C. Toltecs and Pueblos.

    D. Olmecs and Iroquois.

97. Which of the following is a locomotor skill?

    A. Bending

    B. Catching

    C. Throwing

    D. Hopping

98. In 2008 the gross state product of Texas was $1.245 trillion—the second highest in the nation. If Texas were an independent nation, its economy will rank _____ in the world.

    A.   5th to 10th

    B.   12th to 15th

    C.   20th to 35th

    D.   40th to 50th

99. A compass rose is a design printed on a chart to

    A.   show the orientation of a map of Earth.

    B.   show the distance between two places in the world.

    C.   represent features such as elevations and divisions.

    D.   show the distance between two corresponding points.

100. Students who develop an understanding of the key components of a story (i.e., the setting, characters, and the resolution) have mastered understanding through the use of

    A.   semantic clues.

    B.   comprehension monitoring.

    C.   story grammar.

    D.   shared reading.

101. Vinegar is composed of two substances—acetic acid (a colorless liquid) and water. This combination of substances is an example of a

    A.   compound.

    B.   mixture.

    C.   chemical.

    D.   substance.

102. In music, the words "up" and "down" are usually associated with

    A.   fast and slow.

    B.   loud and soft.

    C.   high and low.

    D.   strong and gentle.

103. Identify the strategies that lead the child from the stage of *learning to read* to the stage of *reading to learn*.

    A.   Expose children to different kinds of literature and vocabulary words specific to the content areas.

    B.   Introduce children to different kinds of texts, and teach how to scan to locate and retrieve information.

    C.   Allow students to read without interruptions for at least 20 minutes a day.

    D.   Introduce the concepts of connotation and denotation in words and phrases.

104. In addition to posting the appropriate rules for laboratory safety, teachers send home a safety contract for parents to sign. What is the purpose of sending this type of document home?

    A.   To be sure that parents follow safety procedures at home

    B.   To make parents responsible for the education of their children and to guide children to develop a commitment to study science

    C.   To make parents aware of rules and guidelines that children must exhibit in the laboratory

    D.   To make parents responsible if children do not follow safety rules in the science laboratory

105. Identify the factor(s) that most likely can affect the development of early literacy among preschool children.

    A.   Parents read frequently to their children and have books available at home.

    B.   Parents teach children to use the dictionary and guide them to select the best definition based on the context of the words.

    C.   Parents have available reference materials and electronic translation programs to promote early bilingualism among children.

    D.   Parents take their children to the library and bookstores to obtain books.

106. What is the main purpose of the Federal Reserve System?

    A.   To promote fiscal stability and provide stimulus money to balance the economy

    B.   To promote economic growth

    C.   To create inflation and deflation

    D.   To keep the banking industry strong enough to ensure a supply of currency

107. Vocabulary development is a key predictor of success in reading in the content areas for all students, but especially for children new to the English language. Identify the best strategy to introduce vocabulary development for ELLs from diverse cultural and linguistic backgrounds.

    A. Teach content vocabulary through direct, concrete experience as opposed to definitions.

    B. Identify key vocabulary words in the content area and provide children with a translation of each word.

    C. Teach content vocabulary in a comparative fashion, contrasting the meaning of vocabulary words in the various languages represented in class.

    D. De-emphasize the importance of lexicon, introduce the words in context, and guide children to derive the meaning using context clues.

108. The main purpose for teaching sight words is to promote instant recognition of characters and words. Instant recognition of words can improve students'

    A. reading fluency.

    B. decoding skills.

    C. reading comprehension.

    D. writing skills.

109. Oftentimes the use of acronyms facilitates the learning process. What is a common acronym for remembering the order of operations?

    A. KPCOGS

    B. PEMDAS

    C. ASAP

    D. WYSIWYG

110. Identify two key historical concepts or characters of the Middle Ages.

    A. The Greek and the Roman Empires

    B. The feudal system and the Crusades

    C. Stonehenge and the rise of Islam

    D. The Renaissance and Alexander the Great

111. The key function of the food chain in the ecosystem is to

    A.   control the number of animals.

    B.   preserve the types of plants in the habitat.

    C.   maintain a balance among organisms.

    D.   maintain a balance between fungi and dead matter.

112. Which of the following were the first mathematicians to impact the development of modern-day mathematics?

    A.   Greeks and the Aztecs

    B.   Egyptians and Babylonians

    C.   Hindus and Aztecs

    D.   Arabs and the Mayans

113. Introducing the multiple versions of stories like *Cinderella* can help students understand how a theme can be developed from different points of views. Moreover, this kind of literature can help students in the development of

    A.   critical reading.

    B.   literal recall.

    C.   repairing understanding.

    D.   retelling checklist.

114. The economy theory that states that prices vary based on balance between the availability of a product or service at a certain price and the desire of potential purchasers to pay that price is known as

    A.   free enterprise.

    B.   supply and demand.

    C.   inflation and deflation.

    D.   economic interdependence.

115. There are 16 more apples than oranges in a basket of 62 apples and oranges. How many oranges are in the basket?

    A.   23

    B.   39

    C.   32

    D.   30

116. The imperial forces of Japan attacked Pearl Harbor on Sunday, December 7, 1941. Once the attack began, the officer in charge called President Roosevelt and notified him of the attack. During the communication, the president was able to hear the noise of the bombs exploding and the struggle of the battle. Recently, a reporter from the *Dallas Morning News* was researching the details of the attack and found a transcription of the official diary of Emperor Hirohito, where he indicated the following: "The Imperial forces of Japan destroyed the American fleet in Hawaii Monday, December 8, 1941." If the attack occurred on December 7, why did the official document from the Japanese government indicate that the attack happened on December 8? Select the statement that best explains this discrepancy.

    A.   The Americans knew that the attack was going to happen and assumed that it had happened the day before.

    B.   The U.S. government had spies in Japan, and they knew when the attack was going to take place.

    C.   There is a one-day difference between the two regions.

    D.   Emperor Hirohito learned about the attack the day after, and he assumed that it happened on that day.

117. How is knowledge of a student's instructional reading level useful when planning reading instruction?

    A.   It can help match the student to the right text for guided reading.

    B.   It can be used to form groups that last all year long.

    C.   It can be used to plan instruction for all subject areas.

    D.   The teacher can read a class set of novels with the entire class.

118. There are two categories of maps: reference maps and thematic maps. An atlas is an example of

    A.   a reference map.

    B.   a thematic map.

    C.   a physical map.

    D.   a population map.

119. During reading group activity, Ms. Lueck often asks her second graders to orally retell the main ideas of a story they have just read together. This is an example of which type of assessment?

    A. Informal

    B. Norm-referenced

    C. Criterion-referenced

    D. Standardized

120. Which of the following is an example of formative evaluation?

    A. End-of-year report card

    B. Results from the standardized achievement test

    C. Miscue analysis from a running record done once a week

    D. An end-of-unit test given at the end of the grading period

121. Which is not a critical step to follow when solving a problem?

    A. Understanding the problem

    B. Choosing a strategy and/or making a plan

    C. Checking your answer

    D. Thinking critically about the solution

122. If in the United States we are enjoying a warm winter, what season are the people of Brazil having?

    A. Spring

    B. Summer

    C. Winter

    D. Fall

123. Identify the set of words representing the concept of antonyms.

    A. small—smaller

    B. small—large

    C. bear—bear

    D. small—little

124. The Fifteenth Amendment of the U.S. Constitution was ratified in 1870 to grant

    A. black women and men the right to vote.

    B. citizenship for blacks.

    C. freedom of slaves.

    D. black men the right to vote.

125. Convergent research on linear versus curvilinear rhetorical patterns shows that Spanish-speaking English language learners and young children in general have a tendency to follow a curvilinear approach in writing. What strategies can teachers use to support these students?

    A. Teach pronunciation and application of grammar structures.

    B. Guide children to develop an outline for the story and provide them with guiding questions to keep them focused on the topic and the audience.

    C. Provide a speaking checklist to help students stick to the topic.

    D. Provide examples of stories written in a linear fashion and ask students to modify them by adding their own information.

126. Marcus can separate a word into its individual phonemes and put it back together to recreate the original word. However, he has problems separating words into syllables and identifying the syllable with the primary stress. Based on this scenario, Marcus needs additional support with

    A. phonological awareness.

    B. phonemic awareness.

    C. syllabication.

    D. word stress.

127. Valerie has a bathtub that she needs to fill with water. To fill the tub, she first needs to fill a bucket with water and then dump this into the bathtub. If the bucket is a cylinder with a radius of 6 in and a height of 12 in, how many buckets will it take to fill the 5 ft × 3 ft × 3 ft tub? Pick the best answer.

    A. 50 buckets

    B. 48 buckets

    C. 57 buckets

    D. 62 buckets

128. The English colonies were established in three regions—the New England Colonies, the Middle Colonies, and the Southern Colonies. The economy of the Southern Colonies was based on

    A.   farming, shipping, fishing, and trading.

    B.   farming and very small industries such as fishing, lumber, and crafts.

    C.   trading.

    D.   crops of tobacco, rice, indigo, and cotton.

129. Traditionally, matter has been classified into three states

    A.   rock, soil, and minerals.

    B.   ice, snow, and water.

    C.   liquid, gas, and solid.

    D.   nickel, lava, and magma.

130. During the "engage" component of the 5-E model, students begin the inquiry process. They are guided to engage in scientific inquiry and discover the concepts on their own through hands-on investigation, observation, and data collection. When teachers guide students to discover the scientific principles on their own, what teaching method are they using?

    A.   The inductive method

    B.   The deductive method

    C.   Hands-on method

    D.   Student-centered method

131. What percentage of a daily diet should be composed of carbohydrates?

    A.   5–10%

    B.   15–25%

    C.   35–50%

    D.   70–90%

132. Students in Mr. Campos' classroom are learning to interpret visual images. As part of Mr. Campos' explanation to his class, he is considering mentioning all of the following benefits of visual media EXCEPT

   A.   visual images can help spark an audience's interest in the topic.

   B.   visual images cannot stimulate thinking because they can confuse people.

   C.   visual images add clarity to the message being conveyed.

   D.   visual images can be used to show step-by-step developments.

133. Why do most countries in the world use the metric system in scientific research and engineering?

   A.   The metric system uses large units of measurement.

   B.   The English system is used mostly in business.

   C.   The metric system is very precise.

   D.   The English system allows for the easy computation of measurements.

134. The state song of Texas is

   A.   *Home on the Range.*

   B.   *Deep in the Heart of Texas.*

   C.   *The Yellow Rose of Texas.*

   D.   *Texas, Our Texas.*

135. Identify the main benefit of the shared book experience.

   A.   Stories are shared in a supportive environment.

   B.   The whole class can read with the teacher.

   C.   Children like big books.

   D.   It contains attractive pictures and big letters.

136. As part of the celebration of Martin Luther King Day, fifth graders are getting ready to implement readers' theater on a book about the Civil Rights Movement. In preparation for the presentation, the teacher guides the students through several activities. Which of the preparation activities is **less likely** to help them get ready to implement readers' theater?

    A. Working in groups to develop the characters in the story

    B. Modifying the story so that they can all play a part in the actual performance

    C. Rehearsing the parts that each student is supposed to read

    D. Watching a video version of the story

137. Living things are classified into five groups: monera, protista, fungi, plants, and animals. Some of these groups are unicellular, while the others are made up of multiple cells; however, there is only one group that has prokaryotic cells. What kingdom contains prokaryotic cells?

    A. Monera

    B. Protista

    C. Fungi

    D. Plants

138. Identify the informal activities/instruments used to assess oral communication skills in Pre-K students.

    A. Teacher observation checklists, retelling stories, and anecdotal records

    B. Multiple-choice tests, cloze tests, and an informal reading inventory

    C. Audio-taped conversations, written cloze tests, and standardized achievement tests

    D. Repetition drills, choral reading, and chants

139. What is the main function of Earth's atmosphere?

    A. Protect and preserve life

    B. Prevent the contamination of Earth

    C. Create a vacuum between Earth's crust and its mantle

    D. Recycle water and gases

140. The Declaration of Independence consists of a preamble or introduction followed by three main parts. The first part stresses natural unalienable rights and liberties that belong to all people from birth. The second part consists of a list of specific grievances and injustices committed by Britain. What does the third part announce?

    A. The creation of the United States of America

    B. The right to worship

    C. The right to vote

    D. The right to congregate and freedom of speech

ANSWER KEY – PRACTICE TEST 1

Question	Answer	Competency	Question	Answer	Competency
1	B	001	31	A	043
2	D	003	32	D	045
3	B	005	33	D	038
4	C	013	34	D	002
5	D	013	35	D	003
6	B	015	36	D	003
7	B	044	37	C	013
8	C	021	38	B	013
9	D	004	39	B	019
10	B	021	40	D	019
11	A	023	41	B	028
12	B	035	42	C	022
13	B	035	43	B	018
14	D	035	44	B	044
15	C	005	45	A	019
16	A	005	46	B	002
17	D	009	47	B	044
18	B	039	48	C	042
19	C	042	49	B	036
20	B	043	50	C	036
21	C	045	51	C	011
22	C	023	52	A	011
23	B	021	53	B	016
24	A	017	54	C	012
25	B	012	55	A	009
26	A	007	56	A	016
27	B	016	57	C	019
28	A	025	58	C	020
29	C	009	59	C	017
30	A	042	60	C	008

Question	Answer	Competency	Question	Answer	Competency
61	C	045	93	A	004
62	A	025	94	A	010
63	C	022	95	D	014
64	A	017	96	B	020
65	B	015	97	D	045
66	D	001	98	B	022
67	B	001	99	A	021
68	A	016	100	C	007
69	A	002	101	B	021
70	C	015	102	C	043
71	C	014	103	B	008
72	D	017	104	C	024
73	B	020	105	A	004
74	B	005	106	D	022
75	A	013	107	A	008
76	C	025	108	A	006
77	B	007	109	B	014
78	C	025	110	B	020
79	D	011	111	C	027
80	C	016	112	B	018
81	D	020	113	A	007
82	B	033	114	B	022
83	D	027	115	A	015
84	B	042	116	C	021
85	B	026	117	A	012
86	B	010	118	A	021
87	C	023	119	A	012
88	B	010	120	C	012
89	B	024	121	D	018
90	D	015	122	B	021
91	D	018	123	B	002
92	A	029	124	D	023

Question	Answer	Competency
125	B	010
126	A	002
127	C	015
128	D	022
129	C	031
130	A	025
131	C	044
132	B	011

Question	Answer	Competency
133	C	024
134	D	043
135	A	004
136	D	006
137	A	034
138	A	005
139	A	038
140	A	023

Practice Test 1, Competency Checklist

Competency 001　　　　_/3
1　66　67

Competency 002　　　　_/5
34　46　69　123　126

Competency 003　　　　_/3
2　35　36

Competency 004　　　　_/4
9　83　105　135

Competency 005　　　　_/5
3　15　16　74　138

Competency 006　　　　_/2
108　136

Competency 007　　　　_/4
26　77　100　113

Competency 008　　　　_/3
60　103　107

Competency 009　　　　_/3
17　29　55

Competency 010　　　　_/4
86　88　94　125

Competency 011　　　　_/4
51　52　79　132

Competency 012　　　　_/5
25　54　117　119　120

Competency 013   _/5

4	5	37	38	75

Competency 014   _/3

71	95	109

Competency 015   _/6

6	65	70	90	115	127

Competency 016   _/5

27	53	56	68	80

Competency 017   _/4

24	59	64	72

Competency 018   _/4

43	91	112	121

Competency 019   _/4

39	40	45	57

Competency 020   _/5

58	73	81	96	110

Competency 021   _/8

8	10	23	99	101	116

118	122

Competency 022   _/6

42	63	98	106	114	128

Competency 023   _/5

11	22	87	124	140

Competency 024   _/3

89	104	133

Competency 025   _/5

28	62	76	78	130

Competency 026   _/1

85

Competency 027   _/2

83	111

Competency 028   _/1

41

Competency 029   _/1

92

Competency 030   _/0

Competency 031   _/1

129

Competency 032 ___/0

Competency 033 ___/1

82

Competency 034 ___/1

137

Competency 035 ___/3

12	13	14

Competency 036 ___/2

49	50

Competency 037 ___/0

Competency 038 ___/2

33	139

Competency 039 ___/1

18

Competency 040 ___/0

Competency 041 ___/0

Competency 042 ___/4

19	30	48	84

Competency 043 ___/4

20	31	102	134

Competency 044 ___/4

7	44	47	131

Competency 045 ___/4

21	32	61	97

Detailed Explanations for Practice Test 1

1.   **B**

     The word *thought* is a long word, even though it is monosyllabic. It has three pho-nemes. The word contains two consonant diagraphs, *th* and *ght*, and a vowel digraph, *ou*, representing one sound each for a total of three sounds. (A), (C), and (D) are incorrect based on the previous explanation. **Competency 001**

2.   **D**

     Emergent readers will make use of various strategies for understanding print and make meaningful use of texts. They begin to develop the awareness of the story's structures. They will also use illustrations to understand what they are reading and use visual imagery to represent their stories. Although some emergent readers may begin to use self-correction, it is typically not a characteristic of emergent readers (D). **Competency 003**

3.   **B**

     The analysis of the structure of the words for decoding and comprehension is definitely part of structural analysis. Choice (A) is incorrect because context goes beyond individual words. (C) is incorrect because pictorial clues describe any kind of visual information, like pictures and charts. (D) is incorrect because syntactic clues use whole sentences and determine meaning based on the position of words within sentences. **Competency 005**

4.   **C**

     When subtraction involves any negative numbers, a good rule to use is, "Don't subtract the second number. Instead, add its opposite." Using that rule, the original expression, $(-36) - 11$ becomes $(-36) + -11$. To be "in debt" by 36, then to be further "in debt" by 11, puts one "in debt" by 47, shown as -47. **Competency 013**

5.   **D**

     The order of operations must be obeyed here. Remembering the saying Please Excuse My Dear Aunt Sally (PEMDAS) allows us to remember the order in which mathematical operations must be carried out, Parentheses Exponent Multiply Divide Add Subtract. Following this one will multiply 6 by 2 to obtain 12. Then, one will divide 3 by 3 obtaining 1. Finally, one will add the two results together to obtain $12 + 1 = 13$. **Competency 013**

6. **B**

An easy way to solve this problem is to use basic algebra. Knowing that there are 16 oz. in a pound and that there are 2,000 lbs. in a ton helps ease the difficulty of the problem. We want to find out the number of cans x it will take to obtain a ton. Therefore, we have $\frac{14}{16}x = 2000$. If both sides of the equation are multiplied by 16 and then we divide both sides by 14, we will obtain the approximate number of cans it will take to obtain one ton. $x = \frac{16 \times 2000}{14} = \frac{32000}{14} \approx 2,285.7$. We see that many of the answers are close to this value. When we round this number, we will obtain 2,286. **Competency 015**

7. **B**

The only answer that is not risky behavior for causing illness and disease is (B) keeping the body hydrated by drinking a lot of water. All other answers put the body at risk for illness and/or disease. **Competency 044**

8. **C**

The Earth is divided into 24 zones based on the meridians of longitude, which are determined using the rotation of the Earth and its exposure to sunlight. This rotation creates day and night, and consequently the concept of time. (A) is incorrect because the International Date Line is only one of 24 meridians of the Earth. (B) is incorrect because the term revolution describes the movement of the Earth around the sun, which affects the seasons but not necessarily the time zones. (D) is incorrect because the parallels of latitude do not affect the time zones. **Competency 021**

9. **D**

A balanced reading program is one in which the teaching of reading requires solid skill instruction, including several techniques for decoding unknown words. However, having students decode words on their own is not considered to be the cornerstone of such a program. Therefore (A), (B), and (C) are all strategies that will be implemented in this program. **Competency 004**

10. **B**

Iraq is a Muslim nation with multiple ethnic groups within its borders. The largest groups are the Arabs, consisting of Shiite and Sunni Muslims. The Kurds are the largest minority group. (A) is incorrect. The multiple groups living in Iraq speak Arabic, Kurdish, Turkish, Assyrian, and other languages. (C) is incorrect because Iraq is located in the Middle Eastern part of Asia. (D) is incorrect because Pakistan is a Muslim country from the region, but there is no political association between the two nations. **Competency 021**

11. **A**

The Mayflower Compact was drawn up and signed by the Pilgrims aboard the *Mayflower*. They pledged to consult one another to make decisions and to act by the will of the majority. It is one of the earliest agreements to establish a political body and to give that political body the power to act for the good of the colony. (B), (C), and (D) are incorrect because these were aspects of colonial life but not the purpose of the Mayflower Compact. **Competency 023**

12. **B**

Using high-interest activities like observing live animals and plants in an aquarium, students can be guided to used scientific inquiry and problem-solving skills. (A) and (C) are incorrect because both describe non-scientific objectives. (D) presents a generic statement that fails to address the main scientific objective. **Competency 035**

13. **B**

A healthy aquatic system should have sufficient space and conditions to support life. Aquarium A has a large number of animals for a small 25-gallon aquarium. Over-population can pollute the environment and affect the balance of the ecosystem. The size of the aquarium (A), the number of plants (C), and the number of fish (D) contribute to the success of the habitat, but individually, they cannot justify the students' decision. **Competency 035**

14. **D**

Fish of the same kind have a better chance of reproducing themselves. Aquarium B contains fish of the same kind, while aquarium A has different varieties. (A), (B), and (C) present elements that can affect the overall habitat, but they do not provide key information about the chances of successful breeding. **Competency 035**

15. **C**

Pointing to the words as they are read is designed to establish the connection between speech and print. However, after the skill has been mastered, it is discontinued so students can engage in fluent reading. (A) and (B) are incorrect because they offer non-substantial reasons for the strategy change. (D) is incorrect because the practice of pointing to the words as they are being read is not archaic; it is indeed an effective practice for beginning readers. **Competency 005**

16. **A**

The use of flash cards with pictures representing concepts and concrete objects can definitely be effective in teaching vocabulary to preschool children. (B) is incorrect because parents can teach a word every day to the child, but the child might not be able to participate effectively because preschoolers generally do not have the vocabulary development to teach parents new words. (C) is also incorrect because preschoolers might not have the necessary vocabulary development to participate in a game dealing with antonyms and synonyms. (D) is incorrect because the practice of memorizing vocabulary is quite boring and ineffective for children of all ages. **Competency 005**

17. **D**

Students who are becoming literate are not yet writing conventionally. However, answers (A), (B), and (C) all represent features and characteristics of emergent writers. As young writers grasp the concept of the alphabetic principle and are able to better map speech onto print in conventional ways, their spelling will become closer approximations to conventional spelling. **Competency 009**

18. **B**

The movement of the plates causes intense seismological activity near the faults, resulting in earthquakes. (A) and (C) have some merit because thermal activity can have some implications, but these choices do not provide specific answers to the question. (D) is totally incorrect; there is no known connection between the rotation of the Earth and earthquakes. **Competency 039**

19. **C**

Two-year-old children are primarily concerned with sensory experiences in their earliest art activities. (A) is incorrect because children do not begin to self-express in their artwork until around age five years. (B) is incorrect because children do not begin to use personal symbols in their artwork until around age four years. (D) is incorrect because children do not begin to repeat themes or be concerned with photographic realism until the middle years of elementary school. **Competency 042**

20. **B**

    The rhythm is typically called the melodic rhythm or word rhythm found in the song. The beginning of *Happy Birthday* ("Happy birthday to you") has the same word rhythm as "Oh, say can you see." (A) is incorrect because the word rhythm "My country 'tis of thee" is not the same as "Happy Birthday to you." (C) is incorrect because the word rhythm "Take me out to the ball game" is not the same as "Happy Birthday to you." (D) is also incorrect because "Oh beautiful for spacious skies" is not the same as "Happy Birthday to you." **Competency 043**

21. **C**

    The ADA requires school districts to place special education children in the least restrictive educational environment; thus, an orthopedic handicapped student would be placed in mainstream classrooms. Students are required to receive physical education using appropriate accommodations to allow their successful participation. (A) is incorrect because only in extreme cases are special education children excluded from participating in the school curriculum. (B) is partially correct, but it fails to mention the need to make accommodations for successful participation in physical education activities. (D) is incorrect because it adopts an extreme position not applicable to limited mobility. **Competency 045**

22. **C**

    The Virginia House of Burgesses was the first legislature established in the English colonies. It was established in 1619 and became the first form of government in the colony. (A) is incorrect because the U.S. government did not exist during this time (1619). (B) is incorrect because England regulated trading with the colonies. (D) is incorrect because, there was no official entity in the colony to regulate the establishment of religions. **Competency 023**

23. **B**

    A globe is a scale model of the Earth shaped like a sphere. Because a globe is the same shape as the Earth, it shows sizes and shapes more accurately than a Mercator projection map (a flat representation of the Earth). (A) is incorrect because a compass rose is a design used to show orientation and not a representation of the Earth. (C) is incorrect because a map scale is used to show the distance between two places in the world. (D) is incorrect because thematic maps are not used to show the size and shape of the Earth. **Competency 021**

24. **A**

There are equal numbers of blue and red marbles in each bag. For a single bag on a single draw, the probability of pulling a red or a blue marble is equal to $\frac{4}{8}$, or $\frac{1}{2}$. Selecting a marble from one bag does not affect the probability of selecting a specific marble from the other bag, therefore these events are said to be independent. When dealing with the probability of independent events, one may multiply the probabilities together to obtain the overall probability. In this case, we know the probability of selecting a blue marble is $\frac{1}{2}$ for the first bag and it is also $\frac{1}{2}$ for the second bag. Therefore, the overall probability of the independent events is $\frac{1}{4}$. **Competency 017**

25. **B**

All three instruments, running records, teacher observations, and the checklist, are examples of informal assessment. (A) is incorrect because at least one of the instruments, running records, is not a teacher-developed instrument. (C) is incorrect based on the information previously stated. (D) is incorrect because all three instruments require some level of subjectivity. **Competency 012**

26. **A**

Research on second language acquisition suggests that a strong literacy development in L1 can facilitate the acquisition of similar levels of proficiency in L2. Some language specific variables together with literacy and metacognitive strategies can also transfer from L1 to L2. Reading skills are not identical in L1 and L2; (B) does not explain the rationale for implementing instruction in L1. (C) is probably an accurate statement, reading can be confusing for ELLs, but this statement does not address the question. (D) represents an opinion that fails to provide the rationale for the implementation of initial reading instruction in L1. **Competency 007**

27. **B**

If you can fold a two-dimensional figure so that one side exactly matches or folds onto the other side, the fold line is a line of symmetry. The figure in the problem is a non-square rectangle meaning two of the sides are longer than the other two. Because of this, the shape only has two lines of symmetry. Folding the object from one corner to its opposite corner would not result in a fold where the sides were on top of each other. **Competency 016**

28. **A**

In the "explore" component of the 5-E Model, students begin to have hands-on exposure to the topic. In this stage, students are guided to make observations and gather data about the scientific project. (B) is incorrect because it describes the initial stage of the process, "engage," in which students begin to conceptualize the topic of the study. (C) describes the process of concept invention or explanation, through which a teacher-guided discussion presents the findings of the study. (D) is incorrect, because it describes the "engage" step of the process, in which students are motivated to learn about the scientific concept. **Competency 025**

29. **C**

Reading a story and asking a child to retell it promotes interest in writing. When the teacher writes down the dictated story, the child can see the connection of oral and written work. (A) and (B) are incorrect because the children at the emerging stage don't have sufficient command of written language to correct their own writing or write a composition based on prompts. (D) is incorrect because reading for 30 minutes a day without any kind of explicit or implicit writing support might not be effective for children at the emerging stage for writing. **Competency 009**

30. **A**

The state curriculum states that experiences in critical evaluation for kindergartners should include expressing ideas about personal artworks, and the artworks of peers or professional artists. Critical evaluation is one of the four strands in the state curriculum for fine arts and visual arts. (B) is incorrect because the standards indicate that experiences in critical evaluation should begin in kindergarten rather than first grade. (C) is incorrect because the standards indicate that experiences in critical evaluation should begin in kindergarten rather than second grade. (D) is incorrect because the standards indicate that experiences in critical evaluation should begin in kindergarten rather than third grade. **Competency 042**

31. **A**

The Orff approach uses both unpitched rhythm instruments (e.g., wood blocks, triangles, etc.) and melodic or barred instruments (e.g., xylophones, metallophones, and glockenspiels). The Kodály Method (B) is incorrect because the primary goal is to teach music literacy and singing is the vehicle to achieve this goal. Mariachi (C) is a group of musicians that play violins, trumpets, a Spanish guitar, and a guitarrón. Tejano music (D) features the accordion, and the Tejano orchestra has been influenced by Mexican, Cuban, German, and Czech brass bands. **Competency 043**

32. **D**

   Fun games involving physical activity are the best way to exercise children in kindergarten. (A) is incorrect because, traditionally, jogging for fitness might be inappropriate for children at this early age. (B) and (C) are incorrect because contact sports and activities that require skill and/or endurance are not developmentally appropriate for kindergarten or first-grade students. **Competency 045**

33. **D**

   The teacher can discuss the theory of continental drift, which gave rise to the current theory of plate tectonics. According to this theory, the crust of the Earth is broken down into several floating tectonic plates, which move and change locations. (A) is incorrect because it describes how organisms evolve throughout history. It also alludes to the work of Charles Darwin. (B) is incorrect because it refers to the religious belief that the universe was created by a supreme being. (C) describes the process by which organisms living on one continent manage to migrate to other continents or to other regions within a continent. **Competency 038**

34. **D**

   As seen in the scenario, Luke is clearly in the telegraphic stage. He is using chunks of words and phrases he has heard others use and is including them in his linguistic repertoire. Based on this explanation, options (A), (B), and (C) are incorrect. **Competency 002**

35. **D**

   Onsets represent the first phoneme of a syllable or a monosyllabic word like the words presented in choice (D). Rimes follow the onset and are linked to the concept of word families. The rime *ank* can be used to create multiple words, like *blank, tank, rank,* and *flank*. Choices (A) and (C) are generally used to represent verb tenses and cannot be considered the typical rime or word family. Choice (B) is incorrect because the two words do not represent onset and rimes. Instead, the example of *very–berry* represents a minimal pair—two words that differ in only one phoneme. **Competency 003**

36. **D**

   Semantic, structural, and visual cuing systems are all used by newly fluent readers to aid in their comprehension of texts. They also make use of graphophonemic cuing systems. These are used to self-monitor what they are reading as well as to begin to correct their errors without much support. **Competency 003**

37. **C**

   To solve this problem, one again must use PEMDAS first on the exponential term. Once this is done, one obtains $(2 \cdot 10)^3 = 11 \cdot 10^3 (2 \cdot 10)^3 = 11 \cdot 10^3$. Then, multiplying the two single-digit numbers (8 and 6), one gets 48. Continuing with the solution, we now can multiply 10^3 with 10^4 to obtain 10^7 by adding the exponents (this can be done because each number has a common base, 10). We are now left with $48 \cdot 10^7$. However, the last step is to write the answer in scientific notation, which is $4.8 \cdot 10^8$. **Competency 013**

38. **B**

   One of the basic properties of addition is that it can be carried out in any order. Therefore, since addition is the only operation that is performed in this exercise, one knows the correct answer is the associate property of addition. **Competency 013**

39. **B**

   The social studies strands are systematically integrated throughout the social studies state curriculum in grades K–12. (A) is incorrect based on the previous explanation. (C) and (D) are incorrect because the social studies strands are used in public education as well as in higher education. **Competency 019**

40. **D**

   TEKS introduces social studies beginning with what the child knows to what the child does not know. Students begin studying about themselves and from there they study the school, community, and, finally, the state. The focus on TEKS for fourth grade is the history of Texas. (A) is incorrect because TEKS is available only in K–12. For prekindergarten, teachers use instructional guidelines. (B) is incorrect because the focus of first grade is the school and the community. (C) is incorrect because in grade 3 the focus is the individual and how each affects the community. **Competency 019**

41. **B**

   The state curriculum requires students to engage in scientific exploration in grades K–12. Hands-on experimentation promotes active learning and is beneficial to all students, but it is especially important and developmentally appropriate for children in grades K–2. Choice (A) is incorrect because the incorporation of foreign language methods is a very broad statement, and it does not say specifically which method will be used or how it will be implemented. (C) is also incorrect because the statement is vague and does not describe the types of sophisticated tools. Traditionally, in K–2, the tools used are very simple and concrete. (D) is incorrect because the state curriculum does not require the use of chemicals and human specimens in the early grades. **Competency 028**

42. **C**

Reducing the production of oil while keeping the same demand for the product creates an imbalance between supply and demand. This imbalance results in a price increase. (A) is incorrect. (B) is incorrect because the statement does not explain the economic principle required in the question. Generally speaking, war increases the demand and prices of many things, not only the price of fossil fuels. (B) just presents a true statement—the American economy depends on foreign oil. (D) presents an opinion that fails to address the true question. **Competency 022**

43. **B**

Using the acronym PEMDAS as a mnemonic device to remember the order of operations, it allows us to see that the first operation required in the problems is multiplication. That is, the acronym calls for the following order: percentages, exponents, multiplication, division, addition, and subtraction. However, since the problem does not contain percentages or exponents, the first operation required in the problem is multiplication. **Competency 018**

44. **B**

The only incorrect answer about metabolism is choice (B) fasting speeds up your metabolism. Fasting does not speed up metabolism; it shuts metabolism down in order to conserve energy due to little or no calories getting into the body. (A) is true because your basal metabolism (basal metabolic rate) is constantly burning calories and converting energy. (C) is correct because physical activity always stimulates metabolic function. (D) is correct in that metabolism slowly adjusts to the demands placed on the body over long periods of time. **Competency 044**

45. **A**

Maps use symbolic representation, and children at that age rely mostly on concrete experiences for learning. The abstraction typical of maps' legends and other symbolic representations might not be developmentally appropriate for this age group. (B) is a plausible statement but not the best answer. Children initially will be inclined to use the globe as toys and pay attention to colors, but eventually they will understand its function through classroom instruction. (C) is incorrect because it presents an opinion not supported in the scenario. (D) is probably a true statement: Children will have problems conceptualizing how the Earth can be represented in a small 12-inch globe, but this choice is not the best answer because it addresses only one component of the question—globe representation. **Competency 019**

46. **B**

Homonyms are words that have the same spelling and pronunciation, but have different meanings. The only pair of words that is a true homonym is (B). In this case, the word *club* can refer to a night club or a wooden stick. Option (A) and (C) are incorrect because they represent two different words. Option (D) represents an example of homophones, words that are pronounced in the same way, have different meanings, and are spelled differently. **Competency 002**

47. **B**

Heat stroke is best recognized and described by red, hot, dry skin due to lack of hydration—a condition not allowing the body to cool itself efficiently. Unconsciousness is another sign of heat stroke in extreme situations. (A) does not include the typical signs of heat stroke rather heat exhaustion which is not as severe. (C) and (D) may accompany heat stroke but are not by themselves primary indicators of the problem. **Competency 044**

48. **C**

Perception, creative expression, historical/cultural heritage, and critical evaluation are precisely the four strands identified in the state curriculum for fine arts and visual arts. (A) is incorrect because, although art production, appreciation, and evaluation may be included in the four strands under slightly different terminology, art advocacy is not. (B) is incorrect because, although sensory awareness, creativity, and art production may be included in the four strands under slightly different terminology, crafts are not. (D) is incorrect because the wording of each strand has been changed. **Competency 042**

49. **B**

Corals are invertebrates that fall under the animal kingdom. These small organisms can reproduce themselves sexually or asexually. (A) is incorrect because unlike corals, the kingdom Monera is made up of unicellular organisms with very rudimentary cellular organization. (C) and (D) are incorrect because corals are described in the question as invertebrates, a classification used exclusively for members of the animal kingdom. **Competency 036**

50. **C**

Corals live in a symbiotic relationship with algae because both exchange nutrients or other kinds of services in order for both to survive. (A) is incorrect because corals are not parasites living off algae. Instead, parasites and corals provide support services to each other for their mutual survival. (B) and (D) might be true statements, but they do not define the term *symbiosis*. **Competency 036**

51. **C**

Newspapers and magazines have been considered print media. (B) is incorrect because images are often used to complement texts being displayed in such mediums. (A) is incorrect because there is no such a thing as "electric" media; the correct term is "electronic" media. **Competency 011**

52. **A**

The most appropriate topic would be for students to research the evolution of billboards on the highway (A). (B), (C), and (D) are incorrect because they represent examples of electronic media, not visual media. **Competency 011**

53. **B**

Angle *xyz* is an inscribed angle (its vertex is on the circle). Angle *xCz* is a central angle (its vertex is at the circle's center). When two such angles intercept (or "cut off") the same arc of the circle, a specific size relationship exists between the two angles. The measure of the central angle will always be double the measure of the inscribed angle. In this case, that means that the measure of angle *xCz* must be 80°. Thus, minor arc *xz* also measures 80°. Every circle (considered as an arc) measures 360°. This means major arc *xyz* measures 280° (360 – 80). The explanation shows that (A), (C) and (D) are incorrect. **Competency 016**

54. **C**

A main disadvantage is that ELLs may have difficulty expressing their thoughts in writing. This means the test may not be a valid way to measure student's knowledge about a particular topic. Option (A) is incorrect because many students and teachers are familiar with rubric-based scoring. Answers (B) and (D) are incorrect because they portray the advantages of using an essay to assess knowledge, rather than disadvantages. **Competency 012**

55. **A**

   In the Language Experience Approach (LEA), the teacher is dictating the ideas and thoughts of the students. As the students share ideas, the teacher writes them down, thus connecting speech to print and also modeling how oral language is related to writing. Answer (B) is incorrect because in this approach, it is the teacher who "has the pen" and does the modeled writing as students contribute ideas. Answer (C) is incorrect because the focus is not on oral reading primarily; the emphasis is on both reading and writing for beginning readers with LEA. Answer (D) is incorrect because it focuses on the teacher's own ideas, whereas LEA focuses on the teacher dictating the ideas of the student or students. **Competency 009**

56. **A**

   Since Mrs. Cameron does not want any seams in her carpet, the carpet must be 20 ft long (at least) to cover the entire space. Since the room is only 14 ft wide and the carpet is 16 ft wide, there will be 2 ft of wasted carpet for the entire length of the room (20 ft). Therefore, the amount of carpet that is wasted is $20 \times 2 = 40$ ft^2 of carpet. **Competency 016**

57. **C**

   Cognitive or academic vocabulary is the vocabulary needed to understand the concepts of school. In other words, it is the vocabulary of teaching and learning. Based on this explanation, options (A), (B), and (D) are incorrect. **Competency 019**

58. **C**

   The Apache and the Comanche domesticated the horse and became skillful hunters and warriors. These skills allowed them to fight the whites for many years for control of the Central and Great Plains of Texas. (A) is incorrect because the tribes from the plains were nomads and did not develop an advanced civilization. (B) is incorrect because both the Comanche and the Apache were nomads and did not leave permanent constructions. (D) is incorrect because the tribes from the area had to hunt for survival and they had to move continuously to find adequate food supplies. **Competency 020**

59. **C**

   Since tossing two separate coins does not effect the outcome of the other coin, we know that the probability of getting a head on either coin is 1/2. The probability of the outcome is then 2/4 or 0.5. **Competency 017**

60. **C**

Brainstorming for ideas and developing an outline of the writing project are paramount for process writing. (A), (B), and (D) are incorrect because they do not contain brainstorming as the initial component of the process. **Competency 008**

61. **C**

Repetition and practice of a movement pattern is the fastest way to master a physical skill no matter the age level. (A) has no relevance to skill acquisition. (B) and (D) could in part attribute to skill development, although not to the same level of guided repetition and practice. **Competency 045**

62. **A**

Students need to have a clear understanding of the evolution of science concepts, so they can develop an appreciation for the status of science today. (B) is incorrect because it addresses only one historical period, the Middle Ages. It also addresses the historical value of the information, which should be excluded from the answer. (C) is incorrect because it only addresses the medical implications of the information. (D) presents an incorrect statement, because at the present time most European countries have well-developed scientific knowledge. **Competency 025**

63. **C**

Cotton and eventually cattle were the main products produced in Texas during the nineteenth and early twentieth centuries. Later, with the discovery of petroleum in the twentieth century, it became one of the most important exports for Texas. In the latter part of the twentieth century and until today, computer and electronics replaced oil as the main products of the state. Based on this explanation, options (A), (B), and (D) are eliminated. **Competency 022**

64. **A**

In a normal deck of cards there are 52 total cards. Of the 52 cards, there are four suits and 13 cards per suit. Therefore, there are four queens in the deck. Additionally, of the four suits, two are black and two are red. So, there are two black fours giving a grand total of six cards of 52 that meet the criteria. **Competency 017**

65. **B**

There are a total of 40 individuals in the group. Of the 40 people in the group, 5 are red heads. This gives a ratio of 5/40, which may be simplified to 1/8. **Competency 015**

66. **D**

A visual analysis of columns 4, 5, and 6 shows that the phoneme /sh/ can be represented by at least four different graphemes—*ch, s, ss,* and *t*—in words like **chef,** **sure, mission,** and **caution.** The grapheme *ch* is also inconsistent. Column 3 shows that the grapheme *ch* represents the sound /k/. This inconsistency affects the ability of ELLs to separate the two phonemes. (A), (B), and (C) are incorrect because the scenario does not provide evidence to suggest that ELLs cannot establish a difference or pronounce the two phonemes, or that they might not be interested in learning the difference between the two. **Competency 001**

67. **B**

The chart provides examples of words that follow grapheme-phoneme correspondence. It also provides examples of words that use different graphemes to represent the sounds. This chart provides students with tangible information to help them deal with graphophonemic inconsistencies. (A) is incorrect because this particular chart places more emphasis on graphophonemic inconsistencies than on consistencies. (C) is incorrect because the chart presents words in isolation; thus, it cannot present information about the intonation pattern used in sentences or larger units. (D) is a plausible answer, but it does not capture the true intent of the activity. The chart is designed to deal with specific, inconsistent sounds only. **Competency 001**

68. **A**

The formula for the volume of a cylinder is $V = \pi r^2 h$. Knowing the radius is 6 m and the height is 8 m gives an approximate value of 904 m^3 for the volume of the cylinder ($V \approx 3.14 \times 6^2 \times 8 = 3.14 \times 36 \times 8 \approx 904$). **Competency 016**

69. **A**

Alliteration is a technique to emphasize the connection between the consonant and the sound that it represents. In this particular case, the tongue twister is used to emphasize the sound of the /r/. (B) is incorrect because the technique goes beyond the use of a tongue twister. Tongue twisters are examples of alliteration, and they emphasize pronunciation and fluency. (C) is incorrect because the utterance does not represent an example of traditional nursery rhymes. Nursery rhymes are short poems, stories, or songs written to entertain children. **Competency 002**

70. **C**

An integer number is a whole number that is either positive or negative. Remembering that a negative times a negative gives a positive means that any of the answers could be possible and we cannot rule any out by process of elimination. Knowing that 8 times 8 gives 64 means both (A) and (B) are true. Similarly, –9 times –9 results in 81 (D) meaning 81 is true. However, 6 times 6 gives 36, not 32. This means that (C) is not a true statement and is the solution to the problem. **Competency 015**

71. **C**

In this problem it is necessary to perform the order of operations as well as look at equivalent representations of numbers. Since there are no exponents in any of the solutions, it may be beneficial to carry this out within the problem before proceeding further. Doing so results in $17(64 + 64) - 64$. This may also be written as $17 \times 64 \times 2 - 64$. Since 64 appears in the first multiplication sequence as well as being a subtrahend, it may be factored to produce $64(17 \times 2 - 1) = 64(34 - 1) = 64 \times 33$. **Competency 014**

72. **D**

Knowing that with a pair of dice there are 36 possible outcomes allows us to view all of the possible outcomes. Of the possible outcomes, half are odd and half are even. **Competency 017**

73. **B**

The convergence of the Tigris and the Euphrates created a fertile region where some of the greatest civilizations of the world emerged. This part of the world has been called the Fertile Crescent, and it is part of the area called the Cradle of Civilizations. (A) is incorrect because the Nile gave birth to the Egyptian civilization, and the Amazon River is located in South America, far away from Mesopotamia. (C) is incorrect because the Indus River is located in modern-day India. (D) is incorrect because the Volga and Danube rivers are located in Europe. **Competency 020**

74. **B**

All language skills are interrelated, including reading and writing. Given appropriate instruction, the skills of reading and writing can be introduced and acquired concurrently. Current research does not support the idea that children learn language skills in a sequential manner (A). Based on the explanation given, options (C) and (D) are incorrect. **Competency 005**

75.   **A**

Learning centers allow children opportunities to explore mathematics reasoning in a play and low anxiety format. (B) is incorrect because it addresses only one component of the benefit—the use of manipulatives. (C) is incorrect because, traditionally, learning centers are not used to teach deductive reasoning. Instead, students learn inductively through the use of manipulatives and the input from teachers. (D) is incorrect because learning centers do not use a highly structured format. On the contrary, learning centers are designed to be a low anxiety environment in which children can explore on their own. **Competency 013**

76.   **C**

Reading and discussing the biographies and the accomplishments of scientists from a variety of backgrounds can minimize the stereotypical views that children may have about them. (A) and (D) are incorrect because both address the gender misconception only. Providing generic information about the diversity in the science field (B) might not be the best strategy for first graders. They might need more tangible evidence of the information. **Competency 025**

77.   **B**

Reading to children in any language can promote interest in reading and decoding skills. Promoting reading comprehension is the next logical step. Once the child masters these basic skills, these can easily transfer to the second language. (A) is incorrect because reading to children should not be interrupted, especially during the preschool years. Reading to children is beneficial even for advanced readers. (C) is incorrect because the scenario does not provide evidence to suggest that the child is ready for more challenging first-grade books. (D) is incorrect because reading skills acquired in the first language can transfer to the second language. Additionally, students should be exposed to reading in the dominant language first. **Competency 007**

78.   **C**

The Texas Essential Knowledge and Skills (TEKS) allows the use of burners and hot plates beginning in fifth grade. Based on this information, the rest of the options are incorrect. **Competency 025**

79. **D**

Charts, tables, and graphs can be used to present, summarize, and/or complement the message being conveyed. These are not designed to provide detailed explanations (C) of topics covered in class. Regardless of their use, students must be aware that their use should never be intended to entertain (B) or contradict (D) any of their information. **Competency 011**

80. **C**

The metric system is a very precise system that allows for the measurement of very small amounts of matter. For example, the metric system uses measurements divided into thousands (millimeters or milligrams), while the English system uses larger units of measurement, like inches and ounces. (A) and (B) contain possible true statements and opinions but they fail to address the question. (D) is incorrect; the English system does not have a simple way to compute measures. On the other hand, the metric system is a base 10 system and the computations are typically easier. **Competency 016**

81. **D**

The country of Iraq is located in the region known as Mesopotamia. (A) is incorrect because the country of Iran is located east of the Tigris River. (B) is incorrect because Pakistan is located further southeast of these rivers. (C) is also incorrect because the State of Kuwait is located southwest of the area and south of Iraq. **Competency 020**

82. **B**

Conduction is a form of heat transfer. The metal of the spoon serves as a conductor of the heat emanating from the open flame. (A) is too generic because radiation describes different kinds of energy produced naturally by the sun and artificially by microwaves and cellular phones. (C) is incorrect because it does not describe the type of transfer of energy presented in the scenario. However, convection is also a form of heat transfer carried through movement of matter. For example, the heating of water in a pan creates movement of the liquid from the bottom to the top, forcing cold water down to the bottom of the pan, where it is heated. Kinetics (D) is a term used to describe movement, not energy transfer. **Competency 033**

83. **D**

Both animals, the crocodile and the bird, benefit from this relationship. The bird gets food and at the same time cleans the teeth of the crocodile. (A) is incorrect because the term *commensalism* describes a relationship in which only one organism benefit, from the interaction, while the second organism is not affected by the interaction. (B) is incorrect because in a parasitism relationship; only one organism benefits from the interaction. The term predator-prey (C) relationship does not describe the interaction between the bird and the crocodile. **Competency 027**

84. **B**

The standards state that second graders should use art principles, like emphasis, patterns, and rhythm to create artworks. The principles of art are included in the curriculum strand of Perceptions. (A) is incorrect because the standards indicate that children's first experiences with art principles should occur in second grade rather than kindergarten. (C) is incorrect because the standards indicate that children's first experiences with the art principles should occur in second grade rather than fourth grade. (D) is incorrect because the standards indicate that children's first experiences with the art principles should occur in second grade rather than sixth grade. **Competency 042**

85. **B**

Learning about computers and search engines (A) is a derivative of the process; it does not constitute the main benefit of the activity. (C) and (D) are incorrect because they represent a generic value and byproducts of the activity. **Competency 026**

86. **B**

The teaching of the writing trait of "voice" can be taught through sharing examples, such as through reading aloud stories by authors who portray and exemplify strong voice in their unique style of writing. Teachers can ask their students what characteristics best exemplify this author's voice across multiple texts. Option (A) focuses less on voice and more on the ways in which the writing is structured. (C) and (D) focus more on syntax, grammar, and punctuation and less on voice, although they are related features to how authors construct voice. **Competency 010**

87. **C**

The U.S. Constitution set up a system so that each branch has the power to control or regulate the power of the other two. (A) is incorrect because judicial review addresses only the power of the judicial branch. Judicial review is the power to review legislation enacted by Congress and signed by the president. If the legislation is unconstitutional, it can be invalidated. (B) is incorrect because it addresses the power of the president to veto or refuse to sign legislation approved by Congress. (D) is incorrect because *habeas corpus* is one of the civil rights that guarantees people the right to a quick trial by jury. **Competency 023**

88. **B**

The use of interactive journals allows children opportunities to communicate in meaningful and real-life situations. (A) and (D) are incorrect because listening and speaking abilities are not emphasized in interactive journals. (C) is incorrect because corrective feedback is not encouraged in communication activities. Teachers can provide indirect corrective feedback through modeling. **Competency 010**

89. **B**

The use of household items in place of pure chemicals can reduce the danger for children. Moreover, its use can make science more relevant and practical for students. Avoiding experiments (A) with chemicals (D) is not an option in the upper grades. True scientific experimentation often requires the use of chemicals, thus, substituting the required chemical with plain water is not an option either (C). **Competency 024**

90. **D**

This problem provides unnecessary information to solve the problem. The fact that Stacy discovers 10 extra nickels in her pocket is inconsequential to the solution of the problem. Since a nickel is $0.05 and she had $9.55 in nickels in her purse, divide $9.55 by $0.05 to obtain the number of nickels she had in her purse. **Competency 015**

91. **D**

An irrational number is a number that cannot be expressed as a fraction. Pi is one of the most well-known irrational numbers. Additionally, the square root of 2 and Euler's number (*e*) are well-known numbers that are irrational (at no known point does a pattern appear in the decimals of these numbers). **Competency 018**

92. **A**

Alternative assessment describes the process of gathering performance data as part of instruction. This type of assessment is student-centered and authentic in nature. (B) is incorrect because alternative assessment is generally formative in nature, and it does not have to use instruments approved by the State. (C) is incorrect because it is difficult to determine if all the data collected is easily collected and evaluated. (D) is incorrect because alternative assessment does not emphasize students' weaknesses only. Instead, it tries to assess the overall performance of students in real-life and meaningful situations. **Competency 029**

93. **A**

Venn diagrams can be used for multiple purposes in education, but in language arts it is commonly used to compare similarities, differences, and common elements between two stories. Traditionally, Venn diagrams are not used to identify the parts of the story (B), nor to identify the main idea of a story (D). Semantic mappings (C), not Venn diagrams, are commonly used to identify key attributes of a given concept. **Competency 004**

94. **A**

Children go through predictable stages of spelling development. During the initial stages, children invent words and use phonics skills as a foundation for spelling, which often results in nonstandard spelling. (B) and (C) are incorrect because spelling might not be the most important element in writing, but it is definitely important for effective writing. (D) is incorrect because it does not address the question. It just indicates that spelling requires phonics and structural rules, but it does not say why a rubric should not place heavy emphasis on spelling. **Competency 010**

95. **D**

A prime number is a number whose only factors are one and itself. Even numbers greater than 2 can always be factored by 2, eliminating (B). (A) can be factored as 3 times 3 and (C) can be factored as 7 times 7. Therefore, (D) must be the right answer as it only has factors of 1 and 67. **Competency 014**

96. **B**

The Maya and the Aztecs occupied the area of Central America and Southern Mexico called Mesoamerica. Both groups were accomplished builders, astronomers, and mathematicians. (A) is incorrect because the Inca civilization was not a Mesoamerican group. They developed an advanced civilization in South America, in present-day Peru and Ecuador. (C) is incorrect because only the Toltecs were from Mesoamerica; the Pueblo Indians were from present-day New Mexico in North America. (D) is incorrect because only the Olmecs were a Mesoamerican group. The Iroquois civilizations developed in North America. **Competency 020**

97. **D**

Locomotor activities describe the types of movement that children use to move from one place to the other. In this case, hopping is the only choice that accomplishes this goal. (A) is incorrect because bending is not a locomotor activity, rather a non-locomotor activity. (B) and (C) are also incorrect because they are manipulative skills requiring interaction with equipment or objects. **Competency 045**

98. **B**

In 2008, The Texas economy ranked 12th in the world. The gross state product competes favorably with the gross national product (GNP) of countries like Mexico, India, Australia, and South Korea. Based on this information, (A), (C), and (D) are eliminated. **Competency 022**

99. **A**

A compass rose is a design printed on a chart or map for reference. It shows the orientation of a map on Earth and shows the four cardinal directions (north, south, east, and west). A compass rose may also show in-between directions such as northeast or northwest. (B) is incorrect because a map scale shows the distance between two places in the world. (C) is incorrect because features such as elevations and divisions are represented by different colors. (D) is incorrect because the ratio of the distance between two points on the earth and the distance between the two corresponding points on the map is represented by a scale and not by a compass rose. **Competency 021**

100. **C**

Story grammar focuses on the key elements in a story. By being able to recollect these key features common to many narrative stories, students can develop their understanding of commonalities across texts as well as their understanding of the specific story they are reading. (A) is incorrect because it focuses mainly on meanings at the sentence or word level rather than across the entire text. (B) is incorrect because it is a specific cognitive strategy the learner uses while reading any text. Shared reading (D) is a way to read a text together and is not specific to analyzing features of a text. **Competency 007**

101. **B**

A mixture is a physical combination of two or more substances that retain their own chemical properties; i.e., the mixture can be separated into the original substances—acetic acid and water. (A) is incorrect because in a compound the substances are chemically combined, and in the case of vinegar the substances are only mixed physically. (C) and (D) are incorrect because they lack the specificity required of the answer. **Competency 021**

102. **C**

Pitch describes how high (up) and low (down) sounds are produced. (A) is incorrect because it describes characteristics of rhythm. (B) is incorrect because it describes characteristics of dynamics. (D) is incorrect because it describes characteristics of weight. **Competency 043**

103. **B**

The main purpose of *reading to learn* is to obtain content information efficiently and effectively. One way to accomplish this task is to make students aware of the format used in the content areas and to guide them to retrieve the information by reading for the main idea or scanning for information. Choice (A) is incorrect because it addresses only one component of the process—vocabulary development. (C) is incorrect because it does not address the issue of the complexity of expository writing. (D) is incorrect because it addresses only the issue of vocabulary development—connotation and denotation. **Competency 008**

104. **C**

The purpose of sending safety or any type of contracts for the parents' signature is to make parents aware of the guidelines and expected behaviors in school. Contracts of this type are developed for school purpose only. These are not traditionally used to guide parents to follow safety procedures at home (A), or to guide children to commit to the study of science (B). The purpose of sending the contract home is to make parents aware of the expected behavior, not necessarily to make parents responsible for the behavior of the children (D). **Competency 024**

105. **A**

Reading to children and having books available for them provide children with reading readiness skills and can promote interest in reading. (B) is incorrect because the use of dictionary skills is not developmentally appropriate for preschool children. (C) is incorrect because the children might not be ready for electronic translation programs, and translation is not the best strategy for promoting literacy development. (D) is incorrect because getting books for children without additional support will not develop early literacy among children. **Competency 004**

106. **D**

  The main purpose of the Federal Reserve System (FRS) is to keep the banking industry strong enough to ensure a supply of currency. When the banking industry is strong and there is an adequate supply of currency, fiscal stability and economic growth are more likely to occur. However, the direct role of the FRS is not to provide stimulus money to balance the economy (A), promote economic growth (B), nor create inflation and deflation (C) in the country. Policies adopted by the FRS can lead to a healthy economy—or a weak economy resulting in inflation or deflation. **Competency 022**

107. **A**

  The best way to teach vocabulary to ELLs is to present the word together with a visual or concrete representation—a word concept. The introduction of word concepts can avoid any possible cultural conflict with similar concepts in the students' cultures. (B) is incorrect because translation can teach the word but fail to teach the concept that the word represents. (C) is incorrect because it would be very difficult to teach every single word in a contrasting fashion. Plus, most ESL classes contain speakers of various languages, which makes this activity impractical. (D) is incorrect because with ELLs, we cannot deemphasize the role of vocabulary development. Using context alone to obtain meaning will not work for children new to the English language. **Competency 008**

108. **A**

  When children don't have to struggle to decode words, reading fluency is facilitated. (B) is incorrect because, by definition, no decoding is necessary when the reader recognizes the word instantly. (C) is incorrect because comprehension goes beyond the instant recognition of words. Readers have to analyze the schema of the writing and evaluate other elements to achieve reading comprehension. Instant recognition of words can improve spelling skills; however, it does not necessarily improve the writing process (D). **Competency 006**

109. **B**

  In mathematics, there is a specific order in which actions must occur in order to successfully reach the correct answer. The guideline used to remember this order is typically stated as *Please Excuse My Dear Aunt Sally* (PEMDAS), which stands for *Parentheses Exponent Multiply Divide Add Subtract*. **Competency 014**

110. **B**

The feudal system characterized life in the Middle Ages. The attacks of the barbaric tribes forced people to live under the protection of a lord, usually within the walls of a castle. Muslim Turks took Jerusalem in 1095, and a year later, Christians began the Crusades to rescue the Holy Land. (A) is incorrect because both the Greek and Roman empires are part of the Ancient World. (C) is incorrect because one of the events is part of the Ancient World—Stonehenge. (D) is incorrect because Alexander the Great ruled the Ancient World. **Competency 020**

111. **C**

An ecosystem needs to have a balance among organisms to ensure the ability of the system to support life. (A), (B), and (D) are incorrect because they merely represent examples of how the system maintains a balance. **Competency 027**

112. **B**

While other groups made significant contributions to mathematics, the Egyptians and Babylonians (third millennium BCE) were the first groups to make an impact on the development of modern-day mathematics. **Competency 018**

113. **A**

Comparing and contrasting variations of a fairly tale, like *Cinderella*, can foster higher order thinking skills and critical reading. Students will have to analyze the new story to determine how it related to the traditional version, and how the theme is treated. (B), (C), and (D) are not focusing specifically on such higher-level reading as it relates to comparing and contrasting across multiple texts. **Competency 007**

114. **B**

The economic theory that states that prices vary based on a balance between the availability of a product or service at a certain price and the desire of potential purchasers to pay that price is known as supply and demand. Free enterprise (A) is a generic term to describe capitalism and entrepreneurship. Inflation and deflation (C) are general terms to describe the price stability in the nation and the purchasing power of consumers. **Competency 022**

115. **A**

This problem is easily solved by using some basic algebraic reasoning. Since we are interested in determining the number of oranges that are in the basket, we will set this as a variable called o. The number of apples, a, and the number of oranges, o, sum to a total of 62. We also know that there are 16 more apples than oranges ($a = o + 16$). This gives $o + (o + 16) = 2o + 16 = 62$. Solving for o yields 23 oranges in the basket. **Competency 015**

116. **C**

There is a difference of one day from Honolulu to Tokyo. Honolulu is located west of the International Date Line (IDL), while Japan is east of the line. That is, if we travel from Honolulu toward the east on December 7 and pass the IDL to get to Tokyo, we would get there on December 8. The attack was recorded on December 7, 1941, in Honolulu, but the equivalent date for Japan was December 8, 1941. (A), (B), and (D) are incorrect because they do not explain the real reason for the date confusion. Additionally, the scenario does not provide information to support the position that Emperor Hirohito was confused about the dates. **Competency 021**

117. **A**

Instructional reading levels are texts that a student can read with at least 90-94% accuracy. Students should be matched with text that has a readability level that is best suited for their instructional level for supported instruction such as in guided reading. (B) is incorrect because teachers should use grouping for instruction in a more flexible fashion. (C) is incorrect because the student may have differing levels of ability in other subject areas. (D) is incorrect because it does not provide an example of more individualized reading instruction. Additionally, whole class reading does not take into account each student's reading level. **Competency 012**

118. **A**

Reference maps show the locations of places, and boundaries of countries, states, counties, and towns. Atlases or road maps are examples of reference maps. (B) is incorrect because thematic maps show a particular topic such as population density, distribution of world religions, or physical, social, economic, political, agricultural, or economic features. (C) is incorrect because a physical map is a thematic map that shows the topography of the land including land features and elevations. (D) is incorrect because population maps are thematic maps that are used to show where people live in a particular region. **Competency 021**

119. **A**

An oral retelling is an informal assessment that seeks to determine what a student can recall about a story. It might be scored using a checklist that the teacher created. (B) is incorrect because norm-reference tests compare a student's achievement to grade- or age-level peers, typically in a bell curve. (C) is incorrect because criterion-referenced tests are often more formal and have a target or uniform criteria that students must meet to "pass" the test. (D) is incorrect because an oral retelling is harder to score objectively and is thus typically not standardized. **Competency 012**

120. **C**

Formative evaluations are the ongoing measures of how students are doing during regular classroom instruction. They are typically given throughout the school year. Summative evaluations are given at the end of a grading cycle or at the end of the school year. Therefore, options (A), (B), and (D) are incorrect because they represent examples of summative assessment rather than formative (ongoing) assessment. **Competency 012**

121. **D**

In order to solve a problem we must understand the problem, choose a strategy and/or make a plan, carry out the plan, and check our answer. The only answer that is not a critical component of the process is (D). **Competency 018**

122. **B**

Brazil is located in the Southern Hemisphere, and the United States is located in the Northern Hemisphere; thus, if the United States is in the winter season, then in Brazil it is summer. (A), (C), and (D) are incorrect based on the previous explanation. **Competency 021**

123. **B**

Antonyms are words that indicate "opposites." The only pair that does so is (B), small—large. The set of words in (A), *small* and the comparative, *smaller*, represent two different words. The words in (C), bear—bear, represent an example of homonyms—words with the same pronunciation and spelling, but with different meanings. (D) represents an example of synonyms, words with equivalent meaning. **Competency 002**

124. **D**

The Fifteenth Amendment granted black males the right to vote. (A) is incorrect because the voting right was given to black males only, not women. (B) is incorrect because the Fourteenth Amendment granted citizenship to former slaves. (C) is incorrect because the Thirteenth Amendment granted freedom to slaves. **Competency 023**

125. **B**

During the prewriting stage, students should be guided to develop an outline that reflects the order of the ideas in the composition. They also can benefit from guiding questions to keep them focused on the topic and the intended audience. Choice (A) is incorrect because learning about grammar structures and pronunciation will not necessarily affect the organization and coherence of the composition. (C) is incorrect because it addresses speaking ability as opposed to the writing process. (D) is a strong distracter but not the best answer. Modeling effective writing is always a good strategy, but examples only might not provide the necessary guidance to make permanent changes in the students' writing style. (B) is a better choice because it provides a strategy that, once learned, can be used in multiple future situations. **Competency 010**

126. **A**

The child is having problems with word stress and syllabication, and both terms are part of phonological awareness. (B) is incorrect because the child is not having problems with phonemic awareness. He has mastered the ability to separate phonemes and blend them back to recreate the word. (C) and (D) are incorrect because neither of them individually can explain the needs of the child. The reality is that the child needs support in both components; thus, (C) or (D) individually cannot be the correct answer. **Competency 002**

127. **C**

This problem requires critical thinking and some basic knowledge of math. Solving for the volume of the bathtub one obtains 45 ft^3 and the volume of the bucket is $\pi \cdot 0.5^2 \cdot 1 \approx 0.7854$ ft^3 To find how many buckets of water it will take to fill the tub, we must divide 45 by 0.7854. This gives approximately 57 buckets. **Competency 015**

128. **D**

The economy of the Southern Colonies was based on the crops of tobacco, rice, indigo, and cotton. Plantations produced agricultural crops in large scale and exploited workers as well as the environment. (A) is incorrect because it was the economy of the Middle Colonies that was based on farming, shipping, fishing, and trading. (B) is incorrect because it was the economy of the New England colonies that was based on farming and very small industries such as fishing, lumber, and crafts. (C) is incorrect because trading was a part of the Middle Colonies economy. **Competency 022**

129. **C**

Matter can change from liquid to solid to gas in a cyclical fashion. (A) is incorrect because all three represent examples of solid matter. (B) is incorrect because it presents only examples of the states and fails to address the stages represented. (D) is incorrect because it presents just examples of solid and liquid matter. **Competency 031**

130. **A**

In the inductive method, teachers guide students to discover principles in an indirect fashion. In this indirect way of teaching, teachers create the opportunities for the students to develop their own learning. (B) is incorrect because it describes a teaching style in which concepts are presented through direct instruction. The term "hands-on" (C) and "student-centered method" (D) is part of the "engage" stage of the 5-E model, but they do not fully describe the type of strategy being used. **Competency 025**

131. **C**

Complex carbohydrates should comprise at least half of the calories consumed for the healthy diet of an active person (a little less for an inactive person). Carbohydrates are the primary and most efficient source of energy for the body. Based on this, choices (A), (B), and (D) are incorrect. **Competency 044**

132. **B**

Visual media provides many benefits to students. Some of these include helping students' spark their audience's attention when they are trying to convey a message (A), adding clarity to their message (C) as they can be used to complement not only their texts but the information they are talking about, and allowing students to show step-by-step development ideas (D). Therefore, the only option that does not offer benefits of visual media is (B). **Competency 011**

133. **C**

The metric system is a very precise system that allows for the measurement of very small amounts of matter. For example, the metric system uses measurements divided into thousands (millimeters or milligrams), while the English system uses larger units of measurement, like inches and ounces. (A) and (B) contain perhaps true statements and opinions, but they fail to address the question. (D) is incorrect; the English system does not have a simple way to compute measures. The metric system is based on 10, and the computations are a lot easier. **Competency 024**

134. **D**

   In 1929, the Texas State Legislature adopted *Texas, Our Texas* as the state song. (A) is incorrect because the song *Home on the Range* is the state song of Kansas. (B) is incorrect because the song *Deep in the Heart of Texas* is a well-known song elaborating on the qualities of the state. (C) is incorrect because the song *The Yellow Rose of Texas* is a well-known song in the state. It is a patriotic song popularized by Texan soldiers during the American Civil War. **Competency 043**

135. **A**

   The overall purpose of the shared book experience is to guide children to be successful in reading and to develop an interest in learning to read. The story is read to the students in a very supportive environment using visuals to enhance comprehension. The main goal is to make reading an enjoyable activity and to motivate children to read on their own. (B) is incorrect because reading with the whole class is a by-product of the shared book experience, but it is not the main goal. (C) and (D) are true statements. Traditionally, books used in shared reading use big letters and attractive pictures, and children like big books, but these features are not the main reason for conducting shared reading. **Competency 004**

136. **D**

   Readers' theater is a student-centered activity. They read the story, summarize it, work in groups, develop the characters and story line, and implement the activity. While watching a video version of the story (D) can help students get into the characters of the story, this activity is not required to implement readers' theater. Thus, options (A), (B) and (C) are typically used as part of the preparation to implement reader's theater. **Competency 006**

137. **A**

   The kingdom Monera is composed of unicellular organisms and primitive cells called prokaryotes. (B), (C), and (D) are incorrect because all three have more sophisticated cellular systems called eukaryotes. **Competency 034**

138. **A**

   Checklists, retelling stories, and the use of anecdotal records are examples of informal assessment measures commonly used to assess the development of communication skills among ELLs. The informal nature of these assessment strategies eliminates the stress associated with formal assessment procedures. Multiple-choice, cloze tests, and informal reading inventory (B) are not generally used to assess oral communication skills. Audiotaping can be used to assess oral language development, but written cloze tests and standardized achievement tests (C) are not. Repetition drills, choral reading, and chants (D) are generally used to assess pronunciation, which is only one component of oral communication skills. **Competency 005**

139. **A**

The main function of the atmosphere is to serve as a buffer between space and the Earth's crust. This buffer provides the ideal conditions to protect and preserve life on Earth. (B) and (D) present two functions that can be linked to the atmosphere, recycling water and gases; however, they fail to highlight the real function of the atmosphere. (C) is completely incorrect; the atmosphere is above the crust, not beneath it. **Competency 038**

140. **A**

The Declaration of Independence pronounced the colonies free and independent states. It consists of a preamble or introduction followed by three main parts. The third part announces the creation of the new country. (B), (C), and (D) are incorrect because these choices stress rights that are not explicitly stated in the Declaration of Independence. The unalienable rights, stated in the first part of the Declaration of Independence, are life, liberty, and the pursuit of happiness. **Competency 023**

Practice Test 2

TExES 191 Generalist EC-6

ANSWER SHEET PRACTICE TEST 2

1. (A) (B) (C) (D)
2. (A) (B) (C) (D)
3. (A) (B) (C) (D)
4. (A) (B) (C) (D)
5. (A) (B) (C) (D)
6. (A) (B) (C) (D)
7. (A) (B) (C) (D)
8. (A) (B) (C) (D)
9. (A) (B) (C) (D)
10. (A) (B) (C) (D)
11. (A) (B) (C) (D)
12. (A) (B) (C) (D)
13. (A) (B) (C) (D)
14. (A) (B) (C) (D)
15. (A) (B) (C) (D)
16. (A) (B) (C) (D)
17. (A) (B) (C) (D)
18. (A) (B) (C) (D)
19. (A) (B) (C) (D)
20. (A) (B) (C) (D)
21. (A) (B) (C) (D)
22. (A) (B) (C) (D)
23. (A) (B) (C) (D)

24. (A) (B) (C) (D)
25. (A) (B) (C) (D)
26. (A) (B) (C) (D)
27. (A) (B) (C) (D)
28. (A) (B) (C) (D)
29. (A) (B) (C) (D)
30. (A) (B) (C) (D)
31. (A) (B) (C) (D)
32. (A) (B) (C) (D)
33. (A) (B) (C) (D)
34. (A) (B) (C) (D)
35. (A) (B) (C) (D)
36. (A) (B) (C) (D)
37. (A) (B) (C) (D)
38. (A) (B) (C) (D)
39. (A) (B) (C) (D)
40. (A) (B) (C) (D)
41. (A) (B) (C) (D)
42. (A) (B) (C) (D)
43. (A) (B) (C) (D)
44. (A) (B) (C) (D)
45. (A) (B) (C) (D)
46. (A) (B) (C) (D)

47. (A) (B) (C) (D)
48. (A) (B) (C) (D)
49. (A) (B) (C) (D)
50. (A) (B) (C) (D)
51. (A) (B) (C) (D)
52. (A) (B) (C) (D)
53. (A) (B) (C) (D)
54. (A) (B) (C) (D)
55. (A) (B) (C) (D)
56. (A) (B) (C) (D)
57. (A) (B) (C) (D)
58. (A) (B) (C) (D)
59. (A) (B) (C) (D)
60. (A) (B) (C) (D)
61. (A) (B) (C) (D)
62. (A) (B) (C) (D)
63. (A) (B) (C) (D)
64. (A) (B) (C) (D)
65. (A) (B) (C) (D)
66. (A) (B) (C) (D)
67. (A) (B) (C) (D)
68. (A) (B) (C) (D)
69. (A) (B) (C) (D)

70. Ⓐ Ⓑ Ⓒ Ⓓ
71. Ⓐ Ⓑ Ⓒ Ⓓ
72. Ⓐ Ⓑ Ⓒ Ⓓ
73. Ⓐ Ⓑ Ⓒ Ⓓ
74. Ⓐ Ⓑ Ⓒ Ⓓ
75. Ⓐ Ⓑ Ⓒ Ⓓ
76. Ⓐ Ⓑ Ⓒ Ⓓ
77. Ⓐ Ⓑ Ⓒ Ⓓ
78. Ⓐ Ⓑ Ⓒ Ⓓ
79. Ⓐ Ⓑ Ⓒ Ⓓ
80. Ⓐ Ⓑ Ⓒ Ⓓ
81. Ⓐ Ⓑ Ⓒ Ⓓ
82. Ⓐ Ⓑ Ⓒ Ⓓ
83. Ⓐ Ⓑ Ⓒ Ⓓ
84. Ⓐ Ⓑ Ⓒ Ⓓ
85. Ⓐ Ⓑ Ⓒ Ⓓ
86. Ⓐ Ⓑ Ⓒ Ⓓ
87. Ⓐ Ⓑ Ⓒ Ⓓ
88. Ⓐ Ⓑ Ⓒ Ⓓ
89. Ⓐ Ⓑ Ⓒ Ⓓ
90. Ⓐ Ⓑ Ⓒ Ⓓ
91. Ⓐ Ⓑ Ⓒ Ⓓ
92. Ⓐ Ⓑ Ⓒ Ⓓ
93. Ⓐ Ⓑ Ⓒ Ⓓ

94. Ⓐ Ⓑ Ⓒ Ⓓ
95. Ⓐ Ⓑ Ⓒ Ⓓ
96. Ⓐ Ⓑ Ⓒ Ⓓ
97. Ⓐ Ⓑ Ⓒ Ⓓ
98. Ⓐ Ⓑ Ⓒ Ⓓ
99. Ⓐ Ⓑ Ⓒ Ⓓ
100. Ⓐ Ⓑ Ⓒ Ⓓ
101. Ⓐ Ⓑ Ⓒ Ⓓ
102. Ⓐ Ⓑ Ⓒ Ⓓ
103. Ⓐ Ⓑ Ⓒ Ⓓ
104. Ⓐ Ⓑ Ⓒ Ⓓ
105. Ⓐ Ⓑ Ⓒ Ⓓ
106. Ⓐ Ⓑ Ⓒ Ⓓ
107. Ⓐ Ⓑ Ⓒ Ⓓ
108. Ⓐ Ⓑ Ⓒ Ⓓ
109. Ⓐ Ⓑ Ⓒ Ⓓ
110. Ⓐ Ⓑ Ⓒ Ⓓ
111. Ⓐ Ⓑ Ⓒ Ⓓ
112. Ⓐ Ⓑ Ⓒ Ⓓ
113. Ⓐ Ⓑ Ⓒ Ⓓ
114. Ⓐ Ⓑ Ⓒ Ⓓ
115. Ⓐ Ⓑ Ⓒ Ⓓ
116. Ⓐ Ⓑ Ⓒ Ⓓ
117. Ⓐ Ⓑ Ⓒ Ⓓ

118. Ⓐ Ⓑ Ⓒ Ⓓ
119. Ⓐ Ⓑ Ⓒ Ⓓ
120. Ⓐ Ⓑ Ⓒ Ⓓ
121. Ⓐ Ⓑ Ⓒ Ⓓ
122. Ⓐ Ⓑ Ⓒ Ⓓ
123. Ⓐ Ⓑ Ⓒ Ⓓ
124. Ⓐ Ⓑ Ⓒ Ⓓ
125. Ⓐ Ⓑ Ⓒ Ⓓ
126. Ⓐ Ⓑ Ⓒ Ⓓ
127. Ⓐ Ⓑ Ⓒ Ⓓ
128. Ⓐ Ⓑ Ⓒ Ⓓ
129. Ⓐ Ⓑ Ⓒ Ⓓ
130. Ⓐ Ⓑ Ⓒ Ⓓ
131. Ⓐ Ⓑ Ⓒ Ⓓ
132. Ⓐ Ⓑ Ⓒ Ⓓ
133. Ⓐ Ⓑ Ⓒ Ⓓ
134. Ⓐ Ⓑ Ⓒ Ⓓ
135. Ⓐ Ⓑ Ⓒ Ⓓ
136. Ⓐ Ⓑ Ⓒ Ⓓ
137. Ⓐ Ⓑ Ⓒ Ⓓ
138. Ⓐ Ⓑ Ⓒ Ⓓ
139. Ⓐ Ⓑ Ⓒ Ⓓ
140. Ⓐ Ⓑ Ⓒ Ⓓ

1. What are the six major linguistic subsystems that appear in any given language?

   A. Phonology, morphology, morpheme, grammar, semantics, and pragmatics

   B. Graphemes, morphology, syntax, lexicon, semantics, and pragmatics

   C. Phonology, morphology, syntax, lexicon, semantics, and pragmatics

   D. Phonology, morphology, denotation, semantics, lexicon, and pragmatics

2. Which of the following numbers CANNOT be used to express probability?

   A. −0.004

   B. 20%

   C. 0

   D. 0.99

3. The New England Colonies consisted of

   A. Virginia, North Carolina, South Carolina, and Georgia.

   B. Massachusetts, Connecticut, Rhode Island, and New Hampshire.

   C. New York, New Jersey, Delaware, Maryland, and Pennsylvania.

   D. North Carolina, Rhode Island, Delaware, and Maryland.

4. What might be the benefit of activating background knowledge (schema) of the students prior to reading about a given topic?

   A. Students become more interested and motivated to learn more about the topic.

   B. Students can make connections to the story and develop a better understanding of the content.

   C. Students can visualize the imagery of the story as they read it.

   D. Students develop fluency and increase the speed of reading while reading the text together.

5. Cesar Chávez and Dolores Huerta were two of the most important Mexican-American leaders of the Civil Rights Movement. They fought for

    A. better educational opportunities for language minority groups.

    B. more employment opportunities for ethnic and racial minority groups in the U.S.

    C. better working conditions and fair compensation for agricultural workers.

    D. the development of more worker unions for Mexican Americans.

6. Identify the most appropriate strategy to introduce the concept of magnetism to English language learners in first and second grade.

    A. Describe the North and South Poles and indicate that the Earth is a giant magnetic field.

    B. Present the following information in English and the students' native language: Magnetism is the force of attraction and repulsion of objects.

    C. Guide children to play with a compass.

    D. Develop a learning center where students are able to play with magnets and metals.

7. Which artist's work is credited with beginning the Impressionist movement of art?

    A. Claude Monet

    B. Edward Manet

    C. Michaelangelo

    D. Salvador Dali

8. Dan is an eight-year-old whose vocabulary has significantly improved over the past two months. He is beginning to use relative pronoun clauses when speaking. Dan's teacher has discovered that he still struggles when using subordinate clauses. Which of the following sentences would be an example of a correct use of a subordinate clause?

    A. I like the cars, but I dislike motorcycles.

    B. He wants to sleep until late in the morning.

    C. If you want me to go, I will need to start getting ready now.

    D. My mom and my dad are real Texans.

9. The alphabetic principle has been described as the ability to

   A. create letters in print and say words out loud.

   B. connect letters with sounds and create words based on such associations.

   C. connect letters and sounds to pronounce words by syllables.

   D. connect sounds with those spoken by others.

10. Daniele is a third grader having problems identifying prefixes and suffixes in the words she reads and writes. When asked to identify the free morpheme of the word *predetermined,* she identified the segment *mine* as the answer. Based on the scenario, what might be the rationale for her answer?

    A. She is confused with suffixes and prefixes.

    B. She did not understand that the segment *mine* is not a free morpheme in that context.

    C. She does not understand the concept of free morpheme.

    D. She did not understand that free morphemes constitute the main component of the word.

11. What is the mode of the data set: 10, 9, 3, 1, 2, 8, 4, 3, 9, 10, 5, 7, 6, 6, 2, 8, 9, 4, 1, 10, 5, 8, 4, 6, 2, 1, 9, 7?

    A. 9

    B. 3

    C. 5

    D. 6

12. What is the median of the data set in question 11?

    A. 6

    B. 7

    C. 6.5

    D. 7.5

13. What strategy can be used to assess reading comprehension for students who are not proficient readers?

    A. Drawing inferences

    B. Graphic organizers

    C. Written reflections

    D. Oral retelling of the story

14. The use of thematic units of instruction is ideal to teach English Language Learners (ELLs) social studies because it

    A.   makes learning fun, interactive, and motivating.

    B.   makes content more cognitively accessible.

    C.   is helpful in teaching new vocabulary.

    D.   exposes children to quality literature.

15. Advanced organizers and graphic representations are commonly used in social studies. What is the advantage of using these strategies to teach content?

    A.   They make content accessible to all children.

    B.   They make learning more interesting.

    C.   They can be used to teach other content areas.

    D.   They can be used to teach high-order thinking skills.

16. The main value of using real-life situations to teach problem-solving skills involving mathematics is that the children in grades K–6 can see

    A.   the connection between the school curriculum and mathematics.

    B.   the value of mathematics in solving daily situations.

    C.   that mathematics is an important part of the Texas curriculum.

    D.   that the use of learning centers has a specific value in life.

17. Some of the advantages of using a think-aloud, while reading to students, are that teachers can model comprehension strategies like making inferences, synthesizing information, and visualization. What is another type of comprehension strategy that teachers might model to help students develop reading comprehension skills?

    A.   Readers' theater

    B.   Confirming predictions

    C.   Segmenting multisyllabic words

    D.   Structural analysis

18. What measurement principle do children in Pre-K through kindergarten sometimes have difficulty with?

    A.   Conversation

    B.   Conservation

    C.   Condensation

    D.   Conversion

19. The main advantage of using hands-on activities in mathematics is to

    A.   enhance students' ability to think abstractly.

    B.   make the lesson more enjoyable.

    C.   lead the students to active learning and guide them to construct their own knowledge.

    D.   promote equity, equality, and freedom for the diverse ethnic groups in the nation.

20. The characteristics of the Language Acquisition Device (LAD) include all of the following EXCEPT

    A.   the LAD is an external mechanism that allows humans to learn multiple languages.

    B.   the LAD enables human beings to produce language and utilize correct language rules.

    C.   the LAD is said to be adaptable as it adjusts to the language being learned.

    D.   Chomsky's work provided the theoretical rationale for the work related to the LAD.

21. A pair of dice is rolled. What is the probability the sum of the dice is less than 13?

    A. $\dfrac{1}{12}$

    B. $\dfrac{35}{36}$

    C. $\dfrac{36}{36}$

    D. $\dfrac{2}{36}$

22. When teaching the grapheme-phoneme correspondence in English, teachers must

    A.   make the activity interesting to all students.

    B.   monitor the children so they do not pronounce the letters with a foreign accent.

    C.   create an atmosphere of cooperation among students from diverse ethnic and linguistic backgrounds.

    D.   control the inconsistency of the grapheme-phoneme correspondence of English by presenting consistent sounds first.

23. If a child is reading an average of 90 percent of the words correctly, he or she is reading at the

    A.   independent level.

    B.   frustration level.

    C.   comprehension level.

    D.   instructional level.

24. In which art movement did science and mathematics most influence art and artists?

    A.   Impressionism

    B.   Baroque

    C.   Rococo

    D.   Renaissance

25. You and your family go out to dinner one night. At the end of the meal you receive a bill for the meal. The total bill, before tax, is $78.60. Assuming tax for the meal is 5%, what would you need to do first in order to find out the amount of tax you need to pay?

    A.   Multiply the total by 5

    B.   Multiply the total by 0.05

    C.   Divide by 5

    D.   Divide by 0.05

26. Latitude and longitude lines are used to locate points on a map. What is the term that best describes this type of geometric figure:

    A. A grid system

    B. A compass rose

    C. A legend

    D. A globe

27. What is a bound morpheme?

    A. A morpheme that occurs in isolation.

    B. A morpheme that occurs in isolation but is sometimes attached to a root word.

    C. A morpheme that occurs in isolation but can never be attached to a root word.

    D. A morpheme that cannot occur in isolation and, therefore, is attached to a root word or another morpheme.

28. The world region of North America consists of

    A. the United States and Mexico.

    B. the United States and Canada.

    C. the United States.

    D. Canada, the United States, and Mexico.

29. This term describes the exchange or transmission of cultural information and life-styles from people around the world.

    A. Diversity

    B. Ethnicity

    C. Culture

    D. Cultural diffusion

30. Which of the following is an expression that represents the following statement: three times one-half of a number less eighty percent?

    A. $3 \times \dfrac{4}{2} - 0.8$

    B. $3 \times \dfrac{x}{2} - \dfrac{8}{100}$

    C. $3 \times \dfrac{x}{2} - 0.8$

    D. $3 \times \dfrac{x}{2} - 80$

31. Identify the statement that BEST describes sight words.

    A. Sight words are prevalent in environmental print.

    B. Sight words occur frequently in print.

    C. Children decode sight words using semantic and structural clues.

    D. Children have difficulty spelling sight words.

32. The first 10 amendments to the U.S. Constitution are known as the

    A. separation of church and state.

    B. Bill of Rights.

    C. Right to Privacy.

    D. Right to Due Process.

33. What is one of the key challenges that children in upper elementary school experience when moving from the stage of "learning to read" to "reading to learn"?

    A. Use graphic organizers effectively to learn and to present information

    B. Understand the organizational patterns of the text to read more efficiently

    C. Develop an understanding of academic English

    D. Predict the content of the writing efficiently

34. Ms. Pompa uses DRTA (Directed Reading-Thinking Activity) regularly during her guided reading groups. What is the main purpose of this instructional activity?

    A. To interpret the text according to one's own background knowledge

    B. To pose questions to students related to the themes in the text

    C. To confirm or correct predictions as one reads

    D. To synthesize information in order to better retell the story

35. Which of the following would NOT be included as a component part of the instructional activity of reciprocal teaching?

    A. Connecting the text to one's own life

    B. Asking a question about the main idea

    C. Clarifying difficult parts of the content

    D. Predicting what will come next

36. What song has the same melody as *Twinkle, Twinkle Little Star*?

    A. *Are you Sleeping?*

    B. *Skip to my Lou*

    C. *Polly Put the Kettle On*

    D. *Alphabet Song*

37. Alliteration is a technique frequently used to begin developing students' reading skills as it aims to strengthen students' phonological and phonemic awareness. Which sentence is an example of an alliteration?

    A. Maria bought a muffin for my mom.

    B. Maria baked a large muffin for my mom.

    C. Maria made muffins for Mom.

    D. Maria baked a muffin in a large oven.

38. Plants and trees that need large amounts of water to survive will thrive in which Texas region?

    A. Gulf Coast and hill country

    B. South Texas Plains and Prairies and Lakes regions

    C. Piney-woods and Gulf Coast

    D. Panhandle plains and Big Bend regions

39. In an introductory unit about force and motion, Ms. Martínez brought to her fourth-grade class the following items: scissors, pliers, a hammer, tongs, and a miniature see-saw. These items are ideal to teach and demonstrate how _____work.

   A. complex machines

   B. simple machines

   C. household items

   D. real-life objects

40. Identify the number of phonemes in the following word—through.

   A. Seven

   B. Two

   C. Four

   D. Three

41. The 112 elements of the periodic table represent the anatomical composition of

   A. matter.

   B. liquid.

   C. solid.

   D. gases.

42. Many of the leaders responsible for the writing of the Constitution were familiar with the leading thinkers of the Enlightenment movement. Due to this influence, one of the key components of the Constitution was the protection of the

   A. religious beliefs of people in the new nation.

   B. natural rights of the individual and limiting the power of the government.

   C. power of the central government and the unification of the nation.

   D. rights to fair trading.

43. Which of the following instruments measures relative humidity?

   A. Barometer

   B. Anemometer

   C. Thermometer

   D. Psychrometer

44. Ms. Thomas introduces new vocabulary words within the context of a sentence and through the use of visuals. Once children understand the concept linked to the word, she repeats individual words, pausing after each syllable. Once children can separate the word into syllables, she guides them to separate syllables into individual phonemes. What skills is Ms. Thomas introducing with the last two activities?

    A.   The intonation pattern of the language

    B.   Phonological awareness

    C.   Vocabulary development

    D.   Pronunciation drills

45. The National Science Teachers Association supports the principles that scientific inquiry should be the cornerstone of science education. The association also supports the idea that students should be actively involved in early exploration of scientific concepts. Additionally, the organization believes that instruction should be

    A.   effective and accurate.

    B.   organized thematically.

    C.   organized from the unknown to the known.

    D.   delivered deductively.

46. The United States uses the English system of weights and measurement (standard) in daily business activity. However, scientists use the metric system to conduct scientific experimentation. Why do American scientists use the metric system in scientific research?

    A.   The system is used in developed countries.

    B.   The standard system cannot be used in scientific experimentation.

    C.   The use of the standard system yields inconsistent experimental results.

    D.   The metric system uses a systematic and precise system of weights and measurements.

47. Joe can place a maximum of 5 apples in a sack. If he needs to put 32 apples in sacks, how many sacks will he need?

    A.   7

    B.   6.4

    C.   5

    D.   8

48. Identify the statement that BEST describes the advantages of using the language experience approach to teach reading to language minority students.

   A. It provides the schema or experiential background to facilitate the comprehension of the story.

   B. It uses the vocabulary and the experience common to both language minority and mainstream students.

   C. It minimizes the possibility of errors due to idiomatic expressions from both L1 and L2.

   D. It facilitates reading by ensuring a positive match between L1 and L2

Use the following scenario to answer the next two questions:

Scenario: Mr. Jones brought a small peach tree with peaches to school to explain the process of photosynthesis. He indicated that the tree takes energy from the sun and converts it into chemical energy. Part of the chemical energy produced is used for its survival and growth. The excess energy is stored in the leaves and in the fruits produced. To close the lesson, he gave students pieces of peaches and guided them to discuss how the process of photosynthesis supports life on Earth.

49. Based on this scenario, what is the main topic of the lesson?

   A. Energy transformation

   B. Survival of the fittest

   C. The importance of conservation and adoption of green practices

   D. The importance of peach trees for survival

50. What was the instructional purpose of using a live plant with fruits to begin the lesson?

   A. To promote interest in the lesson

   B. To provide concrete evidence that plants produce energy

   C. To provide concrete evidence that without peaches life will not be possible on Earth

   D. To promote hands-on science experimentation

51. Which of the following artistic movements occurred in the twentieth century?

    A.   Impressionism, Expressionism, and Realism

    B.   Rococo, Hellenistic, and Classical

    C.   Photorealism, Cubism, and Surrealism

    D.   Baroque, Renaissance, and Medieval

52. The basic states of matter are

    A.   liquid, plasma, and solid.

    B.   gas, liquid, and solid.

    C.   liquid, water, ice, and gas.

    D.   plasma, liquid, solid, and gas.

53. When it is winter in North America, it is because

    A.   the Earth is farther away from the sun in its orbit.

    B.   the North Pole is tilted toward the sun.

    C.   the Earth is tilted on its axis with the North Pole tilted away from the sun.

    D.   the Earth is moving in an elliptical orbit around the sun.

54. Ken Goodman used the term *miscues* in reading to describe the type of

    A.   variation that occurs when children attempt to put words into writing.

    B.   variation that occurs when children try to decode and guess the meaning of printed words.

    C.   errors that occur when children try to communicate orally in their native language.

    D.   discrepancy that occurs between the schemata of the child and the one intended by the author.

55. Crystal needs to buy bread for her party. She knows that one loaf will feed 8 people, and there are 371 people coming to her party. How many loaves of bread does she need to buy?

    A.   33

    B.   48

    C.   46

    D.   47

56. Ms. Jefferson has guided first-grade students to read polysyllabic words until they can read them fluently. Later, students are asked to separate the words into syllables, and finally she guides students to identify the main stress in each word. What skill is Ms. Jefferson emphasizing?

    A. Alphabetic awareness

    B. Reading fluency

    C. Phonological awareness

    D. Syllabication

57. According to U.S. copyright law, which song can you legally copy?

    A. *Happy Birthday*

    B. *Cowboy Song*

    C. *Texas, Our Texas*

    D. *I'm a Little Teapot*

58. The use of phonics instruction in conjunction with components from the whole language approach are typically used to create a

    A. skills-based approach.

    B. balanced-reading approach.

    C. meaning-based approach.

    D. humanistic approach.

59. Which of the following is a nonlinear function?

    A. $f(x) = 3x - 1$

    B. $f(x) = x$

    C. $f(x) = \dfrac{x}{5}$

    D. $f(x) = \dfrac{x}{5} - \sqrt{x}$

60. Mr. Martínez is going to be introducing the Dolch words to his first-grade students. Before showing the list of words to his students, Mr. Martínez explains that these words are the most frequently used words in English. Which of the following words SHOULD NOT be included in the list that Mr. Martínez is going to show to his students?

   A.   a

   B.   had

   C.   but

   D.   awesome

61. What is the correct expansion of $(a + b)^3$?

   A. $a^3 + b^3$

   B. $a^3 + 3a^2b + 3ab^2 + b^3$

   C. $a^3 + 6a^3b^3 + b^3$

   D. $3a^2 + 3b$

62. In the past, mercury was commonly used in household thermometers. Why was this substance ideal for thermometers?

   A.   It is easily accessible and available in most countries.

   B.   The substance expands when heated.

   C.   It is a high-volatile and flexible substance.

   D.   It is the only substance approved by the U.S. Department of Energy.

63. Which of these sets of numbers represents a true statement?

   A. $5 < 7$

   B. $10 > 11$

   C. $9 \leq 8$

   D. $3 \geq 5$

64. What type of singing group consists of violins, trumpets, a Spanish guitar, and a guitarrón?

   A.   Mariachi

   B.   Tejano

   C.   Marching band

   D.   Orchestra

65. When people think about radiation, they conceptualize the arms of mass destruction like the atomic bombs used in Hiroshima and Nagasaki during World War II. However, radiation is currently being used for peaceful purposes in nuclear medicine and in household items like

   A.   refrigerators.

   B.   radios.

   C.   gas stoves.

   D.   microwaves.

66. Why is the lowest average temperature in New York City higher than the lowest average temperature of Lincoln, Nebraska, when these cities are at approximately the same latitude?

   A.   New York City is farther south resulting in warmer temperatures.

   B.   New York City is surrounded by water, which moderates the temperature.

   C.   New York City is full of industries that warm the atmosphere.

   D.   New York City is near the Appalachian Mountains, which trap sunlight and heat.

67. The invention of cell phones has revolutionized the communications industry. However, it has also become a health concern because these electronic devices

   A.   distract people and cause automobile accidents.

   B.   emit radiation that has been linked to cancer.

   C.   make children easy targets for sexual predators.

   D.   affect the growth of the traditional phone industry.

68. For what value of x is the expression $\dfrac{5}{x}$ undefined?

    A.   9

    B. $-1,000,000,000.1123$

    C.   0

    D.   0.00000000000001

69. Petroleum products come from nonrenewable fossil fuels. These types of energy sources are nonrenewal because they come from

    A.   the melting of rocks and other minerals.

    B.   decayed remains of animal and plants.

    C.   the bones and flesh from prehistoric lizards.

    D.   the residue produced from volcanic activity.

70. Asking students to make use of visual elements, such as graphics, while they are reading a piece of text allows them to identify ways in which these elements can be used as strategies to interpret and make sense of the information they are reading. Based on this information, which of the following statements best supports this idea in instructional practice?

    A.   Students will collect illustrations to create a group collage.

    B.   Students will talk about the author and illustrator of a picture book.

    C.   Students will create a chart in which they identify the reasons why the author of a newspaper article may have chosen to include pictures in his/her story.

    D.   Students will compare and contrast main characters in a story.

71. The development of fatty tissue and hibernation typical of bears is a system _____ _____ for survival.

    A.   of adaptation

    B.   to avoid competition with other predators

    C.   to keep a healthy balance in the ecosystem

    D.   to prevent the migration of bears to residential areas

72. What is an algorithm?

    A.   A computer program used to evaluate students

    B.   A system of discovering students' abilities

    C.   A step-by-step procedure for evaluating students

    D.   A step-by-step procedure for solving problems

73. Which of the following are objects in our solar system?

    A.   Asteroids, planets, moons, and comets

    B.   Planets, asteroids, moons, and black holes

    C.   Planets, meteoroids, asteroids, and black holes

    D.   Asteroids, milky way, quasars, and comets

74. Mr. Michel provides guiding questions to guide Tamara's writing. A couple of the questions are "What evidence do you need to prove your thesis to skeptics?" and "What would you say to convince them?" Based on this information, what type of writing is Tamara developing?

    A.   Narrative writing

    B.   Expository writing

    C.   Descriptive writing

    D.   Persuasive writing

75. What is another way to write $4 \times 4 \times 4$?

    A. 4^3

    B. 3^4

    C. 4×3

    D.   12

76. The scientific concept that best explains the formation of mountains and mountain ranges on Earth is

    A.   the movement of underground water.

    B.   the movement of tectonic plates.

    C.   erosion.

    D.   the effect of the moon and the resulting waves of the oceans.

77. Which strategy would LESS LIKELY support students' understanding of writing for different audiences?

   A. Having a group of students role play a given audience and asking them to react to a piece of writing

   B. In a persuasive writing, guiding students to revise the writing based on possible arguments from the intended audience

   C. Identifying the audience prior to beginning writing

   D. Telling students they will be writing narrative text

78. Ms. Pérez is planning a lesson that she can implement to increase her students' understanding of viewing and representing. She decides that one of the key issues for her students is to be able to identify how the visual materials they will be using must directly respond to the audience and their needs. As part of the lesson, she intends to have students work on this as a group project. Which of the following group project ideas would be a good choice for her students to select?

   A. Students can discuss their own travel experiences and bring pictures from home to make a chart.

   B. Students can search the Internet for clip art.

   C. Students can create a video directly responding to issues raised by a reporter in a newspaper article and share their response on YouTube.

   D. Students can select an illustration from a book they are reading and act it out in class.

79. Knowledge of the two words used to create compound words can help students in the interpretation of the compound word. However, there are examples of compound words in which the meaning of the two components does not contribute to, and often interferes with, the interpretation of the new word. Identify the set of compound words that fall into this category.

   A. Doghouse, autograph, and boathouse

   B. Greenhouse, White House, and mouthwash

   C. Butterfly, nightmare, and brainstorm

   D. Hotdog, birdhouse, and underground

80. One of the main reasons for the strong Texas economy of the last 20 years is the number of corporations that have moved to Texas. Corporations moved to Texas to enjoy the state's beneficial corporate tax structure and for the

    A. climate conditions of the state.

    B. history and development of the state.

    C. state's proximity to Mexico and Central America.

    D. state's lack of a state personal income tax.

81. Which type of writing focuses mainly on composition of information text that is primarily intended to inform the reader about a topic or subject while explaining and clarifying ideas?

    A. Narrative writing

    B. Expository writing

    C. Descriptive writing

    D. Persuasive writing

82. Identify the instructional activity for viewing and representing for first-grade students that also involves higher-order thinking.

    A. Sketching an image of what a character might be thinking or feeling during a story

    B. Developing a PowerPoint presentation with embedded clip art

    C. Creating a video response to a story

    D. Designing a newsletter related to a social studies unit

83. In a two-week period (including weekends and holidays), Max spent $71.47 on lunch. About how much money did Max spend on his daily lunch?

    A. $5.00

    B. $4.50

    C. $5.50

    D. $4.75

84. Select the answer that contains the correct sequence of Kodály rhythm syllables for this song line, *Twinkle, Twinkle Little Star*.

    A. Ta Ta Ta Ta Ti ti Ta

    B. Ta ti Ti ti Ta Ta Ti

    C. Ti ti Ti ti Ti ti Ta

    D. Ti ti Ta Ta Ta Ta Ti

85. Which of the following best illustrates a teacher using multimedia as a model or "mentor text" for her students in a writing workshop to teach the concept of "presentation"?

    A. Reading aloud from a chapter book and discussing rich imagery and style

    B. Providing electronic storybooks on a CD-ROM as a listening center during guided reading

    C. Bookmarking links to websites with video clips for students to watch during guided reading

    D. Using a digital picture book to model and analyze visual coherence or sense of unity in a text's layout

86. What is a good principle to consider when using formal and informal assessment data to inform literacy instruction in small groups in the classroom?

    A. Grouping should be fairly static and unchanging as change is stressful to students.

    B. Grouping should be based on one assessment measure only.

    C. Grouping based on assessment data should be flexible and consider individual differences in students.

    D. Grouping should be based on last year's assessment data.

87. Mr. Lee models using writing conventions as he writes using an electronic projection system. He says things like, "I use quotation marks here to indicate that I am quoting someone directly. Here's how I write the quotation marks and punctuation surrounding the words someone actually says." The main reason Mr. Lee talks out loud while writing is to

    A. use prewriting strategies to achieve their purposes.

    B. demonstrate the use of conventional grammar, spelling, capitalization, and punctuation.

    C. address a topic or write to a prompt creatively and independently.

    D. organize writing to include a beginning, middle, and end.

88. A teacher notices multiple bruising marks on a child. The teacher should

    A.   ask the child about their home life for more information.

    B.   do nothing.

    C.   talk with the parents about child abuse.

    D.   report the evidence immediately.

89. Mr. Lawrence read a story to his kindergarten students in a very pleasant and natural tone of voice. Later, he uses a series of connected pictures representing events in the story. In addition to helping children understand the story, what other element is he teaching?

    A.   The teacher is introducing the sound-symbol correspondence of the story.

    B.   The teacher is filling the experiential gaps to be sure students can understand the story.

    C.   The teacher is introducing sequencing and the story structure.

    D.   The teacher is using developmentally appropriate practices since children at this stage cannot read on their own.

90. What is currently the most economic activity in the Dallas/Fort Worth region?

    A.   Cotton and oil

    B.   Cattle and oil

    C.   Defense and technology

    D.   Technology and agriculture

91. What was the most important economic implication of the discovery of oil in Texas in 1901?

    A.   It made the United States the leading producer of fossil fuel of the twentieth century.

    B.   It moved Texas from its rural and agricultural economy to petroleum and the industrial age.

    C.   It made Texas the No. 1 producer of textiles and cattle.

    D.   It made the United States the No. 1 economy in the world.

92. Volcano eruptions can cause other natural physical events like earthquakes, avalanches, mudslides, and

    A. human death.

    B. tsunamis.

    C. hurricanes.

    D. tornados.

93. Convergent research on linear versus curvilinear rhetorical patterns shows that Spanish-speaking English language learners and young children in general have a tendency to follow a curvilinear approach in writing. What strategies can teachers use to support these students?

    A. Teach pronunciation and application of grammar structures.

    B. Guide children to develop an outline for the story and provide them with guiding questions to keep them focused on the topic.

    C. Provide a speaking checklist to help students stick to the topic.

    D. Guide children to develop a checklist of the topics to be covered in the writing sample.

94. The Civil Rights Movement sought equality for African Americans. Even after the Thirteenth, Fourteenth, and Fifteenth Amendments were added to the Constitution, blacks were denied full civil rights. Discrimination existed throughout the nation. Jim Crow laws were enforced in the

    A. South.

    B. North.

    C. East.

    D. West.

95. Texas has been identified as a regional economy. That is, each region has a dominant economic activity. For example, timber is one of the most important economic activities in

    A. South Texas.

    B. North Texas.

    C. East Texas.

    D. West Texas.

96. Marcos is a five-year-old student in the process of first language acquisition. He often produces statements like: This lollipop is the *bestest* Mom. Based on this speech sample, this child is

    A. applying language rules.

    B. experiencing language interference.

    C. applying the concepts from L1 to L2.

    D. imitating the speech sample of cartoons on television.

97. The Andes mountain range and the Amazon River are two of the key physical features in

    A. North America.

    B. Central America.

    C. South America.

    D. Central and South America.

98. Inactivity can increase the risk factor of contracting which of the following diseases or conditions?

    A. heart disease.

    B. anemia.

    C. sleep apnea.

    D. psoriasis.

99. Ms. Fuentes frequently leads students in choral reading to promote reading fluency. She also takes declarative statements from the story and asks students to change them to questions or exclamations. Students have fun generating these changes. What is the main purpose of the latter activity?

    A. To emphasize listening and speaking skills

    B. To teach the intonation pattern of the language

    C. To teach singing and music skills

    D. To make the class more enjoyable

100. When analyzing and interpreting assessment data from culturally and linguistically diverse (CLD) students, what must assessors take into account?

    A.   The main objective of assessment is to make students feel valued and wanted in school.

    B.   Students go through different stages of development, and these stages should not affect the way that children are assessed.

    C.   The students might express potential differently due to linguistic and cultural influences.

    D.   Students may have culture and language deficits which can preclude them from effective participation in the testing process.

101. The "E" in the acronym RICE, a treatment process for sprains, represents

    A.   exercise.

    B.   elevation.

    C.   evaluation.

    D.   expose.

102. Ms. Becerra uses a strategy with her sixth graders to help students monitor their own comprehension as they read independently. She instructs students to stop and check if they understand the main ideas in the story before moving on to the next section. This type of comprehension practice fosters which of the following?

    A.   Metacognition

    B.   Fluency

    C.   Decoding

    D.   Vocabulary

103. The movement of planets around the Sun creates what is known as a calendar year. Based on this information and the relative location of the planets in reference to the Sun, what is the planet with the shortest year?

    A.   Jupiter

    B.   Earth

    C.   Venus

    D.   Mercury

104. Story retelling inventories are generally used to assess students'

  A.   comprehension, sentence structure knowledge, and vocabulary development.

  B.   oral language development and writing skills.

  C.   listening skills, speaking, reading, and writing skills.

  D.   knowledge of literary pieces and the writing styles used in literature.

105. Volcanoes are formed with the motion of the tectonic plates. When the plates collapse, the motion creates cracks in the crust of the Earth, which eventually causes an eruption to release the excess heat, gases, and melted rocks and minerals from the center of the planet. The best indicator of the severity of the volcanic explosion is

  A.   the amount of magma inside the Earth.

  B.   the amount of lava available within the tectonic plates.

  C.   the amount of gas in the magma.

  D.   the number of faults in the area.

106. Steve is told that milk must remain at 50°F so it will not spoil and that a turkey must be cooked at 375°F for 2 hours. What is the difference in temperature of the milk and the turkey (while it is cooking)?

  A.   315°F

  B.   335°F

  C.   320°F

  D.   325°F

107. When plants take solar energy from the sun and transform it to usable energy, we say that energy was transformed to

  A.   chemical energy.

  B.   oxygen.

  C.   chlorophyll.

  D.   carbon dioxide.

108. In upper elementary grades, reading becomes more challenging and meaningful for students because at this stage

    A.   interests in reading fade as students find other activities they prefer.

    B.   students are still developing skills in fluency and decoding.

    C.   children use reading to obtain information to be successful in the content areas.

    D.   students have a harder time self-selecting books to read on their own.

109. What is the scientific explanation of the popular saying "once in a blue moon"?

    A.   An extra full moon period that occurs every two or three years.

    B.   A stage of the moon that precedes a lunar eclipse.

    C.   An idiomatic expression not directly linked to the stages of the moon.

    D.   An idiomatic expression implying that people are blue or sad.

110. This symbol represents the official declaration of patriotism in the United States.

    A.   United States of America National Flag

    B.   Liberty Bell

    C.   Pledge of Allegiance

    D.   Statue of Liberty

111. The state curriculum officially introduces children to the people and places of the contemporary world in

    A.   third grade.

    B.   fourth grade.

    C.   fifth grade.

    D.   sixth grade.

112. Which civil rights group challenged the laws of segregation with the *Brown v. Board of Education of Topeka* Supreme Court case?

    A.   The Civil Rights Organization

    B.   The National Association for the Advancement of Colored People

    C.   The Civil Rights Leadership Organization

    D.   The Southern Christian Leadership Conference

113. By ages four and five, children are generally able to stack cups in a pyramid, dribble a small ball, and tap their foot to a rhythm. They also begin dressing themselves using buttons and zippers. These kinds of activities represent an example of

    A.   gross motor skills.

    B.   required curriculum components in school.

    C.   fine motor skills.

    D.   a transition point from early childhood to adulthood.

114. Prior to taking classes of students outdoors, the physical education teacher inspects the fields and contacts the buildings and grounds department to fill in holes. The teacher takes this action to

    A.   help students feel safe while playing or jogging.

    B.   confirm that someone else is responsible for the upkeep of the field.

    C.   minimize the risk of injury and liability presented by unfilled holes.

    D.   ensure continuous play without the interruption of dodging holes.

115. What economic impact did the emergence of railroad transportation have on the last decades of the nineteenth century?

    A.   It expanded farmers' and ranchers' markets.

    B.   It moved Texas from its rural economy to an industrial era.

    C.   It connected the East and West.

    D.   It made Texas the number one economy of the nation.

116. What type of informal assessment instrument would best be used when reporting information about how students work together in discussion groups during a book club?

    A.   Running records

    B.   Portfolios

    C.   Summative evaluations

    D.   Anecdotal records

117. Solve the following problem. Express the answer as a mixed number. $1.6 - \dfrac{3}{8} =$

    A. $\dfrac{49}{40}$

    B. 1.225

    C. 1.23

    D. $1\dfrac{9}{40}$

118. The state curriculum officially introduces children to U.S. history in

    A. second grade.

    B. third grade.

    C. fourth grade.

    D. fifth grade.

119. What will come next in the following sequence: ○○◇○○◇◇○○◇◇◇○○···?

    A. ○◇◇○

    B. ○◇○◇

    C. ◇◇○○

    D. ◇◇◇◇

120. Children can be guided to develop a sense of citizenship beginning in

    A. prekindergarten.

    B. kindergarten.

    C. first grade.

    D. second grade.

121. An isosceles triangle is a polygon with two equal sides. What else does this imply?

    A. It is equilateral.

    B. Its angles sum to greater than 180°.

    C. It is also scalene.

    D. It has two equal angles.

122. A world region is an area identified based on

  A. topographical features.

  B. cultural features, political boundaries, and natural resources.

  C. political features.

  D. sharing similar, unifying cultural or physical characteristics.

123. The Fourteenth Amendment declared that all persons born in the U.S. were citizens and that all citizens were entitled to equal rights, and that their rights were protected by due process. A group of people living in the U.S. was not included. Which group was excluded from the equal rights provisions?

  A. Blacks

  B. Women

  C. Children

  D. Native Americans

124. Geographers have divided the world into ten regions: North America, Central and South America, Europe, Central Eurasia, the Middle East, North Africa, Sub-Saharan Africa, South Asia, East Asia, and Australasia. These divisions are based on

  A. location and the presence of body of waters.

  B. language.

  C. climate.

  D. physical and cultural similarities.

125. Which of the following best describes a lesson plan for elementary physical education students who need additional development and practice with a locomotor skill?

  A. Introduction to traveling pathways such as straight, curved, or zigzag

  B. Activities such as aerobics and circuit training

  C. Refining flexibility, strength, and muscular endurance

  D. Spotting during gymnastics and using nonskid footwear

126. Dr. Martin Luther King Jr. founded the Southern Christian Leadership Conference (SCLC) with other African-American leaders. His famous *I Have a Dream* speech took place during the march in Washington in support of the Civil Rights Act of 1964. This speech

    A. motivated a riot.

    B. prompted the creation of the Montgomery Improvement Association.

    C. resulted in the lost of supporters.

    D. gained more supporters for the cause.

127. In compliance with NCLB legislation, Texas adopted an instrument to assess the English achievement of ELLs—the Texas Observation Protocol (TOP). The TOP assesses the listening, speaking, reading, and writing components of English. In addition to the writing samples required, this instrument uses _____ to assess the linguistic performance of children in English.

    A. a rating scale containing three options (agree, disagree, uncertain)

    B. a multiple-choice test with four choices (A, B, C, and D)

    C. a series of open-ended questions to guide the teacher in the collection of data

    D. a checklist identifying specific literacy components

128. Which of the following would be the best set of units to use when measuring a football field?

    A. Centimeters

    B. Inches

    C. Meters

    D. Miles

129. A second-grade student began writing a composition about his friend in the following way: (1) George is my friend. (2) Mary is my best friend. (3) Rachel are my friends too. What type of support does this child need to write a more cohesive and standard writing sample?

    A. Spelling and agreement instruction

    B. Use of active and passive voices

    C. Agreement and sentence connectors

    D. Use of appropriate capitalization and punctuation

130. The system most affected by aerobic activity is the

    A.   muscular system.

    B.   digestive system.

    C.   cardiovascular system.

    D.   skeletal system.

131. President John F. Kennedy proposed new civil rights laws as well as programs to help the millions of Americans living in poverty. After Kennedy's assassination in Dallas in 1963, President Lyndon B. Johnson urged Congress to pass the laws. As a result of the leadership of these two men, which piece of legislation was passed?

    A.   The Civil Rights Act

    B.   The Equal Education Act

    C.   The Fair Employment Act

    D.   The Desegregation Act

132. What are minimal pairs used to teach and assess?

    A.   Morphology

    B.   Phonology

    C.   Syntax

    D.   Lexicon

133. The ice cap of the North Pole is melting at an alarming rate. The melting of the ice cap is an example of a

    A.   chemical change.

    B.   physical change.

    C.   chemical reaction.

    D.   natural yearly process.

134. How many faces does a cube have?

    A.   7

    B.   6

    C.   5

    D.   4

135. Dan and Stacy live on a farm where they are no longer allowed to let their cattle roam free. They need to add a fence around their land which has a shape like the figure below. How many feet of fence do they need to buy in order to fence in all of their land?

223 ft

467 ft

A. 103,341 ft

B. 104,141 ft

C. 1,380 ft

D. 1,280 ft

136. Warm- and cold-blooded animals need heat to survive; however, only warm-blooded animals produce heat. Cold-blooded animals obtain heat from

A. the food that they eat.

B. the sun.

C. the moon.

D. the water that they drink.

137. What is the formula for the relationship between the number of faces, vertices, and edges of a cube?

A. $F + E = V + 2$

B. $E + V = F + 2$

C. $F + V = E - 2$

D. $F + V = E + 2$

138. While teaching a basketball unit to an elementary school class, the best way to develop skills would be to

A. give a written test to assess students' knowledge of strategy.

B. use smaller balls and lower the baskets.

C. teach the foul shot before the jump shot.

D. play full court, five-on-five games.

139. The principles of art describe

    A. the guidelines that artists follow to create art and to deliver their intended message.

    B. the individual components that combine to create artwork.

    C. the ideas, emotions, and experiences that can be communicated through art.

    D. the sequence of artistic concepts that are presented in grades kindergarten through 6.

140. What is one of the key advantages of using integrated thematic instruction?

    A. The four literacy skills—listening, speaking, reading, and writing—are introduced sequentially.

    B. It is used to introduce and practice basic computation skills.

    C. It eliminates the artificial boundaries created through traditional course scheduling.

    D. It allows for the teaching of the content areas using the inductive method.

ANSWER KEY – PRACTICE TEST 2

Question	Answer	Competency	Question	Answer	Competency
1	C	001	31	B	005
2	A	017	32	B	023
3	B	020	33	B	008
4	B	007	34	C	008
5	C	020	35	A	008
6	D	028	36	D	043
7	B	042	37	C	002
8	C	002	38	C	021
9	B	003	39	B	030
10	B	001	40	D	002
11	A	017	41	A	031
12	A	017	42	B	023
13	D	007	43	D	026
14	B	019	44	B	002
15	A	019	45	B	025
16	B	013	46	D	024
17	B	007	47	A	018
18	B	013	48	A	004
19	C	013	49	A	032
20	A	001	50	A	025
21	C	017	51	C	042
22	D	003	52	D	031
23	D	005	53	C	026
24	D	042	54	B	004
25	B	018	55	D	018
26	A	021	56	C	003
27	D	011	57	B	043
28	D	021	58	B	004
29	D	021	59	D	015
30	C	018	60	D	005

Question	Answer	Competency	Question	Answer	Competency
61	B	015	93	B	006
62	B	032	94	A	023
63	A	015	95	C	022
64	A	043	96	A	005
65	D	032	97	D	021
66	B	040	98	A	044
67	B	032	99	B	006
68	C	015	100	C	012
69	B	033	101	B	044
70	C	011	102	A	007
71	A	037	103	D	041
72	D	014	104	A	004
73	A	041	105	C	038
74	D	010	106	D	014
75	A	014	107	A	037
76	B	038	108	C	008
77	D	010	109	A	041
78	C	011	110	C	023
79	C	005	111	D	019
80	D	022	112	B	020
81	B	010	113	C	045
82	A	011	114	C	045
83	A	014	115	A	022
84	C	043	116	D	012
85	A	011	117	D	014
86	C	012	118	D	019
87	B	009	119	D	015
88	D	044	120	A	019
89	C	007	121	D	016
90	C	022	122	D	021
91	C	022	123	D	023
92	B	038	124	D	021

Question	Answer	Competency
125	A	045
126	D	020
127	D	012
128	C	016
129	C	009
130	C	044
131	A	020
132	B	012

Question	Answer	Competency
133	B	031
134	B	016
135	C	016
136	B	036
137	D	016
138	B	045
139	A	042
140	C	013

Practice Test 1, Competency Checklist

Competency 001 ___/3
1 10 20

Competency 002 ___/4
8 37 40 44

Competency 003 ___/3
9 21 56

Competency 004 ___/4
48 54 58 104

Competency 005 ___/5
23 31 60 79 96

Competency 006 ___/2
93 99

Competency 007 ___/5
4 13 17 89 102

Competency 008 ___/4
33 34 35 108

Competency 009 ___/2
87 129

Competency 010 ___/3
74 77 81

Competency 011 ___/5
27 70 78 82 85

Competency 012 ___/5
86 100 116 127 132

Competency 013   __/4

16	18	19	140

Competency 014   __/5

72	75	83	106	117

Competency 015   __/5

59	61	63	68	119

Competency 016   __/5

121	128	134	135	137

Competency 017   __/3

2	11	12

Competency 018   __/4

25	30	47	55

Competency 019   __/5

14	15	111	118	120

Competency 020   __/6

3	5	110	112	126	131

Competency 021   __/7

26	28	29	38	97

122	124

Competency 022   __/5

80	90	91	95	115

Competency 023   __/6

22	32	42	94	109	123

Competency 024   __/1

46

Competency 025   __/2

45	50

Competency 026   __/2

43	53

Competency 027   __/0

Competency 028   __/1

6

Competency 029   __/0

Competency 030   __/1

39

Competency 031   __/3

41	52	133

Competency 032   __/4

49	62	65	67

Competency 033   __/1

69

Competency 034   __/0

Competency 035   __/0

Competency 036   __/2

1	136

Competency 037   __/2

71	107

Competency 038   __/3

76	92	105

Competency 039   __/0

Competency 040   __/1

66

Competency 041   __/2

73	103

Competency 042   __/3

7	24	51

Competency 043   __/5

36	57	64	84	139

Competency 044   __/4

88	98	101	130

Competency 045   __/4

113	114	125	138

Detailed Explanations for Practice Test 2

1. **C**

    The six language subsystems are phonology, morphology, syntax, lexicon, semantics, and pragmatics. Morphemes, grammar, graphemes, and denotation are not major linguistic subsystems but rather components or terminology linked to these subsystems. **Competency 001**

2. **A**

    A probability can be expressed as a number from 0 to 1, or with percentage or decimal numbers. A percent is a representation of a decimal number relative to 100. Therefore, the only number shown which does not fit is the negative number. **Competency 017**

3. **B**

    The New England Colonies consisted of Massachusetts, Connecticut, Rhode Island, and New Hampshire. (A) is incorrect because Virginia, North Carolina, South Carolina, and Georgia formed the Southern Colonies. (C) is incorrect because New York, New Jersey, Delaware, Maryland, and Pennsylvania formed the Middle Colonies. (D) is incorrect because this answer represents a combination of some of the Southern Colonies and some of the Middle Colonies. **Competency 020**

4. **B**

    Activating schema, or background knowledge related to a topic, helps students to make connections between new information and what they already know. Teachers can help students to activate the correct schema as a pre-reading strategy so that students can better understand new ideas and terminology. While motivation is important (A), it does not activate their schema of the topic. (C) and (D) are related comprehension strategies; however, they are not the primary reason for a teacher to activate prior knowledge in students. **Competency 007**

5. **C**

    Cesar Chávez and Dolores Huerta founded the United Farm Workers union (UFW). Through UFW they fought for better working conditions and fair compensation for agricultural workers. (A) is incorrect because, while this was an important issue at the time it was not the center of the United Farm Workers union. (B) is incorrect because this was not the focus of their work. (D) is incorrect because the development of more workers' unions was not their intent. **Competency 020**

6.   **D**

Allowing children to have first-hand experience with magnets will allow ELLs, and students in general, opportunities to internalize the concept. The explanation provided in (A) might not be developmentally appropriate for children in first and second grade. The use of explanations in the students' native language and in English (B) might not be sufficient to teach the concepts to young children. Playing with a compass (C) alone might not be sufficient to understand the concept of magnetism. **Competency 028**

7.   **B**

Edward Manet was the first artist to experiment with the impressions of light in nature. (A) is incorrect because, although Claude Monet is probably the best known of the Impressionists, his work was initially influenced by Manet. (C) is incorrect because Michelangelo was a Renaissance artist. (D) is incorrect because Salvador Dali was a Surrealist. **Competency 042**

8.   **C**

Technically, a subordinate clause is a dependent clause that must be attached to a main clause to complete the intended meaning. (A) contains a relative clause that provides additional information in the question. (A), (B), and (D) do not use subordinate clauses. **Competency 002**

9.   **B**

The alphabetic principle has been described as the ability to connect letters with sounds and to create words based on these associations. The only option that completely captures these two components is (B). Therefore, (A), (C), and (D) are incorrect. (C) describes the process to identify and create syllables—syllabication. **Competency 003**

10.   **B**

The word *mine* is a free morpheme when used in isolation; however, it is not a free morpheme in the word *predetermined* (B). There is no evidence to suggest that the student is having problems with suffixes or prefixes (A). Since she recognized that the segment *mine* can be classified as a free morpheme in certain conditions, there is no evidence to suggest that she does not understand the concept of free morphemes (C) and (D). **Competency 001**

11. **A**

> The mode is the number that occurs most often in a number sequence. If we place the numbers in order, we can see that the number 9 occurs 4 times while all other numbers occur fewer than 4. **Competency 017**

12. **A**

> The median is the middle number when the numbers are lined up from the greatest to the least. If this is done, one can see that since there are 28 total numbers, there is no clear "middle number." The middle number falls between the fourteenth and fifteenth numbers which happen to be 6 and 6, respectively. Therefore, the two numbers are averaged obtaining the median of 6. **Competency 017**

13. **D**

> Oral retelling is a good strategy to use when having emergent and beginning readers recall the main elements of the story. It allows students opportunities to recall key events and details of the story, even before they become fluent readers. (A), (B), and (C) describe informal assessment techniques used with students who are already reading and writing at the intermediate and advanced levels. **Competency 007**

14. **B**

> Thematic instruction is ideal to teach social studies to ELLs because the multiple components of the theme are presented in multiple disciplines and contexts. This redundancy facilitates the understanding of the multiple components of a theme. (A), (C), and (D) are probably true statements, but they individually do not represent the true advantages of using thematic instruction with ELLs. **Competency 019**

15. **A**

> Information in social studies can be presented in graphic form through the use of graphs and charts. This makes the content accessible to all children, including ELLs. (B), (C), and (D) describe possible ways to use advanced organizers and graphic representations, but individually these options do no fully explain their value. **Competency 019**

16. **B**

> Children can see that knowledge of mathematics has a functional value in their lives. (A) and (C) are incorrect because most children generally cannot make a connection between the content studied and the mathematics curriculum. (D) is incorrect

because children in K–6 generally cannot make extrapolations between activities in the learning centers and their intrinsic value in life. **Competency 013**

17. **B**

Confirming predictions is one of the most common ways to engage students in reading, focus their reading, and help them read with comprehension. By thinking aloud a teacher can explicitly model the procedures used when reading a text. Reader's theater (A) is a technique designed for the purpose of building fluency through repeated reading, while (C) and (D) focus primarily on decoding words or word meanings. **Competency 007**

18. **B**

Children that are four and five years old may not understand that changes in the appearance do not necessarily change the characteristics of an object. For example, if an apple is cut in half the children may not understand that there are two pieces of one apple. Instead, many students may say that there are now two apples. The difficulty these students face is with the concept of conservation. **Competency 013**

19. **C**

Hands-on activities can make the curriculum more relevant and guide children to construct their own knowledge. Hands-on activities can probably lead children to think abstractly (A), but the activity is not designed exclusively to accomplish this goal. Hands-on activities can make the class more interesting and enjoyable (B), but they are not the reasons for the activities. (D) is incorrect because there is no evidence to suggest that hands-on activities can promote equity, equality, or freedom among students. **Competency 013**

20. **A**

The LAD is said to be an internal mechanism that allows human beings to produce language and to make use of their own internal grammar. Of particular interest is Chomsky's work, which led to understanding that the LAD is adaptable to the language that is being learned. **Competency 001**

21. **C**

On a single die there are six numbers, 1–6. On a pair of dice, the values of the sums range from 2–12. All values are clearly less than 12. Therefore, all rolls will be less than 13. Additionally, with a pair of dice, there are 36 possible outcomes (6 each) and, therefore, the answer is C. **Competency 017**

22. **D**

Teachers have to present the consistent sounds of English first to develop self-confidence among children. Once children master those initial grapheme-phoneme correspondences, they can attempt more challenging components. (A) is incorrect because it deals with a generic well-accepted practice, but it does not address the question. (B) is incorrect because the alphabetic principle does not specifically deal with the issue of the development of foreign accents. (C) is incorrect because it failed to address the question. It is always important to create an atmosphere of collaboration among students, but this statement does not address the linguistic nature of the question. **Competency 003**

23. **D**

When children miss about 10 percent of the words in a passage, comprehension problems will occur. Children at the instructional level need continuous support and guidance from the teachers. (A) is incorrect because students at the independent level of reading are able to understand 95 percent of the words. (C) is incorrect because the term *comprehension level* is not a technical descriptor for reading levels. (B) is incorrect because students at the frustration level can read less than 89 percent of the words correctly. With this low level of word recognition, they will have severe comprehension problems. **Competency 005**

24. **D**

Mathematics and science flourished during the Renaissance period and naturally influenced work in the arts. (A) is incorrect because Impressionism focused on the perception of light in nature, as opposed to the scientific properties. (B) is incorrect because the Baroque movement focused on drama, tension, and detail. (C) is incorrect because the Rococo movement focused on creativity and the creation of idyllic landscapes. **Competency 042**

25. **B**

Since a percentage represents a part of 100, a tax of 5% is equal to a decimal value of $\frac{5}{100} = 0.05$. To find out how much tax is added to a bill of $78.60, we must multiply this total by the percentage of tax. **Competency 018**

26. **A**

A grid system is a network of horizontal and vertical lines used to locate points on a map or a chart by means of coordinates. This grid shows the location of places.

Latitude and longitude lines form divisions in this grid system. These divisions consist of geometrical coordinates used in designating the location of places on the surface of the earth in a globe or map. The lines measure distances in degrees. Based on this explanation (B), (C), and (D) are incorrect. **Competency 021**

27. **D**

The word *bound* in this type of morpheme should immediately indicate that this type of morpheme cannot occur in isolation; that is, it is bound to "something else." In this case, a bound morpheme must always be attached to a root word or another morpheme. This explanation makes (A), (B) and (C) incorrect. **Competency 001**

28. **D**

The world region of North America consists of Canada, the United States, and Mexico. (A) is incorrect because it is missing Canada. (B) is incorrect because it is missing Mexico. (C) is incorrect because it is missing Canada and Mexico. **Competency 021**

29. **D**

The term *cultural diffusion* describes the exchange or transmission of cultural information and lifestyles from people around the world. *Diversity* describes differences among people around the world (A). *Ethnicity* (B) is a term used to describe people based on historical and cultural background, including religion, language, and other features. *Culture* (C) is a term to describe the learned and common behavior of a group. **Competency 021**

30. **C**

The statement "three times one-half of a number less eighty percent" implies that we do not know the actual number. Therefore, it must be represented by a variable. This fact eliminates (A). Knowing that 80% is equivalent to 80/100 or 0.8 eliminates (B) and (D). Therefore, the only choice that is left happens to be (C). **Competency 018**

31. **B**

Sight words occur frequently in writing, and often the best way to teach them is by instant recognition. (A) is not correct because environmental print does not necessarily contain sight words. Street signs and store names can have long and very unique names that cannot be taught as sight words. (C) is incorrect because sight words are taught to be recognized instantly, without analyzing their structural or semantic representation. (D) is incorrect because most sight words are short and easy to spell. Because they occur so frequently in reading, spelling is facilitated. **Competency 005**

32. **B**

Civil rights are the legal and political rights of the people who live in a particular country. In the United States, the Constitution and the Bill of Rights guarantee civil rights to American citizens and residents. The first 10 amendments to the U.S. Constitution are known as the Bill of Rights. (A), (C), and (D) are incorrect because these name certain rights included in the Bill of Rights and fail to address the question. **Competency 023**

33. **B**

When reading informational text, students have to analyze the type of text structure and organizational pattern used in the writing. The faster they learn to decipher the structure, the faster they will be able to retrieve information and read with greater efficiency. Using graphic organizers (A) and developing academic English (C) are important but secondary strategies that children need to master to move to the stage of "reading to learn." Predicting the content (D) is an effective strategy for narrative text, but it loses its effectiveness with expository writing. **Competency 008**

34. **C**

The main purpose of DRTA is to enable students to make ongoing predictions and confirmations of those predictions while reading a text. The teacher models this during a read-aloud or shared reading and instructs students to do the same as they read. (A), (B), and (D) focus on activities that will enhance and develop students' comprehension; however, they are not centrally related to the specific instructional focus of DRTA. **Competency 008**

35. **A**

Reciprocal teaching requires students to participate in cooperative learning groups where each student has a role in discussing the key aspects of the text in terms of posing questions, clarifying confusing sections, and making predictions. While making connections to one's life may enhance students' connections to the background knowledge and schema, it is not a central process of reciprocal teaching. **Competency 008**

36. **D**

Melody is the "tune" or singable part of a song. The *Alphabet Song* has the same "tune" as *Twinkle, Twinkle Little Star*. As a matter of fact, *Baa, Baa Black Sheep* also employs the same melody. (A), (B), and (C) have different "tunes" than *Twinkle, Twinkle Little Star.* **Competency 043**

37. **C**

    Alliterations are created when words in a sentence or poem begin with the same phoneme. The option that best represents this concept is (C). Four of the five words in option (C) begin with the phoneme /m/. The rest of the options do not consistently use the same phonemes at the beginning of the words. **Competency 002**

38. **C**

    The regions with the highest annual rainfall are the Piney-woods and the Gulf Coast regions. Thus, these types of plants and trees will flourish in these two regions. The hill country region (A), South Texas Plains and the Prairies and Lakes regions (B) have a relatively low rainfall, when compared with the rainfall from the Piney-woods and Gulf Coast regions. The panhandle plains and the Big Bend regions (D) have the lowest rainfall in the state. **Competency 021**

39. **B**

    All the items listed are classified as simple machines. Based on this answer, (A) is incorrect. (C) and (D) describe in general fashion the types of items brought to class, not the purpose of bringing them to class—to demonstrate the concept of simple machine. **Competency 030**

40. **D**

    The word contains seven graphemes (letters), but only three phonemes (sounds). Based on this explanation, the rest of the options are eliminated. **Competency 002**

41. **A**

    The periodic table represents the 112 elements that constitute matter. Liquid (B), solid (C), and gases (D) are forms or states of matter. **Competency 031**

42. **B**

    The ideas of the Enlightenment quickly reached the British colonies. Many of the leaders responsible for the writing of the Constitution were familiar with the leading thinkers of the movement, and framed the Constitution protecting the natural rights of the individual and limiting the power of the government. (A) is incorrect because it addresses only one aspect of the natural rights of the individual. (C) is incorrect because the purpose of the Constitution was actually to limit the power of the government and not to protect it. (D) is incorrect because it does not represent the ideals of the Age of Reason. **Competency 023**

43. **D**

An instrument called a sling psychrometer is used to measure relative humidity. **Competency 026**

44. **B**

Separating syllables into individual phonemes calls for syllabication and phoneme segmentation. Both concepts are part of phonological awareness. (A) is incorrect because sentence analysis was not the primary concern in the scenario. The intonation pattern describes the rhythm and pitch used in phrases and sentences. (C) is incorrect because in the latter activity, the issue is the phonological analysis of words. Vocabulary development was emphasized in the first part of the scenario only. (D) is incorrect because the scenario does not address pronunciation at all. **Competency 002**

45. **B**

Science instruction should be thematically organized through key science concepts. The delivery of effective and accurate instruction (A) was not specifically in the proclamation because it is a given that instruction in general should be delivered in this fashion. (C) and (D) are similar in nature. Both options call for the presentation of content from the known to unknown, which is a form of deductive teaching. The concept of scientific inquiry uses firsthand exploration of scientific concepts, and this approach is typical of inductive methods of teaching. **Competency 025**

46. **D**

The metric system uses a decimalized system for measurement. The consistency of the system, together with its ability to deal with small amounts of matter, make it ideal for scientific experimentation. (A) is incorrect because the metric system is an international system used in industrialized (developed) as well as in developing countries. (B) is incorrect because both the standard system and metric system can be used in scientific experimentation. (C) is incorrect because the use of the standard system does not automatically result in inconsistent test results. **Competency 024**

47. **A**

To find out how many sacks are required, we can divide the amount of apples that Joe has by the number that fit in a sack. The result of the division is 6.4. So, it could be assumed that (C) and (D) are not correct from this. However, (B) is also incorrect because it is not physically possible to obtain 0.4 of a bag. Therefore, one should round up to 7. **Competency 018**

48. **A**

The main reason for the creation of the language experience approach (LEA), also known as language charts, was to eliminate the discrepancy between the background knowledge that the child brings to the reading process and the experiential background required to understand the story, i.e., the schema of the author. (B) is incorrect because it eliminates the need to discuss the schema of the story by exposing children to a common experience and guiding them to dictate a story using the experience. (C) is incorrect because students will use their own vocabulary in the story; if they use idioms, these are probably known to children in the group. (D) is incorrect because the main purpose of LEA is not to contrast L1 and L2. **Competency 004**

49. **A**

The survival of the fittest (B) or the conservation efforts (C) are not addressed in the scenario. (D) is a very simplistic answer, and it does not address the main purpose of the lesson. **Competency 032**

50. **A**

Bringing concrete objects to class are generally used to build interest in the lesson. In lesson planning, this segment of the lesson is called focus activity or motivation. (B) and (C) provide a generic rationale for the answer. (D) is incorrect because there is no evidence to suggest that the tree was used for experimentation. **Competency 025**

51. **C**

All three of these movements (Photorealism, Cubism, and Surrealism) emerged in the twentieth century. (A) is incorrect because these three movements (Impressionism, Expressionism, and Realism) began and peaked during the nineteenth century. (B) is incorrect because the Hellenistic and Classical movements occurred in ancient Greece, and the Rococo movement occurred in the eighteenth century. (D) is incorrect because the Medieval movement occurred between 800 and 1200 CE, the Renaissance movement occurred between 1400 and 1600 CE and the Baroque movement occurred in the seventeenth century. **Competency 042**

52. **D**

The traditional states of matter found in the Earth are liquid, solid, and gas. In space, the most common form of mass is plasma. Plasma cannot be identified as a solid, liquid, or gas; thus, this new classification was created to describe it. **Competency 031**

53. **C**

   The Earth's 23½ degree tilt causes the seasons, and in winter in the Northern Hemisphere, the earth is tilted away from the sun along its north pole. **Competency 026**

54. **B**

   Miscue analysis describes the variation that students produce in their attempts to read or decode words. Goodman suggested that only those miscues affecting meaning should be taken into account. (A) is incorrect because miscues is a term to describe reading not necessarily writing attempts. (C) is incorrect because Goodman does not identify miscues as errors, plus the concept does not apply to attempts to communicate orally, such as conversation. (D) is incorrect because there is no connection between miscues and the schema theory. **Competency 004**

55. **D**

   In this problem we know there will be 371 people at the party and one loaf of bread will feed 8 people. Dividing 371 by 8 gives 46.375 which is not listed as an option. If she were to purchase 46 loaves of bread she would not have enough bread for everyone. Therefore, she must purchase at least 47 loaves to feed everyone. **Competency 018**

56. **C**

   Syllabication and word stress are part of the concept called phonological awareness. (A) is incorrect because the activity goes beyond establishing the connection between letters and sounds typical of the alphabetic principle. (B) is incorrect because the development of fluency goes beyond the analysis of individual words. The development of phonological awareness is a prerequisite for the development of fluency. (D) is incorrect because the concept of syllabication is only one of two elements presented in the scenario—syllabication and word stress. **Competency 003**

57. **B**

   A *Cowboy Song* typically is in public domain and can be reproduced without obtaining permission. (A), (C), and (D) are protected under the Copyright Protection Law. Just because everyone knows a song (such as *I'm a Little Teapot*) does not mean that it is in public domain. Always verify sources before reproducing music. **Competency 043**

58. **B**

   A balanced-reading approach uses best practices from both phonics and whole language. It also places emphasis on the use of authentic literature and the literature-based approach to construct meaning. (A) is incorrect because the skills-based approach emphasizes mostly phonics instruction. (C) is incorrect because the meaning-based approach emphasizes mostly the whole language approach. (D) is incorrect because there is no connection between humanistic psychology and the question. **Competency 004**

59. **D**

Recalling that the definition of a linear function is $f(\alpha x) = \alpha f(x)$ and $f(a + b) = f(a) + f(b)$, we may view each of the options. We see that applying these rules will mean that (A), (B), and (C) are all linear functions. After further investigation we see that (D) is nonlinear. **Competency 015**

60. **D**

The introduction of sight words can expedite students' decoding skills and it can also help develop fluency among early readers. From the options presented, the only word that is not in the Dolch's list is (D) awesome. **Competency 005**

61. **B**

Using the F.O.I.L. method, we know that there should be more than two terms in the resulting expansion. Therefore, we may eliminate selections (A) and (D). After expansion, we realize that (B) is correct. **Competency 015**

62. **B**

Mercury is one substance that reacts to heat, which facilitates its measuring. Mercury is available throughout the world (A), but that is not the main reason why the substance is used in thermometers. (The U.S. stopped mining it in the 1990s.) Mercury is not a volatile substance (C). (D) is highly irrelevant. In the past, the U.S. Department of Energy did not regulate the use of mercury, but it has regulated it since 2008. **Competency 032**

63. **A**

The *less than* symbol resembles an "alligator mouth" opening and moving away from the smaller number. "It is also helpful to notice that the smallest end in the sign will always point to the smallest number ($5 < 7$). (A) is the correct answer because it correctly states that: 5 is less than 7. (B) is incorrect because it incorrectly states that the number 10 is greater than 11. (C) and (D) are eliminated because both contain an extra line representing the concept of "equal to"; thus, the symbol in (C) incorrectly states that "9 is less than or equal to 8" and (D) states than "3 is greater than or equal to 5." **Competency 015**

64. **A**

Mariachi is a group of musicians playing the instruments listed in this question. Tejano music (B) features the accordion, and the Tejano orchestra has been influenced by Mexican, Cuban, German, and Czech brass bands. Marching bands (C) consist of traditional band instruments (e.g., flutes, clarinets, saxophones, trumpets, trombones, tubas, percussion, etc). An orchestra (D) consists of the four families of musical instruments (woodwinds, brass, string, and percussion). **Competency 043**

65. **D**

Microwaves use a form of radiation to cook meals. Refrigerators and gas stoves do not use radiation to function. Radios use electromagnetic waves to transmit sounds. **Competency 032**

66. **B**

Water cools down and heats up more slowly than any substance on Earth. Therefore, in the winter the average low temperature would be warmer in New York City—a coastal city, than it would be in Nebraska. The warm water (warmed from summer's sun and heat) keeps the air over the water warm and moving toward the city for a longer period of time than the air inland. **Competency 040**

67. **B**

Cell phones emit a type of radiation that has been linked to brain tumors. Current research suggests that heavy, long-term cell phone usage has also been linked to infertility among men. (A) and (C) are incorrect because they present non-medical effects attributed to cell phone usage. **Competency 032**

68. **C**

Until more advanced mathematics are incurred, the standard definition of division states that an expression is undefined if it contains division by 0. Although (D) will approach an undefined answer, it is not equal to 0. Therefore, the answer which best corresponds to the question is (C). **Competency 015**

69. **B**

Fossil fuels like natural gas, coal, and oil come from the remains of living matter, and by definition, they are nonrenewable resources. **Competency 033**

70. **C**

    With the exception of (C) all the other three options focus primarily on the text or images created and less on the role that the graphics have in complementing the message being conveyed. Having students actually create a chart while or after they discuss the author's reasoning for choosing visual elements does provide students with an opportunity to understand that there is a direct connection between the use of the graphics and the text that accompanies it. **Competency 011**

71. **A**

    Bears add fatty tissue to their body in preparation for hibernation during the winter months. Hibernation is a survival mechanism and a system of adaption to avoid starvation during the winter months. It is highly improbable that hibernation is done to avoid competition with other animals (B), to maintain a healthy ecosystem (C), or to prevent the movement of animals to residential areas (D). **Competency 037**

72. **D**

    An algorithm is a step-by-step procedure for solving problems. Although algorithms are often implemented using computers and can be used to evaluate students (A), this does not give the fundamental property of an algorithm. (B) and (C) are not appropriate answers for the definition of an algorithm, although they may be true. Therefore, (D) is the correct answer. **Competency 014**

73. **A**

    Asteroids, planets, moons, and comets are all objects in the solar system. Black holes and quasars are theorized objects in distant galaxies, and the Milky Way is the name of our own cluster of stars or galaxy in which the solar system (sun, planets, dwarf planets, comets, asteroids, and meteoroids) reside. **Competency 041**

74. **D**

    In trying to convince the reader of something, posing a question relating to reasons why the argument might be convincing will help the writer to see the reader's point of view. In narrative writing, expository writing, and descriptive writing, the need to convince may be present; however, it is more essential in the very nature of persuasive writing. **Competency 010**

75. **A**

Recalling that exponential notation is used when numbers are multiplied by themselves numerous times, we may try to simplify the expression. (B) is not correct because this implies 3 is multiplied by itself 4 times. (C) and (D) are the same answer in different representations, but both are incorrect. Since 4 is multiplied by itself 3 times in this problem, we know it should be (A). **Competency 014**

76. **B**

When the tectonic plates collapse, they can create mountains and mountain ranges. The movement of underground water (A) does not have an effect on the formation of the mountains. Erosion (C) refers to the movement of sediment from one location to the other; however, this movement cannot account for the formation of mountains. The effect of the moon on tides (D) does not have a direct effect on the formation of mountains. **Competency 038**

77. **D**

Telling the students the mode of writing is likely not sufficient to support students' understanding of writing for an audience (D). Revising a piece of writing based on feedback provided from the audience (B), and asking students to role play and react to it can guide children to adjust the writing (A). (C) helps students internalize that a specific audience will be reading their paper and that they need to develop the writing accordingly. **Competency 010**

78. **C**

While students implementing all of these project ideas may need to use visual materials to complement their message, students considering implementing (A), (B), and (D) would actually not be involved in selecting these for a specific audience, as is the case in (C). Moreover, none of these three options provide specific information to identify the audience, thus they will not be the best options. **Competency 011**

79. **C**

The words *butterfly*, *nightmare*, and *brainstorm* may confuse students because they do not provide a reliable point of view to comprehend their meaning. (A), (B), and (D) are incorrect because they contain information to help children in the comprehension process. Words like *doghouse*, *underground*, and *mouthwash* provide clear indications of the intended meaning. **Competency 005**

80. **D**

    The state of Texas does not have a state personal income tax. The personal and corporate tax structure, together with the technological development of the state, attracts corporations and investors to the state. The climate (A) and the history (B) play minimal roles in the decision of corporations to relocate in Texas. The proximity with Mexico and Central American (C) might play a role, but not as strong as the financial incentives offered in the state. **Competency 022**

81. **B**

    Informative writing is also known as expository writing. The purpose of expository writing is to explain and clarify ideas. (A) focuses on text that is more "story-like" and is often told from a first-person or third-person perspective about an account or series of events. (C) is more often associated with narrative text, poetry, and advertising than informational text, per se. (D) primarily aims to convince the reader of something and provides arguments and counterarguments instead of mainly writing for the purpose of informing. **Competency 010**

82. **A**

    Sketching a character is developmentally appropriate for students in first grade for viewing and representing and involves creating a visual depiction of a character that can then be discussed. (B), (C), and (D) are more appropriate activities for students in grades 3–6. **Competency 011**

83. **A**

    There are many ways to approach this problem. One way is to realize that there are 14 days in a two-week period. Then, take the amount of money Max spent on lunch ($71.47) and divide this by 14. However, this may result in a messy solution when all we need is an approximation. Instead, try to find a number that, when multiplied by 14, gets you pretty close to the total Max spent. In this case, if $5 is selected, this will approximate an expense of $70 over the two-week period. **Competency 014**

84. **C**

    The question addresses the basic understanding of the Kodály rhythm syllables. The two syllables included in this example are *ta*, which would be notated as a quarter note on the staff, and *ti*, which would be notated as an eighth note on the staff. If a person were to keep the beat and sing the song *Twinkle, Twinkle Little Star*, it should be apparent that the answer is C. (A) and (B) begin with the wrong note (*ta*), and (D) ends with the wrong note (*ti*). **Competency 043**

85. **A**

The teacher is explicitly modeling the features of visual design that will assist students in their own creation and authoring of multi-media. (B), (C), and (D) are incorrect because they focus more on passive viewing rather than discussion and a focus on naming and analyzing specific features of media that makes a piece have a strong presentation. **Competency 011**

86. **C**

Unique differences in students suggest that one assessment measure is not sufficient for one test to be the basis for groups in literacy instruction. Moreover, multiple assessment measures should be used when considering grouping students by ability or skill levels. Based on this information, (A) and (B) are incorrect. (D) is incorrect because recent assessment data should be used to monitor progress of students and for grouping purposes. **Competency 012**

87. **B**

Mr. Lee is modeling conventional use of punctuation. By thinking aloud he is making his own knowledge about conventions explicit and thereby scaffolding the understanding of his students. The students know they will also be expected to use the same conventions in their own writing. (A), (C), and, (D) focus less on mechanical conventions and writing and focus more on the writing and composing process itself in terms of selecting ideas and organizing them into a coherent piece of writing. **Competency 009**

88. **D**

If a teacher notices abuse or neglect of a child, he/she should calmly and immediately report it to the proper authorities at the school (i.e., principal or assistant principal). Although (A) and (C) may appear to be natural for humanistic educators, it is not a good course of action for a variety of reasons. One, the teacher is not trained in the field(s) of counseling or psychology. Two, the teacher will not be as familiar or knowledgeable with the leadership policies and procedures regarding abuse as the principal. Three, the teacher no longer remains anonymous and/or protected by the school district in case of legal issues. (B) is not an option as the teacher has a legal responsibility to advocate for (act on behalf of) the child and to report the case to the appropriate authorities. **Competency 044**

89. **C**

The use of pictures to represent events in the story can be used to represent the sequencing of events in the story. It can also be used to introduce visually the parts of the story, i.e., characters, setting, plot, climax, and resolution. (A) is incorrect because the teacher is not connecting directly the pictures with the written text and the appropriate pronunciation. Teachers can fill the background knowledge of the students through visuals (B); however, this activity is usually done as a pre-reading activity. Since the visuals were used as a post-reading activity, we can believe that filling the gaps was not the primary purpose of the activity. The teacher is definitely using developmentally appropriate practices (D), but the real intent of the activity goes beyond that. **Competency 007**

90. **C**

The most important economic activity of the metroplex (Dallas/Fort Worth) is technology and defense. The area holds about 43% of the state's high tech jobs. Lockheed-Martin in Fort Worth has numerous contracts with the Department of Defense. It provides services and products in aeronautics, electronic systems, information systems, global systems, and space systems. **Competency 022**

91. **C**

The discovery of oil and the economic and technologic development that followed moved Texas from a rural/agrarian society to a modern industrial state. During the twentieth century the production of oil in the United States has never been large enough to supply local and international demands (A). The discovery of oil has not had a direct impact in the production of textiles and cattle in Texas (B). The discovery of oil helped the development of the American economy, but it was not the only element that helped the nation in its economic development (D). **Competency 022**

92. **B**

Volcanoes, especially those underwater, can cause tsunamis or tidal waves. Volcanoes can indeed cause death (A); however, it is not an automatic occurrence. Volcanic eruptions happen continuously without human casualties. Moreover, early evacuation can prevent human casualties. The development of hurricanes (C) and tornados (D) are not linked to volcanic activity. **Competency 038**

93. **B**

Students who follow curvilinear rhetorical and writing patterns need to be provided with a structure to keep them focused on the topic and to write following a linear format. One of the best ways to accomplish this goal is to guide them to develop an outline prior to the actual writing (pre-writing). They can also benefit from guiding questions to keep them focused on the topic and the intended audience. (A) is incorrect because learning about grammar structures and pronunciation will not necessarily affect the organization and coherence of the composition. (C) can help in developing a coherent oral presentation, but it might not affect the development of writing. Developing a check list (D) of the topics to be covered will not guarantee that children will follow a linear progression in the writing. (B) is a better choice because it provides a strategy that, once learned, can be used in multiple future situations. **Competency 006**

94. **A**

Jim Crow laws enforced strict separation in the South. Segregation rules restricted blacks to separate facilities in public places such as theaters, restaurants, buses, restrooms, and schools. (B), (C), and (D) are incorrect because in other parts of the country this separation was not law. **Competency 023**

95. **C**

Timber is the most important activity in East Texas. Based on this explanation, all the other options are incorrect. **Competency 022**

96. **A**

When children over generalize like in the example—*bestest*—they are in reality applying grammar rules which indicate that they have passed the stage of mere repetition, and they are beginning to decipher the grammar of the language. This overgeneralization is typical of English native speakers acquiring a language, and does not show any kind of interference from a language. This statement eliminates (B) and (C). (D) is incorrect but it can be confusing because cartoons such as "Rugrats" often use this kind of overgeneralization to mimic the speech of children; however, the continuous overgeneralization typical of children cannot be attributed to cartoons on television. **Competency 005**

97. **D**

The Andes and the Amazon River are geographical barriers that separate the many ethnic groups in Central and South America. **Competency 021**

98. **A**

Sedentary lifestyle behavior is a primary risk factor for heart disease as well as other preventable diseases. (B), (C), and (D) are not directly caused by inactivity. **Competency 044**

99. **B**

When children change declarative sentences to questions or exclamations, they have to change the intonation pattern of the language. (A) is incorrect because sentence transformations are not designed to teach listening skills. (C) is incorrect because there is no connection between the linguistic transformation requested and teaching singing and music. Conducting sentence transformation can be an enjoyable activity; however, making the class more enjoyable is just a derivative of the process. Therefore, (D) is incorrect. **Competency 006**

100. **C**

Culture shapes the way that children behave and perform in school. Linguistic limitations can also affect the ability of children to demonstrate capabilities and potential. The option of making students feel valued and wanted (A) is a noble cause, but it should not be the main concern when assessing CLD learners. (B) presents a true statement when it indicated that students go through different stages of development, but invalidated the answer by saying that these *should not* affect the way in which they are assessed. The term *cultural deficit* used in (D) invalidates the answer because CLD learners cannot be considered culturally deficient since they already bring with them their language and culture. **Competency 012**

101. **B**

Elevation is a key component to the RICE treatment process for sprains. The other components are rest, ice, and compression. Elevating the sprained limb allows for better circulation of blood, which leads to less swelling and faster recovery. (A) is incorrect because one should not return to exercise until significant healing has been achieved; although bearing a tolerable amount of weight on the sprain has been shown to help quicken the healing process slightly. (C) is incorrect because *evaluation* is not a technical term used in the treatment of sprains. (D) is incorrect because the sprain should be bandaged properly to achieve compression and support the injured joint. **Competency 044**

102. **A**

Metacognition encompasses being aware and self-regulating one's own thinking as comprehension takes place. Self-monitoring, or stopping to self-assess and check one's own understanding is most related to metacognition. (B), (C), and (D) focus on reading skills that are important to comprehension; however, they are not directly related to self-monitoring. **Competency 007**

103. **D**

The year is calculated based on the time needed for the planet to go around the sun (revolution), and the distance from the Sun determines the length of the year. Since Mercury is the closes planet to the Sun, it takes shorter time to complete the revolution. **Competency 041**

104. **A**

Story retelling inventory is generally organized as an informal checklist that teachers administer to check for comprehension and to assess language development. In addition to assessing the story line and the plot, the instrument checks for correct language usage, sentence structure, and vocabulary development. The instrument assesses oral language development but does not address the listening and writing components, thus (B) and (C) are incorrect. Technically, students will develop some knowledge of literary pieces and will be exposed to different writing styles (D), but the main purpose of the story retelling is not to address these issues. **Competency 004**

105. **C**

The amount of gas determines how violent the eruption can be. When the accumulation of gas reaches its peak, violent explosions can occur. The amount of magma inside the Earth (A) is a contributing factor, but not the primary factor. (B) is incorrect because technically, there is no lava inside the Earth. The term *lava* is used to describe when the magma reaches the surface and becomes solid creating volcanic rocks. The number of faults in the area (D) can contribute to eruptions, but it cannot explain why some eruptions are more violent than others. **Competency 038**

106. **D**

In this problem we are not concerned with negative or positive results because we are only asked about the relative difference between the two temperatures. So, the difference between 375° and 50° is 325°. **Competency 014**

107. **A**

Plants take energy from sunlight and convert it to produce chemical energy. Through the process of cellular respiration, this type of energy in converted into ATP—the type of fuel used by living things. As part of the process of photosynthesis, plants take carbon dioxide (B) from the environment and convert it into oxygen (D). Thus, these two elements are part of the process, not the final product. Plants contain a pigment called chlorophyll (C), which also plays a role but does not constitute the product of photosynthesis. **Competency 037**

108. **C**

   Students in fourth grade and up typically have a harder time when it comes to "reading to learn" as it requires having a basic understanding of the format used in expository writing. This is especially important as students need to learn the content areas to succeed academically. Losing interest in reading (A) and lacking fluency and decoding (B) are challenges that children face in upper elementary grades; however, these options individually do not represent the most important challenge experienced in upper elementary grades. Experiencing problems selecting books to read on their own (D) is not a real challenge for students in upper elementary grades. **Competency 008**

109. **A**

   A full moon occurs 12 months a year. Because the year contains about eleven extra days, these days accumulate, in such a way that every two or three years, we have an extra full moon a year. This extra full moon is called a blue moon. (B) is incorrect because a blue moon does not necessarily precede a lunar eclipse. (C) and (D) are incorrect because they do not provide a scientific explanation for the saying. In (C), the idiomatic expression makes reference to a strange rare event in general. (D) incorrectly links this expression to another idiomatic expression that links the color blue with sadness. **Competency 041**

110. **C**

   The Pledge of Allegiance is a declaration of patriotism. It was first published in 1892 in *The Youth's Companion*, and was believed to be written by the magazine's editor, Francis Bellamy. The original purpose was for the pledge to be used by school children in activities to celebrate the 400th anniversary of the discovery of America. The Pledge was widely used in morning school routines for many years and received official recognition by Congress on 1942. In 1954 the phrase "under God" was added and a law to indicate the proper behavior when reciting the pledge, which includes standing straight, removing hats or any other headgear, and placing the right hand over the heart. (A), (B), and (D) are incorrect because while they are all American patriotic national symbols, (C) is an actual declaration of patriotism. Therefore, (C) is a better answer. **Competency 023**

111. **D**

   The state curriculum officially introduces children to the people and places of the contemporary world in sixth grade. (A) is incorrect because in third grade the social studies curriculum covers how individuals change their communities and the world but does not include places of the contemporary world. (B) is incorrect because in fourth grade students become familiar with the history of Texas. (C) is incorrect because in fifth grade the curriculum centers on the history of the United States. **Competency 019**

112. **B**

The National Association for the Advancement of Colored People (NAACP) challenged the laws of segregation with the *Brown v. Board of Education of Topeka* case. In 1954 the Supreme Court ruled that racial segregation in public schools was unconstitutional. (A) and (C) are incorrect because there were no civil rights associations by those names. (D) is also incorrect because while the Southern Christian Leadership Conference was an association led by Dr. Martin Luther King Jr., it was not the group that challenged the Topeka Board of Education. **Competency 020**

113. **C**

Stacking cups, dribbling a small ball, and tapping their foot to the rhythm, as well as dressing themselves require children to master fine motor skills. Based on this explanation, (A) is incorrect because gross motor skills include the use of large muscle groups in the body to perform big movements like running. (B) is a plausible answer but it is too generic in nature and does not address the question. (D) also is incorrect because all of the skills outlined in the question should be achievable long before any transition into adulthood. **Competency 045**

114. **C**

Injury prevention should always be at the forefront of any planned activity in a physical education setting. Therefore, the purpose of inspecting the playing field is to protect the students, minimize the risk of injury, and reduce the overall liability of the educator, class, and school. (A) assumes the teacher is helping the students feel better about participating when in affect the risk of injury still exists because nothing has been done to fix the holes. (B) is incorrect because the teacher is simply passing the responsibility of safety to other school staff when the responsibility is in fact their own. (D) is also incorrect because simply dodging holes is not part of a developmentally appropriate activity during outdoor play. **Competency 045**

115. **A**

The expansion of the railroad system made transportation of cattle and agricultural products easier for Texas' farmers and ranchers. (B) is incorrect because the railroad facilitated the industrialization of the state but this development did not happen in the nineteenth century. Connecting the East and the West (C) is not necessarily a relevant economic development. (D) is a false statement; the economy of Texas in the latter part of the 19th century was still developing. **Competency 022**

116. **D**

Anecdotal records are notes a teacher takes while observing students as they work on tasks in the classroom. It provides insight into the processes and interactions the group is using during their discussion and work on activities. The teacher can also provide feedback to the students at a later time using the anecdotal record for reference. (A) is incorrect because running records are used mostly for assessing miscue analysis, reading accuracy, and fluency. (B) is incorrect because portfolios focus more on looking at student work products and/or self-assessments and reflections over time, while summative evaluation (C) is more for end-of-term evaluations on students. **Competency 012**

117. **D**

This problem can be solved by converting the decimal to a fraction, or the fraction to a decimal and then subtracting. If the decimal is converted to a fraction, 1.6 becomes $1\frac{6}{10}$. In order to subtract, we should now get a common denominator. The lowest common denominator between 8 and 10 is 40. Therefore, the problem becomes $1\frac{24}{40} - \frac{15}{40} = 1\frac{9}{40}$. **Competency 014**

118. **D**

The TEKS introduces the history of the United States in fifth grade. (A) is incorrect because in second grade the social studies curriculum covers local communities. (B) is incorrect because in third grade the curriculum centers on how individuals change their communities and the world. (C) is incorrect because in fourth grade students become familiar with the history of Texas. **Competency 019**

119. **D**

In the presented pattern we see two circles followed by one diamond. Then, there are two circles followed by two diamonds. Next, we see two circles, three diamonds, and then two circles again. We take note that every time circles appear they only appear in pairs. Therefore, we know the next set should not be a circle right away. If we look at the diamonds, we see that at first we had one diamond, then two, and finally three. They are increasing by 1 each time they appear. Therefore, we should expect to see four diamonds. **Competency 015**

120. **A**

   Children as early as prekindergarten can be guided to develop civic responsibility. Teachers can promote this sense of responsibility by involving students in real-life situations in which they take civic responsibility. Citizenship is introduced in different ways in all grade levels, but there is no need to wait until the child gets to kindergarten to begin the process. **Competency 019**

121. **D**

   In any triangle, the sum of the angles must equal 180°. If a triangle has two equal sides, the third side cannot be unique and must be a set length. The lines associated with the equal sides will intersect the third side at the same angle. Therefore, the only answer that can be determined true from the information is (D). **Competency 016**

122. **D**

   A world region is an area of the world that shares similar, unifying cultural or physical characteristics, which are different from those of surrounding areas. (A) is incorrect because topographical characteristics like elevation, rivers, and mountains are part of the unifying elements of a world region but not the only ones. (B) and (C) present partial descriptions of a region, but failed to capture all the elements linked to the concept of a region. **Competency 021**

123. **D**

   The Fourteenth Amendment declared that all persons born in the U.S. were citizens, that all citizens were entitled to equal rights, and that their rights were protected by due process. The amendment, however, excludes Native Americans. (A) and (B) are incorrect because while blacks and women did not enjoy the benefits of full equal rights, such as voting rights, until later on, the amendment did not specifically exclude them. (C) is incorrect because the rights of children were not mentioned in the amendment. **Competency 023**

124. **D**

   These divisions are based on physical and cultural similarities. (A), (B), and (C) are partial answers, but individually they do not constitute an appropriate answer. **Competency 021**

125. **A**

   Locomotor skills are general movement skills done through space (i.e., skipping, running, jumping, etc.). To increase the challenge when practicing these skills, a physical education teacher would instruct learners to perform them via different directions, levels, and pathways. (B), (C), and (D) have nothing to do with performing locomotor movements. **Competency 045**

126. **D**

   Dr. Martin Luther King Jr.'s famous *I Have a Dream* speech took place during the march in Washington in support of the Civil Rights Act of 1964. The eloquent speech and orderly demonstration gained more supporters for the cause. He was assassinated in 1968 in Memphis, Tennessee, but his work resulted in the official Civil Right Act in 1964. (A) is incorrect because the speech did not prompt a riot. (B) is incorrect because the Montgomery Improvement Association was formed after Rosa Parks refused to give up her seat on a bus in 1955. (C) is incorrect because the speech did not result in a loss of supporters. **Competency 020**

127. **D**

   The TOP contains a checklist of specific skills for teachers to document when these behaviors occur during observation. (A) and (B) are incorrect because the TOP does not contain rating scales or multiple-choice questions. (C) is incorrect because the TOP is a checklist identifying the specific linguistic features for observation. **Competency 012**

128. **C**

   While all of these units will accurately express the length of the football field, centimeters and inches would not be a convenient scale to use, as the resolution of the measurement would be too great resulting in an extremely large number (or a long time to measure). Miles are another inconvenient method to measure a football field, as a mile is much larger than a single football field. **Competency 016**

129. **C**

   The three sentences can be combined with appropriate connectors to avoid repetitions. In this particular case, the conjunctions can be used to create compound sentences. Sentence 3 shows faulty agreement, which suggests that the child can also benefit from this kind of instructional support. (A) and (B) are incorrect because the writing sample does not show problems with spelling or the use of active and passive voices. (D) is incorrect because the writing sample does not show problems with capitalization and punctuation. **Competency 009**

130. **C**

Although (A) and (D) are largely necessary for aerobic kinds of activity, it is the cardiovascular system that works the hardest to support and sustain the energy and oxygen necessary for continuous activity (via blood circulation). (B) is not directly relevant to aerobic activity. **Competency 044**

131. **A**

The Civil Rights Act passed in 1964 prohibited segregation in all public facilities and discrimination in education and employment. President John F. Kennedy proposed new civil rights laws as well as programs to help the millions of Americans living in poverty. After his assassination in Dallas in 1963, President Lyndon B. Johnson urged Congress to pass the Civil Rights Act in honor of Kennedy, persuading the majority of Democrats and some Republicans. (B), (C), and (D) are incorrect because these were important aspects of the Act but not the name of the Act. **Competency 020**

132. **B**

In minimal pairs, students are required to identify whether two sets of words are different or the same based on the phoneme sequence contained in each word. For example, the words *vine* and *fine* are different because they differ in at least one phoneme, i.e., the /v/ and /f/. (A) is incorrect because morphology is not taken into account when comparing the two words. (C) is incorrect because there is no connection between minimal pairs and syntax. (D) is incorrect because lexicon deals with vocabulary development, and minimal pairs attempt to test whether children can understand how phonemes change the meaning of the words. **Competency 012**

133. **B**

The melting of the ice caps represents a physical change. It changes from solid to liquid, and it can revert to solid again. There are no chemical changes (A) or chemical reactions (C) when the ice turns into liquid, because the chemical composition of the liquid (water) remains unchanged. Ice melting occurs every summer, but the rate of melting of the last decade has surpassed previous years; thus, we cannot say that it is a natural yearly process (D). **Competency 031**

134. **B**

    Remembering that a face is a plain region of a geometric body, one can determine that since there are six sides to a cube that there are also six faces. **Competency 016**

135. **C**

    This problem deals with finding the perimeter of the rectangle. Since the two short legs of fence have the same length and the two long legs have the same length, we know $P = 2l + 2w$. This gives us a value of $2 \cdot 223 + 2 \cdot 467 = 1380$ ft. **Competency 016**

136. **B**

    Cold-blooded animals, like snakes and turtles, get their heat from solar energy. **Competency 036**

137. **D**

    Recall that the Face (F) of a cube is a plain region of a geometric body, the Edge (E) is a line segment where two faces of a three-dimensional figure meet, and a Vertex (V) is the union of two segments or the point of intersection of two sides of a polygon. Knowing this we can see that for a cube there are 6 faces, 8 vertices, and 12 edges. Substituting these numbers into the appropriate spot in each formula allows us to determine (D) as the only correct answer. **Competency 016**

138. **B**

    Developmentally speaking, children in elementary school do not have the strength or the ability to play with official basketball equipment (i.e., basketballs and baskets). Therefore, the only way to instruct a basketball lesson would be to modify the types of balls used (i.e., lighter and smaller) and lower the baskets so the students can be successful with the game. (A) does not apply because few children at that level understand the strategy of the game. (C) is partly correct in that you would teach the foul shot before the jump shot for developmental progression reasons, although not enough information is given that the shots have been modified for elementary students. (D) is incorrect for the same reasons as above. **Competency 045**

139. **A**

    Artists use the principles of art to create and communicate through their artwork. (B) is incorrect because it describes the *elements of art*, as opposed to the principles of art. (C) is incorrect because subjects are communicated through art. (D) is incorrect because there are several different artistic concepts presented in the standards for kindergarten through grade 6. **Competency 042**

140. **C**

Integrated thematic units are organized around a common theme. Thus, the lesson can contain basic mathematics objectives in conjunction with science and social studies concepts. (A) is incorrect because thematic instruction does not require the introduction of literacy skills in a sequential fashion. (B) is too limited in scope; it addresses only one of the possible topics that can be covered in thematic instruction. (D) is also too limited in scope, because thematic instruction can be delivered in both ways—inductively (from the specific to the general) or deductively (general to specific). **Competency 013**

Index

REA's Study Guides

Review Books, Refreshers, and Comprehensive References

Problem Solvers®

Presenting an answer to the pressing need for easy-to-understand and up-to-date study guides detailing the wide world of mathematics and science.

High School Tutors®

In-depth guides that cover the length and breadth of the science and math subjects taught in high schools nationwide.

Essentials®

An insightful series of more useful, more practical, and more informative references comprehensively covering more than 150 subjects.

Super Reviews®

Don't miss a thing! Review it all thoroughly with this series of complete subject references at an affordable price.

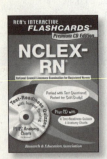

Interactive Flashcard Books®

Flip through these essential, interactive study aids that go far beyond ordinary flashcards.

Reference

Explore dozens of clearly written, practical guides covering a wide scope of subjects from business to engineering to languages and many more.

For information about any of REA's books, visit
www.rea.com

Research & Education Association
61 Ethel Road W., Piscataway, NJ 08854
Phone: (732) 819-8880

REA's Test Preps
The Best in Test Preparation

- REA "Test Preps" are **far more** comprehensive than any other test preparation series
- Each book contains full-length practice tests based on the most recent exams
- **Every** type of question likely to be given on the exams is included
- Answers are accompanied by **full** and **detailed** explanations

REA publishes hundreds of test prep books. Some of our titles include:

Advanced Placement Exams (APs)
Art History
Biology
Calculus AB & BC
Chemistry
Economics
English Language & Composition
English Literature & Composition
European History
French Language
Government & Politics
Latin
Physics B & C
Psychology
Spanish Language
Statistics
United States History
World History

College-Level Examination Program (CLEP)
Analyzing and Interpreting Literature
College Algebra
Freshman College Composition
General Examinations
History of the United States I
History of the United States II
Introduction to Educational Psychology
Human Growth and Development
Introductory Psychology
Introductory Sociology
Principles of Management
Principles of Marketing
Spanish
Western Civilization I
Western Civilization II

SAT Subject Tests
Biology E/M
Chemistry
French
German
Literature
Mathematics Level 1, 2
Physics
Spanish
United States History

Graduate Record Exams (GREs)
Biology
Chemistry
Computer Science
General
Literature in English
Mathematics
Physics
Psychology

ACT - ACT Assessment

ASVAB - Armed Services Vocational Aptitude Battery

CBEST - California Basic Educational Skills Test

CDL - Commercial Driver License Exam

CLAST - College Level Academic Skills Test

COOP, HSPT & TACHS - Catholic High School Admission Tests

FE (EIT) - Fundamentals of Engineering Exams

FTCE - Florida Teacher Certification Examinations

GED

GMAT - Graduate Management Admission Test

LSAT - Law School Admission Test

MAT - Miller Analogies Test

MCAT - Medical College Admission Test

MTEL - Massachusetts Tests for Educator Licensure

NJ HSPA - New Jersey High School Proficiency Assessment

NYSTCE - New York State Teacher Certification Examinations

PRAXIS PLT - Principles of Learning & Teaching Tests

PRAXIS PPST - Pre-Professional Skills Tests

PSAT/NMSQT

SAT

TExES - Texas Examinations of Educator Standards

THEA - Texas Higher Education Assessment

TOEFL - Test of English as a Foreign Language

USMLE Steps 1,2,3 - U.S. Medical Licensing Exams

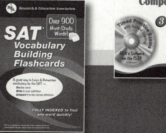

For information about any of REA's books, visit www.rea.com

Research & Education Association
61 Ethel Road W., Piscataway, NJ 08854
Phone: (732) 819-8880